THE
EXCEPTIONAL INDIVIDUAL

THE
EXCEPTIONAL INDIVIDUAL

second edition

Charles W. Telford • James M. Sawrey

San José State College

Prentice-Hall, Inc., Englewood Cliffs, New Jersey

Prentice-Hall Psychology Series

© 1972, 1967 by Prentice-Hall, Inc., Englewood Cliffs, New Jersey

ISBN: 0–13–293779–4

Library of Congress Catalog Card Number: 74–178133

Printed in the United States of America

10   9   8   7   6   5   4   3

PRENTICE-HALL INTERNATIONAL, INC., *London*
PRENTICE-HALL OF AUSTRALIA, PTY. LTD., *Sydney*
PRENTICE-HALL OF CANADA, LTD., *Toronto*
PRENTICE-HALL OF INDIA PRIVATE LIMITED, *New Delhi*
PRENTICE-HALL OF JAPAN, INC., *Tokyo*

Contents

**INTRODUCTION TO
EXCEPTIONALITY**

1

1

Some Basic Psychological
and Social Considerations   3

2

Deviance and Stigma   27

3

The Care and Education
of the Exceptional   56

4

Family and Personal Problems
of Exceptional People   96

v

INTELLECTUAL
EXCEPTIONALITY

II

5
The Intellectually Superior   127

6
Creativity   154

7
The Mentally Retarded:
Some General Considerations   182

8
Mild Mental Retardation   225

9
Severe Mental Retardation   253

10
Learning Disabilities   273

THE SENSORIALLY
HANDICAPPED

III

11
The Visually Handicapped   301

12
The Aurally Handicapped   329

MOTOR AND SPEECH HANDICAPS

IV

13
The Orthopedically Handicapped and the Epileptic   361

14
Speech Handicaps   391

SOCIAL DEVIANCE

V

15
Social Deviance   419

16
The Culturally Disadvantaged   446

PROBLEMS OF THE AGED

VI

17
The Aged   505

APPENDIX:
Specialist Organizations and Agencies, 533

Name Index   541

Subject Index   553

Preface

The second edition of this textbook reflects the shift in the attitude of our culture toward deviant people. The 1967 edition anticipated this shift in the general direction of a decreasing emphasis on the specific categories of exceptionality, the diminishing importance of etiological classifications in social and educational remedial programs, and an increasingly humanistic point of view in dealing with the socially devalued classes of deviant people.

Like most textbooks written in one's teaching area, this book grew out of a conviction that a different conceptual framework, selection and organization of material, and manner of presentation would be superior to the then current ones. While our claims to originality in these respects are limited, this second edition continues to have some unique features:

§ the inclusion in a single text of the highly creative, the culturally disadvantaged, and the intellectually borderline as categories of exceptional people;

§ the consideration of persons beyond childhood and adolescence;

§ the consisitent use of a cultural frame of reference in defining exceptionality and in identifying and dealing with the problems of exceptional people;

§ the handling of the problems of exceptional people as essentially the magnified problems of individual differences among people in general;

§ the emphasis on the generality of most of the problems of exceptionality.

All classifications of exceptional people are arbitrary, and they are useful only with reference to the times and purposes they serve. Our inclusion of the highly creative, the culturally disadvantaged, and the intellectually borderline reflects current interest in these categories of people.

Our extension of the age range to include adults, and our use of the terms "exceptionality" and "exceptional people" rather than "exceptional children," reflects our conviction that exceptionality is often more the problem of the entire family and culture—the tone of which is set by the adults—than it is the property of a unique individual. Moreover, there are more adults than children in many categories of exceptionality.

The acceptance of a dominantly cultural frame of reference in dealing with exceptional people results in an emphasis on the relative nature of the deviations and a recognition of the extent to which the problems of exceptionality cut across categories. It is for this reason that the first four chapters of the book deal with those problems that are common to exceptional people in general, irrespective of the nature or origin of their exceptionalities.

Major revisions in this second edition include a more explicit development of the topic of deviance and stigma and the addition of two completely new chapters, one on learning disabilities and one on the aged. We have collapsed the topics of the orthopedically handicapped and the epileptic into a single chapter and have reduced the section on mental retardation by one chapter. Minor revisions and up-dating of all sections have also been done.

This book is intended for use at the upper division or graduate level as an introduction to the problems of exceptional people. It is intended as a survey course both for people who will specialize in one of the specific areas of exceptionality and for the prospective or current teacher, principal, supervisor, superintendent, occupational therapist, physical therapist, nurse, or physician who will work with a wide variety of deviant individuals but who will not become a specialist in the field.

Every book has many hidden contributors. Our wives, Una Mae Sawrey and Aldene E. Telford, have contributed through their encouragement, their tolerance of our neglect of family obligations, and their critical reading of the manuscript. Instructors, colleagues, students, and clients too numerous to recall or to mention have, over a period of some 45 years, contributed to the writers' knowledge of exceptional people while they were students, teachers on the elementary, secondary, and college levels, clinicians, school psychologists, and consultants. We would also like to thank Professor William G. Wolfe and Professor Richard B. Dever for their helpful comments on the second edition.

C. W. T.

J. M. S.

THE
EXCEPTIONAL INDIVIDUAL

INTRODUCTION TO EXCEPTIONALITY

1

Some Basic Psychological and Social Considerations

In this chapter we shall discuss the criteria of exceptionality. The historical and current conceptions of the nature of exceptional people will be reviewed, and the basic psychological concepts necessary for understanding exceptional individuals will be developed and discussed. We shall concentrate on those characteristics and processes which are common to all or most of the categories of exceptional people. While our concern is principally with children and youth, much of this chapter will deal with exceptional people in general.

Since all of the conventional categories of exceptional people, except those of the intellectually gifted and the creative, are categories of disability, we shall be concerned in this section of the book primarily with the handicapped. Despite the apparent disparateness of the categories of exceptional people, there is a set of concepts and principles which can integrate and unify our thinking about these groups.

The Problem of Individual Difference

To be exceptional is to be rare or unusual. The unusual, the bizarre, and the unexpected have always attracted attention and have often aroused awe and wonder. A change from the accustomed order of things arouses man's curiosity and causes him to ask why. Science has originated largely from man's attempts to explain the unexpected. The commonplace, on the other hand, poses no problems for the uninitiated: It takes some sophistication to see problems in the obvious.

When the regular movements of the sun, moon, and stars were taken for granted and seemed to require no explanation, comets, meteors, and eclipses still attracted attention and led to an interest in astronomy. Errors of astronomical observation led to investigation of the sources of these errors, which resulted in a long series of reaction-time experiments in psychology. The discovery that the sources of variations in reaction time could be identified led to the investigation of the more complex psychological processes. Speculation concerning the origins of more obvious errors of observation and belief, such as illusions and delusions, led John Locke to a consideration of the origins of knowledge in general and the nature of ordinary perceptual experience. The irrational and bizarre behavior of the mentally ill (the psychotic) and the mentally retarded (the feebleminded) attracted attention and seemed to require explanation, while the behavior of the normal person apparently went on by itself and seemed self-explanatory. The occurrence of sporadic dwarfism and gigantism helped to focus attention on the problems of physical growth in general. Instances of precocious puberty (*pubertas praecox*), which have resulted in girls eight and nine years of age bearing children, as well as female virilism characterized by excessive hairiness, loss of the feminine body configuration, and amenorrhea, have stimulated interest in the problems of sex determination and the sexual development of normal people.

Regular, everyday occurrences not only seem to require no explanation; they also cause society relatively little trouble. It is possible to anticipate the regularly recurring events of life, and one may profit by them, avoid them, or endure them. On the other hand, unpredictable catastrophes, such as cyclones, floods, droughts, unusual events, such as eclipses of the sun or moon, and comets, irrational behavior, such as of the psychotic, the epileptic, and the mentally retarded, deviant developmental patterns, such as of the midget and the acromegalic, precocious sexual development of children, and adult feminization of males and masculinization of females—all these not only attract attention, they also become matters of personal and public concern. They threaten the personal security and social status of the afflicted persons and create trouble for their families, for other individuals, and for society. The occurrence of unusual events and circumstances stimulates individual efforts and social movements concerned with the understanding, care, prevention, and control of these conditions and events.

While it may be going too far to claim that most of the significant developments in science in general, and in psychology in particular, have arisen from the curiosity aroused by the unusual events in life and the social needs resulting from them, nevertheless many socially significant lines of investigation and matters of public concern have so originated. We have already mentioned Locke's investigation of the origins and nature of cognitive experiences. Freud's conception of the nature of motivation, his interpretations of dreams, and his beliefs concerning the psychodynamics of everyday behavior grew out of his studies of the mentally ill. The first intelligence tests were developed and initially used for the identification and classification of intellectually exceptional individuals first the mentally retarded, and later the gifted. The existence of blind and deaf people focussed attention on the problems of normal vision and audition and the role of these senses in ordinary life. The personal, family, and social problems resulting from blindness and deafness have stimulated research efforts, educational movements, and social welfare programs concerned with the prevention and amelioration of these conditions.

Prescientific Conceptions of Deviant People

Although the existence of deviant human behavior and development aroused curiosity and focussed interest on normal behavior and development, mystical and supernaturalistic interpretations of deviations persisted long after naturalistic explanations of the more ordinary behavioral events and developmental sequences had been generally accepted. As long as the normal mind was conceived of as an independent *animas* (i.e., power, force, or immaterial entity) controlling the body, deviant behavior and development were even more readily explained in terms of evil or benign powers or spirits (i.e., demons). A more scientific conception of the nature of deviant behavior and physique had to wait for the development of a naturalistic explanation of normal behavior and physique.

The fact that trephining (cutting a hole in the skull) was practiced by prehistoric man suggests that he accepted a demonological conception of the nature of illness—probably mental illness. Historically, trephining has been done to permit the escape of evil spirits from the body. It is therefore assumed that prehistoric man had a demonological conception of the nature and origin of mental deviations (Nowrey, 1945). Certainly man's belief in evil or benign spirits as the cause of deviant behavior has been evident from the beginning of recorded history. The substitution of naturalistic for supernatural explanations of the unusual in human behavior and development has been a slow process and is not complete even today. Historically, philosophers and medical men have been most influential in promoting this transition.

The Greek philosophers were apparently the first to develop something akin to a naturalistic conception of the nature of the mind and its functioning. Anaxagoras (c. 528–500 B.C.) conceived of the mind, or *nous*, as consisting of a finer and more attenuated material than ordinary inert matter. Diogenes (412–323 B.C.) took a similar step toward a naturalistic view of mind when he conceived of *nous* as an attribute of air, which was, for him, the basic element. Aristotle (384–322 B.C.) conceived of mind as bearing the same relationship to body as function does to structure. Mind, for Aristotle, was an attribute or organization of matter itself, not something above and beyond it—a conception as modern as any of the formulations which preceded the modern naturalistic period (Brett, 1962; Weber, 1925).

Hippocrates (460–375 B.C.) and Galen (second century A.D.) were Greek physicians who departed from the prevalent supernatural conceptions of the nature of deviant behavior. Hippocrates insisted that epilepsy, which had been known as the "divine disease," was no more divine or sacred than any other disease. He claimed that it had a natural cause, that men regarded it as divine "from ignorance and wonder," and that medical men had used its supposed divinity as a pretext for their own inability to offer any assistance. Galen located the "psychic functions" in the brain and believed that its operations and resulting activities were determined by the dryness and softness of the nerve tissues. He conceived of stimuli in material terms. Mental aberrations—he called them "dementia" and "imbecility"—resulted from the rarefaction and reduction in the amount of the "animal spirits" and from changes in the temperature and humidity of the brain. These notions seem rather queer today, but they were positive steps forward in the development of a naturalistic conception of the nature of deviant behavior (Brett, 1962; Nowrey, 1945).

The thousand years of the Middle Ages were the dark ages for science. Supernaturalism in general, the practice of magic, and intercourse with demons came to be accepted dogma. Man was considered the victim of invisible powers for good or for evil (Lea, 1957). The early Christian attitude toward the deviant individual was not a consistent one, however. Certain psychotic symptoms were thought to be the work of the devil, but some manic states were interpreted as ecstatic trances in which prophecies were made that indicated divine rather than demoniacal possession. Demoniacal possession was treated by exorcism and incantation.

Toward the end of the Middle Ages, the attitudes toward the deviant person became even more inconsistent and vacillating. Some of the mentally ill were admitted to hospitals for treatment while many of the possessed were still being burned as witches. Some evidences of kind and considerate attitudes appeared, but when psychopathy became epidemic, chains, floggings, and burning faggots became the tools for dealing with them.

The deviant individual came to be feared, and the terrors of the Inquisition caused the mental patients' families and friends to disown them. They were left to wander over the countryside and fend for themselves. It is estimated that three hundred thousand persons were put to death for practicing witchcraft or for demoniacal possession during the Middle Ages, and the concept of demoniacal possession has not yet been put to rest. Executions for this offense continued in Scotland until 1722, and trials are still held in some parts of the world (Nowrey, 1945; Lea, 1957).

During the Renaissance, some physicians raised objections to the mistreatment of the possessed. Paracelsus (1493–1541) became famous for a treatise in which he advocated the use of medicine in the treatment of mental aberrations, in place of exorcisms and incantations (Weber, 1925). The more or less accidental establishment of community care for mental defectives at Gheel, Belgium, took place in this period. Saint Vincent de Paul (1576–1660) maintained an establishment for the care of unfortunates, including the feebleminded (Baker, 1959). During the Renaissance there were many evidences of a change in attitudes toward the deviant individual.

The year 1792, when Pinel became superintendent and struck from the insane at the *Hospice des Bicetre* the chains which bound them, marked the beginning of an enlightened attitude toward the mentally ill. With the founding of the first successful school for the treatment of mental defectives, in 1837, the difference between the mentally deficient and the mentally ill was clearly recognized, and their treatment was correspondingly differentiated. There were, of course, some minor movements in this direction before 1837.

Qualitative versus Quantitative Conceptions of the Differences between Exceptional and Normal People

The substitution of a naturalistic for a supernatural explanation of the origins and nature of the deviant characteristics of an individual did not solve the problem of the nature of the exceptional person. In some respects, the demonological conception of the exceptional person was a qualitative as contrasted with a quantitative one.

A qualitative conception of exceptional individuals conceives of them as constituting separate and, in many ways, distinct categories or classes of people. As separate categories of people, they are considered to have traits and characteristics which make them fundamentally different from the general run of mankind. The titles of certain books and courses—the "psychology of" the gifted, or the mentally retarded, or the blind, or the deaf—suggest that there is a separate kind or brand or category of psychology which explains these deviant types and that such explanations are fundamentally different from the "psychology of" normal people. Such a view implies that a separate and unique set of conceptual categories or ways of thinking is required to understand and deal with exceptional individuals. They are supposed to learn, perceive, think, and adjust in ways which are unique to them; therefore they cannot be understood in terms of those principles of learning, thinking, perceiving, and adjusting which have been derived from and are applicable to normal people. The trend of thinking over the last hundred years has been away from qualitative conceptions, and toward a quantitative frame of reference. However, there are still many unanswered questions concerning the fundamental nature of the differences between the exceptional and the normal.

The quantitative conception of exceptionality holds that the differences between the deviant groups, on the one hand, and the normal, on the other, are only differences of degree and not of kind. Thus the perceptual, conceptual, learning, and ideational processes of all people—whether normal or deviant—are fundamentally the same. We all learn, retain, recall, perceive, think, and make personal and social adjustments according to the same general principles and patterns, but some of us do these things faster, better, more accurately, or more appropriately than others. In its extreme form, the quantitative conception of the mentally retarded is that they are intellectually inferior to the normal by designated amounts, as roughly indicated by test performances, school achievement, and social competence, and that they are essentially normal in ways unrelated to intellectual competence. Except as a consequence of their intellectual deficiencies, their personalities, characters, physical characteristics, and social characteristics are normal—or, at least, their deviations from the normal in these respects are not necessarily or inherently a part of their intellectual deficiencies.

Some people who believe in a modified form of the qualitative conception claim that different *patterns* of traits characterize the various classes of deviant individuals and that these distinctive syndromes, or profiles of abilities and disabilities, constitute a difference in *kind*. This view is counterposed to the quantitative one, which views deviance as a difference in the degree to which the deviant individual possesses a single capacity or attribute. This argument typically takes the following form: Although the differences between the various types of deviant people—blind, deaf, crippled, epileptic, mentally retarded, gifted, and so forth

—and the normal are differences of extent or degree when each attribute (intelligence, sensory capacity, locomotion, aptitude, or creativity) is taken singly, each category of exceptionality will show a deviant and characteristic *pattern* of traits and aptitudes. For example, as is illustrated in Figure 1, the intellectually gifted group scores highest in the area which defines its exceptionality—here intellectual aptitude; it scores almost equally high in academic achievement, slightly above average in physique and motor aptitudes, and slightly more above the norm in personal and social adjustment. The typical pattern of the mentally retarded is virtually the reverse of this. To the extent that these profiles are characteristic of the intellectually gifted and retarded and are unique to these groups, these differences are considered to be *qualitative*.

Social influences are undoubtedly responsible for some of the components of the patterning of traits characterizing the various categories of exceptional people. Deviations from the norm in the various ways labelled "exceptional" may not, of themselves, result in characteristic personality and behavioral patterns; they do so because of the social or personal *meanings* attached to the deviations. For example, children who are chronologically 10 years old and mentally 15 (and thus intellectually gifted) may differ significantly from children who are chronologically 15

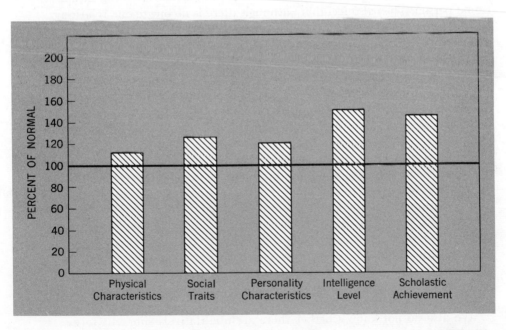

FIGURE 1
Profile of a Typical Intellectually Gifted Individual

and mentally 15 (and thus intellectually normal) because society perceives them as different, labels them as different, treats them differently, and expects them to act differently. The children, in turn, accept these social judgments, perceive themselves differently, and act in accordance with these self-perceptions. The argument is that, although the inherent differences between the normal and the various categories of exceptional people may be largely confined to the area of their exceptionality, these differences invariably spread to other areas as the result of social learning.

Thus, while most workers who deal with the broader concepts of individual differences, abnormality, and exceptionality emphasize, and to some degree are committed to the notion that differences among people and groups of people are quantitative in nature, they are not willing to go all the way in terms of the implications of a purely quantitative theory. For example, the extreme quantitative view is that the ordinary mentally retarded child can be understood solely in terms of his mental age and the environmental conditions that have conditioned his motivational system. The orthopedically handicapped child can be dealt with as a normal child who has limited locomotion. The blind child is simply a child with a narrowed range of sensory input. Few people working with exceptional individuals accept these extreme positions, but they do emphasize the large component of normality in the makeup of every exceptional person. They also feel that, although there is no one-to-one relation between types of exceptionality on the one hand and patterns of social and personal adjustment on the other, there is a common set of problems and, at least, a quantitatively different set of personal and social reactions which run through all the forms of exceptionality. There is mounting evidence that while there are important relationships among organic and intellectual deviations, and among social values and personal adjustment, the social origins of the deviant behavioral patterns are of paramount importance.

It seems likely that the question of whether the differences between the normal and the exceptional are quantitative or qualitative will have to wait for an answer to the same question with reference to different people within the normal ranges of physique and aptitude. For example: Are two people of the same chronological age intellectually equivalent because they have the same IQ's, if their patterns of scores are quite different? In Table 1–1, both A and B have obtained IQ's of 100, as measured by the WISC, and their scores are as shown. Many people would claim that these two people are quite different, even though their IQ's are identical.

We also do not know whether there are qualitatively different forms of learning among normal people or even within the same person. We do not have agreement about whether or not the learning of young children

TABLE 1–1
Scores Obtained by Two People on the Weschler Intelligence Scale for Children

	Scores of A	Scores of B		Scores of A	Scores of B
Information	10	5	Picture Completion	11	4
Comprehension	8	4	Picture Arrangement	9	1
Arithmetic	11	18	Block Design	8	15
Similarities	9	10	Object Assembly	12	13
Vocabulary	11	13	Coding	10	17

is only quantitatively different from that of adults. A recent survey of the comparative learning of children and adults indicates that the laws of learning derived from research on adults hold reasonably well for young children. There is also close correspondence between the variables which influence the learning of children and adults (Keppel, 1964). The following sampling of opinions of workers in the field is typical of current thought on this question. "The laws governing adjustment to disability are the same as those governing adjustment to any other condition. There is little justification for the development of a separate psychology of the disabled" (Loquist, 1960). This same author states that, although disability increases the likelihood of occurrence of certain classes of events (e.g., frustrations and conflicts), these are not unique to the disabled individual. He is simply likely to experience them more often than his nondisabled peers. Loquist also insists that the "styles of life" found in blind individuals, in deaf individuals, and in the orthopedically disabled are as varied as those found in nondisabled individuals, and are of essentially the same types. Myerson (1963) claims, as does Ross (1964), that even in motor or sensory loss—blindness, or deafness, or crippling—the psychological significance of the condition has to do in large measure with such matters as actual or threatened social isolation, personal independence, and acceptance of personal limitations, experiences which all human beings have. The incidence of emotional disturbance is unusually high in the physically disfigured, but it is claimed that the forms that the disturbance takes are in no way unique to this group (Myers et al., 1960; Wright, 1960). Fiedler (1952) believes that the basic needs of deaf and hard-of-hearing children are identical with the needs of all children, and has proposed that these basic needs can be best set for all children in much the same way. From his study of deaf children, Fiedler concludes that children handicapped by loss of hearing present no evidence of any unique patterning of personality or adjustment. He finds just about the same varieties of adjustment as one finds in a similar group of hearing children. The difficulties of growing up and the problems of adjustment that are found are problems that are unrelated to hearing loss as such. The problems of the deaf and the hard-of-hearing, as of hearing children, seem deeply rooted in the patterns of family living and parent-child relationships and have no direct relationship to the hearing loss, although they may often be exaggerated or accentuated by this handicap. Wenar (1953) claims, in the same vein, that there is no evidence that a motor handicap produces a particular kind of deviant thinking in the child, nor that it necessarily forces him to extremes of deviant thinking.

While none of these opinions is focussed primarily on the question of the quantitative versus the qualitative nature of the differences between exceptional and normal people, they all lend support to a quantitative emphasis. The findings are suggestive, but not definitive. Probably the question of the basic nature of the intellectual differences between exceptional people and normal people is a part of the larger question of the nature of individual differences in general, and may not even have a meaningful answer. If we conceive of different patterns of abilities and characteristics as qualitative differences, then every person is qualitatively different from every other person. It may be that when single differences become very great, they at some point become qualitative in nature.

If disproof of the qualitative conception of the difference between the disabled and the normal is difficult, eradicating the widespread acceptance of the idea will be even harder. When a disabled person achieves commensurately with a normal person despite his handicap, he is perceived as overcompensating. The overdependency of a similarly disabled person is also seen as a direct expression of his defect. Much of what the deviant individual does is seen as a manifestation of his deviancy. When a blind, deaf, crippled, or mentally retarded individual gets into trouble or has an accident the difficulty is readily ascribed to his defect. The same experiences of normal people are seen as either situation evoked or as ordinary events in a normal life requiring no explanation.

Few people can accept the notion that a handicapped person's under- or overachievements can arise from ordinary motives and serve the identical functions in his life as they do in the lives of ordinary people. The belief that the achievements of the handicapped require some unique explanation is so widespread that such people are expected and required to develop a special rationale to explain their "normal" behavior. They are supposed to have a special philosophy to account for their achievements. The handicapped are expected to have a unique philosophy to explain why they want the same things as the nonhandicapped and work for them in similar ways. Handicapped individuals respond to these expectancies by statements of their philosophies, which are largely reflections of the prevalent stereotypes concerning their particular disability (Chevigny, 1946).

Current Conceptions of Exceptionality

What is normal and what is abnormal in human behavior and development? What determines whether an individual is usual or unusual, normal or exceptional? Exceptionality and abnormality are popular concepts with variable meanings. Except as they are defined operationally for certain administrative or research purposes, they will always have to be understood in the particular social context in which they are used.

STATISTICAL DEFINITIONS OF EXCEPTIONALITY

Many operational definitions of exceptionality are statistical and quantitative in nature. The mentally retarded can be defined operationally as persons with IQ's below 70 as measured by the Stanford-Binet Intelligence Test. They can alternatively be defined as the intellectually lowest 2 or 3 per cent of the population as indicated by test scores or some other criteria. The intellectually gifted can similarly be defined in terms of test scores or of demonstrated performance, or as the upper 1 or 2 per cent of the general population as measured by some designated intelligence test. The hard-of-hearing and the deaf can be identified in terms of hearing loss as measured in decibels by a standard audiometer. Blindness is typically defined legally as visual acuity of 20/200 or less in the better eye after maximum correction or as possession of a visual field limited to 20° or less. There are no conventional quantitative indices of most other types of deviant individuals, such as the orthopedically handicapped, the socially maladjusted, the emotionally disturbed, the epileptic, and the individual with speech defects. In most of these conditions the diagnostic judgment of trained specialists replaces quantitative measurement. However, it is at least theoretically possible to devise statistical criteria of exceptionality in these areas also.

PRAGMATIC, SOCIAL DEFINITIONS OF EXCEPTIONALITY

While it is often legally and administratively necessary to use independent quantitative criteria for the identification of exceptional individuals, the final test of the validity of these criteria is that of social usefulness. If an IQ of below 70 is accepted as the arbitrary criterion of mental retardation for placement in special classes, but it is found that many children with IQ's of 75 can profit equally by placement in such classes, the 70 limit loses much of its usefulness as a criterion. It then becomes necessary either to change the limit or expand the criterion so as also to take into consideration demonstrated school achievement and physical and social maturity. The audiometric criterion for deafness or partial deafness and the visual acuity criterion for blindness or partial sightedness are meaningful and valid only insofar as experience proves that individuals thus designated are correspondingly handicapped educationally, socially, and vocationally. The judgments of specialists as to the degree of exceptionality represented by the orthopedically handicapped, the speech defective, and the socially and emotionally maladjusted are validated to the degree that individuals so identified do require, and are found to profit by, special education and treatment specifically designed for them. Because of the priority given to the pragmatic social criteria, the term "exceptional individual" usually refers to those people who differ from the average to such an extent that they are perceived by society as requiring special educational, social, or vocational treatment. True, such criteria lack specificity and vary from culture to culture and from one generation to another, but they seem to be the most meaningful yet suggested. Such a relative, social conception of the exceptional individual finds quantitative criteria to be useful only insofar as they correlate with the social. If it is found that all or most of the test-identified exceptional children also meet the educational and social criteria, test performance can be used for identification purposes. But when educational methods and requirements change, when social demands vary, and when occupational opportunities are modified, the tests' usefulness will also change.

Critics can find considerable fault with a definition of the exceptional individual as that person who deviates from the norm in physical, mental, emotional, or social characteristics to such a degree that he requires special social and educational services in order to develop his maximum capacity. In actual practice, a combination of traditional practice, cultural values, social needs, and even political pressures determines what dimensions and degrees of individual differences are sufficiently significant for something to be done about them.

The Variable Nature of Social Criteria of Exceptionality. In a primitive culture, where survival and effectiveness depend upon one's skill in hunting, physical handicaps are serious defects, whereas the inability to learn to read, write, calculate, and handle abstract concepts is much less significant. Where individual and tribal survival and prestige are determined by sensory acuity and by physical agility, strength, and endurance, physically defective infants may be abandoned even though they may be intellectually superior. In an agricultural community which is sparsely settled and unmechanized, a psychotic, mentally retarded, or socially inadequate individual may be a problem to his immediate family without becoming a matter of general social concern. The rural boy who fails to learn in school can still do useful work under the supervision of his father and brothers and can become a contributing member of the family.

Variations among people are universal, but society determines which deviations will be considered disabilities or assets, impairments or enhancements of personal worth. Assets and disabilities are dictated as much by the tasks a culture demands or expects of its members and by the meanings it attaches to deviations from the norm as by the objective facts of exceptionality.

Today's increasing social concern for the extreme intellectual deviates (the mentally retarded, the intellectually gifted, and the creative) is, in part, a reflection of our cultural expectancies and values. A discussion of the reasons for the increasing social problems of mental retardation and the current interest in the gifted and the creative will point up the cultural frame of reference within which all categories of exceptional children are perceived.

In present-day America, the need for unskilled and semiskilled workers is rapidly declining, while the demand for professional, managerial, scientific, and technically trained workers is increasing. The bulk of the work requiring good hands and a strong back is being automated, and we are experiencing the substitution of knowledge for strength. Inventiveness, creativity, and intellectual activity are becoming the real human assets. An advanced industrial culture requires a well-educated, creative, and adaptable labor force. The young students of today can expect to see a complete technological revolution during the course of their lifetimes. The jobs they might hold today will probably not exist when they are fifty. As adults they may well be working with processes not yet developed and using machines still to be designed. In such a highly automated and rapidly changing industrial society, the need is for people to invent, design, install, monitor, and service equipment. The man who offers manual dexterity, brute strength, and endurance is no longer truly productive. Adaptability rather than a specific skill, creativity rather than rote information, the capacity for change rather than a given fund of information in one limited area are the assets valued by such a culture. The concept of a position or industrial occupation as a specialized activity is being replaced by an emphasis on the more general and abstract occupational and professional aptitudes. The demand for the greater plasticity and adaptability which is characteristic of higher intelligence is becoming imperative.

One result of these cultural changes is that mentally retarded individuals, for example, are increasingly becoming a social liability. Even the farm is changing. The demands of scientific farming, the rational use of complicated modern farm machinery, the pressures of mechanized, large-scale, efficient production have forced the marginal farmer and farm worker out of the market. The reduction in the absolute number of farm laborers, as well as the even greater decrease in their relative number, has driven hordes of marginal farm workers, tenants, and owners to the cities, where they gravitate to the slums and swell the rank of the urban culturally disadvantaged.

In the urban centers, the persons with marginal intelligence come to the attention of the educational, public health, police, and public welfare agencies designed to help them, and their intellectual limitations become obvious and public concern is aroused. With increasing numbers of people becoming intellectually marginal and inadequate in terms of the social and occupational demands of the culture, the need for special school classes, welfare programs, and institutions to care for them increases tremendously. People of low mental level become more significant as exceptional individuals with handicaps sufficient to require special programs and facilities. Handicaps are always relative to the social context.

Area or Mode of Deviation

The first classification of exceptional individuals is the *area* or *mode* of primary deviation. This is a qualitative type of classification. The modes or areas selected for consideration reflect the current cultural values of the society. We have selected six general areas or modes of deviation for primary consideration.

Intellectual Deviance.   The first area of deviation considered is the intellectual one. We shall deal with intellectual deviations in both directions from the mean. On the lower end of the scale of intelligence are the mentally retarded, the borderline, and the dull; at the high end of the intellectual scale are the gifted. Creative and potentially creative persons, although they probably do not possess the same kind of exceptionality as the intellectually gifted, the normal, and the retarded, are probably a subgroup of the gifted, but they will be considered separately because of the current interest in them. A certain minimum of intellectual capacity is necessary to be creative, but creativity seems to correlate only moderately with general intelligence. Therefore we will deal with the creative and the intellectually gifted as two overlapping, but not identical, categories.

Sensory Deviance.   The sensorially exceptional—the hard-of-hearing and the deaf, the partially sighted and the blind—constitute a second area of exceptionality. There are, of course, people who have no sense of pain (analgesia), who lack all sensitivity in local skin areas (cutaneous anesthesia or anaphia), and who have no sense of smell (anosmia). There may also be people without a sense of taste, or gustatory sensitivity, and without motor sensitivity, or kinesthesis, although the authors have never heard of them. Such conditions are exceptional in a statistical sense and often constitute medical and psychological curiosities, but they do not pose social problems and therefore are not typically considered in discussions of exceptionality.

Motor Deviance. The third mode of exceptionality is in the motor area. In this group we shall consider the crippled, or orthopedically handicapped, the speech defectives, and the epileptics. While no one will question the first subgroup as being principally motor deviants, many will insist that most speech disorders are functional rather than organic in nature. However, speech defects have their motor aspects, and we shall subsume them under the motor deviants rather than placing them in a class by themselves. Epilepsy is recognized and identified largely in terms of its motor manifestations, although it could be considered basically a neurological deviation. However, since the same thing can be said of most orthopedic defects, we have placed epilepsy in the motor category.

Personality Deviance. The fourth area or mode of exceptionality is the emotional or personality category. This mode resists definition and delimitation even more than the intellectual, sensory, and motor modes of deviation. We can, of course, conceive of a theoretically normal range of emotional and personality adjustment. This normal range of adjustment grades imperceptibly into the minor personality maladjustments, which in turn pass into the more serious personality disturbances the neuroses and the psychoses. The simplest view of the fundamental nature of the personality maladjustments is a quantitative, social-learning conception. Its proponents consider personality deviations to be the end results of the process of social learning. Psychosis and neurosis are thought to be understandable in terms of excessive anxiety, frustrations, conflict, and repression, which are basic processes common to all people. The personally distressing and socially handicapping neurotic and psychotic manifestations are considered to be the end results of the many defensive mechanisms which develop as a consequence of the individual's attempts to handle life's stresses (Sawrey and Telford, 1971). There are, of course, other ways of viewing personality maladjustments. The 1950s and '60s have witnessed an increasing public concern with problems of mental health and mental illness.

Social Deviance. The social deviant has traditionally been the primary concern of law enforcement agencies. Juvenile delinquents and adult criminals are, by definition, social deviants. However, society has become increasingly aware of the existence of subcultural groups—ethnic minorities and the culturally disadvantaged or deprived—who, for a variety of reasons, deviate so far from the dominant social norm that they constitute educational and social problems. The bulk of these people live in poverty, and when cross-cultural studies are made of such people the world over, they seem to possess sufficient common characteristics to cause one to wonder if there does not exist a world-wide "culture of poverty."

Partly for historical reasons and partly because of the need for focussing attention on certain critical areas, juvenile delinquents and the culturally deprived will be discussed as two categories of exceptional people. They constitute the two subdivisions of our fifth area of exceptionality.

Problems of the Aged. Selecting a particular age range as a sixth category for special consideration is quite arbitrary. All of the five modes of deviation are found among the aged and many of these are discussed under the appropriate categories. However, there are some more general problems of adjustment that are unique to this age range. These problems are only beginning to receive the attention they deserve. Since we have committed ourselves to consider exceptionality throughout the entire age range, we feel it is appropriate to include a separate discussion of the problems of elderly persons.

THE OVERLAPPING OF AREAS OR MODES

The enumeration of discrete categories of exceptional individuals over-simplifies the facts of life. Many, or even most, exceptional people are exceptional in more than one area. Everyone knows of people who are both blind and deaf; there are somewhere between three and four thousand such people in the United States today (Rothschild, 1962). Most individuals with cerebral palsy have speech, sensory, or intellectual defects in addition to their motor handicaps, and it is very difficult for an extremely physically, sensorially, or mentally handicapped individual not to become, to some degree, a social or personality deviant. It is also true that people who are handicapped in one way may excel in another. The cripple may be a genius or an artist.

It is obvious that an almost infinite number of possible combinations of abilities and disabilities will be found in a typical population. One of the primary tasks of this book is to indicate the relationships commonly found among the many modes of socially significant deviations. We shall attempt to unravel some of the genetic, organic, social determinants, and relationships of these deviations.

WHY ONLY THESE AREAS OF DEVIATIONS?

It is obvious that there is no consistency in our selection of the particular areas and direction of deviation for consideration. We deal with both the exceptionally bright and the exceptionally dull, but we limit ourselves to the negative deviants, the handicapped, in all the other areas.

Why are we not just as concerned with the child who has *superior* sensory or motor capacities as we are with the child who has a motor or sensory handicap? There are several partial answers to this question. One is that the physically superior people do not constitute social problems; they do not cause trouble. We also are not aware of any possible public costs or social losses resulting from our failure to develop and capitalize on the supernormal abilities of these individuals. Perhaps our society is such that it cannot profit significantly from the superior sensory and motor capacities of its citizens. The telescope and the microscope have so extended the limits of human vision that the difference between the average person and the person with the most acute vision is relatively unimportant. It may be that artificial devices—amplifiers of sensory capacities—and the natural adaptability of the sense organs can bring the sensory aptitude of all but a small percentage of people above a certain minimum, and that differences above this level are not socially and economically critical.

In a way, we do recognize and reward motor facility, even though the physically and athletically superior are not usually considered in texts on exceptional children. In college, and to a lesser degree in high school, we hire and pay large salaries to people who follow the athletic records of prospective students, scout their games, and actively recruit, train, and coach them. We award the selected students scholarships purely on the basis of athletic aptitude; we provide special housing, "training tables," tutoring services, and special medical care, to ensure that they will remain in school and will either maintain or increase their athletic prowess. Their uniforms, equipment, and accessories are given to them. Athletic teams are provided with special transportation over great distances, so that they can compete with other, similarly subsidized teams. Special post-season games are held in exotic places in order to provide the teams with vacation trips at public expense. Star performers receive special awards, testimonial dinners, and public acclaim. And the termination of the athlete's collegiate program may be the beginning of a professional career with similar monetary and social rewards.

So without labelling it as such, we do provide very special programs for the physically superior. But such programs are seldom rationalized, like the programs for the intellectually talented, in terms of the "development and utilization of human resources." Intercollegiate athletic programs are considered part of the physical education program, but the principal justifications for such programs are monetary reward, personal and institutional prestige, and entertainment.

Some interest in individuals who are above average in terms of personality integration and social adjustment has recently developed. Mental health is still largely conceived of as an absence of mental illness, but there have been several attempts to define superior social and personal adjustment. There have also been some studies of the antecedents of superior mental health (Sawrey and Telford, 1971). However, we do not yet have enough relevant information to justify the inclusion of individuals with superior social ability and personality in our discussions of exceptional people. Similarly, we consider the problems of the culturally disadvantaged without giving comparable attention to the culturally advantaged.

Degree or Intensity of Exceptionality

Exceptional people differ in the *degree* of their deviation as well as in the mode of their exceptionality. Deviation has intensity as well as direction. We have already made incidental reference to this factor. It is obvious that people range intellectually from the extremely gifted (IQ's of 200 have been reported) to low-grade, totally dependent individuals with IQ's near zero. It is obvious that the extent of deviation required for designation as exceptional will always be relative to one's purpose. The current practice is to designate as intellectually gifted those individuals who score above a designated point, usually somewhere between 120 and 140, and who meet certain other criteria. The intellectually inferior are usually broken down into several subgroups for most purposes. At the lowest end of the scale (formerly called the "idiot" level) are the most severely retarded individuals—the "total-care," "custodial," or "institutional" cases where IQ's are below 20 or 30. The next higher group, previously the "imbecile" category, are now called the "trainable," the "moderately retarded," or in some classifications, the "severely retarded," whose IQ's are typically between 30 and 50. These are followed by the "mildly mentally retarded" (formerly the "moron" group) or "educable mentally retarded," whose IQ's range from 50 to 70. There is less agreement as to the most appropriate names and IQ ranges for the higher categories; but those with IQ's of 70 to 90 are often called the "slow learners." This range includes the groups previously labelled "dull" or "dull normal" (IQ's of 80 to 90) and the "borderline" (IQ's of 70 to 80). There is considerable variation in terminology, but it is usually clear from either the general context or the data presented which categories are under consideration.

It is clear that the degree, or intensity, of mental retardation may be as important as the fact of retardation. The *degree* of mental retardation is the primary difference between the slow learner, who will be a grade or two retarded in school, but who may eventually finish high school, learn a trade, marry, raise a family, and live a reasonably normal, independent existence and the total-care case, who will require supervision and nursing care comparable to that of a young infant for his entire lifetime. The *fact* of retardation may be less significant than its intensity.

The intensity of exceptionality is just as important in the physical as in the intellectual area. Educationally, minor auditory and visual deficiencies seem to be relatively unimportant. Even the hard-of-hearing (audiometrically defined) and the partially sighted can be educated and can live essentially like children with normal sight and hearing, whereas those whose visual or auditory acuity is below a certain critical point (usually the legally blind and deaf) require special techniques and facilities for their education and vocational training.

It is harder to indicate objectively intensity or degree of deviation in the remaining types of exceptional individuals. However, it is important to know the extent and location of motor involvement. Designations such as monoplegia, diplegia, triplegia, and quadraplegia indicate the number of limbs involved in cases of paralysis. It is just as important to know the degree of functional impairment of locomotion and manipulation resulting from the motor disability.

Specialists in speech pathology have made considerable progress in indicating the severity of speech defects. Speech defects can range all the way from articulatory deviations that are hardly noticeable to the unintelligible vocalizations of the extremely impaired cerebral-palsied or aphasic individual.

The intensity of deviation present in epilepsy is related to the form that it takes (*grand* or *petit mal*), the frequency and severity of the seizures, and their relative responsiveness to medication. Epilepsy can range all the way from a minor inconvenience, when it is of the mild *petit mal* form which may be entirely controlled by appropriate medication, to an incapacitating disorder, when the individual suffers from uncontrollable frequent *grand mal* convulsions.

We have already indicated that the degree or intensity of personality maladjustment can be conceptualized as "minor personality disturbances," "neuroses," and "psychoses." These terms indicate differences in intensity as well as possible qualitative differences.

The social deviant is placed in the broad general diagnostic categories of the delinquent or the culturally deprived, but some indication of the adequacy of his personal and social competence is equally helpful. Conceivably, the degree of social delinquency can be roughly indicated by the types of crime (major or minor) and the number of delinquencies. The extent of cultural deprivation can be inferred from the person's cultural background, which can be roughly quantified by the use of rating scales, or from his behavior. The latter is judged largely by subjective evaluation, although "social maturity" scales might conceivably be useful.

It is obvious that intensity refers to the *degree of individual differences*, not only as between the groups of people designated as exceptional and the normal but also within the deviant groups. The uninformed always overestimate the homogeneity of the identified groups of exceptional people. That the individuals making up a designated category of exceptional people have a narrowed range of aptitudes in one respect does not necessarily make them any more alike in other ways than the general run of people.

Extensity or Breadth of Exceptionality

Extensity, a third way in which exceptionality may be characterized, is used here to refer to the degree of specificity or generality of the handicap or asset in terms of which the individual is exceptional. Extensity is indicated by the degree to which the primary deviation affects other aspects of one's personality and behavior. As we suggested earlier, the average person probably overestimates the breadth or spread of exceptionality. The belief in a broad syndrome of behavior traits characteristic of the various classes of exceptional individuals has been widely held. These popular beliefs are typified by the conception of the intellectually gifted child as a socially inadequate and physically weak individual who is predisposed to physical and mental illness and likely to "burn out" and die at an early age. The mentally retarded individual is likewise stereotyped as a big, dumb brute, likely to be oversexed and criminally inclined. The deaf child was thought to be withdrawn, unsocial, morose, suspicious, and unhappy. Epileptics are alleged to display a characteristic personality syndrome, the "epileptic personality." The orthopedically handicapped individual is typically considered to be a mental as well as physical cripple. The failure of the blind to see and the deaf to hear is generalized into a general syndrome of disability. So we shout at the blind, expect others to speak for them, and attempt to lift them into streetcars as if they are crippled. These beliefs assume that there is an inherent relationship between deviation in one area and corresponding behavioral and personality deviations in other areas.

Research studies have provided little support for these social stereotypes. Where relationships between the conventional categories of physical deviations and personality traits or other behavioral characteristics have been found, the evidence does not support the belief in an inherent *causal relationship* between the two. There are some exceptions, and the topic will be discussed in more detail in connection with each class of exceptional individuals, but the following broad generalizations are probably justified.

Research studies regularly find a greater incidence of social withdrawal, overaggressiveness, personal unhappiness, and all types of defensive behavior patterns among people who deviate from the norm in ways culturally defined as undesirable than among those individuals who are either closer to the group norm or who deviate in socially approved directions. Consistent, but low, correlations are found between many physical handicaps and various measures of personal and social adjustment. However, in most cases, the assumption of a direct causal relationship between the two variables is questionable. The relationship between the physical variable and the behavioral trait is usually the result of intervening social variables. While there are important relationships between physical deviations on the one hand and social values and personal adjustment on the other, there is no one-to-one relationship between form of deviation and type of personal adjustment. Exceptional people have few psychological experiences and problems that are peculiar to them. The personality and behavioral problems of exceptional people—even those who are completely blind or deaf or crippled—arise from such matters as actual or threatened social isolation, personal dependency, and the denial or acceptance of personal limitations, experiences which all people have.

Terminology

There is relatively little standardization of terminology in the field of exceptionality. Only recently terms such as *insane, blind, deaf, crippled,* and *criminal,* as well as the term *feebleminded* and its subdivisions—*moron, imbecile,* and *idiot,* were used to refer to various categories of exceptional individuals. The present tendency is to substitute less stigmatizing, gentler, and less emotionally toned terms for the older ones which have acquired connotations of helplessness and hopelessness.

Mental deficiency was first substituted for *feeblemindedness;* still more recently, *mental retardation* has become the term approved by the American Association on Mental Deficiency. It is recommended that degrees of retardation be indicated by the terms *borderline, mild, moderate, severe,* and *profound.* However, in educational contexts, the term *educable* refers to the level called *mildly retarded* by the American Association, and the educators' *trainable* group roughly approximates the *moderately retarded* as defined by the Association. The matter is further complicated because the educators often refer to the educable and the trainable as "mildly" and "severely" retarded, respectively, thus departing from the Association's recommendations.

The terminology used for the other categories of the exceptional is not quite so involved. However, it is considered better to speak of the "orthopedically handicapped" than the "crippled." Although it is more awkward, the blind are often called the "sightless" or the "visually impaired." The deaf or the partially deaf have become the "aurally handicapped." The older terms *lunatic* and *insane* have been replaced by *psychotic* and *personality deviants*, which cover a broad, indefinite spectrum of deviant behavior in the same general area.

Originally, these categories of deviant people were all referred to as *disabled* or *handicapped*. However, when the intellectually superior were included along with the intellectually and physically handicapped, the term *exceptional* was adopted to refer to the entire group. This nonspecific designation, having no connotations of inferiority or inadequacy, is now used to refer to any or all of the deviant categories, although the general public often objects to this usage because the term is often understood in terms of its common dictionary definition as "uncommon; hence, superior." Occasionally, we find the terms *unusual child* or *special child* used in place of *exceptional child*.

While a part of the renaming of old categories reflects changing conceptions and greater precision in definition and classification, it is more a reflection of our cultural emphasis on the democratic belief in all men as being created equal and of our attempt to avoid the connotations of inherent inferiority which eventually accrue to the terms applied to groups of people perceived as handicapped. One author has suggested that we act as though by changing the label every few years we can keep certain ugly facts from catching up with us (Ross, 1964).

Summary

The problem of exceptional people is a part of the larger problem of individual differences in general. Prescientific conceptions of the origins and nature of the more extreme forms of development deviation and behavioral aberration tended to be supernatural and mystical. The current conceptions are quantitative and conceive of the differences between the normal and the exceptional to be one of degree only. The emphasis today is on the large core of normality found in every deviant individual. Understanding a handicapped child means first understanding him as a child, and only then understanding the ways in which his deviations may influence his development and behavior.

The basic social, psychological, and educational needs of exceptional children are identical with the needs of all children and can be met in much the same general ways. Only the specifics differ. There are probably few psychological experiences that are peculiar to exceptional people. The basic motivations for affection, acceptance, and approval exist whether the IQ is 50 or 150, whether the body is beautiful or a caricature, whether the movements are graceful or made awkward and incoordinate by crippling disease or accident, whether speech is melodious or guttural. The exceptional child, like any other child, can be comfortable and secure when he feels that he is accepted, appreciated, and liked. He will be equally uneasy and insecure when he is rejected and depreciated. Disability increases the probability of occurrence of certain frustrations and conflicts for the disabled, but these experiences are not unique to the disabled person. He simply experiences them more often than his nondisabled peer.

Deviations are conceived as having several aspects: (1) area (sensory, motor, intellectual, emotional, social); (2) intensity (degree of the deviation, from mild to severe); and (3) extensity (the range of behavior that is affected). The visibility or obviousness of a deviation also influences its personal and social significance.

R e f e r e n c e s

BAKER, H. J., *Introduction to Exceptional Children* (3rd ed.). New York: The Macmillan Company, 1959.

BRETT, G. S., *History of Psychology* (rev. ed.); ed. and abr. R. S. Peters. New York: The Macmillan Company, 1962.

CHEVIGNY, H., *My Eyes Have a Cold Nose*. New Haven, Conn.: Yale University Press, 1946.

FIEDLER, M. F., *Deaf Children in a Hearing World*. New York: The Ronald Press Co., 1952.

KEPPEL, G., "Verbal Learning in Children," *Psychol. bull.*, LXI (1964), 63–80.

LEA, H. C., *Materials Toward a History of Witchcraft*. New York: Thomas Yoseloff, 1957.

LOQUIST, L. H., ed., *Psychological Research and Rehabilitation*. Washington, D.C.: American Psychological Association, 1960.

MYERS, E., et al., "Motivational Patterns in Patients Seeking Elective Plastic Surgery," *Psychosom. med.*, XXII (1960), 193–203.

MYERSON, LEE, "Somatopsychology of Physical Disability," in *Psychology of Exceptional Children and Youth*, ed. W. M. Cruickshank. Englewood Cliffs, N.J.: Prentice-Hall, Inc., 1963.

NOWREY, J. E., "A Brief Synopsis of Mental Deficiency," *Am. j. ment. defic.*, XLIX (1945), 319–57.

ROSS, A. O., *The Exceptional Child in the Family*. New York: Grune & Stratton, Inc., 1964.

ROTHSCHILD, J., "Deaf-blindness," in *Psychological Practices with the Physically Disabled*, ed. J. F. Garrett and E. S. Levine. New York: Columbia University Press, 1962.

SAWREY, J. M. and C. W. TELFORD, *Psychology of Adjustment* (3rd. ed.). Boston, Mass.: Allyn & Bacon, Inc., 1971.

WEBER, A., *History of Philosophy*, trans. F. Thelly. New York: Charles Scribner's Sons, 1925.

WENAR, C., "The Effects of a Motor Handicap on Personality: I. The Effects on Level of Aspiration," *Child devel.*, XXIV (1953), 123–30.

WRIGHT, B. A., *Physical Disability: A Psychological Approach*. New York: Harper & Row, Publishers, 1960.

2

Deviance and Stigma

Social attitudes concerning the education, care, and rehabilitation of deviant individuals, and public provision for them, are largely a reflection of a set of more general, culture-wide beliefs and attitudes concerning the obligations of society as a whole to its individual citizens. Ever since the 1930s, the axioms of social obligations in the United States have shifted toward a constantly increasing responsibility of society to provide environmental circumstances conducive to the development of good physical and mental health, to make it possible for every adult to become gainfully employed, and to provide maximum opportunities for the development of one's potential. The assumptions basic to the providing of universal opportunities for educational advancement, vocational outlets, and self-actualization for the "normal" have been expanded to include all people simply because as human beings they are worthy of respect and consideration and are deserving of the entire range of opportunities previously afforded to only a part of the population.

The failure of society to provide facilities and opportunities for deviant individuals as appropriate to their needs as those made available to the normals has not been the result of conspiracies contrived by evil men to deprive certain segments of the population of their rights. Failures to provide educational and vocational programs and opportunities appropriate to the capacities and needs of the deviant minorities resulted incidentally from the efforts of reasonable, well-meaning people directed at other socially useful purposes.

The promise of universal educational opportunities has usually meant, in practice, one educational program which was available to all those able and willing to profit by it. The inability of deviant individuals, and groups of individuals, to take advantage of the programs provided because of sensory, motor, emotional, or intellectual limitations was explained in terms of demoniacal possession, retribution for parental sins, inborn perversity, punishment for individual delinquencies, inherent moral weaknesses, defective genes, or the inevitable accidents of normal life, according to the prevailing beliefs of the times. The inability of deviant individuals to profit by the educational and vocational opportunities provided to the bulk of the citizenry was seen as the result of deficiencies, defects, or weaknesses within the individuals and not of society's failure to provide programs and opportunities appropriate to the special needs of these people. In the apportioning of blame for the social failures of deviant citizens, the responsibility was predominantly that of the deviant himself. In a less moralistic framework, the question was, "Why isn't this person able to take advantage of the opportunities which his society provides?" rather than, "Why doesn't society provide educational, rehabilitative, and vocational facilities and programs appropriate to this individual's needs?"

The climate of the times that progressively has provided more adequately for the blind, the deaf, the orthopedically handicapped, the mentally deficient, and the emotionally disturbed, has expanded to a similar concern for the culturally disadvantaged (Afro-Americans, Mexican-Americans, Puerto Ricans, many rural whites, and ghetto dwellers of all colors and ethnic origins). Studies of the culturally disadvantaged have disclosed the fact that large segments of the population were born into and reared under circumstances which inevitably imposed handicaps upon them. Furthermore, it is now evident that these handicapping circumstances were created and perpetuated by the practices arising from the basic assumptions and beliefs of the larger society.

Society increasingly has assumed the obligation of providing help for all individuals and groups who for whatever reason require assistance. It has also become concerned with changing those conditions, practices, and erroneous beliefs contributing to the handicaps of these people.

The emergence of a widespread concern for handicapped and disadvantaged people has resulted in the state assuming increasing responsibility for extending the rights and privileges of full citizenship to all people. This extension of responsibility has manifested itself in the civil rights movement, the "war on poverty," the "Head Start" programs, and judicial decisions extending the rights, privileges, and immunities, once available to only the affluent or knowledgeable, to all citizens. Many Supreme Court decisions that have been widely criticized as coddling or protecting the criminal are really designed to extend to the poor, the ignorant, and the disadvantaged the same legal protections and rights previously available to only the more advantaged segments of the population. When the Court insists that every person taken into custody as a criminal suspect must be informed of his rights concerning self-incrimination and legal counsel, it is simply making available to the lowliest citizen of the nation the same protections and privileges previously enjoyed by only the more advantaged segments of the population. The well-informed, the better educated, and the more affluent criminals, with legal counsel prompting them at each critical point, know that they need not give self-incriminating testimony and are able to obtain legal counsel and advice. The ignorant "Bowery wino," the poorly informed first offender, and the disadvantaged delinquent are not aware of their legal rights and privileges and consequently may be convicted and punished, not because they are guilty but because they are ignorant, ill-informed, or poor.

The recent redefinition of mental illness as failure in social living, and the development of a community-wide public health approach to those problems of personal and social maladjustment previously viewed as purely personal afflictions, have accompanied increasing public concern for deviant and, particularly, disadvantaged people. There is an increasing professional and public recognition of the existence of a complicated and thorny set of interrelationships among poverty, unemployment, crime, physical illness, emotional disturbance, personality disorganization, mental deficiency, and educational retardation.

One manifestation of the changing climate of our times is the increase in public espousal of humanistic as well as humanitarian values. Historically, special programs for the handicapped—the blind, the deaf, the orthopedically handicapped, the mentally deficient, and the emotionally disturbed—were designed to reduce the level of dependency of the disabled, on the one hand, and to serve as an expression of our humanitarian concern for people less fortunate than ourselves on the other. Rehabilitative and educational procedures were designed to increase the productive efficiency of disabled individuals and thus make them less of a financial and personal burden on society.

Programs for the intellectually gifted and the potentially highly creative were conceptualized as maximizing the superior individual's contributions to society. The aptitudes and capacities of superior people were conceived as community assets to be utilized to the fullest possible extent so as to maximize their value to the state. In the 1960s a surge of interest in the intellectually superior and the creative individual was motivated, at least in part, by the "space race" and the belief that it was necessary for us to utilize the intellectual potential of these people to the maximum if we were to make the scientific and technological advances necessary to attain or maintain national superiority.

To a degree, people were a national commodity to be managed for maximum productivity. The intellectual capacities of citizens constituted tools for the realization of personal—but more importantly—social and nationalistic goals. Education has always served a dual function. It contributes to self-actualization on the one hand and serves as a source of socialization and increased public worth on the other. Recently, the goal of education has been conceptualized more in terms of self-realization and less in terms of productive efficiency. The failure of any individual to realize his potential is seen as more of a personal disappointment than as a social loss.

Some Philosophical Considerations

The way a society handles the problems posed by the presence of handicapped and disadvantaged minorities reflects its fundamental conception of the nature and worth of man and its basic assumptions concerning its communal obligations to the individual citizen. Americans have traditionally seen themselves as devoid of social class bias and have conceived of their society as a uniquely open and fluid one. For the most part, they have taken the oft repeated statements concerning all men being born free and equal as factual. They have assumed that making free public education available to all citizens provided equality of educational opportunity to all people.

Over the last generation Americans have become acutely aware of the discrepancy between their philosophical commitments and preachments on the one hand and their practices on the other. They are discovering that uniformity of opportunity is not necessarily equality of opportunity. Supplying unlimited numbers of free books to all children does not provide educational opportunity equally to blind, trainable mentally retarded, and sighted children of normal mentalities. Educational opportunities equivalent to those provided to normal children by ordinary educational procedures require that alternatives be provided to deviant individuals that are as appropriate to their special characteristics as the ordinary school curriculum and methods are to the average child. The freedom and equality to which all men are entitled are those of equity in law, equal rights to life, and to self-realization. The ideal of maximum opportunities for each person in terms of his unique constellation of traits and characteristics is replacing that of uniformity of opportunities. Each person has equal rights to dignity, courtesy, respect, and the maximum possible provision for him to develop whatever potential he has, not because these will make him a more productive being and a more socially acceptable person, but because these are his birthright as a human being. The notion of maximum opportunity for self-realization for all requires the use of all resources available to capitalize on the assets and minimize the deficits of each individual. Optimum human development rather than maximum productivity becomes the primary goal of educational and rehabilitative efforts. Of course, it is only on the level of concrete goals and specific programs and procedures that such an abstract tenet can be realized.

Reactions to Deviancy

In this book we are principally concerned with the individual who is sufficiently different from his peers to warrant special consideration of some type. However, we consider the minor differences found among "normals" and the deviations of "exceptional" individuals to constitute a continuum. As previously indicated, we believe that the reactions of people along this continuum to their differentness can be understood and handled within a single conceptual framework. The individual differences of ordinary people, people whose deviancies are borderline, the officially labelled deviants, and those individuals whose behavioral deviancies are designated as either exceptionally meritorious or criminal are matters of degree. Furthermore, there is considerable evidence that all degrees and kinds of deviancies have something in common.

Freedman and Doob (1968) in an interesting series of experiments have studied the effects of deviancy per se, without regard to the particular deviant characteristic, and have demonstrated that deviancy or the feelings of deviancy have marked effects on an individual's behavior. The research was carried out in controlled laboratory situations with "normal" subjects. The studies were deliberately designed to study deviancy more or less in a vacuum without the confounding effects of particular types of deviancy.

The research design consisted in giving a group of reasonably normal people an impressive series of tests; then each of them was given feedback from these tests which were alleged to show that their scores, compared to the normal range of scores—and particularly to the small group they were in—were extremely deviant. The tests and test scores were nonevaluative and never labelled in any way. Every effort was made to "decontaminate" the tests and the deviant test scores of any evaluative significance. The subjects were made to feel deviant by discovering that almost all of their test scores were at either extreme of a distribution. The scores might be at either the right or the left end of the distribution, but always at the ends. In contrast, the rest of the group had more or less average scores on the tests. They all bunched fairly close together around the mean.

Using this general research design, these workers have shown that they were able to induce feelings of deviancy in their subjects which were similar to the feelings of people who were "really" deviant in a statistical sense. The subjects receiving deviant feedback rated themselves as more deviant than did comparable subjects who had received nondeviant scores under the same circumstances. The subjects made to feel deviant preferred associating with other deviants more than did nondeviants. The preference of deviants for other deviants held true even for deviants who are unlike themselves. Persons made to feel deviants but whose deviancy is unknown to others minimize social contacts and avoid being conspicuous in situations where their deviancy might become obvious. Deviants were found to be treated better by similar deviants than they were by nondeviants. Deviancy was found to be an important determinant of how a person is treated. In experimental situations where subjects were given free choice of subjects upon whom to bestow rewards or punishments, nondeviants chose known deviants more often for punishment than for reward while deviants chose other deviants more often for rewards than for punishment. The findings indicate that the deviant subject is strongly concerned about minimizing his deviancy and behaves in ways that will produce this effect. In studies of social influence, these same workers found that the deviant is excessively concerned about possible mistreatment and is therefore reluctant to expose his differentness publicly. The more intimate and threatening the situation, the greater this reluctance becomes.

The experimental evidence as well as anecdotal evidence and self-observation all indicate that individuals who are deviant in physique, behavior, or beliefs are subject to a variety of internal and external pressures to reduce the extent or perceptibility of their differentness (Asch, 1952). Feelings of deviancy have important effects on people's behavior independent of the dimension of his deviancy or the social evaluation of the differentness. Everyone who feels deviant is to some extent affected in similar ways and is motivated to behave in similar ways. Although most people prefer not to be exactly the same as the norm of their reference groups, they also prefer not to be too different. Exactly where individuality turns into anxiety-arousing deviancy varies tremendously for different people, circumstances, and dimensions. However, at some point most people begin to be concerned about their deviancy.

In addition to deviancy as such, each dimension or category of deviancy carries with it an assortment of social and personal meanings and values. While each category and degree of differentness can be considered to be either positive or negative in value, it seems necessary to assume that, on balance, deviation is dominantly considered negative. This seems to follow from the experimental findings, already reported, in which statistically "normal" subjects who were fed information which made them believe that they were deviant, with no specification of the personal or social significance of their differentness, behaved in the same way as do people who are deviant in personally and socially devalued ways. Thus it seems from anecdotal evidence, research studies, and introspection that deviancy itself causes people to be concerned about possible diminished social acceptance, personal devaluation, or actual mistreatment because of their deviancy.

Except in the controlled conditions of the laboratory, significant deviancy involves social evaluations and consequences of a negative or positive sort, self judgments of a similar type, and sometimes, institutionalized and legalized sanctions, prohibitions and punishments. Since all of the categories of exceptional people considered in this book, except the gifted and the creative, are handicapped and hence negatively valued, the rest of this chapter will be devoted to the psychological and behavioral consequences of stigmatizing exceptionality.

The Distinction between Disability and Handicap

Writers in this field commonly distinguish between a disability and a handicap. The objectively defined impairment of structure or function is a *disability*. The loss of vision in one eye, or of hearing in one ear, for example, is a disability, but it may not constitute a handicap. The visual field of the person who is blind in one eye is somewhat constricted, and his perception of distance may be slightly impaired; the auditory acuity of the person deaf in one ear may be reduced a little and his perception of the direction of the source of sound may be measurably diminished. However, these inherent disabilities are so small and so easily compensated for that such people are not handicapped. A *handicap* arises from the cumulative effects of the disability and the personal and social consequences which have a detrimental effect on the individual's functional level (Wright, 1960). While this distinction may seem to be pedantic, and one which we may not maintain consistently, it is an important one. Not all medically defined disabilities operate as handicaps. One of the authors is color-blind; this is a disability but it has not been a handicap in his work as a psychologist. In his teaching of psychology he can demonstrate the determinants of perception and of the distinction between the objective and the phenomenal world in ways that a person with normal color vision cannot. On the whole, his disability has been more of an asset than a handicap in the situation in which he has worked.

A handicap must be defined in terms of the situation. A blind person is not handicapped in the dark nor in doing work which does not require vision. The person confined to a wheelchair is not handicapped on a bench job which does not require locomotion. Variations in physique and aptitude have meaning only within a given cultural and occupational context. A disability becomes a handicap when the lack of an aptitude or characteristic makes an individual, or is perceived by the culture or himself as making him, less able, less adequate, or less worthy. The person's handicap results from the combined effects of the limitations imposed by the disability itself, the limitations imposed by society, and the self-imposed limitations.

In this context, a person may be, or at least feel, handicapped by physical characteristics or aptitudes which are statistically and medically normal. In Olympic competition, the person of only normal physique may be hopelessly handicapped. The aspiring young opera singer may be handicapped by a good voice which is not superior enough. The facial asymmetry which would not handicap the average girl may be a serious impediment to a would-be starlet. Many people who think themselves disfigured and seek plastic surgery are physically normal (Nadan, 1962; Hill and Silver, 1950). An attribute may be handicapping, not because it is physically limiting but because it either adversely affects social relationships or operates as a barrier to achievement. Big feet and a prominent nose may be an asset to a male comedian but a serious liability to an ordinary female. A deviation from the normal is a handicap or an asset only in terms of a particular goal.

The intense interest in physical beauty in America makes even people who are statistically normal quite concerned about their own minor deviations from the ideal physique. Indeed, most people are quite unaware that the ideal is culturally defined. Society's conception of the desirable is a mixture of present or past cultural utility and of current values which manifest themselves in social stereotypes. Mass communication—television, radio, newspapers, magazines, and books—helps to inculcate, disseminate, and perpetuate the current conceptions of the ideal in appearance, build, and personal attributes.

Americans spend billions of dollars annually and invest tremendous amounts of time and effort in an attempt to bring themselves closer to the culturally specified physical ideal. They use foundation garments, bustles, brassiere pads, and shoulder pads, wigs, hair dyes, tints, bleaches and restorers, artificial eyelashes, mascara, eye shadow, and contact lenses (even colored ones), powder, rouge, and lipstick, artificial fingernails and fingernail polishes of many hues, built-up shoes, and facial and skin creams and lotions whose types—foundation, vanishing, lubricating, mois- turizing, vitamin-enriched, hormonal, precleansing, cleansing, and wrinkle removing—are limited only by the advertising writer's imaginative vocab- ulary. The billons of dollars invested yearly in these sundry devices and remedies, advertised as beauty aids, bear evidence to a widespread con- cern with a set of less-than-ideal physical attributes. Broadly speaking, all plastic surgery is cosmetic and is similarly motivated (Nadan, 1962).

The culturally limited nature of the ideal physique is becoming less obvious because of the increasing homogeneity of cultures resulting from increased travel and communication. However, the practice, in certain primitive tribes, of feeding girls large quantities of curdled milk in order to fatten them sufficiently to make them desirable brides, the removal or filing of their front teeth to sharp points, and the scarification of the body to increase their beauty is a far cry from the ideal sylphlike Amer- ican female figure with unblemished skin and intact, perfectly matched teeth. The saber cut on the cheek of the prewar German college student may have been a mark of honor, but the same cut on the cheek of the American college student is only a facial disfigurement.

The American ideal of beauty has also changed with the years. The hourglass figure of the 1890s gave way to the straight boyish figure of the 1920s, when the breasts were bound and compressed so as to diminish their prominence, and in the 1950s a fully developed breast became the ideal to be achieved, when necessary, by the use of padding. Each gen- eration of parents is disturbed to find that their children's conception of what is desirable and proper in dress and physique is different from their own.

Exceptionality and the Self-Concept

In most cultures, physique and general appearance are matters of con- siderable concern and may have a decided influence on an individual's self-concept. The effect of a person's physique on his behavior is more indirect than direct, being mediated via social evaluation and the indi- vidual's response to this cultural judgment. A person's level of aspira- tion is intimately related to his self-concept. The kind of a person he con- siders himself to be is an important determinant of what he thinks he is capable of doing, what he expects himself to do, and what he tries to achieve. A person's self-concept is, in turn, largely a product of other people's evaluations of him.

One's general culture, the important groups of people in one's life, and even the significant individual people with whom the developing individual is in contact, all contribute something to his self-concept. Other people are continually telling an individual something about himself, in many nonverbal as well as in the more obvious verbal ways. To take an extreme example: How does the congenitally blind child learn that he is blind, what it means to be blind, and that he is a handicapped individual? Obviously, other people provide him with this information. Similarly, the behavior of others may teach a disabled child that he is more helpless than his physical disability may warrant his being.

How other people react to one's exceptionality, then, may be more important than the fact of difference. Individuals can be more handicapped by their self-concept than by the disability itself. The significance attached to a difference may be more important than the fact of the difference. Rehabilitation workers have found that predictions of the outcome of rehabilitation programs based on the extent of the physical disability itself are very inaccurate, for the actual extent of disability is overshadowed by the patient's unique perception of his disability and his self-concept (Fishman, 1962). In other words, an individual's handicap is often disproportionate to his disability.

The Anxiety Level of the Deviant Individual

In addition to inducing unrealistic self-concepts and levels of aspiration, being disabled may, by inducing excessive anxiety about status, lower one's ability to achieve. The answers supplied by the important individuals and social groups in a person's life to the questions "Who am I?" and "What am I?" are never unequivocal. The exceptional child is likely to receive more conflicting answers to these questions than the more normal individual. What he learns about himself from father may not be the same as what he learns from mother. What he learns about himself in the home he may unlearn on the playground. What his teachers say about him may contradict what his playmates say about him. When a person experiences many confusing and contradictory evaluations of himself, his anticipations become ambivalent and his level of aspiration vacillates. His failure to find a firm and reasonably consistent answer to the question "What kind of a person am I?" produces inner weakness. He lacks self-confidence and becomes anxiously concerned about his exceptionality.

Thus the deviant individual is more vulnerable to anxiety than the average person. He is more threatened by the ordinary demands of his culture. High levels of anxiety resulting from such threats reduce his ability to cope realistically with his environment, and he tends to react impulsively, compulsively, rigidly, constrictedly, and fragmentarily. Such reactions result in a high incidence of socially inappropriate, self-defeating, and blind-alley solutions to many of life's problems. The individual develops defenses which unnecessarily restrict his activity, maintain his aspirations at a low level, and induce a minimal self-definition. The defense mechanisms serve to minimize the threat of failure and reduce anxiety.

The stigmatized individual sometimes tries to "pass" as normal, sometimes he withdraws from competition, and sometimes he becomes either defensive or aggressive concerning his stigmatizing characteristic. All of these reaction patterns are likely to be accompanied by status-anxiety.

The More Limited Range of Experience of the Disabled

Several categories of exceptional people are defined in terms of their limited range of experience or activities. The blind child has one avenue of learning closed to him, the deaf has another, the crippled child's powers of locomotion are restricted, and the mentally retarded person's capacity for profiting by experience is reduced. While these limitations can be compensated for, to a degree, the average disabled child does not have the variety of experiences of the nondisabled. And his more limited experience, combined with higher levels of anxiety, often result in a decreased flexibility of behavior and ideation and a less coherent approach to life situations. The person with a disability is more likely to engage in fewer and simpler activities and to function in a more limited area. Again, this restriction is dictated partially by the nature of his disability, but it is also partially the result of social attitudes and cultural expectancies. When any child has many things done for him, when he does not have to use his own initiative, and when his social relations are limited and stereotyped, he has less opportunity and motivation for free and adventuresome ideation and activity. When any child, disabled or not, finds more simplified and easier approaches to life's problems to be adequate, he is not motivated to master the complexities of a more expanded world.

The limitation of experiences imposed by a disability is, to a great extent, an index of the degree to which society has devised and provided compensatory educational, vocational, and social experiences for these people. There is considerable evidence that the social and personal compensatory and restitutive mechanisms available to the disabled child are often either underestimated or neglected (Wenar, 1953). 'As we have already suggested, the result is that the secondary handicaps become greater than the basic disability requires. Children who could learn to feed themselves are often spoon-fed, both literally and figuratively, for many unnecessary years. Socially engendered fearfulness and self-pity encourage a dependence upon others. Devoted but unwise care may similarly nurture helplessness and dependency beyond that dictated by the primary disability.

Visibility of a Disability as a Handicapping Variable

Historically, the original emphasis in the understanding and care of exceptional individuals was on the nature and extent of the basic impairment of organic structure or aptitude. The focus was on the extent of the sensory, motor, neurological, or intellectual deficit, and problems of physical care and rehabilitation were of paramount concern. More recently, the attitudes of the family, peers, and society, as well as cultural attitudes, feelings, and expectancies, have been perceived as equally important variables. Personal and social attitudes toward exceptional people often have little relationship to the physical mode or extent of the exceptionality; they are more closely related to such superficial things as the visibility or identifiability of the deviation.

Blindness and orthopedic disabilities have high visibility. Consequently these conditions have practically always been matters of individual and social concern. Deafness and intellectual deviations, being less obvious deviations from the normal, elicit less sympathy and understanding from the general public. Deafness, particularly if only partial, and mental retardation, when not extreme, are often equated with inattention and lack of interest or apathy. It is assumed that the partially deaf and the mildly mentally retarded could be normal if they would only try hard enough. The low visibility of their deficiencies delays identification and hampers the development of an understanding of their conditions.

While high visibility may help to focus public attention on a problem, it may also be a source of feelings of aversion. Social acceptance, particularly initial acceptance, is related to visibility. The differential significance of a scar or mark, for example, may depend on its location. A scar on the trunk is much to be preferred to one on the legs, and the latter is better than a comparable blemish on the face. A scar on a girl's leg is more of a burden than the same defect on a boy's leg. Facial scars assume great significance both because of high visibility and because tradition has long regarded the face as the mirror of the personality. Consequently, the facially disfigured are often regarded as deviant in personality as well as in looks (Hill and Silver, 1950).

Much effort is directed toward decreasing the visibility of deviations considered undesirable. The resistance occasionally encountered to the use of canes, crutches, eyeglasses, and hearing aids often arises from the fact that these devices proclaim the presence of a disability even though they diminish the accompanying functional impairment. Contact lenses and disguised hearing aids owe part of their appeal to their decreased visibility. Many individuals attempt to decrease the obviousness of a deformity by special clothing, gestures, or postures. For example, one mother put a large cap on her child even in the hottest weather, to hide his ear defect. Another mother had an artificial ear constructed and required her child, who lacked a pinna, to wear it. A person may try to show only one side of his face, to hide the defect on the other.

Among amputees, the cosmetic problem is often critical. Amputation changes one's appearance, both in the victim's eyes and in the eyes of others. The visibility of the defect is greater when an upper limb is amputated, and the amputation of a lower limb is more visible in the female than the male. Most amputees profit both functionally and psychologically from prosthesis. A part of the psychological profit from prosthetic devices derives from the decrease in visibility of the loss of limbs, although some people feel that the prosthetic device *increases* the visibility of their defect (Fishman, 1962).

The visibility of a defect is often an important consideration in making educational plans for an exceptional child. In the eyes of the parents, attendance in a regular classroom decreases the social identifiability of the deviant child.

Denial versus Acceptance of a Disability

The person with a disability, as well as those who work with the disabled, have problems in two related areas. One area involves the problem of capacities and aptitudes, abilities and disabilities. The second has to do with levels of motivation and the setting of realistic levels of aspiration. The problem of abilities and disabilities, as previously indicated, can be attacked with tests and other measuring devices. Medical, psychological, educational, and sociological testing instruments and rating devices make it possible to indicate roughly the extent of organic, educational, psychological, and social impairment.

However, the problem of establishing realistic levels of aspiration in the social, personal adjustment, educational, and occupational areas is much more complex. It not only involves the individual himself, particularly his self-concept, but also his family, school, and community—indeed, his whole society. The point of crucial impact of all of these social influences is the individual's self-concept, which is largely a distillation of other people's evaluations of him. Each person comes to conceive of himself as adequate or inadequate as he sees himself reflected in the evaluations of others.

Because so many disabled people's lives tend to revolve about their disabilities rather than their abilities, their self-concepts are often unrealistically low. Consequently, their self-expectations, levels of aspiration, and general motivational levels are unnecessarily diminished. Recognizing this fact, many people are motivated and encouraged by others to *deny* the fact of their disability. When an entire culture puts a high premium on a given ideal state, there is a great deal of reinforcement of behavior which conceals, minimizes, or denies the existence of deviations from that ideal. To associate with the normal on their own terms, to act normal, to compete with the normal, then becomes the ideal pattern of one's life. The person with a disability observes that the rewards in this world go, not to the person who accepts those limitations which are seemingly dictated by his condition but to the individual who either refuses to accept the disability as a handicap or who strives for the cultural ideal in spite of his condition.

Because of the advantages of being considered normal almost every person who is able to do so will "pass" on certain occasions. People with epilepsy under control, the hard-of-hearing person, and the partially blind can and often do pass for normal. Homosexuals, drug addicts, and prostitutes as social deviants, conceal their identities (pass) with the general public, and particularly with the police, but in various ways disclose their identities to special classes of people—clients, connections, pushers, and fellow-members. One solution to the problem of denial versus acknowledgement of a deviancy is to divide one's world into an in-group who "know" and a larger group within which the handicapped individual passes. Nonperceptible handicaps may be known only to one's doctor and immediate family. Those "in the know" protect the handicapped in his passing. Those sharing a common stigma often provide mutual aid in passing. Homosexual overtures are made in ways nonhomosexuals will not recognize. Ex-prisoners and ex-mental patients assist each other in concealing their previous status to people on the "outside" (Schur, 1965).

However, there are certain genuine limitations which are not to be denied. The blind person cannot enjoy the beauties of the landscape. The use of auditory cues is denied to the deaf. The trainable child cannot master calculus. To expect these people to strive for such goals is asking them to try for the impossible. To deny completely the existence of a disability requires that the person act as if the condition did not exist. And to do this, the individual, as well as those about him, must pretend that he is something or someone other than himself. He must become an actor, and acting for twenty-four hours a day is hard work. Concealment indicates shame and involves strain. Despite eternal vigilance and constant work, the person with a disability often cannot get away from his disability. The individual who either verbally or by his actions says "Treat me just like a nondisabled person, no matter what!" often finds himself in impossible situations.

For example, the blind host who elects to deny his blindness may be faced with the problem of pouring cocktails for his guests. None of the alternatives open to him permit him to act like a seeing person. The usual way for a blind person to fill a glass is to hook one finger over its edge and then pour until the liquid reaches the finger. In this way the glasses can be uniformly and properly filled. However, this method is not available to the person who is acting like a sighted individual; besides, some people object to having another person's fingers in their cocktails. Another method of pouring, which follows the pattern of the sighted, is to pour the liquid from a sufficient height so that it makes a noise as it flows into the glass. The fullness of the glass can be estimated from the change in sound and the weight of the glass as it fills. But this method is not very accurate; it is hazardous to pour from a distance without visual guidance and difficult to judge when the glass is properly filled. There is no possible way for a blind person to fill glasses as do the sighted.

Again, a person who is hard of hearing may try to act as if his hearing were normal. Such a person tries to listen hard. He must never say "What?" He tries to watch other people's faces and gestures for cues. In dimly lit rooms he pretends to be in revery or asleep. He develops ways to get people to repeat without actually asking them to. He invents humorous stories to account for mistakes which result from his failure to hear accurately. He fakes daydreaming, absentmindedness, boredom, and indifference. In situations where hearing is difficult, he talks all the time. Frances Warfield (1948) gives a vivid autobiographical account of these and other defensive maneuvers of the partially deaf individual who tries to deny his disability. A post-polio adolescent who denied his orthopedic handicap was Raymond Goldman (1947), who would swim early in the morning to prevent others from seeing his legs. When girls were present, he would not walk. When his braces were first fitted, he hated them and refused to wear them. When he was in the fifth grade he took his cue from a telephone repair man and referred to his braces as "tree-climbers."

One solution to the problems posed by socially devalued deviancy is to accept the reality of the deviancy but to deny the stigma, diminish the stigmatizing effect by pointing out the greater defects in "normals," or insist that the deviant individuals really possess special positive values. The Garveyites, the Black Muslims, and other black separatists have propounded a mlitant segregationist or secessionist ideology for the blacks of America. The black separatist emphasizes the special values, distinguishing characteristics, and unique contributions of his kind. He flaunts the stereotypical attributes such as color (black is beautiful), distinctive dress ("native" costumes and "natural" hair style), and articles of diet ("soul food"). The orthopedically handicapped sometimes develop the concept of the greater defects in supposedly "normal" people. The outwardly healthy and robust body hides an inwardly crippled and corrupt mind. The blind sees the normally sighted as having eyes but failing to see. They are blind to the real meanings and significances of the things they experience. People with normal ears are deaf to the pleas of other people. The socially devalued deviant may convert the stigmatized component of his self into a symbol of superiority. This effect can be facilitated by a derogation of the "normal" referent group.

The price of "passing" is high and the effort is often futile. When a person must constantly be vigilant in order to deny his disability, it becomes the central focus of his life. He may resort to partial social isolation in order to help conceal his defect and thus fend off possible discovery.

If denial is not feasible, what about accepting one's disability? The mental hygienists are insisting upon the virtues of acceptance of oneself as a prerequisite of mental health. But acceptance of one's disability involves a lowering of one's level of aspiration and a renunciation of many of the goals of the nondisabled. In a culture which places a high value on either the normal or the ideal, the acceptance of one's disability often carries with it an acceptance of a generally inferior status—a devaluation of the disabled individual as a person.

Acceptance of one's handicap includes the acknowledgement of the contaminated aspects of his social identity. The acknowledgement of the handicap implies acceptance of the fact that some of his attributes warrant his social derogation. If the person accepts all of the implications of his disability, he may so succumb to his condition that he becomes just as unrealistic as the person who elects to deny his disability. When the disabled person concludes, because of his condition, that "It is not worthwhile to live," when he tries "to go into hiding and never show his face for the rest of his life," when he feels so sorry for himself that he expects others to do for him many things that he can well learn to do for himself, he is succumbing to his disability.

Goffman (1963) points out the paradox that when the handicapped individual is urged to accept himself and either explicitly or implicitly is told that as a member of the genus he is entitled to full acceptance and respect from others as a whole person, he is also told that he is different and that it is foolish to either deny or ignore this difference. The normal's acceptance of the handicapped is always conditional. Satisfactory social relationships between normals and deviants is dependent upon the latter voluntarily refraining from "cashing in" on the claim of acceptance beyond the point that normals find comfortable. Positive relationships are dependent upon the implied promise that the extended credit of complete acceptance will never be fully used.

Goffman (1963) also shows that a previously stigmatized person does not attain complete acceptance as a whole human being following remediation or repair of his defect. The full restoration of function does not typically result in his acquisition of fully normal status. The change of status is from that of one with a defect to someone with a history of having corrected a defect, but the stigma of having been defective still persists. The "reformed" alcoholic and the "cured" drug addict are still perceived as more vulnerable and less complete human beings than are individuals with no such histories of deviancy.

Any show of anger by an ex-convict or an ex-psychotic is seen as a direct expression of his basic criminal or psychotic nature. A sarcastic remark to a companion, a heated argument with a spouse, or a sudden change in mood is perceived as a manifestation of his defectiveness. These same responses by a nonstigmatized person are seen as the normal reactions of ordinary people signifying nothing in particular.

In this connection it may be helpful to make clearer certain distinctions which have long been implicit and are now becoming explicit in our thinking concerning the disabled. Just as we found the distinctions between the concepts of disability and handicap to be useful, similar distinctions between *denying* one's disability and *coping* with it, on the one hand, and between *accepting* one's limitations and *succumbing* to them, on the other, may be equally helpful.

ACCEPTING A DISABILITY WITHOUT SUCCUMBING TO IT

How to accept one's limitations without succumbing to them is the problem. To accept one's disability and oneself as a person with a disability requires a clarification of what one can and cannot do. When this is achieved, the individual renounces the goals that are closed to him and devotes himself to the achievement of the possible. When a person is able to say to himself and to others "This is my limitation; these things I cannot do," he eliminates a big area of uncertainty and ambiguity from his life. He is now free to study the requirements of new or different situations realistically and objectively in terms of his abilities and disabilities. Acceptance does not require that the *status quo* be rationalized in a Pollyannish way as the most desirable, nor does it require a flight into apathy, egocentricity, or hypochondria. The disability can be perceived as inconvenient and limiting without being debasing, and the person can strive to improve his condition in a realistic way. Beatrice Wright

(1960) has developed the concept of the "acceptance of loss" very well. Interested readers will find her book very helpful.

One difficulty with those charitable agencies and individuals who are dominantly sentimentally helpful in their approach to people with disabilities is that they may unwittingly reinforce a tendency toward succumbing. Pity and charity, as approaches to rehabilitation, often do not focus on acceptance and coping. The more helpless and dependent the individual, the more he is worthy of sympathy, compassion, pity, and charity—but these may operate to reinforce his dependent behavior.

Secondary Gains from a Handicap

Despite the social derogation which disability entails there are secondary gains available which if capitalized on may result in making the handicap exceed the disability. The disability may serve as a socially and personally acceptable excuse for all of one's inadequacies, procrastinations, and disappointments. It can be used as an escape from threatening competition and as a way of avoiding social responsibility. Even the promise of limited success may be threatening. There is always the thought: "If I succeed I may then have to compete on equal terms for previously renounced goals. By succeeding I may be giving up a good excuse for not achieving."

The correction of a defect may pose problems for the deviant person who has enjoyed many of the secondary gains of disability. The correction of a disability deprives the individual of many of the protections and immunities previously enjoyed. The surgical repair of the cleft-lip, the operation that straightens the misshapen nose, the repair of the damaged middle ear which restores hearing, or the obtaining of a functionally adequate prosthesis may set the individual adrift from his previous anchorages and defenses. Much to his surprise and discomfort, the rehabilitated individual finds that life does not become conflict-free and success-laden when he becomes "normal." Deprived of his previous defenses, he may develop a set of more subtle, but functionally similar, psychosomatic or psychoneurotic symptoms.

Coping with a Disability without Denying It

The difficulties which arise from denying the existence of a disability have already been indicated. Concealing the disability does not eradicate it. The too strenuous striving for acceptance by others negates itself. Denial grows out of the individual's inability to accept himself, and acceptance of one's limitations is a prerequisite to coping with them. Having accepted one's disability without succumbing to it, the individual no longer needs to deny his limitations; he is free to cope with life to the best of his abilities. Coping involves making the most of what one has, and arranging one's life according to one's abilities. The person deprived of vision copes by learning to read and write in Braille; he learns to type; and he learns to use a cane or a seeing-eye dog. He acquires those skills which are open to him. He investigates and makes use of all of the educational and social facilities that are available to him. He does not disregard his difficulties (that would be denial) nor is he overwhelmed by them (that would be succumbing). But *how* to cope with one's disability without denying its existence and *how* to accept an infirmity without succumbing to it are two major problems of the disabled.

When the disabled person cannot get away from his disability, the question becomes one of how he can best get along with it. Overcompensating in the area of one's disability, even when possible, may drive the individual to outward success, but not to personal adjustment. It is only when a person feels guilty about his disability that he has something to disprove or make up for. It is only when one feels especially bad in one respect that he must be especially good in another to counterbalance it and thus disprove that he is an unworthy person. The successful person copes with the problems of status by engaging in activities in which the prospects of satisfactory achievement and personal satisfaction are greatest, rather than feeling compelled to do better in the area of his disability (in order to deny his handicap) or in a closely related area (in order to make up for his deficiency). For the person with serious disabilities to insist on competing and winning over the nonhandicapped may mean that the individual has not adjusted to his infirmity and is overmotivated to achieve in this particular area just to prove the extent to which it does matter—the extent to which it is overvalued.

Ideally, the handicapped person sees himself as a full human being, one who, at worst, happens to be excluded from a limited area of social or occupational life. He is not a type or category but a unique human being in the same way as the nonhandicapped. He should fulfill the obligations of the nonhandicapped as fully as he can, stopping short only when the effort required to overcome or deny his defectiveness increases his obviousness.

The Minority Status of Exceptional Individuals

Several people have likened the status of exceptional individuals to that of the disadvantaged minority ethnic and religious groups (Barker, 1948; Tenny, 1953; Wright, 1960). While there are many ways in which exceptional people, particularly those with disabilities, resemble certain underprivileged racial minority groups, there are also some significant differences.

The nondisabled majority tend to maintain a certain social distance, often treating the disabled as outsiders. Many normal people feel uncomfortable in the presence of a disabled individual. They find it very difficult to accept and mingle with the disabled as they do with other people, and since they have the greater prestige and power, they can restrict the opportunities of the handicapped. Nearly two-thirds of a sampling of college students stated that they would not marry an amputee (one leg), and half would not date such a person. Nearly three-fourths would not date a deaf person (Rusk and Taylor, 1946). The handicapped are thus often forced either to associate with each other or become socially isolated. They are frequently segregated—physically, psychologically, and socially. The disabled person, sensing social discrimination, gravitates to his own kind who can accept him without reservation. And, like a member of a minority racial group, he resents his group identification even though he feels more comfortable there. Noreen Linduska indicates in her autobiography, *My Polio Past* (1947), that she first resisted new group identifications by refusing to answer letters from her readers who had disabilities, but gradually came to realize that she had slipped into a different category of society (that of the disabled) even though she did not like it.

There are some advantages to identification with a group of similarly disabled people. Within such a group the individual is, to a degree, protected from the frustration, conflict, anxiety, and disappointment which might result from trying to compete with and to gain acceptance from the more able majority. Within the world of the disabled he may find understanding and acceptance, friendship and love, respect and status in a way which is impossible when he remains a marginal person in the culture of the more able majority. He is no longer motivated to act as if he were not disabled.

In the larger urban centers there are many organizations and clubs for particular types of exceptional people, particularly the blind and the deaf. In New York City, for example, the Union League of the Deaf rents an entire building for its use. The deaf publish their own journals and newspapers, own their own insurance company, and periodically hold a World Conference of the Deaf and a World Deaf Olympics. They have their own church and largely take care of their own social work. They have even lobbied *against* additional income tax exemptions for the deaf similar to those allowed the blind (Myerson, 1963). In this respect the deaf are behaving like many minority racial groups.

Some social and behavioral deviants develop subcultures, that, like the ethnic and racial ghettos, constitute havens where the individuals can live openly and with mutual support and insist that they are just as good as anyone else. Social deviates such as homosexuals and drug addicts may congregate in enclaves or live in small communities and take the line that they are not only just as good as, but actually better than "normals," and that the lives they lead are superior to those led by the majority. The socially stigmatized individual, by entering a subculture, accepts his alienation from the larger society, and by identifying himself with like souls claims that he is a full-fledged normal or even a superior human being and that it is "the others" who are not truly human. The members of the deviant minority are superior, and the only problem is the unjust outside world which unfairly labels and stigmatizes them. This type of adjustment is more available to ethnic minorities such as Jews, Amish, and Black Separatists and to stigmatized social deviants such as Bohemians, drug addicts, and homosexuals than it is to the blind, the deaf, and the orthopedically handicapped. The socially devalued deviant who is able to pass presents this fact as evidence of the absurd and contradictory claims of the normals who stigmatize him. The fact that he, the deviant, is able to pass proves that all their claims concerning his stigmatizing differentness are mere fabrications. Goffman (1963) points out that the deviant "passer" may delight in bringing conversations with the normals around to where the latter will make statements concerning such deviants which the presence of the unrecognized passer completely disproves.

The disabled, like disadvantaged ethnic groups, experience vocational discrimination. While it is true that the vocational outlets for the disabled may be realistically circumscribed, the restrictions are often extended to areas where the limitations are not inherently confining. Failure to graduate from high school, for example, may keep a boy from even being considered for a job requiring only manual labor; the absence of significant physical defects may be a prerequisite for employment in a company which has jobs in which many disabilities would not be at all handicapping. Unrealistic requirements close the doors of employment to many of the disabled.

And, as we have already mentioned, the disabled are subject to the consequences of group stereotyping. Like minority racial and ethnic groups, the persons with disabilities are often discriminated against on a wholesale basis.

Disabled people are supposed to feel and act inferior, and other people expect them to act accordingly. People see in others what they expect to see and resist modifications of these expectancies. The person with a disability who acts in a normal or superior manner is considered to be compensating or overcompensating for his inferiority. Each individual is perceived in terms of the presumed characteristics of the group to which he is assigned. Chevigny, in his autobiography (1946), indicates that when he became blind, people expected him to act like a tragic figure. They are disconcerted and disbelieving when a blind person insists that he is not a tragic figure. In the same way, people are disturbed when disadvantaged ethnic groups fail to act inferior and even indicate that they feel as worthy as any other group. People are expected to keep their places and play the roles dictated by cultural stereotypes!

Conversely, it should be pointed out that, unlike certain ethnic minorities, the disabled do not constitute organized threats to companies, organizations, and groups which discriminate against them. They do not man picket lines and create dramatic social crises. The disabled typically do not have the group support of others like them, as do the members of other minority groups. Except within the organizations found in large cities, the individual with an infirmity is often a single isolated individual among the more able majority, and unable to acquire the ready-made and shared reactions to prejudice and discrimination which are available to members of the minority racial groups.

DISCRIMINATION VERSUS PREJUDICE

Most people are not prejudiced against the disabled in the same way as they are against certain disadvantaged, racial, or religious groups, however. There can be negative discrimination without prejudice. Negatively discriminated behavior on the basis of valid first-hand experience is not prejudice. However, social discrimination on the basis of vicarious experience (primarily language), when these discriminating responses are the opposite of what would normally result from adequate actual first-hand experiences, is prejudice (Zajonc, 1968).

Much of the avoidance of the disabled by the nondisabled results from anxiety as well as from realistic evaluations of the consequences of association with the deviant individual. When a person has been repeatedly punished for being different, when his motor incoordination has had painful personal consequences, he will respond with anxiety at the mere sight of other people's deviant behavior. When being significantly different from other people regularly brings personal discomfort, the perception of differentness either in oneself or in others eventually arouses anxiety and a person may then avoid contact with exceptional people because of his own anxieties. The negative discrimination reduces identification and hence the anxiety aroused as a consequence of one's own social history. A person may intellectually perceive disability as a condition for which the individual is not responsible, recognize that the person is neither bad nor inferior, and yet be disturbed by his presence or his behavior (Bord, et al., 1968).

Similarly, a girl may prefer not to date an orthopedically disabled boy because she loves to dance. She is no more prejudiced against the orthopedically handicapped than she is against the nondisabled boy who either does not know how to dance or who will not dance because of religious beliefs. A realistic appraisal of the situation may dictate a negative choice which is not necessarily a prejudiced one.

There are also other unprejudiced bases for discrimination against the disabled. The average person has considerable uncertainty about how to behave toward the disabled. For many people, associating with a handicapped person is an ambiguous situation and even a threatening experience. The nondisabled will often check with each other to learn how to act with the disabled. Whether to help or not to help, how much to help, and when to offer help are recurring problems to the inexperienced. When situations are vague and uncertain, contacts may become stilted and formal. The awkwardness and uncertainty of social relationships with the disabled can be reduced by avoiding them or by keeping them at arm's length in formalized situations. One can also contribute funds to organizations devoted to the care of the handicapped (Eisenberg, 1968).

Of course, this difference between prejudice as displayed toward all members of certain minority racial and ethnic groups and the negative discrimination with reference to people with a disability is a relative one. They both have emotional overtones and both may be rationalized in a defensive way, but the social avoidance of disabled people is more likely to result from individual, first-hand experience and be less the result of a culturally transmitted stereotype than is racial or religious prejudice (Jordan, 1963; Lukoff and Whiteman, 1961; Smith, 1969).

A part of the segregation imposed on the handicapped is for the purpose of best providing for their education and training and for their protection, whereas the segregation of minority ethnic and religious groups is principally motivated by prejudice. The segregation of the handicapped into special classes, schools, and institutions is seldom for the purpose of limiting their contacts with other people, nor does it arise from the prejudices of the nondisabled. Handicapped people are segregated because this is perceived as the most effective way of providing for their special needs. One study found a positive relationship between people's tendency to feel pity for the disabled and their espousal of segregated facilities for the handicapped (Lukoff and Whiteman, 1961). This suggests that an advocacy of segregation for the disabled may be a manifestation of a desire to help, rather than a wish to minimize one's contact with them.

Activities designed to help the handicapped, but which may require their segregation, are socially sanctioned, whereas segregation arising from prejudice is generally condemned (Jordan, 1963). And where the isolation of ethnic groups is socially sanctioned, efforts to help these disadvantaged minorities are discouraged; whereas efforts to help minority handicapped groups, and thus reduce their segregation, are socially approved. Handicapped groups are seldom used as scapegoats by the nondisabled, while the disadvantaged ethnic groups are often so used. The disabled are infrequently manipulated economically, socially, and politically for the benefit of the more able majority, whereas minority ethnic groups are often used in this way.

On the other hand, the disabled are in a better position than are the ethnically, religious, or socially disadvantaged groups to manipulate government, educational, and welfare agencies, as well as sympathetic private individuals, for their own advantage. The handicapped are also more able to avoid responsibility, to fail to achieve in accordance with their abilities, and to obtain other secondary gains because of their disabilities than are the minority ethnic groups.

Providing Assistance to the Disabled without Demeaning Them

The perennial dilemma faced by those who would help the disabled or the disadvantaged is how to render assistance without generating dependencies. When a normal, socially advantaged, and emotionally sensitive individual has intimate contact with an organically impaired or socially disadvantaged person his reactions are likely to be a mixture of sympathetic concern, compassionate involvement, and social guilt, which he is motivated to reduce. Emotionally motivated and sustained nurturant assistance is likely to reinforce dependency and perpetuate a self-derogating role which the proffering of assistance implies. Self-humiliation and condescension are not constructive components of a helping relationship. On the other hand, making impossible demands and expecting normal or superior performance by a truly handicapped person makes failure and disappointment inevitable.

The attempts of the white man in America to help blacks have been caught up in this dilemma. When the white liberals displayed attitudes of tolerance, understanding, and acceptance of the blacks, when they overlooked or excused Negroes for defects and delinquencies that they condemned in whites, it carried inevitable overtones of condescension. The whites seemed to be saying, "These blacks are children. They have to go through this stage in growing to maturity, and so we have to overlook their deficiencies." This kind of talking down to blacks often results in needed help being rejected because its acceptance demeans the recipients. (Note that even "tolerance" has overtones of magnanimous condescension. We never speak of being tolerant of people who we think of as superior to ourselves.)

Many colleges are adopting "open admittance" policies for disadvantaged minority students. This policy admits to college and to graduate schools minority ethnic students who cannot meet the usual scholastic requirements. However, such efforts to help may become self-defeating if these students are simply moved up the educational ladder and graduated regardless of accomplishments. When such students are judged in terms of less demanding standards than are the more advantaged students, their inferiorities are confirmed and the special allowances do nothing to better their self-concepts or their relative levels of competence. Providing special tutoring and other aids to minority students also requires extraordinary tact and skill to prevent the recipients of aid from either feeling weaker and depending on the tutors to get them through or rejecting the proffered help because it demeans them (Smith, 1969).

The Differential Treatment of Exceptional Children and Adults

There also seems to be a greater discrepancy between the treatment afforded disabled children and adults than is true for minority ethnic groups who experience discrimination. Many handicapped children live in a more permissive atmosphere than do their more normal peers. They typically receive more sympathy, pity, and charity, they are free of many normal responsibilities, they are disciplined less rigidly, and their misdemeanors are overlooked more often. The special educational facilities provided them often shield them from excessive competition. They are rewarded for less than normal effort or achievement.

When they become adults, the situation often changes radically. The disabled adult is often required to meet, or even exceed, the standards of the nondisabled in order to obtain employment. Because of minimum wage laws and other employment requirements, the handicapped must compete with and meet the production standards set for the normal. The person with a disability may feel that he must even out-produce the normal person in order to prove his worth and make up for his deficiency.

Many employers who support summer camps for handicapped children, contribute to hospitals for crippled children, and favor special education programs for disabled children will not employ handicapped adults. Because of this, it is possible to train and educate handicapped children for positions which may be closed to them as adults. Because the educational world is more accepting and permissive than is the world of employment, it is possible for physically, emotionally, and socially deviant individuals to finish college and obtain advanced degrees but be unable to find employment either because of their real physical limitations or because of unwarranted social attitudes and beliefs.

The treatment of the disadvantaged minority racial and religious groups as children and as adults appears to be less discrepant than that of the disabled. Racial discrimination is probably more consistent educationally, socially, and occupationally. As long as the young child's contacts are largely limited to his own family, racial discrimination is not a part of his life, but as soon as he mingles with people of the dominant majority, the facts of discrimination impinge upon him. The total impact of prejudicial attitudes may not be felt until he grows older, but they are present on the playground and in the schools, as well as in the broader adult social and occupational spheres. Therefore, there is probably less difference in the discrimination against members of racial minorities, as children and as adults, than is met by the disabled.

The Extent of the Problem of Exceptionality

If, in addition to the exceptional individuals themselves, we include the families and professional personnel involved, the problems of exceptionality affect a sizable fraction of the total population. If we include within the category of exceptional people those individuals who become dependent upon others for special assistance, care, treatment, or education at any time in their lives, they will number in the millions and include most of the population. Such a broad interpretation of exceptionality would cover children who are born "too soon," people who live "too long," and those in between who, either because of hereditary factors or environmental influences, deviate in socially significant ways from the norm.

As advances in medicine and nutrition reduce the percentage of the handicapped who are either stillborn or die in infancy, on the one hand, and increase their longevity, on the other, the problems of exceptional people, and particularly of the handicapped, will increase. There are probably few people whose lives are not touched, directly or indirectly, either by physical, intellectual, emotional, or personality disability or by the challenge of the exceptionally able.

When the problems of exceptionality are viewed in terms of people's self-concepts and in a social-psychological context, they become even more extensive. This is a social world, and man's destiny is probably determined as much by what others think of him and what he, in turn, thinks of himself as by the characteristics which he "truly" possesses. Many of the problems of exceptional people are also the lot of those who, for reasons which may be quite invalid, *perceive themselves as handicapped or otherwise exceptional.*

It was noted earlier that many people who are statistically within the normal range perceive themselves as handicapped in view of their levels of aspirations and the groups with which they compare themselves. In addition to these, a large percentage of people who are statistically normal have, at some time, experienced feelings of inferiority about their physiques (Frazier and Lisanbee, 1950; Wright, 1960). To the extent that the adjustment problems of the handicapped stem from their feelings of inadequacy or inferiority, they are universal problems.

The child with sexually inappropriate physical characteristics has many of the experiences of the more extreme physical deviates. The late-maturing boy who finds himself considerably below the norm of his age group in size, strength, and general manliness often suffers from feelings of inferiority (Jones and Bayley, 1950). Similarly, the early-maturing girl who finds herself not only the biggest and tallest girl in her group, but actually larger than most boys her own age, experiences the consequences of a sexually inappropriate physique. The late-maturing girl may deviate just as far as does her physically precocious classmate, but she can still be perceived as cute and feminine, for it is sexually appropriate for girls to be small, and to be petite is to deviate in the direction of femininity. Conversely, the boy who matures early may be statistically as deviant as his late-maturing peer, but his precocity is in a sexually appropriate direction for males. He is perceived as muscular, athletic, masculine, and more attractive than the average male of the same age (Jones and Bayley, 1950; Sawrey and Telford, 1968). Whatever the context, the problems and challenges of exceptionality are of concern to everyone. Any discussion of exceptional children should be addressed to everyone.

Summary

A *disability* consists of the objectively defined impairment of structure or function; a *handicap* is the sum total of the personal and social limitations arising from the disability. There is no one-to-one relationship between disability and handicap.

Denial of a disability (acting as if it does not exist) is distinguished from *coping* with a disability (developing the most adequate substitute alternatives). *Accepting* a disability (learning to live with it) is differentiated from *succumbing* to it (being overwhelmed by the threat).

If the category of exceptional people is expanded to include all individuals who at some time or in some respect *perceive themselves* as exceptional, it will encompass almost everyone. The problems of exceptional people impinge upon the lives of everyone.

References

ASCH, S., *Social Psychology*. Englewood Cliffs, N.J.: Prentice-Hall, Inc., 1952.

BARKER, R. G., "The Social Psychology of Physical Disability," *J. soc. issues*, IV (1948), 28–38.

BORD, M., D. BYRNE, AND G. L. DIAMOND, "Effect of Occupational Prestige and Status Similarity on Attraction as a Function of Assumed Similarity of Attitude," *Psychol. rep.*, XXIII (1968), 1167–72.

CHEVIGNY, H., *My Eyes Have a Cold Nose*. New Haven, Conn.: Yale University Press, 1946.

EISENBERG, S., "Ethnocentrism and the Face of the Stranger," *J. soc. psychol.*, LXXVI (1968), 243–47.

FISHMAN, S., "Amputation," *Psychological Practices with the Physically Disabled*, eds. J. F. Garrett and E. S. Levine. New York: Columbia University Press, 1962.

FRAZIER, A., AND L. K. LISANBEE, "Adolescent Concerns with Physique," *Sch. rev.*, XXXVIII (1950), 397–405.

FREEDMAN, J. L. AND A. N. DOOB, *Deviancy: The Psychology of Being Different*. New York: Academic Press, 1968.

GOFFMAN, E., *Stigma: Notes on the Management of Spoiled Identity*. Englewood Cliffs, N. J.: Prentice-Hall, Inc., 1963.

GOLDMAN, R., *Even the Night*. New York: The Macmillan Company, 1947.

HILL, G., AND A. G. SILVER, "Psychodynamics and Esthetic Motivations for Plastic Surgery," *Psychosom. med.*, XII (1950), 345–55.

JONES, M. C., AND N. BAYLEY, "Physical Maturing among Boys as Related to Behavior." *J. educ. psychol.*, XLI (1950), 129–48.

JORDAN, S., "The Disadvantaged Group: A Concept Applicable to the Handicapped," *J. psychol.*, LV (1963), 313–22.

LINDUSKA, N., *My Polio Past*. Chicago, Ill: Pellegrini and Cudahy, 1947.

LUKOFF, I. F., AND M. WHITEMAN, "Attitudes toward Blindness," *The new outlook for the blind*, LV (1961), 39–41.

MYERSON, L., "A Psychology of Impaired Hearing," in *Psychology of Exceptional Children and Youth* (2nd ed.), ed. W. M. Cruickshank. Englewood Cliffs, N.J.: Prentice-Hall, Inc., 1963.

NADAN, R., "Facial Disfigurement," in *Psychological Practices with the Physically Disabled*, eds. J. F. Garrett and E. S. Levine. New York: Columbia University Press, 1962.

RUSK, H. A., AND E. J. TAYLOR, *New Hope for the Handicapped*. New York: Harper & Row, Publishers, 1946.

SAWREY, J. M., AND C. W. TELFORD, *Educational Psychology* (3rd ed.). Boston, Mass.: Allyn & Bacon, Inc., 1968.

SCHUR, E. M., *Crimes Without Victims*. Englewood Cliffs, N.J.: Prentice-Hall, Inc. 1965.

SMITH, M. B., "The Schools and Prejudice," in *Prejudice U.S.A.*, eds. C. Y. Glock and E. Siegelman. New York: Frederick A. Praeger, Inc., 1969.

TENNY, J. W., "The Minority Status of the Handicapped," *Except. child.*, XVIII (1953), 260–64.

WARFIELD, F., *Cotton in My Ears*. New York: The Viking Press, 1948.

WENAR, C., "The Effects of a Motor Handicap on Personality: I. The Effects on Levels of Aspiration," *Child developm.*, XXIV (1953), 123–30.

WRIGHT, B. A., *Physical Disability: A Psychological Approach*. New York: Harper & Row, Publishers, 1960.

ZAJONC, R. B., "Attitudinal Effects of Mere Exposure," *J. person. soc. psychol.*, IX (1968), 1–27.

3

The Care and Education
of the Exceptional

Although exceptional people are a heterogeneous lot, they do have some common problems. They all have certain personal, social, and educational needs which, to a degree, have been met in similar ways. Residential institutions of various types, hospitals, special day schools and classes, resource teachers, itinerant teachers or consultants, home or hospital teachers, vocational rehabilitation programs, day-care centers, boarding or foster homes, or sheltered workshops have been provided for most of the handicapped groups. Since these facilities and services are similar in purposes and administrative organization, irrespective of the type of exceptional people they serve, we shall consider them as a group, and thus avoid repetitions in the discussions of each of the special categories of exceptional people which follow. In succeeding chapters we will consider only those problems, facilities, and practices that are unique to the specific types of exceptional individuals under discussion.

Residential Institutions

The first facilities for the handicapped either were or soon became residential hospitals or asylums. Typically, they were built in relatively rural areas and often became segregated, isolated, sheltered asylums with little community contact. Now most countries, and all of the states of the United States, provide residential institutions for various types of handicapped children and adults—the mentally retarded, the mentally ill, the blind, the deaf, the delinquent, and in some cases, the epileptic and the orthopedically handicapped. These residential institutions are both publicly and privately supported and administered, and they may be administered at the national, state, regional, county, or municipal level. They range all the way from schools which provide relatively short-term care, rehabilitation, education, and training for the mildly handicapped individuals to schools which provide lifelong custodial care for the totally dependent. Sometimes the entire range of care is given within one institution.

MULTIPURPOSE AND SPECIAL PURPOSE INSTITUTIONS

Several types of residential facilities can be distinguished in terms of their functions (AAMD Project, 1964). One of these is the *multipurpose* residential institution. Such a facility may serve all ages, both sexes, all degrees of disability; while typically designated primarily for one type of disabled individual, it may accept many multihandicapped individuals. Some multipurpose facilities house those who are both blind and deaf, as well as other mixed groups of handicapped people.

A second type of residential facility is the *special purpose institution*. The first level of institutional specialization is in terms of the mode or areas of the exceptional individuals they accept—mentally retarded, psychotic, blind, deaf, and so forth. In addition, some facilities are restricted in terms of age (children or adults only), sex (males or females only), extent of disability (severely handicapped or ambulatory only), or handicapping conditions (sexual delinquents or psychopathic delinquents only).

SHORT-TERM FACILITIES

A third type of residential facility for exceptional individuals provides *short-term* diagnosis, care, treatment, training, or rehabilitation. Individuals of the following categories may take advantage of short-term care facilities: (1) those awaiting admission to long-term facilities; (2) individuals transferred from long-term public or private facilities who require an additional period of adjustment before release to the community (short-term facilities are usually smaller and closer to the local communities); (3) persons requiring temporary care during a period of family emergency or crisis; (4) children placed in a residential facility on a trial basis in order to determine if their families really wish or can accept their permanent or long-term institutional placement; and (5) exceptional children whose primary need is for diagnostic, short-term medical, surgical, educational, or rehabilitation services.

SOME INSTITUTIONAL MODIFICATIONS

There are certain disadvantages to the large residential institution for most exceptional children. Institutionalization involves the prolonged removal of the child from his home and community, and long-term institutionalization makes his later return to normal society difficult. There is an overemphasis on the disability in the institution where life revolves about one's disabilities rather than one's abilities. The excessive cost of providing good institutions and adequate personnel limits the availability of institutions. Various modifications of residential facilities have been introduced to overcome some of their disadvantages.

One of these innovations is the *cottage plan*. In this arrangement, groups of children (typically from eight to twenty) live with a married couple in cottages on the institutional grounds, in a simulated family situation. A second modification, less often used, is the establishment of *colonies* at some distance from the parent institution. In these colonies, groups of individuals live and work either on farms or on industrial projects under the supervision of a married couple. The colonies differ from the cottages in being larger (thirty to forty children), they may be at a considerable distance from the parent facility, they are more work-centered, and more often constitute a kind of halfway house between the large institution and the free community.

The Indictment against Institutions

There has been an ever-increasing volume of criticism of the large residential institutions dating from the 1940s. Of course, there were many investigations and exposés of prisons, reformatories, mental hospitals, and residential institutions for the blind, the deaf, and mentally retarded before the 1940s. As early as 1880 there was a National Association for the Protection of the Insane and the Prevention of Insanity (Alexander and Selesnick, 1966, p. 264) which lasted only four years. Several organizations such as the American Association on Mental Deficiency, The National Association for Mental Health, and the National Council on Crime and Delinquency have periodically surveyed institutions, pointed out their shortcomings, and drawn up specifications for their improvement. Innumerable local, state, and national committees and boards have done likewise. While improvements have been made over the decades, many people believe that there are forces within and without the large residential institutions which make their effective reorganization virtually impossible. Some are saying that they are beyond reform and should be torn down, that they are doing more harm than good.

The criticisms of residential facilities made by such people as Vail (1967), Goffman (1961), and Kugel and Wolfensberger (1969) have focussed on the dehumanization of institutional inmates. Although directed at something quite different, many institutional procedures depersonalize and dehumanize the inmate and strip him of much of his individuality. Institutional routines treat the patient more like a thing than a human being. As a consequence of the admitting procedures in which he is fingerprinted, photographed, undressed, bathed, deprived of many of his possessions in which he has incorporated many of his significant self-feelings, and the institutional procedures which deprive him of the opportunity to function in his most significant roles, he becomes largely a nonperson. The least personal of characteristics—height, weight, color of hair and eyes, fingerprints, social security number and ward number—become his significant identifying characteristics. The inmate is stripped of most of his sources of individual identity and many of the significant components of his self-concept.

The enforced routines of institutional life deprive the inmate of those things most uniquely characteristic of a human being—self-determination, decision-making, and freedom of action. Our large residential institutions have largely been placed where great numbers of similarly situated individuals live and work. They are typically cut off from the larger society, and the inmates lead a restricted and formally administered life. When humane treatment on an individual basis, on the one hand, and institutional efficiency and convenience, on the other, conflict, the institutional needs win out. When overcrowding and understaffing are the rule rather than the exception, individualized and humane treatment is impossible. In such situations, instead of people, whose capacities for autonomy and self-realization should be maximized, being ends in themselves, they become facilitators or hindrances to the institutional ends of smooth and economical operation.

Institutions providing for the education, training, rehabilitation, or custodial care of the handicapped are no different from other large organizations in the extent to which their operations become dictated by their needs for efficiency rather than for the maximum achievement of the purposes for which they were originally designed. Thus, it is better if inmates have few or no personal possessions to be accounted for at entrance and exit. It is easier if all clothes are pooled when laundered and redistributed not according to ownership or individual preference but according to sex and approximate size. Visits off grounds may be restricted or discouraged because of possible runaways or misconduct (with its attendant trouble and possible blame for the institution). Institutions rationally designed and organized to reform, rehabilitate, train, and educate may become efficient machines for realizing the internal needs of the institution and its staff.

The inmate is shaped by the institutional practices and eventually accepts and internalizes the institutionalized self as a mode of adaptation to his new environment. The behavior required or expected within an organization, without intending to do so, implies a conception of the nature of the individual inmate. The institutionally generated assumptions concerning individual autonomy and identity, the simplified environment, the single source of authority which limits individual decision making, the restricted range of social contacts, and the orderly prearranged schedules all contribute to making the institutional inmate less capable of managing his life on the outside, if and when he returns to it.

Present and Future Role of Residential Institutions

Because of the disadvantages of the large residential institutions for those exceptional individuals who will at some time return either to their own or to foster homes in the community, as well as the high cost of hospitalization, the role of these facilities is diminishing. They will undoubtedly continue to exist, however. On a limited scale, they will provide education and training for children residing in such sparsely settled areas that no other provisions are feasible. They will continue to provide for the lifelong care of the severely handicapped—particularly the multihandicapped custodial patients. They will become the principal centers for research on problems of exceptional children. They may also provide specialized clinics to which handicapped children can be brought for short-term diagnostic study or remedial treatment.

The residential institutions can also serve as training centers for such professional personnel as nurses, medical doctors, psychologists, social workers, rehabilitation specialists, and educators who desire to work with exceptional people. By sponsoring seminars, colloquia, conferences, and demonstrations, such facilities may assist in the education of professional personnel who are not working principally with the handicapped. The fostering and promoting of a general understanding of exceptional people should be a key purpose of the institution.

It seems to be the consensus of experts that most existing residential facilities are too large, that more special-purpose, smaller and short-term care facilities, strategically located in local communities, should be provided; that family-care services and facilities for caring for small groups should be used more extensively for individuals requiring intensive and prolonged medical and nursing care (AAMD Project, 1964). Since approximately 95 per cent of exceptional individuals spend most of their lives either in their own homes or in substitute homes in their local communities, more adequate programs need to be provided on the local level (AAMD Project, 1962; Greenblatt, 1960). Today the residential institutions are achieving a closer integration with other community programs and services. They often serve as centers which stimulate cooperation between related social, educational, medical, and lay organizations. They constitute information centers and provide specialized consulting and counseling services (Stevens, 1956; Alt, 1960; Giliberty, 1961; Bergman et al., 1962).

The currently favored residential facility for exceptional people is the *community hospital*. The previous isolation of the institution is thus disappearing; the hospital is now in close touch with the community and guides it in its entire program for the disabled. Such hospitals discourage the expectation of long-term hospitalization and dependency on the institution for the bulk of the disabled (Greenblatt, 1960). An increasing amount of the educational, therapeutic, and rehabilitation work and custodial care is being offered in such facilities as outpatient clinics, day-care centers, day hospitals, short-term treatment facilities, vocational rehabilitation programs, halfway houses, and various private and public educational programs.

Formerly, the large residential facilities provided most of these services, but more and more these activities are being taken over by the smaller, specialized, community-based centers. Several of these facilities provide aftercare and serve as a transition between the residential institution and the community.

Nonresidential Institutions

DAY HOSPITALS OR DAY TREATMENT CENTERS

Day hospitals have been used principally for psychiatric patients. Such hospitals are for those who need intensive treatment and who are able to spend their nights elsewhere—usually in their own homes. The day hospitals are less expensive than the usual residential facility, and they keep the patient related to home and community rather than separated and isolated from them. The first such hospital was established in Moscow in 1932. Since that time similar facilities have been established in many countries. In 1960, 5,000 patients a year were receiving care in twenty-six American day hospitals (Winich, 1960); California has established three such centers (MacMillan and Aase, 1964).

The day hospital reduces the likelihood of the patient becoming over-dependent on institutional life. Many individuals adapt to institutional life too readily. They feel secure in the hospital and become fearful of a return to their homes and community. The day hospital reduces this "hospitalization effect." Experience indicates that some patients respond to treatment more readily in a day hospital than they do in a residential setting which offers total care.

The day hospital also seems to incur less stigma than does the regular psychiatric facility, partly because the patients continue to live at home and partly because legal commitment is avoided (Kramer, 1960). Day hospitals must be in or near larger population centers and have adequate public transportation.

In addition to physical therapy, pharmacotherapy, and individual and group psychotherapy, there is usually provision for occupational therapy, school classes, libraries, and recreation. Occupational training or retraining is also offered in almost all day centers. Patients may be transferred to outpatient departments, halfway houses, day-care centers, or other facilities upon completion of treatment, or, when they do not respond or are judged to be too ill for the day hospital, they may be transferred to a custodial institution (Boag, 1960; MacMillan and Aase, 1964). The day hospital has been used more for adults than for children. One study reports that only 10 percent of the patients were below the age of twenty. Day hospitals have also been used primarily for the more seriously emotionally disturbed patients—the neurotics and psychotics (Kramer, 1960).

DAY-CARE CENTERS FOR THE HANDICAPPED

The disabled child who is either too young or too severely handicapped to take advantage of the special education and other training programs of the community often places a tremendous strain on the personal and financial resources of the family. When such children remain isolated at home they also lack the social contacts and experiences which are necessary for maximum development. To lessen the burden on the family and to provide some social contacts for these children, day-care centers have been established in most larger communities. Private day-care centers have been operating for many years, and publicly supported agencies have recently been established.

The original day-care programs provided physical care alone, but more recently self-help and socialization training have been added. Massachusetts, through its Division of Mental Hygiene, has established a statewide nursery school program for preschool mental retardates, and Delaware has a day-care program for the severely mentally retarded (Jubenville, 1962).

The advantages of day-care centers for the handicapped are: (1) the parents are relieved of the twenty-four-hour task of caring for the handicapped child; (2) nonhandicapped siblings will not be neglected because the excessive demands of the handicapped child will be diminished; (3) the rest of the family can live a more normal social life because the emotional strain is diminished and a more wholesome family atmosphere facilitated; (4) the parents may be able and willing to keep the child at home instead of placing him in an institution or boarding home; and (5) the training received in such centers may raise the child's level of functioning to the point where he can attend special classes, become partially self-supporting, or, at least, be less of a burden to others. The day-care centers for many types of the handicapped stand midway between the traditional outpatient clinic and inpatient hospital services. The day-care facility provides more constant and intensive supervision, care, and treatment than does an outpatient service. It combines care, treatment, and rehabilitation. In some cases, a single administrative organization may operate an inservice unit, a day-care program, an outpatient department and, either on its own or in cooperation with other agencies, provide vocational rehabilitation services (Pfantz, 1962).

OUTPATIENT CLINICS

Another community-based facility serving the disabled which is expanding rapidly is the outpatient clinic. Individuals no longer requiring the supervision and intensive treatment of the residential facility or the day-care center may report to an outpatient clinic daily or weekly, as required, and receive treatment or counseling. The community outpatient clinic may serve as a diagnostic center, as a limited treatment facility, and as a referral agency. Currently, nearly three-quarters of a million people are being served by outpatient facilities in the United States; in the five-year period from 1955 to 1959, during which the population grew by 8 per cent, there was a 32 percent increase in the number of people served by such centers (Norman, Rosen, and Bahn, 1962). Two-fifths of the patients seen in such clinics in 1959 were children. Between 1946 and 1962, the number of psychiatric outpatient facilities in the United States increased more than threefold, from 500 to 1600 (Rosen, Bahn, and Dramer, 1964). It is predicted that the future will witness still more significant changes in the development of comprehensive community-based services for exceptional people. Many such centers, to provide for all the needs of the handicapped, including preventive, diagnostic, and rehabilitative care and consultative and educational needs, are being planned.

FOSTER HOME OR FAMILY CARE FACILITIES

Most states provide some type of family care for handicapped children. Appropriate public agencies normally approve or license and supervise the homes and children involved. Children so placed can take advantage of community education and training programs, to the extent of their ability to profit from them, and foster homes or families provide a more normal and stimulating life than the average residential institution. This type of placement is particularly advantageous for the child who cannot live in his own home but who has the potential for living an at least semi-independent life in the community. Families providing homes for such children are usually paid by the state or county. Some families accept several handicapped children of a given type and operate what is, in effect, a boarding home for small groups of children.

Halfway Houses

Sometimes the boarding home is used much like a dormitory in a residential institution. In Wisconsin, for example, the handicapped from sparsely settled rural areas board in selected homes in communities where special educational programs are available (Voelker, 1958). An extension of the boarding home is the halfway house provided for older adolescents and adults, in which handicapped persons may live for varying periods of time preparatory to going out into the community entirely on their own. People residing in such facilities may be working in a sheltered workshop or on competitive jobs; they may be receiving vocational rehabilitation or simply seeking employment. The halfway home is typically an intermediate step for individuals who will soon return to the community following a period of institutionalization; but, like family care and the boarding home, it can serve as an alternative to institutionalization.

The halfway house, as an aftercare facility which has been used primarily for discharged patients, is designed to assist the patient's transition from hospital to community life. It is used for alcoholics, criminals, the mentally ill, and juvenile delinquents. It facilitates the movement of the individual from his dependent existence in an institution in which he received total care to the free community, by providing an intermediate situation—a more independent, but still relatively simple life in a supervised residential facility (Huseth, 1961). One state, Vermont, is establishing a network of such houses as a transitional facility between the state mental hospital and a rehabilitation agency (Wechsler, 1960b). The halfway house provides a sheltered social environment in which new roles and behaviors can be tried and developed. Most provide professional counseling and supervision (Wechsler, 1960a). The period of residence is typically limited to from three months to a year.

Similar facilities in rural settings are sometimes known as "work camp houses." In such settings, jobs are available on the grounds and the residents are usually there twenty-four hours a day (Wechsler, 1960a; 1961).

Vocational Rehabilitation Programs

All the states of the Union provide vocational rehabilitation programs for disabled adults. The public program of vocational rehabilitation had its beginnings in World War I, was started officially in 1920, and has expanded tremendously since World War II. This program is not concerned primarily with children, and we shall not discuss it in any detail. However, many state rehabilitation programs have recently been expanded to include mentally retarded and psychiatrically disabled adults, as well as the physically handicapped. Rehabilitation personnel are also cooperating with the schools. They take those individuals who either finish the school program or who exceed the age limits for school attendance and provide them with additional vocational training, counseling, and supervision.

To be eligible for the services of the Vocational Rehabilitation Agency the person must be substantially handicapped as a result of a physical or mental disability; he must be of employable age by the time the rehabilitation services are completed; and he must show promise of becoming employable or of attaining a higher level of vocational adequacy as a consequence of the service. These requirements limit the program to older adolescents and to those with milder handicaps.

The vocational rehabilitation agencies have no training facilities of their own, but purchase such services from existing resources. The financial help provided by this service has facilitated the development of training centers, sheltered workshops, and on-the-job training programs for the handicapped.

Sheltered Workshops

As the name indicates, a sheltered workshop is a facility providing training or employment geared to the capacities and need of people who cannot satisfactorily be trained or employed in normal competitive job situations because of special disabilities. Such workshops are found in public and private residential institutions and as independent endeavors in the community. Like the vocational rehabilitation programs, they are primarily for adults.

The individuals working at sheltered employment may, at the lowest level, spend their days in the workshop, keeping busy. Even with maximum assistance and supervision, these people produce little of economic importance, although they act like ordinary employed adults. The workshop serves somewhat the same function for these people that the day-care center does for younger children. The work done by individuals with greater aptitude—the "sheltered employable" group of persons—can contribute significantly to their own support. People functioning on this level may be partially self-supporting in the workshop, but they can probably never compete in an ordinary environment. Individuals with greater potential—the "deferred employable" group—use the sheltered workshop purely for training, preparatory to their placement in ordinary employment. On this level, the sheltered shop mediates between idleness and regular employment. The workshop is primarily a means of controlling the stress on the workers and of assisting handicapped people to increase their self-sufficiency. The shop often provides training in skills which can be used in other jobs; in addition, it may serve to inculcate general work habits, attitudes, and self-confidence which, it is hoped, will carry over to future employment even in different jobs. It is assumed that the disabled person in a sheltered workshop can develop a "work personality" consisting of such things as punctuality, cooperative work habits, ways of relating to authority, as well as favorable attitudes toward a job, a boss, fellow workers, and earnings (Olshansky, 1960).

People in sheltered workshops may make new things for sale, repair or recondition used articles for resale, or contract or subcontract work from private industry. Such workshops have long provided employment and training for the auditory, visually, and orthopedically handicapped and more recently, some workshops have also accepted the mentally retarded and the mentally ill. Many separate workshops have also been established solely for the mentally retarded or emotionally disturbed (Doll, 1958; Dubin, 1956; Niehn, 1958; Stevens and Blumberg, 1957; Zehnder, 1954; Blue, 1964). In 1960, there were more than 600 sheltered workshops in the United States. Over 100 of these were operated by one organization, Goodwill Industries (Olshansky, 1960).

Social and Recreational Programs

The handicapped child, like every child, needs a social life and recreation. The overprotection provided in some homes, the failure of ordinary groups and organizations to accept the handicapped, and the inherent limitations of the uniquely disabled make special provision for the social and recreational needs of the handicapped necessary. In communities where special educational programs, training facilities, vocational programs, and occupational outlets for the disabled are either not available or are very limited, recreational and social programs may provide the handicapped with their sole opportunities for social contacts.

While many handicapped individuals can participate in the regular social and recreational programs of the community, many others cannot. Recreational programs for the handicapped may not differ markedly from those provided for the general public, but it is often necessary to provide some special equipment, training, and supervision. In addition to regular, supervised playground activities and group games, these programs may include conducted field trips, day and summer camps, social groups, and clubs. The programs are often provided or sponsored by city or school recreational departments, voluntary groups and agencies, churches, the YWCA and YMCA, the Boy Scouts and the Girl Scouts, and similar organizations.

One type of cooperative self-help organization contributing to the recreational and social life of some types of handicapped adults is the expatient club. Such clubs were first started in England in 1940. By 1959 an estimated seventy clubs were operating in the United States, the largest concentration of such clubs being in California (Olshansky, 1962).

Programs of Home Training and Counseling

Most parents of handicapped children do not have the knowledge and skills needed to train them effectively. Yet home training services, although they are an essential part of a comprehensive program for the disabled, are available in few communities. The John Tracy clinic in Los Angeles provides information concerning home training techniques for the parents of deaf children; it conducts a nursery school for deaf children and special training classes for parents; and it has hundreds of parents enrolled in its correspondence course. Similar services are provided by the Chicago Hearing Society and Clinic. The Volta Bureau in Washington is another good source of information for parents, and it also teaches special educational techniques to parents of deaf children. There are similar sources of information and training available to the families of the blind. The National Association for Retarded Children, which has its headquarters in New York and has many state and local affiliates, serves as a clearing house for information about the mentally retarded. The United Cerebral Palsy Association, Inc., and its local affiliates perform a similar function for victims of cerebral palsy. The United States Children's Bureau in Washington, D.C. is a good source of information on all types of exceptional children.

The counseling facilities available to the parents of the mentally retarded and most of the other categories are still quite inadequate. Clinic staffs, private physicians, city and county health officials, social workers, nurses, and school personnel all provide some counseling and information for parents of exceptional children, but this is usually sporadic and not followed up. Most parents need and welcome assistance in understanding the significance of their child's condition and would benefit from more information and counseling about handling and training the child.

The exceptional person himself needs special counseling and guidance. Achieving self-understanding, establishing goals consistent with one's abilities and disabilities, and making realistic life plans are major problems in everyone's life, but they are especially critical and difficult for the exceptional individual. While there seems to be nothing distinctive and unique about the personalities of exceptional people, the handicapped do have more severe problems of adjustment and are thus in greater need of counseling. The evaluation of the aptitudes of exceptional children is difficult, and their educational programs are often different. Their vocational opportunities are somewhat unique, and the need for specially trained counselors is great.

Education of the General Public Concerning Exceptional Children

One of the greatest needs of exceptional people is increased public awareness, acceptance, and understanding of exceptionality—particularly of disabling exceptionality. In the first place, unless a substantial part of the public recognizes the needs of the handicapped, the disabled will not be provided with the necessary facilities, programs, and opportunities. Second, unless the general public understands the nature of the difficulties and the needs of the various types of disabled persons, even the available resources and opportunities may be denied them.

The handicapped person does not need sympathy and pity. He needs understanding and acceptance as a person with certain limitations. There is little use in training a handicapped child to become socially adept and aware if fearful and anxious neighbors will not let their children play with him. It is not helpful to teach him to play games, or to sing and dance, if he remains socially unacceptable. Occupational and vocational training programs are wasted if employers will not give the handicapped an opportunity to demonstrate their competence. As we mentioned earlier, many a man will send a handicapped boy to summer camp but not employ him when he grows up. There has been a significant increase in public awareness and understanding of the disabled, but there is still much to be done and too few agencies to do it.

Special Day Schools

Many large school systems provide special schools for certain kinds of exceptional children, especially the severely orthopedically handicapped, the socially maladjusted, the severely mentally retarded, and the multiply handicapped. The large cities, and some counties, often transport the eligible children for considerable distances to a school where special facilities and equipment are provided and where professional nonteaching personnel, as well as specially trained teachers, provide care and instruction for these children.

ADVANTAGES OF SPECIAL SCHOOLS

Some advantages of the separate day school are as follows:

1. The special school is an administrative convenience. It is easier for the administrative officer or staff in charge of special education to administer a single school or center than to supervise and administer a number of special classes held in different school buildings—or even in different school districts, which would involve administrative problems arising from dual jurisdiction and responsibility.
2. The separate school simplifies the control and supervision of the exceptional children. The extra protection and supervision required by many handicapped children are more easily provided when all the children in the school are similarly handicapped. When the handicapped mingle with the nonhandicapped in busses, on the play ground, in extracurricular activities, and in class, it is difficult to provide the additional or differential supervision and protection they require.
3. Providing a separate school or center for a given type of exceptional children makes it easier to utilize the aptitudes of the specialized teachers and other personnel. Individual teachers can exchange or combine classes for certain periods, and some departmentalization is possible. Team teaching is being used in some classes of exceptional children, and this is practical only in the special day school or residential institution (Taylor and Olsen, 1964).

SOME DISADVANTAGES OF SPECIAL SCHOOLS

Some of the disadvantages of the separate schools for exceptional children are:

1. The problem of transporting handicapped children great distances is magnified in the special school arrangement. Because of the rela-

tively small numbers of exceptional children of a given type, it is often necessary to transport children from over a large area, in order to obtain enough enrollment. The long rides on school busses are often a severe strain on the handicapped child.

2. Since the handicapped minority are going to live their lives among the nonhandicapped majority, some people think that it is desirable for them to be educated with normal children. The oversimplified school life of the child in the special school may not be the best preparation for later life.

3. There is often a stigma attached to the children attending the special school. This is especially true for children who attend schools for the mentally retarded, the socially maladjusted, and the emotionally disturbed. The families of exceptional children are often sensitive to the social implication of special schools and feel that special classes in the regular school, or even regular classes are preferable because they do not label the child and cause his life to revolve so completely around his exceptional characteristics.

Special Classes for Exceptional Children

There is a trend toward the organization of special class programs within the regular school, toward some degree of integration with the regular classes, and away from the special school organization, for most types of exceptional children. Separate classrooms for most types of exceptional children are often established within a regular school. The separate classroom has the required equipment, and the class is taught by a specially trained and sometimes separately accredited teacher. The special class often is self-contained, and it may be under different supervisory and administrative control from the rest of the school.

The alleged advantages and disadvantages of the special class over the separate school organization for exceptional children are largely the converse of those listed for the special school. Briefly, the advantages are: (1) the environment of the special class is more normal than that of the completely segregated school; (2) the special class is closer to the child's home and thus transportation problems are lessened; and (3) the stigma of the special class is less than that of the separate school. There is also the additional possibility that the special classes can be partially integrated with the regular classroom, when they are in the same building.

Conversely, the disadvantages of the special classroom organization are: (1) the partial physical and social isolation of the special-class students and their teacher (their teacher is often low man on the totem pole of professional prestige); (2) the greater cost of special equipment and facilities for a number of classrooms in different buildings, as compared with a number of classes in one building; (3) the inconvenience of supervising and administering geographically separated classrooms, sometimes including the difficult problems of dual administration.

MODIFICATIONS OF THE SPECIAL CLASS

Certain modifications of the special class have been introduced in an attempt to minimize some of the disadvantages of the separate, self-contained class for exceptional children and to utilize more effectively the special-class teachers, who are chronically in short supply. Two of these are the partially integrated class and the resource room.

Partially Integrated Classes.   Children who attend partially integrated classes are with the special-education teacher for a part of the day, and in the regular classroom with the rest of the children the rest of the time. This plan is more applicable to the departmentalized junior and senior high school levels than to the self-contained elementary classroom. The arrangement allows both the educable mentally retarded and the intellectually gifted, for example, to participate in regular classes in art, music, physical education, shop work, or home economics. They study more intellectually demanding subjects, such as mathematics, reading, English, natural science, and social science in their home rooms with their special teachers.

The Resource Teacher.   The *resource room* is a school room in which the special-education teacher serves the exceptional children only in the specific ways in which they need help. For example, the resource teacher for the blind can teach and provide help in writing and reading Braille, and provide them with the initial orientation and guidance they need in order to find their way around the school buildings and grounds. He will also see that the children are supplied with readers, Braille books, or talking books, as required. The resource teacher for the deaf can teach lip reading and provide speech training. The special teacher can serve as counselor for the exceptional students; he also serves as consultant and assistant to the regular teachers who have the exceptional children in their classes. He sees that the regular teachers understand the problems of the exceptional children and that they have any special instructional materials or devices which are necessary.

The partially integrated classroom and the resource classroom differ only in degree. In the former arrangement, the exceptional child is carried on the register of the special education teacher, and is her primary responsibility. The regular classrooms are utilized only insofar as the special teacher deems it advisable. In the resource room setup, the exceptional student owes primary allegiance to his regular classroom, his normal peers, and to the teacher of the regular class. The resource teacher is available to him and his teacher only when she is needed.

The resource room is used most widely with the blind, the partially sighted, the deaf, and the hard-of-hearing. It has not been found so appropriate for the other types of exceptional children. The partially integrated class is very widely used for practically all types of exceptional children.

The Itinerant Teacher or Consultant. The itinerant teacher typically serves a number of schools and assists the regular teachers and the exceptional students in somewhat the same way as the resource teacher does. Exceptional children who need special help are enrolled in the regular classes in their home schools, and their particular needs are met through the combined efforts of their regular teacher and the itinerant special education teacher. The itinerant teacher is used when there are too few exceptional children of a given category in any one school to warrant the employment of a resource or special-room teacher for each school, on the theory that it is better for the teacher to travel from school to school than to transport the children to a central location. Because of the small number of children in a given school, the itinerant teacher is likely to work with individual children and teachers on a consulting and tutorial basis.

The itinerant teacher program has been used most for the blind and partially sighted, and somewhat less with the deaf and the hard-of-hearing. It is rarely used for the other types of exceptional children.

Hospital Instruction

Children receiving educational instruction in regular hospitals are of several types, including (1) reasonably normal children hospitalized for prolonged periods because of accidents (e.g., burns or multiple fractures) or recurring attacks of such disorders as rheumatic fever or nephritis; (2) those suffering from chronic conditions (such as tuberculosis or congenital heart disease) requiring long periods of hospitalization; (3) those for whom observation, diagnostic procedures, and the determination of appropriate combinations and dosages of drugs require prolonged hospitalization; and (4) those bedridden, ill, or handicapped children who cannot be provided for in their home. Of these, the chronically ill or bedridden children are often referred to convalescent homes for long-term treatment or to institutions for lifelong care.

The hospital child population is varied. At one extreme, the educational aims may be to maintain teacher-pupil associations and to provide help and supervision to children who are working on assignments received from their regular home teacher. These children will be in the hospital for only a few days or weeks. At the other extreme are the children who, because of the chronic or permanent nature of their disabilities, may be hospitalized indefinitely and who will receive a considerable part of their education in the hospital. There are, of course, all gradations between these extremes.

The physical arrangements for the education of children in hospitals will vary from an entire separate building or wing used solely for school to a single "classroom" consisting of a teacher's chair and a student's desk in one corner of a hospital ward. Generally teachers are assigned to the hospital by the local school system and are under its administration. In small hospitals a single teacher may teach the children individually while in the very large hospital many of the children can be taught in classes.

Some of the more obvious problems of education in hospital setting are these:

1. The interruptions of the school program by hospital demands and the requirements of medical treatment
2. The irregularities of attendance at classes and the skipping of tutorial sessions because of the child's temporary incapacity
3. The necessity of cooperating with nurses, doctors, and other hospital personnel
4. The rapid turnover of pupil population
5. The emotional complications arising from the child's separation from family, home, and friends, and the child's anxieties about his own conditions
6. The tremendous diversity of the children in a hospital
7. The educational retardation and frequent low level of educational motivation of the chronically ill
8. The lack of vigor characteristic of the hospital population.

Home Instruction

Many school systems provide home instruction for children who are unable to leave their homes to attend the public school. The regular room teachers have always assisted homebound students by sending assignments to them and correcting their written lessons, and have often made occasional home visits. However, an increasing number of children who are unable to leave their homes are included in the regular public school program through the use of regularly designated "home teachers." Teachers trained to work with the handicapped are best equipped to provide education for such children. Such teaching assignments require training and experience with a wide variety of exceptional children, adaptability, and the ability to work and plan independently. Since such teaching requires the cooperation of doctors and parents, sensitivity to such relationships is necessary. Teachers providing home instruction need to be generalists rather than specialists. Normally they will teach many subjects, a wide range of grades, and many different types of handicapped children.

Some of the groups requiring home instruction are: (1) the physically weak orthopedically disabled children who cannot attend school because of the difficulties and strain of travel, or because transportation is not available, or because the building is inappropriate to their needs; (2) children suffering such severe cardiac disorders that they cannot attend school, but who do not require hospitalization; (3) children whose physical or mental health would be endangered by the excitement, infections, or injuries involved in mingling with normal active youngsters; (4) children who must remain at home while concurrent psychiatric treatment is provided; and (5) children with such frequent and severe uncontrollable seizures that school attendance is inadvisable.

In some communities, where the public schools operate educational television stations or where educational closed-circuit television is provided, television instruction can supplement the work of the home and hospital teachers. It is also possible for the homebound students to participate in the instructional programs of the regular classes via telephone hookups. This arrangement consists of a microphone and speaker unit in the classroom, and one in the child's home, connected by telephone wires. The homebound child hears the teacher and the children in the classroom and, by turning a switch, can be heard in the classroom and thus participate, in a limited way, in the classroom recitation.

Correspondence course work may also be supervised by a home teacher, but this seems to be done infrequently.

In 1958, almost a thousand school districts in California were providing home or hospital instruction for more than ten thousand handicapped children (Connor, 1961).

Some Assumptions and Principles of Special Education

Despite the great diversity of the special educational programs for exceptional children, there are some basic assumptions underlying them all. With millions of children and hundreds of thousands of parents, teachers, and administrators involved, there are, inevitably, wide differences of opinion about the procedures and details involved in the education of exceptional children (Hodgson, 1964). However, we shall attempt to summarize the assumptions and principles which seem to be basic to much of the past and current thought and procedures in special education. Currently, many of these are being questioned.

THE GOALS OF SPECIAL EDUCATION ARE NOT UNIQUE

The goals of education for exceptional children are, for the most part, similar to those for all children and can best be attained in much the same way. Special education programs are a part of the larger educational endeavor extending all the way from kindergarten to college, and to adult education and vocational training programs. The commonly listed purposes of education—self-realization, improving human relationships, developing economic efficiency, and fostering a sense of civic responsibility (Educational Policies Commissions, 1938)—apply to special as well as to other types of education. All education aims at the best utilization of one's physical and mental aptitudes in socially useful ways.

Special education attempts to provide exceptional children with educational programs equivalent to, even though different from, those available to more normal children. The democratic way of life implies a commitment to educate all individuals, and such a commitment requires that society devise and provide special facilities and methods which make it possible for those children who deviate markedly from the normal to be educated commensurately with the normal. Special education is committed to the proposition that each child should be enabled to learn as much as he can, should be taught to contribute to his own maintenance as much as possible, and should be helped to become as completely as possible a personally and socially adequate person.

SPECIAL EDUCATION IS DIFFERENT

Although there is a large core of normality in every exceptional individual, special education takes particular cognizance of the child's exceptionality. The exceptional child may be first a child, but he is also a child who is different. It is the difference that makes special education necessary. Because of the deviations of exceptional children, special legislation, special facilities, special methods, and special teachers are necessary. It is necessary to provide special transportation, even a bus with an elevator, wheelchairs, walkers, crutches, protective helmets, buildings with ramps instead of stairs, and parallel bars and handrails for the orthopedically handicapped. The hard-of-hearing and deaf require hearing aids, training in lip reading, auditory and speech training, soundtreated rooms, and large mirrors. The blind need special paper, Braille writers, embossed globes of the world, Braille dictionaries, Braille music, Braille typewriters,

Braille slates, and talking books. The child with speech handicaps requires tape recorders, large mirrors, and trained speech correctionists. In
addition to special buildings, rooms, equipment, and teachers, exceptional
children as a group require an excessive amount of auxiliary services, such
as medical, psychiatric, nursing, psychological, social work, counseling,
and teaching assistance. The classes for exceptional children are small—
typically from ten to twenty. Since all of these special requirements are
expensive, additional financial support—often state aid—is necessary.

Exceptional children require special teaching methods, equipment,
and physical facilities in order to meet their personal and social needs.
Special education aims, by means of these special provisions, to enable
exceptional children and youth to realize their potentialities for development as fully as possible, and to minimize the handicaps arising from
their disabilities.

SPECIAL EDUCATION ENTAILS SELECTIVE PLACEMENT

The various organizational plans for exceptional children—the residential
institution, the special school, the special class, the resource room, and
the itinerant teacher—all assume selective placement beyond that involved
in the regular grade and class arrangement. Such selective placement involves the complete assessment of the child, as well as of his social environment, by professionally qualified personnel from many disciplines.

Complete physical examinations and detailed evalutions by competent
specialists—ophthalmologists, otologists, audiologists, speech pathologists,
psychiatrists, pediatricians, neurologists, psychologists, and educational
specialists—are essential for the proper selective placement of many types
of exceptional children.

THE HANDICAPPED ARE A HETEROGENEOUS GROUP

The disabled, even within each category, are a decidedly heterogeneous
group and present a diversity of problems. The education of a handicapped group of children involves all the problems of a heterogeneous
group of nonhandicapped children plus all the special problems arising
from their handicaps.

SPECIAL EDUCATION REQUIRES MANY AUXILIARY SERVICES

The orthopedically handicapped often require physical therapy, occupational therapy, and periodic physical examination so that their braces,
supports, and crutches can be adjusted. Many exceptional children may
be under constant medical care and supervision. Periodic examination

and continual care of eyes and ears may be necessary for children who are partially blind or hard-of-hearing. Psychiatric and psychological services, occupational and physical therapy, and nursing are required much more by exceptional children than by their more normal peers.

The special equipment, additional training required for teachers, and the small classes make education of the handicapped expensive. However, neglect of the handicapped is more expensive than adequate training. The excess cost of educating these groups is returned, multiplied several times, as a consequence of their increased capacity for self-support. Society cannot afford the luxury of a large group of totally dependent handicapped adults because of its failure to provide the required facilities for their education as children and their vocational training as adolescents.

INTEGRATION IS RECOMMENDED FOR THE HANDICAPPED

The trend of thinking in special education is toward as much integration of exceptional children with the general population as is possible. This means that such children will be institutionalized less. More of them will attend some classes in regular school buildings. Whenever possible, the integrity of the family will be preserved and the child's contact with his normal community will be maintained.

The various programs and services for exceptional people need to be integrated. Currently there are a large number of public agencies, bureaus and organizations on the national, state, and local levels functioning independently of each other. Sometimes such agencies even operate competitively. The immediate need is for strategically placed, multidisciplinary organizations capable of providing a complete service to the handicapped of a given area. Since the bulk of the handicapped remain in the community, such programs should be community centered.

Integrating the Diagnostic and Remediation Services

Partially because of the close historical ties of special education to psychology and medicine, an excessive proportion of the available resources has been devoted to identification and diagnosis as compared with intervention and remediation. Wolfensberger (1965a) has documented the fact that in the area of mental retardation, diagnostic services are often overdeveloped in comparison to other available resources. Many retardates undergo repeated and redundant evaluations which, in many places, are available at relatively little cost to the families. Wolfensberger (1965a) describes one person in his experience who, in a five-year period, was subjected to eight complete evaluations. The senior author of this text, while serving as a consulting school psychologist, has been asked several times to make reevaluations of children when the records showed that they had already undergone repeated evaluations at great expense to the school districts. What was needed was not more test and other diagnostic information but some hard decisions as to which of the available remediation services would best serve the student's needs, or what additional services or combination of services could be arranged, adapted, or devised to meet the demands of these particular children.

Program planners are often very specific about diagnostic needs and elaborate and expensive diagnostic services are usually the first, and for years the only, resource to be developed. Professional people planning programs for the handicapped have traditionally accepted the medical model of diagnosis, prescription, and treatment. Within this framework, it is essential to make precise diagnosis before appropriate remediation can be applied.

Wolfensberger (1965a) points out that diagnosis is an activity which the professional neurologist, psychiatrist, and clinical psychologist have learned in their training programs. Diagnosis can be carried out in the office, laboratory, and clinic. In diagnosis the professional feels fairly adequate and secure. The diagnostician can marshal his findings, make his report with a feeling of accomplishment. However, when the professional tries to relate diagnosis to remediation in educational rehabilitative terms he finds neither security nor a sense of accomplishment. The rewards of "correct" diagnosis are immediate while the satisfactions of rehabilitative and special educational procedures with the handicapped are slow in coming and relatively small. Visible progress is in terms of months or years and not from one therapy session to another. The psychiatrically oriented clinic or the dynamically oriented clinical psychologist is likely to perceive the mental retardate or the sensorimotor deviant as a disturbed psychiatric case and in need of psychotherapy. To borrow an example from Wolfensberger (1965a): A mother of four children, the oldest still in diapers, really needs instruction in how to toilet train her defective child; but she is perceived as needing psychotherapy to help her with her feelings about feces.

If the object of diagnosis is the identification of service needs and the appropriate matching of service needs and the available service resources, the two should be firmly tied together. Preferably both should be within the same agency. The diagnostic services and the service continuum need constant feedback from each other.

Many agencies and clinics routinely administer elaborate diagnostic procedures, even when a preliminary interview would indicate that the service needs are relatively clear and are either available or totally lacking. When the service needs are clear and available a phone call to a volunteer agency may obtain a needed mother's helper to come for two afternoons a week to relieve an overburdened mother from the care of her handicapped child, or placement of the child in a day-care center if more prolonged and extensive relief is necessary. Providing regular visits by a public health nurse, enrollment in a class for the trainable mentally retarded, or referral to a sheltered workshop may provide adequate services when the nature and extent of the handicap are obvious or when previously obtained relevant diagnostic data are already available. If it is obvious that the handicapped individual's needs cannot be met, the only function of complicated diagnostics is to rid the staff of its feelings of futility by providing a complete case work-up instead of turning the case away categorically.

When diagnosis and classification are divorced from the remedial, educational, and treatment services available the former can become an exercise in futility. When educational codes and administrative regulations define eligibility for special help on the basis of psychological or medical criteria rather than in terms of educational needs, psychologists and physicians become dominantly involved in diagnosing and certifying eligibility. Because, in practice, psychological and medical clinical classifications often have little relation to learning disabilities, the limits of these supposedly discrete entities of disabilites are either stretched or contracted to bring them more into line with educational needs.

In practice, good teachers and administrators, as well as service-oriented psychologists and physicians, never let labels and artificial code limitations get in the way of providing for the educational needs of the children. Where only those children who meet the strict definition of a category can profit by the special services provided, rigid requirements are adhered to. However, when the defining and limiting characteristics such as extent of orthopedic handicap or etiology of a disorder are not essential to the purposes of classification (treatment, training, or education) the category is operationally defined loosely and flexibly. It is easy to mistake the products of our diagnostic and classification procedures for groupings defined by "nature."

The definitions and boundaries of special classes and their names should be appropriate and contribute maximally to the purposes of classification. Many of our educational and rehabilitative categories are historical groupings maintained for the purpose of defining and controlling administrative and legal requirements.

Wolfensberger (1965b) has shown how diagnosis and labelling can lead to dead ends unless they are tied to appropriate treatment or educational services. He describes a typical case in his experience which involves a fruitless series of diagnostic examinations and cross-referrals that ended with the boy still at home with no service whatever. Over a short period of time the boy, a mildly mentally retarded teenager, was passed back and forth among a regular school program, a special class for the mentally retarded, two state institutions for the mentally retarded, a state psychiatric hospital, a child guidance and residential treatment center, and the state vocational rehabilitation service. During this time he was judged to be too retarded for the regular grade placement, too emotionally disturbed for the special class, too retarded for the outpatient service, and too old for the in-service of the child treatment center. He was found to be too homosexual for the children's ward of the state psychiatric hospital and too young for the adult wards. He was not sufficiently mentally retarded for the state institutions for the retarded and too effeminate for the programs of the state vocational rehabilitation service. Six of the facilities recorded the case as a successful close-out, and all considered him a successfully terminated case since each referral was considered to have been appropriate. The senior author of this book contrasts such cases with the situation he encountered in 1967 when visiting the facilities for the mentally retarded in Holland.

In southwestern Holland thirteen service facilities for the mentally retarded had combined to form "Samivoz," the Dutch abbreviation of cooperating establishments for mental deficients. The entire cooperating group provided a range of services from occupational training provided in workshops, farms, nurseries, dairies, and truck gardens through educational facilities for the educable mentally retarded, the blind mentally retarded, the deaf mentally retarded, and the "doubly handicapped" (mostly orthopedically handicapped and mentally retarded) to day-care. Services were provided for all individuals above the age of two. A central coordinating and cooperative purchasing center was maintained at 's-Hertogenbosch and an observation-clinic was recently established at Oisterwik.

The observation-clinic was really the diagnostic classification center for the entire group of institutions. While visiting these facilities the writer was impressed with their commitment to providing care, education, and training for all the mentally retarded within their service area who needed such services and the close tie-up provided between diagnosis on the one hand, and the educational, rehabilitative, and vocational training services on the other.

The aim of the diagnostic clinic was to see that each child received the most appropriate care, treatment, training, and education possible within the range of services provided by any or all of the cooperating agencies. Although the observation-clinic was a centralized facility, all of the clinic staff members regularly visited and rendered services to the other agencies. These services consisted of reevaluations of children assigned to the various facilities and systematic follow-ups of the children.

Such contacts kept the clinic staff members in touch with the specific possibilities and limitations of the various establishments so that the most appropriate assignments could be made.

The writer was also impressed with the extensive treatment services provided within the clinic itself. In addition to offering the diagnostic and classification services of physicians, psychiatrists, neurologists, biochemist, psychologists, and "orthopedagogues," a kindergarten and special school was operated. Physiotherapists, occupational therapists, and speech therapists were also a part of the clinic staff. A special course for training nurses for work in facilities for the mentally retarded was also provided.

The close relation between diagnosis and service was evident both within the clinic and between the clinic and its cooperating institutions. Within the clinic the children were placed in the most appropriate service departments while undergoing observation and diagnosis not only because the service was considered to be appropriate to their treatment but also because their response to treatment was an integral part of the diagnostic procedure. Occasionally following diagnosis a child was kept indefinitely in the observation-clinic center when it was decided that the center had services which were more appropriate for the child's needs than those provided by any of the other institutions.

On one occasion, the writer asked how long children were kept at the observation clinic. He was told that some children had been there as long as three years. When he asked if that wasn't a long time for a short-term diagnostic-classification center he was told that there were no rigid time limits imposed and that they could keep individuals indefinitely at their discretion. It seemed that the children were kept there because the facilities and services available at the clinic met their unique needs better than did those of any of the other cooperating establishments. When asked how long they would keep such children the answer was, "Until we find a more appropriate place for them."

Such a circumstance seems far removed from the situation often found in the United States where diagnosis, instead of leading to the most appropriate service available, often results only in a frustrating series of fruitless cross-referrals as typified by a case recorded in the literature (Krush, 1964) of a boy being passed back and forth among eighteen different physicians, four teachers, two mental health clinics, two hospitals, one chiropractor, and seven different schools. Following this, the boy became increasingly "uncooperative, untidy, and disturbed." The parents stated that "not even the worst prognosis he had received in all our long years of searching for help had prepared us for this." Similar comparisons between other European and American programs have been made by Wolfensberger (1965b).

Diagnosis and classification must be relevant to the needs of the individual child and to the care, treatment, rehabilitative, training, and educational facilities available. The real test of diagnostic procedures and schemes of classification is how well they serve the individuals involved. If the procedures merely provide more sophisticated labels for the child's conditions, they are not useful. Redundant diagnostic labels with no operational utility are typified by an in-house joke going the rounds of professional psychological personnel that goes as follows:

> *Teacher to psychologist*: "Please take a look at Henry. He is very withdrawn and avoids all contacts with other people. He also is unable to read or perform simple arithmetic calculations."
>
> *Two weeks later: Psychologist to teacher*: "It was a good thing you referred Henry to the clinic. We have found him to be autistic as well as being dyslectic and dyscalculic."
>
> *Teacher*: "That sounds terrible. What does it mean?"
>
> *Psychologist*: "Well, it means that you will find him to be withdrawn and to avoid other people. You will also find that he can neither read nor do arithmetic."

In America, as elsewhere, diagnostic and service progress are being more closely integrated and both are shifting from uncoordinated and piecemeal affairs to a full circle of facilities and services constituting a comprehensive, integrated program covering the entire chronological age range from birth to death and the whole spectrum of disabilities. These services are increasingly designed to make it possible for more of the disabled to remain in their homes and communities with minimal segregation and without becoming the ward of state.

The Administration of Special Educational Services

In the larger school system with special educational programs, there is a variety of special education administrative patterns. Most of these follow either the old classical *line* or *staff* form of organization. In the *staff* setup, the special education supervisor or coordinator has supervisory staff relations with the personnel involved in educating exceptional children. The special education leader is directly responsible to the administrative head, usually the superintendent or district superintendent. The special education department is an operational rather than an administrative division in the staff arrangement. Administrative responsibility for the special education programs remains with the district or assistant superintendents. In the *line* administrative organization, the special education head may be an assistant superintendent. Principals, vice-principals of the special schools, supervisors of special education, and the teaching personnel hold responsibility under him.

Authorities in the field do not agree about which is the preferred form of administrative organization (Hodgson, 1964). In the absence of objective data, most studies of the administration of special education programs have been surveys of current practices and opinions. In one such study, a questionnaire was sent to 48 state departments of education, 26 universities having a department of special education headed by a director or coordinator, and 117 professors of school administration in colleges and universities throughout the United States. The findings indicated a high level of agreement on the following points:

1. The special education program should be the responsibility of a department of special education.
2. The following categories of students, classes, and services should be the direct responsibility of such a department: the blind, partially sighted, deaf, hard-of-hearing; cerebral palsied, orthopedically handicapped, mentally retarded, chronically ill, and emotionally or socially disturbed; lip reading, speech correction, and hospital and home teaching.
3. The final authority for pupil placement should be an educator, rather than medical, psychiatric, or psychological personnel.
4. A centralized pupil placement plan is desirable for the larger school systems.
5. With the exception of the mentally retarded group, exceptional children should be included in the regular elementary school's age promotion plan.
6. Principals of special-education schools should have a special education credential.

No single administrative framework was favored by a majority of the respondents (Los Angeles City School Districts, 1960).

The Exceptional Child in the Regular Classroom

Despite the existence of a wide array of special educational facilities and services for exceptional children, a large percentage of such children are still the primary responsibility of the regular classroom teacher. Since the current tendency is to increase rather than decrease their number, this arrangement will probably continue. The teacher of a regular class which also contains a number of exceptional children is, in many ways, confronted with a bigger problem than is the teacher of a special class. Although the need is great, it is hard to offer specifically relevant information and recommendations. To a large extent, the suggestions offered are primarily good general teaching procedures. Recommendations concern the individuation of instruction, flexibility of programming, the acceptance of and respect for each child as a person, the fostering of independence, the maximum integration of the child into regular classroom activities, counseling, parent-school cooperation, and the use of other auxiliary disciplines—and these are good educational practices for all children, normal as well as exceptional. The only difference is that the exceptional child has a greater need for exceptional instructional procedures and requires a wider variety of special facilities, skills, and practices.

To insure full acceptance of and respect for the handicapped child requires more than giving him the freedom and opportunity to earn them through his own efforts. For example, it is often desirable for blind and crippled children to visit the school before the first day of instruction, in order to learn the physical layout and plan how to get from place to place. It is often necessary to prepare the other children to accept and work with the child who is markedly deviant from the others. The other children may need guidance and instruction about whether or not to help him. If help is indicated, they need to be told how much to help, and in what ways to offer and give it. Moreover, the enrollment of a handicapped child in a regular classroom for the first time constitutes either a threat or a challenge to the average teacher. The teacher is also often uncertain about how to handle the child. She is not sure how to maintain a classroom atmosphere that will recognize and make allowance for the child's genuine limitations without fostering overdependence.

The presence of exceptional children in a classroom requires extra planning and ingenuity. The need for conferences with parents, for making use of representatives of other disciplines—general medicine, psychiatry, psychology, social work, nursing, and counseling—is greater. When resource teachers, consultants, or itinerant teachers are available, they constitute the primary sources of assistance and advice. When none of these are available, the teacher will have to turn to his supervisor, principal, or coordinator for assistance. In the absence of any school or community assistance, the isolated teacher will have to turn to his state department of education, the United States Office of Education, and the various agencies, public and private, state and national, which supply information and assistance to people working with exceptional children.

Not all teachers are temperamentally suited to work with the extremely exceptional children. Where there is an alternative, exceptional children should not be thrust upon teachers who are unable to accept them fully. Consultations with the parents, other professional personnel, and prior teachers will help the inexperienced teacher in his initial planning for the child.

Since the special classes are usually less than half the size of the regular classes, it would seem reasonable for a class to be reduced in size when it contains exceptional children with special needs. At times it is advisable to place the handicapped child with a slightly younger group, whose expectations may be more consistent with his potentialities. When a disabled child needs regular assistance of a rather specific type, a "buddy system" may be used—that is, a classmate is assigned to each of the handicapped to render assistance when needed. Such a system obviously requires care in the selection of the assistants and the permission of all concerned, including the parents of the children.

Nonprofessional teaching assistants have been used successfully with special classes for exceptional children (Cruickshank, 1967). Such assistants might help teachers who have a few exceptional children enrolled in their regular classes. Assistants typically relieve the teacher of some of the more routine nonteaching duties, such as taking attendance, keeping records, making reports, supervising playgrounds, and taking charge of bank deposits and milk money, making it possible for the teacher to devote more time to the professional task of teaching. In some cases, the assistant may assume some responsibility for teaching some of the exceptional children. If the instructional tasks cannot be delegated to the assistants, they can prepare and take care of equipment, help take care of the physical needs of the handicapped, and provide special supervision as required. Such teaching assistants may be paid employees or volunteers.

It seems probable that in the future the self-contained special classroom or school for children with deviant educational needs will become less common. People specializing in the education of the special categories of the handicapped will still be needed, but they will be going into the regular classrooms as resource people to assist the regular teachers work with the children who have special needs and will no longer be segregated in special classrooms.

No matter how many special classes we provide, and no matter where we draw our diagnostic lines for removal of individuals from the regular classes, there will always remain a large number of borderline deviant children in need of special help. The regular educational services will always be required to provide programs appropriate to a wide range of deviant children. The only question is how much heterogeneity within the regular classroom is consistent with providing for individual differences.

Providing an ever-increasing number and variety of special classes may even retard changes needed in the regular curriculum and teaching methods to meet the large range of individual differences in a class of normal children. The availability of special programs may result in the teachers attempting to get rid of all the children who do not fit the regular program rather than changing the program to fit the children.

Placement of children in special classes may unfortunately be perceived as the solution to all difficult educational problems. Special class placement does not, in itself, solve any problems. It may simply shift the problem from one location to another. If the special class only provides a more tolerant teacher, a lower teacher-student ratio, and more individualization of instruction, these can be provided in the regular classroom. The existence of a large range of special services may permit the teacher in the regular classroom to shift the responsibility for providing for the needs of all deviant children and for all problems of classroom management to someone else. When there are available a broad spectrum of special programs and a wide array of psychologists, psychiatrists, physicians, counselors, supervisors, and social workers, the solution to every classroom-management, teaching-learning, and personal-social problem may be to turn it over to the proper specialist or refer the child to the appropriate special program. No class is ever homogeneous and the problem posed by children with a wide range of individual differences will always require the ingenuity of a good teacher to deal with them.

The increasing humanistic emphasis in the culture, extensions of the civil rights movements, and the implications of several court rulings will all contribute to a decrease in the special class and special school placement of exceptional children. Civil rights workers have pointed out that in a school population containing socially disadvantaged ethnic groups, homogeneous grouping on the basis of conventional measures of aptitude or achievement results in de facto segregation. The courts have held that the track system should be abolished because it discriminates against the racially or economically disadvantaged and therefore is in violation of the Fifth Amendment of the Constitution of the United States. While these rulings referred to teaching and homogeneous grouping within regular school grades, special schools and classes are clearly a form of homogeneous grouping and involve the same type of discrimination.

One may object to the courts' dictating educational practices. We can also argue that to deny a child the benefits of a special high-cost program, taught by a highly trained teacher, in a class not of thirty or forty but of ten or twelve, where a lot of individual instruction is possible, and to require him instead to remain in the regular class where he has made no visible progress for several years because he is racially or culturally disadvantaged is also discrimination and in violation of the Fifth Amendment. To provide these special advantages for the genetically or organically impaired upper- or middle-class child and deny them to the equally handicapped, ethnically disadvantaged child because the latter's disabilities were, at some point in time, preventable is hardly social justice or sound educational practice. However, the issue is not quite this clear cut. In practice, it has been very difficult to prove the greater efficacy of the special class or school as compared with regular class placement for exceptional children.

Similar people are segregated in special institutions, schools, and classes for a variety of reasons. Some individuals are placed in institutions because they constitute intentional dangers to innocent people or in punishment for their willful misdeeds. Prisons are institutions of this type. Other people are forcibly segregated because they constitute unintentioned threats to other people. Psychotics and typhoid carriers are members of this category. However, mentally ill individuals and people with contagious diseases are hospitalized partially for their own good; they may harm themselves as well as others. We also provide treatment for their ailments. Finally, large groups of people are placed in partially or completely segregated facilities primarily for their own good. The presence of such people in the general population poses no intentional or unintentional threat to others. Residential institutions, special schools, and classes for the blind, deaf, orthopedically handicapped, emotionally disturbed, educationally handicapped, mentally retarded, and culturally disadvantaged children are in this last category.

In practice, the distinctions among the three categories listed above are not as clear as our characterization suggests. Although the ethical and moral overtones and official stigmatization are most extreme in criminal behavior, they are found to lesser degrees in our evaluations of people with physical deformities, blemished personalities, and behavioral or intellectual deficits. Some degrees of personal guilt and social shame are almost universal components of socially devalued deviancy. Our conceptualizations and treatment of the mentally ill and mentally retarded have typically fallen about midway between those of convicts and normal students. Like the criminal, the institutionalized psychotic and mentally retarded person is forcibly segregated with like deviants. He is deprived of his personal possessions, and experiences a kind of "civil death." He cannot vote, hold public office, or be employed in many places.

Children placed in special classes for educational purposes are segregated "for their own good." These specialized, high-cost programs are designed to provide for the unique educational needs of deviant children so as to reduce the extent of their handicap and make it possible for them to more nearly realize their potential. Most of the people concerned with selecting children and certifying their eligibility for placement in special facilities and programs are reasonably competent, well-intentioned people who are sincerely interested in providing deviant children with the best possible education for them.

However, in practice, there are many informal and unacknowledged selective factors operative in the actual placement of children in special education classes. Children certified as eligibles by committees who screen candidates for special class or special school placement are almost universally referred by teachers initially. Children referred as possibly mentally retarded, educationally handicapped, neurologically impaired, or emotionally disturbed are so nominated for a variety of reasons. For example, a child technically within one of these categories has an increased probability of being referred for possible removal from the regular class if, in addition to his primary disability, he is also male rather than female, socially lower- rather than middle- or upper-class, colored rather than white, and hyperactive or delinquent rather than docile and well-behaved. Practically every school system has more equally handicapped children in the regular classes with no special provision for their education than they have enrolled in their special classes or schools. The likelihood of a child also being transferred back into a regular class from the special class or schools decreases as the child has an increasing number of these same socially devalued identifying characteristics.

While the rationale for referring children for special class placement is that special placement is in the child's best interests, it is often done to favor the teacher by removing some of the tensions and pressures placed on the regular class and teacher. Anyone who has served on special education screening committees is well aware of the many situations in which the alternatives posed by the referring teacher are, "Either he goes or I go"; and the "he" is most often male, culturally disadvantaged, colored, overaggressive, and disruptive of class routines, in addition to the primary characteristic that technically qualifies him for special class or special school placement. Research studies have documented the operation of such accessory selective factors.

One study of 749 sixth and seventh grade children who were placed in three different lanes, on the assumption that such homogeneous grouping enhances learning, showed that placement in and shifting from one lane to another was significantly related to the socioeconomic level of the child's family. When standardized achievement and aptitude test scores were used to determine the correctness of placements in the various lanes, errors in placement were found to be definitely social class related. Among all students technically qualified by aptitude and performance for the superior lane, only one out of five (20%) upper socioeconomic children placed in a lower lane, one in four (25%) children from the middle socioeconomic level were in a lower lane, while half (50%) of the children from the lowest socioeconomic level were in a lane below that indicated by their test performances. In contrast, out of the entire group qualified by test scores for the lowest lane, one-third of the middle-class children were placed above that level, while only one-seventh of the lower socioeconomic children were misplaced upward.

During the year corrections in assignments to lanes were made on recommendation of the teachers. Of the changes made, 93 percent of the changes of the upper-class children were upward changes, while 68 and 61 percent of middle- and lower-class children changes were upward. These differences are magnified beyond their apparent size by the disproportionate number (over two times the number) of lower-class children initially placed *below* their appropriate lane. (Brookover, Leu, and Kariger, 1969). Passow, (1967) has confirmed these general findings in another study. Children are placed in learning groups for reasons that are presumably not educationally relevant.

For a long time there has been a decreasing dependence on segregated facilities for the care, training, and education of the visually, auditorially, and orthopedically handicapped and epileptic children. However, there has been an increase in the segregation (homogeneous grouping) of the gifted, the mentally retarded, the emotionally disturbed, the neurologically impaired, children with learning disabilities, and the culturally disadvantaged. The segregation of these children is based on the assumption that learning is enhanced by such homogeneous groupings. However, children are often transferred to the special schools and the self-contained special classes because they are misfits in the regular classes, because they are disciplinary problems and constitute a threat to orderly classroom management, and because they belong to stigmatized segments of the population. Consequently, many special classes have become a repository for a large segment of our problem children, irrespective of their specific educational characteristics.

The studies of the relative efficacy of the special classes for children with special disabilities have provided even more telling arguments in favor of integration and against segregation. Despite having especially trained teachers, better equipment, greatly increased per capita costs, small classes, programs presumably designed to provide for their unique needs, and more individualized instruction, evaluative studies have consistently shown that mentally retarded children in special classes accomplish the objectives of their education on the same or on a lower level than do equally mentally retarded children who remain in the regular classes (Dunn, 1968; Kirk, 1964; Johnson, 1962; Hoeltke, 1966; Smith and Kennedy, 1967).

We have not been much more successful in our attempts to demonstrate the superior efficacy of special classes for emotionally disturbed children (Dunn, 1968; Rubin, Senison, and Betwee, 1966). The research studies have been only slightly more favorable to special classes for the intellectually gifted (Martinson, 1961). Goldberg (1958), Goldberg and Passow (1962), and Hildreth (1966) have summarized the research findings and have been unable to discover any consistent pattern of increased effectiveness of special classes for the gifted. In spite of the general assumption of educators for the past half century that the special classes for the intellectually gifted are beneficial to the students, there is little convincing evidence that this is true. Hildreth (1966) concludes that the chief value of special class homogeneous groupings in school may reside more in instructional convenience than in any remarkably significant educational outcomes from their segregation and separate instruction. She remarks there is no evidence that the separate grouping of intellectually gifted children for educational purposes has produced any lasting harmful effects.

Currently, the entire question of homogeneous grouping for educational purposes is being critically evaluated. The most extensive recent surveys have failed to find any convincing evidence for the increased educational effectiveness of homogeneous groupings on the basis of age of the pupils or ability level (Goldberg, et al, 1966; Harshman, 1969; Siegel, 1969).

The most rapidly expanding segments of special education are those provided for the education of the culturally disadvantaged and for children with learning disability. Like all special class or special school programs, these are forms of homogeneous grouping and often constitute de facto segregation in terms of their ethnic group and special disability. These groups overlap the conventional category of the educable mentally retarded so extensively that it will be surprising if homogeneous grouping and segregation, as such, will facilitate learning by these children any more than it apparently has done for the mentally retarded.

If the advantages of special class placement are solely the result of smaller classes, more individualized instruction, more adequately trained teachers, and better equipment, these can all be provided in the regular class and are good educational practices for all children. Maybe every class should become a "special" class. If the full potentials of team teaching, ungraded rooms, flexible grouping, prescriptive or clinical teaching, learning centers with diagnostic facilities designed to generate the most effective prescriptions for teaching children with special problems, better trained regular classroom teachers (who are more willing and able to deal with individual differences), the majority of the children now segregated in special classes could be continued within the general education program.

In such a program, special educators will spread their special skills and competences more broadly by serving as members of diagnostic teams responsible for identifying specific learning deficits, developing instructional materials, and devising prescriptive procedures for effective remediation and teaching. Special education personnel will also serve as members of teaching teams, as resource or itinerant teachers, and as consultants, with the regular teachers retaining the central responsibility for all but the most severely handicapped. This is essentially what Dunn (1968) has proposed for the mentally retarded and is an extension of what has been happening in our handling of the special educational problems of the sensory and motor handicapped. Just as we are moving toward the time when our jails and mental hospitals will cease being primarily huge containment facilities for the warehousing of our social misfits, so special education classes may cease to serve as centers which often provide little more than holding operations for troublesome children.

One recommendation calling for the elimination of special classes proposes a resource learning center as an alternative (Ferrara, Iyengar, and Hyman, 1970). In such a program, all children experiencing learning difficulties would be assigned to a regular classroom along with the normal children. They would report to their homerooms in the morning and leave with their respective homeroom groups at the end of each school day. They would eat, play, and participate in as many of the regularly scheduled daily school activities as they are able.

Located in adjacent rooms of buildings will be learning centers with supportive personnel, services and material for those children with special learning difficulties of any type. In the center will be the special teachers properly trained and qualified in the various specialites of special education. Within the learning center differential diagnosis can be made and educational programs designed specifically for each child can be prescribed and carried out. In such a plan each child can identify with the mainstream of the student body while receiving the help of the required supportive services provided by the learning center.

Summary

A comprehensive program for exceptional children, as presently conceived, would include the following:

Basic Supportive Components

   I. Research—both basic and applied
  II. The recruiting and training of personnel
 III. Case finding
 IV. Public education concerning the exceptional
  V. Programs of prevention
     a. Genetic counseling
     b. Improved prenatal care
     c. Improved medical care
     d. Improved nutrition
     e. Improved cultural conditions

Service Components

    I. Provisions for diagnosis, and for corrective medical and surgical treatment

   II. Residential and hospital care
      a. Long-term residential care
         1. Large custodial institutions with multipurpose and special purpose facilities
         2. Smaller colony arrangements
         3. "Cottage" facilities
         4. Foster homes, boarding homes, and group-care homes
      b. Short-term residential care
         1. Twenty-four-hour custodial care
         2. Day hospitals
         3. Day-care centers
         4. Outpatient clinics

 III. Educational and training programs
      a. Home training programs
      b. Academic education at all levels, nursery through adult
         1. Special schools
         2. Residential schools
         3. Day schools
         4. Special classes in a regular school
         5. Resource teachers
         6. Itinerant teachers
         7. Home teaching
         8. Hospital teaching
         9. Training and counseling programs for parents of the exceptional child
      c. Vocational training and placement
         1. Vocational counseling services
         2. Vocational training centers
         3. Sheltered workshops
         4. On-the-job training
         5. Vocational rehabilitation programs
         6. Public and private employment services

 IV. Social and recreational programs
      a. Social adjustment centers
      b. Social and recreational clubs
      c. Recreational and social programs

Some of the assumptions and principles of current special educational programs are:

1. The goals of special education are essentially the same as those of education in general and are attained in much the same ways.
2. Exceptional children require special facilities, methods, and techniques. This is what is "special" about special education.
3. The education of exceptional children requires selective placement and auxiliary personnel and services.

4. The integration of exceptional children into the regular school program and the community, as far as practical, is considered desirable.

References

AAMD Project on Technical Planning in Mental Retardation, "A Manual on Program Development in Mental Retardation," *Amer. j. ment. defic.* LXVI (1962) , Monog. Suppl. 4.

————, "Standards for the Residential Institutions for the Mentally Retarded," *Amer. j. ment. defic.*, LXVIII (1964), Monog. Suppl. 4.

Alexander, F. G., and S. T. Selesnick, *The History of Psychiatry*. New York: Harper & Row, Publishers, 1966.

Alt, H., *Residential Treatment for the Disturbed Child*. New York: International Universities Press, Inc., 1960.

Bergman, J., et al., "A Community Focused Institutional Approach to Mental Retardation," *Amer. j. ment. defic.*, LXVII (1962), 94–100.

Blue, C. M., "Trainable Mentally Retarded in Sheltered Workshops," *Ment. retard.,* II (1964), 97–99.

Boag, T. J., "Further Developments in the Day Hospital," *Amer. j. psychiat.,* CXVI (1960), 801–6.

Brookover, W., D. Leu, and H. Kariger, "Research Notes," *Phi Delta Kappan,* (1969), 358.

Connor, L. E., *Administration of Special Education Programs*. New York: Bureau of Publications, Teachers College, Columbia University, 1961.

Cruickshank, W. M., "The Exceptional Child in the Elementary and Secondary Schools," in *Education of Exceptional Children and Youth* (2nd ed.), eds. W. M. Cruickshank and G. O. Johnson. Englewood Cliffs, N.J.: Prentice-Hall, Inc., 1967.

Doll, E. A., "Occupational Education for the Adolescent Mentally Deficient in a School Program," *Except. child.*, XXV (1958), 51–53.

Dubin, H. N., "The Sheltered Workshop," *Amer. j. ment. defic.*, LX (1956), 508–14.

Dunn, L. M., "Special education for the mildly retarded—Is much of it justified?" *Except. child.* XXXV (1968), 5–22.

Educational Policies Commission, *The Purposes of Education in American Democracy*. Washington, D.C.: National Education Association, 1938.

Ferrara, R. P., K. S. Iyengar and D. J. Hyman, "Learning Centers: An Alternative to Special Classes," *Focus on except. child.*, I, No. 3 (1970), 11–12.

Giliberty, F. R., "Changing Role of Public Institutions," *Amer. j. ment. defic.*, LXVI (1961), 2–5.

Goffman, E., *Asylums*. Chicago, Ill.: Aldine Publishing Co., 1961.

Goldberg, M. L., "Recent Research on the Talented," *Teachers' College Reccord*, LX (1958), 153–54.

————, and A. H. Passow, "The Effects of Ability Grouping," *Education*, (1962), 482–87.

———— A. H. PASSOW, AND J. JUSTMAN, *The Effects of Ability Grouping*. New York: Teachers College Press, 1966.

GREENBLATT, M., "The Transitional Hospital: A Clinical and Administrative Viewpoint," *J. soc. issues*, XVI (1960), 62–69.

HARSHMAN, H. W., "Toward a Differential Treatment of Curriculum," *J. spec. educ.*, III (1969), 385–89.

HILDRETH, G. H., *Introduction to the Gifted*. New York: McGraw-Hill Book Company, 1966.

HODGSON, F. M., "Special Education: Facts and Attitudes," *Except. child.*, XXX (1964), 196–201.

HOELTKE, G. M., *Effectiveness of Special Class Placement for Educable Mentally Retarded Children*. Lincoln, Neb.: University of Nebraska Press, 1966.

HUSETH, B., "What Is a Halfway House? Functions and Types," *Ment. hyg.*, XLV (1961), 116–21.

JOHNSON, G. O., "Special education for mentally handicapped—a paradox," *Except. child.*, XIX (1962), 62–69.

JUBENVILLE, C. P., "A State Program of Day-Care Centers for Severely Retarded," *Amer. j. ment. defic.*, LXVI (1962), 829–37.

KIRK, S. A., "Research in education," in *Mental Retardation*, eds. H. A. Stevens and R. Heber. Chicago, Ill.: University of Chicago Press, 1964.

KRAMER, B. M., "The Day Hospital: A Case Study," *J. soc. issues*, XVI (1960), 14–19.

KRUSH, T. P., "The Search for the Golden Key," *Bull. of the Menninger clinic*, XXVIII (1964), 77–82.

KUGEL, R. B., AND W. WOLFENSBERGER, *Changing Patterns in Residential Services for the Mentally Retarded*. Washington, D.C.: U.S. Government Printing Office, 1969.

Los Angeles City School Districts, *Major Report, Special Education Study: Definition, Function, Organization, and Administration of the Special Education Program*. Los Angeles, Calif.: Office of the Superintendent, 1960.

MACMILLAN, T. M., AND B. H. AASE, "Analysis of the First 500 Patients at the San Diego Day Treatment Center," *California mental health research digest*, II (1964), 11.

MARTINSON, R. A., *Educational Programs for Gifted Pupils*. Sacramento, Calif.: California State Department of Education, 1961.

NIEHN, B. F., "Study of Sheltered Workshops for the Mentally Retarded," *Train. sch. bull.*, LVI (1958), 67–71.

NORMAN, V. B., B. M. ROSEN, AND A. K. BAHN, "Psychiatric Clinic Outpatients in the United States," *Ment. hyg.*, XLVI (1962), 321–43.

OLSHANSKY, S., "The Transitional Workshop: A Survey," *J. soc. issues*, XVI (1960), 33–39.

————, "Social Life," *Ment. hyg.*, XLVI (1962), 361–69.

PASSOW, A. H., *A Summary of Findings and Recommendations of a Study of the Washington, D.C. Schools*. New York: Teachers College, Columbia University, 1967.

Pfantz, H. W., "The Function of Day-Care for Disturbed Adolescents," *Ment. hyg.*, XLVI (1962), 223–29.

Rosen, B. M., A. K. Bahn, and M. Dramer, "Demographic and Diagnostic Characteristics of Psychiatric Clinic Outpatients in the U.S.A.: 1961," *Amer. j. orthopsychiat.*, XXXIV (1964), 455–68.

Rubin, E. Z., C. B. Senison, and M. C. Betwee, *Emotionally Handicapped Children in the Elementary School.* Detroit, Mich.: Wayne State University Press, 1966.

Siegel, E., *Special Education in the Regular Classroom.* New York: John Day, 1969.

Smith, H. W., and W. A. Kennedy, "Effects of Three Educational Programs on Mentally Retarded Children," *Perceptual and motor skills*, XXIV (1967), 174.

Stevens, H. A., "The Residential School's Contribution to the Coordination of Services for the Mentally Retarded," *Amer. j. ment. defic.*, LXI (1956), 20–23.

————, and A. Blumberg, "A Preliminary Report on the Establishment of a Sub-contract Sheltered Workshop in a Residential School for the Mentally Retarded," *Amer. j. ment. defic.*, LXII (1957), 470–75.

Taylor, H., and K. Olsen, "Team Teaching with Trainable Mentally Retarded Children," *Except. child.*, XXX (1964), 304–9.

Vail, D. J., *Dehumanization and the Institutional Career*: Springfield, Ill.: Charles C. Thomas, Publisher, 1967.

Voelker, P. H., "Administration and Supervision of Special Education Programs," in *Education of Exceptional Children and Youth*, eds. W. M. Cruickshank and G. O. Johnson. Englewood Cliffs, N.J.: Prentice-Hall, Inc., 1958.

Wechsler, H., "Halfway Houses for Former Mental Patients: A Survey," *J. soc. issues*, XVI (1960a), 20–26.

————, "The Expatient Organization: A Survey," *J. soc. issues*, XVI (1960b), 47–53.

————, "Transitional Residences for Former Mental Patients: A Survey of Halfway Houses and Related Rehabilitation Facilities," *Ment. hyg.*, XLV (1961), 65–76.

Winich, C., "Psychiatric Day Hospitals: A Survey," *J. soc. issues*, XVI (1960), 8–13.

Wolfensberger, W., "Diagnosis Diagnosed," *J. ment. subnormality*, XI (1965a, Part 2), 62–70.

————, "General Observations on European Programs," *Ment. retard.*, III (1965b), 6–11.

Zehnder, J. R., "Sheltered Workshops for the Mentally Retarded Adults," *Except. child.*, XX (1954), 216–22.

4

Family and Personal Problems
of Exceptional People

The Dynamics of Family Relations

Deviancy is not a problem that resides solely in an individual; rather it is an event that occurs in a given family, community, subculture, and society. We have repeatedly pointed out that deviancy can be understood only with reference to the social reactions it evokes and its meaning to the individual deviant. Just as people with different stigmas must face similar problems and adjust to them in similar ways, the problems of a family with a mentally retarded, blind, deaf, orthopedically handicapped, or epileptic child is an instance of a universal experience, i.e. how the family copes with unexpected disappointment and trauma. Famliy crises, frustrated ambition, and occasional high levels of stress are experiences common to most families.

We have also previously insisted that exceptional and normal people have basically the same general mental make-up—the standard one for their culture. There is no separate "psychology" of deviant people. The normal individual, who occasionally experiences a feeling of psychological distance between himself and a significant reference group or finds himself temporarily in a precarious social situation, and the stigmatized deviant, who lives constantly devalued by his culture and whose life situation is chronically precarious, form a continuum. Their situations and their reactions to them differ only in degree and can be conceptualized similarly. Likewise, the basic problem faced by the families of exceptional individuals is essentially that of all families—how to cope with the problems of living in ways that will enhance rather than hinder the family members' growth and development. The behavior of the deviant is shaped by the actions and attitudes of others, and the adjustments of the family of an exceptional child can either limit and distort or encourage and facilitate the child's potentiality for growth.

When working with the handicapped, it is easy to focus attention so completely on the defective individual that we forget he is a member of a family and that the family may be as much a casualty as is the handicapped member. The family, in turn, is a part of a still larger social context. As we have indicated in earlier chapters, the dominant cultural patterns of society, the subculture in which the individual has membership, and the local community where one resides all have their impact on the handicapped individual. However, the individual family is the primary mediating agent through which these larger social units exert their influences on the individual. This is particularly true of the young child and of the person with a disability.

While the family's impact on the exceptional child has been stated repeatedly, there has been less recognition of the effect of the child on the family. The family is a small interdependent social system with still smaller subsystems within it. The number of subsystems found in any family will depend upon its size and its own unique alignment of members and role relationships (Bell and Vogel, 1960). The smallest of these subsystems is a social dyad—a two-person interaction. In this context, the mother-child pair is typically the focal subsystem embedded in the larger family system. Whatever happens to a family member affects the subsystems of which he is a part, and anything that affects the subsystem is reflected in the system as a whole. Conversely, any stress on the family will have its repercussions on the subsystems and on the individual. There are interacting and reciprocal effects throughout the family, and beyond it. This means that when we discuss the exceptional child and his relationships with his parents or siblings we are artificially isolating the individual or subgroup for purposes of discussion.

What the individual child is, and what he does, affects all the members of the family; their behavior, in turn, affects the child. When the child acts the mother reacts, and the child in turn reacts to the mother in a circular fashion. The father, in turn, reacts to his perception of the child-mother interaction, and thus the father-mother-child subsystem reverberates to both the child's behavior and to the mother-child interaction.

Freedman and his co-workers (1957) have described this circularity in an intensive study of fourteen children suffering from a chronic physical disorder. In every case studied they found emotional disturbances superimposed on the physical disease, with the functional component being perpetuated and aggravated in a vicious circle. This study graphically documents how the hyperactivity, impulsive behavior, and constant restlessness which presumably arise from the children's physical disorders arouse anxiety and result in periodic displays of hostility by the parents. The parents feel guilty and compromise with and make concessions to the children. Reacting to the parents' increased permissiveness, the children continue to manipulate the parents. The children became disturbed by the parents' helplessness and inconsistencies. The children's manipulation of their parents only adds to their own anxiety and feelings of insecurity, and the parents' attempt to appease the children only adds to their feelings of helplessness.

Each family is a unique unit. As a small group interposed between the culture and the individual, it screens the broader cultural influences and, in terms of its own norms, values, and role definitions constitutes almost a unique culture. Family members have certain meanings and role relationships to each other. The family can thus be viewed as a group of interacting personalities which is both sustained and altered through these interactions.

Families, like most social groups, develop internal patterns of alignment and relationships. Because the mother has historically been the central figure in the family, she is typically considered to be the focus of the most significant family alignments. When it becomes necessary to extend investigations of a problem child beyond the child himself, the focus of attention in child counseling and psychotherapy shifts to the mother-child relationship. Indeed, many counselors and psychotherapists refuse to work with a problem child unless the mother will undergo concurrent therapy or counseling. This has been a long-standing rule for many clinics and individual clinicians, although in some clinics concurrent parent-child psychotherapy is being replaced by entire family therapy.

The widespread belief that the family—particularly the mother-child relationship—is in large part responsible for the mental health of the child is a compelling one. However, it is difficult to substantiate this belief with research findings. The evidence of a significant relationship between *specific* maternal child-rearing practices and personality characteristics in the children is meagre and contradictory (Orlansky, 1949; Behrens, 1954; Johnson and Medinnus, 1969). It is becoming increasingly clear that individual acts and practices become significant only as part of a larger social context. For example, while Marjorie Behrens found no correlation between the personality of children and *specific* child-rearing practices in feeding, weaning, and toilet training, she obtained highly significant correlations between the child's adjustment and indices of the "total mother" as seen in the mother-family relationship. Specific child-rearing practices and parent-child relationships became significant only when viewed in the context of a larger pattern.

These data support Rogers' (1939) claim, made over twenty-five years ago, that if we were predicting the outcome of the treatment of a problem child and had to base our predictions on a single factor, we would do best to disregard the child entirely and base our forecast on the "emotional climate" of the home as indicated by the way the parents accept the child and the way they act toward him. A minor study of the same period (Witmer, 1933) also indicated that the one factor showing the closest relationship to success in working professionally with "problem children" is the "emotional tone" of the home and the parents' attitude toward the child. When the parents are well-adjusted themselves, when the home atmosphere is reasonably calm, and when the parents have normal affection for the children, the probability that the problem child will ultimately be making a satisfactory adjustment is very good.

This emphasis on the importance of such broad global factors as "emotional tone" or "emotional climate" of the home, as contrasted with specific child-rearing practices, is supported by more recent studies. Sears, Maccoby, and Levin (1957) found that the mother's personality and the general atmosphere of the interaction were more important to the child's development than any specific practice associated with feeding and toilet training. These same authors, as well as Radke (1946), found child behavior to be most significantly related to the broad permissiveness-restriction and autocratic-democratic rating scales for parental behavior. Schaefer (1959) found that two major characteristics of parental behavior could be derived from the results of a large number of studies of parent-child relationships and arranged meaningfully on an autonomy (freedom)–control (passive) and a hostility (rejecting)–love (accepting) scale. Later Schaefer (1961) presented some support for the significant relation of these very general maternal characteristics to significant categories of children's behavior.

Because of these findings, attention has shifted from the mother-child relationship to the entire family constellation (MacGregor et al., 1964; Satir, 1964). The unique family pattern, rather than either the individual child or the parent-child relationship, has become the primary focus of concern. Consequently, we find individuals and agencies recommending that counseling and psychotherapy should involve the whole family as a group. Changes in the complex interrelationships among family members and subgroups within the family inevitably arise as the result of effective counseling, psychotherapy, or the removal of a member of the family by death or institutionalization. No matter how disturbing the deviant be-havior of a family member, if the behavior pattern has persisted for a time and the family constellation has remained intact, some stability has been established. Even conflict-laden equilibrium and stability have their rewards. The removal of the deviant individual from the home, or a marked change in the individual's behavior resulting from counseling, psychotherapy, or more active intervention from without, disrupts the existing relationships. Sometimes these changes operate to the detriment of other family members; more often they are beneficial. Smith, Ricketts, and Smith (1962) have provided some dramatic illustrations of the pos-sible consequences of institutional placement of a handicapped sibling. In one case cited, Mary, a mentally retarded, deaf, brain-damaged, ten-year-old was institutionalized. No attention was paid to Mary's jealousy of her sister or to the statement of this sister that the mother was institu-tionalizing Mary to get rid of her. The family's life had centered around Mary's condition. Her hyperactivity and temper tantrums had kept the family in a perpetual turmoil. A follow-up interview a year later indi-cated relief and satisfaction with the move by all family members, except the older sister. The sister had become obsessed with the belief that the placement of Mary was cruel and that she was being mistreated in the institution. The sister's depressed agitation, apparently based on her feelings toward Mary, were sufficiently severe for her to require psychiatric treatment.

Modifications in the family constellations are most disturbing when such changes are rapid. For example, the death or institutionalization of a child may require the modification of the patterns of separateness and connectedness which underlie every family relationship. Mother and child, or father, mother, and handicapped child, may have constituted a somewhat independent subgroup from which the other siblings have either withdrawn or have been excluded. When the deviant child leaves the family, or when, as the result of counseling, the parents try to establish new relationships with the other children and with each other a reorgan-ization of all interrelationships ensues. The existence of reasonably stable family alignments and clearly defined roles reduces the amount of con-stant decision-making concerning family relationships. Each person in a well-structured family knows the part he is to play and how he is expected to behave. Any marked change in family constellation necessitates a re-alignment of individuals and a redefinition of their roles. A lot of addi-tional decision making is required before the family is restructured. For example, in the situation mentioned above, where child and mother, or child, mother, and father, have constituted a somewhat independent dyad or triad with the handicapped child as the principal focus of this sub-group, the removal of the child from the home or a decision to break up the cohesive subgroup may be a disturbing factor to the normal siblings as well as to the handicapped child. With one or both parents dominantly concerned with the exceptional child, the siblings may have been quite free to take care of themselves and act independently. When the focus of the parents' life shifts from the dependent child and they then insist upon exerting more direction and supervision of the other children, a major reorganization of the family life becomes necessary. If the family is large, the older children may have assumed the major responsibility for the care and supervision of the younger normal siblings while the parents were preoccupied with the disabled family member. When the parents suddenly elect to reassert their authority and control over all family members, considerable conflict may follow while new lines of authority and control are being established.

The authors have been impressed with the parents' exclusive concern with the handicapped child's probable reaction to prospective foster-home or institutional placement. Many times the adjustment of the parents and siblings is much more difficult than that of the institutionalized child. The separation is more traumatic to them and requires more of a read-justment of their lives. This is particularly true when the care of a severely handicapped child has been a major concern of the family. Family members are seldom aware of the extent to which mutual dependencies and reciprocal relationships have dominated their lives. The removal of the child from the home requires many of the other family members to make other commitments and establish new roles for themselves. We will return to this topic later when the problem of mutual dependency between parent and disabled child are discussed.

PATTERNS OF PARENTAL REACTION
TO A DEFECTIVE CHILD

While there are almost as many different patterns of reaction to evidences of inadequacy in one's offspring as there are parents with such children, certain types of reactions are sufficiently common to warrant description. Some of the more common reactive patterns to the advent of a defective child into a family are: realistic coping with the problem; denial of the reality of the handicap; self-pity; ambivalence toward or rejection of the child; projection of the difficulty as the cause of the disability; feelings of guilt, shame and depression; and patterns of mutual dependency.

None of these reactions is peculiar to parents in general or to the parents of defective children; they are the common reactions of normal people to frustration and conflict. The average parent will, in the course of his lifetime, display or experience these reactions to his nondisabled children as a part of normal life processes, and it is helpful to the parents of handicapped children to be aware of the universality of their reactions. Many parents of deviant children not only experience feelings of guilt and shame but feel guilty and ashamed of themselves for doing so. That is, in addition to feeling guilty, they feel guilty about feeling guilty. Such guilt is a secondary source of emotional disturbance to parents who are already overladen emotionally. The presence of a handicapped child in the family constitutes an additional stress, and defensive reactions are likely to occur more often and to a greater degree in such families than in families all of whose members are reasonably normal.

One source of conflict arises from the fact that the presence of a severely handicapped child in a family arrests certain components of the family cycle. The severely disabled child may permanently occupy the social position of the youngest child in the family. He does not develop the independence and autonomy of adulthood. Farber (1959) has described this situation in the family with a severely mentally retarded child. There the parental role is fairly constant regardless of the child's birth order position; the severely mentally retarded individual is the permanent infant and never emerges from his infantile or childish status.

Coping Realistically with the Problems of the Exceptional Child. Because of our concern with the problem parent as well as the problem child, we can easily overlook the fact that many parents are able to cope in a healthy and constructive way with the problems presented by the presence of a defective child. Many people meet the initial decisions and the additional stresses in a realistic, well-integrated way, just as they meet the other crises and stresses in their lives.

Denial of the Child's Disability. Except for the most obvious disabilities, most parents react with some denial to evidence of their child's inadequacy. There are powerful social and personal forces motivating a parent to deny evidences of disability in his offspring. Many of these factors were discussed in earlier chapters. The cultural stereotype of the ideal child, the parents' expectation that their offspring will successfully play the roles that society and his parents assign to him, the parents' hopes that their child will attain or surpass their own accomplishments all contribute to their "it just can't be so" reaction when the child is apparently defective. Because parents identify with their children, participate in their successes and failures, bask in their reflected glory, and are belittled by their shortcomings, they inevitably experience a loss of self-esteem when one of their offspring is less than expected. A defect in the child is partly that of the parent.

When the initial realization of an infants' defectiveness comes suddenly and traumatically, the more unconscious defensive reactions may occur. One mother actually believed that she had *only imagined* that she had held her physically deformed, day-old, child in her arms when the nurse took the infant back to the nursery. Later on she was unable to recall the first six weeks at home with her defective child. One father reports that when asked how many children he had he would say "two." He actually had three but the third was a badly deformed thalidomide child. One father of a thalidomide infant was unable to take a second look at his deformed infant for three whole days.

The parents of a physically disabled child seem to identify more completely with their child's physique than do the parents of the non-handicapped. One study finds the attitudes of dislike and dissatisfaction with their *own bodies and the bodies of their physically handicapped children,* as measured by a Body-Cathexis scale, correlate around .50, whereas the corresponding correlations attained from similar measurements on the parents of nondisabled children are approximately zero (Centers and Centers, 1963). In other words, the parents of physically disabled children who are greatly disturbed over their children's physical attributes are also dissatisfied with their own physiques, and vice versa, while no such relationship exists between parental attitudes toward their own and their children's physiques among the parents of the nondisabled. It is not surprising that perceptual distortion, misinterpretation of evidence, and all the defenses in one's repertoire will be used to deny evidences of inferiority in one's offspring. Sometimes this denial takes the form of a prolonged trek from doctor to doctor and from clinic to clinic, in search of a more favorable diagnosis. Failing this, the parents claim that the specialists are all wrong. Any parent knows his own child better than all the professionals!

Sympathetic friends, relatives, and even professional people often unwittingly support the parents' denial of their child's inadequacy. They stress the child's assets and minimize his limitations. They emphasize the difficulties of diagnosis, the uncertainties of developmental trends, and the limitations of our knowledge. There are no certainties in this world! Telling a parent bluntly and with certainty that he has a defective child is a hard task for any counselor and is often postponed, or temporized, or modified in the hope that it will be easier on the parents and in the certainty that it is easier on the counselor.

Many parents never get beyond the stage of partial acceptance. They may accept the diagnosis but reject its prognostic implications. How about the miracle drugs, a new operation, a novel form of psychotherapy, or unlimited amounts of parental love?

Self-pity.   Except when the parents are able to assume and maintain a realistic and objective attitude toward their child's disability, some feelings of self-pity are likely to be experienced. "What a terrible thing to happen to me," "Why did this happen in my family?" "What have I done to deserve this?" are either said or thought. The threat to the parents' and the family's prestige represented by the presence of a defective child looms large in most middle- or upper-class households.

When the emotional reaction is extreme, the devout religionist may question his fundamental religious beliefs. "How could a benign Diety permit such a thing to happen? Why did He do this to me?" As the result of such questioning and doubt, the parent may become embittered and atheistic. Of course some people find *solace* in their religious beliefs. Although the evidence is conflicting, some studies find Catholic mothers, who are generally more religious than Protestants, to be more accepting of their defective children than are comparable non-Catholics (Zuk, 1962; Boles, 1959; Telford, 1950).

Ambivalent Feelings toward the Handicapped. Even the best parents are ambivalent in their feelings toward their normal children. Parental attitudes, while dominantly positive, always have overtones of resentment and rejection. The restrictions of activities, the additional responsibilities, the minor disappointments of parenthood, the anxieties, and the irritations which are a normal part of the bearing and rearing of offspring inevitably produce ambivalent parental reactions. Parents accept and love, but they also reject and dislike their children.

It is inevitable that the negative components of this ambivalence will be accentuated when the child is handicapped. These negative reactions vary all the way from consciously and overtly wishing that the child would die or had never been born to repressed, unacknowledged, veiled, and symbolic hostility and rejection. In any case, ambivalent feelings give rise to guilt reactions which in turn often result in overprotection, oversolicitousness, and a parental life of martyrdom which constitutes an attempt to deny or compensate for the hostile feelings of which the person is ashamed.

Parental ambivalences are often involved in the *treatment* of disabled offspring. Trying to find and tread that narrow path between withholding the realistically necessary care and assistance on the one hand and doing too much and nurturing helplessness and overdependency on the other is always difficult. In trying to find this path, many parents are more demanding and less tolerant of excuses from their disabled child than they are of their normal offspring. When the disabled child asks the parent to do something for him, the parent hesitates and asks himself, "Can he do it for himself?" He often does not do for the disabled child many things that he does immediately and without question for his more able offspring because he is less aware of the dangers of instilling overdependencies in the latter.

Projection. Projection is a common defense against feelings of anxiety. Anxiety concerning personal guilt, or unacceptable feelings of resentment and hostility, can be diminished by blaming someone other than oneself for the threatening situation. Parents made anxious by the conditions arising from the handicapped child will often project the causes of the child's deficiencies onto convenient scapegoats. Resentment and hostility may be directed at the other children, the spouse, the doctor, the teacher, the counselor, or society in general. Professional people working with such parents can expect to serve as the innocent victims of this process. Unprovoked attacks against others often represent displaced hostility resulting from the chronic frustrations engendered by the defective child.

Guilt, Shame, and Depression. Guilt and shame are components of several of the reaction patterns already discussed. However, they are sufficiently important in themselves to warrant further discussion. Shame, as used here, refers to the "What will other people think and say?" reaction, whereas guilt refers to the individual's own feelings of self-reproach or self-condemnation. Shame is more other-people oriented; guilt, more self-directed. Shame involves the expectation of ridicule or criticism from others, while guilt involves self-blame, personal regret, and a feeling of decreased personal worth. Shame and guilt both involve anxiety, and popular usage does not differentiate them. Empirical studies indicate that guilt and anxiety, as indicated by self-report, are highly correlated (Luxer, 1964). Feelings of guilt, or self-blame, with their accompanying anxiety and lowered self-concept, result in depression. Shame and its accompanying anxiety, on the other hand, may protect the self-concept by directing hostility outwardly.

Some feelings of guilt or shame are common experiences of the parents of handicapped children. When the parental reaction is dominantly that of shame, the threat to one's personal prestige and the family's social status looms, often realistically, like an ever-present shadow. *Actual* social rejection of the child with a disability ranges all the way from a slight uneasiness on the part of the neighbors when they are in the presence of the disabled individual to thinking of the handicapped person as subhuman and dangerous. The parents of disabled children are aware of many beliefs centering around the sins of the parents and "bad blood," as well as such notions as that neglect or carelessness of the parents are possible causes of many disabilities, particularly when the etiology is either obscure or unknown.

The anticipation of social rejection, ridicule, and loss of prestige, when extreme, may result in an immediate and drastic solution to the problem. To avoid social rebuffs, some parents try to withdraw from social participation. Other parents assume the role of martyr in order to allay any suspicion of lack of parental concern or inadequacy of parental role as a possible cause of the child's defect. By devoting one's entire life to the child, the parent says to the world, "See what a dedicated and devoted parent I am! How can anyone suggest that the child's difficulties arise from my carelessness or inadequacy?"

Attempts at immediate foster-home or institutional placement of the defective child may be the parental reaction to the threat of social ostracism. Less drastic attempts to keep the child from public exposure is a common reaction. The defective child, in either case, becomes the traditional skeleton in the closet, the forgotten child. The fear of social disclosure may force parents to prefer private to public institutional placement even when they can ill afford the additional expense.

Every institution housing the severely disabled—particularly the psychotic and the severely mentally retarded—contains a sizable group of children who are never visited by their parents or other relatives. The writers have been impressed by the large number of severely handicapped children in the higher-priced private institutions whose families reside in distant parts of the country. Many of the children in private institutions in California, for example, come from without the state, some from New York, Pennsylvania, and Florida. The only contacts many of these families have with their children is to send a Christmas present, possibly a birthday present, and mail monthly checks to the institution. The implication is that these children are the forgotten ones and that excessive distance from home is an advantage to the family. Private institutions with ambiguous names, such as Pleasant Hill Manor, The Pines, Yorktown Hall, or The Hudson Country School, are often preferred to public institutions whose names are indicative of the types of children enrolled.

Feelings of guilt and self-accusation, like shame, may result in a parental life of martyrdom. However, the martyrdom resulting from shame is an attempt to prove to other people that the parent is competent and adequate, while the same behavior motivated by guilt is directed at defending the parental *self-concept*. The guilt-motivated parent is trying to deny or compensate for his feelings of hostility and rejection. Overconcern, oversolicitousness, excessive care, and protection are ways in which the parent may *reassure himself* that he is a good parent. Showering the child with presents, clothes, and other material things, sacrificing in order to send the child to expensive schools and to provide care beyond his needs may be motivated by the parent's need to prove to himself what a good and devoted parent he is.

The guilt-ridden parent is always in danger of giving the child more protection than the realities of the situations demand. Of course, the handicapped child *realistically* requires more protection than does a normal child. The parent with little, if any, prior experience with the disabled does not know how much extra care and protection the child requires. It is therefore easy for him to rationalize the expenditure of enormous amounts of time, energy, and money, and the bestowal of excessive affection and care which really represent compensations for feelings of rejection.

Feelings of depression are frequent experiences of either shame or guilt-laden people. Grief reactions typical of the loss of a loved one are to be expected. Whenever anxiety mounts and the stresses of life seem overwhelming, despondency and depression are likely to ensue.

Patterns of Mutual Dependency. In an earlier section, the interaction and circularity of effects in family relationships were mentioned. Parent and child, most often mother and disabled child, develop self-perpetuating patterns of mutual dependency. We have indicated the ways in which the parent—particularly the overanxious parent—can foster overdependency in the handicapped child. It is less obvious that the parent can become almost equally dependent on the disabled child (Blodgett and Warfield, 1959). Whenever a parent invests a large part of himself, both materially and emotionally in the care of a handicapped child, a condition of circular dependency can easily develop. The child, either through his real needs or his parent's exaggeration of his needs, becomes dependent on the parent. The parent, in turn, needs the excessive care and dependency of the child to prove his adequacy as a parent. At times the excessive supervision, protection, and care provided by the oversolicitous parent increases and perpetuates the child's dependency. These reciprocal needs may be perpetuated indefinitely. The parent, by devoting so much of his time and energy to the handicapped child, invests so much of himself in the project that his entire life becomes centered in the child. When this occurs, parents may actually resist efforts to relieve them of the burden because of the void it would leave in their lives. Sometimes the handicapped child's lack of motivation is the result of an adult-fostered dependency and immaturity which is sustained by the neurotic satisfaction the parent derives from the child's dependency. The child for his part, feels secure within the protecting parental arm. There is evidence that when such a neurotically sustained relationship involving a severely handicapped child has persisted for several years, it is very difficult to reverse (Miller, 1958).

Neurotic dependency can also develop in the disabled member of a dyad. This is particularly true when a predisposed adult develops a disability. A paralyzing stroke may accentuate or crystallize processes of surrender, dependency, and resignation already in progress. The neurotically inclined adult can exaggerate his incapacities, relinquish activities he is capable of doing, become more demanding of others, and institute a cycle of functional dependency. The cycle is self-perpetuating in more than one way. The failure to use one's remaining physical capacities results in their atrophy which, in turn, increases the organic disability and the real dependency. There is a dynamic interplay of physiological, psychological, and social factors in all aspects of exceptionality.

SIBLINGS' REACTIONS TO THE EXCEPTIONAL CHILD

The available evidence indicates that the siblings largely adopt the parents' attitudes toward the disabled child (Bansch, 1961). When the parents view the defective child with shame or hostility, the siblings do likewise. When the family has been helped by counseling, the presence of a young mentally retarded child need not have an adverse effect on teen-age siblings (Graliker, Fishler, and Koch, 1962). The family may be so concerned with an obviously handicapped child, however, that a less obviously deviant sibling who is more seriously emotionally disturbed and more in need of help than the more visibly disabled child may be overlooked (Shere, 1956).

When the nonhandicapped siblings are required to supervise, care for, defend, and protect the handicapped child, resentment often develops. When the defective child receives excessive attention and affection, when the additional expense incurred by the deviant child deprives the others of educational and recreational opportunities, the resentment is aggravated. The overprotection of the handicapped is often accompanied by varying degrees of neglect of the other children. The sibling and his possessions may suffer directly at the hands of a demanding, hyperactive, and destructive handicapped child.

The Significance of the Age in Life at Which a Disability Is Acquired

The time in life when a person acquires or becomes aware of his handicap makes considerable difference in the way he meets the problems posed by these events. The individual with a congenital defect and the child who becomes disabled while still very young become socialized within the framework of their deviations in the same way that the normal child develops socially and forms his self-image as a part of the normal developmental process. The person who becomes disabled or discovers that he is handicapped later in life must alter his previous normal self-concept, learn to see himself as defective, and develop new ways of coping with the altered situations.

The socialization of the significantly deviant person involves:

(1) Learning about the norms of his culture: Each individual develops some conceptions of the statistical norms of his culture or subculture or

both. He also learns about the value norms of his society—its conceptions of the ideal.

(2) Becoming aware of his own self-concept: While the child's view of himself never mirrors precisely that of the significant others around him, it is extracted from these sources. If one's culture devalues an individual, it is almost impossible for that person to perceive himself as worthwhile; and as we have already indicated, negative self-viewing may be as handicapping as physical disability or mental defect.

(3) Learning about his self-ideal—self-discrepancy: This is a part of the person's development of his self-concept. However, for the individual who deviates significantly from societal norms, the nature, degree, and social significance of the ways in which he fails to conform to these norms become crucial in determining achievement through the mechanism of the self-concept.

(4) Learning how to cope with the discrepancy between his perceived status and the ideal cultural norms: These adjustments vary from renunciation and acceptance at the one extreme to overcompensations, denial, and passing at the other.

The child with a congenital disability who is fortunate enough to have accepting and understanding parents learns the standards of his culture, the ways in which he deviates from those standards, and acquires ways of coping with these deviancies in precisely the same way that his normal siblings learn these things. On the other hand, the deviant child reared by parents who covertly reject either him or his deviancy and who react defensively to public devaluation of their child may have a protective wall built around him. Such a child may be so protected from the socially devaluing definition of himself that he grows up seeing himself as a completely normal person. Instead of attending a regular school where he would be faced with the judgments of the outside world, the deviant child may be sent to a private special school where he lives with "his own kind." In the special school, he may learn that his previous self-image was erroneous, but he is still protected from the more drastic consequences of his deviancy.

If such a protected child gets through the elementary school years without learning of the cultural devaluation of people like him, the onset of dating and job-hunting will surely make him aware of his status. Whenever the discovery of his stigmatized status occurs, a radical reorganization of his self-concept as well as his view of his past and his perception of those about him takes place.

The person who becomes disabled late in life is faced with a somewhat different situation. Such a person has already learned about normal and deviant people as a part of his socialization. He has learned to perceive himself as reasonably normal and adequate. He now sees himself as defective. To a degree, he develops a new self-concept. For some time such an individual may feel like a dissociated person. Many aspects of his life are continuous and consistent with his old nondefective self but now he must live also in the psychological world of the handicapped. He is faced with all the problems of denial vs. acceptance, succumbing vs. coping, just as is the congenitally handicapped person.

The altered situation introduces feelings of uncertainty into social relationships with old acquaintances. Pre-disability friends are unable to relate to the person he once was and are unsure of how to relate to the new, handicapped person. The former easy relationship of full acceptance is now replaced by excessive tactfulness, guarded references, the avoidance of common words which have now become taboo, artificial levity, or awkward seriousness. The performance of previously ordinary acts takes on a special significance. Accidents, changes in mood, and minor failings are now perceived as the expression of the person's newly acquired differentness. The newly disabled person becomes uncertain as to whether people really still accept and like him or are just being pleasant and pretending to in order not to hurt him. He may become ambivalent concerning his self-concept and his public image.

Counseling the Parents of Exceptional Children

In a good discussion of the problems of parents of the mentally retarded, Sarason (1959) stated that, with the obvious exception of the specific cause of the mental retardation, the failure to inform parents about the nature and implications of their child's condition probably causes more unnecessary suffering than any other factor. A more recent book (Ross, 1964) which is designed to help the parents of exceptional children is based on the conviction that the unhappiness, conflict, and emotional disturbance of such parents can be significantly reduced if every professional person who interacts with the parents shares the responsibility for intelligent counseling. Practically every systematic study of exceptional people and their families stresses the need for more and better counseling. In their fervent search for solutions to their dilemma, the parents of exceptional children are perpetually looking for counsel.

THE GOALS OF PARENTAL COUNSELING

The goals of counseling are essentially the same irrespective of who is being counseled. The nature of the information imparted, the ways in which the person is informed, and the methods used may vary, but the purposes of counseling remain constant. Counseling goals are intellectual, emotional, and behavioral in nature.

In the intellectual realm, the parents of exceptional children need information concerning the nature and extent of the child's exceptionality—diagnostic information. They want to know the probable cause of their child's condition—etiological information. They require information concerning facilities and services available for the care, treatment, and education of these children—information concerning remediation. They should be informed of what the future may hold for the handicapped child, as well as of the specific programs which are most appropriate to the needs and capacities of their child—prognosis.

However, the imparting of information is seldom enough. The purely intellectual or factual approach to problems involving emotionally laden relationships is notoriously insufficient in itself. The feelings of people often carry more weight than do their intellects. Therefore, it is just as important to help parents with their attitudes and feelings as it is to provide them with adequate information. Counselors must concern themselves with the parents' fears and anxieties and their feelings of guilt and shame. They should attempt to reduce the emotional vulnerability of the family members. While the strains and tensions suffered by the family of the exceptional child cannot be eliminated, it is often possible to increase their ability to tolerate tension. Adequate counseling will also result in modified behavior by parents. Every counseling program should involve specific plans for the family and the handicapped child.

The goals of counseling for the parents of exceptional children are considerably more modest than are those of psychotherapy. Counseling is not intended to change the personality of the counselee. It is intended to help reasonably well-integrated people to understand and to deal more adequately with the problems growing out of the presence of the deviant child in the family. Work with the families of handicapped children is closer to social work than to psychotherapy. It is more concerned with environmental manipulation and the handling of practical problems than with the personalities of the family members.

SOME ELEMENTARY PRINCIPLES OF PARENTAL COUNSELING

Interested readers and prospective professional counselors should consult the professional literature on family counseling. We shall present only a list of suggestions for the nonprofessional counselor who either elects to or must counsel the parents of exceptional children. Many different professional people counsel the parents of the handicapped—physicians, psychologists, social workers, school administrators, teachers, speech and occupational therapists, and physical therapists—and few of these people are professionally trained counselors.

The Importance of Listening.   Most counselors, particularly teachers, talk too much. They have faith in the efficacy of instruction and exhortation, and they commonly assume that beliefs and actions derive directly from information and that people behave inappropriately simply because they don't know any better. To be effective, however, counseling must be appropriate to the feelings, attitudes, and personality of the counselee, as well as to his intellectual and informational level. The only way to determine the counseling needs of a given person is to let him tell you, and the best way for him to tell you is in his own way.

In the initial interview the counselees should be permitted to lead. They should do most of the talking and dominate the interview. If both parents are present—as they should be—much can be learned by permitting and encouraging them to talk about their problem child, the nature of the problems with which they want help, what has been done for the child, the plans they have made, and their expectations.

Permitting the counselees to tell these stories in their own ways provides clues to the stage of thinking they have attained in their concern for their children. It will indicate whether they are still concerned about diagnosis or the acceptance of diagnosis. The terms they use and their general vocabulary may indicate the level of sophistication and understanding they have attained. A listener can usually get some idea of the feelings and attitudes of the speaker. He can deduce something concerning the degrees of guilt, conflict, and confusion the counselees are experiencing.

The Problem of Terminology.   Most of the parents of exceptional children are laymen and do not understand professional jargon. Communication must be in terms of the counselee. If the parents talk first, the counselor learns the vocabulary level of the counselees and the terms that they find acceptable. Laymen often perceive professional terminology, even when they understand it, as stigmatizing and threatening. If parents refer to their child as a "slow developer" or as "nervous" or "handicapped," the counselor can adopt and use these terms in discussing the child. Their meaning will become clearer as the exact nature of the child's condition becomes clearer. Terms such as "crippled," "moron," "psychotic," "feebleminded," or even "mentally retarded" and "orthopedically handicapped" may well be set aside in an attempt to determine specifically the child's developmental status—what he can and cannot do. As we pointed out earlier, the fact that a disability exists—whether it be a language deficiency, an orthopedic handicap, a disorganization of personality, or mental retardation—may be less significant than the degree of the disability and the extent to which the person is handicapped by the deficiency.

Professionals will improve their relationships with parents by treating each handicapped person as an individual rather than as a "case" no matter how unusual and interesting. Referring to a child by name, or at least as "your son" or "your daughter," makes the person something more than a statistic. The counselor should be interested in learning about the abilities and disabilities and the unique characteristics of the individual under study, rather than in simply classifying, categorizing, and labelling him.

The Problem of Acceptance. The counselor will remember that while his primary concern is for the exceptional child, the parents are also emotionally disturbed. They are in conflict. They have feelings of shame and guilt. They are subject to terrific social pressures and are vulnerable to criticism. Many parents have developed self-defeating and blind-alley resolutions of their conflicts. Their attitudes and practices may actually be aggravating their child's condition.

To merely judge, disapprove of, or condemn parental attitudes and practices does not help, however. Overt or implied criticism of parental practices only adds to the emotional load of people who are already overwhelmed by their problems. Criticism from the counselor therefore is often met with hostility; the parents become defensive and invite counterhostility. Understanding, acceptance, and empathy is considered to be a fundamental requirement of a helpful counseling relationship. Unconditional acceptance of the family as worthy and deserving of regard and assistance—the parents as well as the exceptional child—is a requisite of a helping relationship.

To be warm and sympathetic, to be understanding and helpful without fostering overdependence, is one of the challenges of counseling. To help parents to a better understanding of themselves, their child, and their relationships and, at the same time, not take over by providing too much advice and assistance, is a critical task. If the counselor is to be most effective, the parents must see that it is primarily their problem and that no one else can solve it for them.

A nonjudgmental, noncondemning, accepting, and understanding attitude toward people does not imply uncritical endorsement and support for whatever is done or proposed. The ultimate goal is to formulate and carry through plans which will most benefit the exceptional child, and with which the family can live at peace. The consequences of current or proposed practices can be suggested, alternatives can be proposed, and appropriate plans can be sanctioned. Additional information can be supplied in such a way as to reinforce certain behavior and discourage others without rejecting or disapproving the individuals involved.

The Importance of Counseling the Entire Family. Some reasons for counseling the entire family have already been listed. Another important reason is that it facilitates communication among members of the family. It is very difficult for a mother—for it is usually the mother who is counseled—to go home and restate, explain, interpret, and answer questions concerning a long and involved counseling session, the nature of which she only partially understands. Selective perception and memory distortion preclude accurate reporting. Emotional tension may be making communication between family members difficult. Effective communication between family members may even have broken down.

Conferences involving all the family may reopen avenues of communication and help to unite the members in the interest of making plans for the exceptional person's welfare. The emotional isolation in which each suffers in silence, is afraid to express his fears, and is reluctant to precipitate the issue is too often a part of the burden imposed on the nondisabled family members.

Effective planning and execution involves the whole family. When all the concerned family members participate in counseling, conflicting beliefs and attitudes come to light, and differences of opinion can be ventilated and possibly reconciled. Family members are more likely to share responsibility and cooperate for a common goal if all are involved in the discussion and planning. Unfortunately, counseling of the entire family is not yet the general practice.

The Importance of Feelings and Attitudes.   Feelings are often stronger than admonitions and logical decisions. Self-pity, anxiety, guilt, and shame are primarily feeling states. While some parents act inappropriately because they don't know how to act in any other way, far more act less adequately than their information dictates because of anxieties, hostilities, and guilt feelings. It is therefore essential that counseling be as concerned with feelings and attitudes as with giving information and making formal plans. Parents need help in clarifying their feelings. They need assistance in wandering through their emotional mazes. When deep-seated emotional disturbances and emotional disorientation are present, however, the problems may be beyond the reach of the ordinary teacher, counselor, physician, or school psychologist, and long-term psychotherapy may be necessary.

The Place of Interpretation in Counseling.   Interpretation can occur at several different levels. At one level, it may be largely a matter of providing information. All parents need information. However, information often requires interpretation; as we indicated earlier, the meaning of the facts of a disability are more important than the presence of the condition.

Some people need self-understanding more than an understanding of the handicapping condition of their child. Some parents need help but do not realize it; others realize they need assistance but cannot ask for or accept it; some seek advice but are unable to follow it. Many parents agree to plans they are unable to carry out. Parents, like all people, often contradict what they say by what they do. All such people can profit by a greater understanding of themselves and their needs. They need to be interpreted to themselves.

Interview questions may point up gross inconsistencies. Questions of concern may be discussed without parental defenses being probed too deeply. Interpretation in depth is hardly practical in counseling which stops short of psychotherapy. Defense mechanisms have value for the individual. To probe deeply and deprive an individual of his defenses without carrying through and helping him to substitute a more adequate adjustment may do more harm than good.

The interpretations of the average counselor will provide information which is as complete and accurate as possible. They will dispel misconceptions. However, even the latter may be carried too far. When the actual causes of the handicapped child's condition are unknown, parents have often developed very positive beliefs about its etiology. These beliefs have considerable value for the parents, for the parents can discuss their child's condition frankly and openly when they are able to present the alleged causes as the real ones. In such cases, so long as the belief does not result in inappropriate treatment for the child, the belief may represent a useful fiction which is just as well left undisturbed.

Imparting Diagnostic Information. One function of counseling is to help parents realize the nature and extent of their problem as early as possible. Many valuable years are often lost because of failures either in diagnosis or in parental acceptance of the factors or implications of diagnostic information. The parents of exceptional children often say "Why didn't someone tell us?" or "If we had only known sooner!" In many cases these parents had been told in various ways, but their ears were not open. Parental attitudes have to develop to a certain level before there is receptivity to the facts and implications of threatening diagnostic information. Understanding and acceptance of diagnosis cannot be forced. Time is required, and counselors can only present the available data as completely and as honestly as possible and hope for its eventual acceptance.

Test data and general impressions must be stated in the counselee's terms. Exact test scores are seldom disclosed. Intellectual status and achievement are usually most meaningful when they are stated in terms of approximate mental age or school grade equivalents. Asking the parents to indicate their estimates of the child's level is often helpful. When the parents' estimate is in approximate agreement with intelligence test scores and other evidence of achievement, a simple confirmation of the parental judgment may be sufficient. When the data are discrepant, additional information may be needed. When parents are reluctant to accept diagnostic information no matter how complete, the counselor may supply the names of several other specialists or agencies from which the parents may select those with whom they wish to consult. One diagnosis or one statement of a diagnosis is seldom enough. It is normal for most parents to want to shop around. Many parents need to nurse their doubt and maintain their defenses until they are able to dispense with them. The initial rejection of many diagnoses and their implications is to be expected. Only the parents can make the critical decisions. Counselors can only assist in the process.

Acceptance of a realistic diagnosis is furthered by accenting positive assets rather than the liabilities of the exceptional individual. The handicapped person is typically under special study because of his disability, and his limitation tends to be the overshadowing fact of his life. But every person has some positive attributes, and diagnosis should be as concerned with what the person can do as with what he cannot do. Plans which are built around what the child is able to do and formulated so as to take maximum advantage of his abilities may be more palatable to the parents than plans which are dominated by the child's disabilities.

The Importance of Plans. Specific plans for the exceptional child should be considered as early as possible. Sometimes an early shift in emphasis from diagnosis to what can best be done for the child immediately will indirectly bring acceptance of an implied status while resistance to an explicit statement is still great. Parents are often able to accept the facts of the child's present level of functioning while rejecting their implications for the child's future attainments.

The typical starting point for planning is the parents' conception of their child's future. A plan which they have considered, together with alternatives suggested by the counselor, is the beginning. Planning for the future is a continuing process and is never complete. Plans are realized one step at a time and need constant revision in the light of the individual's progress. If the parents leave a conference with nothing more than a commitment to attend a meeting of parents with similar problems and exchange information and plans with these parents, they have taken an important first step. Reading suggested literature on their child's condition may be an additional small step toward making long-range plans for their child.

Group Counseling. Group counseling ranges all the way from an informal exchange of information and experiences among a group of parents with common problems to formal counseling by a trained and experienced leader. Group counseling directed by a leader can range from lecture, lecture and discussion, directed discussion, or free discussion to directive or nondirective psychotherapy.

Group guidance, counseling, and psychotherapy were originally used and justified because they saved the time of the counselors and psychotherapists who are in such short supply. However, experience indicates that working with groups may have some unique advantages over individual counseling or psychotherapy. Recently there has been a tremendous growth in group approaches to many training, guidance, counseling, and psychotherapeutic problems (McGowan and Schmidt, 1962).

Some of the advantages of group counseling of the parents of exceptional children are:

1. The group gives the parents emotional support. Groups of people with common experiences and similar needs feel free to express their feelings, attitudes, and beliefs. The group identification which typically develops as the result of shared experiences and common feelings seems to lessen the individual's emotional burden. The mere discovery that many other reasonably normal and adequate parents have similar conflicts and frustrations helps many parents to put their own problems in a different perspective.

   In the group situation the parent is free to proceed at his own rate. He can bring up and focus on problems that are most significant to him. In group discussion he is able to clarify his own ideas and feelings. Self-pity, guilt, and shame diminish when a parent discovers that others have shared and surmounted his problems.

2. In the group situation, parents educate each other. The typical group of parents of exceptional children have, *in toto*, accumulated a tremendous amount of information about exceptional children and the resources available for their diagnosis, care, and treatment. They are able to save each other a tremendous amount of time, money, and emotional stress by the exchange of information and experiences. And parents are generally more receptive to information, advice, and counseling coming from people like themselves than they are to the same information provided by professionals.

3. Programs for action are more likely to succeed as the result of group endeavors than when individuals act alone.

Many times the greatest service that a counselor can provide the parents of exceptional children is to put them in touch with a local group of parents, and perhaps follow through and see that they meet with the group at least once. Such parents can also profit from membership in the state and national organizations concerned with exceptional people.

Counseling as a Continuing Process. Whenever possible, counseling services should be continuously available. Parents who are not receptive to counseling at one time may be so later. The problems of exceptional children change with age. A program for a handicapped child which is quite adequate so long as the child is of school age must be replaced by another when he is older. Changes in the family constellation bring new problems. While the aim of counseling is to help the parents to help themselves, an overdependency on counselors is discouraged. Parents should leave counseling with the feeling that they can return if subsequent problems become overwhelming.

FAMILY AND PERSONAL PROBLEMS OF THE GIFTED

Because counselors spend such a disproportionate portion of their time with the subnormal and the inadequate, the problems of the intellectually superior and potentially creative individuals are often overlooked. The parents of the mentally and physically deficient look with envy on the families of the physically and mentally superior and are surprised to discover that they also have problems.

Intellectual superiority provides no immunity to personal and family problems. Most studies show a lower incidence of personal and social maladjustment among the gifted than among those of normal or below-normal intelligence. However, it is possible that in studies such as Terman's, in which the gifted subjects were originally selected largely by teacher nominations, an excess of high achievers and social conformers are obtained (Hughes and Converse, 1962). Personal and social problems are found at all intellectual levels, and although the number of problems and the nature of the difficulties encountered may differ, the superior child and his parents are often in need of help (Laycock, 1951–52).

The Superior Individual's Adjustment to a World Dominated by Normalcy and Mediocrity. Parents usually expect to have normal children and marked deviations in any direction from this expectancy are disconcerting. When the parents themselves are superior, however, the discrepancy between the expectations and the reality is probably reduced and the potential problems of accepting and understanding the gifted offspring are diminished.

Social institutions are geared largely to the average person. Consequently, the superior individual is often out of step with his peers and the cultural norm. In a world in which the more visibly deviant individuals are handicapped, there is a tendency to see all deviant people as pathological misfits. Because so much of deviant behavior brings social disapproval, there is a tendency for people to look on all deviant behavior and development as undesirable. The democratic emphasis on the equality of men is accompanied by a belief in compensatory justice—that is, that marked superiority in one area goes with corresponding deficits in other areas. This belief is typified in the old conception—now disproven —that the intellectually superior individuals are personally and socially maladjusted and are physical misfits who burn out and die at an early age. Many of the problems of the intellectually superior child grow out of his difference from the stereotype of a child. The nature and significance of the gifted child's uniqueness is often misunderstood.

Some Parents Cannot Understand and Are Afraid of Their Gifted Offspring. When the parents and siblings are only normal, the intellectually superior child is often misunderstood. His precocious behavior and speech are seen as impertinent and officious. His questioning and his skepticism are viewed as a lack of proper respect. The child's ability to outwit his elders or circumvent their rules threatens their status as parents or teachers. His apparent premature willingness to express his opinions shows that he is a smart aleck. Parents and teachers are sometimes frightened by the child's giftedness. This fear may cause them to repress the child's initiative and creativity in an effort to keep him properly controlled.

Parents and teachers may feel insecure and threatened by the child's challenge to their authority. These are the people who see gifted children as smart alecks who need to be kept in their places. Other adults stand in fearful awe of the exceptionally gifted child for a different reason. They perceive him as another *kind* of person. This misunderstanding makes them afraid to do anything, lest they stifle the child's creativity. They abdicate their roles as parents and teachers for fear that rules, regulations, and disciplinary procedures will stifle the child's giftedness. They are so afraid of doing the wrong things that they relinquish all responsibility for direction and guidance.

Such adults need assurance that the gifted, like all other types of exceptional children, are first of all children and in most ways can be treated like other children. Superior children need acceptance, affection, and security. They also require motivation, guidance, and challenge if they are to develop well, just as do children of other intellectual levels. Gifted children are no more delicate or subject to the ill effects of excessive restrictions and repressions than any other children. They likewise are no less in need of encouragement and challenge.

Parents May Either Exploit or Neglect the Superior Child. Overambitious parents have sometimes idolized and at the same time exploited their gifted children. By exhibiting the child's superiority and publicizing his accomplishments, they strive for family recognition and status. In the guise of nourishing his talent, parents may ceaselessly push and overstimulate the child.

Conversely, the superior child may be neglected. Either because of failure to recognize the child's high potential or because of the belief that talent will out and that the superior child can fend for himself, adults may deprive gifted children of the required nurture and opportunities for development (Thom and Newell, 1945).

The Discrepancy between the Child's Intellectual Status and His Physical and Social Developments. Certain of the gifted child's problems arise from the discrepancy between his superior intellectual level on the one hand and his more normal physical and social development on the other. While studies have shown that the intellectually superior are also physically and socially superior to normal children of the same

chronological age, their intellectual precocity greatly exceeds their physical and social acceleration. This means that when gifted children associate with children of approximately their own mental age—and research
studies have consistently shown that they do this—they will be much
smaller and less socially mature than their associates (Barbe and Chambers, 1964). Because the intellectually superior are unable to compete
athletically and socially with their intellectual equals, they are in danger
of becoming social loners. They sometimes prefer sedentary leisure activity to the more active social and athletic activities.

The discrepancy between the intellectual levels and physical status
of the gifted diminishes with age and, of course, becomes of no importance at maturity.

Counseling the Parents of the Gifted Child. The parents of the gifted
need help in understanding the extent and nature of their child's superiority. They often require assistance in accepting the fact of the child's
status without excessive anxiety or pride. They need to be aware of the
possibilities and dangers of exploiting the child's cleverness on the one
hand, and of neglecting or rejecting him on the other. Rejection and
favoritism, either of the gifted child or of his less gifted siblings, are
always possibilities. Sometimes the superior child is favored because he
can be exploited for parental glory, and his less favored siblings are
neglected; less often, he may be neglected because his parents believe that
he can look out for himself and therefore needs less than the others.
Sometimes neglect of the superior child results from parental attempts
to somehow compensate the more normal siblings for their lack of giftedness.

Counseling will indicate to the parents that giftedness carries with it
no immunities or special privileges. Gifted children should be expected
to assume family responsibilities, do their share of housework and chores.
They need to become involved in all matters of family concern and ultimately to become healthily independent of parents, just like other children.

The unusual questions and ideas of the gifted and creative child
should be respected, encouraged, and dealt with to the extent that the
parents are able. As far as possible, the home of the gifted, as of every
child, should provide a model of curious, open, enthusiastic, and creative
behavior. Such a home provides a nourishing environment as well as a
possible refuge from estranged peers and teachers.

S u m m a r y

The individual exceptional child can best be understood in terms of
the entire family constellation. Family and child exert reciprocal effects
on each other, and changes in either affect both. Parental and family

reactions to the advent of a child with a disability do not differ in kind from people's reactions to other types of stress. Parental reactions to the problems of the exceptional range from complete denial to realistic coping with the situation. Self-pity, ambivalence, projection, guilt, shame, depression, self-punishment, and the development of patterns of mutual dependency are common parental reactions to the presence of a less-than-adequate child in the family.

The general reactions of children to a handicapped sibling largely reflect those of the parents, but must always be considered in counseling the families of exceptional children. Working with the families of exceptional children involves no unique counseling techniques or principles. However, the nonprofessional counselor is admonished to heed these precepts:

1. Let the counselee talk.
2. Use the terminology of the counselee.
3. Accept the counselee as an individual but do not necessarily approve of and endorse his ideas, practices, and plans.
4. See both parents, preferably the entire family.
5. Deal with feelings and attitudes as well as with intellectual matters.
6. Keep interpretation on a fairly elementary and superficial level.
7. Give diagnostic information according to the individual's ability to understand and accept it.
8. Include specific plans for the future.
9. Remember that group counseling is often useful for the parents or families of exceptional children.
10. Keep your door open. Counseling should be a continuing process.

References

BANSCH, R., "Explanations Offered by Parents and Siblings of Brain-Damaged Children," *Except. child.*, XXVII (1961), 286–91.

BARBE, W. B., AND N. S. CHAMBERS, "Where Do Gifted Children Find Friends?" *School counselor*, V (March, 1964), 148, 176, 329, 343.

BEHRENS, M. L., "Child Rearing and the Character Structure of the Mother," *Child devel.*, XXV (1954), 225–38.

BELL, N. W., AND E. F. VOGEL, eds., *A Modern Introduction to the Family*. New York: The Free Press, 1960.

BLODGETT, H., AND G. J. WARFIELD, *Understanding Mentally Retarded Children*. New York: Appleton-Century-Crofts, 1959.

BOLES, G., "Personality Factors in the Mothers of Cerebral-Palsied Children," *Genet. psychol. monog.*, LIX (1959), 159–218.

CENTERS, L., AND R. CENTERS, "Body Cathexis of Parents of Normal and Malformed Children for Progeny and Self," *J. consult. psychol.*, XXVII (1963), 319–23.

FARBER, B., "Effects of a Severely Mentally Retarded Child on Family Integration," *Monog. soc. res. child devel.*, XXIV (1959), 210.

FREEDMAN, A. M., et al.; "Psychiatric Aspects of Familial Dysantonomia," *Amer. j. orthopsychiat.*, XXV (1957), 96–104.

GRALIKER, B. V., K. FISHLER, AND R. KOCH, "Teenage Reaction to a Mentally Retarded Sibling," *Amer. j. ment. def.*, LXVI (1962), 838–43.

HUGHES, H. H., AND H. D. CONVERSE, "Characteristics of the Gifted: A Case for a Sequel to Terman's Study," *Except. child.*, XXIX (1962), 179–83.

JOHNSON, R. C., AND G. R. MEDINNUS, *Child Psychology: Behavior and Development* (2nd ed.) New York: John Wiley & Sons, Inc., 1969.

JORDON, S., "The Disadvantaged Group: A Concept Applicable to the Handicapped," *J. psychol.*, LV (1963), 313–22.

LARVE, C. M., "The Equivalence of Guilt and Anxiety as Psychological Constructs," *J. consult. psychol.*, XXVIII (1964), 553–54.

LAXER, R. M., "Relation of Real Self-rating to Mood and Blame and Their Interaction in Depression," *J. consult. psychol.*, XXVIII (1964), 539–48.

LAYCOCK, S. R., "Helping Parents to Accept Their Exceptional Children," *Except. child.*, XXIX (1951–52), 515–20.

McGOWAN, J. F., AND L. D. SCHMIDT, *Counseling: Readings in Theory and Practice.* New York: Holt, Rinehart & Winston, Inc., 1962.

MacGREGOR, R., et al., *Multiple Impact Therapy with Families.* New York: McGraw-Hill Book Company, 1964.

MILLER, E. A., "Cerebral-Palsied Children and Their Parents," *Except. child.*, XXIV (1958), 298–302.

ORLANSKY, H., "Infant Care and Personality," *Psychol. bull.*, XLVI (1949), 1–48.

RADKE, M. J., *The Relation of Parental Authority to Children's Behavior and Attitudes,* University of Minnesota Institute of Child Welfare Monograph, Series 22. Minneapolis, 1946.

ROGERS, C. R., *Clinical Treatment of the Problem Child.* Boston, Mass.: Houghton Mifflin Company, 1939.

ROSS, A. O., *The Exceptional Child in the Family.* New York: Grune & Stratton, Inc., 1964.

SARASON, S. B., *Psychological Problems in Mental Retardation* (3rd ed.). New York: Harper & Row, Publishers, 1959.

SATIR, V. M., *Conjoint Family Therapy.* Palo Alto, Calif.: Science and Behavior Books, Inc., 1964.

SCHAEFER, E. S., "A Circumplex Model for Maternal Behavior," *J. abnorm, soc. psychol.*, LIX (1959), 226–45.

————, "Converging Models for Maternal Behavior and for Child Behavior," in *Parental Attitudes and Child Behavior,* ed. J. E. Glidewell Springfield, Ill.: Charles C. Thomas, Publisher, 1961.

SEARS, R. R., G. E. MACCOBY, AND H. LEVIN, *Patterns of Child Rearing.* New York: Harper & Row, Publishers, 1957.

SHERE, M. O., "Socio-emotional Factors in Families of the Twin with Cerebral Palsy," *Except. child.*, XXII (1956), 197–99; 206–8.

SMITH, E., B. M. RICKETTS, AND H. SMITH, "The Recommendations for Child Placement by a Psychiatric Clinic," *Amer. j. orthopsychiat.*, XXXII (1962), 42–52.

TELEFORD, C. W., "A Study of Religious Attitudes," *J. soc. psychol.*, XXXI (1950), 216–30.

THOM, D. A., AND N. NEWELL, "Hazards of the High IQ," *Ment. hyg.*, XXIX, (1945), 61–77.

ULLMAN, M., *Behavioral changes in patients following strokes.* Springfield, Ill.: Charles C. Thomas, Publisher, 1962.

WITMER, H., "The Outcome of Treatment in a Child Guidance Clinic," *Smith coll. stud. soc. wk.*, III (1933), 399–408.

ZUK, G. H., "The Cultural Dilemma and Spiritual Crises of the Family with a Handicapped Child," *Except. child.*, XXVIII (1962), 405–8.

INTELLECTUAL
EXCEPTIONALITY

II

5

The Intellectually Superior

As the general level of intelligence increases, the number of people possessing the higher levels of intellect increases. The brilliant do not comprise a very large proportion of the general population, but their potential for productivity in the culture is relatively great. The need for scientists, linguists, technicians, and artists gets greater every year. The specific nature of outstanding ability demanded by society tends to vary over the years, but the demand for the contributions of the intellectually superior is always high.

The ever-increasing complexity of society and the expanding horizons of scientific investigation have served to emphasize the necessity for early identification and training of the brilliant. It is theorized that early identification and subsequent training will help to bring about more complete utilization of the potential of these people for making significant contributions to the culture and will also be of personal benefit to the brilliant themselves. Investigations of the characteristics of the brilliant are essential to their identification and training. The contributions of the very bright portion of the population should serve to enhance the quality of existence for all. The culture in general should be improved by the contributions of the brilliant. Concern for the human condition will not allow us to overlook or fail to develop this potential for human betterment.

Historical Background

Concern for the identification and training of gifted children is not a recent one. Plato was concerned about discovering the most able youth so that they might be educated for state leadership and suggested tests of native ability for their selection.

Early studies of gifted children and adults tended to be largely anecdotal and descriptive. Some of the early reports were of children who learned to read and converse at very early ages, but no follow-up studies of their later development are available. Similar case descriptions in the relatively recent past (Bridgmann, 1938) detail the precocious behavior of the children. They report remarkable speech development by one year of age, and subsequent very early and outstanding ability to read, to converse, and to acquire and recite information. Many similar reports of precocious children and prodigies, made before the era of intelligence testing (Dolbear, 1912), comprised the literature on the gifted throughout the last century and the early part of this one.

The scientific investigation of the gifted can be readily traced to Galton's (1869) reports of his genetic and statistical studies of the gifted. These were really the first quantitative studies of human abilities. Galton attempted to show that man's natural abilities derived from inheritance in much the same way as such features as height and other physical attributes. By carefully examining the biographies of men of outstanding achievement he indicated that the principal elements contributing to achievement were "ability, zeal, and readiness to work." He felt that each of these was in part a result of inheritance, but that the most important factor was the "gift of high ability." He devoted his book to the study of the ability of gifted men. From his studies he recognized two kinds of ability. The more important one was a single "general ability" that was basic to all of a man's thoughts and actions. A number of "special aptitudes," each of limited scope, were also recognized, but Galton insisted that these special factors were of secondary importance and contributed only slightly to the attaining of eminence. He asserted that without a special gift for a particular kind of achievement one would not achieve in that area, but that to become great in a given area one needed a high degree of general ability. He emphasized the great versatility that he found in the early years of the future genius. This point has been emphasized more recently and it has been indicated that the *direction* of endeavor results chiefly from interest or accident (Burt, 1962). According to Galton, those of outstanding ability to achieve possess a greater *quan-*

tity of their particular abilities. They possess the same *qualities* as do others, but they have them in greater quantity (a position that has been discussed in an earlier chapter of this book).

Much interest was aroused by these reports and by subsequent investigations of social influences on the gifted as well as the role of genetic factors in giftedness (Ward, 1906; Cattell, 1915). Reports of leadership, mental health, and ability were made, and genius was presented as superior mental ability by Terman (1904, 1905, 1906).

With the advent of the Binet tests and their utilization, it was soon discovered that the range of performance on intelligence tests was great and that those scoring very high on the tests were, indeed, exceptional children. Early investigations by Terman (1915, 1925) served to initiate the attack on many of the then current beliefs about the brilliant and on the attitudes toward them. The reports of Terman et al. (1925) constitute an important landmark in the investigations of giftedness. He investigated more than a thousand gifted children and reported on their development and behavior. These children were studied well into adulthood, and these investigations have provided a large volume of data about the gifted (Terman and Oden, 1947, 1959; Oden, 1968). Investigations of the gifted have been numerous, and a substantial body of literature in this area has accumulated. A general view of the gifted, their problems, and their promise will be presented in this chapter.

Problems of Definition and Terminology

Definitions of intelligence have been offered by a great number of investigators. These definitions have perhaps reflected the divergence of interests and theoretical orientations of persons interested in intelligence as much as they have contributed to any clarification of the concept. The way in which intelligence is defined is a partial determinant, at least, of the way in which the intellectually gifted or exceptionally intelligent will be defined. It is to be expected, then, that uniformity of definition of the exceptionally brilliant will not be found. This problem is further confounded when the same criterion is used differently by various investigators. This is the case in attempting to delineate the brilliant.

A commonly used method of defining the brilliant is in terms of scores on a test of intelligence. This is not as simple a method as it might appear at a first glance. Not all investigators have employed the same tests of intelligence. Some have used individual tests while others have employed group tests of ability. Those using individual measures have not always used the same instrument, and a tremendous variety of group measures has been employed. In addition, the investigators have differed about the score above which an individual would be designated as brilliant, gifted, talented, or superior.

In Terman's notable investigations, the IQ as measured by the Stanford-Binet intelligence test (Terman, 1925) was the criterion used. The minimum score originally set for the gifted was 140, although some children scoring as low as 135 were later included in his group. Subsequently, other investigators have employed other scores as being the minimum for the gifted child. Perhaps the most popular figure has been an IQ of 130. IQ's lower than 130 have been used to select children for special classes. Heck (1953) indicated that an IQ of 125 was an approximate point for determining admission to classes for the intellectually superior, and children with IQ's of 120 whose performance is consistently outstanding in areas of value to society have been considered as eligible for special classes (Otto, 1957). The normally bright child has been considered to have a minimum IQ of 110 (Bentley, 1937).

The use of the IQ in defining the gifted has the advantage of objectivity. It can also be applied relatively early in life. This gives it an advantage over the earlier definitions, which defined the gifted as those who had achieved outstanding stature in one of the professions and thus identified them after their education and training was completed. Although Hollingworth (1931) has asserted that the IQ is the only way to identify gifted children with certainty, using it as the sole basis has come under severe attack. Children from low socio-economic backgrounds and from certain ethnic backgrounds tend not to score well on verbal tests and may be excluded when such instruments are used as the basis for selection. Some children who do not score exceptionally high on tests of intelligence later tend to excel in music and the arts. In order to include these individuals, the definition of the gifted was broadened to include the "talented" and those whose performance is consistently remarkable in some potentially valuable activity (Witty, 1958). Further elaboration of definition to include creativeness as a part of giftedness has become popular (Frierson, 1969). Creativeness has received sufficient investigative attention to be treated in a separate chapter of this text. Research on the gifted published in professional journals shifted from 61 percent dealing with gifted children in 1961 to 64 percent dealing with creativity in 1966 (Frierson, 1969).

The profusion of definitions of the brilliant is great. Abraham (1958) reported that one of his students uncovered 113 different definitions of the gifted while preparing a term paper. In spite of this diversity and the confusion in terminology, there is some general agreement as to who the exceptional are. In spite of the shortcomings of conventional IQ tests, scores on these instruments provide a handy frame of reference for thinking about the gifted, and most investigations of the gifted have dealt with children with high IQ's. As a working hypothesis, we shall consider those with high IQ's or those who in other areas of performance are consistently outstanding. The words *gifted, brilliant,* and *exceptional* will be used interchangeably.

Identification of the Brilliant

Before any systematic effort can be made to provide adequate educational programs or personal guidance for those with high levels of intellect, they must be identified. If gifted students require different curricula and methods of instruction than do the average students, these people must be discovered so that appropriate measure can be taken for their academic welfare. The same thing is true in the personal and social realms. If development of the gifted as persons is to receive any unique consideration, they must be known to those who can make the necessary provisions.

For educational purposes, a systematic program for identification can be developed. Classroom teachers can use measuring devices with all of their students as a first crude step. Such a preliminary screening program can save time and effort, and reduce the complex task of final selection by well-trained personnel.

Standardized tests of achievement can be employed systematically in the school. Those who score high enough above the norms for their age or grade to be considered outstanding can be further examined. A danger in the use of tests of achievement as the sole criterion for selection for special attention is that a number of children who are not particularly brilliant, but who are highly motivated to do good work in school, will be found to score high. These children may be doing very well in their current situation, and should not be expected or encouraged to excel beyond their current status. Tests of educational achievement do not detect the individual who has the potential for high-level achievement but who is not achieving at a rate beyond that of his classmates.

Group tests of intelligence can be employed as a rough device in the discovery of those individuals who are not achieving at a high level. At the same time, those who are achieving at high levels but do not score high on the group tests of intelligence can be referred for more intensive investigation.

Reliance on group tests of intelligence for adequate classification is sometimes necessary due to the lack of adequately trained personnel. It has been found that when this procedure is employed there are several dangers that are encountered (Martinson and Lessinger, 1960; Pegnato and Birch, 1959). Martinson and Lessinger found that less than half of a group of 332 pupils scoring over 130 on the Stanford-Binet scored as high as 130 on a group test of intelligence. Pegnato and Birch reported similar findings; in order to identify 92 percent of those scoring above 135 on an individual test, it was necessary to consider all who had exceeded 115 on the group test. This discrepancy between the results of employing group and individual intelligence tests points up the necessity for thorough examination if the detection procedures are to be effective.

Individual intelligence tests are to be administered by trained individuals. Interpretation of test results is not a routine matter. The trained psychologist has available to him the use of more valid measuring instruments than does the untrained individual. He also has had special training in the interpretation and utilization of such scores once they have been derived. The sophistication of the trained psychologist makes his services in this area imperative. He has knowledge of a variety of tests and testing devices, and can make better estimates of the procedures to be used in an individual evaluation. Individual examination is usually to be preferred over group testing as a procedure. Many of the group tests depend for their validity upon their agreement with the individually administered ones, and greater attention can be paid to the examining situation when it is done on a one-to-one basis.

An interesting attempt to identify the gifted by evaluating school children's creative responses has been reported (Martinson and Seagoe, 1967). In this investigation a high-IQ group (Stanford-Binet IQ mean = 142.7) produced more products that were rated as creative than did a lower-IQ group (mean = 107.5). In this investigation the traditional IQ proved to be a better predictor of creative production than did a measure of divergent thinking!

School grades have also been employed as a rough device for screening. As a generalization, it is safe to say that students who obtain a preponderance of A and B grades are more likely to be brilliant than are those who get lower grades, but school grades reflect a lot of things besides achievement. (It has already been indicated that achievement measures, by themselves, are not adequate.) High grades are sometimes given to increase morale and motivation, and biases are bound to creep into the situation as a result of personality, as well as social and cultural factors which are involved in the complex schoolroom situation.

Teachers' ratings have also been used. When teachers have been asked to designate the children in their classes who are gifted, however, they have not been able to do so very accurately. This is particularly true when no operational definition of giftedness is supplied and each teacher is left free to use his own judgment in determining giftedness. In one investigation (Pegnato and Birch, 1959) it was found that teachers did not refer about 55 percent of the children who were later found to be gifted by the criteria established by the investigators. Thirty-one percent who were not gifted by the criteria employed were referred. If checklists of behavioral characteristics of the gifted are supplied, however, the teachers' ratings improve. Rather extensive lists which have been published (Abraham, 1958; Kough and DeHaan, 1955) cite characteristic behavior of the gifted, either defined by the constructors of the lists or based on large numbers of investigations of the characteristics of gifted individuals. Precocity in a number of physical and intellectual areas combined with breadth of activities and interests is usually indicative of brilliance.

The value to the culture of stimulating, directing, and educating the brilliant is so great that the importance of the task of identifying them should not be underestimated. The utilization of the best available techniques for this purpose is to be encouraged. A variety of procedures can be employed and the best trained personnel available should be utilized.

Incidence[1]

The frequency of occurrence of the brilliant depends on the definition used. The frequency of occurrence in the general population is automatically determined if the brilliant are defined as comprising a given percentage of the population. On such a basis, estimates of frequency among school children have ranged from 0.5 to 20 percent. If the estimate includes those who are not necessarily intellectually superior but do have unusual skill in some particular area, such as the musically and artistically talented or those with mechanical, or motor skills, it will be higher, of course. Using such a definition, 15 percent of a group of Illinois children were found to be gifted (DeHaan and Havighurst, 1957). Workers using other criteria that included creativity estimate that between 5 and 10 percent of the student population should be considered gifted (Sumption and Luecking, 1960).

Operational definitions of the gifted based on intelligence test scores have been followed by a great amount of research. Obviously, the number of persons considered gifted will be determined by the location of the score which constitutes the criterion. If an IQ of 130 on the Wechsler Intelligence Scale for Children is employed, about 2 percent will be considered gifted; if the cutoff score is reduced, this percentage will increase. It has been estimated (Conant, 1959) that as many as 15 to 20 percent should be considered gifted.

[1]Although epidemiologists define *incidence* as the occurrence of new cases during some specified time period and *prevalence* as the total number of active cases in the population at a specified time, we shall use the terms interchangeably as referring to the total number in the population.

Differences among schools in the number of brilliant students have been found to be rather extensive. Malherbe (1921), examining a group of private school children with the Stanford-Binet, found that 13 percent of the students in grades 1 to 8 had IQ's of over 140. Terman (1916) reported that only .55 percent of a group of 905 children in the same grades scored 136 or over.

The socioeconomic level of the community has been found to be an important variable in determining the percentage of children who score at various levels on tests of intelligence. In an average community, 16 to 20 percent of the elementary school population can be expected to have IQ scores above 115, whereas in a high-income area 45 to 60 percent will be found above the same score. If a higher IQ is considered, the same general proportion of difference is found. For children with IQ's above 140, the percentages for the average community are between 0.5 and 1 percent, for the favored community, between 2 and 3 percent (Gallagher, 1959). It seems that between three and six times as many children in the elementary schools in a superior community will have IQ's above either 115 or 140 than will children in a school in an average area.

There are no definitive answers to the question of how many children in the schools should be considered to be brilliant or be classified as gifted. The particular operational definition of giftedness to be employed is likely to be determined by the educational facilities available and by the amount of interest and enthusiasm for providing education and training for the superior groups. If the school district under consideration is relatively small, a larger percentage of the population must be included in order to justify the cost of special classes or facilities; if there is a larger student population from which to select, a smaller percentage will fill whole special schools. Variability of prevalence data is to be expected when practical programs must be devised in school districts of various sizes and socioeconomic classifications employing various definitions of giftedness.

Characteristics of the Brilliant

In discussing the characteristics of gifted children as a group, there is always the danger of falsely assuming that individual differences among them are small. There are many differences between one highly intelligent individual and the next, and these differences are not to be ignored when considering the gifted as a group. To assume homogeneity among the gifted would be to ignore the fact that the restriction of any one variable does not have an equally restrictive effect on other variables, even though they may be highly correlated. For example, if a group of people, all of whom are 6 feet or over in height, is selected for investigation, it is true that there will be also some selection on the basis of weight. Tall people tend to weigh more than short ones. But the restriction of the variability of weight will not be as great as the restriction imposed on height, even though the two are positively correlated.

Variability in factors other than intelligence is to be expected among the gifted as a group. Among the gifted will be found the short, tall, active, and lethargic, as well as high-achievers and low-achievers. It should be remembered, in reading the following paragraphs, that the intellectually superior are being considered as a group and that the characteristics indicated are not all applicable to each and every gifted person.

PHYSICAL CHARACTERISTICS

As a group, the gifted tend to exceed the average on measures of physical traits (Terman, 1925; Witty, 1930; Miles, 1954). Burks, Jensen, and Terman (1930) report that a study of Terman's gifted group showed them to have superior ratings on thirty-four anthropometric measures, including height, weight, and general physical development. Witty's (1930) six-year investigation of another group of gifted children found them to be of better than average bodily development. Superior neuro-muscular capacity (Monahan and Hollingworth, 1927) and infrequent physical defects (Jones, 1925) among children of superior intelligence have been reported.

Terman and Witty both secured health histories of their samples. Consistent health examinations showed that the general physical health of both the child and his parents was better than average. The children were slightly heavier at birth. They cut their first tooth about two months earlier, and walked and talked about two months earlier than the average child. The children in these investigations were more precocious in speech development than they were in other areas. Later development seems to follow an accelerated program, and pubescence is reached earlier by the gifted.

Both major and minor physical defects are found less frequently among groups of gifted children than among the unselected population. They are, in general, fine physical specimens who enjoy good growth and health. These findings, when they were first reported, were in sharp disagreement with popular opinion. It had been thought that the brilliant were typically frail and weak. Research has indicated that, in fact, they are likely to be large, robust, and healthy.

SEX

The question of whether giftedness occurs more frequently in girls or boys really has not been satisfactorily answered. In many of the investigations of children with high IQ's, an excess of boys over girls is reported. Terman et al. (1925) found 121 gifted boys and 100 gifted girls in a sample of 643 preschool and elementary school children. Jones (1925) reports a similar finding. Jenkins (1936) reported an excess of girls over boys in a Negro population. The adequacy of the sampling procedures in all these studies can be questioned, if they are to be used for investigating the frequency of the sexes among the gifted. In the Terman studies, volunteers were permitted and teachers were asked to nominate individual students for examination. Such a procedure apparently produces a disproportionately large number of boys. Some evidence of this can be garnered from the fact that when all children of given birth dates were examined in Scotland, the sample was found to contain a ratio of 4 boys to 5 girls with IQ's of 140 and over (Macmeeken, 1939). Other investigators using samples more adequate for this purpose have reported similar findings (Lewis, 1940).

In view of the conflicting data, it would seem safe to assume that there is no large discrepancy in the frequency with which the sexes occur among the gifted. This is particularly true in view of the fact that the experiences of the sexes become more and more divergent with age, so that we cannot be certain of the fairness of a given test for both sexes. Early examination of intelligence is contaminated by differential development schedules for the sexes and the lower reliability of the scales at the earlier ages.

EDUCATIONAL ACHIEVEMENT

The importance of educational achievement among the intellectually superior has been emphasized by a great many individuals. The highly superior can make considerable and significant contributions to the culture, and it is felt that they must become educated to a relatively high degree in order to maximize their productivity and possibly to ensure their own personal happiness and welfare.

The results of research on the educational attainment of the gifted indicate that, as a group, they achieve highly in most areas. They do not tend to be one-sided, as had been thought. They tend to be remarkably versatile, and their accomplishments in educational areas are found to be rather universally high. This tends to refute the old supposition of the compensation of abilities. The mass of research data indicate that there is no compensating area of weakness for the areas of demonstrated strength in educational achievement.

Early studies of the school progress of the gifted have been in general agreement that they make rapid strides in academic areas (Terman et al., 1925; Witty, 1940). Terman reports that 3 out of 5 of his gifted group attended kindergarten before entering the elementary grades at an average

age of six years and three months. This was in the early 1920s, when kindergartens were not as prevalent as they are currently. One out of 10 in his sample was placed in the second grade on beginning school, and 1 out of 5 skipped half of the first grade. By the end of grade school, his group was found to have skipped one entire grade. Still, the gifted children were found to be below the placement that would be made on the basis of mental age. This is commonly found among gifted children in school. It has been pointed out (Miles, 1954) that if the average gifted child were promoted according to his mental age, (MA), he would be at least 2.8 years advanced by the age of seven and 5 or more years accelerated by the age of eleven. This would seem to be an unwarranted expectation of performance by these students, however. It has been pointed out that the MA progressively overestimates the potential of students as their IQ increases, and that this may be due to the lack of opportunity to receive either school or life experiences essential to performance at their level of MA. It has been suggested that 0.3 of a year of achievement be subtracted from the MA prediction for each 10 IQ points above 100 (Los Angeles City School Districts, 1955; Lucito, 1963). This would materially reduce the predictions made from MA alone. Even then, the predicted acceleration may be difficult for superior students to attain.

Whether the achievement of the gifted is assessed by the grades assigned to their schoolwork or by achievement tests, the results tend to be the same (Witty, 1940). They tend to excel in the academic aspects of education. Teachers rate them as superior in such areas as reading, arithmetic, grammar, science, literature, composition, history, and geography. They excel to a lesser degree in areas that are not correlated so highly with intelligence, such as penmanship, shopwork, sewing, and art. The gifted tend to receive a larger proportion of A's and B's than do the students of average intellectual ability. This seems to hold true even when the children have been accelerated and are competing for grades with older classmates (Barnette, 1957; Shannon, 1957).

On standardized tests of achievement, the gifted have consistently scored higher than their classmates of average intellectual ability. Terman et al. (1925) pointed out that the measured achievement of the gifted in grade school correlates more highly with intelligence when age is held constant than it does when years of attendance in school are used. Correlations between achievement and intelligence have been found to be higher for moderately superior children than for highly superior children (Cohler, 1941; Johnson, 1942). This is to be expected in view of the increasing overestimation of achievement as IQ increases. When classroom instruction is about the same (Hollingworth and Cobb, 1928) or when groups with lower IQ's receive special coaching (Hildreth, 1938) the differences in IQ continue to affect the achievement scores. Those with high

IQ's tend to retain their superior status on measures of achievement, especially on tests measuring more complex abilities.

In the winning of honors and scholarships, the same general picture of superior achievement is apparent. The gifted are more often winners in essay contests and of class honors in elementary and high school. They obtain more scholarships to college than do the less adept, and once in college they contribute a disproportionately higher number of members to honor rolls and honorary organizations. A higher percentage of the gifted group pursues work at the graduate level in college than is characteristic of the average college graduate (Terman and Oden, 1947).

EXTRACURRICULAR ACTIVITIES

Gifted children learn to read earlier than do children of average ability. Roughly half the children in both Terman's (1925) and Witty's (1930) groups of gifted children learned to read before attending school. Reading is a favored pastime of gifted children, and one of their favorite school subjects. The gifted read twice as many books as a control group over a two-month period (Terman et al., 1925).

The gifted express as much liking for games and for playing with other children as do average boys and girls. They are likely to prefer playmates somewhat older than themselves. They spend somewhat less time in active play with other children than do the average, and somewhat more time at games that involve reading and greater mental maturity. Lehman and Witty (1927) report that gifted girls engage in a somewhat larger number of play activities than average girls and that the reverse is true for boys. They report that the gifted less frequently engage in certain kinds of vigorous physical games, and more often in games and activities in which reading is an element. The games and activities that are enjoyed most and played most frequently by the gifted are about the same as those of the average child, with some preference being given by the gifted to thinking games and those that tend to be mildly social.

Gifted children typically display a very strong liking for school and are active in the various sponsored clubs, organizations, and special-interest groups. They enjoy games and sports and rate them highly as school activities. This, again, is contrary to the long-held notion of the solitary and sedentary nature of the gifted.

PERSONAL AND SOCIAL CHARACTERISTICS

The personality traits and character development of the gifted have been investigated in some detail. There seems to be general agreement among the early investigators that the gifted, as a group, differ in a favorable direction from unselected children. Terman et al. (1925), using a wide range of tests and rating devices, investigated the personal and social characteristics of a group of 500 gifted children and a like number of children in an unselected control group. Witty (1930) studied the characteristics of 100 gifted children. The results of these studies were equally favorable to the gifted and served to challenge the once widely held belief that intellectual superiority was associated with social and personal maladjustment.

Terman et al. (1925) report that their investigation shows that gifted children have much more favorable social characteristics than the control group. The gifted showed more favorable social preferences, less boastful exaggeration, less cheating, and greater trustworthiness under stress. Sixty to 80 percent of the gifted exceeded the median scores on the separate tests of the battery employed. The gifted were found to be significantly freer from psychopathic trends and significantly more emotionally stable than were control children. The superiority of the gifted in emotional stability was maintained for a number of years when they were reexamined (Burks, Jensen, and Terman, 1930; Oden, 1968).

Teachers' and parents' ratings of the personal characteristics of the gifted tend to agree with the results of measures of intellectual and volitional traits and are somewhat less in agreement on physical and social traits. Teachers report gifted children to be above average in many desirable traits (Specht, 1919), including courtesy, cooperation, willingness to take suggestions, and sense of humor (Johnson, 1923). The superiority of the gifted as a group on personality traits is given support by other investigations of personality traits in intellectually superior children as compared with children of average IQ. Social adjustment of the gifted as a group tends to be above average. Even children who have been accelerated in school and are young for their grade placement have been reported as well adjusted (Miller, 1957). Sociometric studies indicate that the gifted are more frequently chosen by their peers in regular classes (Gallagher, 1958). On projective tests as well as on rating scales, the lower frequency of emotional problems has held up (Gallagher and Crowder, 1957). Investigations using teachers' rating, sociometric procedures, personality inventories, and projective techniques have reported superiority in emotional stability of the gifted as a group. There is evidence that this superiority continues into adulthood (Barbe, 1957; Terman and Oden, 1959).

The studies so far cited have dealt with gifted children as a group, and various other factors have not been controlled. Bonsall and Stefflre (1955), working with a group of gifted and a group of nongifted high school boys, found the usual pattern of superiority for the gifted as a group. However, when they analyzed the data so that only gifted and nongifted students from the same economic levels were compared, little or no differences were found between the two groups. Although it is without doubt true that the intellectually superior make better personal and social adjustments than do the intellectually average, part of this superiority is apparently due to class differences.

SOCIAL AND CULTURAL BACKGROUND

The social and cultural background of the gifted as a group tends to be considerably better than that of the general population. Gifted children tend to come from homes where the socioeconomic level is above average (Terman et al., 1925; Gallagher and Crowder, 1957). Results of investigations uniformly indicate that the parents of gifted children are found most frequently among professional and managerial groups (Cole, 1956). In Terman's sample, 81.4 percent of his subjects had parents whose occupational status was classified as either professional, semiprofessional, or business, and only 6.8 percent had parents who came from the ranks of semiskilled and unskilled labor. This was an interesting finding, in that it had been known for some time that the occupational status of parents was positively correlated with the achievement of the offspring. But this investigation was not dealing with the later achievement of the offspring, but rather with their measured intelligence while they were still in early childhood. Such measures of intelligence during early childhood should not reflect the cumulative results of opportunity for achievement to nearly the same extent as they would be reflected in adult achievement. It was found (Cattell and Brimhall, 1921) that 43.1 percent of the fathers of 885 leading American men of science came from among the professions, and that the same was true for the fathers of 49.2 percent of 666 American men of letters (Clarke, 1916). Terman and Oden (1947) report that the fathers of their gifted group came from the professions in 31.4 percent of the cases.

These investigations are not, of course, directly comparable, because different means of classifying occupational status were employed and the ages of the children in the samples were different. It is interesting to note, however, that from 12 to 18 percent more of the parents of the prominent individuals investigated came from the professions than was true of the gifted sample. There is no doubt that social influences were operative on children examined by Terman and his associates, but it could hardly be argued either that social influence on eventual accomplishment ceases at rather early ages or that the social influence on Terman's sample was as extensively involved in the measures of intelligence employed as they were in the development of adult achievement. If one looks at these data uncritically, they might be interpreted as suggesting the relative influence of intelligence and social factors in the production of outstanding men in the culture. Such a ratio would be at least 2-to-1 or 3-to-1 in favor of the factor of high-level intelligence. When Terman divided his group into high- and low-achievers on the basis of achievement in early adulthood and examined the family background of the two groups, a marked discrepancy was noted (Terman and Oden, 1947). The proportion of professional fathers of the high-achievers was 38 percent, and only 18.5 percent of the low-achievers. The parental education of these two groups was really quite different. Over three times as many fathers of the group of high-achievers had graduated from college. These data tend to indicate that occupational and educational background are much more important than the data just previously cited would tend to indicate. At the present state of our knowledge about the relative influence of high level intelligence and socioeconomic background on achievement, no very accurate statement can be made. That social, educational, and occupational background does have a profound influence on the adult achievement of the gifted cannot be denied, but its ratio of contribution to outstanding achievement remains unknown.

If the gifted are treated as a group, the superiority of their general social and cultural background is rather apparent. Terman's sample of gifted came from parents whose average formal education exceeded that of the general population by four or five years. These parents had more often graduated from college and received Ph.D. degrees. The median income of families in a random sample of gifted was twice as high as that of California families in general, although extremely high incomes were infrequent. The families of the gifted were rated as superior by investigators (4.5 on a 6-point scale). The homes themselves were distinctly superior to the other homes in their neighborhoods, and the incidence of divorce and broken homes was less among the gifted than among an unselected sample. The gifted tend to come disproportionately from urban, as opposed to rural, environments. This may indicate that urban homes provide more intellectual stimulation.

Intellectually superior children come, in relatively high proportions, from parents who have a good education and fathers who have a high-prestige occupation. The upper and upper-middle classes, jointly, produce nearly twice as many children with IQ's in the top quartile as are produced by the average family, and less than one-half as many children in the lowest quartile (Havighurst, 1962). The home environments from which the intellectually superior come can be described as more intellectually stimulating than the average. The homes tend to be superior on a number of bases. The families tend to be less autocratic, read more and better books and magazines, travel more, and in general have greater energy and stability. The cultural patterns of the families tends to encourage education and achievement (Stouffer and Shea, 1959).

The importance of general cultural influence on achievement and on opportunity is indicated by the fact that a librarian's son is one thousand times more likely to win a National Merit Scholarship than is a laboring man's son (Bond, 1957). Studies in England and in New Zealand lend further support to the important role of general cultural factors in the production of scholars (Burt, 1962). Follow-up measures of intellect of the Terman group indicate that as adults they rank about as far above the mean of the population as they did in childhood (Oden, 1968). When 1,571 of their offspring were examined, a mean IQ of 133.2 was obtained (Oden, 1968).

Education of the Brilliant

Gifted students typically do rather well in school, and there has been little concern about such matters as their keeping up with the class. They usually have little or no trouble measuring up to age or grade levels for achievement. This, combined with their general tendency to be well-behaved and emotionally controlled, may cause them to go unnoticed in the classroom. They create no particular classroom disturbances. They have plenty of ability. They can be left to fend for themselves and will still do all right in the school. An attitude about the gifted seems to be crystallized in the expression "Don't worry about him; he is a very bright boy and he's going to do all right."

There is no immediate and apparent characteristic of the gifted that serves as a basis for an emotional appeal for special consideration. Special consideration for the gifted does not have the emotional appeal or the urgency that training for the physically handicapped, the blind, the deaf or the mentally retarded possess. Rarely does one hear a plea for special facilities or programs for the exceptionally brilliant based on democracy in education. Democracy in education has a strong appeal in this country and has been employed as an argument for special facilities for those who are handicapped in some way. Contrariwise, it has been argued that special consideration for the gifted would be undemocratic, in that it would give advantage in training and education to those who are already ahead of their classmates and result in a kind of intellectual aristocracy or privileged group. Guarding against privilege has perhaps absorbed more attention and effort in our educational structure than have plans and procedures for providing for individual differences. Actually, a desirable slogan for the individual education of students might be "special privilege for all." In the final analysis this is what a program based upon meeting the educational needs of individuals, as well as the culture, strives to do.

In recent years there has developed a genuine concern on the part of many professionals and laymen for the education of the gifted. This concern has, in part, been generated by the rapid advancements in science and technology of the past decade or so. The necessity for the training of scientists becomes rather obvious and imperative in a rapidly expanding scientific world. Few would deny that we must provide educational facilities that will develop achievement in these areas, as well as in the areas of social and literary accomplishment. However, there is a great deal of disagreement as to how this can best be done. Disagreement among so-called experts in the area of curriculum and methods is easy to find. This no doubt stems from our current lack of information in these fields. Research in this area is proceeding. An unfortunate delay in doing anything about the problem stems from our not knowing what to do. In the meantime, various programs are being developed out of a perceived necessity for doing something to insure that better utilization of ability is made by the culture. It seems to be much wiser to develop such programs than to delay doing anything for fear of not doing the "right" thing.

Some rather interesting results that should encourage giving special attention to the education of the gifted have been reported by Martinson (1961). The findings of her investigation of various educational and administrative programs, special classes, cluster grouping, and independent study are quite encouraging. In measured results, including academic achievement and social adjustment, children given special services exceeded those who did not get them. Perhaps any systematic program considered to be adequate by professionals familiar with the characteristics of the gifted produces better results than no program at all. The percentage of gifted children in the United States, however who are in special programs or for whom any systematic program is provided has been reported to be amazingly small (Dunn, 1963). Research has indicated that gifted students can develop new problem-solving skills through the use of autoinstructional materials, and teachers can teach gifted students to approach problems creatively (Parnes, 1966). Improvement in evaluative thinking abilities of gifted children who received special instruction for only one month has been reported (Hauck, 1967).

EDUCATION AND UNDERACHIEVEMENT

It has long been recognized that within school groups in general there are those whose academic achievements are more nearly appropriate to their potentiality for contributing to the culture. It has been fairly well recognized, and it seems to be a reasonable enough expectation, that those of average or nearly average intelligence should achieve at a grade level approximately equal to the expected attainment as predicted from their MA's. Those who score above the average range (who have IQ's over 110) have not, however, achieved at the level predicted by their MA's with any degree of consistency. It is true that these children manage to reach school standards relatively easily, and even exceed age-grade expectancy in most instances. They do achieve at high levels, but the question is whether their achievement is close enough to the level to be expected on the basis of their mental age. It has been argued that as long as these individuals are achieving adequately for their chronological age and grade placement and even exceeding this level, there is little to be concerned about. Others have deplored the lag between the achievement to be predicted on the basis of the bright child's mental age and his actual achievement. If MA is used as the criterion for estimating achievement (without any correction to compensate for the tendency of this group not to meet this criterion), the brilliant can be labelled as underachievers. Formulas for making some correction for this tendency have been developed (Horn, 1941), and tables which make corrections for the limitation in experience of very bright children have been constructed (Los Angeles City School Districts, 1955). These tables make a downward adjustment in expected achievement of about 0.3 of a year for each 10 IQ points beyond 100 for age groups common to the elementary school. The rationale for reducing the level of performance predicted by the MA for brilliant children has to do with the difficulties of providing the stimulation and experience that might result in such rapid achievement. The MA offers a standard for achievement that is not typically found among the brilliant. For example, an 8-year-old child with an IQ of 150 would have an MA of 12, and would thus be expected to function in school at a level comparable to the average 12-year-old with an IQ of 100 who has made normal progress in school and is now in the seventh grade. But 8-year-old children with IQ's of 150 do not function at the beginning seventh-grade level. It is argued that they cannot reasonably be expected to do so, and that the MA does not yield a valid estimate of their potential achievement.

Although even gifted children who have been accelerated by a year get better grades than their older classmates (Barnette, 1957; Shannon, 1957), there has been concern over a number who are definitely underachievers. Meeker (1968) reported that gifted children from a special program in the elementary school tended to do much less well when they moved into a traditional secondary school where they received less than adequate attention.

The number of gifted who do not attend college has been considered alarmingly high (Wolfle, 1960), and there are others who do not live up to the cultural standards expected of them (Terman and Oden, 1947). The loss to society that occurs when some of the gifted become definite underachievers and the loss that may be occurring because insufficient challenge, stimulation, opportunity, or facilities are provided for still more of the gifted, have produced some interesting investigations of achievement and underachievement.

Terman and Oden (1947) and Oden (1968) report some interesting data on achievement from their follow-up investigations of gifted children at adulthood. They divided their gifted group into what they called an "A" group on the basis of adult achievement and what they called a "C" group on the same basis. The A group was comprised of those who had lived up to their earlier promise; the C group was comprised of those who for one reason or another were not doing so well as earlier data had indicated. The principal criterion for assignment to one of the two groups was the extent to which a subject had made use of his superior intellectual ability. Comparisons were made on the basis of 200 items of information secured for 150 subjects in each group between 1921 and 1941.

Both the A and C groups had been outstandingly good elementary school students. Their achievement test scores had fallen above the norms in about one-third of the instances, and the overall achievement of the groups had tended to be highly similar in every school subject except language usage and art information, in both of which the A group slightly exceeded the C group. The C group was about a third of a year older at the time of completion of the eighth grade. The A group was reliably younger when they graduated from high school (9.6 months) and when they graduated from college (15.6 months). Differences in achievement had not really become apparent until they attended high school, and then the grades attained by the A's were significantly better than those of the C's. This difference was also found to exist among those who went to college.

In adulthood, the A's were found to have higher levels of vocational interest and broader interests than the C's. They were particularly more interested in politics, social life, and literature. The family backgrounds of the two groups were somewhat different. The parents of those in the C group had less formal education, as did their brothers and sisters, than was characteristic of the A group. The proportion of those whose fathers had graduated from college was three times as high in the A group as in the C group. The fathers' occupational status was also different. The fathers of those in the A group were professionals over twice as frequently as in the C group. The additional education of the fathers of the A group was reflected in the number of books reported to be in the home library. Nearly twice as many books were reported to be in the libraries of parents of those in the *A* group. The educational tradition of the families of those in the *A* group was also much stronger.

Separation and divorce were about twice as common among the parents of those in the *C* group as among the parents of those in the *A* group. On measures of both personal and social adjustment, the *C* group itself did not do as well as did the subjects in group *A*. These findings, coupled with the stronger educational tradition in the families of those in the *A* group may account for a considerable amount of the differences in achievement. Factors other than intellect appear to be highly involved in achievement, and among these factors social and personal adjustment seem to be relatively important.

An investigation of tenth- and twelfth-grade students of high ability sheds additional light on the problem of achievement among the gifted (Pierce, 1962). The upper 30 percent of children who took ability tests in a midwestern high school were chosen for investigation. These 222 boys and girls were divided into four groups: high-achieving tenth-grade boys; high-achieving tenth-grade girls; low-achieving twelfth-grade boys; and low-achieving twelfth-grade girls. High- and low-achievers were designated as being above or below the median of a sample drawn from each grade and sex.

When adjustment was measured by the California Psychological Inventory (CPI), the high-achievers were found to be better adjusted than were the low-achievers. The ratings of peers and teachers confirmed that the high-achievers had greater qualities of leadership and were less aggressive. All three of these methods of evaluating adjustment indicate that the high-achievers tend to be better adjusted than the low-achievers. From interviews with the students it was concluded that high-achieving students were more scholastically ambitious, liked school better, read more, and identified themselves with an adult of the same sex who valued education. The high-achievers were more positive toward school-related activities and toward individuals who value education.

When the subjects were examined for motivation to achieve by analyzing stories they had written, the high-achieving boys scored somewhat higher than the others, but the difference is rather small. The same thing was found to be true for twelfth-grade girls, but it was reversed for tenth-grade girls. That is, tenth-grade girls who were high-achievers scored as having less motivation to achieve than did the low-achievers. This instrument has not proved useful in discriminating between high- and low-achieving girls.

The parental attitudes differed. Mothers of high-achieving boys were found to be less authoritarian and controlling than mothers of low-achieving boys. Mothers of low-status, low-achieving boys were the most authoritarian and controlling of the mothers studied. There is no evidence that mothers of high- and low-achieving girls differed with respect to authoritarianism and control. These maternal attitudes do not keep girls of low social status and high ability from achieving to the same extent that they seem to deter the boys.

Differences have been found in the child-father relationships of underachievers and overachievers. In a rather extensive investigation of 223 children in grades 2 through 5 who had IQ's of 120 and above, Karnes et al. (1963) found some interesting data. They selected the top and bottom 16 percent of their sample on the basis of achievement in relation to ability, and compared them. The attitude and relationship of the child to the father appeared to play a significant role. The fathers of the underachieving children showed more hostility toward and rejection of their children than did the fathers of the overachievers.

In an extensive investigation of underachievers in grades 4, 7, and 10 in thirteen districts of one California county, underachievers with IQ's of 115+ on the California Test of Mental Maturity were selected for study (Shaw, 1961). Those with a B average or better were called achievers. The groups were given various personality tests, from which it was discerned that the underachievers exhibited a greater negative self-concept and a generally more negative outlook on life. Overt expressions of aggression and hostility were greater among the underachievers. The overachievers apparently experienced feelings of hostility, but tended to suppress them. Underachievers tended to have general feelings of inadequacy and this was not characteristic of the achievers.

Individual differences in performance among the brilliant are great. It is rather well established that a certain level of general intelligence is essential for high-level performance in socially useful areas. The level of intellect necessary has not been agreed on, but it is known that individuals with IQ's of 120 have sufficient intellect for most pursuits if they possess the requisite motivation and opportunity is provided. There are enough individuals of very high intellect who do not perform at high levels to indicate that general intelligence alone does not insure performance commensurate with ability. The problem of the grossly underachieving among the brilliant is one for social concern, as well as one of individual welfare and happiness. It is thought that individual welfare is enhanced by many of the same kinds of achievement that are of benefit to the culture. It is to these ends that educational provisions of various kinds have been made. If the brilliant all achieved well up to their level of ability in the usual school situation, there would be no problem about their education. Underachievement does exist and there is considerable concern about it. Therefore, the problems of education have been investigated and provisions of one kind or another have been made for special attention to the education of the gifted.

EDUCATIONAL PROVISIONS

The empirical data provided by the research done in the area of the gifted have yielded some basis for planning for their education. It would be better if more were known about the individual personal characteristics of the gifted. More research needs to be done before we can have definitive ideas about the most appropriate educational processes, procedures, and plans for the education of the gifted, but as we have already observed, many programs have been effectuated nevertheless. Unfortunately, in some instances the administrative structure has been decided on before either educational objectives or procedures were adopted. Both the objectives and educational experiences that are deemed desirable should be determined first, in order that administrative procedures that are most compatible with the kind of educational program desired can be developed.

Educational provisions for exceptional children have been discussed in an earlier chapter, and it is encouraging to note that attempts are being made to evaluate the relative effectiveness of certain procedures. An investigation of the effectiveness of two plans for increasing the achievement of underachieving intellectually gifted children has yielded some differences (Karnes et al., 1963). Children from grades 2 to 5 who had Stanford-Binet IQ's in excess of 120 and who were achieving one standard deviation or more below the mean of their grade level were selected. The group was divided into two treatment conditions. The members of one group were placed in what were called homogeneous groups (classes with only gifted, high-achieving students). Members of the other groups were placed in heterogeneous groups (classes with children ranging from dull normal to intellectually gifted). After two or three years, the gifted underachievers in the homogeneous arrangement were found to have gained in academic achievement more than the heterogeneously placed children. They also were found, through a test of creativity, to have gained more in fluency. Interestingly, although the children in the homogeneous classes gained greater parental acceptance, both groups lost some acceptance by their peers.

This kind of investigation is difficult to execute, and unfortunately the number of gifted underachievers in each treatment condition was small. However, the results suggest that there may be advantages to the homogeneous grouping of the gifted, as opposed to their placement in regular classes. It is possible that the added stimulus provided by being surrounded by achievers is an important factor in increasing the educational progress of gifted underachievers as well as gifted achievers.

It has been found that special provisions for the education of the gifted tend to enhance their achievement. It would seem that almost any program conceived and executed by enlightened and trained personnel serves to enhance the educational achievement of the gifted (Martinson, 1961).

The effectiveness of grouping has been given much investigative effort. The extensive reviews of these investigations present a confusing pattern of advantages and disadvantages. Most reviewers indicate that grouping, in and of itself, is of little advantage unless the academic program is designed to accommodate the various ability levels.

Summary

A brief history of the interest in and investigations of giftedness was presented in this chapter, and some problems of definition and termi nology were discussed. Concern for the brilliant child is not of recent vintage, but quantitative studies of the gifted are a relatively recent development. The pioneering work of Terman and his associates, who investigated the characteristics of gifted children and conducted extensive follow-up studies at later periods in life, has contributed a large body of data to the area. The various definitions of the brilliant have contributed to some of the confusion that exists in terminology employed in this area. The definition of the gifted is partially determined by the definition of intelligence that is employed. Intelligence has, of course, been defined in a variety of ways.

The importance of the possible contributions of the gifted to the culture, as well as a cultural concern for individual welfare, make the problem of identifying the gifted among us an imperative one. Ability and talent cannot be adequately utilized unless they are identified. The early detection of superiority among children is deemed essential in order to make the earliest provisions for their development and education.

Intellectually superior children tend to be superior in a number of ways that are not closely related to intellectual performance. In general they tend to be larger, healthier, happier, and have more extensive interests and hobbies than their normal peers. They particularly enjoy reading and develop this skill rather early and with a minimum of difficulty. Their educational achievement tends to be uniformly high, and they engage in extracurricular activities rather extensively. The gifted tend to have better educated parents than the average, and to come from better socioeconomic backgrounds and to have parents of the higher occupational levels.

The providing of special educational programs and facilities for the gifted has not developed as rapidly or as extensively as have special programs for the handicapped. The gifted do not create serious problems in the home or school. They are not as noticeable as certain of the handicapped groups nor do they arouse compassion. Concern has developed for the welfare of the highly gifted underachiever, and some research in this area has been reported. Programs for the education of the gifted need to be undertaken at the earliest possible moment and should be sufficiently flexible so that they can be changed when additional research findings so indicate.

References

ABRAHAM, W., *Common Sense about Gifted Children*. New York: Harper & Row, Publishers, 1958.

BARBE, W. B., "What Happens to Graduates of Special Classes for the Gifted," *Educ. res. bull.*, XXXVI (1957), 13–16.

BARNETTE, W. L., "Advance Credit for the Superior High-School Student," *J. higher educ.*, XXVIII (1957), 15–20.

BENTLEY, J. E., *Superior Children*. New York: W. W. Norton and Company, Inc., 1937.

BOND, H. M., "The Productivity of National Merit Scholars by Occupational Class," *Sch. and soc.*, LXXXV (1957), 267–68.

BONSALL, M., AND B. STEFFLRE, "The Temperament of Gifted Children," *Calif. j. educ. res.*, VI (1955), 195–99.

BRIDGMANN, A. S., *My Valuable Time*. Brattleboro, Vt.: Stephen Daye Press, 1938.

BURKS, B. S., D. W. JENSEN, AND L. M. TERMAN, *The Promise of Youth: Follow-up Studies of a Thousand Gifted Children (Genetic Studies of Genius*, Vol. III) . Stanford, Calif.: Stanford University Press, 1930.

BURT, C., "The Gifted Child," in *The Yearbook of Education*, eds. B. Bereday and P. Lauwerys. New York: Harcourt, Brace, Jovanovich, Inc., 1962.

CATTELL, J. McK., "Families of American Men of Science," *Pop. sci. mo.*, LXXXVI (1915), 504–15.

————, AND D. R. BRIMHALL, "Families of American Men of Science," in *American Men of Science* (3rd ed.). New York: Science Press, 1921, pp. 781–808.

CLARKE, E. L., "American Men of Letters: Their Nature and Nurture," *Columbia University Studies in History, Economics and Public Law*, LXXII (1916), 1–169.

COHLER, M. J., "Scholastic Status of Achievers and Nonachievers of Superior Intelligence," *J. educ. psychol.*, XXXII (1941), 603–10.

COLE, C. C. Jr., *Encouraging Scientific Talent: A Report to the National Science Foundation*. Princeton, N.J.: College Entrance Examination Board, 1956.

CONANT, J. B., *The American High School Today*. New York: McGraw-Hill Book Company, 1959.

DEHAAN, F., AND R. J. HAVIGHURST, *Educating Gifted Children*. Chicago, Ill.: University of Chicago Press, 1957.

DOLBEAR, K. E., "Precocious Children," *Pediat. sem.*, XIX (1912), 461–91.

DUNN, L. M., ed., *Exceptional Children in the Schools.* New York: Holt, Rinehart & Winston, Inc., 1963.

FRIERSON, E. C., "The Gifted," *Rev. educ. res.*, XXXIX (1969), 25–37.

GALLAGHER, J. J., "Social Status of Children Related to Intelligence, Propinquity, and Social Perception," *Elem. sch. j.*, LVIII (1958), 225–31.

————, *The Gifted Child in the Elementary School.* Washington, D.C.: National Education Association, Department of Classroom Teachers, 1959.

————, *Teaching the Gifted Child.* Boston, Mass.: Allyn & Bacon, Inc., 1964.

————, and T. H. Crowder, "Adjustment of Gifted Children in the Regular Classroom," *Except. child.*, XXIII (1957), 306–12, 317–19.

GALTON, F., *Hereditary Genius.* London: Macmillan & Co., Ltd., 1869.

HAUCK, B. B., "A Comparison of Gains in Evaluation Ability between Gifted and Nongifted Sixth-Grade Students," *Gifted child*, XI (1967), 166–171.

HAVIGHURST, R. J., *Growing Up in River City.* New York: John Wiley & Sons, Inc., 1962.

HECK, A. O., *The Education of Exceptional Children.* New York: McGraw-Hill Book Company, 1953.

HILDRETH, G., "The Educational Achievement of Gifted Children," *Child devel.*, IX (1938), 365–71.

HOLLINGWORTH, L. S., "How Should Gifted Children Be Educated?" *Baltimore bull. educ.*, L (May, 1931), 196.

————, and M. V. Cobb, "Children Clustering at 165 IQ and Children Clustering at 145 IQ Compared for Three Years in Achievement," *Yearb. nat. soc. stud. educ.*, XXVII, Part 2 (1928), 3–33.

HORN, A., *Uneven Distribution of the Effects of Specific Factors*, Southern Calif. Educ. Monog. XII. Los Angeles, Calif.: University of Southern California Press, 1941.

JENKINS, M. D., "A Socio-psychological Study of Negro Children of Superior Intelligence," *J. Negro educ.*, V (1936), 175–90.

JOHNSON, H. G., "Does the Gifted Child Have a Low AQ?" *J. educ. res.*, XXXVI (1942), 91–99.

JOHNSON, O. J., "Teachers' Judgments of Qualities of Gifted Pupils as Related to Classroom Activities," *Sch. and soc.*, XVII (1923), 466–69.

JONES, A. M., "An Analytical Study of One Hundred and Twenty Superior Children," *Psychol. clin.*, XVI (1925), 19–76.

KARNES, M. B., et al., "The Efficacy of Two Organizational Plans for Underachieving Intellectually Gifted Children," *Except. child.*, XXIX (1963), 438–46.

KOUGH, J., AND R. F. DEHAAN, *Teacher's Guidance Handbook.* Chicago, Ill.: Science Research Associates, Inc., 1955.

LEHMAN, H. C., AND P. A. WITTY, *The Psychology of Play Activities.* New York: A. S. Barnes & Co., Inc., 1927.

LEWIS, W. D., *A Study of Superior Children in the Elementary School*, Peabody Coll. Contr. Educ., No. 266. Nashville, Tenn.: Peabody College Press, 1940.

Los Angeles City School Districts, Evaluation and Research Section, *Expected Achievement Grade Placement Tables*, Division of Instructional Services Publication G.C.-6. Los Angeles, Calif., 1955.

Lucito, L. J., "Gifted Children," in *Exceptional Children in the Schools*, ed. L. M. Dunn. New York: Holt, Rinehart & Winston, Inc., 1963.

Macmeeken, A. M., *The Intelligence of a Representative Group of Scottish Children*, Pub. Scot. coun. res. educ., No. 15 (1939).

Malherbe, E. H., "New Measurements in Private Schools," *Survey*, XLVI (1921), 272–73.

Martinson, R. A., *Educational Programs for Gifted Pupils*. Sacramento, Calif.: California State Department of Education, 1961.

———, and L. M. Lessinger, "Problems in the Identification of Intellectually Gifted Pupils," *Except. child.*, XXVI (1960), 227–31.

———, and M. V. Seagoe, *The Abilities of Young Children*. Washington, D.C.: Council for Exceptional Children, 1967.

Meeker, M., "Differential Syndromes of Giftedness and Curriculum Planning: A Four-Year Follow-Up," *J. spec. educ.*, II (1968), 185–194.

Miles, C. C., "Gifted Children," in *Manual of Child Psychology*, ed. L. Carmichael. New York: John Wiley & Sons, Inc., 1954, pp. 984–1063.

Miller, V., "Academic Achievement and Social Adjustment of Children Young for Their Grade Placement," *Elem. sch. j.*, LVII (1957), 257–63.

Monahan, J. E., and L. S. Hollingworth, "Neuromuscular Capacity of Children Who Test above 135 IQ (Stanford-Binet)," *J. educ. psychol.*, XVIII (1927), 88–96.

Oden, M. H., "The Fulfillment of Promise: 40-Year Follow-up of the Terman Gifted Group," *Genet. psychol. mono.*, LXXVII (1968), 3–93.

Otto, H. J., *Curriculum Adjustment for Gifted Elementary School Children in Regular Classes*, Bureau of Laboratory Schools Publication 6. Austin: University of Texas Press, 1957.

Parnes, S. J., *Programming creative behavior*. U.S. Department of Health, Education, and Welfare. Office of Education, Cooperative Research Project No. 5-0716. Buffalo: New York State University, 1966.

Pegnato, C. V., and J. W. Birch, "Locating Gifted Children in Junior High Schools," *Except. child.*, XXV (1959), 300–4.

Pierce, J. V., "The Bright Achiever and Under-achiever," in *The Yearbook of Education*, eds. B. Bereday and P. Lauwerys. New York: Harcourt, Brace, Jovanovich, Inc., 1962.

Shannon, D. C., "What Research Says about Acceleration," *Phi Delta Kappan*, XXXIX (1957), 70–73.

Shaw, M. C., *The Inter-relationship of Selected Personality Factors in High Ability Underachieving School Children: Final Report*, Project 58-M-1. Sacramento, Calif.: California State Department of Public Health, 1961.

Specht, L. F., "A Terman Class in Public School No. 64, Manhattan," *Sch. and soc.*, IX (1919), 393–98.

Stouffer, S. A., and P. D. Shea, *Your Educational Plans*. Chicago, Ill.: Science Research Associates, Inc., 1959.

SUMPTION, M. R., AND E. M. LUECKING, *Education of the Gifted*. New York: The Ronald Press Company, 1960.

TERMAN, L. M., "A Preliminary Study in the Psychology and Pedagogy of Leadership," *Pediat. sem.*, XI (1904), 413–51.

————, "A Study of Precocity and Prematuration," *Amer. j. psychol.*, XVI (1905), 145–83.

————, "Genius and Stupidity," *Pediat. sem.*, XIII (1906), 307–73.

————, "The Mental Hygiene of Exceptional Children," *Pediat. sem.*, XXII (1915), 529–37.

————, *The Measurement of Intelligence*. Boston, Mass.: Houghton Mifflin Company, 1916.

————, *Mental and Physical Traits of a Thousand Gifted Children (Genetic Studies of Genius*, Vol. I). Stanford, Calif.: Stanford University Press, 1925.

————, AND M. H. ODEN, *The Gifted Child Grows Up*. Stanford, Calif.: Stanford University Press, 1947.

————, *The Gifted Group at Mid-life*. Stanford, Calif.: Stanford University Press, 1959.

————, et al., *Mental and Physical Traits of a Thousand Gifted Children*. Stanford, Calif.: Stanford University Press, 1925.

WARD, L. F., *Applied Sociology*. Boston, Mass.: Ginn and Company, 1906.

WITTY, P. A., "A Study of One Hundred Gifted Children," *Univ. Kan. bull. educ., State t. c. stud. educ.*, I, No. 13 (1930) .

————, "A Genetic Study of Fifty Gifted Children," *Yearb. nat. soc. educ.*, XXXIX, Part 2 (1940), 401–8.

————, "Who Are the Gifted?" in *Education for the Gifted: Yearb. nat. soc. stud. educ.*, ed. N. D. Henry, LVII, Part 2 (1958).

WOLFLE, D., "Diversity of Talent," *Amer. psychologist*, XV (1960), 535–45.

6

Creativity

Creativity has been the focus of much recent interest and research by psychologists and educators. Much of the earlier work on creativity was done under a variety of topic headings. Investigations into insight, imagination, and artistic ability have been reported in the psychological literature for many years, and much of this work was concerned with what now might be labelled "creativity." The recent interest of researchers in the field of creativity, in part at least, appears to parallel a literary concern with the subject of conformity. Many people believe that our culture is becoming less and less tolerant of independent or socially divergent behavior (Whyte, 1956). The social and cultural dangers of overconformity in both the ideational and overt behavioral realms have been given emphasis by social theorists. The rewards for conformity, and the relative absence of rewards for independent thinking and acting, have been a possible stifler of individuality and a deterrent to self-expression (Sawrey and Telford, 1971). Government, industry, and educational institutions have become concerned with the identification and development of creative potential. It is reasoned that, in order for our society to make the burdens of existence as light as possible and for as many as possible, new horizons must be opened and the frontiers of knowledge pushed back. To accomplish these things, it will be necessary to call upon the ingenuity and originality of the best minds available. People must be free to be creative without social sanctions and should be rewarded for their culturally relevant original ideas and innovations.

Recent technological advances have made it possible to solve within minutes problems that previously would have taken years. Electronic computers not only have taken the drudgery out of certain kinds of problem solution, but they have made it possible for people to formulate problems that heretofore were not even considered. The ingenuity of man can now be applied to utilizing machines to perform further analyses, the results of which may lead to still further hypotheses to be investigated. Our modern electronic age seems more and more to reject man as performer of routine tasks and a solver of routine problems. Machines can perform a great number of tasks and solve many problems with much greater efficiency than can man. Such a technological culture, if it is to continue its growth, demands less of man's physical energy and more of his ideational processes. Unique ideas, and original problems and new ways of solving them, are the grist of an innovating society. Continued social, political, industrial, and educational progress is dependent, in large part, on the creativity of the members of society.

Defining Creativity

Definitions of creativity are numerous, and they vary according to the particular emphasis given to the concept. If one focusses on the process or processes of creating, his definition might be at variance with that of one who focusses on the end-product of creative endeavor. If one is concerned with the personal or phenomenological aspects of behavior, his definition will include the behavior and feelings that were unique to a particular individual under specified conditions. If the focus of concern is the socially significant and unique responses of individuals, an external frame of reference evolves and leads to a different kind of definition, one which involves a comparison with some cultural norm.

One of the problems involved in defining creativity is to distinguish it from originality. It might be possible, if one used number of uncommon responses to a stimulus as the criterion, for a hospitalized psychiatric patient to be classified as highly creative or original. Without denying that some patients might indeed be highly original or creative, it seems more sensible to apply some criterion of relevance to the responses. In other situations, where novelty of production is employed as an indicator or measure, it would seem advisable to have some criterion of social utility as well. This is probably necessary in order to distinguish among the bizarre, original, and creative. Many unique solutions to problems may not be very useful or socially constructive. This kind of responding has not generally been included as among those designated as original. In order for a response to be termed original, the probability of that response occurring must be low (Maltzman, 1960; Mednick, 1962). Maltzman has added that it must also be relevant to the situation, Mednick that it must also be useful. By these standards, a person may be highly original, but not qualify as highly creative. This is obviously true as they are considered by Mednick. Maltzman contends that creativity depends not only on originality, but also on societal recognition and approval. And because creativity is dependent on society's approval, Maltzman contends that originality is the facet of creativity that is most readily investigated in the laboratory.

Guilford (1959) has distinguished between originality and creativity on the basis of his factor analytic investigations of creativity. Originality is one of several traits contributing to creativity. Creativity is a more general trait that includes not only originality, but flexibility, fluency, and motivational and temperamental traits as well.

There are three basic approaches to the investigation of creativity: focus can be on the *creative process*, the *creative person*, or the *creative product* (Rock et al., 1969).

The personal or phenomenological definitions of creativity involve novelty or uniqueness, but place it in a personal frame of reference. A product may be a creative one if it is new or novel to the individual involved, if it is his own creation, if it is expressive of him rather than dictated by someone else. It need be neither useful nor unique. Its social recognition and cultural impact may be zero, but if it is a unique personal experience, it is creative (Maslow, 1959; 1970; Rogers, 1959; Barron, 1968). Maslow (1970) distinguishes between *special-talent* creativeness of the Mozart type and the creativeness of all people. He indicates that creativeness is a universal characteristic of persons. That each has his own originality or inventiveness that has unique characteristics. The creativeness of the self-actualized person he indicates as being like the naive creativeness of unspoiled children. All people are said to possess the potentiality for creativeness at birth, but most lose it as they become enculturated.

Those who use a cultural frame of reference insist that a creative product must be novel to both the individual and the society and that, in addition, it must be useful. In order to be called "creative," an activity must result in something that is culturally, as well as individually, novel and useful (Torrance, 1962). Creativity has to do with the production of original ideas, novel problems, novel solutions, and utilizable innovations. Originality is basic to creativity, which is the more inclusive concept. The exercise of originality is essential to creative enterprise, whether it be in the area of science, literature, mathematics, art, or home management.

Identifying the Highly Creative

Problems of central importance in the investigation of creativity involve identifying the creative person and determining his level of creativity (Taylor, 1959, 1960; Stein and Heinze, 1960). If the highly creative are to be studied in a scientifically meaningful fashion, they must be identified. In order to do this, some criterion of creativity must be invoked. The particular criterion employed must be culturally significant and have considerable reliability. It is generally agreed that creativity is not an all-or-none phenomenon, but a characteristic that is possessed by all individuals in varying degrees. Obviously, those individuals who are renowned for their creative work must be investigated if we are to determine the possible characteristics that contributed to their creativity. Not only must these characteristics be determined, but if we are to encourage the development of creative potential in the young, we must discern those patterns of early treatment that contributed to or detracted from their eventual creativity. If the potentially highly creative can be identified early in life, it may be possible to provide them with the kinds of experiences that will insure the best development of their creative talent.

IDENTIFYING HIGHLY CREATIVE ADULTS

A general approach to the study of creativity is to investigate the characteristics of individuals in the culture who are recognized by others in their field as being highly creative. Groups of scientists, writers, architects, artists, and so forth can be asked to nominate individuals within their discipline who are the most highly creative, and these nominees can be investigated. Such a procedure has been followed by the Institute for Personality Assessment and Research (IPAR) at the University of California at Berkeley (MacKinnon, 1953, 1962; Barron, 1963). IPAR has been particularly active in the investigation of creativity in adults, and the general methods of their investigation reflects the considerable creative ability of the investigators.

An investigation of creative architects (MacKinnon, 1962) is reported to be typical of the procedures employed at IPAR (Barron et al., 1965). Subjects were selected for this investigation by a nomination and voting procedure. Five senior architects of the faculty of the College of Architecture at the University of California, Berkeley, were each asked to nominate the forty most creative architects in the United States. A loose definition of creativity in architecture was provided the nominators as a working guide:

> Originality of thinking and freshness of approach to architectural problems; constructive ingenuity; ability to set aside established convention and procedures when appropriate; a flair for devising effective and original fulfillments of the major demands of architecture, the demands of technology, visual form, planning, human awareness, and social purpose.

The five nominators provided a list of eighty-six architects, and since only forty were desired, the most frequently nominated were selected to be subjects in the study. Sixty-four persons were invited to be subjects in the investigation before forty acceptances were obtained. This presented an additional problem. Was there a tendency for the more creative, or for the less creative, of the nominees to turn down the invitation to take part in the investigations? To check on this possibility, eleven editors of the major American architectural journals were asked to rate the creativity of the sixty-four nominees initially invited, and later the forty under investigation were asked to rate the creativity of the sixty-four, including themselves. In both the ratings of the eleven editors and the forty cooperating architects, there was no significant difference in the creativity of the twenty-four who did not accept the invitation and the forty who did. Two control groups of architects were selected for investigation, in order to make certain that the characteristics of the creative architects could be distinguished from the characteristics of architects in general. The two comparison groups were of the same age and from the same geographic area as the creative architects. One group was composed of architects who had had two years of work experience and association with one of the originally nominated creative architects; the other group was composed of architects who had never worked with any of the creative nominees.

The architects were invited to come to Berkeley for a weekend of intensive study in the Institute for Personality Assessment and Research. They were housed in a comfortable house, along with the investigators, for a weekend of intensive evaluation. They were studied in groups of ten with standard psychometric devices as well as instruments developed for the specific study. They were searchingly interviewed about their life histories and present functioning, and they were observed in contrived, stressful social situations. The general method has been described as a "living-in assessment method." The results of the tests, ratings, interviews, and observations were analyzed by appropriate statistical techniques in order to discern the characteristics of the creative, as opposed to the less creative, groups.

The successful architect has a complicated task to perform that combines many of the aspects of other professions. He has to exercise the diverse skills of the author, psychologist, journalist, educator, businessman, lawyer, and engineer in order to become a successful and effective architect. His expression of creativity must have many aspects if he is to become a noticed architect. The choice of architects for the study of creativity was probably a very wise one.

Creative writers, scientists, mathematicians, and artists also have been studied by these techniques of selection and assessment. Such investigations serve to provide descriptions of the highly creative and to give a retrospective glimpse of their development. Of particular importance is the personalized picture of the highly creative that is thus obtained. The characteristics of those who are presently designated as highly creative can yield hypotheses about the background and development of creativity that can be investigated through longitudinal studies.

Historical methods have been employed in the investigation of the intelligence of men of eminence (Cox, 1926). Biographical investigations of the personalities of contemporary scientists have also been reported (Cattell and Drevdahl, 1955). Though this method of investigation is quite different from that employed at IPAR, the conclusions drawn about the personal characteristics of the individuals investigated are markedly similar.

No attempt will be made to describe or discuss the numerous investigations of the characteristics of eminent adults, although, at a later point in this chapter, a composite description of highly creative adults will be presented.

IDENTIFYING HIGHLY CREATIVE CHILDREN

If proper procedures for the nurturing of creativity are to be developed, it is necessary to identify those who have the greatest creative potential. It has long been known that when procedures are instituted for the development of a particular facet of performance, those individuals already possessing some skill profit proportionately more from a given amount of training than those who are relatively unskilled. Therefore, the highly creative youngster might be expected to develop rapidly. It is reasoned, too, that those with strong tendencies toward creativity have a greater capacity for making culturally utilizable innovations.

If the characteristics of children who will later become highly creative adults can be determined, it may be possible to provide them, at a very early age, with experiences that will develop those characteristics and minimize those that lead to low productivity and creativity. A great deal of effort has been expended in attempts to discern the cognitive and other personality variables in children that might be predictive of adult creativity. Tests designed to measure various aspects and correlates of creativity in children have been developed. One of the serious problems encountered in the development of such instruments is that of validity. Test questions that tend to evoke novel or unusual responses or solutions to problems, and questions that are designed to measure originality or uniqueness of response may or may not be indicative of later creative activity.

Long-range studies of people who, as children, were designated as highly creative have not been reported in the research literature. Terman and Oden's (1959) follow-up studies of gifted children at adulthood have indicated that the highly *intelligent*, as determined by IQ, tend to become highly productive adults, but we do not know whether these individuals were creative either as children or adults.

DEVELOPING TESTS OF CREATIVITY

An elaborate battery of tasks has been developed by Guilford and his associates (Guilford and Merrifield, 1960) for the assessment of creativity. Guilford has attempted a factorial analysis of the intellect and its measurement. In his presidential address to the American Psychological Association (1950), he outlined a group of objections to existing measures of intellect and indicated that the "structure of intellect" was complex, and required a variety of measures. He hypothesized that the thinking abilities involved in creativity were those he had defined as "divergent productions and transformations," as opposed to the "convergent functions" that he indicated were being measured by the then-current measures of intellect. Although Guilford has subsequently modified his thinking on this issue, much emphasis was given to *convergent versus divergent thinking*. Guilford's subsequent designation of components of creative thinking includes not only divergent productions, but the redefinition of abilities of the convergent-production category of his structure of intellect as well as sensitivity to problems which fall in his "evaluation" category. Thus a great number of thinking abilities are designated as involved in creativity, and a goodly number of tests have been designed for their measurement (Guilford, 1959; Guilford and Merrifield, 1960; Taylor and Holland, 1962).

Getzels and Jackson (1962) used five different measures of creativity in their research. Some of their ideas were borrowed from Guilford, and others were of their own creation. One measure was a word-association test in which students were required to give as many definitions as possible of a fairly common word, such as "bolt" or "sack." The score depended on the absolute number of definitions and the number of different categories into which they could be placed. A second measure was a uses-of-things test. This test is similar to tests used by Guilford in his studies of cognitive ability. The subject gives as many uses as he can for a common object, such as a brick or a toothpick, and he is scored on the basis of both the number and the originality of the uses given. "Brick can be used as a bed warmer" is a more original answer than "bricks can be used to build houses." A third measure was the hidden-shapes test, from a previously developed test battery (Cattell, 1956). In this test, the subject is shown a card with a simple geometric figure on it. He is then required to find that figure hidden in a more complex form or pattern. A fourth was a fables test. In this test, the subject is presented with short fables from which the last line was missing. He is required to compose three different endings for each fable: a "moralistic" one, a "humorous" one, and a "sad" one. The score depends upon the number, appropriateness, and originality of the endings. A final test was termed *make-up prob lems*. In this situation, the subject was presented with a number of complex paragraphs. Each paragraph contained many numerical statements, and the subject was required to make up as many mathematical problems as he could with the information given. The score depended on the number, appropriateness, complexity, and originality of the problems.

The Torrance tests of creative thinking (Torrance, 1966) have been used rather widely as measures of creativity. Some of the tasks are: an ask-and-guess test, a product-improvement test, and unusual-uses test, and a just-suppose test. These tests present problems that emphasize unusual or clever ideas. The battery also contains the picture-construction test, the incomplete-figures test and the parallel-lines test. There are four scoring criteria for the Torrance tests. They are: fluency—the number of relevant responses made; flexibility—number of shifts from one category of meaning to another; originality—the infrequency of the responses offered; and elaboration—the detail and specificity of the responses. All of the tasks call for the production of divergent solutions, multiple possibilities, and some type of thinking theoretically involved in creative behavior.

Unfortunately the correlation between scores obtained on this test of creative thinking and scores on intelligence test are rather high (Wallach, 1968). It has been indicated that the use of these tests as measures of creativity, as the tests are currently scored, is really open to serious question (Harvey et al., 1970). Fluency, defined as number of responses elicited, has been described as a pervasive element in measures of creativity. This measure may, in part, account for the high correlations found among measures of creativity (Clark and Mirels, 1970).

Divergent and Convergent Thinking

The distinction between divergent and convergent thinking can be shown by some examples taken from commonly used tests of creativity. A task designed to assess *divergent thinking* may involve the listing of as many uses as possible for some common article such as brick or a paper cup. Performance on such tasks is evaluated in terms of the number of separate uses and categories of uses given. Performance on word-association tests is determined by the number of different associations evoked by a list of common words. An individual may be asked to formulate as many different problems as he can from information and data provided by the examiner, or he may be required to think of all the questions he can about a picture shown to him. An unusual-uses test requires the student to indicate as many unusual uses as he can for a familiar object such as a tin can, a toy, or a book (Torrance, 1962, 1966; Getzels and Jackson, 1962). Tests of this kind are not scored for the "correct" answer but according to the number, diversity, and uniqueness of the responses. The thought processes required to score well on such tests as these have been labelled *divergent*, as contrasted with the *convergent thinking* involved in situations where the production of the one correct solution or answer is required, as, for example, in a multiple-choice test. One, and only one, answer is the appropriate one in such situations. Divergent thinking is required when one is confronted with a problem that has many possible solutions.

The kinds of processes required by divergent, as opposed to convergent, thinking may appear to be quite different at first glance, but they probably have many elements in common. The emphasis placed on divergent thinking in early speculations about the nature of creativity may have produced a tendency to attribute less importance to convergent processes than they possess. Divergent and convergent components are both to be found in most forms of thinking. For example, in a completion type of question, where the problem is to provide the best completion (convergence), the individual reads the statement and a large number of associations occur as he reads it (divergence). When he completes the reading of the statement and realizes the nature and form of the required completion, he typically thinks of several possible ones (divergence). He then tries out and rejects each one in turn until he comes up with the one which seems to fit best. This item he accepts and uses (convergence).

The divergent aspect of this process may not be as obvious as it is when the instructions require the individual to give as many different associations or uses as possible; however, a wide variety of possible completions provides a larger pool of hypotheses from which to select. There are some divergent components even in the most formal problem.

Convergent components are apparent in creative thinking, if some criterion of success other than number and diversity of responses is applied. If personal acceptability or social usefulness is desired, convergence will occur before the creative process is completed. Typically, the creative process does not terminate with the emission of as many associations, hypotheses, or solutions as possible. Some implicit or explicit standard of acceptability is applied, and one of the alternatives is used as the most appropriate basis for decision or action.

In actual life, the creative process does not end, as it does in the test situation, with the listing of all the possible uses of a brick or the verbal solution of a problem. One may think of many uses for a brick because a brick is at hand and one desires to make use of it. Thought, then, is given to all the possible uses for it, so that the most appropriate one can be selected. This process involves both divergent and convergent ideational processes. Even in the production of the most free and self-expressive art, where social standards may be largely disregarded, there is some convergence in terms of the artist's own sense of appropriateness. Out of the infinite array of possible combinations of colors, forms, and figures, he finally selects and produces the one combination which best expresses his feelings or ideas. Self-imposed selectivity still involves convergence. And when the creative process involves the development of a new process, convergence occurs in terms of the relative utility of the many ideas, propositions, or hypotheses available. Most ideation contains both divergent and convergent components.

The dichotomy of divergent and convergent elements is analogous to the older dichotomy of inductive and deductive reasoning. Inductive reasoning is said to proceed from particular instances to general rules, while deduction supposedly begins with the generalizations and derives specific conclusions therefrom. Inductive reasoning is said to proceed from the particular to the general, while deductive reasoning moves from the general to the particular. In certain respects, induction is divergent thinking and deduction is convergent thinking.

In practice, of course, reasoning is neither purely inductive nor deductive; it always has elements of each. The interested layman or scientist may begin with repeated observations of a related nature and then generalize from these specific instances (convergence, hypothesis formation, or inductive reasoning). From the generalization, a number of inferences are then drawn. If A is true, then $B, C, D,$ and E should follow (divergence or deductive reasoning). If inferences *B, C, D,* and *E* are verified, the generalization is confirmed.

IQ and Creativity

Much has been written on the values and the shortcomings of measures of general intelligence. The measurement of general intelligence has a long and useful history and such tests have proven to be useful devices for the purposes for which they were intended. The general idea involved has been to measure current intellectual functioning in a variety of ways, in order to use this as a basis for prediction of future performance in essentially intellectual areas. Indeed, this has been an ambitious undertaking! Documentation of the relative success of such an approach has been provided in the preceding chapter of this book. Enthusiasm for intelligence tests stems from their apparent usefulness. The apparent usefulness of the various measures in the prediction of academic success, however, probably led to unrealistic expectations of the utility of tests of general intelligence.

Some investigators (Holland, 1961) have urged that nonintellectual criteria be employed for the selection of students for fellowships and scholarships. Such statements, which imply the ignoring of the IQ as such, have contributed to the confusion surrounding the relationship between the IQ and creativity. If the selection of students for fellowships and scholarships were really to be made without reference to their IQ's or to variables which are related to their IQ's, a very different group might be selected. However, if selection were to be made on the basis of the measured creativity of the top 1 or 2 percent in measures of general intelligence, little could be said about the overall relationship between the two measures under consideration. Many reports of limited relationships between creativity and intelligence have been made by generalizing from samples containing a restricted range of both intelligence and creativity. The meaning of correlation under such circumstances is difficult to discern. It has long been known that the IQ, above a given level, is essentially unrelated to even such an intellectually challenging area as collegiate success. Many factors are involved. Such things as health, motivation, study habits, and family finances are considerations. On the other hand, unless there is a certain minimum level of measured intelligence, academic failure becomes highly predictable. There *are* individual differences among the highly intelligent. Restriction of the range of one variable does not equally restrict other variables, even though they are highly correlated in the general population. Creativity, if it is a complex of individual differences among the highly intelligent, should not be expected to correlate highly with IQ. The study of individual differences is most desirable, and studies of individual differences among the highly intelligent, including creativity as a variable, is to be encouraged. The concept of creativity should serve to enhance our knowledge of people and their performances. Enthusiasm for the concept should not be carried to the point of making it into a panacea for the woes of society. The implied, and sometimes stated, abandonment of the concept of general intelligence may be a matter of throwing the baby out with the bath. Although it may well be true that we must look beyond the limits of the IQ in order to understand creativity (Guilford, 1950), it does not follow that intelligence can be ignored in our quest for such understanding. Creativity has been defined as involving social usefulness, and it appears logical that most of the useful creative ideas are likely to come from the most intelligent. High intelligence does not guarantee creative activity, but low intelligence certainly militates against it.

CORRELATIONAL INVESTIGATIONS AND SPECULATIONS

It has been estimated, as the result of correlational studies of creativity and intelligence among the designated highly creative, that the correlation between the two variables is low but positive (Barron et al., 1965). In these instances, the range of both creativity and intelligence has been restricted. The amount of restriction of ranges is variable from one investigation to the next, and the exact curtailment of range of creativity is really not known. For highly creative writers, the correlation between IQ and creativity has been estimated to be around .40 (Barron, 1963). In a study of architects designated as creative, a correlation of near zero is reported, but the author speculates that, over the entire range of creativity and intelligence, there is a positive relationship between the two variables (MacKinnon, 1962). From a study of the better high school students (upper 1 percent), it has been estimated that intelligence has little or no relationship to creative performance in arts and science (Holland, 1961). In addition to the problem of curtailment of range, it has been pointed out that creativity in a given area may require quite different abilities than creativity in another. Among architects, creativity may reflect the ability to engineer structural innovations, in which case it should be a correlate of intelligence. If the creativity depends on new artistic designs, intelligence would probably be less important (McNemar, 1964). The kind of creativity involved, then, may be a factor in the size of correlation to be expected. The highly creative writers were reported to have an average IQ of about 140. Creative writers apparently are very bright! From groups of so restricted a range of intelligence, conclusions about the general relationship of intelligence and creativity cannot be drawn.

The serious problem of attempting to predict later creativity from tests of creativity in childhood has been mentioned. Actually, the childhood characteristics of creative adults have only been studied restrospectively. Tests administered during childhood, and scored for uniqueness and novelty of response, may or may not be highly related to adult creative activity. We do not now have creative adult subjects who, as children, were given the current tests of creativity. This problem of validity is a hard one, but it cannot be ignored. However, if tests of creativity are administered to children, and if these subjects are subsequently investigated as adults, data on validity will then be available.

Users of tests of creative thinking for elementary school children and adolescents have reported little relationship between scores on such measures and scores on tests of intelligence (Torrance, 1962; Getzels and Jackson, 1962). The extensive investigation of Getzels and Jackson (1962) has been cogently criticized by a number of other workers (Burt, 1962; De Mille and Merrifield, 1962; Marsh, 1964; McNemar, 1964; Ripple and May, 1962). Their statistical procedures and their manner of describing their research have been attacked. They used, as a measure of creativity, the sum of scores of five tests of creativity. Using their reported data, McNemar (1964) discerned that creativity and the IQ's in their sample correlate to the extent of .40. This r has been greatly attenuated by the usual measurement errors, by the restriction of the IQ range (the mean was 132), and by the variety of intelligence test scores employed. He concluded that their creativity tests and intelligence tests have far more common variance than is indicated by the authors' report. Getzels and Jackson's use of Chi Square as a statistical procedure has been criticized by Marsh (1964) because of Chi Square's insensitivity to interaction. Marsh concludes that the IQ may still be the best single criterion for creative potential.

An empirical demonstration of the possible effect of restriction of the range of IQ's has been reported by Ripple and May (1962). By correlating Otis IQ's and scores on creative thinking tests administered to several seventh-grade groups, homogeneous or heterogeneous with respect to their IQ's, they demonstrated that the low correlation of these measures reported by other investigators may well be due in part to the restricted range of the IQ's in their samples. Barron (1968) asserts that beyond a minimum IQ creativity is not a function of intelligence as measured by IQ tests. A minimum IQ would appear to be about 120, which has to be considered a pretty high IQ.

An unfortunate designation of the groups investigated and reported by Getzels and Jackson has contributed to the confusion. Basically, they reported on two groups of adolescents. One group was composed of individuals scoring in the top 20 percent on measures of intelligence but not in the top 20 percent on measures of creativity. The other group scored in the top 20 percent on measures of creativity, but not on measures of intelligence. They excluded those who were in the top 20 percent on both. The group scoring in the top 20 percent on measures of creativity but not on intelligence was labelled the *high-creative* group, and the other group was labelled the *high-IQ* group. The mean IQ of the high-IQ group was 150, whereas the mean IQ of the high-creative group was 127. Now an IQ of 127 most certainly is not as high as an IQ of 150, but it is still a high IQ when the total range is considered. Their high-creative group was still pretty bright. The labeling of the two groups as *high-IQ* and *high-creative* has probably contributed to the tendency to overlook its high level of intelligence.

The correlation between IQ and creativity obtained in an extensive investigation of a carefully chosen sample of 7,648 fifteen-year-old boys and girls in Project Talent (Shaycoft, et al., 1963) was reported to be .67. This *r* becomes .80 when corrected for attenuation (McNemar, 1964).

It would seem that the extent of the relationship between IQ's and measured creativity depends on the nature of the tests of creativity employed, among other things. The nature and size of the relationship remains speculative, however. It would appear that the early speculations that the relationship is slight may have been exaggerated and may have led to considerable confusion. Creativity of certain kinds may be highly related to intelligence, while creativity in certain areas may not be so highly dependent on intelligence. That some intelligence is essential for the production of cultural, scientific, technological, or artistic innovation would appear obvious.

Highly Creative Adults

Adults designated as highly creative by one means or another have been studied rather intensively by several groups of investigators by the methods already described. Perhaps the most usual means of designation as highly creative has been that of nomination by contemporaries. As a consequence of the investigations of creative scientists, writers, artists, architects, and mathematicians, a rather large body of descriptive material is available. A general picture of the highly creative person is difficult to discern, however, because of the complexity of bright adults in general and because of the diversity of creative endeavor. Individual differences among the highly creative are to be expected.

We will try to review some of the more consistently reported characteristics of the groups investigated. A variety of techniques for describing the highly creative has been employed. Self-rating scales, self-inventories, and ratings by trained observers have been employed, as have adjective check lists, interviews, and interest measures and personality measures of various kinds.

There does seem to be some agreement among various investigators as to the characteristics of outstanding men of science. They are generally described as being highly intelligent, emotionally sensitive, self-sufficient, of independent judgment, dedicated, introspective, confident, ideationally productive, and somewhat unconventional. On the Allport-Vernon-Lindzey Scale of Values, they score high in "Theoretical and Aesthetic" values and low in "Religious, Social, and Economic" values (Gough, 1961). Barron (1965) presents a unified picture of the productive scientist gleaned from the research of a number of individual investigators. Productive scientists are depicted as having a high degree of intelligence, emotional stability, ego strength, personal dominance, forcefulness of opinion, and liking for precision and order. They are challenged by the unknown, by contradictions, and by apparent disorder. They appear to be somewhat distant and detached in personal relations, and prefer to deal with things or abstractions rather than people. Productive scientists are further depicted as having a strong need for independence and autonomy. They appear to be self-sufficient and self-directing, and they enjoy abstract thinking. They resist pressure to conform in their thinking. In brief, they seem to be personally strong, dedicated, independent, somewhat adventurous, and scholarly.

These characteristics of the productive scientist appear to be those that would rationally be expected (Taylor and Barron, 1963). The scientist, in order to be productive or creative, must be bright, orderly, and thorough. If he is to make a contribution to science, his efforts must be unique and at the frontiers of knowledge. Novelty and uncertainty are of necessity involved in such endeavors. The scientist must be willing to take risks and be enthusiastically dedicated to the pursuit of his own ideas and directions.

Scientists judged to be highly original express preferences for some of the same factors that are preferred by artists (Gough, 1961). Creative scientists and artists both appear to prefer complex, asymmetrical figures, both are highly imaginative, and both enjoy esthetic qualities. The scientist may enjoy the esthetic qualities of his theories, whereas the artist may be inclined to appreciate the esthetic qualities of objects.

An earlier investigation (Cox, 1926) of the characteristics of 300 geniuses, divided into several subgroups according to area of accomplishment, provides some interesting data for comparing scientists and imaginative writers. Their personal and moral qualities, as well as their intellectual ones, were depicted.

The scientific geniuses were estimated to have an average IQ of over 170. This represents a very high level of intellect, as might be expected. Compared with eminent individuals from all of the subgroups, the scientists had very great strength or force of character and balance, and were very active. They were less sociable, excitable, and sensitive to criticism than the other subgroups. These scientists were described as the strongest, most forceful, and best balanced people in the study.

The artists in the study were estimated to be of somewhat lower, but still very high, intelligence, their average IQ probably being well over 135. They were rated as having a high degree of esthetic feeling, desire to excel, belief in themselves, originality of ideas, and as being able to strive for distant goals.

Imaginative writers (poets, novelists, and dramatists) were judged to have an average IQ of 165. These people were notably high in imaginativeness and esthetic feeling, effort directed toward pleasure, originality of ideas, strength of memory, and keenness of observation. They ranked lower on common sense and the degree to which their actions and thoughts were dependent on reason than did the other groups.

The descriptions of eminent men of science and the arts have some common, as well as some distinguishing, features. Individual differences among the highly creative are to be expected as much as are individual differences among the highly intelligent, and it is difficult to put together a composite picture of creative adults. In one rather large investigation of physical scientists (Taylor, et al., 1961), a list of 150 criteria of scientific productivity and creativity was developed. Even when this number was reduced to 48 categories, and then by factor analysis further reduced to 14, the picture of potential creativity remained extremely complex. Torrance (1962) compiled a list of 84 characteristics found in one or more studies to differentiate highly creative persons from less creative ones. This list includes such apparently contrasting items as: courageous and timid; self-assertive and introversive; appears haughty and self-satisfied at times and is outwardly bashful; reserved and spirited in disagreement; receptive to the ideas of others and stubborn; emotional and somewhat withdrawn; and, finally, quiescent, self-satisfied at times, and discontented. When such diverse descriptions of productive and creative people are at hand, one is tempted to say that the only communality discernible in persons designated as creative is that they have attained eminence—that is, adults designated as creative have been creative. The complexity of the category or the vagueness of the concept tends to make a composite description of the "creative" extremely tenuous.

The most consistent findings in the literature appear to be those of

MacKinnon (1960). Other investigators have since reported essentially the same patterns of interest on the Strong Vocational Interest Blank and the Allport-Vernon-Lindzey Scale of Values. The more original or highly creative rated high on the interest scales for architect, psychologist, author-journalist, and specialization level. They scored low on scales for purchasing agent, office manager, banker, farmer, carpenter, veterinarian, policeman, and mortician. MacKinnon interprets these findings as indicating that creative individuals are less interested in small details or the practical, concrete facets of life, and more concerned with meanings, implications, and the symbolic equivalents of things and ideas.

All of MacKinnon's highly creative groups scored high on theoretical and esthetic values and high on several scales of the Minnesota Multiphasic Personality Inventory. His groups of highly creative males scored high on the masculinity-femininity scale, although they were *not* effeminate in manner or appearance. Their elevated masculinity-femininity scores apparently derived from their openness to their feelings and emotions, a sensitive awareness of self and others, and a wide range of interests. Their interests included many which are regarded as feminine in our culture.

Various researchers have emphasized conflicting motives among the highly creative (MacKinnon, 1960; Palm, 1959; Torrance, 1962) and their ability to tolerate the tensions arising from such conflicts. Torrance depicts the creative person as one who enjoys intense, sustained, and vigorous effort to surmount difficulties and who has a need to dramatize and display his ideas and prove his personal worth. He indicates that these tendencies are held in check by the creative individual's self-awareness, awareness of the feelings and experiences of others, and detached intellectualization. The total picture is one of a person alive and open to his own experiences and to those of others, who tries to organize and see meaning in them.

Highly Creative Adolescents

In the study of the personal characteristics of creative children and adolescents, an assumption must be made about the future creativity of the subjects. Retrospective studies of the childhood of creative adults yields some justification for assuming that creativity in childhood and adolescence is predictive of adult creativity. Such an assumption seems warranted, too, in the light of investigations of other psychological variables. Most psychological variables in adults can be seen to have their roots in earlier development and experience. In essence, the quest is for answers to the question, "What are the early signs of adult creativity?"

An investigation of the personality characteristics of highly creative adolescents was conducted by Getzels and Jackson (1962). In this investigation, the adolescents selected for study and comparison were in grades 7 through 12. They were separated into a high-creative group (26 children) and a high-IQ group (28 children), in the manner previously described. When the two were contrasted, some interesting findings resulted.

The values of the two groups appeared to be grossly different. Both groups were given an Outstanding Traits test. Thirteen descriptions of hypothetical children displaying a desirable personality quality or trait were given to the subjects. They were required to rank the thirteen descriptions of children in three ways. First, they ranked the descriptions according to the degree to which they would like to be like the child described. The data from this procedure provided a measure of the "self-ideal" of the subjects. Second, they ranked the descriptions according to the degree to which they believed the various children would succeed in adult life. A "success image" of the subjects was thus obtained. Third, they ranked the descriptions according to the degree to which they believed the children described would be liked by their teachers. This provided a measure of the subjects' "teacher perception."

Analyses of the data revealed that both groups agreed on the qualities that make for adult success in our society and on the qualities which teachers prefer in their students. However, there was little agreement between the two groups about what qualities they wanted for themselves, in spite of their agreement about the qualities considered desirable by the adult world. The high-IQ group preferred for themselves the personal traits believed to be predictive of adult success. The high-creative group had but little preference for these traits. In other words, the high-creative group seemed not to be highly success-oriented. The high-IQ group preferred traits for themselves that were highly similar to those personal traits they believed to be favored by teachers. Not so the high-creative group. They tended to place high personal value on qualities which they feel teachers value least! "Sense of humor" was ranked near the top, above "high marks," "high IQ," and "goal directedness." The high-IQ group ranked "sense of humor" near the bottom, below high marks, high IQ, and goal directedness. A sense of humor seems to be highly characteristic of creative adolescents and it is expressed in a variety of ways, but both groups perceived the teachers as ranking it rather low. The highly creative adolescents know what makes for conventional success and what teachers like, but these are not necessarily the qualities they want for themselves.

When projective materials were used as testing devices, some rather interesting data were garnered. The two groups do not differ on need for achievement, but the highly creative adolescents scored significantly higher in the use of stimulus-free themes, unexpected endings, humor, incongruities, and playfulness. They also showed a tendency toward more violence in the stories they related and exhibited a mocking attitude toward conformity and conventional success. This mockery did not appear in the stories of the high-IQ group.

The attempt to determine something of the ultimate goals and aspirations of the two groups made it apparent that there were differences here as well. The techniques used by Getzels and Jackson uncovered differences in both the quantity and quality of occupational goals. The number of occupational possibilities mentioned by the high-creatives was significantly greater than the number mentioned by the high-IQ's, nearly twice as many. And the occupational choices of the high-IQ group were more conventional (i.e., doctor, lawyer, professor), while the high-creative group made unconventional choices (i.e., adventurer, inventor, writer) a significantly greater proportion of the time. In other words, the highly creative adolescents had more diffuse occupational goals. They appeared to be more willing to deal with a greater range of career possibilities, and with careers in which success is problematic. The results of the Getzel and Jackson research with adolescents is fairly generally supported by other workers who find that highly creative adolescents tend to be more intelligent, adventurous, and self-confident than the less creative ones. They have a less favorable attitude toward school with highly creative boys being more accepted by their peers than are highly creative girls (Kurtzman, 1967).

FAMILY BACKGROUND OF HIGHLY CREATIVE ADOLESCENTS

Data on their subjects' families were obtained by Getzels and Jackson (1962) with a questionnaire directed at parents and by a two-to-three hour conference with each mother. Parents of the high-IQ children tended to have somewhat more education than the parents of high-creative children. Mothers also tended to be housewives more exclusively, that is, without holding any other jobs. It was the opinion of the interviewers that the parents of the high-IQ children were more insecure than the parents of the high-creative children, and thus were more concerned about correct and proper child rearing. Finances and financial hardship were mentioned more frequently in the mother's memory of her own home by the mothers of the high-IQ children than by the mothers of the high-creative children.

Questions about reading habits revealed that the homes of the high-IQ group subscribed to and read more magazines. Specifically they subscribed to more children's magazines and fewer magazines of liberal political comment. The authors observed that the families of the high-IQ children were more conventional, more child-centered, and put greater pressure on the child to do well scholastically.

The mothers of the high-IQ group tended to be somewhat more satisfied with their own child-rearing practices than the mothers of the high-creative sample. Getzels and Jackson indicate that these mothers have a right to self-satisfaction if their intent was to rear children who do well in school, accept conventional values, are liked by their teachers, and aspire to career in the prestige professions. The two groups of mothers differed about the kinds of friends they preferred for their children. The mothers of the high-IQ group tended to emphasize such external factors as good family, good manners, and studiousness. The mothers of the high-creative children valued such attributes in their children's friends as a sense of values, interests, openness, and maturity of interpersonal relations. The family of the high-IQ child was characterized by Getzels and Jackson as one in which individual divergence is limited and risks minimized; the family of the high-creative child as one in which individual divergence is permitted and risks accepted.

A rather detailed study of five creative adolescent artists who were compared with two groups (equally limited in size) of young artists who were not rated as being truly creative, yields descriptions of creative individuals that essentially conform to the data on creative adults and to the Getzels and Jackson reports on creative adolescents (Hammer, 1961). The highly creative young painters, as opposed to the merely facile young painters, showed greater depth of feeling, greater need for self-expression, a greater range of emotions, stronger determination and ambition, more tolerance for discomfort, more independence, more rebelliousness, more self-awareness and a balance of feminine and masculine components in their natures.

Highly Creative Children

Studies of the personality characteristics of children who either score high on tests of creativity or are rated high in creativity by their teachers are of great interest to parents, psychologists, and educators. It is understood full well that many young children who are creative will no longer be so at adulthood and that some children who are not classified as creative may turn into creative adults. However, it would seem that children designated as highly creative have a better chance of being creative in later life than those not so designated. If children classified as creative do not turn out to be creative adolescents or young adults, it would also be interesting to determine why this is so. Either way, the study of creativity in children certainly seems justified.

An investigation of the personalities of highly creative children by Weisberg and Springer (1961) is reported by Torrance (1962). This was a rather extensive investigation, using materials from the Minnesota test battery, psychiatric interviews, Rorschachs, and the Draw-a-Family Technique. As compared with less creative children, the highly creative scored higher on strength of self-image, ease of early recall, humor, availability of Oedipal anxiety, and uneven ego development. The more creative children could recall their earlier experiences more readily even when they were unpleasant. Torrance reports that the same highly creative child might love Shakespeare and dolls, and that self-control appropriate to a young adult might be interspersed with impulsive, almost infantile behavior, during one interview.

Projective tests showed a tendency toward unconventional responses, and fanciful and imaginative treatment of the material. The results were interpreted as reflecting both a greater independence of the environment and a greater readiness to respond emotionally to it. The creative children were seen as more sensitive and independent than the less creative children.

The families of the highly creative children were described as not overly close, with little clinging to one another. There was little stress on conformity to parental values, and the marriage was not a particularly well-adjusted one. Emotion was often openly expressed. Both parents interacted strongly with the creative child, who was allowed to regress. The mothers were sometimes ambivalent toward their children. There was no overevaluation of the child's abilities.

Torrance (1962) conducted a rather well-controlled investigation of the personalities of a group of elementary school children. He chose the most creative boy and girl from each of twenty-three classes in grades 1 through 6, and matched them with control subjects in sex, IQ, race, classroom teacher, and age. He states, from an analysis of his data, that certain personality characteristics differentiate the highly creative from the less creative children. Teachers and peers agree that the highly creative, especially boys, have wild and silly ideas. Their work is characterized by the production of ideas "off the beaten track, outside the mold." Their work is also characterized by humor, playfulness, relative lack of rigidity, and relaxation. These findings are in essential agreement with those of other investigations of the personality traits of creative children and adolescents.

Development and Fostering of Creativity

The course of the development of creativity in children in our culture is not an easy one. Torrance (1962; 1965) has been particularly interested in the development of creativity and has studied developmental patterns throughout the elementary grades. Creative children in the early grades in school often have the reputation among their peers for having silly or naughty ideas and are thought of as wild by their teachers. By the end of the third grade, they have usually learned to keep their wild ideas to themselves and thus some of their originality goes unrecognized and unrewarded. During the subsequent few years, they learn to conform more or less to the conventional demands of the school, but without enthusiasm for the conformity demanded.

Getzels and Jackson's (1962) study of adolescents indicated that teachers preferred their high-IQ adolescents to their high-creative adolescents, whose more unconventional occupational interests may lead them to explore areas that do not particularly fit into the curriculum. Their sense of humor, which to them is quite important, may not always be exercised in the most proper ways. All in all, they possess some personal characteristics that may not endear them to teachers. They may be overly energetic, highly independent, somewhat rebellious, and emotionally expressive. These characteristics can be a source of annoyance to the busy teacher, and unless he is fully appreciative of the potentialities of the children, he may be tempted to overcontrol the situation and suppress the expression and exercise of creative talent.

Rogers (1959) has listed two general conditions as favorable to creative activity. He calls these two conditions "psychological safety" and "psychological freedom." He considers acceptance of the individual to be one of the most important factors conducive to psychological safety, but it may be one of the things of which the creative youngster is deprived in our culture. Creative children, as a group, are aware of those traits which their culture, teachers, and peers revere, but they do not particularly want those traits for themselves (Getzels and Jackson, 1962; Torrance, 1962). Highly creative individuals deviate from the culture norms in both ideation and overt behavior, and they recognize this fact. The very nature of creativity dictates that creative activity must be different; it must be deviant behavior. When acceptance of the person is made conditional on conformity, creative individuals will be devalued and their deviant ideas will be discouraged. A society which provides a wide variety of socially approved roles for its citizens will be acceptant of the deviant individual. In a culture highly tolerant of a minority of one, the deviant individual can be what he is without posing and pretending. He would not feel less worthy because he is different. In an educational environment that is tolerant of many approaches to the acquisition of information and accepting of deviant methods of problem solving, the creative individual would feel more accepted and be freer to pursue his own paths to educational goals. In a nonthreatening social environment, the creative individual should experience less anxiety, and his principal sources of motivation could become the positive satisfactions of exploration and discovery rather than the reduction of his anxiety. When the individual feels psychologically safe, he is not afraid to develop and express his divergent ideas.

When the creatively deviant individual associates with people who are able to understand and appreciate his own personal world, he can be comfortable and need not waste time and energy protecting himself. He can be divergent without being defensive and can be a nonconformist without suffering social disapproval. In such an environment, creative ideation and creative problem solving may become well-established behavior, and originality and creativity could be habitual ways of responding.

"Psychological freedom," as described by Rogers (1959, 1963) is, in many ways, a consequence of "psychological safety." Some of the characteristics of the person who is psychologically free are as follows:

1. He is able to accept himself for what he is, without fear of being laughed at or ridiculed.
2. He can give at least symbolic expression to his impulses and thoughts, without having to repress, distort, or hide them.
3. He can handle percepts, concepts, and words playfully and in unusual ways, without feeling guilty.
4. He sees the unknown and mysterious either as a serious challenge to be met or as a game to be played.

Studies of highly creative people indicate that the prevailing cultural and educational climate in America does not reward creative individuals commensurately with their potential value to society. Indeed, according to Torrance (1962), "Society is downright savage toward creative thinkers, especially when they are young." It is suggested that to promote creativity, we need to provide a friendly and rewarding environment in which it can flourish. To accomplish this, we will have to recognize a wide range of ideational divergence as being a part of the nature of things, rather than as being bizarre or abnormal. We will have to recognize the value of a wide diversity of talents, encourage children to perceive things in a variety of unconventional ways, increase our tolerance of people who perceive and think in ways which are different from ours, and develop specific methods for teaching and for encouraging creativity.

Studies have demonstrated that certain procedures consistently facilitate the frequency and appropriateness of original responses (Maltzman, Bogarty, and Breger, 1958a; Maltzman et al., 1958b; Maltzman, 1960; Maltzman et al., 1960; Mednick, 1962; Covington and Crutchfield, 1965; Denny, 1968). Maltzman and his associates have conducted a series of laboratory experiments demonstrating that practice in giving unusual responses to a list of words in "free association" produced an increase in the number of unusual associative responses to a different list of words presented at a later time. They also showed that instructions to give unusual or original responses produced a significant increase in such associative responses. Training in giving unusual word associations also increased performance on an unusual-uses test in which the subjects were asked to give as many different uses as they could think of (other than their common, everyday uses) for six common objects. Practice and instruction were both effective in increasing the number of original responses. Practice in giving the same associative responses to words produced a smaller number of original responses to different words at later times. Certain training techniques can significantly *decrease* originality, and others can *increase* originality. Training in original responses appears to be transferable. Rewarding unusual responses by saying "good" when they occur increases the number of such responses. These findings have been supported in a large number of verbal conditioning experiments.

A special curriculum in creative problem solving, using an autoinstructional program, has been devised by Covington and Crutchfield (1965). This program is being tested within the school system itself, rather than in the laboratory. Initial reports are that the special training increased creativity in the experimental group, as compared with an appropriate control class, and the investigation is continuing. This should provide some indication of the permanence of the increased creative responding resulting from such training.

Systematic attempts can and should be made to reward original behavior when it occurs. The experimental studies on the training of originality indicate that originality can be increased by instructions, encouragement, and reward. Research workers are inclined to agree that freedom to explore, to make errors, and to pursue tangential ideas is essential for the development of creativity. The teacher's, parent's, peer's, and community's approval of genuinely original efforts in a great variety of areas is to be encouraged (Mearns, 1958; Torrance, 1962).

Summary

Concern with the development and encouragement of creativity has become widespread in our culture. Government, industry, and education have all become concerned with the identification and development of creativity. Rapid technological advances have made routine problem solving the province of machines. Man can be free from this drudgery to engage in more productive and creative enterprise.

Creativity may be defined in two essentially differing frames of reference. The personal and phenomenological frame of reference results in an emphasis on the subjective originality of response: If it is novel, new, or different for the individual, it is creative. Creativity may also be defined in the light of its end-product: To be creative, the innovation must not only be novel to the individual, but useful and novel to the culture as well. The emphasis in this chapter has been largely on the latter concept. Originality is usually designated as being an essential part of creativity, but it does not involve social recognition. Originality becomes, then, more amenable to laboratory investigation than does creativity.

A variety of means have been employed to identify highly creative individuals. In the identification of creative adults, a method of nomination by peers can be used or a listing of culturally relevant productions can be made. Identifying creative children is more tenuous. Teachers may make nominations or tests designed to measure originality can be employed. A great deal of effort has gone into the development of tests of creativity for both children and adults. The criteria for creativity seem to be elusive, especially for creativity among children and adolescents. Long-range studies should improve the validity of measures being developed.

The relationship between measured intelligence (IQ) and creativity over the entire range of both variables is not known. Low positive estimates of the size of the correlation may be unrealistically low. Some intelligence is obviously essential for creative activity, but a high level of intelligence does not guarantee creativity. The concept of creativity may encompass a host of individual differences among the brilliant.

The personalities of creative adults have been investigated by a number of researchers. The descriptions of the highly creative are complicated, and attention must be paid to the area of creative activity in order to present a meaningful composite of creative persons even within a given discipline. Tests of creativity have been devised and given to groups of children and adolescents. Descriptions of children and adolescents thus designated as highly creative were presented.

Various procedures for fostering creativity in children and adults have been investigated. Many of these procedures appear to be promising and should be of considerable interest to parents and educators.

References

BARRON, F., *Creativity and Psychological Health*. New York: Van Nostrand Reinhold Company, 1963.

———, "The Dream of Art and Poetry," *Psychology today*, II, No. 7 (1968). 18–23, 66.

———, et al., *New Directions in Psychology*, Vol. II. New York: Holt, Rinehart & Winston, Inc., 1965.

Burt, C., "Creativity and Intelligence," *Brit. j. educ. psychol.*, XXXII (1962), 292–98, Critical notice.

Cattell, R. B., *Objective-analytic Test Battery.* Champaign, Ill.: Institute for Personality and Ability Testing, 1956.

———, and J. E. Drevdahl, "A Comparison of the Personality Profile of Eminent Researchers with That of Eminent Teachers and Administrators and That of the General Population," *Brit. j. psychol.*, XLVI (1955), 248–61.

Clark, P. M., and H. L. Mirels, "Fluency as a pervasive element in the measurement of creativity," *Educ. measure,* VII (1970), 83–86.

Covington, M. V., and R. S. Crutchfield, "Experiments in the Use of Programmed Instruction for the Facilitation of Creative Problem Solving," *Programmed Instruction* (January, 1965), pamphlet.

Cox, C., "The Early Mental Traits of 300 Geniuses," in *Genetic Studies in Genius,* Vol. II. Stanford, Calif.: Stanford University Press, 1926.

De Mille, R., and P. R. Merrifield, "Creativity and Intelligence," *Educ. psychol. meas.,* XXII (1962), 803–8.

Denny, L. A., "Identification of Teacher-Classroom Variables Facilitating Pupil Creative Growth," *Amer. educ. res. j.,* V (1968), 365–83.

Getzels, J. W. and P. W. Jackson, *Creativity and Intelligence.* New York: John Wiley & Sons, Inc., 1962.

Gough, H. G., "Techniques for Identifying the Creative Research Scientist," in *The Creative Person,* ed. D. W. MacKinnon. Berkeley, Calif.: University of California Extension, 1961.

Guilford, J. P., "Creativity," *Amer. psychologist,* V (1950), 444–54.

———, "Traits of Creativity," in *Creativity and Its Cultivation,* ed. H. H. Anderson. New York: Harper & Row, Publishers, 1959.

———, and P. R. Merrifield, *The Structure of Intellect Model: Its Uses and Implications,* Rep. Psychol. lab., No. 24. Los Angeles, Calif.: University of Southern California, 1960.

Hammer, E. G., *Creativity.* New York: Random House, Inc., 1961.

Harvey, O. J., J. K. Hoffmeister, C. Coates, and B. J. White, "A Partial Evaluation of Torrance's Test of Creativity," *Amer. educ. res. j.,* VII (1970), 359–72.

Holland, J. L., "Creative and Academic Performance among Talented Adolescents," *J. educ. psychol.,* LII (1961), 136–47.

Kurtzman, K. A., "A Study of School Attitudes, Peer Acceptance and Personality of Creative Adolescents," *Except. child.,* XXXIV (1967), 157–62.

MacKinnon, D. W., "Fact and Fancy in Personality Research," *Amer. psychologist,* VIII (1953), 138–46.

———, "What Do We Mean by Talent and How Do We Test for It?" in *The Search for Talent.* Princeton, N.J.: College Entrance Examination Board, 1960, pp. 20–29.

———, "The Nature and Nurture of Creative Talent," *Amer. psychologist,* XVII (1962), 484–95.

McNemar, Q., "Lost: Our Intelligence? Why?" *Amer. psychologist,* XIX (1964), 871–82.

MALTZMAN, I., "On the Training of Originality," *Psychol. rev.*, LXVII (1960), 229–42.

———, W. BOGARTY, AND L. BREGER, "A Procedure for Increasing Word Association Originality and Its Transfer Effects," *J. exp. psychol.*, LVI (1958a), 392–98.

———, et al., "The Facilitation of Problem Solving by Prior Exposure to Uncommon Responses," *J. exp. psychol.*, LVI (1958b), 399–406.

———, et al., "Experimental Studies in the Training of Originality," *Psychol. monog.*, LXXIV, No. 493 (1960).

MARSH, R. W., "A Statistical Re-analysis of Getzels and Jackson's Data," *Brit. j. educ. psychol.*, XXXIV (1964), 91–93.

MASLOW, A. H., "Creativity in Self-actualizing People," in *Creativity and Its Cultivation*, ed. H. H. Anderson. New York: Harper & Row, Publishers, 1959.

———, *Motivation and Personality* (2nd ed.). New York: Harper & Row, Publishers, 1970.

MEARNS, H., *Creative Power: The Education of Youth in the Creative Arts*. New York: Dover Publications, Inc., 1958.

MEDNICK, S., "The Associative Basis of the Creative Process," *Psychol. rev.*, LXIX (1962), 220–32.

PALM, H. J., *An Analysis of Test-score Differences between Highly Creative and High Miller Analogies Members of the Summer Guidance Institute*, Res. memo, BER-59-13. Minneapolis, Minn.: Bureau of Educational Research, University of Minnesota, 1959.

RIPPLE, R. E., AND F. B. MAY, "Caution in Comparing Creativity and I.Q.," *Psychol. rep.*, X (1962), 229–30.

ROCK, D. A., F. R. EVANS, AND S. P. KLEIN, "Prediciting Multiple Criteria of Creative Achievements with Moderator Variables," *J. of educ. meas.*, VI, No. 4 (1969), 229–36.

ROGERS, C. R., "Toward a Theory of Creativity," in *Creativity and Its Cultivation*, ed. H. H. Anderson. New York: Harper & Row, Publishers, 1959.

———, "Learning to Be Free," *N.E.A.J.*, LII (1963), 28–31.

SAWREY, J. M., AND C. W. TELFORD, *Psychology of Adjustment* (3rd ed.). Boston, Mass.: Allyn & Bacon, Inc., 1971.

SHAYCOFT, M. F., et al., "Project Talent: Studies of a Complete Age Group Age 15." Pittsburgh, Pa.: University of Pittsburgh, 1963. Mimeographed.

STEIN, M., AND S. HEINZE, *Creativity and the Individual*. New York: The Free Press, 1960.

TAYLOR, C. W., ed., *The Third (1959) University of Utah Research Conference on the Identification of Creative Scientific Talent*. Salt Lake City, Utah: University of Utah Press, 1959.

———, "Identifying the Creative Individual," in *Creativity: Second Minneapolis Conference on Gifted Children*, ed. E. P. Torrance. Minneapolis, Minn.: Center for Continuation Study, University of Minnesota, 1960.

———, AND F. BARRON, *Scientific Creativity: Its Recognition and Development*. New York: John Wiley & Sons, Inc., 1963.

————, AND J. S. HOLLAND, "Development XXXII and Application of Tests of Creativity," *Rev. educ. res.*, XXXII (1962), 91–102.

————, et al., *"Explorations in the Measurement and Predictions of Contributions of One Sample of Scientists,"* USAF ASD tech. rep., 61–96. Washington, D.C., 1961.

TERMAN, L. M., AND M. H. ODEN, *The Gifted Group at Mid-life.* Stanford, Calif.: Stanford University Press, 1959.

TORRANCE, E. P., *Guiding Creative Talent.* Englewood Cliffs, N.J.: Prentice-Hall, Inc., 1962.

————, *Rewarding Creative Behavior.* Englewood Cliffs, N.J.: Prentice-Hall, Inc., 1965.

————, *Torrance Tests of Creativity.* Princeton, N.J.: Personnel Press, Inc., 1966.

WALLACH, M. A. Review of *Torrance tests of creative thinking. Amer. educ. res. j.*, V (1968), 272–81.

WEISBERG, P. S., AND K. J. SPRINGER, "Environmental Factors Influencing Creative Function in Gifted Children." Cincinnati: Department of Psychiatry, Cincinnati General Hospital, 1961. Mimeographed.

WHYTE, W. H., Jr., *The Organization Man.* New York: Simon and Schuster, Inc., 1956.

7

The Mentally Retarded:
Some General Considerations

Definitions

The American Association on Mental Deficiency proposes the following definition of mental retardation:

> Mental retardation refers to subaverage general intellectual functioning which originates during the developmental period and is associated with impairment in adaptive behavior (Heber, 1961).

A more recently proposed modification of the official definition (Kidd, 1964) reads:

> Mental retardation refers to significantly sub-average intellectual functioning which manifests itself during the developmental period and is characterized by inadequacy in adaptive behavior.

These definitions are quite different from the older ones. Doll (1941), in a widely quoted statement, indicated six criteria as essential to an adequate definition of mental deficiency: Social incompetence, due to mental subnormality, resulting from developmental arrest, which obtains at maturity, is of constitutional origin, and is essentially incurable.

The principal distinguishing characteristics of the A.A.M.D.'s definition, as contrasted with Doll's, are: (1) the current definition refers to level of present intellectual functioning rather than to inferred potential; (2) no statement of cause is implied, whereas the older definition specified that the impairment was "of constitutional origin" (that is, rooted in some enduring organic impairment or deficiency); (3) the newer definition says nothing about curability. Incurability is dependent on the prevailing medical, educational, and rehabilitative methodology. Currently, prediction of the course and outcome of a given condition is not considered to be an essential component of a definition of mental retardation. Determinations of cause and the predictions of outcome are important, but they are divorced from the problem of initial identification of the mentally retarded.

According to the A.A.M.D., all three conditions—subnormal intellectual functioning, originating during the developmental period, and impairment of adaptive behavior—must be present for a person to be designated mentally retarded. Persons cannot be labelled mentally retarded just because their adaptive behavior is impaired. There are many causes other than mental retardation for slow maturational development, poor school progress, and inadequate social and vocational adjustment. They likewise cannot be designated as mentally retarded solely because of a low IQ. A low IQ, plus impaired adaptive behavior, which originates before maturity, are all required.

The A.A.M.D.'s definition is stated in functional terms—impairment in adaptive behavior. This impairment may take the forms of: (1) maturational retardation as indicated by slowness in acquiring help skills such as sitting, crawling, standing, walking, talking, habit training, and interacting with age peers; (2) deficiencies in learning, principally poor academic achievement; and (3) inadequate social adjustment, principally adult social and economic inadequacy (Heber, 1959). The individual's adequacy of adjustment must be judged in relation to that of the general population. This definition makes "mental retardation" a term descriptive of the current status of the individual's adaptive behavior, irrespective of etiology or curability. Deficiencies are also relative to the culture. A person may meet the criteria of mental retardation at one time or in one culture or subculture, and not at another time or place.

Although this definition and its proposed modification (Kidd, 1964) are broadly functional in nature, in practice they rely on quantitative standards. "Subaverage general intellectual functioning" is indicated by scores on intelligence tests. The A.A.M.D. suggest that an IQ of at least one standard deviation (15 IQ points) below the mean of the general population indicates subaverage general intellectual functioning. This makes an IQ of 85 the upper limit for the mentally retarded, thus including the old "borderline" group and a part of the "dull normal." Children in these ranges have been called "slow learners" in educational terminology. Of course, mental retardation is a matter of degree, and the term can be applied to anyone below the mean of the population. If we classify the mentally retarded as exceptional, and define as exceptional those individuals who deviate from the norm sufficiently to warrant special treatment or education, we can either extend the range of the mentally retarded to include these intermediate categories or we can designate them by the older terms. Since most of the studies made and the statistics on prevalence are based on the older classifications, we shall use an IQ of 70 (two standard deviations below the mean) as the upper limit for the mentally retarded, and shall refer to the 70 to 80 IQ group as borderline or dull normal.

Identification of the Mentally Retarded

The A.A.M.D. definition of mental retardation assumes a psychometric criterion for the determination of the level of intellectual functioning, developmental information to indicate maturational status, school records to indicate learning ability, and evidence of social and economic competence to serve as an index of social adjustment when the person involved is an adult.

THE PSYCHOMETRIC CRITERION

With the advent of intelligence testing, psychometric criteria came to the fore as diagnostic of mental retardation. The first individual intelligence tests were developed as a means of identifying the mentally retarded, and today there are on the market literally hundreds of tests which can be used to identify the intellectually retarded individual.

Mental retardation, defined in terms of test performance, is a fairly objective finding. Tests can be given and scored according to prescribed procedures designed to reduce to a minimum the biases, prejudice, and expectancies of the examiner. Numerical scores can be defined in terms of IQ's or mental-age equivalents—easily understood concepts. Mental retardation can be defined in terms of IQ or mental-age limits, and diagnosis is based on the individual's test performance in terms of these limits. This is apparently a very simple and straightforward procedure. However, it is also true that what psychometric data gain in ease of definition and clarity of statement, they lose in terms of social utility as compared with social criteria. Follow-up studies of mildly mentally retarded children show that test scores, by themselves, are poor prognosticators of adult occupational and social adjustment.

THE DEVELOPMENTAL CRITERION

When a person's level of educational or social functioning and his psychometric indices are consistent with a diagnosis of mental retardation, the developmental history of the individual often helps to make possible a more positive statement that this is the case. While the correlation between preschool development and later academic potential is not high, consistently subnormal general development and extensive retardation of development are supportive indications of mental subnormality.

The mentally retarded, as a group, have consistently been shown to be slow in learning to walk, talk, feed themselves, and develop toilet habits (Gesell and Amatruda, 1947). They are, in fact, retarded in practically all aspects of anatomical, physiological, motor, and social development, as well as in intellectual development. Sometimes retardation in age of sitting, standing, feeding oneself, walking and talking are sufficiently marked and consistent for a diagnosis of mental retardation to be made on these bases alone. This will of course be true only when motor disabilities (crippling), sensory defects (blindness or deafness), or lack of opportunity and absence of training are not sufficient to account for the retardation.

Conversely, a history of normal development, in the absence of accidents, disease, or evidence of deterioration, makes a diagnosis of mental deficiency questionable even though social and psychometric data so indicate. Developmental data provide useful supplementary information in the identification of the mentally retarded.

THE LEARNING-ABILITY CRITERION

Failure in educational endeavors as a criterion of mental retardation can be subsumed under the broader social criterion just as logically as placing it by itself. However, the fact is that academic success and social and economic competence are not highly correlated. The two are positively related, but discrepancies between them are sufficiently great so that social or economic failure cannot be predicted on the basis of lack of academic success alone. The A.A.M.D.'s clarification of its definition of mental retardation also distinguishes the two.

Formal education is part of our culture, and intellectual achievement has considerable prestige value. Intellectual skills are also a prerequisite to admittance to many trades and professions. The individual who does not progress in school has failed in an important social area. The school's situation is also the first place in which objective comparisons are systematically made, and the child finds himself in a rather definite position in a prestige hierarchy based largely on intellectual achievements.

Failure in school is often their first symptom of inadequate intellectual functioning. In view of this, school failure, when not the result of sensory or motor handicaps or absence from school, has been suggested as a criterion of mental retardation. Two or three years retardation in school achievement, in the absence of other causes, has sometimes been considered indicative of mental retardation.

THE SOCIAL-ADJUSTMENT CRITERION

Although it has its limitations, the test of social adequacy is the most basic of all. It is the elementary datum from which we start in establishing the fact of mental retardation. If a person is functioning adequately socially and economically as compared with his peers, a diagnosis of mental retardation can hardly be justified, irrespective of low test scores, demonstrable lack of normal neural development, or the presence of brain damage. The observation of social deficiency is the starting point of the inquiry and the primary point of reference in dealing with most cases of mental retardation.

THE ASSESSMENT OF MENTAL RETARDATION

The diagnosis of mental retardation is always made in terms of the criteria accepted as basic to the definition of mental defectiveness. We have already indicated that multiple criteria are involved in the practical diagnosis of mental defectiveness.

The assessment of the mentally retarded individual is an inevitable process. It is also a never-ending process. It goes on informally and haphazardly when done by relatives, friends, and acquaintances. It becomes more systematic and formal when done by teachers, counselors, and psychologists for purposes of school promotion, demotion, or retention, or for placement in special classes or institutions.

The overall assessment of the mentally retarded individual typically serves several purposes. First, it provides as accurate an estimate as possible of the individual's present level of functioning. It is a statement of the person's status in terms of test performance, social adjustment, school achievement, and physique. Second, the assessment of the mentally retarded should provide information concerning the causes of the individual's inadequacies. Deductions concerning possible or probable etiology are an important part of the assessment process. Third, determination of the causes of functional inadequacies normally implies something concerning possible care and treatment. Fourth, information about the nature, cause, and possible treatment of a mental defective also makes possible some prediction of the probable outcomes of treatment.

In summary, complete assessment of a mentally retarded individual should provide: (1) a classification of the individual in terms of mental level; (2) a statement of probable causes of the condition; (3) an indication of possible care or treatment; and (4) some prediction of the probable outcome.

Except for very special purposes, the immediate occasion for the assessment of mental status is some social circumstance, and the ultimate purpose of diagnosis is the solution of some social problem. In addition, the final test of the accuracy of diagnosis and the effectiveness of treatment is the extent to which the social circumstance is improved.

THE RELATION OF IDENTIFICATION TO CRITERIA

It is obvious that identification of the mentally retarded individual involves the acceptance of certain criteria. We have already indicated that, in practice, multiple criteria are commonly used. The relative weight given to the psychometric, educational, social, economic, and developmental criteria will vary with the purpose of the assessment process. Whereas combined school achievement (educational criteria) and mental test scores (psychometric criteria) are most valid for the identification of the mentally retarded of school age when exclusion from the regular class or special class placement are being considered, the broader criteria of adequate social adjustment and economic sufficiency are more crucial in the evaluation of the out-of-school adult, and general developmental status is the most relevant information for the preschool child.

Since the various criteria do not correlate highly with each other, we can have the paradox of a child who was classed as intellectually retarded while in school and who, as an adult, functions in a socially adequate way. The available data on the incidence of mental retardation according to chronological age suggest that this happens with a fairly large number of individuals. Table 7–1 shows such data based on two different surveys.

Table 7–1 shows that relatively few children below school age are diagnosed as mentally retarded, that the percentage of defective individuals increases tremendously during the school-age period, and that in adulthood the percentage drops to a comparatively low level. Part of the large difference between children and adults is attributed to the higher death rates among the mentally subnormal and the greater ease of case-finding while the children are of school age, but it is probable that the biggest single factor is the lesser weight given to abstract verbal facility in the adult situation. Many retarded individuals of the higher mental levels (the mildly mentally retarded), who probably make up 75 percent of the children of school age so diagnosed, find formal education an unsurmountable hazard, but once they are out of school a large percentage of them are not defective in terms of social and economic criteria (O'Conner and Tizard, 1956).

TABLE 7–1
Incidence of Mental Retardation and Chronological Age
(Per 1,000 of the General Population)

Age in Years	England and Wales*	Baltimore†
0–4	1.2	0.7
5–9	15.5	11.8
10–14	25.6	43.6
15–19	10.8	30.2
20–29	8.4	7.6
30–39	5.7	8.2
40–49	5.4	7.4
50–59	4.9	4.5
60 and older	2.9	2.2

*Based on Wood Report as reported by O'Conner and Tizard
(1956, p. 22).
†Data from Lemkau, Tietze, and Casper (1942).

An extensive survey in New York (New York State Department of
Mental Hygiene, 1955) shows that the reported incidence of mental retardation in that state rises with increasing age, reaches a peak at about
fourteen to eighteen years, and then drops off sharply. The upper limit
for compulsory school attendance is in this age range.

Terminology and Classification

The American Association on Mental Deficiency has recommended a
standard set of terms, but there is still great variation in the terminology
used in the field of intellectual subnormality both in the United States and
abroad. In the older American terminology, *feebleminded* was the generic
term for all persons sufficiently intellectually subnormal to warrant special consideration, and the terms *moron, imbecile,* and *idiot* designated
various degrees of subnormality. At a later date, *mental deficiency* replaced *feebleminded* as the generic term, while the older terms were
retained for the three subcategories. The A.A.M.D. more recently has
proposed that *mental retardation* become the preferred generic term,
and that the various degrees of subnormality be indicated as *borderline,
mild, moderate, severe,* and *profound.* Additional sets of roughly equivalent terms are used in Great Britain, by the World Health Organization,
and by the American Psychiatric Association. There are also separate
educational terminologies, both in Great Britain and in America. Table
7–2 indicates the relationships among these various sets of terms.

TABLE 7-2

Some Terminology for Mental Retardation

Organization	Generic Terms	More Specific Designation				
American clinics (earlier)	Feeblerninded			Moron	Imbecile	Idiot
American clinics (later)	Mental deficiency			Moron	Imbecile	Idiot
World Health Organization	Mental subnormality			Mild	Moderate	Severe
American Psychiatric Association	Mental subnormality			Mild	Moderate	Severe
British clinics	Amentia			Feeblerninded	Imbecile	Idiot
American, educational	Mentally retarded			Educable	Trainable	Idiot
British, educational	Amentia			Educational subnormal	Backward	Custodial
Approximate IQ-equivalent of British educational terminology	0–70			50–70	20–50	Below 20 or 30
American Association on Mental Deficiency	Mental y retarded		Borderline	Mild	Moderate	Severe	Profound
Recommended IQ-equivalent of A.A.M.D.	0–85		70–84	55–69	40–54	25–39	Below 25
Standard score ranges of A.A.M.D.	−1.01 to below −5.00		−1.01 to −2.00	−2.01 to −3.00	−3.01 to −4.00	−4.01 to −5.00	Below −5.00

189

The diversity of roughly equivalent terms is the result of the different criteria used to define and identify individuals with intellectual impairments, the varying purposes served by the diagnosis, and the never-ending attempt to get away from the negative connotations of the names given to handicapping conditions. The older terms—*feebleminded, moron, imbecile*, and *idiot*—came to have a clinical and psychometric frame of reference. Definitions were largely in terms of IQ ranges, heredity was considered to be the primary causal factor, and the prognosis was considered to be poor. These terms, descriptive of significant intellectual impairment with the connotations of hopelessness, became emotionally toned and stigmatizing. The newer terms—*mental retardation* as the general term and *borderline, mild, moderate, severe*, and *profound* as varying degrees—are less emotionally toned and commonly imply the use of multiple criteria. Maturational rate (developmental data), information about learning ability (school achievement), and social adjustment (social and economic competence) are used for purposes of identification and classification. The terms *educable, trainable*, and *custodial* to indicate degrees of mental retardation obviously refer more to the practical problems of administrative classification than to the broader questions of etiology and prognosis. All these terms refer to classes of intellectual subnormality which relate to the degree of impairment. A second classification is based on the principle causes of the low level of intellectual functioning.

Etiological Classification

When the mentally retarded are classified according to the cause of their deficiency, the basic division is into endogenous and exogenous causation.

Endogenous is roughly equivalent to *primary, familial, hereditary*, and *cultural familial*. This term and its counterpart, *exogenous*, are not used consistently by different writers. Endogenous literally means originating within the body, and should refer to those forms of mental retardation that are genetically determined (English and English, 1958). This would include the relatively rare cases of single-gene determined mental retardation as well as the biggest etiological subgroups, which are often referred to as the "ordinary familial" or "common garden variety" in which multigenetic *and* disadvantageous culturally related factors combine to produce mental retardation. When the ordinary familial mentally retarded are classified as endogenous, we imply that heredity is the primary causal factor. To be consistent, those who consider environment to be the primary cause of the deficiency of this group should classify it as exogenous. In practice, "endogenous" has often been used as synonymous with "ordinary familial." Most authorities today probably believe that multigenetic and environmental factors both contribute significantly to ordinary familial mental retardation, so it should be placed in a "mixed" category.

One limitation of etiological classifications is that in many cases the causes are not known. This may reflect the limitation of our knowledge of etiologies or the inadequacy of our information on the cases to be classified. At any rate, when we find that about one-third of the institutionalized mentally retarded are usually placed in the "causes unknown" category, the limitations of etiological classifications become obvious (Yannet, 1957).

Exogenous, the second major etiological classification, is also called "secondary," "acquired," or "environmental." Sometimes the exogenous causes are subdivided into the "organic" and the "environmentally or culturally deprived." The intellectual inadequacy of the exogenous mentally retarded person is primarily the result of environmentally induced organic impairment. The causes may be traumatic injury, disease, toxins, or anoxia, on the one hand, or extremely restricted or deviant cultural experiences, on the other.

In a literal sense, the level of intellectual functioning is always the result of the combined effects of endogenous (genetic) and exogenous (environmental) factors. Causation is never an either-or proposition. In this sense, etiology is always "mixed." There are also conditions which can be produced primarily by either exogenous or endogenous causes. Microcephaly can result from a genetic defect or from high levels of irradiation during the fetal period. Cretinism can be genetic or result from a limited intake of iodine (Rundle, 1962).

GENETIC CAUSATION

Mental Retardation Caused by a Dominant Gene. Mental retardation which is due to a single defective dominant gene is quite rare. Some conditions apparently of this type are Huntington's chorea, tuberous sclerosis, neurofibromatosis, hereditary cerebellar ataxia, and Freidreich's ataxis (Roberts, 1963). It is obvious that severe mental defectiveness due to a single dominant gene will be self-limiting because the parents must also be defective. Since most of the severely mentally retarded do not reproduce, either because of sterility or lack of opportunity, the transmission of the defective dominant gene from one generation to the next is very limited. No recipient of a dominant "lethal" gene can beget offspring. Some of these genetically determined conditions may occur in a mild form in one generation or in certain members of a family, and in a more severe form in other generations or in other members of the same family. The less severely affected individual can produce and transmit the defective genes to succeeding generations. The occurrence of sporadic cases is sometimes attributed to a mutation in a germ cell (Kugelmass, 1954). The average age of onset of Huntington's chorea is thirty-six (Gottesman, 1963), so that this condition can be perpetrated indefinitely and in some cases unknowingly. But if we are to be consistent, those conditions of mental subnormality which appear after maturity should not be called "mental retardation."

The characteristics of mental subnormality which is determined by a single dominant gene are as follows:

1. The affected and unaffected members of a family are usually sharply differentiated.
2. Every defective individual has at least one affected parent.
3. Where only one parent is affected, and is heterozygous, approximately one-half of the offspring will be affected; when the affected parent is homozygous all the offspring will be mentally defective.
4. When both parents are affected and are heterozygous, approximately three-fourths of the offspring will be defective (Penrose, 1963; Roberts, 1963).

Mental Retardation Caused by a Recessive Gene.   Much more often mental retardation is due to a single recessive gene. Such defective children typically come of apparently normal parents. The defect is typically the result of the child's receiving two similar recessive genes, one from each parent. The phenotypically normal parents are carriers of the defective gene but are not themselves affected. Some conditions which are generally considered to be due to a single defective recessive gene are: Tay-Sach's disease, gargoylism, galactosuria, phenylketonuria, and genetic microcephaly. Most of these types of mental retardation are found rarely and the sum of all of them does not represent a very large proportion of the total population of the mentally deficient. However, many types have been discovered quite recently, and new ones are currently being identified, which indicates that this category may be larger than was formerly realized.

Many of these genetically determined mental deficiencies are, in turn, due to inborn defects of metabolism. The genes produce defective metabolism which in turn affects the development and functioning of the nervous system (possibly through other agencies), resulting in lowered mentality.

Where mental deficiency is the result of a single recessive gene

1. the affected and unaffected members of a family are usually clearly differentiated;

2. many times the parents and immediate ancestors are unaffected;
3. the offspring are more often affected when the parents are related to each other by blood than when they are not;
4. when neither parent is himself affected, but some of the offspring show the defect, approximately one-fourth of the children will be defective (Penrose, 1963).

Chromosomal Aberrations. Improved techniques for studying chromosomes led to the discovery, in 1956, that the true number of chromosomes in man was forty-six rather than forty-eight (Tijo and Levan, 1956). Soon after this it was disclosed that mongols (Down's syndrome) had forty-seven chromosomes in place of the normal complement of forty-six (Lejeune and Turpin, 1961). It has since been established that mongolism is associated with an extra chromosome (trisomism) at pair number 21. Cases of extra chromosomes in positions other than number 21 have been reported, but almost none of these individuals, although usually mentally retarded, are mongols (Therman et al., 1961; Gottesman, 1963). Some cases of mental retardation have been found associated with a chromosomal count of 45, one less than the normal number (Moorhead, Mellman, and Wenan, 1961; Gottesman, 1963). Trisomy of their chromosomes is associated with multiple congenital anomalies, including mental retardation (Robinson and Robinson, 1965; Jarvik, Falek, and Pierson, 1964) In mongolism resulting from a trisomy of chromosome number 21, there is apparently a failure of the two chromosomes of the pair to separate (nondisjunction) during the maturation process (meiosis) prior to fertilization. This produces an ovum with twenty-four (one more than normal) chromosomes, which then unites with a normal sperm to produce the forty-seven chromosomes characteristic of such individuals.

The discovery of these chromosomal anomalies discloses the fact that we can have genetic disorders that are not necessarily inherited. To further complicate the picture, there is a rare familial type of mongolism caused by a translocation (the attachment of one chromosome to another). This produces an excess of chromosomal material, but one of the number 21 chromosomes is attached to another chromosome, usually number 15, but sometimes number 22. Either the father or the mother may be the carrier of the translocation. Some such translocations have been traced through three generations (Carter et al., 1960; Forssman and Lehmann, 1962; Penrose, Ellis, and Delhanty, 1960; Penrose, 1963). The ages of the parents of mongoloid children of this type do not differ from the norms of the population, whereas mothers of the nondisjunctive type are considerably older than the mothers of nonmongoloids. There is evidence that parents who are carriers of the translocation can be detected (Rundle, Copper, and Cowie, 1961; Rundle, 1962; Jarvik, Falek, and Pierson, 1964).

Finally, there is another type of chromosomal anomaly known as mosaicism, which also produces a very rare type of mongolism. This condition is apparently not present at conception, but in the division of an early embryonic cell there occurs a nondisjunction of chromosome number 21 resulting in two daughter cells, one of which has forty-seven and the other forty-five chromosomes. The cell with only forty-five chromosomes dies, but the one with forty-seven develops into a new line of cells parallel to the normal lines of cells which did not experience nondisjunction. Individuals resulting from such deviations have some body cells with forty-six chromosomes, and some with forty-seven (mosaicism). Not all individuals with mosaicism are mongols, but some are (Hannah-Alava, 1960; Fitzgerald and Lycette, 1961; Clarke, Edwards, and Smallpace, 1961). Some significant differences among mongols of these differing etiologies have been demonstrated (Gibson and Pozsonyi, 1965).

These three types of chromosomal anomalies—nondisjunction, translocation, and mosaicism—none of which is hereditary in the ordinary sense, all result in developmental deviations (including mental retardation) which are genetically linked to dominant single genes, and, at least three of which are due to chromosomal abnormalities. There have been tremendous advances in genetics since the 1950s, and we can anticipate that additional light will continue to be thrown on the big category of the mentally retarded designated "causes unknown." The discovery of chromosomal deviations in chimpanzees and other species of nonhuman primates with clinical, behavioral, and chromosomal features similar to those in human mongolism makes possible experimental studies of these conditions (McClure, et al, 1969).

Mental Retardation Involving Many Genes. The ordinary familial, undifferentiated, nonclinical, or common garden variety mental defectives are at the low end of the distribution curve of intelligence. The factors determining the intelligence of these individuals are the same as those affecting the intelligence level of the normal and the superior. It is certainly a mistake to treat this group of mentally retarded as a well-defined and isolated category for, in reality, they are simply the arbitrarily defined tail end of a normally distributed population.

Unlike the mentally retarded whose deficiency results from a single gene, the ordinary familial mentally retarded individual does not differ markedly from his parents or siblings. He has no obvious distinguishing physical characteristics. He is more likely to be smaller in stature, lighter in weight, have defective vision and hearing, poor health, and greater susceptibility to disease than his peers of normal or superior mentality, but many individuals in this group are actually superior in these areas. Postmortem gross and microscopical examinations of the nervous systems have failed to disclose significant special characteristics of the brains of the typical familial mental defective. Most of the histological studies showing characteristic neural pathology in mental defectives have been carried out upon the low-grade cases who are predominantly of the secondary, or exogenous types.

CHANGING CONCEPTIONS OF
THE IMPORTANCE OF HEREDITY

Following the rediscovery of Mendel's work in 1900 and its uncritical application to humans, heredity came to be stressed as the primary factor in the etiology of mental retardation. Estimates of the incidence of mental retardation in which heredity was considered to be the principal cause averaged around 80 percent. Tredgold, in 1929, gave 80 percent; Hollingworth, in 1920, 90; and Goddard, in 1914, 77 (Hutt and Gibby, 1965). Around 1930, there was a reaction against the extreme hereditarian emphasis, and it has since been carried to the point where some workers seem to be denying that heredity plays any significant role in determining the mental level of the ordinary familial type of mental retardation (Sarason and Gladwin, 1958; Lewis, 1933).

Wallin (1956), in a review of some twenty-three studies in which estimates of the extent of hereditariness among the mentally deficient were made, gives values ranging from 90 percent to 1.7 percent. One noticeable trend in the studies is the decreasing emphasis on the role of heredity. Wallin presents data based on 9,187 first admissions to public institutions for mental defectives in the United States which indicate that hereditary factors are dominantly responsible for deficiency in 44.2 percent of morons, 22.7 percent of imbeciles and 11.4 percent of idiots. Doll's (1934) estimate that approximately 30 percent of the defectives (of all mental levels) of the Vineland Training School are hereditary cases, 30 percent are of secondary causation, and 40 percent are of unknown causation is fairly typical.

The wide diversity of views and percentages given in the studies of this topic arises partly from the nature-versus-nurture bias of the individual authors, partly from the different kinds of cases constituting the groups studied, and partly from the varying criteria used in assigning causative factors in individual cases.

THE NATURE-NURTURE PROBLEM

It seems likely that most attempts to determine the proportional contribution of heredity and environment in the determination of intellectual level have oversimplified the problem. There is evidence that the influence of each factor depends upon the other. Thus, the contribution of heredity to the variance of a given trait will itself vary according to the environmental conditions.

Similarly, environmental difference may produce considerable change in the functional level of a person with one level of inherited potentiality and practically none in someone with a much lower potentiality. For example, the type of home in which a child is raised may have considerable effect on a potentially normal child and relatively little effect on a low-grade custodial case. Heredity determines the range of variation within which environmental differences determine the actual outcome. In some conditions this range is very narrow, while in others it is very broad. At one extreme we have such conditions as amaurotic idiocy, in which the physical conditions necessary for normal intellectual development are lacking as the result of inherited deficiencies. There is no known environmental factor or change that can in any appreciable degree compensate for this deficit. The individual inheriting the defective genes responsible for this condition will be mentally retarded regardless of the environment in which he is raised. The range of variation produced by environment is very small.

Next to these extreme conditions are such syndromes as phenylpyruvic amentia, in which an inherited inability to metabolize phenylalanine (an amino acid) normally results in a severe degree of mental deficiency. However, if the child is raised on a diet free of phenylalanine, he may develop quite normally. In this condition an environmental change (restriction of diet) may counteract the effects of a hereditary defect.

In a less specific way, the handicap of hereditary deafness may likewise be largely offset by adequate training. In a later chapter we suggest that the degree of intellectual backwardness of the deaf is an index of the state of development of special instructional facilities for their training. Here the range of environmentally produced variations is very broad.

However broad or narrow the *possible* environmentally produced variations, the range of actual variation may be greatly narrowed because of particular social circumstances. One of these circumstances may be the handicap of being born into a culture which artificially limits behavioral possibilities because of social stereotypes. In many regions of the world, inheritance of a given skin color or certain other physical characteristics may determine where and how one shall live, the educational and vocational opportunities open to one, and many other important behavioral variables. These restrictions range all the way from legal prohibitions and physical coercion to the more subtle but no less real determinants, such as social attitudes and expectancies, and their acceptance and internalization by the individual. It has been suggested that in a culture which considered carriers of blood group AB to be aristocrats and those of O-type blood to be laborers, the blood group genes would become important determinants of behavior (Anastasi, 1958; Dobzhansky, 1950). It is obvious that in these cases the narrowing of behavioral possibilities is not due to biological inheritance itself, but that it results from the social stereotypes which use the inherited characteristic as an identifying one. The restrictions are in the culture rather than within the individual.

If these examples seem remote from the problems of intellectual retardation, we need only to point out that apart from any inherited biological deficits, the social and economic level in which a child is raised may be an important determinant of the range and nature of his intellectual stimulation, his interest in formal education, his level of aspiration, and his orientation to time. All these contribute to his lack of interest and low motivational level toward many things which our culture values highly. Terman found that, within his gifted group, achieving in accordance with one's potential was decidedly influenced by the social, professional, and family backgrounds of the subjects. The greatest contrasts between the high, as contrasted with the low, achievers were in the areas of interest and in drive to achieve (Terman and Oden, 1947).

There is also considerable evidence that the failure to learn to read and write or to graduate from elementary or high school or college may close certain job possibilities to many individuals who could perform quite adequately in these positions if given the opportunity. It is also very likely that the overall devaluation of the individual who fails academically, and his incorporation of this valuation into his own self-concept, lowers his level of aspiration and his ultimate achievement. In these instances it may be society, more than the individual's inherited incapacities, that limits his performance levels. This topic is developed more fully in the chapter on the culturally disadvantaged.

In addition to the facts that the contribution of environment to functional level varies with inherited potentiality and that cultural stereotypes may artificially limit the expression of such potentialities, the weight to be assigned to a given environmental change may vary with the age of the child. Studies have shown that the child's exposure to a superior environment may have a greater effect at an earlier age than at a later age (Freeman, Holzinger, and Mitchell, 1928). For example, the regular administration of thyroid extract to a potential cretin, if started at birth, may result in a reasonably normally developed individual. If similar medication is delayed until after adolescence, the individual will be mentally deficient. Cretinism usually is not inherited, but it illustrates the point. Both nature and nurture contribute to all behavior traits, and their respective contributions can never be specifically weighted.

On the other hand, in a general way, we are probably justified in speaking of certain given conditions, such as the single-gene-determined mental deficiencies, as inherited. In these conditions, the range of environmentally produced variations is very narrow. In the ordinary familial, higher-level types of mental defectives, both heredity and environment affect the ultimate level of attainment over a considerable range. We never feel that we can speak of these deficiencies as either environmental or inherited, since variations in either can have a significant effect on functional level.

When the heredity is presumably normal, but an environmental factor such as brain injury so lowers the individual's capabilities that he functions defectively both socially and psychometrically, we can legitimately speak of the deficiency as environmentally induced. In these cases the range of variation has been so narrowed by an environmental factor that the person's original inheritance has relatively little influence on his functional level.

In the last group are those individuals who, because of environmental restrictions, emotional conditioning, or personality disorganization, function at a level comparable to the mental retardates in the other groups. These individuals still have potentialities, and their deficiencies are presumably remediable. Adequate training or psychotherapy can often greatly increase their functional level. Such people are discussed more fully in the chapter on the culturally disadvantaged.

THE NATURE-NURTURE CONTROVERSY REVISITED IN THE 1960s

The questions of the relative heritability of intelligence and the validity of inferring the causes of cross-cultural differences from measures of heritability were raised anew in the late 1960s by the publications of Arthur Jensen of the University of California. Jensen (1968, 1969) derived heritability values from the statistical analysis of intelligence test scores and claimed that these values were sufficiently high to indicate that intelligence is overwhelmingly the result of genetic inheritance rather than environmental influences. Jensen also contended that compensatory educational programs, such as "Head Start," had failed to reduce the educational deficits of the disadvantaged children, particularly of the blacks, because these children were incapable of the higher levels of conceptual learning as the result of their genetic limitations.

Predictably, the appearance of Jensen's articles in the *Harvard Educational Review* evoked many critical reactions. Interested individuals will find the McCord and Demerath (1968), Thoday and Gibson (1970), and Bodmer and Cavalli-Sforza (1970) articles among the better objective evaluations. Our major objections to Jensen's interpretations and extrapolations are implicit in the preceding discussion. However, since Jensen has raised the racial issue, we will summarize the research findings which cause us to question the Jensen genetic interpretation of the origin of racial differences in intelligence.

1. Heritability values are based on individual differences within a specific group and have nothing to do with mean differences between groups. Therefore, the percent of heritability based on the variances within one population cannot be extrapolated to another population or to differences between populations. The values obtained on one population or subpopulation may differ markedly from those from another. A heritability figure is not a value that can be applied to a trait in general but only to a trait as found in a particular population and under a particular set of environmental circumstances.

2. The ranges of environmental and genetic variations in the groups and environs investigated are also critical variables in determining heritability values. A given behavioral characteristic may be uninfluenced by environmental variations within a particular range but be extremely sensitive to changes outside that range. For example, Cooper and Zubek (1958) found that the large difference between "bright" and "dull" strains of rats disappeared entirely when the rats were reared either in a very restricted or enriched environment. Large, genetically determined differences in rates of learning present under one set of environmental circumstances disappear entirely under different developmental conditions.

3. A given environmental change may exert marked effects at one stage of development but have relatively little influence if present during other developmental periods—the critical-period phenomenon. A child born without a functional thyroid gland (a potential cretin), who receives a small amount of thyroxin from birth can develop into a mentally normal adult instead of a low-grade mentally retarded individual. However, the same amount of thyroxin will have no appreciable effect on mental level when administered to an adult cretin. Bloom (1964) and others believe that the first four years of a child's life constitute a critical period for mental development and that environmental enrichment or improvement has a much greater effect during this period than later in life.

4. The overall difference between the mean intelligence tests scores of blacks and whites in America is about one standard deviation or 15 IQ points (Jensen, 1968). Jensen believes that this difference cannot be accounted for in terms of environmental differences. However, it has been shown that environmental differences commonly encountered in contemporary society can produce larger differences. The mean difference between the IQ's of identical twins reared under contrasting "favorable" and "unfavorable" conditions is about 20 points (Newman, et al., 1937; Bloom, 1964). Siblings reared apart under similar conditions differ by approximately the same amount (Sontag, et al, 1958). Bloom (1964) believes that 20 points is a conservative estimate of the effects of extreme social environments on measured intelligence. Thus it seems that the social, economic, educational, and color-related caste differences between blacks and whites in America *can* account for the black-white intelligence-test-score differences and does not necessitate the postulation of intellectually related genetic differences.

5. The heritability of a trait within a population and the hereditary origin of a difference between two populations are not the same and are not necessarily related. Some extreme examples will make this

point clear. The genetic variability of pure strains (identical twins, etc.) is zero and the heritability values obtained within such strains is also zero. All variations within strains are due to environment. However, if the contrasting strains have been selectively bred and developed for differing specific behavioral characteristics such as maze "brightness" and "dullness," the differences between the two populations, reared under the same environments, are entirely hereditary. Heritability values are zero but group differences are entirely hereditary. Conversely, if two groups of identical genetic endowment are reared under very different circumstances, the resulting group differences will be entirely of environmental origin with zero heritability within each group. The etiology of differences between two populations has no necessary relation to the heritability within the populations and cannot be inferred from it.

6. The fact that a large percentage of the variance of a trait within a population is attributed to hereditary factors does not preclude the production of significant group changes due to changing environmental variables. Estimates of the percentage variance in height due to genetic factors run as high as 90 percent. However, this does not prevent major illness or inadequate diet during critical growth periods from exerting significant effects on adult height. In the early years of this century, children born in the United States after their immigrant parents had resided here for four or more years were considerably taller than their siblings born and reared partly or completely in Europe (Boas, 1911). The second-and third-generation American-born children of pure Japanese extraction are several inches taller than their parents or grandparents born and reared in Japan (Tanner, 1955).

7. The available evidence suggests that if all relevant environmental variables could be equated, the black-white difference in intelligence tests scores would disappear. Some evidence supporting this contention is as follows:

a. The first intelligence test (Army Alpha) administered to a nationwide sample showed that the average score of Northern World War I Negro army recruits was considerably above that of Southern blacks. The median scores of Negroes in Pennsylvania, New York, Illinois, and Ohio were above those of white recruits in Mississippi, Kentucky, Arkansas, and Georgia. However, these latter differences were small and based on small numbers of cases and attracted little attention when first reported. (Yerkes, 1921).

b. The superiority of Northern as compared with Southern Negroes found consistently in the early studies, was shown not to be a result of a selective migration of the superior individuals to the North (Klineberg, 1935; Lee, 1951).

c. The children of Negro migrants from the South showed increases in intelligence test scores directly proportionate to length of residence in the North (Klineberg, 1935, Lee, 1951). Earlier studies had found a similar relationship between the Army Alpha test scores of foreign-born immigrants and length of residence in the United States (Brigham, 1923).

d. If a battery of tests ranging from a heavily culturally loaded test

at the one extreme, through those less culturally related, to relatively
culture-free tests at the other extreme are administered to blacks,
American Indians, and whites, the relative superiority of the whites
diminishes as the cultural component of the tests decreases (Telford, 1938).

e. The more closely the socioeconomic and educational backgrounds
of black and white comparison groups are equated, the smaller the
test score differences become (McCord and Demerath, 1968).

f. When groups are equated on such specific things as proportions of
broken homes, time spent with children in educational related
activities, and "housing crowdedness" factors, in addition to the
conventional indices of socioeconomic and educational status, the
customary test score discrepancies practically disappear (Tulkin,
1968).

During the last fifty years, opinion has shifted from a preponderance in
support of heredity as being the major cause of the superior achievements
in test-score performances of whites as compared with blacks to a small
dissonant minority who still hold this belief. Current arguments in support of the contentions of this latter group are given by Garrett (1962)
Shuey, (1966), and Jensen (1968; 1969). For recent, more balanced reviews
of the problem see Dreger and Miller, (1960; 1968).

ENVIRONMENTAL CAUSES OF MENTAL RETARDATION

There is a wide variety of possible environmental causes of mental retardation. It is easy to list these and indicate how they may conceivably
lower the mental level. It is also possible to find individual cases in which
each of these alleged causes is apparently operative. However, when quantitative studies start with a fairly large, heterogeneous group of mentally
deficient individuals, and comparisons are made of the incidence of the
alleged causes in the deficient group and in a comparable group of intellectually normal people, significant differences often fail to appear. In
other words, that various environmental factors produce mental retardation seems to be fairly convincing on the clinical, individual case level,
but their functioning as statistically significant factors in causing mental
retardation in general is often hard to establish.

Prenatal Environmental Causes

The differentiation of cases of mental retardation due to prenatal
environmental causes from those produced by rare genetic determiners
is very difficult. Both groups are congenital. Presumably a genetically
normal fetus or embryo can be injured by mechanical, chemical, nutritional, glandular, actinic, and infectious agents, but there are few data
and few informed guesses about the extent to which any or all of these

factors actually produce mental retardation. Kugelmass (1954) estimates that such prenatal factors produce 10 percent of the mental retardates.

Prenatal Physical Trauma. It is quite possible that unsuccessful attempts at abortion and accidents to the pregnant mother may so injure the fetus as to lower the child's mental level. There are clinical records of defective children being born to mothers following such occurrences. However, a causal relation between the two events is very difficult to establish. Workers in the field feel that direct injury to the embryo or fetus from blows, falls, or unsuccessful attempts at abortion by means of mechanical instruments are relatively unimportant in producing mental deficiency (Wallin, 1956; Robinson and Robinson, 1965).

Prenatal Nutrition. Many authors recognize the possibility that "nutritional amentia" may occur (Tredgold and Soddy, 1956; Fraser, 1964).

A larger number of studies, but without controls, suggest that the nutritional status of the pregnant mother may significantly affect the mental level of the offspring. Some two decades ago it was shown that congenital malformations in mammals could be experimentally produced by putting the pregnant mother on a deficient diet. The first such congenital malformations were produced by vitamin deficiencies (Kalter and Warkany, 1959). Since that time a bewildering array of congenital malformations has been produced by feeding to the pregnant mothers diets which were deficient in any one of the following: vitamin A; vitamin D; riboflavin; folic acid; thiamin; niacin and pantothenic acid. On the other hand, deficiencies of pyridoxine, choline, biotin, or vitamin K have failed to produce congenital malformations. Paradoxically, congenital anomalies have been produced by feeding animals excessive amounts of vitamin A.

The experimental evidence concerning humans is much less complete, but one large-scale (N = 2,400) experiment with good controls has been reported. In this study, two groups of pregnant women, one eating a deficient diet and the other a diet judged adequate, were each subdivided into two equated subgroups. The two control subgroups received placebos, while the members of the experimental groups received vitamin supplements. The supplements consisted of thiamine, ascorbic acid, or a polynutrient supplement. The offspring were tested with the Stanford-Binet, Form L, when they were three or four years old. There was no significant difference between the offspring of the mothers whose diet was deemed adequate and those on supplemented diets. The group born of mothers eating a deficient diet, but supplemented, averaged 3.7 IQ points above the children born to the mothers of the control (placebo) group. While this difference does not seem large, it was highly significant statistically. There were no significant differences among the three types of supplements (Harrell, Woodward, and Gates, 1955; 1956).

While a difference of 3.7 IQ points is hardly sufficient to produce a large number of mentally retarded in potentially normal individuals, dietary deficiencies of greater magnitude than those involved in the above study would presumably produce greater differences in intellectual level and, in extreme cases, could produce mental retardation. It seems that in at least one well-controlled, large-scale study of humans, a measurable intellectual deficit was produced in children by deficiencies in the diets of the pregnant mothers.

Surveys of human populations have no definitive value because of their lack of controls, but they are suggestive. Reports of a high rate of congenital malformation among the offspring of Jewish women who spent periods of internment in German concentration camps prior to World War II are common. One study of 1,430 offspring born in 1946 to 1948 of Jewish mothers who had gone through the hardships of concentration camp life prior to their marriages showed a disproportionate number of congenital defects (Benda, 1952). Mongolism, hydrocephalus, club feet, polydactylism, anencephaly, and other similar conditions occurred many times as often as would be expected. Such data are difficult to interpret because of the multiple factors involved—such as the influence of general starvation, specific dietary deficiencies, mental and emotional stress, and possibly age (Robinson and Robinson, 1965).

Prenatal Infections. The evidence that diseases of the mother during pregnancy may affect the physical and mental development of the fetus is quite convincing. Congenital syphilis has been recognized as a clinical entity for a long time. The child may be infected either prenatally, through the placental circulation, or in the passage through the birth canal during delivery. It has been established that a syphilitic mother undergoing treatment *can* give birth to an uninfected child.

The proportion of mentally retarded children resulting from syphilitic infection has long been in dispute, but it has certainly declined in recent years. Prenatal infection with syphilis from infected mothers is today a relatively infrequent cause of mental deficiency in children. Surveys conducted before 1935 showed that about 6 percent of institutionalized mental defectives had a history of congenital syphilis. This figure had fallen to about 4 percent in the 1950s (Wolf and Cowen, 1959).

Rubella, or German measles, in the first trimester of pregnancy has also been established as a cause of multiple maldevelopments in the fetus. The most common congenital defects so caused are those of the eyes, heart, and the central nervous system. Microcephaly, deafness, blindness, and epilepsy have all been reported (Wolf and Cowen, 1959). Mental retardation may be an accompaniment of such maldevelopment. It is not known just how rubella affects the developing embryo, but the critical time is the organogenic period—the first three months of pregnancy.

The studies of the extent to which maternal rubella is responsible for congenital malformations are quite divergent, depending upon whether they are among the earlier reports which were largely retrospective (starting with the malformations and working back in attempting to determine possible causes) or prospective (starting with a medical diagnosis of maternal rubella and determining the incidence of malformation in the resulting offspring). The earlier studies reported 50 to 100 percent of maldeveloped offspring; the later, better controlled, studies claim only about 10 to 15 percent of congenital defects (Gregg, 1941; Swan et al., 1943; Swan, 1947; Greenberg and Pelleteri, 1957; Wolf and Cowen, 1959; Skinner, 1961; Robinson and Robinson, 1965). There is a sharp gradient in susceptibility. One study (Michaels and Mellin, 1960) found 47 percent, 22 percent, and 7 percent of injured infants born to mothers infected in the first, second, and third months of pregnancy respectively.

A vaccine for rubella is now available which makes it possible to eliminate this source of potential damage to the unborn child. An effort is being made to administer the vaccine to prevent another epidemic otherwise predicted for the 1970s. The last major epidemic in 1964–65 resulted in an estimated 20,000 damaged children being born, an additional estimated 30,000 were stillborn and an unknown number were spontaneously aborted (Horstmann, 1965).

Prenatal infection of the fetus by protozoa does occur, but it is apparently a relatively uncommon phenomenon caused by a one-cell parasite in the mother's blood. The parasite may enter the fetus through the placental barrier. It has been observed in the lower animals since about 1900, and was first reported in humans in 1942. Since that time several hundred cases have been reported. An infected mother may infect her fetus and give birth to a child with various abnormalities of the nervous system, including hydrocephalus, microcephalus, and intracerebral calcification. Any organ or tissue of the body may be affected, but the central nervous system suffers most severely in the congenital condition (Weinman and Chandler, 1956 Robinson and Robinson, 1965).

Congenital cases are often stillborn; others show obvious symptoms at birth but survive for various periods; and sometimes symptoms do not appear for weeks, months, or even years. Most of the congenital cases are mentally retarded. The few surveys which have included a search for toxoplasmosis indicate a very few cases of mental deficiency apparently caused by toxoplasmosis, even though serological studies indicate that the population is widely infected (Minto and Roberts, 1959; Masland, Sarason, and Gladwin, 1958; Wolf and Cowen, 1959).

Various other protozoan, bacterial, and infectious viral diseases have been suspected of either being transmitted from the pregnant mother to the developing embryo or fetus, or of otherwise interfering with normal development. Among these are Asiatic cholera, typhus, typhoid, Asian influenza, malaria, and mumps. Individual case studies seem to indicate that all the above may be implicated in occasional cases, but no large-scale study with adequate controls has yet been made to provide evidence of the extent to which the various maternal infections may be responsible for mental retardation in the offspring (Doll, Hill, and Sakula, 1960). In one extensive survey of 20,000 pregnancies, all the virus diseases taken together were found to have occurred ten times as frequently among mothers of malformed infants as in the whole sample. Mumps produced the worst record, with five malformed infants and one abortion out of thirty-four cases (Penrose, 1963). The fact that a fetus can apparently be injured by a virus which caused no evident maternal illness greatly complicates the task of assessing the importance of maternal infections during pregnancy as etiological factors in mental retardation. It is claimed that a virus can injure a fetus via the pregnant mother's blood stream, even when the mother herself is immune to the virus (Masland, Sarason, and Gladwin, 1958; Robinson and Robinson, 1965).

Blood Incompatibility. Since 1939, it has been known that Rh incompatibility between the maternal and fetal blood may result in the newborn child being severely jaundiced, and that mental deficiency is a possible accompaniment.

It is estimated that Rh incompatibility is the cause of the mental retardation of 3 to 4 percent of the institutionalized mentally retarded (Yannet and Lieberman, 1948). The proportion of Rh-negative mothers in a large group of undifferentiated mentally retarded is significantly larger than that reported in the literature for large random samplings (Glasser, Jacobs and Schain, 1951). There seems to be one case of Rh incompatibility in every 150 to 200 births (Waters, 1958).

Replacement blood transfusions for the jaundiced, Rh-positive child born of an Rh-negative mother are now saving many of these children from the more serious effects of Rh incompatibility (Waters, 1958). However, one study found that children who had had severe anemia and jaundice, and who had received replacement transfusions so that there was no detectable nervous system defect, still scored 23.1 IQ points below their normal siblings. The lowering of the IQ was significantly related to the degree of jaundice (Day and Haines, 1954).

Additional help is now available for Rh-negative women whose husbands have Rh-positive blood. Anti-Rh gamma globulin can be used to block the sensitizing process which produces antibodies to an Rh-positive baby's incompatible blood. The administration of the appropriate gamma globulin immediately following the birth of each Rh-positive baby gives the mother a temporary passive dose of antibodies which destroys any Rh-positive blood cells which may get into the mother's blood stream during the delivery. This prevents the mother from producing her own permanent antibodies. If the mother has already built up her own anti-bodies the gamma globulin will not protect future children. Currently the supply of gamma globulin is a problem since it can be obtained only from rare blood donors whose blood plasma has a high level of Rh-posi-tive antibodies.

The development of spectrophotometric methods for the examination of the amniotic fluid making possible more accurate determinations of the severity of the condition, the use of exchange transfusions at birth, the institution of premature delivery in critical cases, the use of new techniques of intrauterine transfusion, combined with the use of gamma globulin have all helped reduce the mental retardation, deafness, and cerebral palsy previously common in the Rh-positive offspring of Rh-negative mothers.

Recent evidence indicates that mother-child blood incompatibility in the classical major blood groupings (A, B, and O) may also be a factor in causing some cases of mental deficiency (Yannet and Lieberman, 1948; Robinson and Robinson, 1965).

Radioactivity. In the late twenties, it was discovered that X-ray ir-radiation of human mothers during pregnancy resulted in abortions or in a wide array of congenital defects including *spina bifida* (cleft spine), deformed skulls, and microcephaly (Murphy, 1928; Goldstein and Mur-phy, 1929; Brent, 1960). Studies of the United States Bomb Casualty Commission have shown that one out of every six unborn children who received substantial doses of radiation at Hiroshima were delivered mal-formed (Oughterson, 1956). These malformations were caused by the direct effect of high levels of irradiation on the young fetus. Present evi-dence indicates that high levels of irradiation to the pelvic regions of pregnant mothers in the first three weeks of pregnancy are usually fatal to the embryo. However, if the embryo survives, it is normal. Comparable irradiation during the next eight weeks results in the most severe abnor-malities involving the entire body (dwarfism) but often centering on the brain (microcephaly) and the sense organs (blindness and/or deafness). Between the 15th and the 20th week of pregnancy irradiation produces minor defects and lesser brain damage. After the 20th week the fetus usually suffers no apparent damage. All of these studies have involved mothers undergoing irradiation for cancer of the pelvic regions, who either did not realize they had become pregnant or their conditions were so serious the doctors and the mothers took the risks of damaging the fetus in an attempt to save the mothers (Cushner, 1968).

A second way in which irradiation may produce mental retardation is by the production of mutations. A mutation is presumably an alteration in the complicated chemical nature of the gene. Mutations occur spontaneously and may be either beneficial or detrimental so far as the propagation of the species is concerned. However, the mutant genes in the vast majority of cases produce some kind of harmful effects.

The possible effects of the increased irradiation of the people of the earth from man-made sources is receiving a great deal of attention. It seems that radiation may affect the germ cells in three ways: They may be killed; their chromosomes may be broken up; or they may mutate. The death of the germ cells would, of course, simply reduce the fertility of the individual. Breakage of the chromosomes may induce abortion or malformation of the offspring, if conception takes place within a few months of irradiation. The last and most important is the increased mutation rate already mentioned (Clarke and Clarke, 1958; Brent, 1960; Rugh and Grupp, 1959).

Since most of the mutations are deleterious, an increase in the number of mentally retarded is to be expected from any significant increase in the general level of radiation. Although the amount of irradiation required to produce malformations such as microcephaly is large, the effects of irradiation are cumulative. For this reason, there is considerable concern over the possible combined effects of natural radiation, X-rays used for dental and medical diagnosis or treatment, and the increased radiation incident to the use of atomic energy for industry and war. The studies of the Hiroshima and Nagasaki atomic bomb explosions show that there was a marked increase in microcephaly and mental retardation as well as in fetal and infant mortality among children born to pregnant mothers exposed to radiation. Many of the survivors of all ages were also found to have chromosomal abnormalities (Miller, 1969; Boffey, 1970). The conservative use of X-ray by dentists and medical doctors in diagnosis and the use of ultrasensitive film and image intensifiers in X-ray procedures minimize the amount of exposure to radiation from these sources.

Toxic Agents. Virtually all drugs and potentially toxic agents pass through the placental barrier and enter the fetal circulation. Thalidomide taken during pregnancy produces mostly limb deformities. However, heart, eye, and ear defects are also common in the offspring of mothers ingesting this drug while pregnant. Apparently little, if any, brain damage occurs. The fetus is particularly vulnerable to toxins because the enzyme systems involved in the metabolic detoxication and elimination of dangerous substances are poorly developed. Consequently toxins can attain high concentrations in fetal tissues. Antithyroid agents such as radioactive iodine administered to the mother, after ten to twelve weeks of pregnancy, when the fetal thyroid has the ability to take up the radioactive iodine, may produce potential cretinism in the offspring. Morphine withdrawal effects are seen in babies born to morphine addicted mothers; and if they are not recognized and treated promptly, the infant may die (Kelsey, 1969).

It is generally believed that toxins, such as lead, nicotine, alcohol, and morphine, in the maternal bloodstream may affect the developing embryo and possibly be responsible for lowering the mental level of the offspring (Tredgold and Soddy, 1956; Wallin, 1949; Robinson and Robinson, 1965). However, it is very difficult to assess the importance of these agents in the actual production of mental retardation. It is generally felt that they do not account for very many of the mentally retarded.

Natal Causes of Mental Retardation

The major hazards of the birth process are prematurity, traumatic injury, and asphyxia.

Prematurity. Extensive long-range studies, with fairly adequate control groups, have established that an abnormal number of people born prematurely are mentally retarded (Masland, Sarason, and Gladwin, 1958).

In one comparative study of over a thousand mentally retarded children and the same number of controls (matched for age, sex, race, place of birth, maternal age, and social and economic status), it was found that the incidence of prematurity was independent of whether or not the prematurity was the result of a complication of pregnancy or parturition (Pasamanick and Lilienfeld, 1955). This same study found that complications of pregnancy, prematurity, and congenital abnormalities were all associated with mental retardation. These same factors were also shown to be associated with stillbirth, neonatal deaths, cerebral palsy, epilepsy, and childhood behavior disorders. The association of these factors is greatest with cerebral palsy and epilepsy, next with mental retardation, and least with childhood behavior disorders.

One group of seventy-three prematurely born children, 5 to 10 years of age, was compared with their siblings who were not premature. The mean IQ of the premature children was 94, as compared with 107 for their full-term siblings. The difference was statistically significant. Nineteen of the premature group were mentally retarded, five were in institutions. None of the normal siblings were mentally retarded (Dann, Levine, and New, 1958). More recent studies have reported comparable findings (Towbin, 1969).

It seems that there is a definite association between prematurity and mental retardation, and that this association persists even when those cases are excluded in which the prematurity and mental deficiency might both be due to some common factor such as disease or accident (Drillien, 1961). Fetuses, otherwise normal, delivered prematurely by Cesarean section develop more normally than do those born equally prematurely by either spontaneous or instrumental delivery. This fact indicates that the stresses of the birth processes are greater and potentially more damaging when both mother and fetus are less ready for the delivery. Over 300,000 premature children are born annually in the United States. The evidence indicates that improved medical procedures have been more successful in increasing the survival rates of premature infants than in preserving the infant from neurological damage (Towbin, 1969). Evidently, the premature fetus, unready for birth and fragile, born through a physiologically unprepared, unrelaxed birth canal, is highly vulnerable to anoxic and mechanical damage sufficiently serious to produce a high incidence of mental retardation, cerebral palsy, epilepsy, and other neuropsychiatric disorders in such children.

Asphyxia. Asphyxia during the birth process may occur if the placenta separates too soon, if the umbilical cord kinks, if the child aspirates excessive amniotic fluid or if the child, for any reason, does not breathe for some time after delivery. There is considerable difference of opinion about the importance of natal asphyxia in producing neural damage and subsequent mental retardation. Present evidence indicates that the newborn is capable of tolerating a relatively severe degree of oxygen deprivation. Anoxia seems to produce a lowering of body temperature and metabolic level which may operate as a protective mechanism.

The studies which have attempted to relate oxygen deprivation at birth to mental level yield inconclusive results. One follow-up study of infants who were known to have a severe degree of asphyxia at birth, but who by the end of the neonatal period were considered to have been normal, showed that they had mean Stanford-Binet IQ's of 88.05 as compared with 100.47 for the control subjects. This difference is statistically significant (Darke, 1944).

On the other hand, in one sample of 250 subjects, no significant correlations were obtained between their IQ's in their preschool years and the oxygen content of their blood during the first three hours after birth (Apgar, 1955). The apparently discrepant data may be due either to the very low correlation between preschool and later IQ scores or it may be produced by the large percentage of infants having oxygen levels above the critical level.

Severe mental retardation often results when resuscitation follows prolonged asphyxia (coma due to oxygen deficiency) from respiratory arrest, carbon monoxide poisoning, or near drowning (Bering, 1969). Protracted coma due to brain concussion results in psychological deficits the severity of which is directly related to the duration of unconsciousness (Bering, 1969). At the present time, both the bulk of the studies and expert opinion indicate that asphyxia is a cause of mental retardation—

but just how important it is has yet to be determined (Graham et al., 1962).

Traumatic Birth Injury. It is estimated that birth injuries are responsible for somewhere between 1 and 5 percent of the mentally retarded (Penrose, 1963). Traumatic birth injury and prematurity are related. The brain structure of the premature infant is more fragile than that of the full-term infant, and therefore more easily damaged. The mother is also not entirely prepared for the birth process; her pelvic structure is not as elastic and does not yield so readily to the pressure of the infant as when the child is born at full term. The increase in pressure necessary to expel the child, and the increased vulnerability of the premature child, result in a high incidence of stillborn and birth-injured children (Benda, 1952; Prechtl, 1961). Mechanical pressure applied directly to the head or strong uterine contractions may injure the brain, may occlude the umbilical cord, and may impede the venous outflow or arterial outflow of the brain. The size of the maternal pelvis, position of the fetal head, and forceps delivery are all correlated with neuropsychological impairment of the infant (Bering, 1969).

It is claimed that most infants, even after a normal birth, show some signs of slight intracranial injury. In most cases the signs of injury rapidly disappear, with no apparent aftereffects.

Postnatal Causes of Mental Retardation

Many of the prenatal and natal causes of mental retardation also operate postnatally. However, there are some additional factors whose effects are primarily postnatal.

Traumatic Brain Injury. Traumatic brain injury from such things as gunshot wounds and falls is a rare cause of mental retardation. There seems to be no informed estimate as to the extent of mental deficiency resulting from such postnatal injuries.

Postnatal Infections. All brain infections involve the hazard of permanent brain damage and mental retardation. These infections include encephalitis of various types, meningitis from various causes, and syphilitic brain infections, as well as some other, rare types. The total number of cases of mental deficiency resulting from these various viruses and bacteria is much greater than those produced by traumatic brain injury.

Encephalitis (inflammation of the brain) is caused by a group of neurotropic viruses, as well as by some viruses which normally have no particular affinity for the nervous system. Its incidence is unknown, but it is believed that many mild cases (some estimate 80 percent of the total) go unrecognized. The postencephalitic symptoms include a large number of motor disturbances (including cerebal palsy and the Parkinsonian syndrome), personality changes, and general mental retardation or deterioration. One study reports a deficit of 16 IQ points in a group of postencephalitic children when compared with their normal siblings (Dawson and Conn, 1929).

About 90 percent of the neurological complications of measles, chicken pox, mumps, and scarlet fever are encephalitic. The prognosis for postencephalitics is not good, since there is a tendency for their intelligence level to decline (Lurie et al., 1937; Robinson and Robinson, 1965).

Meningitis (literally an inflammation of the coverings of the brain) may be caused by almost any pathogenic microorganisms. The most common organisms involved are the meningococcus, streptococcus, pneumonoccus, and the tubercle bacillus. There is also a viral form of meningitis. The permanent after-effects of meningitis are varied, but blindness, deafness, and arrest of mental development are common (Eichenlaub, 1955; Nickerson and MacDermot, 1961). The incidence of mental retardation caused by meningitis is not known, but it is probably a less important cause than encephalitis. Meningitis responds to treatment with the modern antibiotics. Protozoa may also occasionally invade the brain (Cerva, Zimals, and Novak, 1969). According to a recent news release, M. S. Artenstein, director of the project, has announced that a vaccine for the prevention of meningitis has been developed after six years of research at the Walter Reed Army Institute of Research in Washington, D.C. The vaccine is not expected to be available for public use until 1973. The number of diagnosed cases of meningitis is estimated to be about 500 among military recruits and 3,000 among civilians.

Diet. When the discussion of mental retardation caused by dietary deficiencies is limited to a few specific types of mental retardation, the evidence is quite clear and convincing. For example, endemic cretinism due to iodine deficiency has been known for a long time. In most of the regions of the world where endemic cretinism is likely to develop, the ingestion of iodized salt usually prevents its occurrence.

The presence of normal amounts of phenylalanine in the diet of a phenylketonuric child will result in his being mentally retarded, while the reduction or elimination of phenylalanine from the diet of such a child makes possible normal mental development. Lactose, in the diet of a galactosemic child, operates in a similar fashion. There may be other dietary elements that operate this way. However, the importance of the more general nutritional factors in determining intellectual level is not so clear.

The research studies of restriction of food intake of rats and mice have shown that a diet quantitatively inadequate, to the extent that it produces considerable bodily stunting, does not decrease the learning ability of the animals. When differences in learning rates have been found, the stunted animals have usually been found to be *superior* to the normal animals

(Fritz, 1935; Biel, 1938; Koch and Warden, 1936; Ruch, 1932; Morgan, 1965). If the risks of inference from rats to humans are not too great, reduced food intake, in itself, would not be expected to reduce mental level. The numerous reports of apparent lowering of human mental level due to a low food intake have practically all involved specific deficits of essential food elements in addition to low caloric intake.

The evidence from experimental studies of the lower animals as well as observational and clinical reports of humans indicates that insufficient intake of protein during early neural development affects adult mental level. The diet of children afflicted with Kwashiorkor may be adequate in calories, but it is grossly deficient in protein. The intellectual levels of children who have apparently recovered from severe episodes of protein deficiency are consequently below those of comparable individuals with adequate diets (Eichenwald and Fry, 1969).

General nutritional status correlates positively with the IQ (Fritz, 1935; Jones, 1939, 1946). However, the correlations largely disappear when the social and economic status is held constant. One exception to this seems to occur with children living close to subsistence. One study of a fairly homogeneous group of children from a slum area found a correlation of only .18 ± .04 between their nutritional status and their IQ (O'Hanlon, 1940).

Attempts to improve the mental level of children by improvements in general diet have been largely unsuccessful (Smith and Field, 1926; Seymour and Whitaker, 1938; Stout, 1937; Jones, 1946). These studies suggest that restricted food intake of moderate extent, in the absence of specific dietary deficiencies (vitamins, and so forth), does not result in lowered intelligence.

Research studies have demonstrated quite clearly that vitamin B complex deprivation reduces the learning ability of rats (Morgan, 1965). However, deficiencies of vitamins A and D have *failed* to produce any consistent decrease in the learning of rats (Moore and Mathias, 1934; Bernhardt, 1936; Maurer, 1935; Frank, 1932).

The few data available from studies of variations in vitamin intake using human beings are conflicting. One worker (Harrell, 1947) reports that thiamin administration increases learning and intelligence, but the improvements found were small and not statistically significant. Other research workers (Balken and Maurer, 1934; Bernhardt, Northway, and Tatham, 1948; Guetzkow and Brozek, 1946; Morgan, 1965) have been unable to demonstrate significant effects of the vitamin B complex on learning in humans. None of these studies have dealt with groups suffering from *acute* deficiencies of this vitamin complex. Likewise, no one has studied the effects of experimentally induced acute deficiencies of these vitamins in human subjects.

Lowering of both mental and physical functioning are said to be part of the syndrome of pellagra and beriberi, which are the result of chronic vitamin deficiencies. The mental deterioration found in these chronic conditions is probably comparable to the decreased learning ability of rats suffering from severe vitamin deficiency. The relative infrequency of pellagra and beriberi in Western culture today indicates that vitamin deficiencies are probably not an important cause of mental retardation.

General Health. It has been estabished that mental and physical handicaps are associated. However, we cannot conclude that one causes the other. Both may be the result of a common cause or set of causes. Studies of the influence on the mental level of children of the correction of physical defects, the elimination of focal infections, and the providing of good dental care have generally shown that there is little or no effect. Studies of the removal of focal infections, such as diseased tonsils, have shown that there is an improvement in school achievement, but no significant effect on measured intelligence (Rogers, 1922; Lowe, 1923; Rickey, 1934; Jones, 1946). Extensive medical and surgical treatment of the 10 percent of children having the largest number of physical defects over a nine-month period is reported to have had no measurable effect upon their mental level (Westenberger, 1927; Jones, 1946). A program of extensive dental treatment and instruction in dental hygiene likewise was without any apparent effect on intellectual level (Kohnky, 1913; Jones, 1946).

In the above studies, changes in physical condition and school achievement were usually found, but levels of general intelligence remained about the same after as before treatment.

General Cultural Factors. The research studies of the past thirty years have shown quite convincingly that measured intellectual level is influenced by the child's cultural background. A long series of studies has shown that children continuously deprived of general cultural stimulation (comparable to that of the average American middle-class child) show progressively greater intellectual retardation as they get older (Gordon, 1923; Jordon, 1933; Asher, 1935; Edwards and Jones, 1938; Tomlinson, 1944; Anastasi, 1956; McCandless, 1964).

These studies have shown quite convincingly that intelligence, as measured by conventional tests, progressively declines in children who lack the general cultural and educational experiences of the norm groups. Many such children will therefore appear mentally retarded by psychometric criteria. However, in the absence of any definitive large-scale long-range studies, the question of the extent to which cultural impoverishment may produce *irreversible* mental retardation still remains unanswered.

In one study, over three thousand children in forty mountain schools of east Tennessee were tested in 1930. In 1940, the children in these same schools were again given the same tests. In the ten-year period between testings, there was marked improvement in the economic, social, and educational status of this mountain area. The test results showed that the children were, in 1940, superior at all ages, and in all grades, to those tested ten years earlier. However, in 1940, as in 1930, there still was found a decrease in the average IQ as one goes up the grades (Wheeler, 1932; 1942).

There may be more than one explanation for this increase in test scores, but the results at least suggest that the improved test performance was incident to improved educational and socioeconomic conditions (Anastasi, 1956).

Home Environment.   There are a number of research studies on the effects of home environment on intelligence level. However, none of these studies separates home influence proper from the broader cultural and educational influences already discussed. Adoption into a home of a given type typically involves being introduced into a given culture, social class, and educational milieu. This means that the studies of the effects of home environment include these other factors as well.

Studies of the effects of being raised in various types of homes on the intelligence test scores of children began in the late 1920s. Since then a number of such studies have been reported (Freeman, Holzinger, and Mitchell, 1928; Burks, 1928; Skeels and Fillmore, 1937; Speer, 1940). From these and similar studies, the following generalizations seem to be warranted:

1. Children adopted into and residing in homes which were superior to their own homes showed an increase in their IQ's over comparable children residing in their own homes.
2. The younger the children when placed in the superior homes, the greater was the increase in their IQ's.
3. The longer the period of residence in the superior home, the greater was the increase in their IQ's.
4. Unrelated children residing in the same home resemble each other in intelligence as much as do siblings raised in separate homes.

The type of home in which a child is raised does seem to influence his intelligence test scores, and certainly contributes significantly to his general level of functioning.

Extreme Environmental Deprivation.   Two types of deprivation are often involved in studies of extreme environmental deprivation. One is an affectional deprivation. Many workers in the fields of mental hygiene, clinical psychology, and psychiatry believe that continuous affectional relationships with other people are necessary for the child's normal emotional, social, intellectual, and even physical development. The reality of permanent intellectual impairment resulting from this type of deprivation has not been established.

The second type of environmental restriction studied is general sensory deprivation. There is evidence, principally from the lower animals, that the individual's functional level is lowered when sensory deprivation is extreme and chronic. The extent to which this lowering of adjustment level is permanent still remains to be determined.

The deprivation characteristic of many of the mentally retarded, particularly those of the familial type, involves both the "maternal," or affectional, and the general environmental or sensory types. There is some evidence that some children who are institutionalized as mentally retarded, and who come from very adverse social conditions, continue to improve mentally beyond the age at which mental development normally ceases (Clarke and Clarke, 1958). This suggests that the deleterious effects of early deprivation may not be irreversible.

A more recent study has extended these findings. Children in an institution were placed into arbitrary groups according to the extent to which their early life was one of deprivation. A follow-up study over a period of six years showed that the group of children whose preinstitutional life had been "most deprived" had gained 16 IQ points on the average, while a group of children judged to have suffered a lesser degree of deprivation gained an average of 10 IQ points in the same period (Clarke and Clarke, 1958). These results also suggest that the deleterious effects of early deprivation may, to some extent at least, be overcome in later life.

The reports of individual children who are alleged to have been permanently retarded as the result of extreme isolation and environmental deprivation are not very helpful. It is impossible to determine whether their isolation was imposed on them because they were originally physically or mentally defective or whether their retardation resulted from their isolation (Davis, 1940; Dennis, 1941; Wallin, 1949). The authenticity of the several published accounts of supposedly feral (wolf) children has also been seriously questioned (Singh and Zingg, 1939; Dennis, 1941; Gesell, 1942; Mandelbaum, 1943).

Diversity among the Mentally Retarded

Mental retardation is not a disease, although diseases may accompany or cause it. It is not a unitary thing. Etiologically it is many things and has a bewildering array of causes. Its physical accompaniments are either many and diverse or practically nil, depending upon the etiological type and the level of retardation. The personalities and temperaments of the mentally retarded are almost as diverse as are those of groups of the population at large. Even when the mentally retarded are placed in so-called homogeneous groups for educational purposes, tremendous scholastic differences still exist within these classes. The mentally retarded are a heterogeneous group who are identified, and to some degree segregated, and given special consideration because of one characteristic—inadequate adaptive behavior resulting from impairment of intellectual functioning.

When people ask "What are mentally retarded people like?" they are asking a meaningless question. They would not ask "What are short or fat people like?" Most people would agree that about the only thing that such physically deviant individuals have in common is their diminutive stature or their obesity. While being mentally retarded has more widespread behavioral consequences than being tall or being fat, the similarities between mental retardates and intellectually normal people exceed their differences. The mentally retarded are almost as statistically variable and individually distinctive as are people whose intelligence is within the normal range.

Summary

The causes of mental retardation are both hereditary and environmental. A few rare types of mental retardation are caused by a single dominant gene. A larger number of types apparently are due to a single recessive gene. Chromosomal anomalies account for certain types of mental retardation. The hereditary components of the ordinary "familial," or nonclinical, class of mental retarded are multifactorial or polygenetic.

The importance assigned to the genetic factor in the determination of mental level has varied tremendously from time to time and from worker to worker. The period from 1900 to 1930 was a time when great emphasis was placed on the hereditary component. From 1930 to 1950, the emphasis shifted to environment as the principal determinant of intellectual level. The problem of assigning specific weights or values to heredity and environment as they influence the intelligence level is almost beyond solution because of the many variables. The concept of a "range of variation" within which either heredity and environment may operate is suggested as a useful frame of reference.

Environmental causes of mental retardation are prenatal physical trauma, nutritional or toxic infections, blood incompatibility, and radioactivity. Natal causes include prematurity, asphyxia, and physical trauma. Postnatal causes are physical trauma, infections, dietary and extreme sensory deprivation, or general environmental deprivation.

Mental retardation is not a unitary thing. It is not a disease. It has diverse causes and physical accompaniments and embraces a rather wide range of mental levels.

References

ANASTASI A., "Intelligence and Family Size," *Psychol. bull.*, LIII (1956), 187–209.

————, "Heredity, Environment and the Question 'How,'" *Psychol, rev.*, LXV (1958), 197–208.

APGAR, V., "Neonatal Anoxia: I. A Study of the Relation of Oxygenation at Birth to Intellectual Development," *Pediatrics*, XV (1955), 652–62.

ASHER, E. J., "The Inadequacy of Current Intelligence Tests for Kentucky Mountain Children," *J. genet. psychol.*, XLVI (1935), 480–86.

BALKEN, E. R., AND S. MAURER, "Variations of Psychological Measurements Associated with Increased Vitamin-B Complex Feeding in Young Children," *J. exp. psychol.*, XVII (1934), 65–92.

BENDA, C. E., *Developmental Disorders of Mentation and Cerebral Palsies*, New York: Grune & Stratton, Inc., 1952.

BERNHARDT, K. S., "Vitamin A Deficiency and Learning in the Rat," *J comp. psychol.*, XXII (1936), 277–78.

————, M. L. NORTHWAY, AND C. M. TATHAM, "The Effect of Added Thiamine on Intelligence and Learning with Identical Twins," *Canad. j. psychol.*, II (1948), 58–61.

BIEL, W. C., "The Effect of Early Inanition upon Maze Learning in the Albino Rat," *Comp. psychol. monog.*, XV, No. 2 (1938).

BERING, E. A., JR., "Mental Retardation Caused by Physical Trauma," *Science*, CLXIV (1969), 460–66.

BLOOM, B. S., *Stability and Change in Human Characteristics*. New York: John Wiley & Sons, Inc., 1964.

BOAS, F., *Changes in Bodily Form of Descendants of Immigrants*. Washington, D.C.: U.S. Senate Document No. 208, (1911).

BODMER, W. F., AND L. L. CAVALLI-SFORZA, "Intelligence and Race," *Scient. Amer.*, CCXXIII, No. 4 (1970), 19–29.

BOFFEY, P. M., "Hiroshima/Nagasaki: Atomic Bomb Casuality Commission Perseveres in Sensitive Studies," *Science*, CLXVIII (1970), 679–83.

BRENT, R. L., "Indirect Effect of Irradiation on Embryonic Development," *Amer. j. dis. child.*, C (1960), 103–8.

BRIGHAM, C. C., *A Study of American Intelligence*. Princeton, N.J.: Princeton University Press, 1923.

BURKS, B. S., "The Relative Influence of Nature and Nurture upon Mental Development: A Comparative Study of Foster-parent, Foster-child Resemblance and True-parent, True-child Resemblance," *Yearb. nat. soc. stud. educ.*, XXVII (1928), 219–316.

CARTER, C. O., et al., "Chromosome Translocation as a Cause of Familial Mongolism," *Lancet*, II (1960), 678–80.

CERVA, L., V. ZIMALS, AND K. NOVAK, "Amoebic Meningoencephalic: A New Amoebic Isolate," *Science*, CLXIII (1969), 575–76.

CLARKE, A. M., AND A. D. CLARKE, *Mental Deficiency*. New York: The Free Press, 1958.

CLARKE, C. M., J. H. EDWARDS, AND V. SMALLPACE, "21-Trisomy/Normal Mosaicism in an Intelligent Girl with Some Mongoloid Characteristics," *Lancet*, I (1961), 1028–30.

COOPER, R. M., AND J. P. ZUBEK, "Effects of Enriched and Restricted Environments on the Learning Ability of Bright and Dull Rats," *Canadian j. psychol.*, XII (1958), 159–64.

CUSHNER, I. M., "Irradiation of the Fetus," in *Intra-Uterine Development*, ed. A. C. Barnes. Philadelphia, Pa.: Lea & Febiger, 1968.

DANN, M., S. Z. LEVINE, AND E. V. NEW, "The Development of Prematurely Born Children with Birth Weights or Minimal Postnatal Weights of 1,000 Grams or Less," *Pediatrics*, XXII (1958), 1037–53.

DARKE, R. A., "Late Effects of Severe Asphyxia Neonatonum," *J. pediat.*, XXIV (1944), 148–52.

DAVIS, K., "Extreme Social Isolation of a Child," *Amer. j. sociol.*, XXXVIII (1940), 554–65.

DAWSON, S., AND J. C. CONN, "Effects of Encephalitis Lethargica on the Intelligence of Children," *Arch. dis. child.*, I (1929), 357–89.

DAY, M. F., AND A. HAINES, "Erythroblastosis Caused by Rh Incompatibility," *Pediatrics*, XIII (1954), 333–38.

DENNIS, W., "The Significance of Feral Man," *Amer. j. psychol.*, LIV (1941), 425–32.

DOBZHANSKY, T., "Heredity, Environment, and Evolution," *Science*, CXI (1950), 161–66.

DOLL, E. A., "Annual Report from the Department of Research," *Vineland train. sch. bull.*, XXXI (1934), 112–23.

————, "The Essentials of an Inclusive Concept of Mental Deficiency," *Amer. j. ment. defic.*, XLVI (1941), 214–19.

DOLL, R., A. B. HILL, AND J. SAKULA, "Asian Influenza in Pregnancy and Congenital Defects," *Brit. j. prevent. soc. med.*, XIV (1960), 167–77.

DREGER, R. M., AND K. S. MILLER, "Comparative Psychological Studies of Negroes and Whites in the United States," *Psychol. bull.*, LVII (1960), 361–402.

————, "Comparative Psychological Studies of Negroes and Whites in the United States," *Psychol, bull. monog. suppl.*, LXX, No. 3, Part 2 (1968).

DRILLIEN, C. M., "The Incidence of Mental and Physical Handicaps in School-age Children of Very Low Birth Weights," *Pediatrics*, XXVII (1961), 452–64.

EDWARDS, A. S., AND L. JONES, "An Experimental and Field Study of North Georgia Mountaineers," *J. soc. psychol.*, IX (1938), 317–33.

EICHENLAUB, J. E., "Meningitis," *Today's health*, LII (1955), 40–42.

EICHENWALD, H. F., AND P. C. FRY, "Nutrition and Learning," *Science*, CLXIII (1969), 644–48.

ENGLISH, H. B., AND A. C. ENGLISH, *A Comprehensive Dictionary of Psychologi-*

cal and Psychoanalytical Terms. New York: David McKay Co., Inc., 1958.

FITZGERALD, P. H., AND R. R. LYCETTE, "Mosaicism Involving the Antosome Associated with Mongolism," *Lancet,* II (1961), 2121.

FORSSMAN, H., AND O. LEHMANN, "Chromosome Studies in Eleven Families with Mongolism in More than One Member," *Acta paediat.,* LI (1962), 180–88.

FRANK, M., "The Effects of a Rickets-producing Diet on the Learning Ability of White Rats," *J. comp. psychol.,* XIII (1932), 87–105.

FRASER, F. C., "Teratogenesis of the Central Nervous System," in *Mental Retardation: A Review of Research,* eds. H. A. Stevens and R. Hebens. Chicago, Ill.: University of Chicago Press, 1964.

FREEMAN, F. N., K. J. HOLZINGER, AND B. C. MITCHELL, "The Influence of Environment on the Intelligence, School Achievement, and Conduct of Foster Children," *Yearb. nat. soc. stud. educ.,* XXVII (1928), 103–218.

FRITZ, M. F., "The Effect of Diet on Intelligence and Learning," *Psychol. bull.,* XXXII (1935), 355–63.

GARRETT, H. E., "The SPSSI and Racial Differences," *Amer. psychol.,* XVII (1962), 260–63.

GESELL, A., *Wolf Child and Human Child.* New York: Harper & Row, Publishers, 1942.

———, AND C. S. AMATRUDA, *Developmental Diagnosis: Normal and Abnormal Child Development* (2nd ed.). New York: Hoeber-Harper, 1947.

GIBSON, D., AND J. POZSONYI, "Morphological and Behavioral Consequences of Chromosome Subtype in Mongolism," *Amer. j. ment. defic.,* LXIX (1965), 807–13.

GLASSER, F. B., M. JACOBS, AND R. SCHAIN, "The Relation of Rh to Mental Deficiency," *Psychiat. quart.,* XXV (1951), 282–87.

GOLDSTEIN, L., AND D. P. MURPHY, "Microencephalic Idiocy Following Radium Therapy for Uterine Cancer During Pregnancy," *Amer. j. obstet. gynecol.,* XVIII (1929), 189–95.

GORDON, H., *Mental and Scholastic Tests among Retarded Children: An Inquiry into the Effects of Schooling on the Various Tests.* Educ. Pamphlets No. 44 (1923).

GOTTESMAN, I. I., "Genetic Aspects of Intelligent Behavior," in *Handbook of Mental Deficiency,* ed. N. R. Ellis. New York: McGraw-Hill Book Company, 1963.

GRAHAM, F. K., et al., "Development Three Years after Prenatal Anoxia and Other Potentially Damaging Newborn Experiences," *Psychol. monog.,* LXXVI (1962), 522.

GREENBERG, M., AND O. PELLETERI, "Frequency of Defects in Infants Whose Mothers Had Rubella During Pregnancy," *J. amer. med. assoc.,* CLXV (1957), 675–77.

GREGG, M. M., "Congenital Cataract Following German Measles in the Mother," *Trans. ophthal. soc. aust.,* III (1941), 35.

GUETZKOW, H., AND J. BROZEK, "Intellectual Functions with Restricted Intakes of B-complex Vitamins," *Amer. j. physiol.,* LIX (1946), 358–81.

HANNAH-ALAVA, "Genetic Mosaics," *Scient. Amer.*, CCII (1960), 119–30.

HARRELL, R. F., "Further Effects of Added Thiamine on Learning and Other Processes," *Teach. coll. contr. educ.*, CMXXVIII (1947), 102.

———, E. WOODWARD, AND A. I. GATES, *The Effects of Mothers' Diets on the Intelligence of the Offspring.* New York: Bureau of Publications, Teachers College, Columbia University, 1955.

———, "The Influence of Vitamin Supplementation of the Diets of Pregnant and Lactating Women on the Intelligence of their Offspring," *Metabolism*, V (1956), 552–61.

HEBER, R. A., "A Manual on Terminology and Classification in Mental Retardation," *Amer. j. ment. defic.*, LXIV (1959), Monog. Suppl.

———, "Modifications in the Manual on Terminology and Classification in Mental Retardation," *Amer. j. ment. defic.*, LXV (1961), 499–500.

HORSTMANN, D. M., "Rubella and the Rubella Syndrome: New Epidemologic and Viralogic Observations," *Calif. Med.*, CII (1965), 397–403.

HUTT, M. L., AND R. G. GIBBY, *The Mentally Retarded Child* (2nd ed.). Boston, Mass.: Allyn & Bacon, Inc., 1965.

JARVIK, L. F., A. FALEK, AND W. P. PIERSON, "Down's Syndrome (Mongolism) : The Heritable Aspects," *Psychol. bull.*, LXI (1964), 388–98.

JENSEN, A. R., "Social Class, Race, and Genetics: Implications for Education," *Amer. educ. res. j.*, V (1968), 1–42.

———, "How Much Can We Boost IQ and Scholastic Achievement?" *Harvard educ. rev.*, XXXIX (1969), 1–123.

JONES, H. E., "Relationships in Physical and Mental Development," *Rev. educ. res.*, IX (1939), 91–103, 134–37.

———, "Environmental Influences on Mental Development," in *Manual of Child Psychology*, ed. L. Carmichael. New York: John Wiley & Sons, Inc., 1946.

JORDON, A. M., "Parental Occupations and Children's Intelligence Scores," *J. appl. psychol.*, XVII (1933), 103–19.

KALTER, H., "Congenital Malformations Induced by Riboflavin Deficiency in Strains of Inbred Rats," *Pediatrics*, Suppl. ("Congenital Malformations"), XXIII (1959), 222–30.

———, AND J. WARKANY, "Experimental Production of Congenital Malformations in Mammals by Metabolic Procedures," *Physiol. rev.*, XXXIX (1959), 69–115.

KELSEY, F. O., "Drugs and Pregnancy," *Ment. retard.*, VII (1969), 7–10.

KIDD, J. W., "Toward a More Precise Definition of Mental Retardation," *Ment. retard.*, II (1964), 209–12.

KLINEBERG, O., *Negro Intelligence and Selective Migration.* New York: Columbia University Press, 1935.

KOCH, A. M., AND C. J. WARDEN, "The Influence of Quantitative Stunting on Learning Ability in Mice," *J. genet. psychol.*, XLVIII (1936), 215–17.

KOHNKY, E., "Preliminary Study of the Effect of Dental Treatment upon the Physical and Mental Efficiency of School Children," *J. educ. psychol.*, IV (1913), 571–78.

KUGELMASS, I. N., *The Management of Mental Deficiency in Children*. New York: Grune & Stratton, Inc., 1954.

LEE, E. S., "Negro Intelligence and Selective Migration: A Philadelphia Test of the Klineberg Hypothesis," *Amer. soc. rev.*, XVI (1951), 227–33.

LEJEUNE, J., AND R. TURPIN, "Chromosomal Aberrations in Man," *Amer. j. human genet.*, XIII (1961), 175–84.

LEMKAU, P., C. TIETZE, AND M. CASPER, "Mental Hygiene Problems in an Urban District: Third Paper," *Ment. hyg.*, XXVI (1942), 275–88.

LEWIS, E. O., "Types of Mental Deficiency and Their Social Significance," *J. ment. sci.*, LXXIX (1933), 298–305.

LOWE, G. M., "Mental Changes After Removing Tonsils and Adenoids," *Psychol. clin.*, XV (1923), 92–100.

LURIE, L. A., et al., "Late Results Noted in Children and Presenting Postencephalitic Behavior: A Follow-up Study of Fifty Cases," *Amer. j. psychiat.*, XCV (1937), 171–79.

McCANDLESS, B. R., "Relation of Environmental Factors to Intellectual Functioning," in *Mental Retardation: A Review of Research*, eds. H. A. Stevens and R. Heber. Chicago, Ill.: University of Chicago Press, 1964.

MANDELBAUM, D. G., "Wolf-child Histories from India," *J. soc. psychol.*, XVII (1943), 25–44.

MASLAND, R. L., S. B. SARASON, AND T. GLADWIN, *Mental Subnormality*. New York: Basic Books, Inc., Publishers, 1958.

MAURER, S., "The Effect of Acute Vitamin A Depletion upon Maze Performance in Rats," *J. comp. psychol.*, XX (1935), 456–58.

McCLURE, H. M., R. H. BELDEN, W. A. PIEPER, AND C. B. JACOBSON, "Autosomal Trisomy in a Chimpanzee: Resemblant to Down's Syndrome," *Science*, CLXV (1969), 1010–1011.

McCORD, W. M., AND N. J. DEMERATH, "Negro Versus White Intelligence: A Continuing Controversy," *Harvard educ. rev.*, XXVIII (1968), 120–35.

MICHAELS, R. H., AND G. W. MELLIN, "Prospective Experience with Maternal Rubella and Associated Congenital Malformations," *Pediatrics*, XXVI (1960), 200–9.

MILLER, R. W., "Delayed Radiation Effects in Atomic Bomb Survivors," *Science*, CLXVI, (1969), 569–74.

MINTO, A., AND F. J. ROBERTS, "The Psychiatric Complications of Toxoplasmosis," *Lancet*, I (1959), 1180–82.

MOORE, H., AND E. MATHIAS, "The Effect of Vitamin A and B Deficiency on the Maze-learning Ability of the White Rat," *J. comp. psychol.*, XVI (1934), 487–96.

MOORHEAD, P. S., W. J. MELLMAN, AND C. WENAN, "A Familial Chromosome Translocation Associated with Speech and Mental Retardation," *Amer. j. human genet.*, XIII (1961), 32–46.

MORGAN, C. T., *Physiological Psychology* (3rd ed.). New York: McGraw-Hill Book Company, 1965.

MURPHY, D. P., "Ovarian Irradiation: Its Effects on the Health of Subsequent Children," *Surgery, gynecol., and obstet.*, XLVII (1928), 201–15.

NEWMAN, H. H., F. H. FREEMAN, AND K. J. HOLINGER, *Twins: A Study of Heredity and Environment*. Chicago, Ill.: University of Chicago Press, 1937.

New York State Department of Mental Hygiene, *Onondaza County Survey: A Special Census of Suspected Referred Mental Retardation*, Technical report: Syracuse, N.Y., 1955.

NICKERSON, G., AND P. N. MACDERMOT, "Psychometric Evaluation and Factors Affecting the Performance of Children Who Have Recovered from Tuberculosis, Meningitis," *Pediatrics*, XXVII (1961), 68–82.

O'CONNER, N., AND J. TIZARD, *The Social Problems of Mental Deficiency*. New York: Pergamon Press, 1956.

O'HANLON, G. S., "An Investigation into the Relationship between Fertility and Intelligence," *Brit. j. educ. psychol.*, X (1940), 196–211.

OUGHTERSON, ASHLEY, W., *Medical Effects of the Atomic Bomb in Japan*. New York: McGraw-Hill Book Company, 1956.

PASAMANICK, B., AND A. M. LILIENFELD, "The Association of Fetal Factors with the Development of Mental Deficiency," *J. amer. med. assoc.*, CLIX (1955), 155–60.

PENROSE, L. S., *The Biology of Mental Defect* (3rd ed.). New York: Grune & Stratton, Inc., 1963.

———, J. R. ELLIS, AND J. D. DELHANTY, "Chromosomal Translocation in Mongolism and in Normal Relatives," *Lancet*, II (1960), 409–10.

PRECHTL, H. F., "Neurological Sequelae of Prenatal and Paranatal Complications," in *Determinants of Infant Behavior*, ed. B. M. Foss. New York: John Wiley & Sons, Inc., 1961.

RICKEY, A., "The Effects of Diseased Tonsils and Adenoids on Intelligence Quotients of 204 Children," *J. juv. res.*, XVIII (1934), 1–4.

ROBERTS, J. A., *An Introduction to Medical Genetics*. London: Oxford University Press, 1963.

ROBINSON, H. B., AND N. M. ROBINSON, *The Mentally Retarded Child*. New York: McGraw-Hill Book Company, 1965.

ROGERS, M. C., "Adenoids and Diseased Tonsils: Their Effect on General Intelligence," *Arch. psychol.*, XII, No. 50 (1922).

RUCH, F. L., "The Effect of Inanition upon Maze Learning in the White Rat," *J. comp. psychol.*, XIV (1932), 321–29.

RUGH, R., AND E. GRUPP, "Exencephalia Following X-irradiation of the Preimplantation Mammalian Embryo," *J. neuropath, exper. neurol.*, XVIII (1959), 468–81.

RUNDLE, A. T., "Etiological Factors in Mental Retardation: I. Biochemical, II. Endocrinological," *Amer. j. ment. defic.*, LXVII (1962), 61–78.

———, A. COPPER, AND V. COWIE, "Steroid Excretion of Mothers of Mongols," *Lancet*, II (1961), 846–48.

SARASON, S. B., AND T. GLADWIN, "Psychological and Cultural Problems in Mental Subnormality," in *Mental Subnormality*, ed. R. L. Masland. New York: Basic Books, Inc., Publishers, 1958.

SEYMOUR, A. H., AND J. E. WHITAKER, "An Experiment on Nutrition," *Occup. psychol.*, XII (1938), 215–23.

SHUEY, A. M., *The Testing of Negro Intelligence* (2nd ed.). New York: Social Science Press, 1966.

SINGH, J. A., AND R. M. ZINGG, *Wolf Children and Feral Man.* New York: Harper & Row, Publishers, 1939.

SKEELS, H. M., AND E. A. FILLMORE, "Mental Development of Children from Underprivileged Homes," *J. genet. psychol.*, LVI (1937), 427–39.

SKINNER, C. W., JR., "The Rubella Problem," *Amer. j. dis. child.*, CI (1961), 104–12.

SMITH, A. J., AND A. M. FIELD, "A Study of the Effect of Nutrition on Mental Growth," *J. home econ.*, XVIII (1926), 686–90.

SONTAG, L., C. BAKER, AND V. NELSON, "Mental Growth and Personality: A Longitudinal Study," *Monog. soc. res. child develop.*, XXIII, No. 2 (1958), 1–143.

SPEER, G. S., "The Intelligence of Foster Children," *J. genet. psychol.*, LVII (1940), 49–56.

STOUT, G. H., "Variations of Normal Children," *J. exp. educ.*, VI (1937), 84–100.

SWAN, C., "Rubella and Congenital Malformations," *Med. annu.* (1947), 303–10.

———, et al., "Congenital Defects in Infants Following Infectious Diseases During Pregnancy," *Med. j. aust.*, II (1943), 210–11.

TANNER, J. M., *Growth at Adolescence.* Springfield, Ill.: C. C. Thomas, 1955.

TELFORD, C. W., "Comparative Studies of Full- and Mixed-blood North Dakota Indians," *Psychol. monog.*, L (1938), 116–29.

TERMAN, L. M., AND M. H. ODEN, *The Gifted Child Grows Up.* Stanford, Calif.: Stanford University Press, 1947.

THERMAN, E., et al., "The D Trisomy Syndrome and XO Gonadal Dysgenesis in Two Sisters," *Amer. j. human genet.*, XIII (1961), 193–204.

THODAY, J. M., AND J. B. GIBSON, "Environmental and Genetical Contributions to Class Differences: A Model Experiment," *Science*, CLXVII (1970), 990–992.

TJIO, J. H., AND A. LEVAN, "The Chromosomal Number of Man," *Heredias*, XLII (1956), 1–6.

TOMLINSON, H., "Differences between Preschool Negro Children and Their Older Siblings on the Stanford-Binet Scales," *J. negro educ.*, XIII (1944), 474–79.

TOWBIN, A. "Mental Retardation Due to Germanal Matrix Infraction." *Science*, CLXIV (1969), 156–61.

TREDGOLD, A. F., AND K. SODDY, *Mental Deficiency* (9th ed.). Baltimore, Md.: The Williams & Wilkins Co., 1956.

TULKIN, S. R., "Race, Class, Family, and School Achievement," *J. person. soc. psychol.*, IX (1968), 31–37.

WALLIN, J. E., *Children with Mental and Physical Handicaps.* Englewood Cliffs, N.J.: Prentice-Hall, Inc., 1949.

———, *Mental Deficiency.* Brandon, Vt.: Journal of Clinical Psychology, 1956.

WATERS, W. J., "The Prevention of Bilirubin Encephalopathy," *J. pediat.*, LII (1958), 559–65.

WEINMAN, D., AND A. H. CHANDLER, "Toxoplasmosis in Man and Swine: An

Investigation of the Possible Relationship," *J. amer. med. assoc.*, CLXI (1956), 229.

WESTENBERGER, E. J., "A Study of the Influence of Physical Defects upon Intelligence," *Cath. univ. amer. educ. res. bull.*, II (1927), 9.

WHEELER, L. R., "The Intelligence of East Tennessee Mountain Children," *J. educ. psychol.*, XXIII (1932), 351–70.

————, "A Comparative Study of the Intelligence of East Tennessee Mountain Children," *J. educ. psychol.*, XXXIII (1942), 321–34.

WOLF, A., AND D. COWEN, "Perinatal Infections of the Central Nervous System," *J. neuropath, exp. neurol.*, XVIII (1959), 191–243.

YANNET, H., "Classification and Etiological Factors in Mental Retardation," *J. pediat.*, L (1957), 226–30.

————, AND R. LIEBERMAN, "Further Studies of ABO Secretion Status and Mental Deficiency," *Amer. j. ment. defic.*, LII (1948), 314–17.

YERKES, R. M., ed., *Psychological Examining in the United States Army*. Memoirs, Nat. Acad. Sci., XV (1921), 890.

8

Mild Mental Retardation

In the next two chapters we discuss two degrees of mental retardation: *mild* and *severe*. We shall use an IQ of 50, the most commonly used dividing line between the *educable* and *trainable* mentally retarded as an arbitrary boundary line between these categories. In doing this, we are including the A.A.M.D. *profound, severe,* and part of the *moderate* groupings in our *severely retarded* category. The A.A.M.D. *borderline, mild,* and part of the *moderate* categories are combined into our *mild mental retardation* group. In this chapter we discuss mild mental retardation.

Mentally retarded children with IQ's above 50 have enough in common to warrant discussing them all together. First, the subgroups within this range merge imperceptibly into each other in terms of most social and educationally significant variables. Second, they represent an arbitrarily designated low end of the normal distribution curve of intelligence. Third, their low intellectual status is generally caused by an interacting combination of handicapping multigenic and/or environmental factors. Fourth, although individuals in this broad category are statistically below average in physique and general health, they are not perceptibly different in these respects from the general population. More specifically, they usually lack the physical stigmata often found in the severely retarded.

Fifth, most of the mildly mentally retarded are first identified as educational retardates and only after extensive study are labelled mentally retarded. Follow-up studies of children in this category indicate that most of them, as adults, merge into society and adjust to out-of-school situations only slightly less satisfactorily than do their intellectually normal age-mates from the same socioeconomic background.

This category of the mentally retarded has traditionally included many of the children now designated *educationally handicapped* or *culturally disadvantaged*. These individuals are handicapped principally by their low academic aptitudes and the ever-increasing demands of their culture.

As the technological complexity of society increases, the level of education required to function adequately similarly increases. In the United States, since the beginning of the twentieth century, first graduation from the eighth grade, then a high school diploma, and finally a college degree have been increasingly required for employment, career advancement, social status, and self-esteem. More and more, the prestigeful occupational and social options available to people funnel through the schools. Thus, increasing numbers of the mildly mentally retarded and educationally disadvantaged are losing out in a technologically oriented society in which higher education is either required or expected.

Incidence

From our earlier discussions, it is clear that estimates of the number of mentally retarded are meaningful only in terms of the criteria applied at a particular time and in a given culture or subculture. Psychometric criteria place roughly one-fifth of the total population in the 70–89 IQ range and about 2.5 percent below this level (Merrill, 1938; Wechsler, 1944, 1949, 1955). This latter figure is fairly consistent with the usual estimate of three percent of people legally or educationally designated mentally retarded. Figure 2 shows this percentage distribution according to a normal probability curve.

When theoretical expectations are compared with actual counts from various sources, the two agree very well for the borderline and mildly mentally retarded, but the estimated prevalence greatly exceeds theoretical expectations for the severely mentally retarded as shown in Table 8–1. The theoretical expectancies are based on the assumption that a person's mental level is produced by a large number of factors combining on the basis of chance. The deviations from normal expectancies at the lower mental levels is thought to reflect the operation of disease, accidents, single dominant or recessive genes, and other infrequently occurring dele-

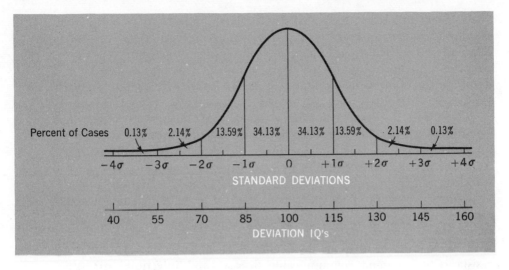

FIGURE 2
Borderline Intellect in the General Population

terious factors which have massive effects and produce a disproportionate number of severely mentally retarded individuals.

Physical Characteristics

We have already indicated that in appearance, physique, and general health the mildly mentally retarded are not noticeably different from their intellectually normal age-mates. However, there is a statistically significant, but low, correlation between intellectual level and various indices of organic status and health (Ingram, 1953; Culley and Jolly,

TABLE 8–1
Departures from Expectations Based on the Normal Distribution Curve

IQ	Theoretical Expectancy	Estimated Prevalence	Excess beyond Theoretical Expectancies	Percentage of Excess
0–20	50	92,750	92,700	185,400
20–50	164,861	371,000	206,139	125
50–70	5,537,710	5,593,360	55,650	1

Data from Dingman and Tarjan (1960) and Robinson and Robinson (1965).

1963; Kugel and Mohr, 1963). All studies show the life expectancy of the mentally retarded to be below that of the general population. The incidence of sensory defects and motor disabilities is greater, and the medical histories of the mentally retarded show a higher incidence of disease and developmental defects than do those of persons of average or more intelligence.

The mentally retarded approach the normal much more closely in physique and general health than they do intellectually, but they do show some inferiority. The physical handicaps of the mentally subnormal are the result of a variety of causes. In some cases, the mental and physical inferiorities have a common basis such as accident, disease, and maldevelopment, which produce widespread organic and intellectual deficits. Some of the organic deficits of the retarded are the result of their generally low socioeconomic status. A wide variety of health-related factors such as poor diet, inadequate medical care, greater contact with and less resistance to common communicable diseases and infections are associated with low socioeconomic status.

FAMILY AND INTELLIGENCE

The intelligence of parents and children is such that a positive relationship is found between the two. In a study at Stanford University (Burks, 1928), a correlation of .46 was found between mothers and their children and a correlation of .45 between fathers and their children. In a Minnesota study (Leahy, 1935) correlations of .51 were found between both fathers and mothers and their children. In an Iowa study (Skodak and Skeels, 1949) a correlation of .44 between true mothers' intelligence and their children was found even though the children were living in foster homes. These correlations are about the same size as one would get from correlating the physical measure of parental height with that of their children. These data lead to the general statement that a large percentage of the borderline population comes from families of like intelligence. If one takes filial regression into account, it is probable that a high percentage of these people are as bright or brighter than their parents.

Studies of family size and intelligence have been reported in the literature in rather goodly numbers. The earlier studies of intelligence and family size are subject to a number of errors. Frequently parental intelligence was estimated from the intelligence of children, or from the father's occupational status, or from general cultural background. An interesting study of size of family in relation to the brightness of children (Lenz, 1927) should be reported. Intelligence test results from 4,330 children in public schools in seven cities in eastern United States and in the middle west were obtained. Different tests were given by different examiners in the different schools. The median IQ for the entire group was 97. It was found that the larger the family, the lower the median IQ of the children. The median IQ of only children was 107.9; of children with three sibs, 97.4; of children with ten sibs, 84.9; and of children with twelve or more sibs, 79.9.

An investigation of the family history of mentally retarded children in the Massachusetts public schools with Binet IQ's of 70 or over (Dayton, 1929) gives the mean number of sibs for these children as 4.52, after correction for sampling errors. This figure is considerably larger than the 2.8 children per mother found in New York.

A study of 9,956 fourth-grade pupils who had attended the public schools in Ottawa, Canada, during the years 1933 to 1942 (Robbins, 1948) indicates a general rise in the family size as the IQ's of the children go down. The specific intelligence test, which was apparently administered by the school department, is not named. The number of siblings in the families of children with IQ's of 130 and over was 3.2; for those with IQ's of 90 to 109, 4.3; and for those with IQ's under 90, 5.3.

From the studies cited and from numerous other studies bearing directly or indirectly on intelligence and family size, it can be said that the mean IQ tends to decrease as family size tends to increase. This being the case, the person with an IQ between 70 and 89 is more likely to have come from a large family than is a person of normal or superior measured intelligence. The person with an IQ between 70 and 89 is likely, then, to have parents who have about the same relatively low level of intelligence, and also to have been reared in a larger family than children in the normal range. Nisbet (1953) has made some interesting speculations as to the effect of differential verbal stimulation on children, which will be discussed later.

The high rate of reproduction among those of lower intelligence is probably not the result of increased fertility as such, or of excessive sex drive. It is probably a product of early marriage and early childbearing (Baller, 1936; Roberts, 1939), coupled with various other factors such as lack of foresight, economic pressures that bring about early marriage for women, and lack of the practice of birth control. The absence of birth-control practices among the mentally retarded has been designated as a prime reason for the heightened birth rate of the group (Wallin, 1956). In Sweden, family limitation began many years ago among the better educated, but it has now permeated the entire population. The differential birth rate in that country, once marked, has been reduced to practically zero (Shield and Slater, 1961). The increase in the size of family as intelligence declines is probably counteracted by a host of other factors, including the facts that, for various reasons, not all the mentally retarded reproduce, many children who are mentally deficient never reach maturity, and most of the severely mentally retarded do not reproduce at all.

Through the middle ranges of intelligence, there is a low negative correlation (—.10 to —.30) between intelligence and the number of children in the family. However, in the upper and lower levels of intelligence there is a slight positive correlation between the intellectual level of parents and the size of the family they produce (Anastasi, 1956; Reed and Reed, 1965; Reed, 1965). If instead of correlating the size of family with the intelligence level of those who marry, we include the childless brothers and sisters of the parents studied and compute the *average* number of offspring for *all* members of the same generation, the picture is quite different. Table 8–2 shows the relationship between the number of offspring *per capita, when both married and unmarried are included,* and the mean IQ of the parental generation.

Including the childless brothers and sisters of the parents cancels the negative relationship between the mean IQ of the parental generation and the mean number of offspring. The mentally retarded who do reproduce have large families, but the average number of children produced by the retarded members of a given generation is *lower* than that of normal people because a large percentage of the mentally retarded do not marry and are childless.

Nisbet (1953) has indicated that there is a distinct environmental influence of the size of the family on verbal ability and, through this, on general mental development. This evidence suggests that there are important variables in family size that tend to bring about differences in language development. There is really little information as to what these

TABLE 8–2

IQ of Parental Generation as Related to
Mean Number of Offspring When Both Married and
Unmarried Members of Parental Generation Are Included

IQ's of Parental Generation	Mean Number of Offspring
70 and below	2.09
71–85	2.30
86–100	2.22
101–115	2.20
116–130	2.49
131 and above	2.98

Data from Higgins, Reed, and Reed (1962); Bajema (1963); and Reed (1965).

variables are or how they operate. Some interesting questions have been raised about the variables which produce this differential language development by Sarason and Gladwin (1958). They suggest that in large families each child is exposed to a great deal of verbal stimulation, but receives less training from adults. They also wonder if the effect of family size on language is less a quantitative one than a qualitative one, having to do more with the content and style of the stimulation.

Nisbet's (1953) and Doll's (1946) work, taken together, may serve as the basis for some further speculation. We have here the indications that social development continues after intellectual development has ceased and the evidence that language development is not as adequate in large families as in small ones. Children of limited intelligence tend to come from larger families. Is it possible that children from larger families get neither the quantity nor quality of verbal stimulation that children in smaller families get? Children in larger families have playmates, but they still must get their verbal training from the adults in the family. There is no doubt a great difference between being talked to by an adult and playing and talking with another child. Only children are likely to receive a great deal of adult verbal stimulation. When there are a number of children in the family, each child probably receives less verbal attention from the adults. The children spend more time talking with each other, but it is probable that they all know the same words anyhow. Either all have learned from their parents, or a younger child has learned from an older (in which case the younger might have some advantage). Conversations among the children probably have a greater social than linguistic value. A great deal of attention has been paid to the importance of language development in concept formation and general intellectual growth (Fowler, 1965; Hess and Shipman, 1965; McCarthy, 1964). This is a very promising area for research and development, and federal support of such research should contribute to the understanding of this complex problem.

It is probable that children who have no, or few, brothers and sisters spend less time in social situations and more time in solitary play. It has been shown (Lehman and Witty, 1928) that the brighter children more frequently participate in solitary activities. They spend more time reading. Is it possible that children of large families receive more social stimulation and less verbal and intellectual stimulation and that they therefore continue to develop socially beyond the time when intellectual growth levels out? And that children from small families receive less social stimulation and more verbal and intellectual stimulation, and therefore continue to develop intellectually beyond the time when social maturity is reached? To contend that these stimulus variables would account entirely for the observed differences would be ridiculous. All that is intended is to indicate that these differential stimulation patterns should be considered along with other variables in attempting to account for the inverse relationship between family size and intelligence and the differential social development of people of various intellectual levels.

SOCIAL AND ECONOMIC BACKGROUND

Social and economic background has been given considerable recent attention as an important variable in mental development. Social anthropologists have expressed strong doubt that cultural behavior can be separated from so-called intellective responses (Davis and Havighurst, 1948). An issue of *Genetic Psychology Monographs* devoted largely to cultural problems in mental subnormality is an excellent review of research in the area. The authors (Sarason and Gladwin, 1958) contribute an analysis of cultural problems and focus attention on these factors as highly relevant variables in the understanding of intellectual development. A brief look at the social milieu that provides the background for a large number of people under consideration in this chapter seems in order.

Education and Mental Level. Ranking adults in terms of educational level typically results in ranking them reasonably well according to levels of intelligence. It was found that the Army General Classification test scores of a sample of 4,330 men during World War II correlated .73 with the highest year completed in school (Sarason and Gladwin, 1958). Results such as these are to be expected for several reasons. The schools are academically oriented to such an extent that those who have difficulty in verbal learning tend to drop out before completing high school. Intelligence tests are highly dependent on verbal ability, and only those with relatively high verbal ability score well on them. It would naturally be expected that the more intelligent would fare better in school and thus obtain greater satisfaction from school-like achievement. Their intelligence is higher and, to add to this, the motivational situation is better for them than for the less intelligent. Those with sufficient intelligence tend to remain in school through high school and college. Those with less intelligence tend to drop out because of failure to achieve, discouragement, or both.

There is a possibility that education raises the IQ. This, of course, would be independent of the tendency for the more brilliant to remain in school. The studies showing positive effects of early schooling on IQ (Wellman, 1945) have been criticized for their technical errors (McNemar, 1945). Other research (Tuddenham, 1948) shows that World War II soldiers had significantly higher IQ's than those of World War I. These results are difficult to interpret, but it is possible that the gain can be attributed to the increase in educational level. The average educational level in World War I was the eighth grade, while in World War II it included two years of high school. Another possibility is that greater emphasis was placed on the importance of doing well on the test in World War II. Still another possibility is that the World War II sample was more familiar with this type of testing than the previous group. If all these factors—increased educational level, greater motivation, and greater sophistication—are considered together, the rise in test scores is probably understandable.

One study related the education of true parents with their children's IQ's and compared this with the relationship of the education of foster parents to the IQ's of foster children (Skodak and Skeels, 1949). The data indicate that a significant, positive relationship exists between the length of the true mother's and father's education and the child's IQ. There was no significant relationship between the foster mother's and father's education and the foster child's IQ. Thus, children reared by their true parents are likely to be reared by parents of the same general educational and intellectual level as themselves. It can be seen that it is likely that children of borderline intelligence are reared by parents of approximately equal intellectual background and a limited educational background.

People of borderline intelligence occupy the lower end of the continuum of educational achievement. They find school difficult and uninteresting. They have in all probability come from a family that does not consider educational achievement very important. Academic achievement is difficult, and the completion of only the compulsory years of education is typical of those of borderline intellect. Those below this intellectual level are likely to avoid, in one way or another, the completion of the usual years of training required of children in most states.

The borderline group seems to be doubly handicapped in a society which places so much emphasis on educational achievement. Not only do they have less intellectual endowment, but they do not receive the years of educational training that brighter people receive. They are the group with less formal training and with less capacity to cope with a complex environment.

Occupation and Mental Level. The interrelationships among intelligence, education, and occupation are such that if we rank people according to occupation we have ranked them fairly well according to intelligence. It is to be expected that a hierarchy of intellect can be established by ranking years of attendance in school, because those who are brighter tend to remain in school, whereas those who are duller, and therefore less successful, tend to drop out. Some occupations require more academic and formal training than others, and are quite naturally reserved for the more educated. Certain occupations are simply not open or available to persons with IQ's between 70 and 89, but the possession of a high IQ does not prohibit a person from entering the less intellectually demanding occupations. We would therefore expect to find greater variability in intelligence within the occupational groups requiring the least intelligence and education, and the least variability within occupational groups requiring the most education and intelligence.

The overlap in intelligence among the various occupations is great. It is certainly not safe to make predictions of an individual's intelligence from his occupation. It probably is safe to say that people with IQ's in the borderline category are more commonly engaged in occupations requiring lower than average levels of education and training.

Geographic Area and Mental Level. Ginzberg and Bray's (1953) analysis of men who were rejected for military service on the grounds of mental deficiency during World War II sheds some interesting light on geographic area as it is related to measured intelligence. According to these data, more than 700,000 men were rejected for military service under the general heading of "mental deficiency." This is about 4 percent of the men examined. This, taken by itself, probably would indicate that the screening standards were such as to reject a few more than are ordinarily considered to be mentally retarded. However, this would not be a very complete picture, because they report that nearly 14 percent were rejected in some states and that only 0.5 percent were rejected in others. They report that the rate of rejection in the southeast was almost ten times as large as that in the far west. The rate of rejection of Negroes was higher than that of whites, but the rate of rejection of Negroes in the northwest and far west was less than the rate of rejection of whites in the southeast and the southwest. They further analyzed the data by the more than 3,000 counties throughout the United States. When this was done, it became apparent that the degree of urbanization was a major factor in the lower rejection rates of both Negroes and whites. Sarason and Gladwin (1958) point out that the majority of people rejected almost invariably came from the lowest social classes, and that their functioning reflected cultural rather than constitutional variables. They indicate that explanations for the increase in measured intelligence with urbanization fall into three major categories: (1) better schools; (2) "selective migration," i.e., the brighter people move to the cities; and (3) the larger number of personal relationships available provides a better opportunity to develop skills important for an intelligence test in school.

It appears that measured intelligence is likely to be lower in certain areas than in others. Urban dwellers score higher on intelligence tests than rural, for whatever reason. We can therefore expect to find a greater percentage of the rural population with IQ's between 70 and 89 than of the urban population. Local variations in rural areas are also to be expected, as there are variances in isolation and educational opportunity.

The generally low level of intelligence, income, occupational level, and education characteristic of families with familially mentally retarded children leads to modes of living and social behavior that causes society to reject them. They frequently become social outcasts. The family background is often enough to turn society against the children from the very beginning. Evidence that this absence of social acceptance is compensated for by the great understanding and acceptance within the family structure is lacking. Actually, the reverse seems to be more nearly true. Rejection by the community is frequently accompanied by parental and familial rejection or neglect. Town (1939) reports from his study of 141 defective families that 28 of the marriages were broken by desertion, abandonment, separation, annulment, or divorce. Illegitimate maternity was found in 51 families, incest in 7 families, and prostitution in 14 families. Imprisonment of one form or another was reported for 38 families. Twenty families had children removed from their custody, and an equal number habitually practiced physical violence toward each other.

Not all studies of parental or maternal care of the mentally retarded are so bleak (Mickelson, 1947), but those that report adequate maternal care tend to deal with supervised cases or to be made in rural areas where adjustments are probably not as difficult to make.

Sarason (1943) found themes of loneliness, desire for affection, fear of rejection, aggression, and ambivalence toward parental figures from an analysis of stories of institutionalized defectives (mainly diagnosed as garden variety) on the basis of the Thematic Apperception test. Abel's (1945) findings were essentially the same. These findings are rather understandable in view of the findings of a study of parental attitudes toward mental defectives (Thorne and Andrews, 1946). There were 291 institutionalized subjects in this study which extended over a five-year period. Twenty-five percent of these children received no gifts or visits from parents during the entire period. Forty-five percent received gifts but had no visitors, and another 8 percent had visits but did not receive gifts. Only 22 percent of the children received both gifts and visits. Sarason (1959) suggests that these data are not only revealing of parental attitudes toward the institutionalized child, but are suggestive of the nature of the parent-child relationships before the period of institutionalization. He formulates hypotheses of child-rearing practices in defective homes that, if proven to be true, would make for an environment in which it would be extremely difficult for any child to develop, even if he were well-endowed. He hypothesizes that the defective mother does not possess adequate knowledge of child care, is negative in her attitude toward the child, does not adequately mother it, and does not respond consistently or promptly to the usual crying signals of childhood distress. He further hypothesizes that the mother's low level of intellect and consequent poor judgment interferes with feeding, care, and the ordinary attention received by most children. The lack of encouragement in verbalization and locomotion, and the absence of stimulating toys, games, and puzzles, add to the maternal ineptness to form a rather gloomy picture of the early life of the familially mentally retarded child. It has been pointed out by various investigators that an early adverse environment has a "crippling" effect on mental development (Clarke and Clarke, 1955).

The classical descriptions of mentally retarded and degenerate families (Goddard, 1912; Estabrook, 1916) are not to be discounted as belonging to the past. More recent authors (Smith and Burks, 1954), describing experiences in teaching retarded children, stated that almost all the children coming to them had been "kicked around." They state that the average retarded child is an exile, not only in society, on the street, in the school, but even in his own home. The home and familial conditions existent for large numbers of the familially mentally retarded are probably comparatively little better now than they were at the time of the early descriptions. All in all, the situation is hardly one that could be said to be conducive to the development of the intellectual and social skills necessary for successful living in our culture, even if the hereditary nature of intellectual functioning were to be completely discounted. This problem is discussed more fully in the chapter on the culturally disadvantaged.

Work and Job Expectancy.   In spite of the ever-increasing emphasis on academic training for employment in a good number of situations, it is still safe to say that a large number of employment opportunities are open to those who possess less formal training. A vast number of industrial jobs can be performed by a person with limited intelligence with a minimum of formal training. Some of the industrial jobs involve a great deal of repetition. With the rapid increases in work mechanization and simplification, the increase in simple jobs has been, and should continue to be, great. The low-level, semiskilled jobs that are constantly created create a great demand for workers of relatively low mental ability. Many workers of relatively limited intelligence do not become bored by the repetitive nature of the task (Wyatt, Langdon, and Stock, 1937). They gain a high degree of proficiency and tend to stay on the job longer than some people of high intelligence. The range of intelligence in various occupations has been studied and reported (Harrell and Harrell, 1945), and the studies indicate that the dull-normal have sufficient intelligence to successfully pursue a large variety of occupations. Large numbers of automotive mechanics, carpenters, cooks, barbers, miners, farmers, and laborers of various kinds have been found to have intelligence test scores equivalent to the dull-normal and borderline categories.

Schaefer (1941) studied the intelligence test scores and accident rates of 6,829 industrial workers. He reports that the accident rate of those who scored low on intelligence tests is about four times as great as that of those who scored high. Other investigators have reported a smaller relationship between accident rate and intelligence. However, the relationship between intelligence and industrial accidents is rather tenuous. It probably depends on the complexity of the situation in which accidents occur. If working conditions are dangerous, it obviously takes a higher degree of intelligence to avoid accidents. The dull worker is not likely to have a higher rate of accidents in situations where the hazards are simple.

As we have already indicated, those of limited intelligence are likely to be employed in jobs requiring less training. These are usually the lower-paying jobs, but there are a lot of them. During times of maximum employment, the dull should encounter no particular difficulty in getting jobs. During slack periods, more of these people will be without jobs, and they will probably be less skillful at finding jobs than the more intelligent workers.

Delinquency and Crime.   Low-level intelligence has frequently been cited as a cause of delinquency or crime. A word of clarification is, perhaps, in order. There is nothing inherent in the possession of limited intelligence that dictates antisocial behavior. The lack of vocational opportunity, too-high social expectations, and the resultant feeling of frustration and failure that are frequent concomitants to low-level intelligence may result in social behavior that is criminal or that could be called delinquent. Then, too, there is always the possibility that the antisocial behavior of those of limited intelligence is more readily detected than the antisocial behavior of the more intellectually sophisticated. Data on intelligence and delinquency are no doubt influenced by the fact that those of lesser intellect are more likely to get caught.

There has been a growing conservatism in the interpretation of data on delinquency over the years. Early studies placed heavy emphasis on the relationship between intellect and delinquent behavior. Later studies have sought to account for the findings in terms of sociological and psychological variables other than intelligence as such. Metfessel and Lovell (1942) concluded, after a comprehensive review of the literature on the correlates of crime published during the 1930's, that the typical delinquent in the studies was dull-normal. The same conclusion had been reached earlier by Wallin (1917) and by Porteus (1922).

More recent studies of the intelligence of delinquent boys (Durea and Taylor, 1948; Wedeking, 1949) confirm these earlier findings. The mean

IQ's of the boys fell in the dull-normal classification, roughly one-third of them scoring between 70 and 89.

Educators have been in essential agreement with an early observation (Wallin, 1917) that the backward pupil was an important source of problems in the school. The school curriculum, as we mentioned, has little appeal for these children, and they have been unable to meet the usual academic requirements. Truancy is greater when no special provision is made to meet their interests and aptitudes. It is reduced to a minimum when special provisions are made for their education and training (Wallin, 1956). Mullen (1950), using either the Stanford-Binet or Wechsler intelligence tests, tested 886 truants and 742 classroom discipline cases and found the mean IQ of younger truants to be 91.1, and of younger disciplinary cases to be 92.7. In an earlier study, Kvaraceus (1945) tested 701 predelinquents and delinquents with the Stanford-Binet and the Kuhlmann-Anderson intelligence tests, and reported 39.3 percent to have IQ's between 70 and 89. A mean IQ of 88.7 was reported for 463 cases in the group.

The intelligence of a group of people that might be termed vocationally delinquent in our society has been investigated. The median intelligence test score for 107 randomly selected destitute men was 89 (Johnson, 1917).

Comparisons of the types of criminal offense committed by people of relatively high and relatively low intelligence have shown that those of relatively low intelligence are more likely to engage in assault and sexual misconduct (Tulchin, 1939; Merrill, 1947). It seems clear that intelligence and delinquency of various kinds are related, and that the type of delinquency probably will depend more on the individual's environment and the opportunities afforded him than on his intelligence. No doubt it takes more intelligence to defraud or embezzle than to commit crimes of violence or become a prostitute or other type of sexual offender.

Social Expectancy.   The level of social expectancy for those of borderline and dull-normal intelligence in our society is fairly high. In spite of the fact that they typically have a poorer background, where values and standards differ from the vast middle class, they are expected to conform to middle-class values and standards. This is often an imposing task, and for a person of limited intellectual facility, it is doubly difficult.

In school there is often no special provisions or special curriculum for those with IQ's in the 80's. Typically, they must struggle through the academic curriculum and are expected to complete a regular high school program. In that they are not formally recognized as being particularly backward, they are sometimes looked on as lazy or shiftless. Because of the ill-adapted curriculum, they not infrequently become disciplinary problems. Unfortunately their being disciplinary problems in the school is frequently seen as an inherent characteristic of those with less than ordinary intelligence, rather than as a function of inappropriate curricular offerings.

Most of these individuals are expected to seek and procure gainful employment and become self-sustaining individuals. This expectancy is more fully realized than the expectancy of adequate academic progress. Gainful employment is the rule, rather than the exception, for these people in our highly industrialized society.

People with IQ's between 70 and 89 have not been considered legally mentally retarded, and there are no legal protective agencies for them as there are for the obviously mentally retarded. They are expected to function adequately in our society without special social or legal protection. If they prove to be gullible and unable to manage their economic affairs wisely, they are subject to the same legal reprisals as others. A low level of intelligence is not an acceptable excuse for social or economic irresponsibility, or for other inadequacies that may develop as the result of existence in a relatively complex culture.

However, the mentally retarded, when they have been recognized as such, are offered some protection by society. The various states have legal structures that provide for the care and education of the mentally retarded. The courts recognize that the individual of subnormal intelligence may violate the law without a real understanding of the wrongfulness or the consequences of his behavior. When this is the case, the mentally retarded are typically placed in institutions for the mentally deficient. The legal protection is twofold: it protects society from the irresponsible behavior of the retarded, and it protects the mentally retarded from being victimized by those individuals who would take advantage of their low intelligence. But because of the difficulty of identifying the high-grade mentally retarded person, the legal protection they get may come after the fact. That is, they are protected after they have been victimized or after they have injured others. This is extremely difficult to avoid, because many mentally retarded individuals are quite capable of making an adequate social adjustment and of earning their own livelihoods. It is not currently possible to predict with any degree of accuracy who will be able to do so, and who may instead become involved in behavior that is neither tolerated nor condoned by the law.

Most of the high-grade mentally retarded are expected to live in society with a minimum of protection. If the families of the mentally retarded can provide a reasonable amount of guidance and protection, a great many can acquire the training that will enable them to make a reasonable adjustment. The various states provide schools and institutions for the mentally retarded, and many provide special classes for those who cannot function adequately in the usual classroom. The limitations imposed by low-level intelligence in a complex social structure are many, and the pitfall of expecting too much from the mentally retarded is probably as great as that of expecting too little. They need help in the form of special training, supervision, guidance, and sympathetic understanding. Under favorable circumstances many can become productive members of society.

Education and Learning. The education and training of people of limited intellectual facility is a challenge to the public schools which has been recognized only fairly recently. The usual and conventional curricula have been designed for those whose learning facility is within the normal range. It is only recently that schoolchildren have been afforded the opportunity of having a curriculum adjusted to their ability and background. Wallin (1949) reports that his experience indicates that dull-normal children tend to be listless and inattentive in school, and that they lose interest in regular school work and soon grow weary. These characteristics can be readily accounted for in terms of curricular offerings that are not meaningful for the individual and are extremely difficult or impossible for the child to master. The child presented with a course of study that is difficult, has little or no appeal, and is unrelated to his goals and purposes must develop some means of coping with the situation. One way is to ignore the situation by being inattentive and uninterested.

The ordinary school designed for the average or better student fails to provide meaningful experiences for those of less intelligence. The school, instead of being a training ground and stepping stone to effective living in the community, becomes the largest single obstacle to the adequate adjustment of a large number of children. Many students find that after they have hurdled the obstacle of conventional school attendance by putting in the appropriate amount of time, they can then live a fairly happy and adequate existence. School becomes an obstacle to effective living rather than an aid to it. Many students faced with an insurmountable and, to them, meaningless curriculum develop habits of indolence rather than effective habits of work. They develop expectancies of failure rather than success. They become discouraged, devalue themselves, regard themselves as failures, and expect to be regarded as failures by others.

Children in the borderline intellectual classification can be expected to master the fundamental skills of reading, writing, and arithmetic. They cannot be expected to do so with alacrity. Neither can they be expected to deal effectively with abstract concepts or with materials that are too distant from their own real-life experiences. They need to be trained to use effectively the powers and capacities they do possess. They need training in motor, occupational, and vocational skills that will equip them to cope with the complex society in which they must function.

Because verbal facility and ability to deal with abstractions are typically more limited than other intellectual and motor facilities, the education and training of the dull should capitalize on other facets of ability that are more nearly normal.

The general academic level of education of the group here under consideration is lower than the educational level of the intellectually normal. More of these individuals drop out of school as soon as it is legally possible than do people from higher intellectual strata, and they do not consider formal education so important.

Level of Aspiration. Level of aspiration is at least a partial function of social status, educational level, and ability. Social and economic status, and educational level, are no doubt a partial function of ability. The group we are considering has less ability than the usual person, and we might expect that its level of aspiration would be lower. Level of aspiration is no doubt related to the concept of self which is developed by the individual. The self-concept of people whose IQ's range from 70 to 89 is undoubtedly more limited than those of higher intellectual status, in that these people have probably experienced failure more frequently than the others. Children of less intelligence have lower and less realistic self-concepts than normal children (Ringness, 1961). In the area of academic accomplishment this would most certainly be true. It is probably also true that in school these people have experienced social failure more frequently than others. Jucknat (1937) has shown that few people raise their level of aspiration after experiencing failure, and it has been shown that the experience of failure may have the effect of reducing level of aspiration.

One can hardly aspire to do that which he knows nothing about. The very nature of a limited intellectual capacity indicates that the less intelligent will know less about the opportunities and possibilities for individuals within the culture. Parental pressures for intellectual achievement are not likely to be as great. The steadiness of a job is more likely to be of concern than the nature of the job itself.

After studying the prevalence of mental subnormality, Tizard (1953) stated that the percentage of children considered educationally subnormal in different countries ranged from about 1 to 4, and that 6 to 9 percent more were so dull as to require special assistance within the normal school system. He further indicates that surveys have revealed a much higher incidence of educational subnormality than any society is known to make provisions for.

In order to establish a meaningful educational program for the educable mentally retarded, it is essential that the characteristic traits of persons of this level be identified. What learning characteristics, other than his inferior mentality as such, tend to set him apart from the others? What are the consequences of low-level intelligence as far as learning is concerned? In what areas is he particularly handicapped and in what areas might he be expected to achieve most readily?

Reporting on the subnormal girl, Abel and Kinder (1942) have pointed out that her restricted vocabulary, improper use of abstract terms, inadequate comprehension of verbal instructions, and poor performance on tests requiring verbal ability are the areas where her limitations are most acutely demonstrated. They further indicate that the subnormal child has trouble in understanding causal relationships, is immature, and is given to unpredictable emotional outbursts. Other writers have pointed out that mentally retarded children are deficient in quantitative thinking (Kirk and Johnson, 1951). It has been pointed out that the retarded are deficient in their ability to think abstractly (Ingram, 1953) and that the attention spans are short and powers of association are small (Magnifico, 1958).

The mentally retarded individual's motivations have been depicted as "inadequate" and their drive as "erratic" (Daly and Cain, 1953). This is understandable when one considers that motivation is, in part, a product of the nature of the experiences of the individuals. The mental retardate, not understanding the nature of his own intellectual limitations, is bound to be frustrated by his inability to master the concepts and skills which others master. It is probable that the mentally retarded have so frequently experienced failure that they have learned that it is less painful not to try, than to try and fail. That their motivations are "inadequate" for academic learning is a way of saying that they are not interested in what is to be learned or in the things that are prerequisite to their learning of more complex tasks. The role of learning in the acquisition of interests has been emphasized in educational psychology (Sawrey and Telford, 1968). One can hardly be interested in those things that are beyond the realm of experience. If rewards are experienced in connection with a certain activity, that activity is likely to be repeated. If no rewards are forthcoming, the activity wanes. If a given activity is rewarded frequently enough, the activity may soon become enjoyable and interesting. The mentally retarded usually gets little or no reward for his academic efforts. He does not develop interests in those activities that invariably result in frustration, failure, and unfavorable comparison with those who are more successful.

Academic Expectancy.   The mildly mentally retarded group is considered *educable.* If the instruction is appropriate and the atmosphere for learning is adequate, these people can be expected to acquire academic skills ranging in level from the second to the fifth or sixth grade. Their maximum academic achievement can be expected to equal that of the average seven- to ten-year-old child. As has been indicated elsewhere (Sawrey and Telford, 1968), the mentally retarded child should not be expected to attain this level of accomplishment at the same chronological age as normal children. The rate of mental growth is not the same for mentally retarded children as it is for normal ones. The normal child of eleven has a mental age of eleven, whereas the mildly mentally retarded child of eleven has a mental age of seven. This is the conventional age for first or second graders, and in all probability the retarded child will be ready to do first or second grade work by the time he is ten or eleven years old.

The academic progress of a group of 163 children with a median IQ of 60.6 who were admitted to special classes at the age of twelve years and seven months yields what is probably rather typical data for academic progress (Phelps, 1956). Most of these people left school at sixteen, with work certificates, or at eighteen, without them. The median time spent in the class was three years and four months. A small percentage (2.5) graduated from the eighth grade; and a still smaller percentage (1.2), from junior high school. The median reading grade level on leaving school was 3.9, and the median arithmetic grade level was 4.3. The median age of 12.7, when they were admitted to the special classes, may seem rather high, but it is likely that many of them were not mature enough to have profited much from academic instruction before that age.

Administrative Provisions. Educational programs are provided for the educable mentally retarded in public and private residential schools, special day schools, special classes in the regular schools, integrated programs, and regular classrooms. Occasionally "resource teachers" are used, and less often home and hospital instruction are provided for the educable mentally retarded. Most of the mentally retarded receiving special educational services are enrolled in special day classes in the regular public schools. A smaller number attend special schools for the mentally retarded. The administrative groupings of these children follow the patterns used for the regular normal students. Table 8–3 shows some of the more common characteristics of these administrative divisions.

There have been relatively few preschool programs for the educable mentally retarded. Most of these children are not identified prior to the first grade. Consequently, most of the educable mentally retarded attend the regular nursery schools and kindergartens. However, some studies indicate the desirability of providing special preschool programs for these children (Kirk, 1958; Conant, 1961). The "Head Start" programs under the Economic Opportunities Act of 1965 have provided preschool education for many of these children.

Elementary-school-level mentally retarded children are usually taught in special self-contained classes. Many, of course, remain in regular classes. Most of the educable mentally retarded children are identified and segregated at the primary elementary school level. Much of the school work

TABLE 8–3

Some Common Administrative Division and
Scholastic Characteristics of the Educable Mentally Retarded

Administrative Units	Approximate Grade Levels	Usual CA's	Usual MA's	Curricular Goals
Preschool	Nursery	4–5	2– 3	Perceptual and conceptual development, elementary language, and social skills
Primary	Kindergarten	6–10	3– 6	Continuation of above
Intermediate	1–3	11–13	6– 9	Basic academic skills and work habits
Secondary	2–7	14–18	8–12	Life adjustment; prevocational and vocational skills
Postschool	3–7	16 and above	8–12	Practical vocational and social skills

at this level is preacademic. The chief criterion for advancing the child from the primary to the intermediate level is his readiness for academic work as indicated by his achievement level and his having attained a mental age of approximately six years.

The intermediate special class program provides formal instruction in the basic skill areas. A good deal of individual instruction is provided, as classes are usually small (twelve to eighteen). Most of the educable mentally retarded acquire academic skills ranging from the second to the fourth grade level before going on to the secondary level. Children are usually moved from the intermediate to the secondary level on reaching adolescence, irrespective of their academic achievement.

The secondary-school mental retardates are typically integrated to some degree with the regular students. Because most secondary schools are departmentalized, integration is administratively simple. The mentally retarded are usually taught the more academic subjects such as mathematics, reading or English, geography, social studies, and science by a single homeroom teacher, but take the less academically demanding subjects such as physical education, home economics, art, music and shopwork in regular classes. The educable mentally retarded are able to mingle quite indistinguishably with the other students in athletics and social affairs.

Preparation for work receives major emphasis in the secondary school curriculum for the mentally retarded. Some type of in-school work experience, in office, shop, cafeteria, or as janitor, is often provided. During the last years in school, part-time placement in community work experiences are becoming standard practice (Syden, 1962; Dunn, 1964).

The postschool education of the mentally retarded makes use of sheltered workshops for job training and on-the-job training, sometimes under the auspices of the schools, the state vocational rehabilitation programs, or private organizations (Dinger, 1961; Mackie, Dahelstein, and Heber, 1959).

Social Training. Social training for the mentally retarded has received the attention of a number of workers in the field. It has been emphasized that the development of socially acceptable attitudes should be a major aim of education of the mentally retarded. They are less capable of managing their own lives and therefore need special training in the social processes. The modern emphasis upon "self-expression" has but limited applicability to the mentally retarded because of their tendency toward emotional outbursts (Goodenough, 1956).

Out-of-school success in jobs frequently depends on social skill as much as or more than on occupational skill (Kirk and Johnson, 1951; Dunn, 1964). Many jobs are sufficiently simple so that they can be rather readily mastered. If the individual has learned the value of promptness, good manners, good appearance, and dependability, he can function in a large number of jobs without too much difficulty. The social training necessary for the development of such characteristics should start early and be intensive enough so that he develops patterns of social response that will become assets rather than liabilities as he matures. Frequently the mentally retarded learn at home precisely the social behavior which will add to the burden of being mentally retarded rather than assist him in social adaptation. The simple social characteristics of honesty, obedience, and kindness, which are accepted as a part of socialization, are often lacking in the mentally retarded simply because they have not received the systematic training by which these are acquired.

Physical and Vocational Training. The mildly mentally retarded individual comes closer to the normal in physical and sensory capacity than in the more intellectual areas. In order to capitalize on this, training in these areas should be undertaken early and be an important part of the educational program. These children should be encouraged by rewards in this area as much as possible, because they must depend largely on their physical and manipulatory skills to fit into the vocational world. The intellectual tasks are largely beyond them, and their jobs will be in the physical areas of employment. Their physical training should teach them to keep themselves healthy, strong, and clean, in order to make themselves as physically acceptable as possible in a society whose attitudes toward them are likely to be unfavorable at best.

Vocational training should be initiated with the intent of making them reasonably proficient in a number of skills. The emphasis on manual training for retarded children is a realistic one. They are more likely to develop skill here than in other areas, and if they are to be employable they most certainly will be employed in a job somewhat dependent on manual skill. Classes in typewriting and driver education have proven practical in the curriculum for mentally retarded students (Daly and Cain, 1953). Most of the educable mentally retarded can be trained adequately to earn their own living. If this is to be done, the individual must have some reasonable proficiency in the academic areas (he should be able to read and write) and in the social areas. The social aspects of getting and holding a job should most certainly be stressed in the vocational training of the mentally retarded.

Occupational instruction in a variety of areas is practical. Training for the mentally retarded in the following areas in public schools was described by Masters (1937): automobile repair, electrical and metal work, pressing, shoe repair, cooking, table service, child care, home nursing, cafeteria, barber and beauty parlor service, garment making, laundry, repair work, industrial training, and other allied areas. Since that time the curricular offerings have been expanded a great deal. Table 8–4 indicates the most common areas of employment for the mentally retarded.

The mentally retarded person can be taught good habits of work and industry and can learn to take pride in doing a job to the best of his abilities. From this he can gain some sense of personal worth, self-sufficiency, and social belonging.

Objectives of Education and Training. The mentally retarded, as a rule, have a greater comprehension of the concrete than of the abstract. The greatest disability of the mentally retarded has been described as

TABLE 8–4

Some Areas of Employment for the Mentally Retarded

General Areas	Specific Job or Task	
Industrial production	Welder	Painter
	Miner	Tailor
	Carpenter	Farm laborer
	Bricklayer	
Transportation and communication	Teamster	Telephone lineman
	Loader	Telephone serviceman
	Truckdriver	
Retail sales and services	Elevator operator	Waiter
	Bus boy	Dishwasher
	Sales clerk	Porter
	Shipping clerk	Laundry worker
Personal services	Janitor	Barber
	Doorman	Domestic servant
	Handyman	Street cleaner
	Caddy	Maid
	Shoe repairman	Beauty parlor operator

his inability to perceive the underlying pattern of things (Devereux, 1956). In view of the limitations of the mentally retarded and the fact that certain of their characteristics are less handicapping than others, special consideration for them as individuals is imperative. There is some agreement that the first goal of education for these people should be that of self-help (Graham, 1956). The state of California has formulated some rather specific and extensive goals for the education of the mentally retarded. These include: begin work without urging; finish what is started; help others; protect health; master tools at ability level; accept limitations; communicate; listen while others speak; prepare to be homemakers; develop and respect hand skills; spend money wisely; and use basic vocabulary necessary for functioning citizenship (Daly and Cain, 1953). These goals are not grossly different from the goals of education for everyone, except that there is a greater emphasis on manual skills.

The broad education and training objectives for the mentally retarded could be said to be: (1) adequate social development; (2) academic achievement to ability level; (3) the development of vocational skill; and (4) personal habits and adjustments satisfactory to society and to its individuals. These goals, too, are not grossly different from those for the education of children in general.

Summary

In discussing the mentally retarded as a group, there is the ever-present danger of minimizing or ignoring individual differences among them. Although their range of intellectual ability is limited, there is still room for rather great individual variance. The restriction in range of intelligence does not restrict other important variables in direct proportion. Each mentally retarded person is an individual, but there is sufficient homogeneity among them to allow their consideration as a group.

The exact extent of mental retardation is not known. Generalizing from data based on a statistical concept of mental retardation, it is probable that there are almost six million mentally retarded (i.e., with IQ's below 70) in the United States. Between 80 and 90 percent of these are mildly mentally retarded (i.e., with IQ's between 50 and 70). An additional one-fifth of the population is sufficiently intellectually handicapped to require special consideration.

The mentally retarded are generally considered to be under par in general physical health and stature. Their life span is shorter and their death rate higher than the normal population. The familially mentally retarded tend to come from homes that are grossly inadequate for normal health and growth. The severely mentally retarded, more than those in the mild category, tend to come from parents of normal intelligence and from average social backgrounds. Not infrequently, mentally retarded people are avoided by their peers, ignored by the community, misplaced in the school, and rejected at home. The social atmosphere for many mentally retarded persons is most inadequate. Many are culturally disadvantaged.

The education of the mentally retarded has received increased attention in the past decade or so. Most of the educable mentally retarded can be educated to lead useful and productive lives. They approach normality more nearly in sensory acuity and motor ability than in other areas. Some can eventually complete academic work equivalent to that of the average fifth- or sixth-grader.

Social and personal training for the mentally retarded can equip them to lead more adequate lives. Vocational training, coupled with social training, can be of great assistance in eventual successful living. There are a great many jobs that can be performed adequately by this group. The adjustment problems of the mentally retarded are about the same as those faced by normal people, except that they are intellectually less equipped to cope with them. They frequently become discouraged, are avoided by those their age, and live lonely, isolated lives. There are relationships among intelligence, delinquency, and crime. Delinquent behavior is related to intelligence but is not directly caused by it. A larger proportion of the mentally retarded become delinquent than is characteristic of the normal population.

The various states have passed laws for the protection of the mentally retarded and have made provisions for their care and training. Special classes in the public schools have been sponsored for their education.

References

ABEL, T. M., "Responses of Negro and White Morons to the Thematic Apperception 'Test,'" *Amer. j. ment. defic.*, XLIX (1945), 463–68.

———, AND E. F. KINDER, *The Subnormal Adolescent Girl*. New York: Columbia University Press, 1942.

ANASTASI, A., "Intelligence and Family Size," *Psychol. bull.*, LIII (1956), 187–209.

BAJEMA, C. J., "Estimation of the Direction and Intensity of Natural Selection in Relation to Human Intelligence by Means of the Intrinsic Rate of Natural Increase," *Eugen. quart.*, X (1963), 175–87.

BALLER, W. B., "A Study of the Present Social Status of a Group of Adults Who, When They Were in the Elementary Schools Were Classified as Mentally Deficient," *Genet. psychol. monog.*, XVIII (1936), 165–222.

BURKS, B. S., "The Relative Influence of Nature and Nurture upon Mental Development: A Comparative Study of Foster Parent-Child Resemblance and True Parent-Child Resemblance," *Yearb. nat. soc. stud. educ.,* XXVII, Part 1 (1928), 219–316.

CLARKE, A. D., AND A. M. CLARKE, "Pseudo-Feeblemindness: Some Implications," *Amer. j. ment. defic.,* LIX (1955), 507–9.

CONANT, J. B., *Slums and Suburbs.* New York: McGraw-Hill Book Company, 1961.

CULLEY, W. J., AND D. H. JOLLY, "Heights and Weights of Mentally Retarded Children," *Amer. j. ment. defic.,* LXVIII (1963), 203–10.

DALY, F. M., AND L. M. CAIN, *Mentally Retarded Students in California Secondary Schools,* Bulletin of the California State Department of Education, No. 7. October, 1953.

DAVIS, A., AND R. J. HAVIGHURST, "The Measurement of Mental Systems: Can Intelligence Be Measured?" *Sc. mo.,* LXVI (1948), 301–16.

DAYTON, N. A., "Order of Birth and Size of Family," *Amer. j. psychiat.,* VIII (1929), 979–1006.

DEVEREUX, G., *Therapeutic Education.* New York: Harper & Row, Publishers, 1956.

DINGER, J. C., "Post-school Adjustment of Former Educable Mentally Retarded Pupils," *Except. child.,* XXVII (1961), 353–60.

DINGMAN, H. F., AND G. TARJAN, "Mental Retardation and the Normal Distribution Curve," *Amer. j. ment. defic.,* LXIV (1960), 991–94.

DOLL, E. A., "Practical Implications of Endogenous-Exogenous Classification of Mental Defectives," *Amer. j. ment. defic.,* L (1946), 503–11.

———, "The Feeble-Minded Child," in *Manual of Child Psychology,* ed. L. Carmichael. New York: John Wiley & Sons, Inc. (1946a), pp. 845–85.

DUNN, L. M., ed., *Exceptional Children in the Schools.* New York: Holt, Rinehart & Winston, Inc., 1964.

DURFA, M. A., AND G. J. TAYLOR, "The Mentality of Delinquent Boys Appraised by the Wechsler-Bellevue Intelligence Tests," *Amer. j. ment. defic.,* LIII (1948), 342–44.

ESTABROOK, E. H., *The Jukes in 1915,* Carnegie Institute Publication 240. Washington, D.C., 1916.

FOWLER, W., "A Study of Process and Learning in Three-year-old Twins and Triplets Learning to Read," *Genet. psychol. monog.,* LXXII (1965), 3–89.

GINZBERG, E., AND D. W. BRAY, *The Uneducated.* New York: Columbia University Press, 1953.

GODDARD, H. H., *The Kallikak Family.* New York: The Macmillan Company, 1912.

GOODENOUGH, F., *Exceptional Children.* New York: Appleton-Century-Crofts, 1956.

GRAHAM, D. F., "So Johnny Can't Read," *Training sch. bull.,* LIII (1956), 36–37.

HARRELL, T. W., AND M. S. HARRELL, "Army General Classification Test Scores for Civilian Occupations," *Ed. psychol. meas.,* V (1945), 229–39.

HESS, R. D., AND V. SHIPMAN, "Early Blocks to Children's Learning," *Children,* XII (1965), 189–94.

HIGGINS, J. V., E. W. REED, AND S. C. REED, "Intelligence and Family Size: A Paradox Resolved," *Eugen. quart.*, IX (1962), 84–90.

INGRAM, C. R., *Education of the Slow-learning Child.* New York: The Ronald Press Company, 1953.

JOHNSON, G. R., "Unemployment and Feeble-mindedness," *J. of delinq.*, II (1917), 59–73.

JUCKNAT, M., "Accomplishment, Level of Aspiration, and Self-consciousness," *Psychol. forsh.*, XXII (1937), 99.

KIRK, S. A., *Early Education of the Mentally Retarded: An Experimental Study.* Urbana, Ill.: University of Illinois Press, 1958.

————, AND D. JOHNSON, *Educating the Retarded Child.* Boston, Mass.: Houghton Mifflin Company, 1951.

KUGEL, R. B., AND J. MOHR, "Mental Retardation and Physical Growth," *Amer. j. ment. defic.*, LXVIII (1963), 41–48.

KVARACEUS, W. C., *Juvenile Delinquency and the School.* New York: Harcourt, Brace & World, Inc., 1945.

LEAHY, A. M., "Nature-Nurture and Intelligence," *Genet. psychol. monog.*, XVII (1935), 235–308.

LEHMAN, H. C., AND P. A. WITTY, "A Study of Play in Relation to Intelligence," *J. appl. psychol.*, XII (1928), 369–97.

LENZ, T., "Relation of I.Q. and Size of Family," *J. educ. psychol.*, XVIII (1927), 486–96.

MACKIE, R. P., D. H. DAHELSTEIN, AND R. F. HEBER, *Preparation of Mentally Handicapped Youth for Gainful Employment.* Washington, D.C.: Government Printing office, 1959.

MAGNIFICO, L. X., *Education for the Exceptional Child.* New York: David McKay Co., Inc., 1958.

MASTERS, E. H., "Occupational Preparation for Mentally-Handicapped Children," *J. psycho-aesthetics*, LVII (1937), 157–65.

MCCARTHY, J. J., "Research on the Linguistic Problems of the Mentally Retarded," *Ment. retard. abst.*, I (1964), 3–27.

MCNEMAR, Q., "Note on Wellman's Reanalysis of I.Q. Changes of Orphanage Pre-school Children," *J. genet. psychol.*, LXVII (1945), 215–19.

MERRILL, M. A., "The Significance of I.Q.'s on the Revised Stanford-Binet Scales," *J. educ. psychol.*, XXIX (1938), 641–51.

————, *Problems of Child Delinquency.* Boston, Mass.: Houghton Mifflin Company, 1947.

METFESSEL, M., AND C. LOVELL, "Recent Literature on Individual Correlates of Crime," *Psychol. bull.*, XXXIX (1942), 133–64.

MICKELSON, P., "The Feeble-minded Parent: A Study of 90 Cases," *Amer. j. ment. defic.*, LI (1947), 644–53.

MULLEN, E. A., "Truancy and Classroom Disorder as Symptoms of Personality Problems," *J. educ. psychol.*, XLI (1950), 97–109.

NISBET, J. D., *Family Environment: A Direct Effect of Family Size on Intelligence,* Occasional paper on Eugenics, No. 8. London: Eugenics Society, 1953.

PHELPS, H. R., "Post-school Adjustment of Mentally Retarded Children in Selected Ohio Cities," *Except. child.*, XXIII (1956), 58–62.

PORTEUS, S. D., *Studies in Mental Deviation*, Training sch. Publ. 24. Vineland, N.J., 1922.

REED, E. W., AND S. C. REED, *Mental Retardation: A Family Study*. Philadelphia, Pa.: W. B. Saunders Co., 1965.

REED, S. C., "The Evolution of Human Intelligence," *Amer. scientists*, LIII (1965), 317–26.

RINGNESS, T. A., "Self-Concept of Children of Low, Average and High Intelligence," *Amer. j. ment. defic.*, LXV (1961), 453–61.

ROBBINS, J. E., "The Home and Family Background of Ottawa Public School Children in Relation to Their I.Q.'s," *Canadian j. psychol.*, II (1948), 35–41.

ROBERTS, J. A., "Studies on a Child Population: III. Intelligence and Family Size," *Ann. Eugen.*, VIII (1939), 178–215.

ROBINSON, H. B., AND N. M. ROBINSON, *The Mentally Retarded Child*. New York: McGraw Hill Book Company, 1965.

SARASON, S. B., "The Use of the Thematic Apperception Test with Mentally Deficient Children: I. A Study of High Grade Girls," *Amer. j. ment. defic.*, XLVII (1943), 414–21; "II. A Study of High Grade Boys," *ibid.*, XLVIII (1943), 169–73.

————, *Psychological Problems in Mental Deficiency*. New York: Harper & Row, Publishers, 1959.

————, AND T. GLADWIN, "Psychological and Cultural Problems in Mental Subnormality: A Review of Research," *Genet. psychol. monog.*, LVII (1958), 3–290.

SAWREY, J. M., AND C. W. TELFORD, *Educational Psychology* (3rd ed.). Boston, Mass.: Allyn & Bacon, Inc., 1968.

SCHAEFER, V. G., *Safety Supervision*. New York: McGraw-Hill Book Company, 1941.

SHIELD, J., AND E. SLATER, "Heredity and Psychological Abnormality," in *Handbook of Abnormal Psychology*, ed. H. J. Eysenck. New York: Basic Books Inc., Publishers, 1961.

SKODAK, M., AND H. M. SKEELS, "A Final Follow-up of One Hundred Adopted Children," *J. genet. psychol.*, LXXV (1949), 3–19.

SMITH, M. F., AND A. J. BURKS, *Teaching the Slow-learning Child*. New York: Harper & Row, Publishers, 1954.

SYDEN, M., "Preparation for Work: An Aspect of the Secondary School's Curriculum for Mentally Retarded Youth," *Except. child.*, XXVIII (1962), 325–31.

THORNE, F. C., AND J. S. ANDREWS, "Unworthy Parental Attitudes toward Mental Defectives," *Amer. j. ment. defic.*, L (1946), 411–18.

TIZARD, J., "The Prevalence of Mental Subnormality," *Bull. world health org.*, IX (1953), 423–40.

TOWN, C. H., *Familial Feeble-mindedness*. Buffalo, N.Y.: Foster and Stewart Publishing Corp., 1939.

TUDDENHAM, R. D., "Soldier Intelligence in World Wars I and II," *Amer. psychol.*, III (1948), 54–56.

TULCHIN, S. H., *Intelligence and Crime*. Chicago, Ill.: University of Chicago Press, 1939.

WALLIN, J. E., *Problems of Subnormality*. New York: Harcourt, Brace & World, Inc., 1917.

————, *Children with Mental and Physical Handicaps*. Englewood Cliffs, N.J.: Prentice-Hall, Inc., 1949.

————, *Mental Deficiency*. Brandon, Vt.: Journal of Clinical Psychology, 1956.

WECHSLER, D., *Measurement of Adult Intelligence*. Baltimore, Md.: The Williams & Wilkins Co., 1944.

————, *Wechsler Intelligence Scale for Children: Manual*. New York: Psychological Corporation, 1949.

————, *The Wechsler Adult Intelligence Scale Manual*. Psychological Corporation, 1949.

WEDEKING, L. P., "A Note on the Intelligence of Delinquents at Indiana Boys School," *J. consult. psychol.*, XIII (1949), 58.

WELLMAN, B. L., "IQ Changes of Preschool and Nonpreschool Groups during the Preschool Years: Summary of the Literature," *J. psychol.*, XX (1945), 347–68.

WYATT, S., J. N. LANGDON, AND F. G. STOCK, *Fatigue and Boredom in Repetitive Work*, Industrial Health Research Board, No. 77. London: His Majesty's Stationery Office, 1937.

9

Severe Mental Retardation

Definition of Terms

For the sake of brevity we are combining the American Association on Mental Deficiency's *severe* and *profound* categories of mental retardation together with the educationally designated *trainable mentally retarded* and *custodial*, into a single group. *The bulk of these people have IQ's below 50.* Except when it is necessary to make finer differentiations, we shall refer to the entire group as the *severely mentally retarded*.

Distinguishing Characteristics

Whereas most of the mildly mentally retarded are of the ordinary familial type and have few if any distinguishing physical characteristics, most of the severely mentally retarded are physically deviant. Most of the "clinical types" of mental retardation, which are typically characterized by distinctive patterns of physical symptoms, are severe mental retardation. The causes or accompaniments of severe mental retardation consist, in most cases, of organic brain injury, endocrinological and biochemical deviations of either genetic or environmental origin, and single pathogenic genes.

Some Genetic Syndromes

CHROMOSOMAL ABERRATIONS

Down's Syndrome (Mongolism). Mongolism constitutes the largest single clinical category of the severely mentally retarded. From 10 to 20 percent of severely retarded children are of this type. In many cases, from a fourth to a third of the students in the classes for severely mentally retarded are mongoloids. Approximately 1 in every 600 to 900 live babies is a mongoloid (Collmann and Stoller, 1962; McIntire, Menolascino, and Wiley, 1965). The incidence of mongoloid births varies markedly with the age of the mother: 1 in 1,500 for mothers between fifteen and twenty-four years; 1 in 1,000 for mothers between twenty-five and thirty-four; 1 in 150 for mothers over thirty-five; 1 in 70 for mothers forty to forty-four; to 1 in 38 for mothers over forty-five (Knoblock and Pasamanick, 1962; Robinson and Robinson, 1965). Even though young mothers run relatively little risk of having a mongoloid child, 1 in every 4 is born to a mother under thirty. This discrepancy between relative incidence and total number occurs because so many more children are born to younger mothers (Smith, 1960; Lilienfeld, 1969).

More than fifty physical signs have been listed as characteristic of mongolism. The problem is that none of these stigmata is peculiar to mongoloids, and no single sign is found in all of them. In addition, some of these characteristics do not appear until the child is several years old, while others disappear with aging (Gibson, Pozony, and Zarfas, 1964; Menolascino, 1965). Gibson, Pozony, and Zarfas (1964), by applying standards of age stability and assessment reliability, have reduced the number of significant diagnostic signs to the following thirteen: (1) a flattened skull which is shorter than it is wide; (2) abnormally upturned nostrils caused by undeveloped nasal bones; (3) abnormal toe spacing (increased space particularly between the first and second toes); (4) disproportionate shortness of the fifth finger; (5) a fifth finger which curves inward; (6) a fifth finger which has only one crease instead of the usual two; (7) short and squared hands; (8) epicanthic fold at the inner corners of the eye; (9) large fissured tongue; (10) a single crease across the palm of the hand (simian crease); (11) abnormally "simplified" ear; (12) adherent ear lobule; and (13) abnormal heart.

Wallin (1949) considers the presence of three or more of these physical anomalies to be indicative of mongolism. Penrose (1963) states that if four or more of these anomalies are present, the individual is "almost certainly a mongolian type of imbecile." Despite considerable variability in the individual identifying characteristics, the overall physical impression in mongolism is usually one of striking similarity (Penrose, 1963).

While rare cases with borderline intelligence have been reported (Wunsch, 1957), most mongoloids are severely mentally retarded (Stemlicht and Wandever, 1962). The mean IQ for various groups is in the 20-to-40 range.

As indicated in an earlier chapter, mongolism was first demonstrated to involve a chromosomal abnormality in 1959. Since then, three types of chromosomal deviations have been identified in mongolism:

1. A trisomy of chromosome number 21 resulting from *nondisjunction*. This is a genetic disorder but not an inherited one. This type is rarely familial. It is the form most commonly born to older mothers.

2. A *translocation* of a chromosome involving the attachment of an extra number 21 chromosome onto another (usually number 15). This type is familial and occurs in the children of younger parents.

3. A rare chromosomal anomaly in mongolism is known as *mosaicism*, which was described in Chapter 7. The range of symptoms, including mental level, varies greatly in this condition.

There is evidence that individuals in the three chromosomal subcategories of mongolism differ in learning ability, mental level, and temperament, as well as in certain biochemical characteristics (Jarvik, Falek, and Pierson, 1964; Gibson and Pozsonji, 1965).

Since the discovery of the chromosomal abnormality in mongolism a large number of chromosomal deviations have been identified. Apparently most chromosomal abnormalities result in early embryonic death. Studies of aborted embryos indicate that approximately one-third display chromosomal aberrations (Bloom, 1970). At least 6.5 percent of newborns possess major chromosome abnormalities sufficient to impair their effectiveness in society (Lubs and Ruddle, 1970).

Samples of amniotic fluid containing cells from the developing fetus can be taken to detect chromosomal abnormalities during the first 12 to 16 weeks of pregnancy. Translocations of chromosomes in "carrier" parents can also be detected by cytogenic study of suspected individuals. Where a mother carries the appropriate chromosomal translocation for mongolism, she has a 33 percent chance of having a mongol child. An infant chimpanzee with clinical, behavioral, and chromosomial features similar to those in mongolism has been described in one study (McClure, et al., 1969).

MENTAL RETARDATION CAUSED BY A SINGLE GENE

Some of these types were listed in Chapter 7, and limitations of space permit only a brief characterization of a few of them. Most are relatively rare. They appear most often in the children of consanguineous marriages and display the other features of single-gene-determined conditions listed earlier. There is no consistency in the naming of the clinical types of mentally retarded. Some are named after the men who first identified and described the syndrome. Others are identified by their etiology. Still others are given the label of some physical stigma which is a part of the syndrome.

BIOCHEMICAL ANOMALIES

Biochemical causes of mental retardation may involve abnormal carbohydrate metabolism or storage, anomalies of protein (amino acid) metabolism or excretion, and similar defects involving lipoid material (fats).

Carbohydrate Metabolism. *Galactosaemia* is the best known of the conditions involving abnormal carbohydrate metabolism. Individuals suffering from this condition are unable to metabolize galactose. This leads to a high level of galactose in the blood and urine, and in some unknown way results in mental retardation. Infants placed on a galactose-free or lactose-free diet before the onset of permanent tissue damage can develop quite normally. Since lactose is a constituent of milk, such a regime requires the elimination of milk from the child's diet (Rundle, 1964). A single recessive gene seems to be the cause of galactosaemia. Carriers of the recessive gene show an abnormal tolerance for galactose and can therefore be identified.

Additional abnormalities of carbohydrate metabolism which may produce mental retardation are:

1. *Sucrosia,* an inability to metabolize sucrose (ordinary beet or cane sugar)
2. *Idiopathic hypoglycaemia,* an error of carbohydrate metabolism producing abnormally low blood-sugar levels
3. *Glycogenosis,* a disturbance of the metabolism of glycogen.

Protein Metabolism. Phenylketonuria (PKU) was the first of the metabolic disorders shown to cause mental retardation. It is the result of a single gene determined defect of amino acid metabolism. The genetic anomaly produces a deficiency of the liver enzyme which normally catalyzes the breakdown of the amino acid phenylalanine to tyrosine. In this condition, phenylalanine accumulates and is eventually metabolized by an alternate pathway, producing *ketonuria*, the characteristic excretion in the urine of above-average amounts of phenylketones (Menkes, 1967). Approximately 60 percent of untreated PKU children have IQ's under 20, more than 80 percent have IQ's below 40, while a few are average or above in intelligence (Menkes, 1967). Behavior syndromes similar to those of untreated PKU children have been produced in monkeys by feeding them high levels of phenylalanine from birth to from three to six months of age (Chamove, Waisman, and Harlow, 1970).

Phenylketonuria is caused by a single recessive gene, although carriers of the defective gene can be detected (Hsia, Paine, and Driscoll, 1957). Tests of the blood and urine can detect the condition, and if a diet low in phenylalanine is instituted early enough, development apparently can be normal. Some states now require routine testing of infants for this condition.

Additional conditions involving abnormal protein or amino acid metabolism are discussed by Rundle (1964); Scheinberg and Gitlin (1952), Patric (1961), and Holt and Coffee (1968).

Metabolism of Fats. The best known group of related conditions involving abnormal lipoid metabolism is *amaurotic familial idiocy.* Various forms of this condition have been given different names, depending primarily on the age of onset. The infantile form (Tay-Sach's disease) has an early onset and progresses rapidly. It is characterized by progressive spastic paralysis, blindness, convulsions, and death by the third year. Juvenile forms have a later onset (three to ten years), with mental deterioration and death within ten to fifteen years. A single recessive gene seems to be the primary cause of this condition.

Additional conditions involving abnormal lipoid metabolism are *Niemann-Pick disease, Gaucher's disease,* and *Gargoylism (Hurler's disease)* (Rundle, 1964. Holt and Coffee, 1968).

MENTAL RETARDATION RESULTING
FROM ENDOCRINE DISTURBANCES

Cretinism. Cretinism is the best known disorder of endocrine function resulting in mental retardation. Cretinism results from insufficiency of thyroid which causes irreversible damage to the central nervous system. There is evidence that a fetus suffering from insufficient thyroid may sustain such brain damage prenatally (Lawson, 1955). Cretinism can be either genetic or environmental in origin. The endemic type of cretinism is the result of an iodine-deficient diet and occurs in geographic regions in which the soil, water, and vegetation are deficient in iodine. (See Fierro, et al. (1969) for a report of an Andean region where cretinism is still endemic.) Cretinism of this type can be prevented by iodine supplements to the diet. Using iodized salt is one way of accomplishing this. Most sporadic cretinism is not genetic.

However, there are at least three separate genetic types of cretinism. All involve recessive genes which seem to interfere with the different enzyme systems of the body involved in the synthesis and secretion of thyroxin. The degree of mental retardation is roughly proportional to the extent of hypothyroidism.

The physical syndrome of cretinism is quite complex and involves physical dwarfism and marked delay in bone development, muscular flaccidity, and a shuffling and waddling gait. The head is large, extremities are short and fat, and the fingers are square at the ends. The neck is short and thick, the skin is dry and scaly, the tongue is thick, and the abdomen protrudes. Basal metabolism and blood pressure are both low. The typical cretin is placid, inactive, apathetic, and severely mentally retarded.

Early identification, and immediate and properly controlled thyroid medication, can prevent the more severe symptoms. In most cases the physical symptoms can be prevented by thyroid treatment, but normal intelligence is seldom attained (Smith, Blizzard, and Wilkins, 1957). Intellectual and physical impairment are generally more severe in the endemic and sporadic forms of cretinism, which are of environmental origin, than in the genetic types. Cretins of the genetic type practically always have goiters, indicating the presence of some thyroid tissue. The genetic types also have not suffered from thyroid deficiency *in utero*, because the normal mother supplies the needs of the fetus. For a good discussion of the genetic basis of cretinism, as well as many of the other metabolic disorders, see Stanburg (1960).

Other Endocrine Disorders.   Some additional endocrine disturbances sometimes associated with mental retardation are *hypoparathyroidism, nephrogenic diabetes insipidus,* and *sexual infantilism and dwarfism* (Horstmann, 1949; Rundle, 1964; Simpson, 1952; McDonald, 1955; Kirman, et al., 1956).

CRANIAL ANOMALIES OF GENETIC ORIGIN

Microcephaly.   Microcephaly may be either genetic or environmental. The genetic form is transmitted by a single recessive gene. The secondary, or exogenous, form results from massive irradiation of the fetus or embryo (Murphy, 1947; Plummer, 1952), or possibly from maternal infections (Wesselhoeft, 1949). Microcephalic individuals are characterized by small, conical skulls; the lower jaw recedes; the skin of the scalp is often loose and wrinkled. The individuals are small in stature but not dwarfed, with a curved spine and stooping posture. The appearance of microcephalics is often like that of monkeys, and their quick, jerky movements remind one of a bird. Genetic microcephalics are severely mentally retarded, but those with the acquired type are more variable both in physical characteristics and mental level (Martin, 1970).

Other Cranial Abnormalities. Two other cranial anomalies of possible genetic origin are *acrocephaly or oxycephaly,* a tower- or steeple-shaped skull, with a narrow forehead which slopes up to a point to form a dome-shaped vertex (Crome, 1961); and *anencephaly,* a partial or complete absence of the cerebrum and cerebellum. Since these individuals live for only short periods of time, their mental level cannot be determined (Penrose, 1957, 1963).

Syndromes of Exogenous Origin Commonly Associated with Severe Mental Retardation

HYDROCEPHALY

Hydrocephaly (water on the brain) consists of an excessive accumulation of cerebrospinal fluid either in the ventricles of the brain (internal hydrocephalus) or on the outside of the brain in the subarachnoid space (the external form). If the internal form develops before the bones of the skull have fused, the head gradually enlarges, sometimes attaining tremendous size. The extreme conditions of hydrocephalus produce various sensory, motor, and intellectual symptoms—mental retardation being one of these. If the excessive accumulations of fluid develop after the cranial bones are mature and the sutures have fully ossified, enlargement of the head cannot occur, but pressure builds up inside the brain. This pressure produces a thinning out of the neural tissue, with resulting motor disability, including paralysis and convulsions, mental deterioration, and eventual death if the condition is progressive. Obstructions in the path of circulation of the cerebrospinal fluid is the most common cause of internal hydrocephalus, and this is the type most frequently associated with mental retardation. Some of the agents or conditions blocking circulation of the cerebrospinal fluid are congenital malformations, tumors, scar tissue, infections (such as encephalitis, meningitis, or syphilis), parasites, and intracranial hemorrhage. It is claimed that about one-third of congenital syphilitic infants develop hydrocephalus.

The mentality of hydrocephalics ranges all the way from low-grade idiocy to superior intelligence. A slight degree of hydrocephaly, which becomes arrested, may be consistent with normal or superior mentality. One of the authors has studied two individuals who, as children, showed pathological head expansion with all of the classical symptoms of hydrocephalus. In neither of these children did the condition progress to a point where any mental effects were noticeable. At maturity, both had test scores comparable to their normal siblings, and the only residual symptoms were poor motor coordination of a nonspecific, generalized sort—including poor articulation. At the other extreme are the severely affected, progressive cases which end up in hospitals and institutions as severely retarded, helpless individuals whose life span is typically short.

Several operative procedures have been developed for early correction of the defect, and treatment with drugs has met with some success (Matson, 1956; Elvidge, Branch, and Thompson, 1957).

CEREBRAL PALSY

Cerebral palsy may occasionally be of genetic origin, but it is usually caused by environmental factors. It is characterized by disturbances of motor function due to brain damage. Cerebral palsy is by far the most common single syndrome associated with severe mental retardation of exogenous origin. Estimates of the total number of cases are in the hundreds of thousands, with an estimated ten thousand new cases added each year (Bailey, 1958; Robinson and Robinson, 1965). While not all of these are mentally retarded, a sizable percentage are. Since cerebral palsy always involves motor disabilities, this condition is discussed in a later chapter on the orthopedically handicapped.

EPILEPSY

Epilepsy may have either a genetic or environmental etiology. It is sometimes associated with mental retardation, but when the retardation is severe both the epilepsy and the mental retardation are usually the result of extensive brain damage or maldevelopment, as in microcephaly or cerebral palsy. Epilepsy is discussed extensively in a later chapter.

BRAIN INFECTIONS

Severe mental retardation may be caused by brain infections, as indicated in an earlier chapter. Meningitis, encephalitis, and syphilitic brain infections can all result in mental retardation. Untreated syphilitic brain infection is progressive (except for remissions), with a wide variety of physical, personality, and intellectual accompaniments. There is nothing unique about mental defect of syphilitic origin, and with the modern methods of treatment it has become a minor cause of mental retardation.

Meningitis. Meningitis usually responds to the modern antibiotics and seldom causes severe mental subnormality. Defects of vision and hearing are probably caused by meningitis more often than is severe mental retardation.

Encephalitis. Encephalitis more often results in permanent brain damage and mental retardation than does either syphilis or meningitis. Mental deterioration and other postencephalitic effects may follow immediately after the acute attack or they may appear several years later. These chronic effects either remain stationary or become progressively worse.

Paradoxically, the severity of the delayed aftereffects is not closely related to the severity of the acute attack. In fact, many times the symptoms and immunity reactions of postencephalitis develop in the absence of any recognized acute attack. For example, 149 of one group of 507 postencephalitics had no history of an acute phase (Wallin, 1949).

The postencephalitic symptoms include a large number of motor disorders and character and personality changes, as well as general mental deterioration. The motor symptoms include all of those found in cerebral palsy—paralysis, muscular rigidity, tremors, tic, athetoid and choreiform movements, and the Parkinsonian syndrome. The latter syndrome is said to develop in about 20 percent of postencephalitics. Parkinsonism includes the expressionless, immobile masklike face, tremors, a stiff and eventually stooped posture, and propulsive gait. Hydrocephalus, epilepsy, and deafness are infrequent sequelae. The incidence of serious aftereffects varies from 10 to 40 percent.

The personality and intellectual changes are more likely to develop when the encephalitis is contracted in infancy or early childhood (DeJong, 1959). In fact, some workers claim that no child who has encephalitis before the age of three ever escapes some intellectual deficit. About half of the postencephalitics are reported as suffering some mental deficit when encephalitis was contracted before the age of fourteen. Behavioral and personality changes include increased emotional instability, hyperactivity, sleep reversals, impulsiveness of action, and even psychosis. Some 20 percent are reported to develop psychotic symptoms.

There have been few well-controlled studies of the extent of mental deterioration or arrested intellectual development in postencephalitics. Enough case studies have been reported to indicate that the term "arrested mental development" can appropriately be applied to some of these cases. The mental deficit resulting from encephalitis ranges all the way from no apparent decline to complete arrest or even marked deterioration.

In one survey of ten studies, mean IQ's ranged from 73 to 91 and individual scores ranged all the way from low-grade custodial to superior (Pintner, Eisenson, and Stanton, 1940). One study reports a deficit of 16

IQ points in a group of postencephalitic children as compared with their normal siblings (Dawson and Conn, 1926). There seems to be a tendency for the intelligence level to decline in successive testings. The prognosis for postencephalitics is not very good (Lurie et al., 1937; Brown, Jenkins and Cisler, 1940).

Culture and Psychological Causes of Severe Mental Retardation

The A.A.M.D.'s etiological classification of the mentally retarded recognizes emotional conditioning and familial-cultural factors as possible causes of mental retardation. Since familial-cultural factors are the major concern of the chapter on the culturally disadvantaged, and emotional maladjustment is considered extensively in the chapter on the social and emotional deviate, we shall deal with them only briefly here. The fairly high incidence of emotional disturbance among the mentally retarded and, conversely, the fact that many of the more seriously emotionally disturbed function as mentally retarded, probably stem from a number of complex relationships. Sometimes the two stem from common causes. Often the two handicaps also intensify each other. Retarded individuals are more vulnerable to emotional problems because they are handicapped, and their emotional problems may further depress their functional level.

Among severely retarded children, there is a high incidence of psychoticlike behavior. Certain behavioral syndromes, such as Heller's disease and childhood autism, have been considered by some workers to be forms of severe mental retardation of either organic or functional origin, and as forms of childhood psychosis (schizophrenia) by others. Those who conceive of these syndromes as functional believe that the children showing these symptoms have suffered such severe deprivation—either affectional or general environmental—that they have failed to develop any but the most primitive responses to their environment.

Although the evidence indicates that severe mental retardation may result primarily from extreme affectional or general environmental deprivation or from pathogenic emotional experiences, the evidence suggests that most cases are not so caused. The family, community, subcultural, and cultural backgrounds of the severely mentally retarded are considerably above that of the mildly mentally retarded. In fact, the family and cultural backgrounds of the most severely retarded (custodial or profoundly retarded) are about normal. The bulk of the parents and siblings of the severely mentally retarded are normal. Within the zero-to-70 IQ range of the mentally retarded, the lower the IQ level of the retarded children, the higher is the mean IQ level of their parents and siblings.

Penrose (1963) reports that the homes of the mildly mentally retarded are definitely subnormal, while those of the severely retarded and custodial are distributed about as in the general population. This same author also reports that 12.1 percent of the parents of a large group (448 cases) of mildly mentally retarded (moron) children were themselves judged to be mentally retarded, while 6.5 percent of the parents of the more severely mentally retarded (imbeciles) and only 2.7 percent of the parents of custodial mentally retarded (idiots) were rated as mentally retarded. This would suggest that the bulk of the severely mentally retarded function so in spite of reasonably normal homes and culture, rather than because of deficits in these areas.

EDUCATIONAL PROGRAMS FOR THE TRAINABLE

Since it is expected that most of the trainable mentally retarded will be dependent or semidependent all their lives, the objectives of their school programs are limited. In general terms, their training programs are devised to develop self-help skills, socialization, and elementary oral language. The materials and methods are not far removed from those of Itard and Seguin, although there is greater emphasis on socialization through group activities—especially group play.

The self-help skills taught are such things as independent eating, dressing, toileting, washing, combing hair, brushing teeth, and using a handkerchief. The children are taught to follow directions and perform simple tasks. In the area of social skills, the children are taught consideration for others (e.g., taking turns), common courtesy, and obedience. A good deal of basic sensory and motor training is provided in order to improve sensory discrimination and develop motor skills. Such household skills as dusting, sweeping, setting and clearing the table, washing and drying dishes, washing and ironing, sewing, elementary homemaking, using common tools, telephoning, and limited traveling in familiar areas are also taught. Considerable time is spent on the development of oral language. Health and safety rules are also taught. The major purposes of these classes are to develop the ability of the child to look after himself and to perform simple tasks about the home or the immediate neighborhood.

Several studies have been made of the effectiveness of the special day classes for the trainable mentally retarded. Dunn (1963) has summarized many of these studies, and while they are rather unsatisfactory, they indicate that not much progress was made during the short periods covered by the reports in attaining the school's objectives.

Follow-up studies of former students of the special classes for the trainable indicate that the outcomes are extremely varied. Practically none of the studies included control or comparison groups of children who did not attend such classes. These studies indicate that, in the years immediately following the termination of their school attendance, about one-fourth of the children are institutionalized and most of the others live under supervision at home. Interviews with parents indicate that they believe the school programs have been a help in reducing the child's dependency on the family (Dunn, 1963). The available data are inconclusive about the value of special classes for the trainable mentally retarded (Kirk, 1957; Cain and Levine, 1961).

The sheltered workshops have demonstrated that some of the trainable mentally retarded can be productively employed. O'Connor and Tizard (1956) have provided some optimistic reports of success attained by boys of this mental level in factory work, following systematic on-the-job training. There is some evidence that Great Britain and certain other countries of Europe are more successful with their work programs, which are oriented toward industrial production, than is the United States, which uses a more educational, mental-hygiene, and social-learning approach (O'Connor and Tizard, 1956). One report of an industrial-production oriented workshop in the United States indicates that many of the trainable mentally retarded can function adequately in such a situation (Blue, 1964).

A study of the work characteristics of mentally retarded adults in workshop-like situations has shown: (1) productivity is significantly related to IQ; (2) an IQ of 20 constituted an approximate limit below which such work is not practical; and (3) tolerance for work is positively related to intellectual level, with the most retarded showing the greatest work decrement from boredom and fatigue (Tobias and Gorelick, 1963).

CUSTODIAL TREATMENT (IQ's BELOW 20–30)

Until recently, the only alternatives open to parents of the custodial-level mentally retarded child (IQ below 20 to 30) were home care and institutionalization. Day hospitals, day-care centers, and boarding or nursing homes are now also becoming alternatives. The public and private residential institutions still take care of the largest group of those profoundly mentally retarded who live outside their own homes.

A 1965 survey of state institutions for the mentally retarded in the United States showed that approximately 192,000 people were residing in such institutions. Table 9–1 shows the resident populations, classified according to degree of retardation.

The data in Table 9–1 indicate that the resident population is predominantly of the lower mental levels. Eighty-two percent are classified as having IQ's below 50, whereas this group represents only 7.4 percent of

TABLE 9–1

Distribution of Institutional Residents According to Degree of
Mental Retardation, Compared to Estimated Prevalence (192,493 Cases)

Degree of Retardation	IQ	Percentage of Residents	Estimated Percentage Prevalence
Profound	Below 20	27	1.4
Severe	20–35	33⎱	
Moderate	36–50	22⎰	6.0
Mild	51–67	13	92.6*
Borderline	68–83	5	

*IQ's of 50 to 70.
Data from Robinson and Robinson (1965); Scheerenberger (1965); and Dingman and Tarjan (1960).

the estimated total number of mentally retarded. This means that the below-50 IQ group contributes to the resident population between eleven and twelve times its proportional numbers, whereas the above-50 IQ category contributes only 15 percent of its proportional numbers. If we extrapolate from Robinson and Robinson's (1965) data and obtain 464,000 as the approximate number of individuals in the United States with IQ's below 50 in 1965, and 157,800 as the resident population, only about one-third of the total number were in public institutions for the mentally retarded. Since public institutions house about 90 to 95 percent of the total institutionalized population in the United States, almost two-thirds of this group reside at home. The proportion residing in boarding homes and other similar facilities is negligible.

Less than 2 percent—a total of 15,941 of the total number of educable mentally retarded of school age—were receiving education in a residential institution in 1965 (Robinson and Robinson, 1965).

THE ROLE OF THE RESIDENTIAL INSTITUTION

In the last ten years, emphasis on the residential institution as the place to take care of the bulk of the mentally retarded has declined. Several developments have contributed to this trend. One, as previously indicated, was the recognition of the fact that segregation was not the solution to the problem of mental defectiveness. Another was the increasing cost of institutional care and the practical impossibility of obtaining funds sufficient to provide institutions for any large percentage of the mentally handicapped. It also came to be recognized that the large residential institution was not the best place to provide care and training for most of the mildly mentally retarded.

Advances in medicine, as well as social changes, have contributed to the change in the makeup of our institutional population. Medical advances now keep alive many low-grade mental defectives who would have died at an earlier period. For example, the death rate in New York State institutions for the mentally retarded decreased from 34.9 per thousand in 1926 to 13.5 per thousand in 1944. Coupled with this decline in death rate are an increase in the proportion of first admissions in the lower mental level and a reduction in the age of first admissions (Goldstein, 1958). These three factors (increased longevity, reduced admission age, and increasing proportions of admissions from the lower mental level requiring life-long custodial care) all combined to give the institutions predominantly a static, custodial, resident population. As a result, the days of trying to provide institutionalization for the bulk of the mentally retarded has passed.

This does not mean that the large public and private institutions will cease to exist. Institutions of this type will continue to be needed in any comprehensive program for the care and training of the mentally retarded. They are needed to receive selected cases requiring custodial, or total, care. Most of these cases will be the severely mentally retarded which the family is unable or unwilling to care for at home, as well as the mentally deficient who have additional handicaps. Finally, the residential *school* facilities may be needed to provide education and training for the educable or trainable child who resides so far away from a day school that commuting is not possible.

If the post-World War II trends continue, we can expect the public residential institutions, which account for 95 percent of the total residential population, to become more custodial centers and less schools or training centers for patients of the higher mental levels. The institutional school will have, as students, more of the trainable and less of the educable retarded. The decrease in patient turnover will reduce the number of first admissions. The per capita cost will increase as the number of higher-grade cases decreases. The increase in cost will result from the need for more attendants to perform the tasks formerly done by the higher-grade patients as well as for an increased number of professionals (M.D.'s and nurses) to care for the large number of custodial cases with organic pathology. The social services and psychological staffs will have less parolable patients to supervise, and will concern themselves more with the personal and social problems of the resident patients and their families (Goldstein, 1958).

As the need for additional professional staff and attendants increases and the per capita costs mount, there is increasing pressure on institutional administrations to let economic considerations temper professional judgment in the admission and retention of patients. The higher-grade patients often do much of the manual work around the institution, and many of them are detailed to help take care of the more helpless, lower-grade patients. Economic considerations will sometimes dictate the retention within the institution of the more skilled and more efficient patient who could be paroled or discharged, but who may be an economic asset or, at least, less of a liability than the low-grade custodial case which may replace him.

This same conflict of interest arises in the operation of the institution's dairies, farms, and workshops. When pressures are exerted to operate these facilities at a profit, there is a tendency to retain the better workers and increase their output within the institutional setting, instead of training them so as to facilitate their early placement outside. It is very easy for institutional personnel to forget that institutions exist for the good of the patients and that low per capita cost may mean that the social function of the institution is being sacrificed to efficient plant operation.

TRAINING THE CUSTODIAL MENTALLY RETARDED

The conditioning methods that have been used to study learning in the lower animals have also been applied with some success to the training of the low-level custodial mentally retarded. Ellis (1962; 1963) developed a theoretical analysis of how toilet training could be accomplished using regular operant procedures. Dayan (1964) later reported some success with the method. Roos (1965) has described an "intensive habit-training unit" established to apply these methods systematically to the training of the profoundly mentally retarded. Bensberg (1965) has reported considerable success with these methods.

These methods vary from simple toilet training, in which each person was placed on the commode every two hours and was rewarded each time he eliminated while he was on the commode (Dayan, 1964), to the development of many self-care habits by a systematic rewarding of successive approximations to the desired behavior—called "behavior shaping" (Bensberg, 1965).

In the latter methods, simple verbal directions and appropriate gestures were used as cues and successive approximations of the desired behavior were immediately rewarded. At first food (pieces of cookies and candy) were used. The food reward was always preceded or accompanied by a social reward (e.g., saying "good boy" or patting the head). As learning progressed, the social rewards were continued but the food was gradually withheld until longer units of behavior occurred and closer approximations to the desired response were attained. Finally the edible rewards were discontinued and only the social rewards were used.

These studies indicate that the principles of operant conditioning used in the training of the lower animals in the research laboratories and by such commercial organizations as the Animal Behavior Enterprises, Inc., of Hot Springs, Arkansas, can be successfully applied to the low-level custodial mentally retarded. These methods can be used by regular institutional personnel after instruction in behavior-shaping methods. Considerable improvement in self-help behavior (toileting, dressing, washing, and brushing teeth) can be obtained in a few months with such systematic training (Bensberg, 1965).

Summary

Most individuals with IQ's below 50 are either *severely* or *profoundly* mentally retarded, according to the A.A.M.D.'s classification, and are either *trainable* mentally retarded or *custodial*, in educational terminology. The bulk of the "clinical types" of mentally retarded, the single-gene-determined cases, and most of the more severely environmentally damaged (the exogenous mentally retarded) also fall into these categories. In this chapter, the severely mentally retarded clinical types, single-gene-determined, and severely environmentally damaged mentally retarded were considered.

The genetic syndromes are the result of either chromosomal aberrations or pathogenic single genes. Mongolism (Down's syndrome) is the most common type of chromosomal anomaly accompanying mental retardation. Three subtypes of mongolism are differentiated in terms of the chromosomal mechanism involved. These are: nondisjunction, which results in the embryo having three number 21 chromosomes (trisomy) instead of the normal two; translocation, in which an extra number 21 chromosome is attached to another one—usually a number 15; and mosaicism, in which at an early stage of embryonic development one cell which will develop into a particular type of tissue (i.e., skin) receives an extra number 21 chromosome. In mosaicism, some of the person's body tissues are made up of cells having 47 chromosomes and others consist of cells with the normal number of chomosomes (46).

Mongolism is characterized by a long list of physical stigmata, and mongoloid persons are usually severely mentally retarded. Biochemical, physical, and mental characteristics seem to vary somewhat, according to chromosomal type.

Biochemical anomalies caused by single genes with accompanying mental retardation may affect carbohydrate, protein, or lipoid (fat) metabolism. Galactosaemia—an inability to metabolize galactose or lactose (milk sugar), phenylketonuria—a failure to properly metabolize phenylalanine (one of the amino acids which is a constituent of most proteins), and amaurotic familial idiocy—involving abnormal lipoid metabolism, are representative of these three categories. Specific dietary restrictions, if instituted sufficiently early in life, can prevent the physical stigmata and mental retardation characteristic of certain types of untreated cases.

Familial cretinism is a form of severe physical and mental retardation resulting from insufficient thyroid. Cretinism can be of either genetic or environmental origin. Untreated cretins display a characteristic physical syndrome and are severely mentally retarded. Most cretinism can be prevented by early and continued administration of supplementary thyroid extract.

Microcephaly (in which the person has an extremely small head) can be either genetic or environmental in origin. Microcephalics are severely mentally retarded and have many characteristic physical stigmata.

Hydrocephaly (water on the brain) is a syndrome which is usually environmentally caused. The most common cause is an obstruction in the ventricular system of the brain which prevents the normal circulation of the cerebrospinal fluid. The abnormal accumulation of cerebrospinal fluid produces an enlarged head, atrophy of brain tissue, and mental retardation. Some cases can be treated surgically.

Severe mental retardation may accompany or be caused by cerebral palsy, epilepsy, and brain infections. General familial and cultural deprivation is not considered an important cause of severe mental retardation, since the familial-cultural background of this type is fairly typical of that of the general population.

The bulk of the severely mentally retarded are cared for in residential institutions, special classes, and at home. A relatively small number work in sheltered workshops and under close supervision in industry. Some are taken care of in boarding homes, halfway houses, and day-care centers. Even the low-level custodial mentally retarded can be trained if appropriate methods are employed.

References

BAILEY, C. J., "Interrelationships of Asphyxia Neonatonium, Cerebral Palsy, and Mental Retardation: Present Status of the Problem," in *Neurological and Psychological Deficits of Asphyxia Neonatonium*, ed. W. F. Windle. Springfield, Ill.: Charles C Thomas, Publisher, 1958.

BENSBERG, G. J., "Teaching the Profoundly Retarded Self-help Activities by Behavior Shaping Techniques," *Amer. j. ment. defic.*, LXIX (1965), 674–79.

BLOOM, S. E., "Trisomy—3-4 and Triploidy (3A-ZZZW) in Chick Embryos," *Science*, CLXX (1970), 457–58.

BLUE, C. M., "Trainable Mentally Retarded in Sheltered Workshops," *Ment. retard.*, II (1964), 97–104.

BROWN, A. W., R. W. JENKINS, AND L. E. CISLER, "Influence of Lethargic Encephalitis on the Intelligence of Children as Determined by Objective Tests," *Amer. j. dis. child.*, LIX (1940), 238–54.

CAIN, L. F., AND S. LEVINE, *A Study of the Effects of Community and Institutional School Classes for Trainable Mentally Retarded Children.* United States Office of Education, Cooperative Research Branch, Contract 589; SAE 8257. Washington, D.C.: Government Printing Office, 1961.

CHAMOVE, A. S., H. A. WAISMAN, AND H. F. HARLOW, "Abnormal Social Behavior in Phenylketonuric Monkeys," *J. abnorm. psychol.*, LXXVI (1970), 62–68.

COLLMANN, R. D., AND A. STOLLER, "A Survey of Mongoloid Births in Victoria, Australia: 1942–1957," *Amer. j. publ. health*, LII (1962), 813–29.

CROME, L., "A Critique of Current Views on Acrocephaly and Related Conditions," *J. ment. sci.*, CVII (1961), 459–74.

DAWSON, S., AND J. C. CONN, "Effects of Encephalitis Lethargica on the Intelligence of Children," *Arch. dis. child.*, I (1926), 357–89.

DAYAN, M., "Toilet Training Retarded Children in a State Residential Institution," *Ment. retard.*, II (1964), 116–17.

DEJONG, R. N., "Diseases of the Nervous System," in *Annual Review of Medicine*, ed. D. A. Rytard and W. P. Greger, Palo Alto, Calif.: Annual Reviews, Inc., 1959.

DINGMAN, H. F., AND G. TARJAN, "Mental Retardation and the Normal Probability Distribution Curve," *Amer. j. ment. defic.*, LXIV (1960), 991–94.

DUNN, L. M., *Exceptional Children in the Schools.* New York: Holt, Rinehart & Winston, Inc., 1963.

ELLIS, N. R., "Amount of Reward and Operant Behavior in Mental Defectives," *Amer. j. ment. defic.*, LXVI (1962), 595–99.

——, "Toilet Training the Severely Defective Patient: An S-R Reinforcemnet Analysis," *Amer. j. ment. defic.*, LXVIII (1963), 98–103.

ELVIDGE, A. E., C. L. BRANCH, AND G. B. THOMPSON, "Observations in a Case of Hydrocephalus Treated with Diamox," *J. neurosurg.*, XIV (1957), 628–39.

FIERRO, B., R. W. PENAFIEL, L. J. DEGROAT, AND I. RAMIREZ, "Endemic Goiter and Endemic Cretinism in the Andean Region," *New England j. med.*, CCLXXX, No. 6 (1969), 296–302.

GIBSON, D., L. POZONY, AND D. E. ZARFAS, "Dimensions of Mongolism: II. The Interaction of Clinical Indices," *Amer. j. ment. defic.*, LXVIII (1964), 503–10.

——, AND J. POZSONJI, "Morphological and Behavioral Consequences of Chromosome Subtype in Mongolism," *Amer. j. ment. defic.*, LXIV (1965), 801–4.

GOLDSTEIN, H., "Population Trends in the U.S. Public Institutions for the Mentally Deficient," *Amer. j. ment. defic.*, LXIII (1958), 599–607.

HOLT, K. S., AND V. P. COFFEY, Eds., *Some Recent Advances in Inborn Errors of Metabolism.* London: E. and S. Livingstone, 1968.

HORSTMANN, P., "Dwarfism: Clinical Investigation with Special Reference to the Significance of Endocrine Factors," *Acta endoc.* (1949), Suppl. 53.

HSIA, D. Y., R. S. PAINE, AND K. W. DRISCOLL, "Phenylketonuria," *J. ment. defic. res.,* I (1957), 53.

ITARD, J. M., *The Wild Boy of Aveyron,* Trans. George and Muriel Humphrey. New York: Appleton-Century-Crofts, 1932. Orig. publ. 1894.

JARVIK, L. F., A. FALEK, AND W. P. PIERSON, "Down's Syndrome (Mongolism): The Heritable Aspects," *Psychol. bull.,* LXI (1964), 388–98.

KIRK, S. A., *Public School Provisions for Severely Mentally Retarded Children.* Albany, N.Y.: New York Interdepartmental Health Resources Board, 1957.

KIRMAN, B. H., et al., "Familial Pitressin-resistant Diabetes Insipidus with Mental Defect," *Arch. dis. child.,* XXXI (1956), 59–61.

KNOBLOCK, H., AND B. PASAMANICK, "The Developmental Behavioral Approach to the Neurological Examination in Infancy," *Child devel.,* XXXIII (1962), 181–98.

LAWSON, D., "On the Prognosis in Cretinism," *Arch. dis. child.,* XXX (1955), 75.

LILIENFELD, A. M., *Epidemiology of Mongolism.* Baltimore, Md.: Johns Hopkins Press, 1969.

LUBS, H. A., AND F. H. RUDDLE, "Chromosomal Abnormalities in the Human Population," *Science,* CLXXIX (1970), 495–97.

LURIE, L. A., et al., "Late Results Noted in Children Presenting Post-encephalitic Behavior: A Follow-up Study of Fifty Cases," *Amer. j. psychiat.,* XCV (1937), 171–79.

MCCLURE, H. M., K. H. BELDEN, AND W. A. PIEPER, "Autosomal Trisomy in a Chimpanzee: Resemblance to Down's Syndrome," *Science,* CLXV (1969), 1010–11.

MCDONALD, W. B., "Congenital Pitressin-resistant Diabetes Insipidus of Venal Origin," *Pediatrics,* XV (1955), 298.

MCINTIRE, M. S., F. J. MENOLASCINO, AND J. H. WILEY, "Mongolism: Some Clinical Aspects," *Amer. j. ment. defic.,* LXIX (1965), 794–800.

MARTIN, H. P., "Microcephaly and Mental Retardation," *Amer. j. dis. child.,* CXIX (1970), 128–31.

MATSON, D. D., "Current Treatment of Infantile Hydrocephalus," *New England j. med.,* CCXXV (1956), 933–36.

MENKES, J. H., "The Pathogenesis of Mental Retardation in Phenylketonuria and Other Inborn Errors of Amino-Acid Metabolism," *Pediatrics,* XXXIX (1967), 297–308.

MENOLASCINO, F. J., "Psychiatric Aspect of Mongolism," *Amer. j. ment. defic.,* LXIX (1965), 653–60.

MURPHY, D. P., *Congenital Malformation* (2nd ed.). Philadelphia, Pa.: University of Pennsylvania Press, 1947.

O'CONNOR, N., AND J. TIZARD, *The Social Problem of Mental Deficiency.* New York: Pergamon Press, 1956.

PATRIC, A. D., "Maple Syrup Urine Disease," *Arch. dis. child.,* XXXVI (1961), 269.

PENROSE, L. S., "Genetics of Anencephaly," *J. ment. defic. res.,* I (1957), 4–15.

———, *The Biology of Mental Defect* (3rd ed.). New York: Grune & Stratton, Inc., 1963.

PINTNER, R., J. EISENSON, AND N. STANTON, *The Psychology of the Physically Handicapped*. New York: Appleton-Century-Crofts, 1940.

PLUMMER, G., "Anomalies Occurring in Children Exposed *in Utero* to the Atomic Bomb in Hiroshima," *Pediatrics*, X (1952), 687–93.

ROBINSON, H. B., AND N. M. ROBINSON, *The Mentally Retarded Child*. New York: McGraw-Hill Book Company, 1965.

ROOS, P., "Development of an Intensive Habit-training Unit at Austin State School," *Ment. retard.*, III (1965), 12–15.

RUNDLE, A. T., "Etiological Factors in Mental Retardation: 1. Biochemical," *Amer. j. ment. defic.*, LXVII (1964), 61–68.

SCHEERENBERGER, R. C., "The Current Census of State Institutions for the Mentally Retarded," *Ment. retard.*, III (1965), 4–6.

SCHEINBERG, I. H., AND D. GITLIN, "Deficiency of Ceruloplasim in Patients with Hepatolenticular Degeneration (Wilson's Disease)," *Science*, CXVI (1952), 484–85.

SIMPSON, J. A., "The Neurological Manifestations of Idiopathic Hypothyroidism," *Brain*, LXXV (1952), 76–78.

SMITH, A., "Maternal Age in Mongolism," *Lancet*, I (1960), 875.

SMITH, D. W., R. M. BLIZZARD, AND L. WILKINS, "The Mental Prognosis in Hypothyroidism of Infancy and Childhood," *Pediatrics*, XIX (1957), 1011–20.

STANBURG, J. B., *The Metabolic Basis of Inherited Disease*. New York: McGraw-Hill Book Company, 1960.

STEMLICHT, M., AND Z. W. WANDEVER, "Nature of Institutionalized Adult Mongoloid Intelligence," *Amer. j. ment. defic.*, LXVI (1962), 301–2.

TOBIAS, J., AND J. GORELICK, "Work Characteristics of Adults at Trainable Level," *Ment. retard.*, I (1963), 338–44.

WALLIN, J. E., *Children with Mental and Physical Handicaps*. Englewood Cliffs, N.J.: Prentice-Hall, Inc., 1949.

WESSELHOEFT, C., "Rubella (German Measles) and Congenital Deformities," *New England j. med.*, CCXL (1949), 258–61.

WUNSCH, W. L., "Some Characteristics of Mongoloids Evaluated at a Clinic for Children with Retarded Mental Development," *Amer. j. ment. defic.*, LXII (1957), 122–30.

10

Learning Disabilities

Historical Origins

THE STRAUSSIAN LEGACY

The category of learning disabilities as known today has developed out of the concept of the "brain-damaged child" formulated by Alfred A. Strauss and Heinz Werner while they were associated for more than a decade at a Michigan institution then known as the Wayne County Training School. Heinz Werner, a developmental and comparative psychologist, and Alfred A. Strauss, neuropsychiatrist, both refugees from Nazi Germany, worked together at this school for approximately thirteen years studying the impact of brain injury on the behavior and psychological development of children.

During this period a number of young psychologists and educators including Newell Kephart, Ruth Melcher Patterson, William Cruickshank, Charlotte Philleo, and Samuel A. Kirk worked in various capacities at Wayne County Training School and became interested in the problems of the brain-injured child. Of this group, Kephart and Cruickshank have most directly perpetuated the work of Werner and Strauss. Most other workers in the area of learning disabilities have, knowingly or unknowingly, borrowed from these pioneers. Werner and Strauss, of course, drew upon the work and concepts of their predecessors. They acknowledge their indebtedness to Itard's and Sequin's early work with the mentally retarded. They also borrowed more directly from the earlier work of Kurt Goldstein with brain-injured adults.

GOLDSTEIN'S CONTRIBUTIONS

Goldstein (1939), a neurologist, drawing on his experience principally with brain-injured veterans of World War I, advanced the notion that cortical injury, particularly when it involved the frontal lobes, resulted in marked changes in personality, and in cognitive and behavioral functioning. The primary deficit stressed by Goldstein was loss of abstract concepts. This deficit resulted in concretistic thinking accompanied by an inability to abstract and generalize from experience, an inability to plan ahead, a deficit in symbolic thought, and in the more extreme cases, generalized linguistic disabilities. Goldstein described the acute emotional upsets which his patients showed as reactions to apparently trivial stresses such as changes in the physical arrangements of their wards or in modifications of the daily routines. These reactions were seen as indications of the patient's need for a well-structured, highly predictable environment. A complex and constantly changing environment required a degree of flexible planning and anticipation and the invoking of higher and more abstract ideational processes, and of this they were not capable (Goldstein, 1939). Many of the characteristics of the "Strauss syndrome" which eventually were incorporated into the category of learning disabilities were identified by Goldstein.

EARLY WORK ON DYSLEXIA AND APHASIA

Strauss paid relatively little attention to linguistic defects in his characterizations of the brain-injured child. However, the professional literature in the fields of speech, hearing, and neurology had for a long time associated certain linguistic and other types of symbolic representational-impairment with brain injury. An impressive list of formidable-sounding terms had been coined to refer to a wide variety of linguistic defects associated with brain injury. These included aphasia and dyslexia. Aphasia refers to an impairment of language functions due to brain injury. Aphasias were subdivided into sensory or reception aphasia when the disorder involved the understanding of the written or spoken word, expressive or motor when the disability centered on the speaking or writing functions, and semantic aphasia when the loss involved the finer meaning components of language (Ewing, 1930). Dyslexia refers to a neurogenic reading disability. The symptoms of dyslexia, in addition to the defining inabilities to read, include difficulties in writing and spelling, memory disorders, inadequate auditory and visual imagery, deviant motor behavior patterns, and other signs of neurological disturbances (Orton, 1937; Mykelbust and Johnson, 1962).

Orton, the pioneer in the area of dyslexia, believed that the study of language losses in brain-damaged adults disclosed the neurological pattern by which reading and other language functions are governed. Orton concluded that linguistic and reading disorders could result from disturbances of cerebral *function* as well as from the destruction of cerebral tissue. He believed that the most severe cortical damage would result in *cortical blindness* in which there was no conscious vision although the subcortical optic neural mechanism was unimpaired. Less severe damage could produce *mind blindness* in which the patient could see objects but was unable to recall their use. With still less cortical damage, *word blindness* could occur in which only the printed or spoken word had no meaning. This latter category constitutes sensory aphasia according to the more conventional terminology.

Although Orton's studies began with the reading problems of children, his interest expanded to special writing disabilities (agraphia), developmental "word deafness," delayed speech (motor aphasia), childhood stuttering, generalized motor discoordination (developmental apraxia) and various combinations of these syndromes.

Orton's book was written in 1937, and he has been dead since 1948. However his descriptions of children's linguistic problems and the techniques he proposed for their remediation still serve as the basis for much that is current. He also contributed significantly to the legacy of the organic basis of specific behavioral, linguistic, and cognitive malfunctioning. While the direct antecedents of the category of learning disabilities are the contributions of Werner and Strauss, the notion that specific educational and particularly linguistic handicaps were neurogenic was found in these earlier works on aphasia by Ewing, and dyslexia by Orton in the 1930s.

BEHAVIORAL TESTS FOR THE IDENTIFICATION OF THE NEUROLOGICALLY IMPAIRED

Strauss and others characterized the behavior patterns of the brain-damaged child and suggested that when the behavior of a given child *resembled that of diagnosed neurologically impaired children*, the child can be presumed to be brain-damaged even though his medical history is negative and no positive neurological signs are present. Such a proposal opened the way for the development of purely behavioral tests for the identification of children of this type.

Goldstein and Scheerer (1941) developed a battery of tests for the identification of the conceptual deficits of the brain-injured individual. A series of studies started by Halstead in the 1930s culminated in the development of a battery of tests consisting of twenty-seven behavioral indicators of brain damage (Halstead, 1947). Neither of these test batteries came into general use but they did contribute to the conviction that it was possible to identify the brain-injured individual by means of behavioral data. It remained for Bender (1938, 1946) to make available a simple and easily administered test which, while not claiming to be limited in purpose to the identification of the neurologically impaired, came to be used predominantly for this purpose. The Bender-Gestalt test made use of nine designs previously developed by Wertheimer (1923) to demonstrate the principles of Gestalt psychology involved in perception. Bender postulated that the perception and reproduction of the Gestalt figures are determined by organic factors dependent on the growth patterns and maturational level of the individual and his neurological impairment either functionally or organically induced.

These tests were important in themselves but they also significantly contributed to the notion that the neurologically impaired constituted a fairly distinct category of people with differentiating behavioral characteristics. The existence of such tests also indicated that brain-damaged individuals can be differentiated from "normals." The educational program described by Strauss and Lehtinen (1947) was specifically designed to remedy the perceptual, cognitive, and behavioral limitations of this category of handicapped children. The brain-injured child thus became, even under its original exponents, a broad elastic category including children with neurological impairment demonstrated by positive neurological signs as well as those with perceptual and conceptual difficulties with no evidence of brain damage but which were assumed to be the result of a postulated neural impairment. The reasoning behind these assumptions seemed to go as follows: since some children with brain injury show certain perceptual, cognitive, and behavioral characteristics, those children with these same characteristics can be assumed to be brain-damaged.

The Divorcement of the Category of Learning Disabilities from Etiology

Skeptics have long insisted that children with functional emotional disturbances display many of the components of the Strauss syndrome. More recently, a large number of "culturally disadvantaged" children have also been shown to have deficiencies in perceptual discrimination, concept formation, and sustained attention and are hyperactive and emotionally labile, much like the diagnosed brain-damaged. Critics have argued quite convincingly that these behavioral symptoms do not necessarily indicate central nervous system damage.

Many people today believe that there will be no loss if the concept of presumed neurological impairment as an intervening variable is dropped and each child's particular perceptual, cognitive, and motor deficits and assets are described or defined so that appropriate psychoeducational programming can be developed for him. Irrespective of etiology, the critical problem is to determine the individual's areas of relative strength and handicap and then to capitalize on the strengths and either remove, diminish, or circumvent the deficits so that the child's intellectual and behavioral functioning may reach the optimal practical level.

The Sudden Popularity of the Concept

Prior to the 1960s the term learning disabilities, if used at all in special education, referred in a generic way to all children who were educationally handicapped for whatever reason. In the early 1960s the term began appearing with regularity largely as a substitute for *minimally brain-injured*. Within a few years the acceptance of the term *learning disabilities* by people in the field of special education was widespread. In the early '60s the term *learning disorders* competed with learning disabilities for acceptance. In 1965 Hellmuth (1965) published *Learning Disorders*, Volume One. The following year the *Review of Educational Research* for the first time reviewed the topic of *Learning Disorders* (Bateman, 1966). The 1969 review of the same area is titled "Learning Disabilities" (Kass, 1969). At the 1965 annual convention of the Council for Exceptional Children the topic of learning disabilities was second only to mental retardation in the number of sessions and papers dealing with the topic. The entire December, 1964 issue of *Exceptional Children* was devoted to the topic of learning disabilities. In 1965 when the local and state organizations of parents of minimally brain-damaged children formed a national organization they adopted the name, "National Association for Children with Learning Disabilities," and by 1969 had over 200 local and state affiliates (McCarthy, 1969). In 1968 the first issue of the *Journal of Learning Disabilities* appeared.

Legal Recognition of the Category

Early in the decade the state legislatures began recognizing the category and started providing additional financial aid for programs so designated. California began providing such state aid in 1963. The designation used for the programs in that state is *Educationally Handicapped* (E.H.). What happened in California is probably typical of what happened elsewhere. The California Association for Neurologically Handicapped Children, consisting largely of the parents of minimally brain-damaged children, sponsored and obtained passage of a bill in the state legislature providing special state aid for the establishment of special classes for such children. A 1968 national survey of programs for children with learning disabilities found that over half of the programs were started largely as the results of the activities of parent pressure groups (Clark and Richards, 1968). Since the differentiation between the neurologically handicapped and the emotionally disturbed is not easily made the authorized programs for the educationally handicapped in California included both categories. California may be unique in the use of the term *Educationally Handicapped* to refer to this group which, by code, includes both the emotionally disturbed and the neurologically handicapped as etiological categories in the same classes. National legislative recognition for the educational category was first given when HR13310, "The Children with Learning Disability Act of 1969" passed the House of Representatives by a roll call of 350 to zero. The bill provided $6 million for the fiscal year 1971, $12 million for 1972, and $18 million for 1973 to support research, training programs, model centers and demonstration programs in the area. By 1967 it was reported that over 35 states had legislation providing financial assistance to school districts for the development of support of special classes or programs for children described as educationally handicapped, perceptually handicapped, neurologically impaired, minimally brain-damaged, and/or emotionally disturbed (Blom, 1969). All such children are now being encompassed within the category of learning disabilities. By the 1970s no area of special education was receiving as much attention as that of learning disabilities.

Definitions and Delineations

The distinguishing behavioral characteristics of the category of neurologically impaired children described by Strauss as *brain-injured* and who came to be known as the *Strauss-syndrome children* and still later as *children with learning disabilities* were characterized by hyperactivity, distractibility, disinhibition, and perseveration. Educational measures proposed to overcome or compensate for these behavioral disturbances or deficits included spacious rooms to accommodate small groups of children without crowding, bare walls with all extraneous sights eliminated, translucent rather than transparent windows, screens to hide extraneous objects, and sound absorbent walls and ceilings to reduce distracting sounds. Masking screens for printed matter, which permitted only one line of print to be seen at one time, were used, thus reducing the distracting effects from the rest of the page while reading. The significant figures in visual material were darkly outlined to aid in the differentiation of figure and ground in accordance with the principles of Gestalt psychology.

Strauss mentioned the necessity of directed and controlled motor activity to reduce the disinhibition and diffuse hyperactivity. However, it remained for Kephart (1960) and Barsch (1965) to develop educational programs which centered primarily around motor activities. Drill was kept to a minimum because of the tendency of these children to perseverate. The teaching of rhythm was recommended. Speech training was required but should be done by specialists.

The Strauss-Lehtinen program and concepts set the patterns and, with shifts in emphasis, still dominates the thinking and practice in the field. Some programs for the neurologically impaired or Strauss-syndrome child were established during the 1940s and 1950s, but it was not until the next decade, as already indicated, that the concept really came into its own. Several things had developed during these years which made the period of the 1960s propitious for this great surge of interest. One was the enlarging of the category.

THE NEED FOR A NEW CATEGORY

Since the 1940s it has been generally accepted by educators, school psychologists, psychiatrists, and neurologists that there is a group of children of normal or superior intelligence who fail to learn because of neurogenic learning disabilities. These children have been variously characterized as minimally brain-damaged, chronic brain syndrome, minimal brain dysfunction, or psychoneurological learning disabilities. However, paralleling these organically oriented designations there has been a corresponding set of *behavioral* terms used to identify these groups of children. Dyslexia (marked impairment of the ability to read), dysgraphia (inability to express ideas in written form) and perceptual handicap, difficulties in figure-ground differentiation, letter and number reversals in reading and writing (poor form recognition) are behavioral syndromes presumably associated with cerebral dysfunctioning. Although originally the correlation of behavior syndromes and neural impairments was assumed, the evidence supporting this assumption was always tenuous. It soon became clear that: (a) Many children with known brain damage do not exhibit the patterns of behavior presumably characteristic of the brain-damaged child. (b) Many children exhibiting these behavior patterns do not show independent signs of neurological impairment. (c) Most of the behavior characteristics ascribed to the brain-damaged are common manifestations of emotional and presumably functional psychiatric disorders so these behavior syndromes can arise from *either* functional or organic causes. (d) Attaching the qualifying adjective "minimal" to the term "brain damage" does not increase the appropriateness of the organically oriented designation. (e) There is little to be gained by postulating the existence of nondemonstrable neurological impairment to account for the observed behavioral deficits.

In the early 1960s the term "learning disabilities" began to appear regularly as a substitute for "brain injured." This term referred to behavior rather than to etiology. Although the new term still carried the implications of brain damage, it seemed more logical to call children who displayed symptoms similar to those with certain neurological impairments learning-disabled rather than brain-damaged. Although originally the term learning disability became the educational alternative to the etiological category of minimal brain dysfunction, there is an increasing tendency to divorce it from etiology and define it entirely in behavioral and educational terms.

DEFINITIONS

This progressive divorcement of the term from etiology is typified in the following sequence of definitions of *learning disabilities*: "Children of near average, average, or above average general intelligence with learning and/or certain behavioral abnormalities ranging from mild to severe, which are associated with deviant function of the central nervous system" (Clements, 1966). ". . . a disorder . . . in one or more of the processes of speech, language, reading, writing, arithmetic, or other school subject resulting from a psychological handicap caused by a possible cerebral dysfunction and/or emotional or behavioral disturbances" (Kirk and Bateman, 1962). ". . . a specific retardation or disorder in one or more of the processes of speech, language perception, behavior, reading, spelling, writing or arithmetic" (Kirk, 1968). These definitions indicate that the deficits mentioned above called "learning disabilities" are not the result of mental retardation, sensory deprivation, or motor handicaps.

We believe that the term learning disability will be maximally useful if used to refer to a marked discrepancy between the child's apparent potential and his performance level as he is engaged in essential learning processes. This is essentially the Kirk (1968) definition. The learning disability itself is not caused primarily by low mental level, emotional disturbance or sensory-motor defects. It is possible for a child with a learning disability *also* to have defective vision or hearing, to be emotionally disturbed or mentally retarded, but the discrepancy still exists when these handicaps are taken into consideration. This is essentially the use recommended by Bannatyne (1968), Haring and Ridgway (1967), Kass (1969), and Kirk (1968).

Except for the exclusionary provisions, such a concept is divorced from etiology and is characterized solely by a significant educational discrepancy between the individual's capacity for learning and his actual functional level. Such a definition will include a sizable group of children in need of special assistance who have previously been denied such help because they failed to meet the specifications of the older conventional categories of exceptional individuals eligible for special aid.

TAKING CARE OF ONE CATEGORY OF "LEFT-OVER" CHILDREN

Educators, psychologists, psychiatrists, and pediatricians, as well as parents, have recognized for a long time that there is a group of children of average or above average intelligence who fail to actualize their potential in school learning. Such children have been a source of puzzlement and frustration to all concerned. They all demonstrate a failure to learn despite apparently adequate intellectual abilities, sensory acuity, and educational opportunities. These are the children who are referred from service to service and from agency to agency in the hope of finding a conventional category for special educational or rehabilitative service where they "fit" and can receive help. The psychologist finds that they are not mentally retarded, the psychiatrist can find no evidence of emotional blockings or other serious disturbance, the neurologist finds no evidence of neural impairment, the internist's findings are "negative," and the child is handed back to the regular classroom teachers and/or parents with the admonition, "I guess it is your problem." One reason for the tremendous popularity of the category learning disabilities is that a large number of people were waiting in the wings who were eligible and anxious to take advantage of the help that such an additional service offered. It promised to reduce the total number of "left-over" children in need of special help.

The Educational Appeal of the Term

Another reason for the popularity of the term and concept of learning disabilities derives from the implications of the term itself. The term and category are educationally oriented. Most of the conventional groupings of children for rehabilitative and special educational purposes have derived from medical and psychological rather than from primarily educational sources. For the most part, quantitative medical, psychological, and legal definitions and criteria have been used in defining and establishing eligibility requirements for educational services. In many cases these criteria and definitions are not maximally useful for identifying educational needs. This often results in interpreting eligibility criteria loosely or strictly and otherwise stretching or redefining terms to make them educationally relevant. This means that many children may be legally and administratively eligible for programs which they do not need while others more in need of the special services are deprived of them because they do not fit the category and are therefore ineligible.

If the category of learning disabilities can be divorced from etiology, it frees special education from being limited by the "medical model" which is probably no more appropriate for special education than it is for mental health.

The term *learning disability* implies diagnosis that is primarily educational and remediation that is teacher-learner oriented. The term also suggests a program of positive action, appropriate teaching. It does not suggest an inherent and largely static condition as the term *mental retardation* does. The name contains a plea for good teaching based on the child's specific needs.

The term is relatively nonstigmatizing and designates a specific deficit in children who are essentially normal and focuses attention on identifying the child's specific needs and applying appropriate remedial procedures rather than becoming excessively concerned with etiology and proper labelling.

Because the same people are intimately involved in both processes, identification and classification will be more closely tied to the corrective, remedial, educative process. An ongoing study and analysis of the child's classroom behavior and his assets and deficits in learning are crucial in the identification of and his response to remedial procedures. Rehabilitative efforts become a part of a continuous diagnostic, evaluative, process. Diagnosis is concerned with identifying the areas of educational deficit, and response to the proposed educational procedures becomes an integral part of the diagnostic and classifying procedures.

Although the concept and category of learning disabilities will not break down the rigid and artificial barriers between the categories of exceptional individuals for whom special services are provided, nor will they entirely divorce special education from its medical and psychological roots and its excessive concern with formal diagnosis and defining etiologies, it does constitute a major step in this direction. The broad category of learning disabilities will assist in providing a full circle of services for all who need it. It constitutes a move in the direction of providing a comprehensive, integrated program extending over the entire range of deviants in need of special services and covering the entire age range.

Educational Programs for Children with Learning Disabilities

The training and educational techniques involved and the rationale for most of the programs designed for children with learning disabilities are either derived or extrapolated from Strauss and Lehtinen (1947)(McCarthy and McCarthy, 1969). The programs are specifically designed to remedy or diminish the behavioral deficits arising from the characteristics of such children presumed to be caused by their postulated, but often nondemonstrable, neural impairment. Breaking down and adding to the original list of the behavioral characteristics provided by Strauss, workers and writers in the field have listed almost a hundred specific behaviors. McCarthy and McCarthy (1969) list the eight most frequently cited.

1. Hyperactivity
2. Perceptual-motor deficits
3. Emotional lability
4. General orientation and laterality defects
5. Disorders of attention such as distractibility and short attention span
6. Impulsivity
7. Disorders of memory and conceptual thinking
8. Specific learning defects, particularly language deficits

These are the behavioral deficits we associate today with learning disabilities. Strauss and Lehtinen (1947) wrote separate chapters on the pathologies of perception, language, concept formation, and behavior and related these deficits to educational or training techniques designed to remedy them.

THE STRAUSS-LEHTINEN-CRUICKSHANK PERCEPTUAL-MOTOR PROGRAM

We have already indicated that the Strauss-Lehtinen conceptualization of the brain-damaged child and their development of a program of education for these children provided the basis for the programs associated today with learning disabilities. Most of the programs in existence today have been largely refinements of this program or of particular components of this program.

Cruickshank, one of the original group of workers with Werner and Strauss, has written extensively and developed a program of his own which largely follows the Strauss-Lehtinen proposals. Cruickshank (1961,

1967) emphasizes that individuation of instruction is essential to an appropriate educational program. This requires a small teacher-student ratio. Even with a relatively homogeneous group a full-time teacher and teacher's aid should have no more than eight children. The major element which must be incorporated into the educational programs for brain-injured children is "structure," and many of the details of methods consist of ways in which structure can be utilized in the training and education of the child. The various components of structure identified by Cruickshank are: (*a*) relationship structure; (*b*) environmental structure; (*c*) program structure; and (*d*) structured teaching material. Motor training is also an essential part of the program.

Relationship structure.   Relationship structure refers to the personal relationship between teacher and child. A satisfactory relationship requires that the teacher understand the child sufficiently well to deal with him in ways that will maximally aid in his development. Properly structured personal relationships are the basis from which all other structuring emanates. If this relationship is satisfactory the child eventually identifies with his teacher, internalizes his goals, and strives to live up to his expectations. Cruickshank believes that this can best be achieved in a structured teaching situation—an adult-dominated teaching situation. Such a situation is not dominated in the sense of constricted but dominated in terms of carefully planned procedures based on the unique needs and nature of the individual child. The adult is the most significant element in the entire concept of structure and too much emphasis cannot be placed in the nature of this personal relationship. Essential elements incorporated into this child-teacher relationship are: (*a*) The setting of limitations for appropriate behavior. The child must know just what is and what is not acceptable behavior. (*b*) Within these limitations the teacher must accept the child and his behavior at all times in terms of the meaning of the situation to the child. (*c*) The final essential is that of consistency of attitude and behavior on the part of the teacher.

Environmental Structure.   The classroom must be a nonstimulating or nondistracting environment. This is achieved by removing as much visually and auditorily distracting stimuli as possible. Walls, woodwork, and furniture are all painted the same color. No bulletin boards or pictures are on the walls. Indirect lighting or translucent rather than transparent window glass is used. Wall-to-wall carpeting and sound-treated walls and ceilings are used to reduce extraneous sounds.

Individual cubicles for each child are recommended. The sound-deadened cubicle is large enough to permit the child and the teacher to sit side by side. The cubicle prevents the child from visual distraction by the other children.

Children in such programs should be in a self-contained classroom with their own toilet and lunchroom facilities immediately at hand. The factor of stimuli-reduction is a significant one for the brain-injured child.

Program Structure.   Program structuring is a further attempt to bring order into the child's "life space." It is essential that the child's daily program be simplified and definitely structured so that routines can be anticipated. With the school program sufficiently simplified and precisely structured, the child and teacher can work together comfortably within a context which insures the child of some degree of success. The program structuring extends to such things as the specific ways in which hats, coats, and overshoes are put on, taken off, and stored, ways of signaling the teacher or assistant for help, the routines established for lunch, toilet, and rest activities and all of the other innumerable routines involved in the course of a normal school day.

Structured Teaching Material.   Teaching materials and their use must be adapted to the child's individual characteristics regarding attention-span, perceptual and conceptual limitations, perseverative and disso-ciative tendencies, and motor capacities. Much of the material used by the child will be prepared by the teacher or assistant to meet the child's specific needs. Most of it is expendable. As with all disabled, it is neces-sary to "teach to the disability." Where figure-ground perceptual diffi-culties are present the stimulus value of the perceptual components which require emphasis must be increased by the use of heavy outlining or con-trasting colors. Tasks must be geared to the child's attention span. For example, to minimize the distracting effects of extraneous stimuli, mask-ing screens which expose only one line of print at a time are prescribed, and instead of giving the child a single page with ten arithmetic problems to be done, he is provided ten pages, one at a time, with one problem on each page.

Motor Training.   In addition to the personal relationship and envi-ronmental structuring, motor training is an integral part of the educa-tional program of the brain-injured child. Daily motor training carried out on an individual basis for approximately thirty minutes is prescribed. It is suggested that properly supervised volunteers can be utilized in the motor-training program. It is also recommended that the total educational program include a speech development or correction program carried out by personnel ancillary to the educational program.

THE KEPHART PROGRAM

Newell Kephart (1960) and Cruickshank (1967) have probably most com-pletely perpetuated the work of Werner and Strauss. While Kephart's program is a perceptual-motor one, he, more than Cruickshank, made the motor component the primary focus of treatment and the perceptual component somewhat derivative. His program is also more developmentally organized. Kephart stresses the effects of motor processes on perception and the effects of perception on the higher cognitive processes in a kind of hierarchical relationship. Kephart also emphasizes the need to develop skills in their "natural order." He believes that perceptual-motor deficits are primarily organic in nature and are best remedied by the development of such basic skills as eye-hand coordination, temporal-spatial relationships, and form perception. Kephart relates the effects of perceptual-motor practice to changes in the central nervous system without as much speculating concerning specific brain mechanism as Delacato (1966) has done. The Delacato program is discussed later in this chapter.

On the physiological side, Kephart believes that perceptual and motor processes are inseparably tied to each other because there is always a motor component accompaniment or consequence of perception. Movements are modified and perceptions molded by the visual and kinesthetic feedback involved in these processes.

Kephart provides a number of nonstandardized tests for measuring the child's stage of perceptual-motor development and for evaluating the child's progress in improving these skills. He also provides specific instructions and procedures for the development of form perception, space and form discrimination, ocular control, and general sensorimotor integration. Kephart's program uses chalkboard training, rail walking, balancing, tracing templates, and music. The Straussian heritage is evident in much of Kephart's work with primary emphasis being placed on the motor and developmental aspects.

BARSCH'S "MOVIGENIC" PROGRAM

While the effects of his early work with Strauss are evident, Barsch (1965) seems to have developed some unique techniques and an orientation to learning which is somewhat novel. "Movigenics" (Barsch, 1965) is the study of the origins and development of the movement patterns which are necessary for ideational learning. Barsch's physiologically oriented curriculum is based on an elaborate set of eight major constructs or hypotheses. Interested readers are referred to the original source for the details of constructs. Using these constructs as a theoretical framework, Barsch has developed his movigenic program consisting of a planned sequence of activities by means of which the child explores his world, orients himself in space, and integrates his activities and experiences into progressively more complex patterns and relationships.

A movigenic classroom is quite different from the ordinary one. All furniture is removed to provide maximum open space for activity. Lines on the floor guide the child upon entering and leaving the room, for work at the chalkboard, and for other activities. A strip of carpeting across one end of the room provides a surface for crawling, creeping, and rolling. The children in class are barefooted or in stocking feet.

Although activities are carefully planned, no rigid schedules are followed. A good deal of equipment such as walking and balancing rails, scooter and teeter boards, and tracing templates are used. Visuo-motor practice involving first one eye, then the other, and then both eyes, with the body in various positions is provided. Practice in visual tracking in darkness is a part of the program. Tachistoscopes are used in visual training. Analogous exercises in auditory processes are also included. While one can recognize the possible influences of Itard, Seguin, and Montessori and much that is derived directly from Strauss, many of Barsch's ideas about movement and vision seem novel.

GETMAN'S VISUO-MOTOR EMPHASIS

Whereas Barsch emphasized visual and general motor training about equally, Getman and his associates (1964, 1965, 1966) have developed a program of visuo-motor training with development of the general motor system as necessary but subsidiary to the former. For Getman, visual perception is the culmination of a developmental motor sequence consisting of seven levels. These levels are suggestive of Delacato's (1966) model to be discussed later. It is necessary to understand all the physiological systems of the body and their developmental sequence if we are really to understand how the child learns. Learning is a process involving the entire body.

The first developmental level of Getman's seven step model is the *Innate Response System*. This is primarily a reflex alerting mechanism, including such things as the light reflex, the grasp reflex, the reciprocal reflexes involved in bilaterality and antagonistic muscular responses, the statokinetic reflexes involved in maintaining postures, and the myotatic reflexes providing muscles with kinesthetic guidance. These response systems are species specific and are innate. However, Getman believes the maximum effective relationship between the different reflex systems is established through activity, awareness of movement, and conscious control of movements which are learned.

Getman's second level is that of the *General Motor System*, which includes creeping, crawling, walking, running, and jumping. These activities extend and further develop laterality and provide for the exploration of the child's world.

The third developmental level is that of the *Special Motor Systems*. This level involves the incorporation and elaboration of the systems of the first two levels in more complex patterns. The special motor systems include visual motor combinations such as eye-hand coordinations, foot-hand relationships, and infinite number of postural-hand-foot-gesture-voice combinations.

The fourth level involves predominantly the development of the *Ocular Motor System*. This system includes the coordinate and balanced movements of the two eyes. Other components of the ocular system are eye-fixations, saccadic movements (back and forth movements of the eyes), visual pursuit movements, and eye rotations (moving both eyes in all directions).

The fifth level of Getman's system is that of the *Speech Motor Systems*. This includes the verbal skills of babbling, imitative and original oral speech.

The sixth developmental level is that of the *Visual System*—really visual imagery. This system involves imagery which is cross-sensory in the sense that one can visualize something that he feels. This imagery also involves recall of the events of yesterday and the projection of similar events into the future. This provides the basis for the recognition of past-present-future relationships. At this level perception occurs.

Single perceptual events generate constructs. Relegating individual percepts to appropriate constructs results in *cognition*, the seventh and highest developmental level in Getman's model.

Getman's discussion focuses dominantly on visual perception and the ocular mechanism. The exercises proposed by him and his associates (Getman et al., 1964) include practice in general coordination, balance, eye-hand coordination, eye movements, form recognition and visual memory (visual imagery).

THE DELACATO PROGRAM

The Delacato (1966) approach, like the Getman model, is developmental and physiological but in a more specific and limited sense. Although Delacato's concepts seem to have developed independently of the Strauss formulations, he agrees with their contention that the neurologically impaired retardate displays clinically observable behavioral symptoms which are characteristic of his organic deficits. However, Delacato has developed a much more specific and elaborate theoretical superstructure to rationalize his diagnostic and remediable procedures. His conceptions of both neurological and behavioral growth and function are hierarchical and developmental. According to Delacato, neurological development progresses vertically from the spinal cord, through the medulla, pons, and midbrain to the cerebral cortex. The developmental progression to this level is also found in animals below man in the phylogenetic scale.

However, the normally developed man goes one step beyond that of the lower animals and achieves unilateral cerebral dominance. When this is achieved, the two cerebral hemispheres, while mirroring each other anatomically, have differentiated functionally. Left hemisphere dominant individuals are right-handed, right-footed, and right-eyed. The dominant cerebral hemisphere also controls language. The evolution of man into an ideating, language-oriented human being was the consequence of his development of cortical laterality. Failure to attain this highest level of human neurological development (unilateral cortical dominance), or brain damage which disturbs this functional dominance, manifests in impaired linguistic processes. Aphasia, delayed speech, stuttering, retarded reading, poor spelling and handwriting, and reading which may be within the normal range but below the individual's level of mathematical performance, are in this descending order reflections of corresponding degrees of decreasing neurological impairment of failures of development of cerebral unilateral dominance. Individuals who have normal language development have achieved this uniquely human level of neurological development.

Lack of adequate neurological development at each of the lower (spinal cord, medullary, pontine, brain-stem, or cortical) levels shows a specific syndrome of behavioral deficits. To illustrate: Spinal cord and medullary deficits result in failures to make the normal precreeping and precrawling movements. The remedial procedures recommended for these deficits consist in passively imposing these movements upon the body of the child until he begins making them spontaneously. For example, while one person holds the child's head, another moves the body in undulating fish-like movements.

The inability to execute homolateral crawling movements at an appropriate age (6 months) and "improper" sleep postures are indicative of inadequate neural organization at the pontine level. For this deficit, homolateral "patterning" is administered by putting the child through the appropriate arm and leg movements. When the child is able to execute these movements spontaneously, daily practice in crawling with the stomach in contact with the floor is prescribed. The child is also taught the "proper" sleep posture which consists of the homolateral position, that is, arm and leg on the same side flexed and the head turned toward the flexed limb.

Failures of neurological integration at the midbrain level manifest themselves as deficits in the cross-pattern activities such as making simultaneous opposite arm and leg movements in creeping. These behavioral defects are treated similarly by imposing the appropriate patterning movements on the child.

Bilateral cortical deficits manifest themselves in the child's failure to develop cross-pattern walking (what other kind is there?). Play exercises involving the large muscles of the body and practice in walking are recommended to remedy this defect.

Failures to develop consistent laterality and "confused" laterality indicate a failure in the deveopment of unilateral cortical dominance. The accompanying symptoms include a long list of linguistic deficiencies; the particular ones found depend on the degree of the lack of cortical dominance of one side of the brain.

According to Delacato, the ontogenetic development of each individual recapitulates the phylogenetic evolutionary development of man. This recapitulation of the evolutionary development begins at conception and normally is complete at six and one-half years of age. The orderly development of neural controls in humans progresses, as indicated, from the spinal cord up to the cerebral cortex and parallels the evolutionary origins of their structures. Adequate development of all lower levels is a prerequisite to the functioning of higher levels and normal behavior requires that each higher level dominate and supersede all those below it. Any obstruction to this ontogenetic recapitulation arrests behavioral development and prevents the development of the higher functions. The recommended procedures are designed to bring about this neurological organization and when this is accomplished the behavioral deficits disappear.

In addition to the "patterning" activities which are unique to the Delacato model, the entire training schedule includes much that is found in the other programs proposed for educationally handicapped children. These recommended procedures include creeping and crawling, walking and trampoline jumping, training in visual and auditory discrimination and perception, reading aloud to the child, encouraging talking, and play activities involving the large muscles.

THE MARIANNE FROSTIG VISUAL PERCEPTION APPROACH

Marianne Frostig has published a test of visual perception (1961), has developed a specific remedial program for the perceptually handicapped (1964), and directs the Frostig Center of Educational Therapy for children with learning disabilities. The test is designed to differentiate the various kinds of visual-perceptual disabilities and to serve as the basis for specific remedial programs. It is a paper and pencil test designed to assess five areas of visual perception: eye-motor coordination, figure-ground, constancy of shape, position in shape, and spatial relationships.

The perceptual training materials developed by Frostig are designed to ameliorate the specific disabilities disclosed by the tests and to provide readiness training in the perceptual abilities normally developed prior to school entrance.

THE FITZHUGH PROGRAM

Kathleen and Loren Fitzhugh (1966) have produced a series of eight workbooks consisting of exercises designed as a remedial or readiness program. The program covers visual-perceptual problems in two workbooks and language and numbers in the remaining five. The workbooks are essentially self-teaching. The visual-perception exercises deal principally with spatial organization and attempt to increase the child's ability to perceive and manipulate shapes and objects in time and space.

The five language and number workbooks are designed to improve the child's ability to identify letters, numbers, words, and pictures. They also are intended to increase the child's understanding of language symbols and arithmetic operations. The advertisement in the April, 1970 issue of *Exceptional Children* indicates that the revision of the program consists of nine instruction workbooks. The authors have not seen the revised program.

SOME GENERAL DIAGNOSTIC-REMEDIAL APPROACHES

In the 1890s Lightner Witmer at the University of Pennsylvania and Grace Fernald in the Clinic School at the University of California at Los Angeles were treating educationally handicapped children in a diagnostic-remedial way.

Witmer's Psycho-Educational Approach. The establishment of the first psychological clinic in the world at the University of Pennsylvania by Witmer in 1896 marked not only the beginning of clinical psychology but also of the diagnostic-remedial approach to problem school children. Each child served by the clinic received an educational program specifically designed for him by an interdisciplinary team in which the teacher was the central figure. Clinical studies were supplemented by classroom observation. Diagnosis was a continuing process growing out of clinical data, classroom experience, and the child's response to treatment. Psychologists, teachers, social workers, and physicians were all involved in the process.

Witmer believed that children with educational problems could not be understood without periods of systematic observations in the school setting during which attempts were made to improve their behavior. Particular emphasis was put on special types of remedial and educative efforts. Much of what Witmer wrote in the journal, *The Psychological Clinic*, which he founded and edited, sounds quite modern and many of his procedures are applicable to the child today designated as having learning disabilities. Like many present-day workers, Witmer was quite interested in the physical and neurological aspects of the cases referred to him (Wolman, 1965).

The Fernald Contribution. Grace Fernald, the first psychologist to work in a child guidance clinic, was dealing in a diagnostic-remedial way with children with learning disabilities in the University of California clinic school long before these children were separately categorized (Fernald, 1943). She insisted that all educational difficulties in children of normal or superior intelligence can be removed or compensated for if proper techniques were employed.

Fernald is best known for her kinesthetic method of teaching reading which is still used with children who have failed to learn to read by other methods. The first step in Fernald's method consists in writing in large letters on a card a word chosen by the child. The child then traces the word with his finger while saying it. He repeats the process until he is able to write the word from memory. It is important that the child trace the word with his finger, and have cutaneous contact with the paper while saying the word in a natural way. This procedure combines visual, kinesthetic, cutaneous, and auditory factors. In the next step, the tracing is dropped, and the child merely looks at and says the word. From then on, the method is fairly conventional except that Fernald believes that children should select the words they want to learn and should begin writing and reading with their own stories rather than those adults have written for them.

OTHER DIAGNOSTIC-REMEDIAL APPROACHES

Currently, a large number of pragmatic diagnostic-remedial approaches to the problems of children with learning disabilities are being developed. Some of these are: Otto and McMenemy's (1966) *Corrective and Remedial Teaching,* Peter's (1965) *Prescriptive Teaching,* Valett's (1967a,b) *Psychoeducational Evaluation of Basic Learning Abilities* and *The Remediation of Learning Disabilities,* and Gillingham and Stillman's (1960) *Remedial Training for Children with Specific Disabilities in Reading, Spelling, and Penmanship.* Bateman (1965, 1966) and Wiseman (1965) have described procedures for the diagnosis and remediation of language problems. There is no paucity of pragmatic and theoretical approaches to the problems of children with learning disabilities.

As the field of learning disabilities evolves, the pragmatic general diagnostic-remedial approaches may prove to be the dominant ones. The entire range of children designated as having learning disabilities may prove to be so varied that educational programs stemming from a single orientation may not be applicable to more than a small segment of the total population, For children with perceptual-motor problems and children whose problems verge in that direction, programs with this emphasis will be most appropriate. Matching each child's disability to the appropriate program is technically feasible but does involve many practical problems.

Evaluative Studies

A few studies have been concerned with the claim of Strauss and his co-workers that brain-damaged children do actually learn differently from non-brain-damaged children. Barnett, Ellis, and Pryor (1960) matched brain-damaged and non-brain-damaged children on a variety of variables and compared their learning of six different types of skills in which differences in favor of the neurologically unimpaired group would support the Straussian theory. The brain-damaged children performed less well on two of the learning tasks but no differences were found on the other four. The authors concluded that the proposition that the brain-damaged learn differently from the neurologically unimpaired must be questioned.

Cruse (1961) found no differences in distractibility between brain-injured and ordinarily familial mental retardates of equal mental levels. Cruickshank et al. (1961) and Rost (1967) found that the use of isolation booths during one semester had no measurable effect on the classroom learning of brain-injured children. On the other hand, Levine, Spivak, and Fernald (1962) did find differences in visual discrimination learning between groups of brain-injured, emotionally disturbed, and normal children, favoring the normal and emotionally disturbed. Haring and Phillips (1962) found that a group of emotionally disturbed, but presumably not neurologically damaged children, profited significantly by a program which was structured along the lines recommended by Cruickshank for the brain-damaged. This study provides support for the proposition that the highly structured programs designed for the brain-damaged are useful for children with behavioral characteristics similar to those who are positively identified as brain-injured.

McCormick, Schnobrick, and Footlik (1966) provide some support for the Straussian hypothesis. They compared two equated groups of first-graders, one of which received perceptual-motor exercises systematically for nine weeks with a group which received an equivalent amount of physical education activity. Subsequent testing revealed no significant differences between the means of the reading achievements scores of the two groups. However, a subgroup of underachievers in the perceptual-motor trained group did show significant greater improvement in reading than did those whose achievements were more in keeping with their aptitudes.

The results of studies designed to test the Delacato hypothesis have also been equivocal. Robbins (1966) could find no evidence that a group of children receiving Delacato exercises in creeping and crawling, maintaining specified writing positions, engaging in sidedness and cross- and homolateral patterning activities did any better in reading and arithmetic than did a control group which continued its normal classroom activities or a group which engaged in activities which were the opposite of those recommended by Delacato. Kershner (1968) in a slightly different type of study reports results which tend, in part, to support the Delacato approach. Painter (1966) using changes in pretest and post-test performances rather than extent of learning as the dependent variable found that twenty-one half-hour training sessions involving activities recommended by Barsch (1965) and Kephart (1960) did significantly increase scores on the Goodenough Draw-a-Man Test, the Beery Geometric Form Reproduction Test, the Illinois Test of Psycholinguistic Abilities and a specially constructed sensory-motor performance test. Jessen (1970) found that training with the Frostig visual-perceptual training materials and additional auditory and kinesthetic training significantly improved the reading readiness of kindergartners and the reading skills of first-graders. However, after a two-year interval the perceptually trained children did not have significantly higher reading achievement test scores than comparable children who received no training.

The limited research on the effectiveness of the various programs developed for the children with learning disabilities is inconclusive. A large number of linguistic, perceptual, and motor remedial programs are available to the special educator concerned with the educationally handicapped child. However, there is little in the evaluative studies to guide the practitioner in selecting the most effective one to use. Perhaps children with learning disabilities are too heterogeneous a group for all to be helped by any program that is dominantly linguistic, perceptual, or motor. It is possible that further research and practice should be directed at the problem of matching student needs and appropriate remediation.

Summary

An increasingly large segment of the school's special education population is being designated as "children with learning disabilities." The term was seldom heard before the 1960s, but by the 1970s it was probably receiving more professional attention than any other category of exceptional children. The term "learning disabilities" first appeared as a substitute for brain-injured in the sense in which the term was used by Strauss. The brain-injured, according to Strauss, was a broad and elastic category including children with positive neurological signs and/or a history of neural trauma on the one hand but also applicable to children characterized by purely behavioral, perceptual, and conceptual deficits *similar to* those with demonstrated neural pathology. There is an increasing tendency to divorce the category from etiology entirely and to define it in purely behavioral and educational terms.

Strauss and Lehtinen proposed a specific methodology for the education of the brain-injured child and most subsequent programs developed for children with learning disabilities have been derived, either directly or indirectly, from their proposals. Cruickshank's program follows very closely the original Strauss model and emphasizes the importance of "structure." Kephart developed a more action and developmentally oriented program. Barsch also emphasized the role of movement but put particular stress on the ocular mechanisms. Wepman's program also emphasized both general motor and visual training with the major emphasis on the latter.

The most controversial program is that of Delacato which claims to modify the nervous system directly. Delacato insists that by imposing certain activities on the child the underlying neural mechanisms are altered in predictable ways. Marianne Frostig and the Fitzhughs have developed programs which emphasize visual perception and provide sets of training materials to be used in their proposed educational procedures. Although not historically related to Strauss and his co-workers, there are available several general diagnostic-remedial approaches which are applicable to the remediation of learning disabilities.

References

AREY, L. B., *Developmental Anatomy*. Philadelphia, Pa.: W. B. Saunders Company, 1934.

BANNATYNE, A. "Diagnosing Learning Disabilities and Writing Remedial Prescriptions," *J. learn. disab.*, I (1968), 242–49.

BARNETT, C. D., N. R. ELLIS, AND M. PRYOR, "Learning in Familial and Brain-Injured Defectives," *Amer. j. ment. defic.*, LXIV (1960), 894–97.

BARSCH, R. H., *A Movigenic Curriculum*. Madison, Wisconson: Bureau for Handicapped Children, 1965.

BATEMAN, B., "An Educator's View of a Diagnostic Approach to Learning Disabilities," in *Learning Disorders*, Vol. I, ed. J. Hellmuth, Seattle, Washington: Special Child Publications of the Seattle Segiun School, Inc., 1965.

———, "Learning Disorders," *Rev. educ. res.*, XXXVI (1966), 93–119.

BENDER, L., "A Visual Motor Gestalt Test and Its Clinical Use," *Amer. orthopsychiat. assoc. res. monog.*, No. 3, 1938.

————, *Bender Motor Gestalt Test: Cards and Manual of Instructions.* New York: The American Orthopsychiatric Association, Inc., 1946.

BLOM, G. E., "The Concept 'Perceptually Handicapped': Its Assets and Limitations," *Seminars in psychiat.*, I (1969), 253–61.

CLARK, A. D., AND C. J. RICHARDS, "Learning Disabilities: A National Survey of Existing Public School Programs," *J. spec. educ.*, II (1968), 223–28.

CLEMENTS, S. D., "Learning Disabilities—Who?" in *Special Education: Strategies for Educational Progress.* Washington, D.C.: The Council for Exceptional Children, 1966.

CRUICKSHANK, W. M., "The Education of the Child with Brain Injury," in *Education of Exceptional Children and Youth* (2nd. ed.), W. M. Cruickshank and G. O. Johnson. Englewood Cliffs, N.J.: Prentice-Hall, Inc., 1967.

————, F. A. BENTZEN, F. H. RATZEBURG, AND M. T. TANNHAUSER, *A Teaching Method for Brain-Injured and Hyperactive Children.* Syracuse, N.Y.: Syracuse University Press, 1961.

CRUSE, D. B., "Effects of Distraction upon the Performance of Brain-Injured and Familial Retarded Children," *Amer. j. ment. defic.*, LXVI (1961), 86–90.

DELACATO, C. H., *Neurological Organization and Reading Problems.* Springfield, Ill.: Charles C Thomas, 1966.

EWING, A., *Aphasia in Children.* New York: Oxford University Press, 1930.

FERNALD, G. M., *Remedial Techniques in Basic School Subjects.* New York: McGraw-Hill Book Company, 1943.

FITZHUGH, K. B., AND L. FITZHUGH, *The Fitzhugh Plus Program.* Galien, Mich.: Allied Education Council, 1966.

FROSTIG, M., *Manual for the Marianne Frostig Developmental Test of Visual Perception.* Palo Alto, Calif.: Consulting Psychologists Press, 1961.

————, AND D. HORNE, *The Frostig Program for the Development of Visual Perception.* Chicago, Ill.: Follett Publishing Company, 1964.

GETMAN, G. N., "The Visuomotor Complex in the Acquisition of Learning Skills," in *Learning Disorders*, Vol. I, ed. J. Hellmuth. Seattle, Wash.: Special Child Publications of the Seattle Segiun School, Inc., 1965.

————, *How to Develop Your Child's Intelligence.* Luverne, Minn.: The Announcers Press, 1966.

————, E. R. KANE, M. R. HALGREN, AND G. W. McKEE, *The Physiology of Readiness.* Minneapolis, Minn.: P.A.S.S., Inc., 1964.

GILLINGHAM, A., AND B. STILLMAN, *Remedial Training for Children with Specific Disabilities in Reading, Spelling, and Penmanship.* Cambridge, Mass.: Educators' Publishing Service, 1960.

GOLDSTEIN, K., *The Organism.* New York: American Book Co., 1939.

————, AND M. SCHEERER, "Abstract and Concrete Behavior: An Experimental Study with Special Mental Tests," *Psychol. monog.*, No. 239 (1941), 151.

HALSTEAD, W. C., *Brain and Intelligence.* Chicago, Ill.: University of Chicago Press, 1947.

HARING, N., AND E. L. PHILLIPS, *Educating Emotionally Disturbed Children*. New York: McGraw-Hill Book Company, 1962.

HARING N. G., AND R. W. RIDGEWAY, "Early Identification of Children with Learning Disabilities," *Except. Child.*, XXXIII (1967), 387–92.

HECKLEMAN, R. G., "A Neurological-Inpress Method of Remedial Reading Instruction," *Acad. ther.*, IV (1969), 277–82.

HELLMUTH, J., ed., *Learning Disorders*, Vol. I. Seattle, Wash.: Special Child Publications, 1965.

JESSEN, M. S., "Reflections on Research Related to Reading Readiness," *J. Calif. state fed. coun. for except. child.*, XIX (1970), 19–21.

JOHNSON, D. J., AND H. R. MYKLEBUST, *Learning Disabilities: Educational Principles and Practices*. New York: Grune and Stratton, 1967.

KASS, C. E., "Learning Disabilities," *Rev. of educ. res.*, XXXIX (1969), 71–82.

KEPHART, N. C., *The Slow Learner in the Classroom*. Columbus, O.: Charles E. Merrill Books, Inc., 1960.

KERSHNER, J. R., "Doman-Delacato's Theory of Neurological Organization Applied with Retarded Children," *Except. child.*, XXXIV (1968), 441–45.

KIRK, S. A., "The Illinois Test of Psycholinguistic Abilities: Its Origin and Implications," in *Learning Disorders*, Vol. 3, ed. J. Hellmuth. Seattle, Wash.: Special Publications of the Seattle Segiun School, Inc., 1968.

———, AND J. J. McCARTHY, *Illinois Test of Psycholinguistic Abilities*. Urbana, Ill.: University of Illinois Press, 1961.

———, AND B. BATEMAN, "Diagnosis and Remediation of Learning Disabilities," *Except. child.*, XXIX (1962), 73–75.

KRUSH, T. P., "The Search for the Golden Key," *Bull. of the Menninger Clinic*, XXVIII (1964), 77–82.

LEVINE, M., G. SPIVAK, AND D. FERNALD, "Discrimination in Diffuse Brain Damage," *Amer. j. ment. defic.*, LXVII (1962), 287–91.

MASLOW, P., M. FROSTIG, W. LEFEVER, AND J. R. B. WHITTLESEY, "The Marianne Frostig Developmental Test of Visual Perception," *Percept. motor skills monog. suppl. II*, XIX (1964), 463–99.

McCARTHY, J. J., AND J. F. McCARTHY, *Learning Disabilities*. Boston: Allyn and Bacon, Inc., 1969.

McCARTHY, J. M., "Learning Disabilities: Where have we been? Where are we going?" *Sem. in psychiat.*, I (1969), 354–61.

McCORMICK, D. D., J. N. SCHNOBRICK, AND S. W. FOOTLIK, *The Effects of Perceptual Motor Training in Reading Achievement*. Chicago, Ill.: Reading Research Foundation, 1966. Mimeographed.

MYKLEBUST, H. R., AND D. JOHNSON, "Dyslexia in Children," *Except. child.*, XXIX (1962), 14–25.

ORTON, S. T., *Reading, Writing, and Speech Problems in Children*. London: Chapman and Hall, 1937.

OTTO, W., AND R. McMENEMY, *Corrective and Remedial Teaching*. Boston: Houghton Mifflin, Co., 1966.

PAINTER, G., "The Effect of a Rhythmic and Sensory Motor Activity Program on Perceptual Motor Spatial Abilities of Kindergarten Children," *Except. child.*, XXXIII (1966), 113–16.

PETER, L. J., *Prescriptive Teaching*. New York: McGraw-Hill Book Company, 1965.

ROBBINS, M. P., "A Study of the Validity of Delacato's Theory of Neurological Organization," *Except. child.*, XXXII (1966), 517–22.

ROST, K. J., "Academic Achievement of Brain-Injured and Hyperactive Children in Isolation," *Except. child.*, XXVIII (1967), 103–07.

STRAUSS, A. A., AND L. LEHTINEN, *Psychopathology and Education of the Brain-Injured Child*. New York: Grune and Stratton, 1947.

VALETT, R. E., *The Remediation of Learning Disabilities*. Palo Alto, Calif.: Fearon Publishers, 1967. (a)

———, *Psychoeducational Evaluation of Basic Learning Abilities*. Palo Alto, Calif.: Fearon Publishers, 1967. (b)

WERTHEIMER, K. N., "Studies in the Theory of Gestalt Psychology," *Psychol. forsch.*, IV (1923), 230–41.

WISEMAN, D., "A Classroom Procedure for Identifying and Remediating Language Problems," *Ment. retard.*, III (1965), 21–25.

WITMER, L., "Clinical Psychology," *Psychol. clin.*, I (1907), 1–9.

WOLFENSBERGER, W., "Diagnosis Diagnosed," *J. ment. subnorm.*, XI, Part 2 (1965), 62–70. (a)

———, "General Observations on European Programs," *Ment. retar.*, III (1965), 8–11. (b)

WOLMAN, B. B., "Clinical Psychology and the Philosophy of Science," in *Handbook of Clinical Psychology*, ed. B. B. Wolman. New York: McGraw-Hill Book Company, 1965.

THE SENSORIALLY HANDICAPPED

III

11

The Visually Handicapped

The blind have always been the favored group as compared with other categories of the handicapped. They have often been granted special rights and privileges. Although at times blindness, like other disabilities, has been looked upon as a curse of the gods, the blind were more generally revered as seers, prophets and soothsayers. They were often educated, respected, and sometimes became poets and transmitters of oral traditions. Although most other categories of handicapped are far larger, there are more special social, legislative, and educational services provided for the blind than for any other group.

Scott has estimated that in 1960 there were over 800 separate organizations, agencies, and programs for the blind in the United States. The total annual expenditures of these agencies were nearly $470 million (Scott, 1969). In 1785 the first special educational programs established were for the visually handicapped.

Some Definitions

As indicated in earlier chapters, there are both quantitative and functional definitions of the visually handicapped. When quantitative definitions are required for legal and administrative purposes, blindness is

301

usually defined as: "Visual acuity of 20/200 or less in the better eye with proper correction, or a limitation in the fields of vision such that the widest diameter of the visual field subtends an angular distance no greater than 20 degrees" (American Foundation for the Blind, 1961). A person is said to have a visual acuity of 20/200 if he must be at a distance of twenty feet in order to read the standard type which a person with normal vision can read at a distance of two hundred feet. The restriction of the visual field to an angular distance of twenty degrees or less is sometimes called "tunnel vision." An individual with such a condition may have normal visual acuity for the area on which he can focus, but his field of vision is so restricted that he can see only a limited area at a time. A person suffering a restriction either of visual acuity or field to this extent is typically considered legally and medically blind.

There has been little demand for medical and legal definitions of *partial blindess* or *partially sighted*. However, the quantitative standard most often accepted is "visual acuity of between 20/70 and 20/200 in the better eye after maximum correction," or comparable visual limitations of other types (Ashcroft, 1963). Some eye specialists have proposed more complex quantitative measures of "visual efficiency" in which visual acuity plays only a part (Hoover, 1963).

Functional definitions vary according to the purposes they are intended to serve. Thus we have "travel vision," "shadow vision," "near vision," and "distance vision," as well as "educational blindness" and "occupational blindness." Because of its practical importance, *educational blindness* has been most systematically studied. The educationally blind are those people whose vision is so defective that they cannot be educated via vision. Their education must be primarily through the auditory, cutaneous, and kinesthetic senses. The educationally blind must read and write in Braille. Functional definitions of the partially sighted or partially blind—we shall use the two terms interchangeably— are less precise. The partially sighted are able to use vision as their main avenue of learning and do not require Braille. But they read only enlarged print, or require magnifying devices, or can read only limited amounts of regular print under special conditions.

Many studies have documented the lack of a close relationship between the quantitative medical and legal definitions and the more functional definitions of visual handicaps. Many legally blind children can read large or even ordinary print. Many more can distinguish large objects sufficiently well to enable them to move around and have a sense of orientation (travel vision), and most have some light perception (shadow vision). Of over 7,000 children enrolled in over 600 classes for the partially sighted, less than one-third had vision within the limits of visual acuity commonly used in defining partial sight—between 20/70

and 20/200 in the better eye after maximum correction (Kerby, 1952).
Table 11–1, based on another study (Jones, 1962), also shows the discrepancies between the quantitative and functional criteria.

TABLE 11–1
Reading Practice as Related to Visual Acuity

	Percentages of Children		
Visual Acuity	Reading Print	Reading Braille	Reading Both Braille and Print
20/200*	82	12	6
15/200*	67	27	6
10/200*	59	32	9

¹The fractions indicate that the person must be 20, 15, or 10 feet distant from a standard type to read the material which a person with normal vision can read at 200 feet. All these groups are legally blind.
Data from Jones (1962).

Symptoms of Visual Impairment

Since regular and complete eye examinations for all children are seldom feasible, initial identification of children for more complete examinations is usually based on behavioral symptoms or rough screening tests. The more common symptoms of visual impairment (selected and modified from Winebrenner, 1952), are as follows:

1. Has chronic eye irritations as indicated by watery eyes or by red-rimmed, encrusted, or swollen eyelids.
2. Experiences nausea, double vision, or visual blurring during or following reading.
3. Rubs eyes, frowns, or screws up the face when looking at distant objects.
4. Is overcautious in walking, runs infrequently and falteringly for no apparent reason.
5. Is abnormally inattentive during chalkboard, wall chart, or map work.
6. Complains of visual blurring and attempts to brush away the visual impediments.
7. Is excessively restless, irritable, or nervous following prolonged close visual work.
8. Blinks excessively, especially while reading.
9. Habitually holds the book very close, very far away, or in other unusual positions when reading.

10. Tilts the head to one side when reading.
11. Can read only for short periods at a time.
12. Shuts or covers one eye when reading.

Tests of Visual Impairment

The National Society for the Prevention of Blindness recommends, as a minimum test for school-age children, an annual test with the Snellen chart. The Snellen test chart consists of rows of letters, or E's, in various positions in lines of different size print. Each row of letters of a given size has a distance designation. For example, the 20-foot row can be read by people with normal vision at a distance of 20 feet. A person reading the 20-foot row at this distance is said to have 20/20 vision. A person who can read nothing smaller than the 70-foot line at the standard 20-foot distance has 20/70 vision.

The Snellen test is the most widely used because it is simple and can be quickly administered by a nurse or a teacher. Despite its widespread use, however, the Snellen test has decided limitations. It tests central vision only. It does not detect hyperopia (farsightedness), presbyopia (impairment of vision due to diminution of the elasticity of the crystalline lens), or strabismus (a deviation of one of the eyes from its normal direction). While most authorities strongly recommend that visual screening programs include tests such as the Massachusetts Vision Test, the Telebinocular, the Sight Screener, and the Ortho-Rater, studies indicate that, when used by teachers, the Snellen chart does about as well as these much more complicated and expensive devices (Crane et al., 1952; Foote and Crane, 1954).

Causes of Impaired Vision

Table 11–2 indicates various causes of visual defects among children of school ages, as well as changes in etiology, over a twenty-five-year period. The category of "excessive oxygen" is of special interest because it accounts for one-third of the 1958–1959 total. The condition or disease known as retrolental fibroplasia was practically unknown before the 1940s. It was identified as a clinical entity and named by Dr. T. L. Terry, a Boston ophthalmologist, in 1942. The condition occurred only in premature infants and increased rapidly until, in 1952–1953, it accounted for over half the blindness of preschool children. In 1952 it was established that the increased concentrations of oxygen to which premature infants were being subjected was the cause. Since the cause was discovered, and it was found that the concentration and duration of oxygen administration could be reduced below the critical level without increasing the mortality rate, blindess of this type occurs only rarely. However, the impact of the several thousand blind children of this type will be felt in the educational systems until the 1970s, when they will have largely completed their education.

TABLE 11–2

Estimated Prevalence of Legal Blindness of Different Etiologies in School Children (per 100,000)

Causes	1933–1934	1943–1944	1954–1955	1958–1959
Infections	6.1	5.0	1.5	1.3
Injuries	1.6	1.5	1.0	0.8
Excessive oxygen	—	—	3.8	11.3
Tumors	0.5	0.8	1.0	0.6
Prenatal causes	10.8	12.1	11.1	16.2
Cause unreported	1.9	2.2	1.3	2.6
Totals per 100,000	21.3	21.9	19.9	34.1
Number of cases	2,702	3,749	4,429	7,757

Data from Hatfield (1963).

Table 11–2 indicates that, except for the marked increase in the 1958–1959 figures due to retrolental fibroplasia, the total incidence of blindness has not changed significantly. However, the relative importance of certain etiologies has changed. Blindness due to infectious diseases has progressively declined, from 6.1 per 100,000 in 1933–1934 to 1.3 in 1958–1959. There has also been a progressive decline in blindness due to injuries. Unspecified prenatal causes remain the major etiological category of the blind. Heredity is undoubtedly the primary cause in many of these cases. Kerby (1958) estimates that 14 to 15 percent of blindness results from genetic factors. Heredity as a cause is difficult to establish, but it is thought to be an important etiological agent.

As the age composition of the population changes, the incidence of blindness and the relative importance of the various causes of visual impairment change. With increased longevity, glaucoma, cataracts, and diabetic retinopathy increase in importance as causes of blindness. In the late 1960s and early 1970s, the blind population was increasing at a rate nearly twice that of the general population. Between 1940 and 1960 the known blind population of the United States increased 67 percent, while the total population increased 36 percent. Except for retrolental fibroplasia, most of this increase is the result of the high incidence of glaucoma (2 percent of the adult population are affected) and cataracts (25 percent of the total blind). With more effective controls for diabetes an increasing number of affected persons are living to advanced ages and develop diabetic retinopathy. This is currently the most rapidly growing cause of blindness. Currently 15 percent of all new cases of blindness are of diabetic etiology (Lowenfeld, 1965).

Incidence of Visual Impairment

The incidence of mild visual defects is very high. It is estimated that one-fourth of schoolchildren have some visual anomaly. In a survey of over 5,000 children in California, 22 percent of the elementary school children and 31 percent of the high school students were found to have visual defects (Dalton, 1943). Of course, the great majority of these defects are correctable and constitute no particular educational or vocational handicap.

There are no dependable statistics on the prevalence of blindness and partial sight as herein defined (Hurlin, 1962). The medicolegal criterion for blindess (corrected vision of 20/200 or less in the better eye) is generally considered to give an incidence of approximately 1 in 3,000 (0.03 percent) of school age children. The number of children with visual acuity between 20/70 and 20/200 (the partially sighted) is estimated to be 1 in 500 (0.2 percent). These figures are much larger than the number of children judged to need special educational services because of visual impairment (the educationally blind or partially sighted). The United States Office of Education estimates that a total of 0.09 percent of school children need special education facilities for the visually impaired. Of these 0.09 percent, two-thirds (0.06 percent) are educationally partially sighted, and one-third (0.03 percent) are educationally blind. If we accept the Office of Education's estimate of fifty million children enrolled in the elementary and secondary schools in 1966, these percentages work out to about 15,000 educationally blind and 30,000 educationally partially sighted children. These are the groups presumably requiring special educational programs. While these are sizable groups, the visually impaired probably constitute the smallest area of exceptionality (Dunn, 1963).

The Handicaps of the Blind

Like all disabilities, the total handicap of the blind person is the cumulative effects of (a) the disability itself and its inherent limitations, (b) the social stigma manifesting itself in cultural stereotypes of the blind, and (c) the self-concept of the blind person.

The inherent limitations of any disability are relative to the extent to which current technology has made available to the handicapped compensatory devices and procedures. Blindness (*a*) prevents direct access to the printed word, (*b*) restricts independent mobility in unfamiliar surroundings, (*c*) limits a person's direct perception of his distant environment as well as objects too large to be apprehended tactually, and (*d*) deprives the individual of important social cues.

The stigmas of blindness which contribute to the total handicap of blindness consist of a set of popular conceptions or misconceptions which result in social practices that are sufficiently consistent with and supportive of these misconceptions to constitute a self-fulfilling prophecy. The popular stereotypes of blindness contain contradictory components. On the one hand are the presumed traits of docility, dependency, helplessness, and despondency. This stereotype is implicit in the application of the term to the nonhandicapped as typified by expressions such as "You are as helpless as a blind man," "Are you blind?," "He is blind with rage." The stereotype of helplessness is also typified by the blind man on the street corner with a tin cup in his hand. On the other hand, we also have the less common popular conceptions of the unusual and almost miraculous aptitudes of blind people—their alleged inner insights which more than compensate for their lack of vision, the supposed increased acuity of their other senses, or their possession of a special extra sense or extrasensory perceptiveness. As mentioned earlier, historically some blinded individuals have been especially revered as seers, prophets, and wise men.

Since the popular stereotype of helplessness and dependency is the dominant one, the treatment of the blind individual often results in social practices which preclude his developing and exercising the skills and competences which will enable him to become independent. There is nothing uniquely inherent in the nature of blindness that requires a person to be docile, helpless, and dependent. He only becomes so through the same basic processes of learning as do the sighted who develop these same characteristics.

Scott (1969) shows how the blind beggar, complying to the popular stereotype of helplessness by superficially conforming to the popular conceptions of the sighted, persuades people to give him money. He behaves as others expect him to and, in exchange, extracts money from the normal. Blind beggars, while capitalizing on the popular stereotype of helplessness, are usually independent, capable, and employable. They typically travel independently, using public transportation, move about freely as street crowds shift, maintain their orientation in crowds, remain composed under stress, and are self-reliant. The causes for which money is solicited by the blind beggar, such as an operation or a new guide dog, are usually fictitious. The blind beg because it is lucrative, they prefer begging to other jobs that are available to them, and they enjoy more freedom than they have when they become or remain the client of official agencies (Scott, 1969). The blind person may succumb to the social pressures and expectancies engendered by the cultural stereotype by either internalizing the role and becoming a helpless, dependent individual requiring and entitled to extensive aid and/or deliberately exploiting for their own economic gain the compassion and guilt feelings of the sighted via begging.

The blind person is deprived of important social cues. Vision plays an important role in interpersonal communication. Instead of maintaining eye contact, as the sighted normally do when conversing, the blind person may turn his better ear toward the speaker thus turning his face away. Turning the face and/or eyes away from the speaker suggests inattentiveness and evasiveness and is disconcerting to the sighted. The blind person is also deprived of the socially communicative cues provided by the facial expressions, gestures, and movements of the other person. His failure to observe and use conventional gestures in communication may result in less complete communication or in the use of gestures which are perceived by others as either contradictory of the oral message or distracting. The blind person uses facial expressions and gestures less often and less appropriately and more often develops stereotyped body movements called "blindisms" which detract from the individual's communicative effectiveness than do the sighted.

Mobility of the Blind

One of the most, if not the most, difficult task for the blind person is that of independent travel. However, the problem has never been systematically investigated. The only aspect of the mobility of the blind that has been comprehensively researched is the "obstacle sense," which is discussed in the next section. Since in moving about independently, the blind person makes use of other senses—especially audition—seldom used by the normally sighted for this purpose, the mobility of the blind is influenced markedly by other handicaps, particularly auditory impairment. It is therefore not surprising to find a significant relationship between the auditory thresholds of blind subjects and their relative mobility. The highest correlations are found with thresholds for the higher frequencies (Riley, Luterman, and Cohen, 1964). This relationship probably derives from the crucial role of the higher frequencies in the detection of obstacles (echo reception).

The restricted mobility of the blind has many causes. The most obvious is their limited capacity to perceive distant objects. Other less obvious causes are in the areas of motivation. The young blind child cannot see objects or people, which he then sets out to reach as does the sighted child. He has to wait for contact, sound, or smell to arouse his curiosity. The blind child cannot see other children moving toward and reaching for toys and other interesting objects. He is deprived of visual models to imitate. The visual incentives which stimulate the sighted child to learn to crawl, creep, stand, walk, and run are not present to the blind. The visually impaired child is much more dependent on auditory, principally verbal, sources for his motivation to move. The many bumps and bruises he will get arouse the anxiety of those about him because of the real as well as the exaggerated danger he invites. This and the overprotection afforded him add to his inherent disability and increase his handicap. Although independent locomotion—the ability to move about freely and independently at home, in the neighborhood, and in traffic—is of primary importance to the blind, it has only recently begun to receive the attention it warrants. It is obvious that these skills, which the sighted individual learns largely incidentally and with little formal instruction, must become a matter of primary concern in the training of the blind.

Such training begins in the home, where situations must be deliberately contrived to encourage the blind child to become curious and explore his world. The blind child needs a wealth of sounds, objects within reach, and even odors which he is encouraged to find and explore. Stimulation of the child to move about the house, rather than to sit quietly in the crib or playpen, is more essential for the blind than for the sighted child. Keeping furniture in the same places and teaching the child the safe routes around the house will minimize the number of bumps and bruises which may discourage independent exploration of his world. Permitting him to follow mother or other family members about, encouraging him to use furniture, utensils, and tools, and to smell and taste vegetables and fruit are a necessary part of the blind child's education.

Normal playground activities require some modification, but with adequate supervision the blind child can participate in most such programs. The blind child can use the sandbox, jungle gym, and most other playground equipment. He can swim, dance, wrestle, and participate in many forms of athletics.

Currently the Veterans Administration, the Seeing Eye Dog organization, the state vocational rehabilitation programs, and the American Foundation for the Blind are all providing training or assistance in training the blind to be mobile. Surveys indicate that most blind adults have relatively little ability to travel independently, are dissatisfied with their level of performance, have not been systematic or purposeful in their mode of travel, have seldom had travel training of any duration, and have no active plans for improvement (Finestone, Lukoff, and Whiteman, 1960).

The goals of these programs are not limited to independent travel, but also involve training in dressing, eating, and personal relations. Specific travel training includes instruction in the use of the cane and experience with the seeing-eye dog, as well as the more general training in motor and mental orientation in travel.

The Hoover technique of cane travel, which was developed in the rehabilitation program for veterans blinded in war, is generally recognized as superior to others. This technique involves moving a long white cane in a pendulum-like, scanning motion, to detect obstacles in one's path. Techniques for various specific situations have been developed, and a specific course of training is provided in the use of the cane.

The use of dog guides by the blind has received a good deal of popular interest, but its practicability has probably been exaggerated. It is esti-mated that the use of guide dogs is practical for only about 5 percent of the blind (Ashcroft, 1963). The seeing-eye dog does not guide the blind to a destination. The person must know his destination and how to get there. His is still the task of orientation. The dog, like the cane, only indicates the spaces into which the blind person can safely move.

Dependence on human guides is seldom satisfactory. It is often costly, and it makes the blind person's mobility contingent on the good health, dependability, and availability of a second person. If he can travel inde-pendently, the blind person is freed of his dependence on the convenience and disposition of family members, friends, or the availability and com-petence of hired guides (Spar, 1955). Studies show that blind persons using human guides travel much less than those who use canes or dogs. The blind who use dogs as guides actually travel more than either of the other groups (Finestone, Lukoff, and Whiteman, 1960).

Independent travel involves mental orientation as well as physical locomotion (Lowenfeld, 1963). Mental orientation is the recognition of an area in terms of its spatial and temporal relations to oneself. This recognition typically consists of a "mental map" of the area, within which the blind person orients himself as he moves toward his destination. As he moves about, he picks up cues—noises, echoes, changes in ground level, air currents, odors—which either confirm or cast doubt on the accuracy of his mental orientation. The blind person also makes use of his "motor memory." This is his sense of direction and distance, a kind of "muscular memory." A destination is perceived as at a certain distance in terms of time or movement. The blind person perceives distances, not by counting steps but more in terms of time and movement (Villey, 1930).

THE OBSTACLE SENSE OF THE BLIND

Many totally blind individuals can sense obstacles in their paths. It is this ability which has generated the belief that the blind have a super-normal sensory capacity of some sort. Theories to explain the obstacle sense have ranged from the occult, which border on the supernatural, through a heightened responsiveness of either known or unknown sense organs, indirect response to remote sensory cues (unrecognized cues arouse fear which produce contractions of the pilomotor muscles of the skin, the person experiences the muscular contractions as an obstacle in his path), to theories which assume a simple direct response to cues from one or more sense organs (auditory, thermal, or pressure).

A series of experiments started in the 1930s and continued over a period of twenty-five years has pretty well established the following facts concerning the obstacle sense:

1. There are large individual differences in the "obstacle sense" of the blind. One study found one-fifth (7 out of 34) of blind students *did not* possess the obstacle sense (Worchel, Mauney, and Andres, 1950).

2. Stimulation of the face or other exposed areas of the skin is neither a necessary nor a sufficient condition for obstacle perception (Supa, Cotzin, and Dallenbach, 1944).

3. Deaf-blind subjects do not possess the obstacle sense and seem to be incapable of acquiring it (Worchel and Dallenbach, 1947).

4. Under most conditions, auditory stimulation is both a necessary and sufficient condition for the perception of obstacles (Worchel and Dallenbach, 1947).

5. Other sensory cues, such as cutaneous and olfactory, are quite inefficient and are utilized only under certain conditions when auditory cues are not available (Ammons, Worchel, and Dallenbach, 1953).

6. Changes in the pitch of a sound or echo are a necessary condition for the perception of obstacles. That the pitch of a sound rises as the listener moves toward the source of the sound is known as the Doppler effect.

7. At normal walking speed, sound frequencies of about 10,000 cycles and above are necessary for obstacle perception. Frequencies below this level are insufficient for such perception (Cotzin and Dallenbach, 1950). The higher frequencies are important in the detection of obstacles because of their better resolution of the echoes reflected from small objects. Bats and other animals who emit and perceive sounds well above the human range use the echoes from such sounds in obstacle detection, and this seems to be the basis for their avoidance of obstacles. Some quantitative measurements have been made of the ability of the human blind to detect echoes (Kellogg, 1962; Rice, Feinstein, and Schusterman, 1965).

8. Blind subjects lacking the obstacle sense are able to develop it with systematic practice (Worchel, Mauney, and Andres, 1950).

9. Blindfolded normally sighted subjects are, with practice, able to develop the obstacle sense (Worchel and Mauney, 1951).

These studies have demonstrated that the "obstacle sense" is largely a reaction to small, unrecognized auditory cues (principally echoes) which warn the individual of obstacles. There is nothing supersensory or mysterious about this responsiveness. It is something that a person with vision could accomplish equally well if he had the motivation, training, and experience. In fact, it is probable that a blind person cannot accomplish anything with his remaining senses that a seeing person could not accomplish equally well if his incentives and experiences were the same.

To assist in the training of blind people to acquire an "obstacle sense" a special sonic echo device has been developed. It consists of a sound source and a miniature loud speaker that can be carried on the chest. When switched on this device emits a succession of sharp clicks of relatively high pitch, producing a more satisfactory echo than either the footsteps or the human voice. The volume of the sound can be increased in noisy environments. People with normal vision, when blindfolded, are reported to learn very quickly to find their way with the aid of this instrument (Taylor, 1965).

Language of the Visually Impaired

There are certainly no language deficits or proficiencies peculiar to the blind. Unlike the deaf, the blind acquire speech in the ordinary way and handle language in ways which are quite normal. However, most studies show that the blind do have speech disorders somewhat more frequently than do the normally sighted. Estimates of the incidence of speech defects range from as high as 50 percent (Brieland, 1951; LeZak and Starbuck, 1964) to 6.7 percent (Rowe, 1958). Tabulations of the types of speech disorders suggest that those categories in which the blind exceed the normal are mostly of the less severe types. For example, Rowe (1958) reported that no blind child in her study was considered to be a stutterer.

Congenitally blind children are somewhat slower in learning to speak, and their language development lags behind that of seeing children. At least a part of this is due to the absence of the visual component of the imitative process which plays a major role in speech development. These children cannot see the lip and mouth movements, nor the bodily movements and gestures which accompany speech. They depend solely upon auditory stimulation and imitation. Some commonly listed speech characteristics of the blind are:

1. The blind speak at a slower rate than the sighted.
2. The blind talk louder, modulate their voices less, and project their voices less appropriately (more of a "broadcast" voice).
3. The blind have less vocal variety.
4. The blind use fewer bodily movements, facial expressions, and gestures in talking.
5. The blind use less lip movement in articulation (Lowenfeld, 1963).

It should be mentioned that not all studies show these differences between the blind and the sighted (Brieland, 1951; Rowe, 1958). Because of his exclusive dependence on auditory cues in the perception of oral speech, the blind person becomes quite sensitive to the nuances of inflections, pitch, loudness, and pacing of the speech of others. He depends upon these auditory cues for indications of tension or relaxation, good will or dissatisfaction, approval or disapproval. These auditory cues, together with physical contacts such as a pat on the back or touching the hand, have great significance for the visually handicapped because of his greater dependence on the auditory and cutaneous cues for information and socialization.

Personal and Social Adjustment

The earlier discussion of the relationship of exceptionality in general to personal and social adjustment applies to the visually impaired. There is no special "psychology of the blind." The blind are characterized by no special personality characteristics or types. The adjustment problems of the visually disabled, like the normal, range all the way from those of everyday social contacts to those of economic dependence. Congenitally blind children left to themselves do not live in a world of blackness or eternal night. They do not yearn for light or feel sorry for themselves because they cannot see. The few that do express such attitudes have acquired them from other people. The social and personal effects of impaired vision are nonspecific, most often taking the form of immaturity and insecurity (Bauman, 1964). The phantasies of the blind concern social acceptance, personal achievement, and withdrawal to a simpler and less demanding life. These are analogous to the phantasies of the normally sighted (Cutsforth, 1951).

Certain "blindisms" are commonly listed as occasionally found in the blind. Blindisms are socially irrelevant and often bizarre repetitive activities which are distracting to other people. The most common ones are rocking or weaving, fingering or rubbing the eyes, waving the fingers before the face, and bending the head forward, as well as the twisting, squirming, and posturing which are characteristic of many nervous or mentally retarded children. None of these activities is peculiar to the blind, and they are important only because they add to the person's exceptionality and decrease his social acceptability. In most cases these activities disappear as the child grows up, although they persist longer in blind children who are also emotionally disturbed or mentally retarded. The socialization and personal development of the blind are being augmented by such things as special museums, exhibits, and gardens designed especially for them. Illustrative of these are the Mary Duke Biddle Gallery for the Blind, a part of the North Carolina Museum of Art in Raleigh, North Carolina, the Garden of Fragrance in San Francisco's Golden Gate Park, and the traveling museum for the blind sponsored by the California Arts Commission.

Intelligence of the Visually Impaired

Practically everything that will be said about the problems involved in evaluating the intelligence of the deaf and the partially deaf apply to the visually impaired. Except in the few instances in which blindness and intellectual subnormality are genetically linked (Tay-Sach's disease) and in those cases where mental deficiency and blindness may result from common environmental causes (disease or accidents), any intellectual deficits which accompany visual impairment are presumably due to the uncompensated limitations of sensory input and mobility. An individual's mental potentiality is neither raised nor lowered by blindness. His functional level may be lowered to the extent to which society has not provided experiences which can offset the limitations imposed by his sensory deficit.

The mental level of the visually handicapped, as measured by existing intelligence tests, does not differ markedly from that of children with normal vision (Bateman, 1963; Karres and Wollersheim, 1963). As early as 1930, the Binet intelligence test was revised by Hayes specifically for the blind. Hayes (1941) tested children in 17 residential schools for the blind and obtained an average IQ of 99. The only significant deviation from the normal was that a larger percentage of blind children scored both high and low (10 percent were above 120 and 9 percent were below 70), and that a correspondingly smaller percentage was in the middle range. Hayes found no relation between the age at which the child became blind and his intelligence level.

The studies indicate that visual impairment produces less of a decrement in intellectual functioning as measured by conventional intelligence tests than does comparable auditory deficit, and that most children with visual defects have normal mental abilities. To the extent that blindness is genetically independent of defective mentality or brain damage, the basic intellectual capacity of the blind is comparable to that of the general population.

Sensory Acuity of the Blind

The popular notion that the blind are endowed with hyperacute hearing, touch, taste, and smell or phenomenal memories is largely erroneous. Studies have consistently shown that persons with vision are either equal or superior to the blind in their ability to identify the direction or distance of the source of a sound, to discriminate the relative intensities of tones, to recognize tactual forms, and to discriminate relative pressures, temperatures, or weights, as well as in their acuteness of smell, taste, and the vibratory sense. They have likewise displayed no superiority in either rote or logical memory (Seashore and Ling, 1918; Hayes, 1941; Axelrod, 1959; Lowenfeld, 1963; Emart and Carp, 1963). Any superiority of the blind in the perceptual areas is the result of increased attention to small cues and greater use of such cues as a source of information and guidance. It is apparently not the result of a lowering of sensory thresholds.

Perceptual and Conceptual Processes of the Blind

Lowenfeld (1963) states that "blindness produces problems *sui generis* only in the area of cognitive functions and mobility." Here we shall be concerned only with the cognitive (perceptual and conceptual) processes. It is obvious that the congenitally blind person experiences (perceives) the objects of the universe and builds up his knowledge of the world in ways that are different from those of seeing children. That is, his percepts and concepts derive from different types of stimuli—which does not mean that his cognition is necessarily less adequate or useful.

It is as impossible for the seeing person to experience the world of the congenitally blind as it is for the congenitally blind to conceive of visual experiences, but it does not necessarily follow that the blind individual thereby has a significantly restricted range of concepts. It is obvious that a person lacking visual perception will have no visual imagery. Studies indicate that adults who became blind before the age of five have no visual imagery (Schlaegel, 1953; Blank, 1958; Lowenfeld, 1962). However, such people do develop and use concepts of forms, space, and distance beyond the range of touch and movement. They function efficiently in conceptual areas which sighted people derive primarily from visual experiences. It is not known if these percepts and concepts, derived primarily from tactual, kinesthetic, and auditory sources, remain on these levels or whether there is a coalescence of impressions and an emergence of concepts from such experiences into something akin to that which the sighted derive from visualization.

Knowledge of the spatial qualities of objects is gained by the blind largely through touch and kinesthesis. Audition provides clues to the direction and distance of objects which make sounds, but it gives no idea of the objects as such. Tactual and kinesthetic experiences require direct contact with, or movement around, objects. Thus, distant objects, such as the heavenly bodies, clouds, and the horizon, as well as very large objects such as mountains and other geographical units, or microscopic objects such as bacteria, cannot be perceived and must be conceived only by analogy and extrapolation from objects actually experienced. While this is a limitation, it is probably comparable to the way in which the sighted person conceives of the size of the world and the other planets which he cannot directly perceive or of interplanetary distances which are far beyond his direct experience. When interplanetary distances are stated in terms of light years, for example, one's conception of such magnitudes depends largely on verbal or written symbols, or is an extrapolation from distances actually traversed. They are hardly perceived in the way that the distant mountain top or the corner grocery store are perceived.

It is surprising that we have few studies directly concerned with the concept formation or the conceptual levels attained by the blind as compared with the normally sighted. One study compared "early blind" and "late blind" children with sighted children on various tactile and auditory tasks (Axelrod, 1959). "Early blind" subjects were inferior to seeing subjects in: (1) abstracting a characteristic common to consistently rewarded members of pairs of objects; (2) solving matching problems involving spatial or temporal sequences; and (3) transferring a principle of solution from one sensory area to another—auditory to cutaneous or vice versa. The "late blind" subjects showed no inferiority to the normally sighted. The differences obtained, while statistically significant, were small and, according to the author, do not suggest marked intellectual impairment. The author also indicates that possible brain damage to the early blind cannot be ruled out.

Research studies have documented the deficiencies of the visually handicapped in the development of spatial concepts (Nolan and Ashcroft, 1969). There is also research evidence indicating that blind persons do not use abstract concepts to the degree that sighted people do, but think much more on a concrete level (Zweibelson and Barg, 1967; Nolan and Ashcroft, 1969).

Much more research has been done in the cognition of the deaf. Since the blind seem to be superior to the deaf in their performances on ordinary intelligence and achievement tests, and since few investigators have been sufficiently concerned to study the problem, we suggest that any deficiencies the blind experience in the conceptual realm is less than that found in the deaf. Certainly the deaf suffer greater linguistic handicaps; their conceptual limitations are thought to be largely in this area.

Educational Achievement of the Visually Impaired

Visual defects of the type found in some 25 to 35 percent of schoolchildren, most of which are not sufficiently severe to require special educational programs, do not seem to affect educational achievement. While hyperopia (farsightedness) and astigmatism (irregularity of the curvature of the cornea) are associated with less than normal progress in reading, myopia (nearsightedness) is associated with above-normal progress in reading (Farris, 1936; Eames, 1955, 1959).

As early as 1918, an educational achievement test was developed for the blind (Hayes, 1941). Since then many achievement tests have been adapted for use with the blind. In addition to offering the tasks in Braille, these tests come with more detailed preliminary instructions, and two and one-half or three times the time is allowed for taking them. Some tests have been adapted for oral administration. Because of these differences, direct comparisons with the norms obtained on the regular tests with the sighted are rather hazardous. However, we can only take achievement test scores as we find them. When seeing and blind children are compared grade-by-grade, the two groups are about equal except in arithmetic, in which the scores of the blind are generally lower. However, blind children are on the average about two years older than seeing children of the same grade. Consequently, comparisons by either chronological or mental age indicate considerable educational retardation (Hayes, 1941; Lowenfeld, 1945, 1963; Ashcroft, 1963). The greater age of blind children seems to result largely from their late entry to school, absence from school because of treatment for eye trouble, lack of appropriate school facilities, and their slower rate of obtaining information from Braille, large type, or audition (Ashcroft, 1963). Persons interested in testing the blind will find *A Manual for the Psychological Examination of the Adult Blind* (Bauman and Hayes, 1951) to be most valuable.

Some incidental facts relevant to the school achievement are:

1. The cause of blindness and age of becoming blind are unrelated to school achievement (Hayes, 1934).
2. Age of school entrance is negatively correlated with school success (Hayes, 1934).

3. Blind children have particular difficulties in arithmetic (Nolan, 1959a).

Education of the Visually Impaired

The aims, content, and subject matter involved in the education of the visually impaired are not essentially different from those involved in normal education. They need a good general education, plus a vocational type of instruction which is in keeping with their special requirements. The education of the visually impaired, like all special education, requires special training of teachers, special facilities and equipment, and some curricular modifications. We shall pass over the teacher-training component and indicate some of the curricular and special equipment required for the education of the visually impaired. Because the educations of the educationally blind and the partially sighted are somewhat different, we will discuss them separately.

SPECIAL EDUCATIONAL NEEDS OF THE BLIND

It is estimated that ordinary educational experiences are 85 percent visual. Since the blind child is deprived of this type of experience, the adaptation required for his education requires a shift from vision to the auditory, tactual, and kinesthetic senses as avenues of instruction, learning, and guidance. These needs have been met by teaching Braille reading and writing, using many audio aids, and constructing and using models, as well as embossed and relief maps, graphs, and geometric designs. Because of the importance of independent mobility for the blind child, instruction in orientation and training and experiences designed to increase his control of the environment and of himself in relation to it are becoming part of special education programs for the blind.

The Teaching of Braille. Learning and developing facility in the Braille system of reading and writing is the greatest single curricular

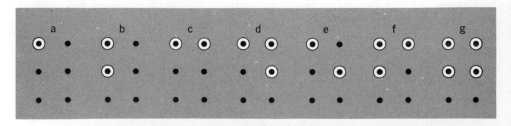

FIGURE 3
Sample of the Braille Letter Codes

modification required for the education of the blind. In 1829, Louis Braille, a young blind student and later a teacher at the Paris School for the Blind, modified a military code used for night communication so that it could be used by the blind. The system has been further modified under various auspices. At one time there were three major systems in use—the New York point system, American Braille, and British Braille. In 1932, a modified British Braille became the Standard English Braille, and since 1950 it has been used quite consistently as the preferred system. In 1950, UNESCO adapted a Braille system for all languages, but many of its details still have to be worked out.

Braille is the most efficient and useful means of reading and writing yet devised for the blind. Using the sixty-three possible combinations of six raised dots in the Braille cell, virtually any literary, numerical, or musical material can be presented. Since unmodified Braille takes a lot of space—each Braille cell requires a quarter-inch of line—many abbreviations, contractions, and signs have been developed. Mathematics makes use of a special Braille notation system, and most scientific symbols can be written in Braille. A type of Braille shorthand for the blind stenographer has also been developed.

Although Braille is a modified military code, it is not merely a code for the blind reader. It is a complete medium for reading and writing. Braille is taught, learned, and read much the same as ordinary writing and reading. Reading Braille is, in many ways, similar to visual reading. The proficient Braille reader uses both hands in reading, but the two function independently, one ahead of the other. The hands move regularly and smoothly, and horizontally along the line, with few vertical regressive movements. The touch is light, the pressure uniform. The activity is not particularly fatiguing, and there seems to be no decrease in the sensitivity of the touch even after several hours of reading.

Developing facility in reading Braille involves a unifying process in which larger and larger units of material are apprehended at a time in a manner similar to the reading of print by sighted persons. Some Braille readers use lip movements or silent speech just as do some visual readers (Fertsch, 1946).

The limitations of Braille as compared with visual reading are its relative slowness, the large size of books printed in Braille, and the restricted range of material available. Braille reading is comparatively slow —about one-third or one-fourth the rate of visual reading. Blind high school students read approximately 90 words per minute in Braille (Ashcroft, 1963). A plane geometry textbook, when put into Braille, required over one thousand pages and cost more than ten times the same text in print. Carl Sandburg's biography of Abraham Lincoln is ten volumes in Braille (Heck, 1953).

Blind children are also taught to write Braille. Braille is written by hand, using a special slate and stylus. The slates come in both pocket and desk sizes. Writing is done by punching holes with a stylus in a paper inserted between two metal strips. Since the material must be read from the underside of the paper, it must be written in reverse by starting at the right margin and writing toward the left. Braille writers or typewriters are available, and a good Braille typist can type forty to sixty words per minute. Blind children are also taught to use a standard typewriter, usually in the third or fourth grade. They find it very difficult to write with pen or pencil, and this is no longer emphasized except to teach each child to write his name. See Lowenfeld, Abel, and Hatten (1969) for a good survey of the studies on Braille reading.

Audio Aids for the Blind.   The education of the blind requires many audio aids. Tape recorders and record players are necessary parts of his school life. Resource or itinerant teachers may give assignments or special instructions on tape. Text material not available in Braille may be taped or recorded. Recordings are normally read at rates of 150 to 170 words per minute—considerably faster than reading Braille. Two studies have shown that sixth-, seventh-, and eighth-grade children can comprehend and retain material read at a fast rate (200 to 275 words per minute) as well or better than comparable material read at the more normal rate of 172 words per minute (Enc and Stolurow, 1960; Bixler et al., 1961; Foulke and Stecht, 1969). Most of the talking books available are fiction or magazines, but school texts are made available through the American Printing House for the Blind, the Library of Congress, and a few private agencies.

Arithmetic Aids for the Blind.   Mental arithmetic is used extensively in the education of the blind. For higher levels of mathematics, calculators, rulers, slide rules, compasses, and protractors have all been adapted for use by the blind. The Braille writer is also used in arithmetical calculations, as are an arithmetic board and adaptations of the abacus (Nolan and Morris, 1964). Modelling clay, pins, and rubber bands are utilized in constructing geometric designs and graphs.

Additional Educational Aids.   Braille relief and embossed maps and relief globes are useful in teaching geography as well as orientation and space perception to the blind child. Maps of the room, school grounds, and the town help the blind child develop a mental map of his surroundings, assist him in his orientation, and aid his independent travel.

VOCATIONAL TRAINING FOR THE BLIND

The educational needs of the blind person are more adequately met today than are his vocational needs. In most of the more advanced countries of the world today, no blind child of normal intelligence need grow up without academic, prevocational, and even some vocational training.

However, many are unable to obtain employment appropriate to their capacities. It is estimated that less than half of the blind individuals capable of working in general occupations are doing so and that only about 20 percent of those who could function adequately in sheltered workshops are so employed (Barnett, 1955).

Specialized vocational training—the teaching of specific skills and knowledge required for employment in regular trades or professions—is seldom provided by agencies for the blind. Only in a few limited areas, such as work with other blind, in the operation of service stands, and in the teaching of special skills such as chair caning, broom-making and weaving have the agencies for the blind developed vocational training programs. For the most part, blind people must obtain their vocational training along with the sighted. No special techniques for placing skilled or professional workers have been developed. The only special problem involved in vocational placement is dealing with the unrealistic prejudices of employers and with unwarranted physical qualifications which may preclude the hiring of the blind.

There are relatively few occupations and professions in which the blind are not successfully employed. However, the sheltered workshop is still the largest single source of employment for blind people. In the most successful instances of industrial job placement, commitments have been obtained from top management for the employment of a given number of blind workers. It is understood that the workers will meet regular production schedules and standards and be paid at regular rates. As long as the company has jobs which can be satisfactorily performed by blind workers, employment opportunities will be maintained for a specified number or percentage of blind workers. Union commitments are sometimes needed to exempt these people from the seniority provisions of union contracts. Agreements to employ a certain *number* of blind, rather than a particular group of blind workers, prevent the loss of those jobs to other blind workers when a particular employment is terminated. To prevent the blind workers from isolating themselves from the larger working group, many placement officers prefer not to place several blind workers in the same department.

EDUCATION OF THE PARTIALLY SIGHTED

The education of the partially sighted is much less of a problem than is that of the blind. For the most part, the partially sighted are basically seeing people and are educated with and prepared for life as such. At one time there were a large number of "sight saving" classes conducted for the partially sighted. The notion of sight saving has been largely discarded because it is generally recognized that the maximum use of even defective eyes will not cause them to deteriorate. Vision is not saved by not using it. The child with poor vision is now encouraged to use his vision to its maximum, to learn to read print, to write, and to acquire as much of his education as possible by sight. In contrast with the sight-saving emphasis of the old classes for the partially sighted, we now find programs, or at least proposals, for their "sight development" or "sight utilization." In such programs, the children are "learning to see," to make full use of their residual vision.

People working with the visually impaired are becoming increasingly concerned with the most effective use of any residual vision. Many legally blind children have potentially useful but undeveloped near vision. Many such children can develop considerable functional vision even though they have very low measured visual acuity. However, these children require planned opportunities and programs to achieve this end. Teaching procedures specifically directed at this end can significantly increase the visual efficiency of partially sighted children (Barraga, 1964; 1970).

The education of partially sighted children makes those adjustments in curriculum and equipment necessary for the education of the handicapped child, but otherwise his education is not unique. He does not have to learn Braille reading and writing. He is capable of independent travel without acquiring special techniques. His spatial orientation and concepts are not unique.

Educational Aids for the Partially Sighted.   For the child with borderline vision, minor adjustments, such as sitting him near the blackboard, placing his desk in a good light, and permitting him to move about so as to be as close as possible to charts and other wall displays may be all that is necessary.

For the more severely handicapped child, books in large type, and magnifying devices of various types, are necessary. There are two companies—American Printing House for the Blind and Stanwix Publishing House—which publish books in large type for the partially sighted, and a fairly wide variety of reading material is becoming available (Nolan, 1959b).

The simplest way to obtain magnification of print is to bring the book closer to the eyes. To see people holding reading very close to the eyes is disturbing to many persons because they believe such close reading damages the eyes. Most authorities believe that reading material may safely be held as close to the eyes as necessary. For many partially sighted individuals, however, holding print close to the eyes is not adequate and other means of magnification may be needed.

Optical magnification is achieved in several ways. Magnifying projectors, and special lenses—both contact and in conventional frames—are available. Telescopic effects are achieved by using contact lenses along with special lenses in conventional frames. A wide variety of special magnifying devices is produced.

Simple enlargement of print or magnification does not make a normal reader out of the partially sighted person. All means of enlarging print reduces the effective field of vision. This means that the amount of material that can be perceived at one time is reduced, and the rate of reading is correspondingly slow. It is therefore necessary to find the most appropriate type and degree of magnification for each person.

ADMINISTRATIVE EDUCATIONAL PLANS FOR THE VISUALLY IMPAIRED

All the administrative plans for the education of exceptional children discussed in earlier chapters are used with the visually impaired. These are: (1) the residential school; (2) the self-contained special day school or class; (3) the special room in a regular school with some degree of integration of the visually impaired with the rest of the school (cooperative plan); (4) the resource teacher; (5) the itinerant teacher; (6) complete integration of the visually impaired with the normally sighted, with little formal arrangement for them; and (7) home instruction (Stephens and Birch, 1969).

The residential schools were the first, and for a long time practically the only, facilities for the education of the visually impaired. With the development of many local facilities, however, the role of the residential schools has lessened. Most educators today believe that the maximum degree of integration of the handicapped child into the regular school and community is the most desirable arrangement. This means that those children who can be educated in regular, unsegregated classrooms should be so placed. Children who can be educated in special classes, or by resource or itinerant teachers, should not be institutionalized. The residential school aims to return the handicapped child to the regular school as quickly as possible.

Education of the Blind with Additional Handicaps

When both vision and audition are seriously impaired, the problems of education and social adjustment of the handicapped person are multiplied. Dr. Samuel G. Howe and Ann Sullivan Macy's pioneering work with Laura Bridgman and Helen Keller, respectively, focussed attention on the education of the deaf-blind in America. The first systematic program for these children was provided at the Perkins Institute for the Blind in Watertown, Massachusetts. Currently, eight schools provide educational programs for the deaf-blind. In 1955 it was estimated that there were 3,000 deaf-blind individuals in the United States, only about 10 percent of whom were children (Frampton and Gall, 1955).

The rubella epidemic of 1964–65 produced many deaf and blind children and has resulted in an increasing concern for these children in the United States. Interested readers are referred to Guldager (1969) and Robbins and Stenquist (1967).

The education of these children is a very demanding, one-to-one, teaching-learning process. The teacher typically becomes a companion to his student and provides constant and intensive social contact and stimulation as well as formal instruction. Education is initially directed at establishing contacts with the world via the cutaneous, kinesthetic, gustatory, and olfactory senses, and arousing a desire for learning. The isolation of the deaf-blind individual is great, and it is only after effective contact is established and his isolation is reduced that formal instruction is possible.

Special educational programs for the blind-mentally retarded have also been established. While these programs require much less modification than do those for the blind-deaf, the instruction is largely individualized and classes must be limited to three to five children (Williams, 1964).

Summary

The blind were the first handicapped group for which social provisions were made. Although the numbers involved are comparatively small, they have enjoyed more public concern and special legislation than any other category of the handicapped. Today the quantitative definitions of blindness and partial sight are being either supplemented or replaced by more situationally relevant, functional definitions. While the blind are quite easily identified, the partially sighted require examinations by specialists.

A wide variety of both genetic and environmental causes produce blindness. Infections and accidents are decreasing in importance as causes, whereas a larger percentage of blindness is attributed to prenatal factors the exact nature of which is largely unknown. It is estimated that among school-age children, 1 in 3,000 meet the medico-legal criterion of blindness, and that 1 in 500 have vision in the 20/70 to 20/200 range commonly designated as partially sighted. The United States Office of Education estimates that about half the medicolegally blind children (1 out of 6,000) are educationally blind (requiring the bulk of their education to be other than visual) and that about twice this number (1 in 3,000) require the special education provided for the partially sighted.

The three big problems of the blind are social understanding, education by other than visual means, and independent mobility. Some type of educational program is available to practically all of the blind in the United States. The problems of social understanding and acceptance of the blind are gradually being reduced. Systematic assistance and training for independent travel is only recently becoming available.

The "obstacle sense" of the blind has been shown to be fundamentally the location of echoes by auditory means. The language of the blind is not noticeably different from that of normal people. Language defects are probably more common, but they are not noticeably different in type from those of the sighted. The same things are true of the personal and social maladjustment of the visually impaired. Their basic intellectual capacities are probably normal. Their restricted sensory input, limited mobility, and greater dependence on other people probably account for any deficits they show in intelligence and scholastic achievement tests. The blind seem to be quite capable of compensating for their visual deficit in the perceptual and conceptual areas. While the congenitally blind lack visual percepts and concepts, they do not suffer any significant over-all deficiency in this area.

All of the different types of administrative arrangements are used in educating the blind. The special educational needs of the blind are the learning of Braille, the extensive use of auditory, tactual and kinesthetic experiences, and special mobility training. The partially sighted are educated essentially as are the normally sighted, but with the aid of large print and magnification of various types.

References

AMERICAN FOUNDATION FOR THE BLIND, *A Teacher Education Program for Those Who Serve Blind Children and Youth.* New York: American Foundation for the Blind, 1961.

AMMONS, C. H., P. WORCHEL, AND K. M. DALLENBACH, " 'Facial Vision': The Perception of Obstacles Out of Doors by Blindfolded and Deafened Subjects," *Amer. j. psychol.,* LXVI (1953), 519–53.

ASHCROFT, S. C., "Blind and Partially Sighted Children," in *Exceptional Children in the Schools,* ed. L. M. Dunn. New York: Holt, Rinehart & Winston, Inc., 1963.

AXELROD, S., *Effects of Early Blindness: Performance of Blind and Sighted Children on Tactile and Auditory Tasks.* New York: American Foundation for the Blind, 1959.

BARNETT, M. R., "Current Problems of the Blind," in *Special Education for the Exceptional,* eds. M. E. Frampton and E. D. Gall, Vol. II. Boston, Mass.: Porter Sargent, Publishers, 1955.

BARRAGA, N. C., *Increased Visual Behavior in Low Vision Children.* New York: American Foundation for the Blind, 1964.

————, "Teaching Children with Low Vision," in *New Directions in Special Education*, ed. R. L. Jones. Boston, Mass.: Allyn and Bacon, Inc., 1970.

BATEMAN, B. D., "Reading and Psycholinguistic Processes of Partially Sighted Children." Unpublished doctoral dissertation, University of Illinois, 1963.

BAUMAN, M. K., "Group Differences Disclosed by Inventory Items," *Int. j. educ. deaf.*, XIII (1964), 101–6.

————, AND S. P. HAYES, *A Manual for the Psychological Examination of the Adult Blind*. New York: The Psychological Corporation, 1951.

BIXLER, R. H., et al., *Comprehension of Rapid Speech*, Part I. Louisville, Ky.: University of Louisville Press, 1961.

BLANK, H. R., "Dreams of the Blind," *Psychoan. quart.*, XXVII (1958), 158–74.

BRIELAND, D., "Speech Education for the Visually Handicapped Child," *Int. j. educ. blind*, I (1951), 9–12.

COTZIN, M., AND K. M. DALLENBACH, " 'Facial Vision': The Role of Pitch and Loudness in the Perception of Obstacles by the Blind," *Amer. j. psychol.*, LXIII (1950), 485–515.

CRANE, M. M., et al., "Study of Procedures for Screening Elementary School Children for Visual Defects," *Amer. j. public health*, XLII (1952), 1430–39.

CUTSFORTH, T. D., *The Blind in School and Society* (rev. ed.). New York: American Foundation for the Blind, 1951.

DALTON, M. M., "A Visual Survey of 5,000 School Children," *J. educ. res.*, XXXVII (1943), 81–94.

DUNN, L. M., ed., *Exceptional Children in the Schools*. New York: Holt, Rinehart & Winston, Inc., 1963.

EAMES, T. H., "The Influence of Hypermetropia and Myopia on Reading Achievement," *Amer. j. ophthal.*, XXXIX (1955), 375–77.

————, "Visual Defects in Reading," *J. educ.*, CXLI (1959), 1–34.

EMART, A. G., AND F. M. CARP, "Recognition of Tactual Forms by Sighted and Blind Subjects," *Amer. j. psychol.*, LXXVI (1963), 488–91.

ENC, M. A., AND L. M. STOLUROW, "The Effect of Two Recording Speeds on Learning," *New outlook for the blind*, LIV (1960), 39–48.

FARRIS, L. P., "Visual Defects as Factors Influencing Achievement in Reading," *J. exp. educ.*, V (1936), 58–60.

FERTSCH, P., "An Analysis of Braille Reading," *New outlook for the blind*, XL (1946), 128–31.

FINESTONE, S., I. LUKOFF, AND M. WHITEMAN, *The Demand for Dog Guides and the Travel Adjustment of Blind Persons*. New York: Research Center, Columbia University, 1960.

FOOTE, F. M., AND M. M. CRANE, "An Evaluation of Visual Screening," *Except. child.*, XX (1954), 153–61.

FOULKE, E., AND T. G. STECHT, "Review of Research on the Intelligibility and Comprehension of Accelerated Speech," *Psychol. bull.*, LXXII (1969), 50–62.

FRAMPTON, M. E., AND E. D. GALL, eds., *Special Education for the Exceptional*, Vol. II. Boston, Mass.: Porter Sargent, Publishers, 1955.

GULDAGER, L., "The Deaf-blind: Their Education and Their Needs," *Except. child.*, XXXVI (1969), 203–6.

HATFIELD, E. M., "Causes of Blindness in School Children," *Sight saving rev.*, XXXIII (1963), 218–33.

HAYES, S. P., "Factors Influencing the School Success of the Blind," *Teachers forum (blind)*, VI (1934), 91–99.

———, *Contributions to a Psychology of Blindness*. New York: American Foundation for the Blind, 1941.

HECK, A. O., *The Education of Exceptional Children* (2nd ed.). New York: McGraw-Hill Book Company, 1953.

HOOVER, R. E., "Visual Efficiency as a Criterion of Service Needs," *Res. bull.*, XII, No. 3 (1963), 116–19.

HURLIN, R. G., "Estimated Prevalence of Blindness in the United States and in Individual States," *Sight saving rev.*, XXXII (1962), 162–65.

JONES, J. W., "Problems Involved in Defining and Classifying Blindness," *New outlook for the blind*, LVI (1962), 115–21.

KARRES, M. B., AND J. P. WOLLERSHEIM, "An Intensive Differential Diagnosis of Partially Seeing Children to Determine the Implications of Education," *Except. child.*, XXX (1963), 17–25.

KELLOGG, W. N., "Sonar System of the Blind," *Science*, CXXXVII (1962), 399–404.

KERBY, C. E., "A Report on the Visual Handicap of Partially Seeing Children," *Except. child.*, XVIII (1952), 137–42.

———, "Cause of Blindness in Children of School Age," *Sight saving rev.*, XXVIII (1958), 10–21.

LAND, S. L., AND S. E. VINEBERG, "Locus of Control in Blind Children," *Except. child.*, XXXI (1965), 257–60.

LEZAK, R. J., AND H. B. STARBUCK, "Identification of Children with Speech Disorders in a Residential School for the Blind," *Int. j. educ. blind*, XIV (1964), 8–12.

LOWENFELD, B., *Braille and Talking Book Reading: A Comparative Study*. New York: American Foundation for the Blind, 1945.

———, "Psychological Problems of Children with Impaired Vision," in *Psychology of Exceptional Children and Youth* (2nd ed.), ed W. M. Cruickshank. Englewood Cliffs, N.J.; Prentice-Hall, Inc., 1962.

———, "The Visually Handicapped," *Rev. educ. res.*, XXXIII (1963), 38–41.

———, *Our Blind Children* (2nd ed.). Springfield, Ill.: Charles C Thomas, 1965.

———, G. L. ABEL, AND P. H. HATTEN, *Blind Children Learn to Read*. Springfield, Ill.: Charles C Thomas, 1968.

NOLAN, C. Y., "Achievement in Arithmetic Computation: Analysis of School Differences and Identification of Areas of Low Achievement," *Int. j. educ. blind*, VIII (1959), 125–28. (a)

———, "Readability of Large Types," *Int. j. educ. blind*, IX (1959), 41–44. (b)

———, AND J. E. MORRIS, "The Japanese Abacus as a Computational Aid for Blind Children," *Except. child.*, XXXI (1964), 15–17.

———, AND S. C. ASHCROFT, "The Visually Handicapped," *Rev. educ. res.*, XXXIX (1969), 52–70.

RICE, C. E., S. H. FEINSTEIN, AND R. J. SCHUSTERMAN, "Echo Detection Ability of the Blind: Size and Distance Factors," *J. exper. psychol.*, LXX (1965), 246–51.

RILEY, L. H., D. M. LUTERMAN, AND M. F. COHEN, "Relationship between Hearing Ability and Mobility in a Blind Adult Population," *New outlook for the blind*, LVIII (1964), 139–41.

ROBBINS, N., AND G. STENQUIST, *The Deaf-blind "Rubella" Child*. Watertown, Mass.: Perkins School for the Blind, 1967.

ROWE, E. D., *Speech Problems of Blind Children: A Survey of North California Area*. New York: American Foundation for the Blind, 1958.

SCHLAEGEL, T. F., JR., "The Dominant Method of Imagery in Blind as Compared to Sighted Adolescents," *J. genet. psychol.*, LXXXIII (1953), 265–77.

SCOTT, R. A., *The Making of Blind Men*. New York: Russell Sage Foundation, 1969.

SEASHORE, C. E., AND T. L. LING, "Comparative Sensitiveness of Blind and Seeing Persons," *Psychol, monog.*, XXV (1918), 148–58.

SPAR, H. J., "Some Special Aspects of an Adequate Vocational Training and Employment Program for the Blind," in *Special Education for the Exceptional*, Vol. II, eds. M. E. Frampton and E. D. Gall. Boston, Mass.: Porter Sargent, Publisher, 1955.

STEPHENS, T. M., AND J. W. BIRCH, "Merits of Special Class, Resource, and Itinerant Plans for Teaching Partially Seeing Children," *Except. child.*, XXXV (1969), 481–85.

SUPA, M., M. COTZIN, AND K. M. DALLENBACH, "Facial Vision: The Perception of Obstacles by the Blind," *Amer. j. psychol.*, LVII (1944), 133–83.

TAYLOR, J. G., *The Behavioral Basis of Perception*. New Haven, Conn.: Yale University Press, 1965.

VILLEY, P., *The World of the Blind*, trans. A. Hallard. New York: The Macmillan Company, 1930.

WILLIAMS, D., "Sunland's Program for the Blind," *Ment, retard.*, II (1964), 244–45.

WINEBRENNER, D. K., "Finding the Visually Inadequate Child," *Visual digest*, XVI (1952), 21–34.

WORCHEL, P., AND K. M. DALLENBACH, " 'Facial Vision': Perception of Obstacles by the Deaf-Blind," *Amer. j. psychol.*, LX (1947), 502–53.

———, AND J. MAUNEY, "The Effect of Practice on the Perception of Obstacles by the Blind," *J. exper. psychol.*, LX (1951), 746–51.

———, AND J. G. ANDRES, "The Perception of Obstacles by the Blind," *J. exper. psychol.*, XL (1950), 170–76.

ZWEIBELSON, L., AND C. F. BARG, "Concept Development of Blind Children," *New outlook for the blind*, LXVIII (1967), 218–22.

12

The Aurally Handicapped

The Significance of Aural Handicaps

Because of the low visibility of auditory defects, and because the hard-of-hearing are often suspected of being unmotivated, inattentive, or mentally retarded, the general public has lacked interest in and sympathy for the aurally handicapped. The normal person can close his eyes and move about in total darkness and get some conception of the nature of blindness. The average individual has been temporarily orthopedically handicapped and obtained some idea of the problems of the crippled. However, one cannot close his ears. Even inserting ear plugs does not approximate the condition of the average person with a serious auditory deficit. The nonhandicapped individual typically is either apathetic or impatient with the acoustically handicapped person.

The young child with defective hearing often does not realize the nature of his problems, and few nonhandicapped adults are aware of the breadth of the problems of the aurally handicapped. The failure of the congenitally deaf child to acquire speech in the ordinary way, and his inability to hear the speech of others, are his most obvious handicaps. However, the oral and aural handicaps of the deaf and the severely hard-of-hearing are much broader than this. Sharing a common language is a prerequisite to full integration of a child into family, community, and society. Adequate hearing and speaking are tremendous aids to cooperative behavior. Sounds—even nonverbal ones—act as guides to behavior and to understanding. Hearing is normally a major source of pleasurable social experience. A common language is man's principal means of social interaction. In addition to being two of our prime avenues of information, hearing and speech contribute to social acceptance as well as to one's feeling of personal security, and they also aid in the learning and maintaining of nonverbal skills. The fact that severely and profoundly deaf, but otherwise normal children, sit up, crawl, and walk later than their normal siblings indicates the importance of hearing and speech in the development of nonverbal habits. The severely aurally handicapped child lacks much more than his ability to hear other people and to acquire speech in the ordinary developmental way. Loss of hearing not only results in an impoverished informational environment; it also entails a restriction of the child's incentives to explore his world, a reduction in the things to become curious about.

Definitions

Within special education, the deaf and the hard-of-hearing are usually differentiated. These two subgroups are not homogeneous, and further subclassifications are often made. Such subgroups are usually based on the degree of hearing impairment, the cause of the deficit, or the age of the person at the onset of the disability.

The two types of definitions of exceptionality mentioned in earlier chapters—the quantitative and the psychological, educational, and social —are found in the literature on the aurally handicapped. The quantitative definitions typically indicate auditory disability as the degree of hearing loss measured audiometrically in terms of decibels (db). (Hearing loss refers to the deficit in the better ear in the speech range of frequencies.) The following definitions and categorization condensed from Streng et al. (1958), are representative of this type.

> *Class 1. Mild losses (20 to 30 db).* People with hearing losses in this range learn to speak by ear in the ordinary developmental way, and are borderline between the hard-of-hearing and the normal.
>
> *Class 2. Marginal losses (30 to 40 db).* People with such losses usually have some difficulty in hearing speech at a distance of more than a few feet, and in following group conversation. Speech can be learned by ear.
>
> *Class 3. Moderate losses (40 to 60 db).* With amplification of sound and the assistance of vision, people with hearing in this range can learn speech aurally.

Class 4. Severe losses (60 to 75 db). People with hearing losses in this range will not acquire speech without the use of specialized techniques. Most such people are considered to be "educationally deaf." They are borderline between the hard-of-hearing and the deaf.

Class 5. Profound losses (greater than 75 db). People with hearing in this range seldom learn language by ear alone, even with maximum amplification of sound.

People in classes 1, 2, and 3 are considered to be *hard of hearing,* while those in classes 4 and 5 constitute the *deaf.* The use of subgroups is a recognition that there are tremendous differences between the hard-of-hearing and the deaf, as audiometrically defined.

An alternative proposal, by a committee of the American Medical Association (1961), is to indicate hearing loss in terms of percentages rather than in decibels.

The more functionally oriented definition proposed by the White House Conference on Child Health and Protection (1931) distinguishes between the hard-of-hearing and the deaf primarily in terms of the *age of onset of the hearing loss.* This formulation defines as deaf: (1) those persons who are born with sufficient hearing loss to prevent the spontaneous acquisition of speech; (2) those who became deaf before language and speech were established; and (3) those who became deaf so soon after speech and language were acquired that these skills have been practically lost. The *hard-of-hearing* are defined as those persons who acquired useful speech and the ability to understand speech *prior to their hearing loss,* and who have continued to use these skills.

This conception violates the common-sense use of "deaf" and "hard-of-hearing," which refers to the degree of loss rather than to the age at which the sense of hearing was lost. According to this definition, an individual with an 80 decibel, congenital loss of hearing is called "deaf"; another person, with the same loss but dating from the age of ten, is called "hard-of-hearing." Such use of the terms does unnecessary violence to the common-sense meanings of the terms.

The definition of the Committee on Nomenclature of the Conference of Executives of American Schools for the Deaf (1938) is simpler and more practical. In their terms, the deaf are those people in whom the sense of hearing is nonfunctional for the ordinary purposes of life, while the hard-of-hearing are those in whom the sense of hearing, although defective, is functional with or without a hearing aid. The deaf are then subdivided into: (1) the congenitally deaf; and (2) the adventitiously deaf who were born with normal hearing but whose hearing became nonfunctional through accident or disease. We shall use the nomenclature of the Executives of American Schools for the Deaf in our discussion.

The aurally handicapped are sometimes subdivided according to whether the hearing loss is purely conductive (conduction deafness) or is the result of sensory-neural impairment (neural deafness). Since conduction deafness usually can be greatly aided by sound amplification systems (hearing aids), whereas sensory-neural impairment is less amenable to such treatment, the difference between the two is of social and educational, as well as of medical, significance.

It is often necessary, for legal and administrative purposes, to use audiometric definitions and classifications of aural impairment. However, the functional criteria, though vague, are more educationally and psychologically meaningful. Of course, there is a fairly high correlation between the two criteria. For example, it is possible to say that most people with hearing losses within designated, pure-tone, audiometrically defined limits have specified functional limitations. But there are exceptions. Individuals with the same threshold for pure tone often vary greatly in their behavioral (social, psychological, and educational) impairment. It is possible for almost any degree of residual hearing to become functional for most of the "ordinary purposes of life." Possibly only total loss of hearing, which is extremely rare, precludes any functional usefulness. This means that functional utility is a matter of degree, and cannot be divided into two discrete categories. With intensive auditory training, children reported to have "99 percent bilateral loss of hearing" have learned to speak spontaneously and to interpret speech aurally (Wedenberg, 1951, 1955). Conversely, children who experience only a partial hearing loss after speech and language are well established may, under unfavorable conditions, have these skills deteriorate and become functionally deaf and unintelligible (Meyerson, 1963). In other words, it is possible, with proper training, for small amounts of residual hearing to become socially and educationally useful. It is also possible for individuals with auditory potentialities well within the useful range to fail to use them, or to cease to use previously acquired language skills and become functionally deaf. The range of individual differences among the aurally impaired is as significant as is the mean difference between the normal and the aurally impaired. Labels and formal categories have some usefulness, but they can never be substituted for information concerning the individual person under study.

Symptoms of Hearing Loss

An infant severely or profoundly deaf from birth experiences emotion, cries, and initially vocalizes much as does a baby whose hearing is unimpaired. Because such a child seems dominantly normal, his auditory defect may not be suspected—or, if it is suspected, it may not definitely be established for some time. Many of the symptoms of deafness, such as poor articulation, delayed speech, and lack of responsiveness are found in mentally retarded, emotionally disturbed, and brain-damaged children, as well as in some otherwise normal children. In the absence of physical signs of pathology, such as malformations of the ears, absence of the ear canal, or chronic discharge from the ears, it is not easy for parents to discover deafness in a child before the age when he normally begins to talk.

The general symptoms of auditory deficit in older children are:

1. Apparent chronic inattention
2. Frequent failure to respond when spoken to
3. Marked delay in age of speaking or unusually faulty articulation
4. Apparent backwardness in school despite adequate tested intelligence

Tests for Identifying the Aurally Impaired

Studies have uniformly shown that a relatively small proportion of children who are aurally impaired are identified by behavioral symptoms alone. One research report indicates that teachers do only slightly better than chance in detecting hearing losses among their students (Curry, 1954). Many studies document the need for audiometric testing for the identification of the majority of children with significant hearing losses (Geyer and Yankauer, 1956; Kodman, 1956; Kodman et al., 1959). The range of testing devices and procedures used in the detection and measurement of auditory loss is very wide.

THE WATCH TEST AND THE WHISPER TEST

It is claimed that the normal person can hear the tick of an Ingersoll pocket watch at forty-eight inches. In testing, one ear is plugged and the watch is placed close to the other ear, being slowly withdrawn until the person ceases to hear it. The reverse procedure is then followed. The average distance obtained provides a rough index of auditory acuity.

In the whisper test, a whisper is made after "emptying the lungs of all normal air and then whispering distinctly with the residual air." The person being tested stands twenty feet away with his back to the tester, and repeats what is whispered. If the testee fails at twenty feet, the tester gradually moves closer until the testee is able to repeat the words whispered. Auditory deficit is estimated from the relative reduction in distance.

Watches and voices differ so much that standardization of norms for the watch and whisper tests is not practical. Although these tests may be used systematically in a few instances, they are used principally for preliminary screening when audiometric equipment is not available. Noise-makers of various types are the oldest devices for testing hearing, and they are still widely used. But because they are not calibrated, they are probably even less useful than the watch and whisper tests.

TUNING FORKS

With a set of appropriately tuned tuning forks, pitch can be systematically controlled in testing hearing. However, loudness is largely uncontrolled unless calibrated, mechanical, activating devices are used. Tuning forks are still frequently used for a quick approximation of hearing ability, but they are most frequently used for differentiating types of hearing impairment.

PURE-TONE AUDIOMETERS

The modern audiometers most frequently used are electronic devices which produce tones of variable frequency (pitch) and intensity (loudness) over a wide range. Today, practically every complete test and analysis of a person's hearing involves the use of the pure-tone audiometer. The testing consists of the systematic sounding of a series of tones varying in pitch and loudness. The person being tested hears the tones through earphones and responds by saying "Now" or by pressing a button whenever the tone is heard. The test results are typically plotted on an audiogram which provides a graphical representation of the acuity of each ear for various frequencies.

THE PHONOGRAPHIC AUDIOMETER

These devices are phonographs with the desired number (from ten to forty) of telephone receivers attached. Calibrated recordings of both male and female voices are played, and the voices grow gradually less distinct until the material spoken—usually digits or words—can be heard only by people with normal or superior hearing. Each ear is tested separately. The child being tested responds by writing in appropriate blanks, checking the proper word, or marking the picture of the object named. Tests with the phonographic audiometer are calibrated and standardized, and make possible the rapid screening of large numbers of children. More recent developments along this line are usually known as "speech perception tests."

SPEECH PERCEPTION TESTS

These tests measure perception for speech somewhat like the whisper test and older phonographic audiometric tests. The American Medical Association has developed tests of the threshold of speech perception. These tests use standardized speech material which is presented either on commercial recordings or via the live voice, monitored and controlled for intensity (O'Niell, 1964). The Central Institute for the Deaf in St. Louis has developed a Social Adequacy Index to indicate the degree of difficulty an aurally impaired individual has in ordinary communication (Davis, 1948; O'Niell, 1964).

THE GALVANIC SKIN RESPONSE TEST

This test makes use of a lie-detector type of instrument, and depends upon the establishment of a conditioned response in the person tested. A slight electric shock is applied to a part of the body, usually the foot, and the shock is preceded by a tone. The shock causes a characteristic deflection of the needle of the galvanometer (indicative of the galvanic skin response) which is in circuit with the subject being tested. After repeated applications of the tone-shock sequence, the tone will produce the galvanic skin response by itself—*provided the person can hear the tone, and provided the learning has taken place as expected*. The galvanic skin response to the tone proves that the person can hear. Failure to respond may be the result of either failure to hear or of failure to learn the necessary association.

This test is often recommended for use with very young children, suspected malingerers, people who are apparently functionally deaf (psychic deafness), and the severely mentally retarded. There is some difference of opinion about its usefulness, and one study has shown that most mentally retarded children who cannot be tested by pure-tone audiometric methods cannot be tested by the galvanic skin response method, either (Moss, Moss, and Tizard, 1961).

OTHER METHODS

A large number of ingenious variations of both the formal and informal methods of testing auditory acuity have been developed. For example, warbled pure tones have been found to be more effective than steady tones with children who have difficulty in attending (Douglas, Fowler, and Ryan, 1961). One test for children uses a simple Go-Game, in which they make a simple motor response whenever the word "Go!" is heard (Dale,

1962). Music, noisemakers, and animal sounds have been used as stimuli, both for measurement and for warm-up exercises which provide rough preliminary assessment of the child's hearing (Reichstein and Rosenstein, 1964).

Conditioned response methods, in which the appropriate response is rewarded, have taken several forms. In one of these, the child looks into a darkened house. When he hears a tone, he pushes a button which illuminates the interior of the house and revolves a group of dolls (Dix and Hallpike, 1947). Another such device yields candy and knickknacks when the child responds to the auditory stimuli (Meyerson and Michael, 1960). Studies indicate that children whose responses are rewarded perform significantly better than children who are not rewarded (Reichstein and Rosenstein, 1964).

Causes of Auditory Defects

Some auditory defects are inherited. There is a hereditary type of degenerative nerve deafness which may be present at birth or develop later in life. Infections such as German measles (rubella) in early pregnancy, as well as influenza and mumps, may cause congenital deafness which is not hereditary. Occasionally, a child is born with an absence or malformation of the ear canal, ear drum, or the ossicles of the middle ear.

Postnatal causes of auditory defects include most of the childhood diseases—scarlet fever, mumps, measles, and whooping cough. Occasionally, typhoid fever, pneumonia, influenza, and meningitis result in injury to the auditory mechanism. A common but decreasingly important cause of auditory loss is chronic infection of the middle ear (*otitis media*). Among adults, intracranial tumors, cerebral hemorrhage, prolonged exposure to tones of high intensity, and degenerative processes in the auditory mechanism are increasingly important causes of deafness. In approximately one-third of all cases, the causes of deafness are unknown (Vernon, 1968a).

The Incidence of Auditory Defects

We have only gross estimates on the total incidence of auditory defects in the United States. Statements such as ". . . less than half the population has perfect hearing" (Wynburn, 1960) mean nothing, since half the population must fall below the statistical norm (the median). O'Niell (1964) estimates that there are 300,000 children and 2,300,000 adults who are hard-of-hearing in the United States. Among adults, progressive nerve deterioration (presbycusis) is the most common type of auditory defect. The relationship between age and the incidence of impaired hearing (principally presbycusis) is shown in Table 12–1.

TABLE 12–1
Incidence of Impaired Hearing as
Related to Age (Per 1,000)

Age	Incidence
45–54	36
55–64	64
65–75	125
Above 75	226

Data from the United States Department of Health, Education, and Welfare (1961).

The aging process is said to produce a hearing loss of 160 cycles per year from the upper frequency limits, so that most individuals past middle age have little hearing above 10,000 cycles (Wynburn, 1960).

Personal Characteristics of the Acoustically Handicapped

Questions concerning the intellectual, personality, and behavioral characteristics of children with auditory defects sound deceptively simple. Such questions typically assume some specific but unspecified criterion for identifying people who are deaf or hard-of-hearing. But "hard-of-hearing" sometimes includes people with measurable, but not necessarily handicapping losses in one or both ears (if a pure-tone audiometric test is used). Sometimes the same term refers to people whose perceptions of speech are functional but defective (a social-utility criterion). Some workers following the recommendations of the White House Conference use the term to refer to any impaired individual who, regardless of the degree of auditory impairment, has developed speech and language in the ordinary developmental way. When we deal with data about groups variously defined, and assume that they are the same population, we get many different and apparently contradictory answers to the same questions. In the absence of a single acceptable criterion of deafness, information about the characteristics of the deaf has limited usefulness.

Obtaining adequate samplings of a defined population is also difficult. Investigators with limited time, money, and facilities have had to study those groups that were available. These groups have practically always been selected populations—students in special schools, special classes, or patients referred to clinics or practitioners. It is probable that children in residential schools contain a disproportionate number of people with multiple handicaps. In addition to their auditory defects, these children are often brain-damaged, aphasic, epileptic, emotionally disturbed, and may have impaired vision bordering on blindness. While these children all have auditory defects, the impairment of hearing is often not their greatest problem, nor is it the primary cause of their placement in residential schools. With the development of more special classes for the acoustically handicapped within the regular schools and the increased integration of handicapped students with the normal, the population of residential schools is changing to such a degree that the students of today are not comparable to those of twenty years ago. Children who attend residential schools are more severely aurally handicapped, are less academically able, have lived in less favorable psychological environments, and have more multiple handicaps than children attending special day-school classes or ordinary public or private schools. Special residential schools and special education classes probably enroll a disproportionate number of problem children, regardless of the degree of auditory impairment (Meyerson, 1963).

Assuming that we have access to a defined group of unselected acoustically handicapped, typical of a designated population, what are the proper questions to ask concerning them? Do we want to know the educational, personality, intellectual, and social characteristics of the acoustically handicapped as a group, irrespective of kind or degree of auditory impairment, linguistic ability, social origins, or place of residence? When the man on the street asks what people with auditory handicaps are like, he seems to be asking some such question. However, the answer would probably be meaningless. Suppose we find, as we usually do, that the acoustically handicapped are somewhat below the average of the non-handicapped population in all of these areas. What would it mean? Analysis might show that the deficit in these areas is contributed almost entirely by a comparatively small group of severely impaired, multiply handicapped, institutionalized individuals. The rest of the acoustically deficient are essentially normal in other respects.

Perhaps the more appropriate question is: "What are the characteristics of people with various degrees of impaired hearing and no other disability?" The authors have found no studies which answer this question. However, if we had an answer, we might then ask, "What, if any, are the additional handicapping effects of institutionalization, and of various degrees of physical and other sensory impairments?" Conversely, we can also ask what types of medical care and treatment, home situations, social provisions, and educational programs minimize these deleterious influences. With these limitations in mind, we will briefly summarize the present state of our information concerning people with impaired hearing.

INTELLIGENCE LEVEL OF
THE ACOUSTICALLY HANDICAPPED

Studies of handicapped groups have typically begun with attempts to determine how the intelligence of the group compares with comparable nonhandicapped persons.

Over a half-century ago, Pintner and Paterson (1915) used a modification of the Goddard Revision of the Binet-Simon Scale to test eighteen deaf children. They obtained a mean IQ of 63. Since that time, dozens of studies have compared the intelligence test performances of various groups of acoustically impaired people with the acoustically normal. Because of the language handicap of the majority of the severely aurally impaired, verbal tests of intelligence have seldom been used in such studies. Surveys of available studies show a great diversity of results. For example, Meyerson (1963) surveyed twenty-five studies. Ten, using individual performance tests, reported lower than normal IQ's for deaf children. The median IQ of the means reported in the ten studies is 91. In twelve studies, no significant differences between the deaf and the acoustically normal were reported. In three, the deaf were found to have higher IQ's. Studies using *group tests* have reported slightly lower mean IQ's for the aurally impaired than have those using individual tests. In the same review, Meyerson surveyed twelve studies using *group* nonverbal or nonlanguage tests. He found the median IQ of the reported means of eight studies to be 85. Four studies reported insignificant differences, and none of them found higher IQ's for the deaf children. Since the 1930s and '40s, interest in the general question of the intelligence of the aurally handicapped seems to have decreased. The authors' tabulation of thirty-six major studies according to year of publication is shown in Table 12–2.

There are probably several reasons for the declining interest in the question of the general intellectual level of people with sensory deficits. Workers in the field have decided that a simple statement of the mean IQ of all people with auditory defects is neither meaningful nor useful. To be meaningful, measurements must be of people with a specified type of handicap, degree of impairment, age of onset of the disability, degree of language deficit, chronological age, and background. The tests used must also be specified as group or individual, language or nonlanguage, omnibus or analytical. The problem of the intellectual level of the acoustically impaired breaks down into dozens of smaller, more specific, but more meaningful subproblems.

TABLE 12–2
Years of Publication of Studies of the
Intelligence Test Scores of the Aurally Impaired

Year	Number of Studies
1910–1919	1
1920–1929	4
1930–1939	16
1940–1949	12
1950–1959	3
	Total = 36

Our changing conceptions of the nature and components of intelligence have also reduced interest in the general question of the intellectual level of people with auditory defects. Before the 1930s, intelligence was generally considered to be primarily a genetically determined, innate ability to learn. If a child was born with little potentiality, there was not much to be done about it. Heredity was thought to place definite limits on achievement, and environmental influences were thought to operate only within these limits.

Starting in the late '20s and continuing through the '30s and '40s, a long series of studies demonstrated that environmental changes have significant effects on intelligence test scores. This change from an extreme hereditarian to a more environmental emphasis was accentuated during the '50s and '60s by a series of studies of the effects of environmental deprivations on intellectual level. Intelligence, as measured, is currently recognized to be a product of both genetic and environmental factors. It is partially a social product. Intelligence test scores are rough indices of functional level, implying no particular information about the determinants of that level.

In the absence of evidence that inferior intelligence and hereditary deafness are genetically linked, we assume that the hereditary determinants of the intellectual level of deaf children are not significantly different from those of their siblings with normal hearing. Differences in their intellectual functioning must then be due to environmental differences. The question of the possible intellectual inferiority of the sensorially handicapped becomes a question of the extent to which the sensory deprivation has influenced the individual's level of intellectual functioning.

Partially because of these considerations, interest has shifted from the general question to that of ways in which the restrictions of auditory input affects the level and pattern of intellectual functioning. In special education, interest focusses primarily on the question of the most effective means of compensating for the auditory deficit. The extent of deficit of intellectual and behavioral functioning in uncomplicated cases of deafness is conceived of as an index of the extent to which the culture has failed to develop or use devices and methods for compensating for the sensory limitatons. Special education assumes that specific methods of training and educating handicapped children do make a difference in their functional level. Deaf children learn, or fail to learn, self-help and independence, as well as the fundamental educational and vocational skills, according to the adequacy and availability of the required specialized educational and training resources. In such a frame of reference, the effect of deafness on intelligence becomes part of the question of its effect on achievement (Reynolds, 1965). For a more detailed discussion of this topic, see Vernon (1968b).

Some workers believe that although the general intellectual level of the aurally impaired child may not be inferior to comparable children with normal hearing, the perceptual and conceptual processes of congenitally deaf children fail to develop in a comparable way (Myklebust, 1953, 1960; Farrant, 1964). This view is supported by some studies (Hughes, 1959) dealing primarily with *verbal* conceptualization, but the bulk of the investigations indicate that in processes not requiring verbalization, or when the verbalizations required are within the vocabulary range and experience of the subjects, the deaf do as well as hearing subjects in abstract conceptualization (Kates et al., 1961; Kates, Yudin, and Tiffany, 1962; Furth, 1963; Nass, 1964; Michael and Kates, 1965; Kates and Kates, 1965; Kates, 1967). Deaf subjects have less adequate verbalization than hearing subjects, and a larger proportion of adequate conceptual categorizations which are accompanied by inadequate verbalizations than do hearing subjects of the same age and IQ. These differences in verbalization disappear when hearing and deaf subjects are equated as to age, IQ, and educational achievement. Educational attainment probably equates verbalization. These studies also find no evidence of greater rigidity (less flexibility in the strategies of concept attainment) in the deaf subjects.

EDUCATIONAL ACHIEVEMENT OF THE AURALLY IMPAIRED

The studies of educational achievement have uniformly shown the deaf to be retarded from three to five years. The absolute amount of educational retardation increases with age (Meyerson, 1963). It is less in the more mechanical skills, such as arithmetic computation and spelling, than in the more intellectual areas such as paragraph meanings, word meanings, and arithmetic comprehension. Language and communication lag behind the motor and computational skills.

Students applying for admission to the preparatory class at Gallaudet College, who probably represent the best students graduating from the residential schools for the deaf, have a mean age of eighteen years and nine months and obtain a median grade of 9.2 on the Stanford Achievement Test. This level is attained by the average fifteen-year-old child (Fusfeld, 1954). This group of students, probably highly selected in terms of educational achievement, is retarded by three to four years. The educational retardation of deaf children may be partially the result of the excessive amount of school time required for them to learn to speak and their subsequent language deficiencies. The development of improved methods for teaching these children, and the increasing number of children who acquire language in the home, nursery school, and kindergarten prior to beginning their academic education, may help reduce the extent of their educational retardation.

PERSONAL AND SOCIAL ADJUSTMENT OF THE AURALLY IMPAIRED

The statements made in earlier chapters concerning the personal and social adjustment of handicapped people in general hold true for the deaf and the hard-of-hearing. Research studies of the personal and social traits of the aurally impaired show a higher degree of emotional instability, neuroticism, and social maladjustment than do the appropriate norm groups (Allbright, 1952; Fiedler, 1952; Levine, 1960).

The deaf child need not be psychologically different from the child who hears. Although the aurally handicapped are more maladjusted than are the normal, they show no distinctive forms or patterns of maladjustment. The adjustment patterns of deaf and hard-of-hearing children are as varied as they are in hearing children. Most of these problems do not derive directly from the hearing loss; they are accentuated by the child's primary handicap but cannot be traced directly to his hearing.

Medical Aspects of Hearing Loss

Routines for the diagnosis and measurement of hearing loss include: (1) otological examinations of the ear canal, tympanic membrane (eardrum) and a qualitative evaluation of the type and extent of hearing function; and (2) audiometric and other evaluations to provide more precise quantitative information of the degree of hearing loss.

Medical care and surgery can also do a lot to improve certain types of hearing loss. Individuals with middle-ear damage have a very good chance of obtaining improved hearing as a result of appropriate surgery or appropriate hearing aids.

SURGERY

Some of the more common surgical operative procedures are:

1. *Fenestration of the labyrinth.* A new oval window is made into the horizontal semicircular canal of the inner ear. The artificial window is closed with a membrane which acts as a sound-sensitive surface picking up the sound waves directly and bypassing the bones of the inner ear.
2. *Mobilization of the stapes.* The plate of the stapes (the bone which attaches to the oval window) is loosened by breaking away the excess bone impeding its action
3. *Artificial replacement of the stapes.*
4. *Covering tympanic drum perforations with skin grafts.*

Today, the otological surgeon can change the shape of the middle ear, rebuild the ossicular chain (the three bones spanning the middle ear), repair, move into a new position, or make a new tympanic membrane, construct new functional membraneous windows into the inner ear, and make a bony canal into the middle ear when an infant is born without one (Proctor, 1961).

At present, there is no known medical or surgical means of significantly improving nerve deafness. The approximately 20 percent of deaf children who are deaf because of meningitis, mumps, acute fevers, or other forms of injury to the inner ear or auditory nerve cannot be helped surgically. Because of the constant development of new surgical procedures, however, every person with a serious hearing loss should have a complete otological examination and be advised of the possibilities of medical or surgical treatment.

HEARING AIDS

Modern hearing aids can be used in place of, or in addition to, surgical procedures to improve the hearing of a large percentage of people with conduction deafness. A hearing aid is primarily a sound amplifier. The earphone simply increases the loudness of sounds; a person must have some residual hearing to profit by sound amplification. The person with conduction deafness (outer or middle-ear impairment) can profit more from hearing aids than can the person with perceptive or nerve deafness (injury to the middle ear or auditory nerve).

Improvements in hearing aids are being made continuously, and every person with some residual hearing should probably consider their use. It is estimated that not more than one person in three who could be helped by a hearing aid owns and uses one (Van Itallie, 1962; Maltzman, 1949; Gentile, Schein, and Hasse, 1967). People with aural impairments fail to use hearing aids for several reasons. Some are unaware of the possibilities offered by modern hearing aids. Many are restrained by vanity or self-consciousness. Some of the deaf and hard-of-hearing have become resigned to their restricted world and are either apathetic or resistant to help. Many people have tried hearing aids and then discarded them. Most of these people can profit from counseling. The first group may simply need information concerning the nature and availability of hearing aids. Those restrained by vanity may be helped to realize that when a person needs and can profit by a hearing aid, he is probably more conspicuous when he does not wear one than when he does. The social blunders of the person who hears only half of what is said are much more obvious than is an inconspicuous hearing aid. The adolescent girl who will not wear a hearing aid when she needs one makes social errors, the consequences of which are far greater than being recognized as a person with a hearing loss sufficient to require a hearing aid, but otherwise normal. Many people who discard their hearing aids after a short trial expect too much and do not realize that a considerable period of adjustment and new learning is required before a hearing aid can be tolerated and used effectively.

The Limitations of Hearing Aids. Some people cannot profit sufficiently from hearing aids to warrant their use, some expect too much from them, and some have developed habits which preclude their effective use. There are people with certain kinds of inner-ear (nerve) deafness who cannot tolerate hearing aids. The person with nerve deafness often has an irregular pattern of auditory loss. A hearing aid with equal amplification of all frequencies will make some sounds unbearably loud while it is making others just audible. Some earphones provide greater amplification of higher tones, but this often produces intolerable distortion. The accentuation of high tones and suppression of the low frequencies sometimes produce such a radical change in patterns of stimulation that the person's habitual patterns of auditory perception are severely disrupted (Anderson, 1967).

Several attempts have been made to provide shifts or transposition of high-frequency speech sounds to lower ranges so as to make them more audible to people with residual hearing in the low frequencies. Since most deaf individuals have some residual hearing in the very low frequencies, the successful devising of practical means of doing this would be of considerable significance (Quigley, 1969). Preliminary studies indicate that selective amplification of particular frequencies to fit individual hearing losses is practical and is superior to the flat amplification of a broad band of frequencies as found in most conventional hearing aids (Reddell and Calvert, 1966; Quigley, 1969).

The average person has to learn to use a hearing aid. Amplification does not restore hearing to normal. It does not necessarily make a hard-of-hearing person hear better. It only provides him with the possibility of hearing better. The deafened person (one who has lost his hearing after having heard normally) has often lost his habits of selective hearing. The congenitally deaf person has never acquired these habits. The deaf or hard-of-hearing person must learn or relearn to screen out irrelevant sounds and "hear out" the sounds that are important to him. The deaf-ened person must also develop a tolerance for the distortions of sound imposed by a hearing aid.

It is advantageous for a person with progressive impairment to begin using a hearing aid before he loses the habits of listening and of selective hearing. Distortions imposed by a hearing aid may be tolerated if the device is used with progressively greater amplification as the hearing loss develops, whereas the degree of distortion ultimately involved may be intolerable if the aid is used for the first time after a loss has become acute. Similarly, babies with congenital hearing losses may be fitted with hearing aids so that they will learn in the ordinary developmental way to use sounds as guides to behavior and to understanding. The severely handicapped child, without a hearing aid, may learn to ignore sounds that he can hear because they are too faint to attract his attention and serve as useful guides. He does not become interested in sounds and re-mains unaware of their significance. If effective amplification is provided, the child will learn to notice and respond to sound. The child who has learned to live in a soundless world is likely to find some sounds disagree-able, and must change from having dominantly visual and cutaneous perception to having dominantly visual and auditory perception.

The Aurally Impaired Child in the Family

In addition to the family problems of handicapped children in general, there are some situations peculiar to the aurally impaired. If the child has any residual hearing—and most children do—every attempt should be made to capitalize on it. After complete otological and audiometric examinations have been made and any surgical or medical treatments completed, hearing aids may be used if there is any useful residual hear-ing, and training should start immediately.

The child should be raised in a speaking environment. Special efforts should be made to reinforce both the child's responses to sounds and his spontaneous vocalizations. If parents look at the child, go to him, attend to his needs and play with him when he cries, coos, and gurgles, he will tend to repeat his vocalizing. Talking carefully, distinctly, and slowly to the child when he is watching one's face and when the face is in full light will encourage him to combine looking and listening as sources of cues to meanings. The aurally handicapped child needs the same kind of opportunities to learn and understand speech as the normal child, but he needs more of them. Special situations may have to be contrived in order to emphasize the relationship of dimly heard sounds and visual cues to their meanings by concrete reference to persons, objects, activities, and situations.

When treatment directed at maximizing the child's use of his residual hearing and his potentiality for speech is combined with a good home-training program, most aurally handicapped children can come to school as talking children. The majority of deaf children who learn to talk have had a good home training from their earliest years (Ewing and Ewing, 1958). If the child is one of the few who are totally deaf, he must learn to understand speech and to talk via sight and touch.

Phrases and short sentences using the pattern of normal speech—spoken a little more slowly and clearly—while maintaining the normal rhythmic pattern of the sentence are more easily followed than are single words. The home is the place where auditory training, lip reading (or the more recent terms "speech reading," "visual communication," and "visual listening"), and learning to speak all begin (O'Niell, 1964). Proper home training with hearing aids is making it possible for a large percentage of aurally handicapped children to learn to understand language and to talk in the ordinary, developmental way.

A modification of a list of suggestions provided by Van Wyk (1959) for the parents of children with severe auditory impairments is as follows:

1. Talk to your child constantly. Provide a rich speaking atmosphere. Don't use signs with him, and when the child uses a sign, supply the proper word.
2. Expect your child to learn speech reading and to speak. Start with simple phrases or meaningful words in specific situations or with reference to concrete objects and activities.
3. Work constantly to increase his vocabulary. Systematically introduce new words and teach different words for the same thing to avoid the development of a stilted, limited speech pattern.
4. Insist that the child speak for himself, first to members of his family, then to friends and relatives, and later to casual acquaintances and strangers. Don't step in to speak and interpret for your child. Encourage independence and self-confidence.

5. Require and expect the handicapped child to accept responsibility, perform household duties, and to participate in family life essentially like the nonhandicapped. Send him on errands as soon as he has sufficient vocabulary to be able to make himself understood.
6. Discourage the use of pencil-and-paper or signs in place of oral speech.
7. Provide as much pleasure and feelings of satisfaction as possible with the use of language. Speech training in the house should never become dull, monotonous, repetitious drill.

Language used spontaneously, in natural situations where it serves a purpose and is meaningful, with the attention, acceptance, and understanding of others operating as rewards, is the ideal situation for the acquisition of speech by the aurally impaired child just as it is for the nonhandicapped. Success in teaching him to understand and to use oral speech depends on the whole family, the characteristics of the child himself, and the use of specialized facilities and help. But of all these factors, the most important is the parents' attitude toward the child and his handicap (Ewing and Ewing, 1958).

Education of the Aurally Handicapped

Although no clear division can be made between the deaf and the hard-of-hearing, many of the problems of their education are sufficiently different to warrant their being educated either separately or by different methods (Ewing, 1960). The primary difference in the education of these two groups is in their learning to speak and to understand speech. The deaf child with no useful residual hearing must depend entirely on vision and the other senses for his education. He must learn to understand speech solely by seeing (lip reading, speech reading, visual communication, or visual listening), and he learns to speak via the visual, cutaneous, and kinesthetic senses. If the child with useful residual hearing is taught, like the deaf child, to rely largely or entirely on visual, cutaneous, and kinesthetic cues for the understanding of speech and for learning to speak, he will eventually neglect his auditory potentialities and become functionally deaf. The profoundly deaf child acquires oral speech by learning to reproduce what he sees on the lips and faces of people talking to him. He can monitor his own speech only via the cutaneous and kinesthetic sensations from his vocal apparatus. The hard-of-hearing child needs auditory training along with his speech reading to increase his use of his residual hearing, so that he develops a combined visual and auditory perceptual system. Except for the ways in which they acquire their communication skills, the education of the profoundly deaf and the hard-of-hearing is not significantly different.

The statements made above assume that the deaf are to be taught oral speech. However, for reasons not entirely clear, some deaf individuals seem unable to master oral speech, and these people must not be neglected. Consequently, many schools use a combination of speech and a manual alphabet (fingerspelling). Few, if any, schools use the manual alphabet entirely, but unless much more effective methods of teaching oral speech are developed, it seems that both the pure oral and the combined oral and manual methods are with us to stay.

There has recently developed an increased interest and research in the use of manual communication by deaf children. The Russians claim that by starting to teach manual communication at the age of two years they are able to develop vocabularies of several thousand words by the time deaf children are six years old. They claim that the use of fingerspelling fosters rather than retards the development of oral speech and speechreading, and that children so taught eventually abandon fingerspelling and rely solely on oral speech and speechreading for communication (Morkovin, 1960; Quigley, 1969).

Two systems of manual communication are used by the deaf. One is the manual alphabet, or fingerspelling, in which the configurations of the hand correspond to the letters of the alphabet. In this system a spoken language is spelled out manually. The other system consists of sign language, in which a set of manual configurations, movements, and gestures correspond to particular words or concepts. There are national and regional variations in sign language that are comparable to those of spoken languages. The American Sign Language (A.S.L.), with certain regional variations, is used by the deaf in North America and has recently been the subject of formal analysis. The A.S.L. is somewhat like pictograph writing in which some symbols are quite arbitrary and some are representational. For example, the sign for "always" is made by holding the hand in a fist, index finger extended as in pointing while rotating the arm at the elbow. This is purely arbitrary. The sign for "flower" is more representational. It is made by holding the fingers of one hand extended, all five fingertips touching (the tapered hand), and touching the fingertips first to one nostril and then to the other as if sniffing a flower. All such signs are arbitrary to a degree. The literate deaf individual typically uses a combination of A.S.L. and fingerspelling in manual communication.

Special educational provisions for the child with impaired hearing are provided, to some degree, from kindergarten through college. Residential schools, special day schools, special classes in the regular schools, resource teachers, and itinerant teachers are all used for the education of the aurally impaired child.

NURSERY SCHOOLS FOR THE AURALLY IMPAIRED CHILD

The young child with useful residual hearing, fitted with a hearing aid and equipped with good home training, will probably develop best in a normal environment where he experiences oral speech all day long and where special efforts are made to talk to him as much as possible. The profoundly deaf child will require supplementary training by a special teacher of the deaf. The special teacher can also instruct and train the mother and the regular teacher so that they can provide supplementary speech and speechreading training for the child. A good, natural, normal nursery-school program, with the aurally handicapped child using his hearing aid, if indicated, and the teachers making special efforts to reach and stimulate him, is probably the best supplement to the home-training program for the three- to five-year-old.

THE SPECIAL SCHOOL FOR THE DEAF

In 1960, there were seventy-two public residential schools for children with auditory impairments in the United States, enrolling about 16,000 children. Historically, the residential school was the first type of facility established for the education of the deaf. The advantages and disadvantages of the residential school for the child with auditory impairment are essentially those listed in an earlier chapter for residential institutions in general. As is true for most categories of exceptional people, there is a decrease in the percentage of children with hearing impairments being sent to the special schools—both residential and day. The special day school for the aurally impaired child has not been a practical facility except in a few large cities. The relatively low incidence of severe auditory impairment (perhaps 1 per 1,000) requires a school to draw from such a large geographical area that transportation becomes a serious problem.

The advantages and disadvantages of the special day school were also listed in an earlier chapter and will not be restated here. The residential school will probably always be needed, although attendance at such schools is decreasing. Children with severe hearing impairments living in isolated rural areas, aurally impaired children with additional disabilities, children with unfavorable home situations, and others with special problems can best be educated in residential schools. For some children, short-term programs may be sufficient to develop their special oral and aural skills to the point where they can function satisfactorily in the regular classroom (Poulos, 1961). Since nearly half the children attending residential schools for the hearing impaired go home each weekend, and 12 percent of the children attending such schools are really day students, the majority of the students maintain contact with their homes, communities, and families (Schunhoff, 1964).

THE SPECIAL CLASS IN A REGULAR SCHOOL

The special class, with some integration with the regular classes or a still greater degree of integration with the assistance of resource teachers, consultants, or itinerant teachers, is rapidly becoming the most common educational arrangement for children with auditory impairments. With maximum surgical remediations and the use of improved hearing aids, many children previously considered hopelessly deaf and placed in residential schools can now function quite adequately in the regular schools.

Although there is a paucity of large-scale and well-controlled studies, the evidence indicates that children in the ordinary school environment mixing with the normally hearing children are superior to institutionalized children, except possibly in the areas of personal adjustment. When institutionalized and integrated groups of children are equated for degree of auditory impairment, age of onset of the disabilities, and mental level, the children educated in integrated classes are generally superior in fluency of speech and in educational achievement (Johnson, 1962; Brereton, 1957). Recent experience indicates that children can manage in the ordinary school with more severe hearing impairments than has been generally considered possible. Such children do require special help.

When the special class for aurally impaired children is part of a regular school, varying degrees and rates of integration can be achieved according to the child's needs. There is evidence that abrupt complete integration may overwhelm some aurally handicapped children (Motto and Wawrzaszek, 1963), and for such children, gradual integration is indicated. Alice Streng (1958) recommends that most handicapped children begin school in a special class. They can later be assigned to a regular classroom—preferably one to a classroom—for a limited time each day, largely for socialization. Still later, they can take such courses as art and physical education with the regular students. As they get older, they are assigned to regular classes in selected additional subjects in which they excel. In high school, the average aurally impaired child can take home economics, industrial arts, physical education, and art, and each year add one additional regular academic subject to his program. By the senior year, such children would be taking all their work in regular classes.

THE AURALLY IMPAIRED COLLEGE STUDENT

In the United States, the deaf high school graduate has a choice of attending a college for the deaf—Gallaudet—or one of the 2,000 regular universities and colleges. Gallaudet is a federally sponsored college for the deaf in Washington, D.C., and the only college exclusively for the deaf in the world.

Many of the problems of the deaf student are magnified in the regular college. There are no special facilities or aids available to him. Classroom instruction is often more oral—sometimes purely lecture or lecture and discussion. The handicapped student is only one among many nonhandicapped, and usually no special consideration is provided him. Students with severe auditory impairments usually watch the lecturer to get the general ideas, but depend upon a carbon copy of the notes of helpful classmates and their own outside readings for details. It is very difficult for people who must read speech to follow the rapid flow of conversation in group discussions. They usually have to rely on the help of a thoughtful friend in such situations, for this problem seems insurmountable.

Vocational Opportunities of the Aurally Impaired

The deaf find employment in almost all vocational areas. Table 12–3 indicates the occupational distribution of the employed deaf in the United States in the late 1950s.

Table 12–3 indicates that the deaf are employed in sizable numbers

TABLE 12–3

Occupational Areas of the Employed Deaf Compared with the Total Employed in the United States

	Employed Deaf (%)	General Population (%)
Professional, technical, and similar workers	6.6	10.6
Managers, officials, and proprietors	3.2	15.5
Clerical, sales, and similar workers	7.2	20.7
Craftsmen, foremen, and similar workers	35.9	13.4
Operatives and similar workers	35.2	20.1
Laborers and service workers	11.9	19.7

Data from Lunde and Bogman (1959).

in all the major occupational groups. There are relatively fewer in the higher professional, managerial, and clerical and sales areas, probably because of the greater necessity for facile communications in these occupations. There are relatively greater numbers employed in the intermediate occupational levels (craftsmen and semiskilled workers), and a decidedly smaller percentage working as unskilled laborers. In the study cited (Lunde and Bogman, 1959), 85 percent of the deaf workers were rated as "successful" in their occupations.

Studies of the occupational success of girls who had attended the Lexington School for the deaf indicate that achievement in the language skills was the keystone to successful careers (Connor and Rosenstein, 1963).

The vocational training of the aurally handicapped is not essentially different from that designed for those who hear. Individual differences in special talents and general intelligence are as great among people with hearing defects as among those with normal hearing. Interests, motivation, and realistic levels of personal aspirations and social expectation are no less important to the aurally impaired than for the acoustically normal, and their occupational possibilities are only slightly more restricted.

Each state has a vocational rehabilitation office and most states have many branch offices, most of which have personnel trained to work with the deaf and hard-of-hearing. Many states also have people in their departments of employment who are selected and trained to work with the handicapped.

The Social Life of the Deaf

The social life of most of the deaf and hard-of-hearing is essentially the same as that of those with normal hearing. The average deaf man has a job, owns his home, marries a girl of his choice, raises a family of reasonably normal children, and participates in the social life of his community. More than other types of handicapped people, they tend to favor social groups of their own kind. Many deaf people are more relaxed and find great satisfaction from associating with those who share their problems and interests. One evidence or consequence of the tendency of the deaf to associate with those similarly impaired is found in a study of 10,000 married adult deaf, which showed that less than 5 percent had married hearing people (Brill, 1961).

In addition to social clubs, the deaf have organized The National Fraternal Society of the Deaf, which writes insurance in the millions, publishes a monthly paper, and has a large ladies auxiliary (Elstad et al., 1955). The deaf have organized the National Association of the Deaf, with offices in Berkeley, California. The Association publishes a monthly magazine, *The Silent Worker*. The deaf hold a national basketball tournament yearly; and less often, they have bowling and football tournaments. The deaf have been a very self-conscious group. They have opposed all types of begging by the deaf. In several states, they have established homes for the aged deaf. The deaf have opposed special preferential legislation for the aurally impaired, just as they have opposed legislation which they feel unrealistically restricts their activities (Elstad et al., 1955).

Prospects for the Aurally Impaired

If we extrapolate from the recent past, the prospect for additional ame-lioration of the conditions of the deaf is good. We can expect continued developments in the medical treatment and surgical remediation of the aurally impaired. Further reduction in the incidence of severe aural im-pairment can result from the decreasing incidence of those diseases of the pregnant mother, or of the child, which may damage the auditory appa-ratus. We can reasonably expect the development of new hearing aids which reduce the handicap of those with impaired hearing.

There is always the possibility that some major breakthrough may occur—the more effective use of the other senses in perceiving speech, or even bypassing the ordinary sensory inputs to get appropriate neural impulses to the brain. The skin has some capacity for transmitting speech information which conceivably could be used in place of, or to comple-ment, speech perception by the other senses. It is possible to convert the frequency and amplitude of speech into an array of tactual vibrations. How practical this might be as a means of perceiving speech has not yet been determined (Pickett and Pickett, 1963).

Summary

Studies of attitudes toward handicapped persons show that while the blind, the orthopedically disabled, the physically ill, and the like are viewed with compassion, the majority of lay people are either indifferent to the deaf or react unfavorably toward them. The individual deprived of hearing from birth, in addition to being unable to hear the speech of other people and to acquire speech in the ordinary developmental way, lacks an important tool for the acquisition of nonverbal skills, a major source of pleasurable social experience, as well as one of the principal means of social interaction. The deaf and the hearing are most meaning-fully differentiated according to whether or not they have hearing which is functional for the ordinary purposes of life.

Because only a small proportion of the deaf and the hard-of-hearing are identified by parents and teachers unaided, a wide variety of tests has been developed for this purpose. These consist of the watch test, the whisper test, the phonographic audiometer and its modern counterpart the speech perception tests, tuning fork tests, the galvanic skin response test, and finally and most importantly, the pure-tone audiometers.

Auditory defects are both endogenous (hereditary) and exogenous (environmental or adventitious) in origin. The causes of a large percentage of cases of impaired hearing are unknown. The exact incidence of impaired hearing is unknown, but conservative estimates indicate that some 300,000 children and 2,300,000 adults are sufficiently aurally impaired to warrant special care and treatment.

There are no personal characteristics or personality patterns peculiar to the aurally impaired. The deaf typically score below the hearing on most intelligence tests, but this can be accounted for in terms other than differences in inherent capacity. The educational retardation of two to three grades commonly found among the severely aurally impaired indicates the extent to which society has failed to develop alternative methods of educating these people. The conceptual deficiencies of the aurally impaired seem to be principally in the verbal areas. Deafness produces no peculiar patterns of personal or social adjustment or maladjustment but, like any handicap, it creates an excessive number of adjustment problems. Special care and treatment of the acoustically impaired involves medicine, surgery, education, and social work, as well as other disciplines. People with middle- or outer-ear damage (conduction deafness) have a very good chance of having their hearing improved by corrective surgery, appropriate hearing aids, and aural rehabilitation. Those with damage to the inner ear or the auditory nerve have a smaller chance of obtaining help in these ways.

The education of the aurally impaired child begins in the home and is continued in residential schools, special day schools, special classes in regular schools, and integrated classes. The consensus seems to be that the aurally handicapped, like most exceptional children, should not be sent to special schools if they can be suitably educated in ordinary schools, and that they should not go to boarding schools if they can be suitably educated in day schools near their homes. The acquiring of adequate language and communication skills constitutes the major problem of the aurally handicapped, whether these are acquired by oral speech and speechreading alone or by speech with the aid of fingerspelling, either with or without the language of signs.

The deaf find employment less often than the aurally unimpaired in the professional, managerial, clerical and sales, and personal service areas, and more often in the skilled crafts and in the technical areas. Some find employment in practically all areas.

The social life of the deaf is essentially the same as that of the rest of the population, although there is a greater tendency for them to form social groups of their own kind than is true for the other types of handicapped people. The prospect for improved surgical, remedial, and educational programs for the aurally impaired is good.

References

ALLBRIGHT, M., "Mental Health of Children with Hearing Impairments," *J. except. child.*, XIX (1952), 110–13.

AMERICAN MEDICAL ASSOCIATION COMMITTEE ON MEDICAL RATINGS OF PHYSICAL IMPAIRMENT, "Guide to the Evaluation of Permanent Impairment of Ear, Nose, Throat, and Related Structures," *J. Amer. med. assoc.*, CLXXVII (1961), 489–501.

ANDERSON, V. M., "The Incidence and Significance of High-Frequency Deafness in Children," *Amer. j. dis. child.*, CXIII (1967), 560–65.

BRERETON, B. L., *The Schooling of Children with Impaired Hearing*. Sydney: Commonwealth Office of Education, 1957.

BRILL, R. B., "Hereditary Aspects of Deafness," *Volta rev.*, LXIII (1961), 168–75.

CONFERENCE OF EXECUTIVES OF AMERICAN SCHOOLS FOR THE DEAF, "Report of the Conference Committee on Nomenclature," *Amer. ann. deaf*, LXXXIII (1938), 1–3.

CONNOR, L. E., AND J. ROSENSTEIN, "Vocational Status and Adjustment of Deaf Women," *Volta rev.*, LXV (1963), 585–91.

CURRY, E. T., "Are Teachers Good Judges of Pupils' Hearing?" *J. except. child.*, XXI (1954), 42–48.

DALE, D. M., *Applied Audiometry for Children*. Springfield, Ill.: Charles C Thomas, Publisher, 1962.

DAVIS, H., "The Articulation Area and the Social Adequacy Index for Hearing," *Laryngoscope*, LVIII (1948), 761–78.

———, "Guide for the Classification and Evaluation of Hearing Handicap in Relation to the International Audiometric Zero," *Transactions amer. acad. ophthal. otolaryng.*, LXIX (1965), 740–51.

———, "Validation of Evoked-Response Audiometry (ERA) in Deaf Children," *Inter. audiol.*, V, No. 2 (1966), 77–81.

DIX, M. AND C. S. HALLPIKE, "The Peep Show," *Brit. med. j.*, II (1947), 719–23.

DOUGLAS, F. M., E. P. FOWLER, JR., AND G. M. RYAN, *A Differential Study of Communication Disorders*. New York: Columbia Presbyterian Medical Center, 1961.

DOWNS, M. P., AND G. M. STERRITT, "Identification Audiometry for Neonates: A Preliminary Report," *J. audit. res.*, IV (1964), 69–80.

———, "A Guide to Newborn and Infant Hearing Screening Programs," *Arch. of otolaryng.*, LXXXV (1967), 15–22.

EIVERTON, H. W. "Teddy-bear screening for babies," *Acta otolaryng.*, LXI (1966), 279–80.

ELSTAD, L. M., M. E. FRAMPTON, AND E. D. GALL, *The Deaf in Special Education for the Exceptional*. Boston, Mass.: Porter Sargent, Publisher, 1955.

EWING, A. G., ed., *The Modern Educational Treatment of Deafness*. Washington, D.C.: The Volta Bureau, 1960.

EWING, I. R., AND A. G. EWING, *New Opportunities for Deaf Children*. Springfield, Ill.: Charles C Thomas, Publisher, 1958.

FARRANT, R. H., "The Intellective Ability of Deaf and Hearing Children Compared by Factor Analysis," *Amer. ann. deaf*, CIX (1964), 306–25.

FIEDLER, M. F., *Deaf Children in a Hearing World*. New York: The Ronald Press Company, 1952.

FURTH, H., "Language and the Development of Thinking." Paper presented at the International Congress of the Deaf, Washington, D.C., 1963.

———, "Conceptual Performance in Deaf Adults," *J. abn. soc. psychol.*, LXIX (1964), 676–81.

FUSFELD, I. S., *A Cross Section Evaluation of the Academic Program of Schools for the Deaf*, Gallaudet coll. bull. No. 3. Washington, D.C., 1954.

GENTILE, A., J. D. SCHEIN, AND K. HAASE, *Characteristics of Persons with Impaired Hearing*. U.S. Department of Health, Education, and Welfare, Public Health Service. Publication No. 1000, Series 10, No. 35. Washington, D.C.: Government Printing Office, 1967.

GEYER, M. L., AND A. YANKAUER, "Teacher Judgments of Hearing Loss in Children," *J. speech hearing disorders*, XXI (1956), 482–86.

HUGHES, R. B., "A Comparison of Verbal Conceptualization in Deaf and Hearing Children." Unpublished doctoral dissertation, University of Illinois, 1959.

JOHNSON, J. C., *Educating Hearing-impaired Children in Ordinary Schools*. Manchester: Manchester University Press, 1962.

KATES, S. L., *Cognitive Structures in Deaf, Hearing, and Psychotic Individuals*. Northampton, Mass.: Clarke School for the Deaf, 1967.

———, AND F. F. KATES, "Social and Nonsocial Verbal Concepts of Deaf and Hearing Children," *J. abn. psychol.*, LXX (1965), 214–17.

———, L. YUDIN, AND R. K. TIFFANY, "Concept Attainment by Deaf and Hearing Adolescents," *J. educ. psychol.*, LIII (1962), 119–26.

———, et al., "Categorization and Related Verbalizations in Deaf and Hearing Adolescents," *J. educ. psychol.*, LII (1961), 188–94.

KODMAN, F., "Identification of Hearing Loss by the Classroom Teacher," *Laryngoscope*, LXVI (1956), 1346–47.

———, et al., "Socioeconomic Status and Observer Identification of Hearing Loss in School Children," *J. except. child.*, XXVI (1959), 176–79.

LEVINE, E., *The Psychology of Deafness*. New York: Columbia University Press, 1960.

LUNDE, A. S., AND S. K. BOGMAN, *Occupational Conditions among the Deaf*. Washington, D.C.: Gallaudet College Press, 1959.

MALTZMAN, M., *Clinical Audiology*. New York: Grune & Stratton, Inc., 1949.

MEYERSON, L., "A Psychology of Impaired Hearing," in *Psychology of Exceptional Children and Youth* (2nd ed.), ed. W. M. Cruickshank. Englewood Cliffs, N.J.: Prentice-Hall, Inc., 1963.

———, AND J. L. Michael, *The Measurement of Sensory Thresholds in Exceptional Children*. Houston, Tex.: University of Houston, 1960.

MICHAEL, J., AND S. L. KATES, "Concept Attainment as Social Material by Deaf and Hearing Adolescents," *J. educ. psychol.*, LVI (1965), 81–86.

MORKOVIN, B. V., "Experiments in Teaching Deaf Preschool Children in the Soviet Union," *Volta rev.*, LXII (1960), 260–68.

MOSS, J. W., M. MOSS, AND J. TIZARD, "Electrodermal Response Audiometry with Mentally Defective Children," *J. speech hearing res.*, IV (1961), 41–47.

MOTTO, J., AND F. J. WAWRZASZEK, "Integration of the Hearing Handicapped: Evaluation of the Current Status," *Volta rev.*, LXV (1963), 124–29.

MYKLEBUST, H. R., *The Psychology of Deafness*. New York: Grune & Stratton, Inc., 1960.

———, "Towards a New Understanding of the Deaf Child," *Amer. ann. deaf*, XCVIII (1953), 345–57.

NASS, M. L., "The Deaf's Conception of Physical Causality," *J. abn. soc. psychol.*, LXIX (1964), 669–73.

O'NIELL, J. J., *The Hard of Hearing*. Englewood Cliffs, N.J.: Prentice-Hall, Inc., 1964.

PICKETT, J. M., AND B. H. PICKETT, "Communication of Speech Sounds by a Tactual Vocoder," *J. speech hearing res.*, VI (1963), 207–22.

PINTNER, R., AND D. G. PATERSON, "The Binet Scale and the Deaf Child," *J. educ. psychol.*, VI (1915), 201–10.

POULOS, T. H., "Short-term Rehabilitation Programs for Hard of Hearing Children," *Hearing news*, XXIX (1961), 4–7.

PROCTOR, B., *Chronic Progressive Deafness*. Detroit, Mich.: Western State University Press, 1961.

QUIGLEY, S. P., "The Deaf and the Hard of Hearing," *Rev. educ. res.*, XXXIX (1969), 103–23.

REDDELL, R. C., AND D. R. CALVERT, "Selecting a Hearing Aid by Interpreting Audiologic Data," *J. audit. res.*, VI (1966), 445–52.

REICHSTEIN, J., AND J. ROSENSTEIN, "Differential Diagnosis of Auditory Deficits: A Review of the Literature," *J. except. child.*, XXX (1964), 73–82.

REYNOLDS, M. C., "The Capacities of Children," *J. except. child.*, XXXI (1965), 344–55.

SCHUNHOFF, H. F., "Bases of a Comprehensive Program in the Education of the Deaf," *Amer. ann. deaf*, CIX (1964), 240–47.

STOKOL, W. C., D. CASTERLINE, AND C. G. CRONEBERG, *A Dictionary of American Sign Language on Linguistic Principles*. Washington, D.C.: Gallaudet College Press, 1965.

STRENG, A., "Public School Programs for Children with Impaired Hearing in Small School Systems," *Volta rev.*, LX (1958), 304–6.

———, et al., *Hearing Therapy for Children* (2nd, rev. ed.). New York: Grune & Stratton, Inc., 1958.

UNITED STATES DEPARTMENT OF HEALTH, EDUCATION, AND WELFARE, *Health Statistics from the United States National Health Survey*, Series B-27, United States Department of Health, Education, and Welfare Publication 584 B-27. Washington, D.C.: Government Printing Office, June, 1961.

VAN ITALLIE, P. H., *How to Live with a Hearing Handicap*. New York: Paul S. Erickson, Inc., 1962.

VAN WYK, M. K., "Some Help with Speech," *Volta rev.*, LIX (1959), 207–8.

VERNON, M., "Current Etiological Factors in Deafness," *Amer. ann. deaf*, CXIII (1968a), 103–15.

———, "Fifty Years of Research on the Intelligence of Deaf and Hard-of-Hearing Children: A Review of Literature and Discussion of Implications," *J. rehabil. deaf.*, I (1968b), 1–12.

WEDENBERG, E., "Auditory Training of Deaf and Hard of Hearing Children," *Acta otolaryng. suppl.*, XXI, No. 94 (1951).

———, "Auditory Training of Severely Hard of Hearing Preschool Children," *Acta otolaryng. suppl.*, XXV, No. 110 (1955).

WHITE HOUSE CONFERENCE ON CHILD HEALTH AND PROTECTION, *The Handicapped and the Gifted*, Report of the Committee on Special Classes, Section 3, Education and Training (*Special Education*, Vol. III). New York: Appleton-Century-Crofts, 1931.

WYNBURN, G. M., *The Nervous System*. New York: Academic Press, 1960.

MOTOR AND SPEECH HANDICAPS

IV

13

The Orthopedically Handicapped
and the Epileptic

Children and adults with orthopedic handicaps are those who have all varieties and degrees of difficulty in physical movement (walking, coordination, and speech). The physical impairment may be due to accidents, disease, or congenital anomalies. Children with cerebral palsy are usually included among those with orthopedic difficulties and are ordinarily so classified for educational purposes. This is true because of the severe nature of the physical involvement in cerebral palsy.

It is obvious that the term *orthopedically handicapped* designates such a broad category of individuals that to attempt to find psychological and other characteristics of them as a group may be an exercise in futility. This extremely heterogeneous category of exceptionality includes individuals who are alike in not being average in physical ability. Beyond this, their likenesses become fewer and fewer because of the tremendous variety of disabling conditions that occur. However, some general characteristics can be gleaned from research findings and from clinical observations, although generalizations from these findings are difficult.

Incidence of Orthopedic Handicap

Any estimate of the number of orthopedically handicapped in the population is dependent on the manner of their definition. Different definitions and different sources of estimates yield varying numbers. The White

House Conference Report (1958) summarizes the data from surveys on the prevalence of crippling disabilities. Some surveys indicate 0.91 per 1,000 of the general population for certain areas and cities, while others go as high as 9.79 per 1,000. There were 755,786 crippled children reported on the registers of states in the United States in 1952 (Garrison and Force, 1965). There has been a continuous increase in the percentage of crippled children being helped by crippled children's programs since 1937 (Saffian, 1962). In 1960, slightly less than half the number listed on the states' registers were involved in such programs. The nature of the disabilities among those being served by programs for crippled children were many, with congenital malformations being the most frequent. Handicaps resulting from bone disorders and organs of movement were the second most frequently mentioned, and cerebral palsy was third. Certain crippling factors have noticeably declined. Poliomyelitis accounted for 14.5 percent of children in official programs in 1950, but by 1960 this figure had declined to 7 percent and soon will probably disappear entirely. Vaccine has reduced the incidence of poliomyelitis drastically, and other medical advances hold promise of still further reduction in the incidence of crippling diseases. At the same time, increased medical skill may result in saving from death some orthopedically handicapped infants who heretofore would have died. Some of these children suffer neural damage that results in physical disability of one kind or another.

There has been a significant decrease in the crippling conditions which result from infectious diseases. Such conditions as poliomyelitis, osteomyelitis, tuberculosis of the bones and joints, and arthritis due to infection have been reduced over the years by advancing medical science. Congenital defects, which include a large variety of disorders, have increased among the newborn. However, because of the early correction of many deformities and the development of effective prosthetic devices, large numbers of congenital defects can no longer be considered handicapping. An unfortunate trend has been toward increased impairment due to accidents of various kinds (Boyles and Calovini, 1960). The National Safety Council (1963) indicates that accidents claim more lives of children, ages one to fourteen years, than the five leading diseases combined. Between 11,000 and 15,000 children are accidentally killed in the United States each year, and it is estimated that over 50,000 other children are permanently crippled and disabled by accident. Over half the crippling accidents occur to children under five years of age (Garrison and Force, 1965).

EMOTIONAL AND SOCIAL ADJUSTMENT

Investigations of the adjustment of physically handicapped people are never very satisfactory, for several reasons. The extent and nature of physical disability within a group of the orthopedically handicapped is extremely variable. It is difficult to determine the intellectual level of the handicapped, and therefore matching them with control groups is always tenuous. Brain damage may be present in some individuals and not in others, and the extent of damage usually is unknown.

The problems of formulating an adequate self-concept are many for the physically handicapped. Self-concept has been considered to be intimately related to adjustment (Wright, 1960; Sawrey and Telford, 1971). The orthopedically handicapped child is different by reason of his disability. He may suffer pain, fatigue from undue exertion, accidents, and fear of injury or social rejection. These factors make it difficult for him to form realistic perceptions of his own adequacies and limitations. As a result of too much parental attention, emotional rejection by parents, or condescending attitudes on the part of society in general, the handicapped child may come to feel inferior and inadequate. The resulting behavior may be maladaptive.

A number of investigators have indicated significant differences in the psychological adjustments of crippled and nonphysically handicapped children, while others have reported that the adjustments of the two groups can be favorably compared (Cruickshank, 1963). There is little doubt that the adjustive problems of crippled children take on different proportions than do those of noncrippled children. That their adjustive problems are different in kind or process is doubtful. In an investigation of the emotional needs of crippled children (Cruickshank and Dolphin, 1949), it was found that there were no statistically significant differences between them and a group of normal children. Cruickshank (1963) later concluded that many of the objective tests used in the early studies of adjustment of crippled and noncrippled children were not sensitive enough to point up differences even if they did exist. More subtle and less personally threatening projective tests found differences between crippled and normal children (Broida, Izard, and Cruickshank, 1950; Smock and Cruickshank, 1952). The differences reported tend to support the hypothesis that a desire for, and a fear of, social participation constituted a source of anxiety and fear in crippled children. It is probable that there are characteristic differences in adjustments between crippled and normal children. Delicate measuring instruments and sophisticated research procedures are needed in order to determine the nature and extent of these differences. Researchers in the field have emphasized that parental and home attitudes may be more significant factors in the adjustment of crippled children than they are for normal children. Such speculations appear to be quite reasonable in view of the fact that the handicapped child is likely to spend more time in the home and be more dependent on the family for social contacts.

The parents with attitudes toward crippled children considered to be most constructive (Coughlin, 1941) are those that had sufficient understanding to accept the child's handicap and turn their attention and energies toward finding means to compensate for it. Such parents fully realize the implications of the orthopedic problem and can accept the problem and the child both intellectually and emotionally.

LIMITING COVERAGE

It is recognized that there are a great number of crippling conditions from which both children and adults suffer. Cerebral palsy, poliomyelitis, osteomyelitis, arthritis, muscular dystrophy, multiple sclerosis, spina bifida, skeletal deformities, birth defects, and various other debilitating conditions are of concern to the student of exceptionality. Children and adults with special health problems, such as epilepsy, heart conditions, asthma, eczema, and diabetes present special problems with their special conditions and are of concern to educators and psychologists.

It is not our intention to give coverage to each of these conditions and their special problems. It has been indicated earlier that many problems are shared by normal persons as well as by persons with orthopedic and special health problems and to cover each of these conditions is beyond the scope of the text. We shall treat two special conditions, cerebral palsy and epilepsy, in this chapter.

Cerebral Palsy

A considerable number of children who are orthopedically handicapped have suffered from early brain damage to the motor area of the brain. This damage results in motor disturbances and incoordination of various degrees of severity. People exhibiting these motor disturbances as the result of brain damage are said to be suffering from *spastic paralysis.*

Spastic paralysis was first described by Little in 1843, hence it has been referred to as "Little's disease." Although spastic paralysis was described rather early, intensive work in the area of cerebral palsy was a long time in coming. Work in this area seriously got under way during the 1930s, and since that time a great deal of research has been done. A particularly great amount of energy has gone into providing services for the cerebral-palsied.

Cerebral palsy has been defined as "a motor defect present or appearing soon after birth and dependent on pathological abnormalities in the brain" (Yannet, 1944). Localization of motor functions and sensory functions in the brain is rather generally accepted. When there is a motor or sensory dysfunction, it is assumed that damage has occurred to the particular part of the brain controlling this function. Damage to the motor area of the brain results in cerebral palsy. It is impossible to determine the extent of any damage beyond that to the motor area and that causing concomitant sensory dysfunction.

CLASSIFICATION AND DESCRIPTION

Cerebral palsy may be classified in several different ways. This leads to considerable confusion. Stephen (1958) lists five basic ways in which cerebral palsy is classified. These are: (1) according to type; (2) according to number of limbs involved; (3) according to time of onset; (4) according to degree of involvement; and (5) according to the extent and nature of the brain damage.

Classification According to Type. Three main types are discerned: the spastic; the athetoid; and the ataxic. They are defined in terms of the dominant symptoms, which in turn are related to the area of the brain that has been damaged.

In *spasticity*, the lesions are in the motor cortex, the premotor area, and the pyramidal tract. Injury to the motor area of the brain results in loss of voluntary muscle control. There appears to be a generalized muscular response to stimulation that results in the simultaneous contraction of both the flexor and extensor muscles. The result is that coordinated movement is extremely difficult. The slightest stimulation causes the person to become very rigid. Jerky and spasmodic movements with "clasp-knife" rigidity and exaggerated reflexes are common. Hypertonicity prevails, and the person can move only with the greatest of difficulty. Severe trembling, unsteadiness, and tense and irregular movements are characteristic. When the patient makes a deliberate effort to control the jerkiness and incoordination, this frequently causes them to be worse rather than better.

In *athetosis*, the lesions are in the extrapyramidal system, particularly in the basal ganglia. Athetosis is characterized by involuntary, slow, writhing, serpentine-like movements of the paralyzed member. The shoulders, face, feet, hands, and arms may be involved. Frequently the hands and arms are the seriously involved members. The rhythmical, writhing movement is slow and persistent. If one were to see only an arm and not the rest of the person, it could easily be mistaken for a deliberate, tense movement. The writhing may start in the shoulder and steadily move outward toward the fingers, involving progressively the elbow, the wrist and then the fingers. Frequently the muscles of the throat and diaphragm are involved, and speech becomes labored, hoarse, and unintelligible. The person may have difficulty in controlling his saliva, and thus add to his own inconvenience and embarrassment. He may start to do something, like reach for a glass, but spill the contents. This causes excitement and an increased effort for control, which may result in increased tension and spasticity. When the patient relaxes or goes to sleep, the athetoid movements disappear.

In *ataxia,* the area of the brain involved is usually the cerebellum or cerebellar tract. The eighth cranial nerve, which is involved with hearing and equilibrium, is sometimes affected. Ataxia is characterized by a disturbance in balance which is reflected in posture and gait. The person moves at a gait that suggests intoxication. His movements are awkward, speech is slurred, and he sways and staggers. His locomotion is such that he appears dizzy and uncertain.

More common than a pure case of either spasticity or athetosis is a combination of the two, involving damage to both areas (Sarason, 1959).

Classification According to Number of Limbs Involved.   Wyllie (1951) has suggested a sixfold classification according to the number and manner in which the limbs are involved:

1. *Congenital symmetrical diplegia,* paralysis in all limbs
2. *Congenital paraplegia,* in which only the legs are involved
3. *Quadriplegia* or *bilateral hemiplegia,* in which the disturbance is greater in the arms than the legs
4. *Triplegia,* a very rare condition in which three limbs are involved
5. *Hemiplegia,* in which both limbs on the same side are involved
6. *Monoplegia,* an extremely rare condition in which only one limb is affected

Stephen (1958) makes the point that such a classification implies a continuum of motor disturbance, rather than clearly defined types of disturbance, and that such a continuum offers a possible explanation for the differences in the reported frequencies of the various involvements.

INCIDENCE

Reports of the incidence of cerebral palsy present a somewhat confusing picture. The usual problems of data collection, analysis, and interpretation are confounded by difficulties in defining the limits of what constitutes cerebral palsy. Milder cases present particular difficulties in this regard.

Phelps (1946) contends that the incidence of new cases is rather constant from year to year and from one part of the country to the next. He contends that for every 100,000 people, 7 cerebral-palsied children are born each year. Of these, one dies in infancy or at an early age. This leaves an expectancy of 6 new cases each year for each 100,000 population. Two of these (or one-third) are definitely mentally retarded and will require permanent custodial care. The remaining 4 will need treatment.

He estimates that there are 40 cases under twenty years of age for each 100,000 population.

Asher and Schonell (1950) and Dunsdon (1952) report the incidence of cerebral palsy in school-age children to be about 1 per 1,000 in England. Investigations in America have yielded slightly higher figures. The United Cerebral Palsy Association has accepted a rate of 3 to 3.5 per 1,000 school-age children in the United States (Baker, 1959).

When the incidence of cerebral palsy is broken down according to types, there is not always uniformity of reports. McIntire (1938) and Phelps (1948) report roughly 40 percent each of athetoid and spastic cases. Dunsdon (1952) reports from England only about 10 percent of athetoid and about 80 percent of mixed athetoid and spastic cases. Asher and Schonell (1950) report about 10 percent athetoids and 80 percent spastics from their cases in England. Hopkins, Bice, and Colton (1954) report about one-fourth athetoid, a little less than one-half spastic, and about one-fourth ataxic rigidity. These discrepancies are probably due to variations in diagnoses because of the difficulty in assigning a given patient to one category or the other.

The incidence according to number of limbs involved and type is reported by Cruickshank and Raus (1955). They report roughly 20 percent each of quadriplegics, right hemiplegics, left hemiplegics, and paraplegics among spastics; and nearly 90 percent of the athetoids were classified as quadriplegics. Roughly one-half of the rigidity cases were quadriplegics, and one-fourth were right hemiplegics. Dunsdon (1952) reports that roughly 60 percent of 474 special-school candidates in England were quadriplegics and about one-fourth were paraplegics. Dunsdon considers her sample to be biased because of the referral of the more severely handicapped. Perestein and Hood (1957) estimate that about one-third of all cerebral-palsied are hemiplegics. They state that only about 10 percent of all cerebral palsy is postnatally acquired, but that nearly one-third of spastic hemiplegia is postnatal in origin. The incidence of cerebral palsy may be on the increase as a result of improved medical techniques that save lives.

The frequency with which the cerebral-palsied are found among the mentally deficient is difficult to discern because of differing diagnoses and differing provisions for the care of cerebral-palsied children. Doll (1933) estimated that 6 to 10 percent of the mentally defective at Vineland had motor handicaps due to birth lesions. It was estimated (Kirman, 1956) that 23 percent of the population of a hospital for certified low-grade mentally deficient children were cerebral-palsied. A preponderance of boys over girls has been reported. McIntire (1946), after studying 500 cerebrally palsied children, found an excess of males over females of 16 percent.

ETIOLOGY

The causative background of cerebral palsy is complex, and only a brief summary of the outstanding features will be attempted here. The causal factors can be classified as to their time of occurrence in the development of the individual. For a more thorough treatment of the background of cerebral palsy, the reader is referred to Benda (1952).

Prenatal Causes. Disease in the mother and developmental lesions are considered to be important factors in the etiology of cerebral palsy. Infections of the fetal brain from diseases of the mother occur. Notable among these are syphilis, meningitis, encephalitis, and German measles. Insufficient oxygen in the mother's bloodstream may result in cerebral damage (Benda, 1952). Anoxia of the brain can occur by the turning of the fetus in such a manner as to twist the cord around the neck. When the oxygen supply is thus disrupted, the brain soon degenerates or fails to develop adequately. Hemorrhages caused by blood incompatibility due to Rh factors may produce brain damage (Yannet, 1944). The most serious cases of cerebral palsy are the result of congenital brain deformities (Gauger, 1950).

Natal Causes. Benda (1952) states that birth injury accounts for 30 to 40 percent of severe cases of mental deficiency occurring in families who could ordinarily expect normal offspring. The mode of birth was not found to be of any particular significance in the production of cerebral palsy. Nearly one-fourth of his sample were premature babies. Prolonged labor was reported in eight of his thirty-seven cases, but normal delivery was reported in nine. Prematurity is dangerous to the child because the mother is not actually ready to give birth, and the pressure on the infant during birth is likely to be increased. The child is less mature, and consequently less capable of resisting the increased pressure than he would be at maturity. Hemorrhages and asphyxiation occur more easily in the premature.

Various other factors are related to, or can produce, cerebral palsy. Mechanical injury at birth through difficult delivery or from the use of forceps is a factor. However, the role of forceps in the production of cerebral palsy has probably been grossly overestimated. The sudden release of pressure during Caesarean delivery may cause the rupture of blood vessels, as may too rapid a birth or too great pressure during a very difficult birth. Interruptions to the oxygen supply and hemorrhages of the brain membranes and tissue are prominent in birth injury. Cerebral palsy resulting from birth injury of one kind or another comprises about 10 percent of the institutionalized cerebral-palsied cases (Sarason, 1959). A continuum theory of brain damage (Meyer, 1957), implying that all brains are more or less damaged at birth, indicates the difficulty involved in identifying brain injury at birth.

Postnatal Causes. Injury to the brain after birth may produce cerebral palsy. Such injuries to the motor area of the brain can be produced by injury to the skull through severe accident. High temperature for a prolonged period, which results in a reduced oxygen intake, can also produce brain damage. The separating of natal from postnatal factors is very difficult when it is considered that some injuries at birth are not detectable for some length of time. Injuries occurring after birth, when the brain has more fully developed, are not associated with mental deficiency to the same extent as are prenatal anomalies.

OTHER FACTORS ASSOCIATED WITH CEREBRAL PALSY

Sarason (1959) indicates that mothers of cerebral-palsied children are significantly older than the average. Yannet (1944) reports no significant difference between the percentage of affected children who were first-born than would be expected by chance, and that a greater proportion are born after the third pregnancy than would be expected by chance. Sarason and Yannet were dealing with the cerebrally palsied mentally deficient.

Dunsdon (1952), investigating cerebral-palsied children of whatever mental level, found 66 percent of 327 cerebral-palsied children were first-born. She reported that 10 percent of her cases had suffered from asphyxia and that 39 percent were premature.

Cerebral palsy cannot be accounted for by any single etiological factor. Cruickshank and Raus (1955) have suggested that a genetic component may be still another variable to consider in cerebral palsy.

INTELLIGENCE OF CHILDREN WITH CEREBRAL PALSY

The task of measuring the intelligence of cerebral-palsied children is fraught with difficulties. The problem of how to best measure the intelligence of children who may have multiple sensory handicaps in addition to paralysis has been attacked by a number of investigators. Most investigators have found it necessary to alter the tasks of standardized intelligence tests in one way or another to fit the handicapped state of the subject involved. Altering standardized tests in any way no doubt has an effect on their validity. In the absence of tests developed particularly for the multiple combinations of disabilities encountered in cerebral palsy, investigators of the intelligence of the cerebral-palsied typically have used the Stanford-Binet or other such tests and prorated the test scores. The items that are inappropriate are not used, and those that are used count an increasing amount. A certain percentage of cases are found to be untestable. Bice and Cruickshank (1955) found 15 percent to be untestable.

Studies of the intelligence of the cerebral-palsied have yielded quite uniform results. Two English studies and two in the United States are in fairly close agreement, and all have involved a sizable number of cases. M. Dunsdon (1952) studied the intelligence of 916 cerebral-palsied children. They were largely candidates for special school in England. She reports that the IQ's of 58.6 percent were below 70, and that only 8.25 percent scored 100 or better. Schonell (1956), after studying 354 cases of English cerebral-palsied children over three years of age, reports that 51 percent had IQ's over 70, and that 23 percent had IQ's between 50 and 69.

In America, Hopkins, Bice, and Colton (1954) reported on 1,000 cases in New Jersey. They reported that 48.8 percent had IQ's below 70; 20.4 percent had IQ's between 50 and 69; and 7.9 percent had IQ's of 110 or more. Miller and Rosenfeld (1952) studied 330 children with cerebral palsy. They report that 50 percent of their cases had IQ's below 70, and that 4 to 5 percent scored 110 or better. In order to assess the possibility of an increase in the percentage of mentally defective children due to the large number of children brought to the clinic from a considerable distance as a "last resort," they evaluated them separately and compared them with the total group. They found "no important differences." A better control would have been to compare them to the remainder of the group. As it is, they were compared to a group over one-third of which consisted of themselves.

The four studies presented tend to agree that the incidence of mental deficiency among the cerebral-palsied is high. The studies indicate that roughly 50 percent have IQ's below 70. The distribution of the intelligence of the cerebrally palsied definitely piles up at the lower end of the intellectual continuum. Only 3 or 4 percent have IQ's above 115, and less than one-fourth have IQ's between 70 and 89. They agree, too, that there is no significant difference between the mean IQ's of athetoids and spastics. This is in contrast with the supposition that intelligence is relatively unaffected in athetosis. The damage in athetosis is subcortical (in the basal ganglia), and intelligence was therefore thought to be less impaired. However, there appears to be no significant difference in general intelligence between the two main forms of cerebral palsy. Dunsdon (1952) and Schonell (1956) both report quadriplegics to be less intelligent than those with a lesser number of limbs involved. The reasons for the lowered IQ of quadriplegics could be that their paralytic handicap keeps them from learning at the rate others learn, or it could be that in quadriplegia the extent of damage outside the motor area of the brain tends to be greater. McIntire's (1938) classification of the intelligence of cerebral-palsied defectives was as follows: 29 percent borderline, 27 percent moron, 22 percent imbecile and 21 percent idiot.

In view of the range, it is difficult to characterize the intelligence of the cerebral-palsied. Intellectually they do not represent a homogeneous group, although the general trend is for intelligence to be low.

ASSOCIATED DEFECTS

Other than motor paralysis and decreased intellectual efficiency, which are characteristic of the cerebral-palsied, a number of defects are commonly found. Roughly 30 percent of children with cerebral palsy are reported to have a history of one or more epileptic seizures (Floyer, 1955; Hopkins, Bice, and Colton, 1954). In a study of certified mentally defective children, Kirman (1956) reported that children with epilepsy tended to be less intelligent than those not so afflicted. Visual defects and speech disorders are common. Speech defects probably occur in about 70 percent of the cases of cerebral palsy (Stephen, 1958). Hearing disabilities have been reported as more frequent than in other populations. Sensory impairment has been reported in 50 percent of cases of hemiplegia (Tizard, Paine, and Crothers, 1954).

Cerebral-palsied children, particularly those who are mentally retarded, have a wide variety of concomitant defects. When the additional defects are added to the already existing ones, they represent a tremendous handicap. The cerebral-palsied child is typically a multiply handicapped child.

TREATMENT AND TRAINING

Special facilities for the treatment and training of cerebral-palsied and other brain-damaged children have grown rapidly during the past 30 years. The training and subsequent rehabilitation of those who are not mentally retarded is very promising. Chapter 10 of this text deals with the treatment of children with learning disabilities. Your attention is directed to that chapter.

The Epileptic

Children and adults with epilepsy are subject to convulsions. They differ from others principally in that they have convulsive seizures or must take medication in order to prevent or control seizures. The word *epilepsy* is derived from a Greek word that means "to be seized," and modern neurologists consider *epilepsy* to be merely a synonym for "seizure" rather than a term representing a specific disease entity (Rupp, 1958). Convulsive states or seizures that tend to be episodic and recurrent are considered to be symptoms of a disorder, rather than a disorder in and of themselves. When these symptoms occur, they are the result of a functional disturbance in a group of nerve cells in the brain. These nerve cells, for some reason, are discharging their electrical energy at an accelerated rate. The precise reasons for these accelerated discharges are not known, but there are a variety of factors that may be considered contributory. Among these are head injuries, infections, interference with normal blood supply or oxygen to the brain, and prolonged high fever.

Convulsive disorders are not uncommon in early childhood. Thom (1942) reported that about 7 percent of the children in Boston had one or more convulsions during their first five years of life but that only a few of these were epileptic. Early childhood seizures are frequently associated with prolonged high temperatures. It is not uncommon for people to experience an isolated seizure. Any interference with the normal supply of blood and oxygen to the brain may cause certain brain cells to discharge electrical energy at an accelerated rate and bring about a seizure in a healthy person. A seizure reflects the normal reaction of a group of neurones to excessive irritation. A seizure which occurs once and is not repeated within a reasonable period of time does not constitute epilepsy (Sakel, 1958).

Seizures associated with epilepsy are recurrent. There is a relatively persistent functional disturbance of the electrical discharge of cells in the brain. Destroyed cells are no longer functional and do not discharge energy. However, slightly damaged cells, or those which are partially damaged and which surround destroyed cells, may function abnormally and produce seizures. The extent and location of brain cells that discharge excessively are determinants of the nature and severity of epileptic seizures. Periodic disturbances of the rhythm of the brain have been termed "cerebral dysrhythmia" (Lennox, 1941). In many instances it is not possible to identify the contributory factors resulting in cerebral dysrhythmia or to locate areas of brain damage, but the pattterns of electrical discharge are disturbed and convulsive behavior does occur. This is *idiopathic epilepsy*. In other instances, contributory factors are identifiable and pathological conditions are present. This is known as *symptomatic epilepsy*.

In symptomatic epilepsy, the convulsions are considered to be a secondary manifestation of a known pathological condition in the brain. Symptomatic epilepsy can be observed in various kinds of mental defectives. The lesions in the brain may be traced to various kinds of injury or infection, or they may represent developmental anomalies. Idiopathic epilepsy is very largely of unknown origin, and by far the greatest number of epileptics are classified as "idiopathic." In these cases there is no detectable structural anomaly. Epileptic seizures are rather common among the mentally retarded, but are considered to be concomitant with the retardism rather than a cause of it.

Epileptic seizures appear in numerous and diverse forms because the electrical disturbance responsible for the seizure may be located within any portion of the brain and may involve few or many abnormally functioning cells. Epileptic seizures of a variety of forms and severity have been described and classified. The typical epileptic seizure comes on suddenly. Unconsciousness occurs, and the person may fall. The patient is unable to control the seizure; it runs its course and is recurrent.

Varieties of Epileptic Convulsion

Epileptic convulsions vary in a great number of ways. They do not all occur with the same frequency, nor are they all of the same duration, comprehensiveness, or severity. It has already been indicated that this variability has a complex background of concomitant variability in the nervous system. Some of the types of epileptic seizures will be discussed, but it should be remembered that seizures may vary almost infinitely in character and number. The origins of epilepsy are numerous and diagnosis is, therefore, difficult. The presence of overt seizures which are recognizable as epileptic is a guide in the clinical diagnosis of epilepsy. The nature and severity of the seizure determines, in large part, the classification that it is given.

GRAND MAL

By far the most frequently reported type of seizure is *grand mal*. A survey of clinic and private patients (Lennox, 1941) reports that of patients having only one type of seizure, 51 percent had *grand mal*. Among the *grand mal* patients, 25 percent had less than five seizures per year, 50 percent less than 15, 75 percent less than 50, 22 percent more than 1,000, and 0.4 percent more than 5,000. Males have more *grand mal* seizures than women. Lennox's data were compiled from questionnaires returned by neurologists, and are based on other than institutional cases.

The typical *grand mal* seizure can be described according to stages, the first of which is an aura. An *aura* may be described as a preliminary experience which constitutes a warning to the patient that he is going to have a convulsion. It may consist of nausea, dizziness, flashes of light, sounds, odors, or any sensory experience. About one-half of epileptic patients apparently experience an aura (Lennox and Cobb, 1933), and it has been reported to be less frequent among children than among adults (Kanner, 1935). The aura, or warning, may precede the loss of consciousness by but an instant, but may be as long as a few seconds, which would enable the person to prepare for the impending seizure. Children, when asked about their seizures, have been known to confine their comments to the aura (Carter, 1947). The aura may be a frightening experience for a child.

The aura is followed by a sudden loss of consciousness. The patient pitches or falls to the floor, as if he had been suddenly struck a heavy blow, and may injure himself. He may emit a cry as he falls. This is caused by the lungs expelling air and has been called an epileptic cry. The patient quickly stiffens. The muscles are contracted violently, and temporarily are held rigid. This is the *tonic* phase of the seizure. The stiffness or rigidity seems to involve the whole body. The head and eyes may turn. The vigorous contraction may force the air from the lungs and inhibit breathing. The skin turns blue and the pupils of the eyes become dilated. The tonic phase of the seizure may last from a few seconds to a minute or two, and is terminated by the beginning of the clonic phase.

The *clonic* phase of the seizure is the most violent portion of it. It is the convulsion proper. It is characterized by the violent alternate contractions and relaxations of the musculature. The legs and arms jerk, the abdominal and chest muscles contort, the face becomes distorted, the chest moves violently as breathing becomes vigorous. Perspiration is often profuse, and the bowels and bladder may be evacuated. This phase of the seizure usually lasts for two or three minutes. The patient may froth at the mouth. This is caused by the violent relaxation and contraction of the facial muscles and the vigorous breathing which may force saliva out of the mouth. It may be blood-stained because the tongue and lips may be bitten during the convulsion. During this phase of the seizure, the patient may seriously injure himself by banging his body and limbs against the floor or other objects. He may chew his lips and tongue, and precautions should be taken against injury and strangulation. The frequency and severity of the contractions gradually diminish, and the patient finally relaxes and goes into a deep sleep or coma which is followed by a natural sleep.

The length of the *coma* and of the natural sleep following it will vary according to the state of exhaustion of the individual after his vigorous seizure, and with the time of day. When he awakens, he does not feel well. He may be very tired, and suffer from headache, sore muscles, vomiting, disorientation, and confusion. He is confused, has an amnesia for the seizure, and frequently feels depressed. Seizures vary greatly from patient to patient in frequency, severity, and aftereffects. The same individual may also show differences among seizures from time to time.

The seizures typically last only a few minutes, but they do not always follow the typical pattern of aura—tonic phase—clonic phase—coma. The patient may go from a semicomatose state back into a tonic phase, followed by a clonic phase, then go back into coma. He may do this several times. This is termed *status epilepticus,* and can be very serious. The attention of a physician is imperative when this occurs. Lennox and Cobb (1933) reported that 40 percent of 1,500 patients studied had seizures either at night or in the daytime. Thirty-six percent had seizures only during the daytime and 15 percent only at night. Patients not uncommonly injure themselves in falling or when thrashing about during the clonic phase of the seizure. They frequently chew their tongue, bite their lips, and are bruised in places by the violence of the attack.

PETIT MAL

This type of seizure is much less severe than *grand mal,* but may occur much more frequently with a given patient. There is typically no aura for this attack. It comes on suddenly and lasts from a few seconds to a half-minute or so. It consists of a short lapse of consciousness. The patient rarely falls or convulses. He suddenly appears dazed; he may grow pale, stare fixedly, drop an object that he is holding, and twitch slightly. His eyelids may flicker. He may continue to do whatever he is doing, rather automatically, or he may stop for a few moments and then resume his activity. He is frequently aware of his short lapses of consciousness. *Petit mal* is most frequently found in children. The attacks may range in frequency from 1 to 200 per day (Bridge, 1949). The seizure begins and ends abruptly and may go unnoticed because of the short period of time involved and the nonspectacular symptoms. *Pyknoepilepsy* is a name frequently applied when children have *petit mal* attacks that seem to cease spontaneously with development. Some varieties of *petit mal* consist of only a single shocklike jerk, without a loss of consciousness (myoclonic jerk). Patients with myoclonic jerks are usually also subject to the more common *petit mal* attacks. Another variety of *petit mal* attack (akinetic epilepsy) involves a sudden postural collapse, with consequent nodding of the head or even falling. Some seizures (autonomic seizures) may consist of periods of sweating, flushing, increased blood pressure, or gagging without apparent cause, with no loss of consciousness. These seizures are rare and can be considered variations of *petit mal.*

JACKSONIAN

Jacksonian seizures are named for the famous English neurologist, Hughlings Jackson. They start in an extremity, or on one side of the face, and gradually move to engulf other portions of the body. If the whole body is involved, it terminates in *grand mal.* In this form of seizure, the extremity

starts to convulse or a progressive anesthesia begins to develop. The patient can observe the twitching or jerking from the contractions or feel the
numbness as it moves to encompass greater portions of the body. In some
cases there is no convulsiveness as such, but a tingling sensation that progressively moves toward greater physiological involvement. These patients
sometimes find that they can prevent the continued spread of the muscular
twitchings by rapidly engaging themselves in some task requiring large
expenditures of physical energy or extensive intellectual involvement.

In some instances the seizure is completely localized. That is, there is
no tendency for progressive bodily involvement. One extremity or one side
of the body is involved. The attack may be convulsive or simply a sensory
phenomenon such as anesthesia (loss of sensation). Sensory seizures may
involve various sensations of the body, or they may involve taste, smell, or
visual phenomena (Lennox, 1947b). Clonic movements of the face or an
extremity are often involved when an attack begins.

PSYCHOMOTOR

This is an ill-defined, rare, and poorly understood condition. Mild tonic
cramps, a stiffening of the extremities, tightening of the jaws, drooling,
and a blueishness of the face may occur. The characteristic part of this
seizure is amnesia. The person may act as if drugged, and move about
rather automatically and deliberately. He may mutter incoherently and go
through various apparently meaningless motions or engage in rather complex and complicated behavior as if he were aware of what he was doing.
He may sit motionless or muttering and chewing or he may be violently
active. The patient does not appear to lose consciousness, but neither does
he seem to be aware of his actions. He will report amnesia for the duration
of the seizure. He may give vent to feelings of hostility through physical
violence or abusive language. When resisted, he may commit violent aggressive acts without apparent provocation. In some cases, only drastic and
abrupt alterations in temperament occur, during which time the person
is extremely aggressive and impulsive. He may commit crimes of violence,
but Turner and Merlis (1962) found only 5 out of 337 epileptics had committed illegal acts during seizures. These attacks may vary in length from
a few minutes to several days. It is difficult to tell, in many cases, whether
the person is having a psychotic episode of some sort, is emotionally distraught, or is having a seizure. Data about the frequency of such attacks
are hard to evaluate because of the failure to make such distinctions.
Epileptic equivalency has been used as a label for the designation of some
such attacks. These attacks have been designated as preceding, taking the
place of, or following an epileptic convulsion. The concept of epileptic
equivalency has been criticized by Foxe (1947), who points out that the

concept may include any kind of pathological behavior in an epileptic individual or in a person with just a family history of seizures. He indicated that epilepsy thus becomes the scapegoat for pathological behavior.

Incidence

It is difficult to estimate the frequency of epilepsy in the general population. It is probable that, in every 1,000 schoolchildren, 1 or 2 have or have had epileptic seizures. In a group of 365 epileptic children, only 10 percent were reported to have had a convulsion in school (Henderson, 1955). The fear and ignorance surrounding epilepsy keep a number of cases from being brought to the attention of medical authorities. Epilepsy has probably existed in all stages of human history, and probably among all races (Penfield and Erickson, 1941). The figure of 0.5 percent of the population is a generally accepted figure for the frequency of epilepsy. Malzberg (1947), after reviewing World War I and II draft figures and other relevant data, feels that about 6 or 7 per 1,000 population would be a better estimate of the incidence. The question of whether or not there are significant differences in incidence between the sexes has not been adequately determined (Pollock, 1931). Institutions usually contain a greater number of male than female epileptics. The fallibility of institutional data relative to sex differences has been discussed previously. It is difficult to tell from these data what the sex differences are.

Lennox (1941) reports that five times as many children under five years of age as adults over twenty had 1,500 *petit mal* attacks per year. The frequency of *grand mal* was three times greater in children. The onset of seizures began before the age of twenty in 71 percent of his cases. Sixty-three percent of the girls and 52 percent of the boys had their first convulsion before fifteen. Lennox also reported (1951) that epilepsy began in the first decade of life of 47 percent of 4,000 epileptic cases he investigated. Epilepsy is essentially a disorder of childhood and youth. The slightly earlier onset in girls may be a function of their earlier maturation.

The incidence of idiopathic epilepsy in institutional defectives is high. Penrose (1963) reports that 16 percent of a group of 1,280 institutionalized defectives had idiopathic epilepsy. Tizard (1958) points out that having convulsions may be the reason for institutional care being sought in some cases.

Convulsive disorders are relatively common among the mentally deficient. The convulsions are, in a majority of the cases, probably secondary manifestations of pathological brain conditions (Sarason, 1959). Whether epilepsy is a concomitant or a cause of low-level intellectual functioning, it is encountered with sufficient frequency among the mentally subnormal that those who are interested in working with them should be reasonably familiar with it.

Etiology

The causes of epilepsy are multiple, and not thoroughly understood. There are a number of sources of brain damage that might result in symptomatic epilepsy. There are so many factors that could possibly produce symptomatic epilepsy that no attempt will be made to enumerate them all. Brain lesions traceable to definite natal or postnatal brain injuries to the motor cortical areas are sometimes causative. Brain injury was found in about half of a group of over 700 epileptic patients. One-half of these injuries occurred during the birth process, and the others resulted from various accidents and diseases in childhood (Bridge, 1949). Developmental anomalies which result in maldevelopment of brain tissue may occur. Mechanical injuries of various kinds may produce lesions, as may various infections, hemorrhages, and interruptions in the supply of oxygen to the brain. Brain tissue is very susceptible to interruptions in the supply of oxygen; deterioration sets in rapidly and brain tissue does not regenerate. In older patients, seizures are associated with arteriosclerosis (hardening of the arteries). There are a great variety of cerebral lesions that may result in seizures, but none of them can be depended upon to do so consistently (Wallin, 1949). Seizures or convulsions are really symptoms which can be produced by a great variety of causes. When it is possible to locate the disturbance in the brain, the epilepsy is termed *focal*. Almost any gross disturbance of cerebral functioning can be accompanied by epileptic convulsions, as is apparent from the large proportion of defectives with cranial malformations who are subject to epilepsy. Generally, the younger the child when seizures first occur, the greater the likelihood of there being a known organic cause. After the age of ten, other causes become more important (Kram, 1963). Forty-four percent of 765 epileptic children in the Detroit school system are reported to have developed their epilepsy during their first four years of life, while only 7 percent started having seizures after the age of twelve (Tenny, 1955). Of 352 epileptic patients in Norway, 40 percent began having seizures before the age of five. In 52 percent of the total sample, possible organic factors were indicated (Mackay, Wortis, and Sugar, 1960). An investigation of epileptic patients in England indicated that most often seizures first occur during the first two years of life (Kram, 1963).

The etiology of idiopathic epilepsy is very perplexing. When there is no detectable structural abnormality and when no other disease condition is present except that the patient is subject to epileptic convulsions, the epilepsy itself has to be regarded as the principal condition.

Investigations of the number of relatives of epileptics who were subject to epilepsy has led to speculations about the hereditary nature of idiopathic epilepsy, but early findings varied considerably. One source of this variance was the closeness of the relationships studied and whether or not the count was restricted to relatives with epileptic convulsions or included other neuropathic disorders which might be predisposing to epilepsy. Another variable was whether institutional or noninstitutionalized cases were used. Lennox (1954), investigating 20,000 near relatives of approximately 4,000 epileptic patients, found evidences of an inherited predisposition to idiopathic seizures. The incidence of near relatives with a history of one or more seizures was 3.2 percent, and of these about half had chronic epilepsy. This would be more than three times the percentage of chronic epileptics in the general population.

Studies indicate that a greater frequency of epilepsy is found among identical than nonidentical twins (Lennox, 1947a; 1954). Lennox investigated 173 pairs of twins who had seizures. Among the 77 pairs of identical twins, 70 percent were both subject to seizures. Among the 96 pairs of fraternal twins, both were affected only 12.5 percent of the time. In an investigation quoted by Penfield and Erickson (1941), epilepsy was found in both identical twins in 86.3 percent of idiopathic cases, and in both fraternal twins in only 3 percent of the cases.

Studies of the electrical brain activity of epileptics have revealed that they have characteristic brain wave patterns. The highly sensitive device which measures this activity is called an electroencephalograph (EEG). Special training is required for the interpretation of the EEG record, on which is traced the amplitude and frequency of the brain waves. Various convulsive conditions reveal their own unique patterns.

The EEG is not always conclusive in epilepsy. From 5 to 20 percent of clinically diagnosed epileptic patients have been reported to have EEG records within the normal range (Penfield and Erickson, 1941; Hefner, 1960). The situation is further complicated by the observation that 10 to 15 percent of the general population have cerebral dysrhythmia while only 0.5 percent of the population is epileptic (Lennox, Gibbs, and Gibbs, 1940).

In spite of the fact that the EEG is fallible, it is an important diagnostic and research tool. Through its use a great amount of indirect evidence about the heretability of epileptic brain wave patterns has been compiled. EEG records of the families of epileptics early received the attention of Lowenbach (1939). Lennox (1947c) has been an important contributor to this field. He found the incidence of epilepsy to be 2.8 percent among a large sample of the parents, siblings, and children of 2,000 epileptics. This figure is 5.5 times greater than its occurrence in the general population. He found dysrhythmia in nearly all his epileptic subjects. The EEG records of over 90 percent of one or the other of the parents of 55 unselected epileptics were found to be abnormal. Abnormal brain waves were found in both parents of 30 percent of the cases. Sixty percent of the near relatives of 94 epileptics showed abnormal brain waves. In 78 percent of over 2,000 cases, no cause other than an inherited predisposition toward cerebral dysrhythmia could be found. In the remaining 22 percent, various other causes may have produced the seizures or have played only a contributory role.

That seizures are frequently related to emotional factors is rather well agreed (Robinson and Robinson, 1965). There is considerable disagreement that epilepsy is caused by emotional and personality factors. Bridge (1949) feels that there is a possibility that in certain instances emotional and personality factors may be the primary agents. It has been suggested that seizures can be interpreted as release of psychic tensions when other avenues of release are inaccessible. Emotional conflict has been found with a high degree of frequency among epileptic children, and release of hostility in psychotherapy has resulted in a decrease in the number of seizures and required amounts of medication (Deutsch and Wiener, 1948).

The background of epilepsy is not clear. Research is needed into the question of why some, but not all, persons with abnormal EEG records have seizures, and why some who have seizures do not have abnormal EEG records. Psychogenic factors in epilepsy need systematic research, as do the various causes and consequences of cerebral damage.

Intelligence

It is to be expected that the frequency of seizures can be associated with severity of mental defects, because almost any gross disturbance of cerebral functioning can be accompanied by epileptic manifestations (Penrose, 1963). The influence of epilepsy on intelligence is not clearly understood. Although many epileptics are below average in intelligence, it is not inconsistent with average or superior ability.

Some of the notable men of history are reported to have been subject to epileptic seizures. Such men as Julius Caesar, Alexander the Great, and Napoleon are reported to have been epileptics, as were such literary lights as Charles Lamb and Guy de Maupassant. These men are frequently cited as evidence of the outstanding ability of some epileptics, but the usual findings are that a group of epileptic persons cannot be expected to be of high-level intelligence.

Investigations of the intelligence of epileptics have varied because some researchers have confined their efforts to institutional cases. These cases usually yield lower IQ's than do noninstitutional cases, possibly because the most severely afflicted and less brilliant are institutionalized.

When epileptics who are not institutionalized have been studied, higher intelligence quotients have been obtained. Some studies, particularly early ones, did not differentiate between symptomatic and idiopathic epileptics. When such distinctions have been made, the lower measured intelligence of the symptomatic group becomes apparent.

Using either the Stanford-Binet, Form L, or the Wechsler-Bellevue, Lennox and Collins (1945) examined 149 nonepileptic twins and obtained a mean IQ of 108. They obtained a mean IQ of 96 for 27 epileptics without evidence of brain lesions, and 77 for 10 epileptics with brain damage. The IQ's of 248 Chicago children with convulsive disorders (Mullen, 1953) were spread over a wide range, with 56.7 percent falling between 50 and 79. The mean IQ of the group was 71.8. A review of the studies of the intelligence of noninstitutionalized cases (Broida, 1955) indicates that their intelligence does not differ significantly from that of the general population. Efforts to establish characteristic subtest patterns for epileptics indicate that there is no typical pattern. Numerous studies of the distribution of intelligence among epileptics have reported no significant difference from the normal. A 1962 summary of the psychological test literature (Geist, 1962) concluded that the literature was replete with conflicting evidence.

The intelligence of the epileptic in general is of only secondary concern to people working with the mentally deficient. The relatively high frequency of convulsions among the mentally retarded is of prime concern to those who work with the mentally retarded. It is difficult to say with precision just how great this frequency is, but convulsions are very common occurrences among the mentally retarded.

The question of intellectual deterioration and its relation to epilepsy has been of rather great concern. Pintner, Eisenson, and Stanton (1940) reviewed various studies and indicated that only a small minority of epileptics show marked deterioration. It is rather difficult, in studying deterioration in an institution, to separate the results of institutionalization from those of the seizures (Sarason, 1959). From the data currently available it is impossible to state whether or not there is a relationship between frequency and severity of seizures and deterioration. Studies have reported less impairment of those with milder seizures, which would seem to be logical when one considers that brain damage is associated with intelligence.

Whether or not the use of anticonvulsant drugs produces impairment is questionable. Several studies of the various anticonvulsants and intelligence have been made. The results are conflicting, but the better-controlled studies tend to discount the adverse effects of the drugs on intellectual functioning.

Personality and Emotional Factors

Early writers in the field described the personality of epileptics in an essentially unfavorable manner. They were described as egocentric, antisocial, unstable, quarrelsome, moody, and criminotic. Enough uniformity in the alleged personality traits was reported so that much consideration was given to the so-called epileptic personality. A stereotype of the personality of people with epilepsy came into being, and the early literature led one to believe that the epileptic was hopelessly antisocial. However, the stereotype of the epileptic personality has not held up under systematic investigation. No doubt some institutionalized epileptics do display unfortunate behavior patterns, but they apparently do not do so with enough consistency to allow for an all-inclusive epileptic pattern.

The theory that differences in personality among epileptics are related to differences in type of epilepsy has, in the case of temporal-lobe epilepsy (excessive electrical discharge from the temporal lobes) received some support (James, 1960). Typically, the behavior of temporal-lobe epileptics has been described in terms of their being underactive, with outbursts of aggressiveness and destructiveness. Personality changes of one kind or another have been identified in as many as 52 percent of temporal-lobe epileptics (Bingley, 1958). In one of the better designed investigations using the EEG to identify the location of discharge focus, frontal-lobe epileptic children were rated as more aggressive than other EEG groups, and their mean "neurotic" score was the lowest (Nuffield, 1961).

The person suffering from the ravages of continuing convulsions has not only the ordinary problems of living to encounter, but the stress and strain of epilepsy as well. Frequently, the epileptic is scorned and discriminated against. He frequently has brain damage that is progressive, and the neural pathology may have direct behavioral consequences. He must take medication to control convulsions. In some cases, the medication may cause general irritability in the patient. In spite of these considerations, the personalities of epileptics are highly diverse. Studies of the personalities of epileptic children, using the Rorschach (a projective test using ink blots), indicate that they have a wide diversity of personality characteristics rather than a single constellation that would comprise a type (Broida, 1955; Tizard, 1962). Studies of the behavior problems of epileptic children indicate that their problems are very similar to those of other children found in a child-guidance clinic. Although epileptics are reputed to be destructive, in a study of seventy epileptic children they were found to exhibit less destructive behavior than a comparable group of nonepileptic children (Deutsch and Wiener, 1948). Strong issue has been taken with the concept of an "epileptic personality."

Investigations of the personality characteristics of epileptics are difficult to evaluate for several reasons. Classifications of epilepsy are inadequate; samples have not been representative or adequately observed; bias is hard to avoid; inadequate diagnoses have been employed; the factor of intelligence level has not always been controlled; and personality-measurement devices may lack reliability (Tizard, 1962).

Treatment and Prognosis

The treatment of epilepsy is very largely medical. Sedative and anticonvulsant drugs have proven very effective in diminishing the frequency and severity of the convulsions. Phenobarbital (a sedative) and Dilantin (a nonsedative anticonvulsant) are frequently used to control seizures. Other drugs have been developed, and new ones are constantly being produced in laboratories around the world. Drug therapy is not considered curative of epilepsy. The drugs are used to control and prevent convulsions. They tend to have no intellectually impairing effects, and the relief from convulsions may cause children under sixteen to actually increase in intelligence test performance (Somerfield-Ziskund and Ziskund, 1940).

Some cases of symptomatic epilepsy, particularly the Jacksonian type, can be remedied by surgery. When the convulsions are due to lesions, pressure, or tumor, surgical procedures have proved effective in a limited number of cases. When surgery is effective, the patient is no longer subject to seizures and can function normally.

Psychotherapy, once considered futile with epileptics, holds considerable promise. Emotional problems and conflicts may serve as precipitating factors in the production of seizures. Through psychotherapy those emotional conflicts may be reduced and the frequency of seizures thus reduced. Efron (1956, 1957) reports the arrest of seizures in a woman with temporal-lobe epilepsy through the use of Pavlovian conditioning procedures. Robinson and Robinson (1965) report the case of a girl who had major seizures in spite of medication until she was placed in an institution at the age of fourteen. Following this and without new treatment she had only one seizure during the next year. When she was sent home her seizures returned and were as severe as ever. The role of psychological factors would seem important here. It has been speculated that psychological factors may actually cause seizures (Bridge, 1949). If this is true, considerable improvement might be expected from psychotherapy. Even when the causes of the seizures are rather definitely physiological, psychotherapy may help the patient to live with the epilepsy, its treatment, and the limitations imposed by it.

In institutions for the mentally retarded, the control of seizures through the use of drugs has proven to be a tremendous help. The patients, relieved of their convulsions, function better and adjust more readily. Some of the mentally retarded may be rehabilitated after their seizures have been brought under medical control.

Medical treatment of epilepsy varies from patient to patient. Some patients require different dosages and different drugs than others. Some patients' seizures can be completely prevented through medication; in others, the frequency or severity of the seizures may be reduced. Prolonged use of anticonvulsant drugs is usually necessary, but the prognosis for alleviation of the convulsions is favorable for large numbers of patients.

Teacher, Parent, and Community Attitudes

Epilepsy is probably one of the older afflictions known to man (Tower, 1960). Its long history is one of interesting contrasts, and the confusions and misunderstandings of the past tend to persist in modified form up to the present time. The persistence of certain attitudes and customs makes the affliction more difficult than it need be. Modern diagnosis and treatment have developed to the point where most people subject to epileptic seizures can be treated so as to control or eliminate the convulsions.

Teachers' attitudes toward epilepsy and the epileptic child in the classroom have improved markedly over the past twenty years. Teachers, however, cannot be of much assistance in the management of epilepsy if they have no way of knowing that a child is epileptic. As parents become better informed, the frequency with which parents of children with epilepsy will inform the teachers of the child's condition will increase.

Public attitudes toward epilepsy have seriously lagged behind scientific information. The result is that many epileptics still face unreasonable discriminatory practices in employment, insurance, automobile driving, and so forth. The public must be brought up-to-date about epilepsy, and research on prevention and treatment must continue. The principal problems for most people with epilepsy are not really in the medical realm. Treatment and control are fairly well advanced. Where most problems arise is in the area of public understanding and acceptance.

The educational problems of children with epilepsy are like those of other children who may be deviant or be so considered. With the medical control of seizures and the enlightenment of parents, teachers, and the public, the educational and social problems of the epileptic can be considered essentially those of any other children.

Summary

THE ORTHOPEDICALLY HANDICAPPED

Children and adults with orthopedic handicaps are those who have problems of physical motility. The orthopedically handicapped include people with a large variety of physical disabilities. Orthopedic handicaps can stem from innumerable causes, and the incidence of such handicaps is relatively high. The relationship between various psychological variables and physical handicap is not a close one. Emotional and social adjustment and intellective status of the physically handicapped were discussed.

Cerebral palsy has a long history, but little systematic work was done until the 1930s. Cerebral palsy is a motor defect present at birth or appearing soon after, and dependent on pathologic abnormalities in the brain. It has been classified and described in a variety of ways. The most common is according to type. Three main types are generally considered. They are spastic, athetoid, and ataxic. Spasticity is characterized by jerky, spasmodic movements. Athetosis is characterized by rhythmical, writhing movements, and ataxia by disturbances in balance.

The incidence of cerebral palsy is probably from about 1 to 3 per 1,000 school-age children. It has been estimated that there are about 40 cases under twenty years of age for each 100,000 people.

Cerebral palsy is caused by brain damage of one kind or another. The causes of brain damage are many. They have been divided into prenatal, natal, and postnatal factors. A number of conditions giving rise to injury before, during, or shortly after birth have been studied and reported.

The intelligence of the cerebrally palsied is rather low. Roughly half have IQ's below 70. The distribution of intelligence is crowded toward the lower end. However, the range of intelligence among the cerebral-palsied is rather large. Sensory defects are common. Concomitant defects in cerebrally palsied mentally deficient are frequent. The cerebrally palsied person typically suffers from a multiplicity of handicaps.

Brain-injured children display a wide variety of physical disabilities and behavioral disorders.

THE EPILEPTIC

Children and adults with epilepsy differ from others principally in that they are subject to convulsions or must take medication in order to prevent or control seizures. Epilepsy may be termed either *symptomatic* or *idiopathic*. The causes of symptomatic epilepsy can frequently be isolated.

The causes of idiopathic epilepsy are essentially unknown. Epilepsy can be classified as to type of seizure. The types of seizure considered were *grand mal, petit mal,* Jacksonian epilepsy, and psychomotor epilepsy. *Grand mal* is the most violent of the varieties of seizure. It is probable that epilepsy in some form occurs in 1 or 2 schoolchildren per 1,000. About 0.5 percent of the general population is probably epileptic. Epileptic convulsions are more common among children and youth than adults. Convulsive disorders are relatively common among the mentally deficient.

The exact causes of epilepsy are not known. Seizures are associated with various forms of brain lesions, but many epileptics have no detectable structural abnormality. An hereditary predisposition is suggested from the measurement of brain waves. An epileptic pattern of brain waves is found in a high percentage of the close relatives of idiopathic epileptics. Seizures are frequently related to emotional factors. There is some disagreement as to whether or not emotional or personality factors might cause some epilepsy.

The influence of epilepsy on intelligence is not clearly understood. The mean intelligence of epileptics is slightly below that of the general population, but the range of intelligence among epileptics is extreme. Whether epileptic convulsions produce mental deterioration has not been fully determined. Perhaps in a small percentage of cases, when seizures are frequent, severe intellectual deterioration does take place.

The range of personality characteristics among epileptics is such that the concept of the "epileptic personality" appears to be a useless one. Treatment of epilepsy by sedative and anticonvulsant drugs is common practice. A great reduction in the frequency and severity of seizures can be brought about by proper medication. Psychotherapy with epileptics has served to reduce conflicts and anxiety and decrease the number of seizures.

With constantly advancing scientific knowledge and increasing sophistication of parents, educators, and the general public, the life of those afflicted with convulsions should become constantly more nearly normal. Medical control of seizures is now sufficiently adequate that the largest problems faced by the epileptic are those of public misunderstanding and restrictions.

References

ASHER, P., AND F. E. SCHONELL, "A Survey of 100 Cases of Cerebral Palsy in Childhood," *Arch. dis. child.,* XXV (1950), 360–79.

BAKER, H. J., *Exceptional Children* (3rd ed). New York: The Macmillan Company, 1959.

BENDA, C. E., *Developmental Disorders of Mentation and the Cerebral Palsies.* New York: Grune & Stratton, Inc., 1952.

BICE, H. V., AND W. M. CRUICKSHANK, "The Evaluation of Intelligence," in *Cerebral Palsy: Its Individual and Community Problems,* eds. W. M. Cruickshank and S. Raus. Syracuse, N.Y.: Syracuse University Press, 1955.

BINGLEY, T., "Mental Symptoms in Temporal Lobe Epilepsy and Temporal Gliomas," *Acta psychiat. neurol, scand.,* kbk., XXXIII (1958), Suppl. 120.

BOYLES, I. J., AND G. CALOVINI, *Statistical Report: Physically Handicapped Children in Illinois.* Springfield, Ill.: Office of Superintendent of Public Institution, 1960.

BRIDGE, F. M., *Epilepsy and Convulsive Disorders in Children.* New York: McGraw-Hill Book Company, 1949.

BROIDA, D. C., "Psychological Aspects of Epilepsy," in *Psychology of Exceptional Children and Youth,* ed. W. M. Cruickshank. Englewood Cliffs, N.J.: Prentice-Hall, Inc., 1955.

———, C. E. IZARD, AND W. M. CRUICKSHANK, "Thematic Apperception Reactions of Crippled Children," *J. clin. psychol.,* VI (1950), 243–48.

CARTER, J. D., "Children's Expressed Attitudes towards their Epilepsy," *Nerv. child,* VI (1947), 34–37.

COUGHLIN, E. W., "Some Parental Attitudes toward Handicapped Children," *The child,* VI (1941), 41–45.

CRUICKSHANK, W. M., ed., *Psychology of Exceptional Children and Youth* (2nd ed.). Englewood Cliffs, N.J.: Prentice-Hall, Inc., 1963.

———, AND J. E. DOLPHIN, "The Emotional Needs of Crippled and Non-crippled Children," *J. except. child.,* XVI (1949), 33–40.

———, AND S. RAUS, eds., *Cerebral Palsy: Its Individual and Community Problems.* Syracuse, N.Y.: Syracuse University Press, 1955.

DEUTSCH, L., AND L. L. WIENER, "Children with Epilepsy: Emotional Problems and Treatment," *Amer. j. orthopsychiat.,* XXVIII (1948), 65.

DOLL, E. A., "The Psychological Significance of Cerebral Birth Lesions," *Amer. j. psychol.,* XLV (1933), 444–52.

DUNSDON, M. I., *The Educability of Cerebral Palsied Children.* London: National Foundation for Educational Research, 1952.

EFRON, R., "The Effect of Olfactory Stimuli in Arresting Uncinate Fits," *Brain,* LXXIX (1956), 267–81.

———, "The Conditioned Inhibition of Uncinate Fits," *Brain,* LXXX (1957), 251–62.

FLOYER, E. B., *A Psychological Study of a City's Cerebral Palsied Children.* Manchester: British Council for the Welfare of Spastics, 1955.

FOXE, A. N., "The Antisocial Aspects of Epilepsy," in *Epilepsy: Psychiatric Aspects of Convulsive Disorders,* eds. P. H. Hock and R. P. Knight. New York: Grune & Stratton, Inc., 1947.

GARRISON, K. C., AND D. G. FORCE, JR., *The Psychology of Exceptional Children* (4th ed.). New York: The Ronald Press Company, 1965.

GAUGER, A. B., "Statistical Survey of a Group of Institutionalized Cerebral Palsy Patients," *Amer. j. ment. defic.,* LV (1950), 90–98.

GEIST, H., *The Etiology of Idiopathic Epilepsy.* New York: Exposition Press, 1962.

HEFNER, R., "Some Unusual Varieties of Visceral Epilepsy," *Missouri med.,* LVII, No. 3 (1960), 289–92.

HENDERSON, P., "The Epileptic Child," *Practitioner,* CLXXIV (1955), 394–99.

HOPKINS, T., H. V. BICE, AND K. COLTON, *Evaluation and Education of the Cerebral Palsied Child.* Washington, D.C.: International Council for Exceptional Children, 1954.

JAMES, I. P., "Temporal Lobectomy for Psychomotor Epilepsy," *J. ment. sci.,* CVI (1960), 543–47.

KANNER, L., *Child Psychiatry.* Springfield, Ill.: Charles C Thomas, Publisher, 1935.

KIRMAN, B. H., "Epilepsy and Cerebral Palsy," *Arch. dis. child.,* XXXI (1956), 1–7.

KRAM, C., "Epilepsy in Children and Youth," in *Psychology of Exceptional Children and Youth* (2nd ed.), ed. W. M. Cruickshank. Englewood Cliffs, N.J.: Prentice-Hall, Inc., 1963.

LENNOX, W. G., *Science and Seizures: New Light on Epilepsy and Migraine.* New York: Harper & Row, Publishers, 1941.

———, "Sixty-six Twin Pairs Affected by Seizures," in *Epilepsy and the Convulsive State,* Assoc. for Res. in Nerv. and Ment. Dis., research publication 26. Baltimore, Md.: The Williams & Wilkins Co., 1947. (a)

———, "The Treatment of the Epileptic Veteran," *Veterans Administration Technical Bulletin.* Washington, D.C.: Government Printing Office, 1947, pp. 5–9. (b)

———, "The Genetics of Epilepsy," *Amer. j. psychiat.,* CIII (January, 1947), 457–62. (c)

———, "The Heredity of Epilepsy as Told to Relatives and Twins," *J. amer. med. assoc.,* CXLVI (1951), 529–36.

———, "The Social and Emotional Problems of the Epileptic Child and his Family," *J. pediat.,* XLIV (1954), 591, 601.

———, AND S. COBB, "Epilepsy: Aura in Epilepsy: A Statistical Review of 1,359 Cases," *Arch. neur. psychiat.,* XXX (1933), 374–85.

———, AND A. L. COLLINS, "Intelligence of Normal and Epileptic Twins," *Amer. j. psychiat.,* CI (1945), 764–69.

———, E. L. GIBBS, AND F. A. GIBBS, "Inheritance of Cerebral Dysrhythmia and Epilepsy," *Arch. neur. psychiat.,* XLIV (1940), 1155–83.

LOWENBACH, H., "The Encephalogram in Healthy Relatives of Epileptics," *Bull. johns hopkins hosp.,* (July, 1939), 125–37.

MACKAY, R. P., S. B. WORTIS, AND O. SUGAR, *The Year Book of Neurology, Psychiatry, and Neurosurgery.* Chicago, Ill.: The Year Book Medical Publishers, Inc., 1960.

MCINTIRE, J. T., "The Incidence of Feeblemindedness in the Cerebral Palsied," *Proc. amer. assoc. ment. defic.,* XLIII (1938), 44–50.

———, "The Incidence of Feeblemindedness in the Cerebral Palsied," *Amer. j. ment. defic.,* L (1946), 491–94.

MALZBERG, B., "The Incidence and Prevalence of Intramural Epilepsy," in *Epilepsy: Psychiatric Aspects of Convulsive Disorders*, eds. P. H. Hoch and R. P. Knight. New York: Grune & Stratton, Inc., 1947.

MEYER, V., "A Critique of Psychological Approaches to Brain Damage," *J. ment. sci.*, CIII (1957), 70–109.

MILLER, E., AND G. B. ROSENFELD, "The Psychologic Evaluation of Children with Cerebral Palsy and Its Implications in Treatment," *J. pediat.*, XLI (1952), 613–21.

MULLEN, F. A., "Convulsive Disorders among Educable Handicapped Pupils," Paper presented at Amer. Educ. Res. Assoc., Atlantic City, N.J., February 16, 1953.

NATIONAL SAFETY COUNCIL, *Accident Facts*. Chicago: The National Safety Council, 1963.

NUFFIELD, E. J., "Neurophysiology and Behavior Disorders in Epileptic Children," *J. ment. sci.*, CVII (1961), 438–57.

PENFIELD, W., AND T. C. ERICKSON, *Epilepsy and Cerebral Localization*. Springfield, Ill.: Charles C Thomas, Publisher, 1941.

PENROSE, L. S., *The Biology of Mental Defect* (3rd ed.). New York: Grune & Stratton, Inc., 1963.

PERESTEIN, J. A., AND P. N. HOOD, "Infantile Spastic Hemiplegia, Intelligence and Age of Walking and Talking," *Amer. j. ment. defic.*, LXI (1957), 534–43.

PHELPS, W. M., "Recent Significant Trends in the Case of Cerebral Palsy," *South. med. j.*, XXXVIII (1946), 132–38.

————, "Characteristic Psychological Variations in Cerebral Palsy," *Nerv. child*, VII (1948), 10–12.

PINTNER, R., J. EISENSON, AND M. STANTON, *The Psychology of the Physically Handicapped*. New York: Appleton-Century-Crofts, 1940.

POLLOCK, H. M., "A Statistical Review of Convulsive Disorders," *Amer. j. psychiat.*, X (1931), 655–61.

ROBINSON, H. B., AND ROBINSON, N. M., *The Mentally Retarded Child*. New York: McGraw-Hill Book Company, 1965.

RUPP, C., "The Management of Epilepsy," *J. amer. med. assoc.*, CLXVI (1958), 1967–70.

SAFFIAN, S., *Program Trends in Crippling Conditions: 1950–1960*, Child Health Studies Branch, Division of Research, United States Department of Health, Education, and Welfare. Washington, D.C.: Government Printing Office, 1962.

SAKEL, M., *Epilepsy*. New York: Philosophical Library, Inc., 1958.

SARASON, S. B., *Psychological Problems in Mental Deficiency*. New York: Harper & Row, Publishers, 1959.

SAWREY, J. M., AND C. W. TELFORD, *The Psychology of Adjustment* (3rd ed.). Boston, Mass.: Allyn & Bacon, Inc., 1971.

SCHONELL, F. E., *Educating Spastic Children*. Edinburgh: Oliver and Boyd, 1956.

SMOCK, C., AND W. M. CRUICKSHANK, "Responses of Handicapped and Normal Children to the Rosenzweig P-F Study," *Quant. j. child behav.*, IV (1952), 156–64.

SOMERFIELD-ZISKUND, E., AND E. ZISKUND, "Effect of Phenobarbital on the Mentality of Epileptic Patients," *Arch. neuro. psychiat.*, XLIII (1940), 70–79.

STEPHEN, E., "Cerebral Palsy and Mental Defect," in *Mental Deficiency: The Changing Outlook*, eds. A. M. Clarke and A. D. Clarke. New York: The Free Press, 1958.

TENNEY, J. W., "Epileptic Children in Detroit's Special School Program," *Excep. child.*, XXI (1955), 162–67.

THOM, D. A., "Convulsions of Early Life and Their Relation to the Chronic Convulsant Disorders and Mental Defects," *Amer. j. psychiat.*, XCVIII (1942), 574–80.

TIZARD, B., "The Personality of Epileptics: A Discussion of the Evidence," *Psychol. bull.*, LIX (1962), 196–210.

TIZARD, J. P., "Individual Differences in the Mentally Deficient," in *Mental Deficiency: The Changing Outlook*, eds. A. M. Clarke and A. D. Clarke. New York: The Free Press, 1958.

————, R. S. PAINE, AND B. CROTHERS, "Disturbance of Sensation in Children with Hemiplegia," *J. amer. med. assoc.*, CLV (1954), 628–32.

TOWER, D. B., *Neurochemistry and Epilepsy*. Springfield, Ill.: Charles C Thomas, Publisher, 1960.

TURNER, W. J., AND MERLIS, S., "Clinical Correlations Between Electroencephalography and Antisocial Behavior," *Medical times*, XC (1962), 505–11.

WALLIN, J. E., *Children with Mental and Physical Handicaps*. Englewood Cliffs, N.J.: Prentice-Hall, Inc., 1949.

WHITE HOUSE CONFERENCE REPORT, UNITED STATES DEPARTMENT OF HEALTH, EDUCATION AND WELFARE, *Summary of Health and Vital Statistics*. Washington, D.C.: Government Printing Office, 1958.

WRIGHT, B. A., *Physical Disability: A Psychological Approach*. New York: Harper & Row, Publishers, 1960.

WYLLIE, W. S., "Cerebral Palsies in Infancy," in *Modern Trends in Neurology*, ed. A. Feiling. London: Butterworth & Co. (Publishers), Ltd., 1951.

YANNET, H., "The Etiology of Congenital Cerebral Palsy," *J. pediat.*, XXIV (1944), 38–45.

14

Speech Handicaps

Concern for the person with a speech defect undoubtedly preceded by centuries the development of an interest in normal speech. Several centuries before Christ, Greek physicians were prescribing cures for stuttering. However, it is largely within the present century that systematic studies of normal speech have been made, and it is only within the twentieth century that scientific investigations of the nature, causes, and treatment of speech defects have been systematically pursued. Special community and school services for the speech-handicapped are relatively new, compared to the services provided for the more dramatic forms of disability such as blindness and orthopedic handicaps. The first statutes providing special services for speech defectives in the United States were enacted by Wisconsin, in 1913. The following year, Dr. Smiley Blanton established the the first university clinic for speech problems at the University of Wisconsin (Irwin, 1955).

Many different professional specialities—general medicine, plastic surgery, otology, oral surgery, dentistry, psychiatry, psychology, education and speech therapy—are involved in the diagnosis and treatment of speech disorders. A wide variety of disciplines is necessarily involved in speech correction, because anatomical, sociological, psychological, and educational factors all contribute to speech impairment and correction. Speech defects may be caused by anatomical defects or deviant physiological functioning of the jaws, tongue, or soft palate, by disturbed feelings, emotions, or attitudes, by inadequate self-concepts, and by faulty language habits arising from unsatisfactory speech models, social pressures, and misguided efforts at speech training or correction.

Definitions of Speech Defects

There have been few attempts to define speech impairment quantitatively. The commonly accepted definitions of speech defects are all largely functional in nature. Three components seem to be common to most current answers to the question: What is defective speech? Speech is considered to be defective when the manner of speaking interferes with communication, when the person's manner of speaking distracts attention from what is said, or when speech is such that the speaker himself is unduly self-conscious or apprehensive about his way of speaking. More concisely, speech is defective whenever the deviant manner of speaking interferes with communication, calls undue attention to itself, or causes the speaker concern to such an extent that special educational or remedial measures are deemed necessary.

These criteria vary according to their social context. The listening ear defines the intelligibility and distractibility of speech. The speaker himself is the measure of his personal concern. One's culture, subculture, and status within the culture, as well as one's age, profession, and role in life enter into a definition of defective speech. The speech of the average three-year-old is defective by adult standards, but normal for his age group. The adolescent from the slum who says "dese" for "these," "dose" for "those," and "dem" for "them" will not usually be labelled a speech defective. A southern drawl, an eastern twang, or midwestern nasality are normal in those geographic regions and become matters of concern outside these localities only to radio announcers, actors, and public speakers. The listener matches the speech that he hears against a varying standard of acceptability and intelligibility, and labels speech as normal or defective accordingly.

There are similarly marked variations in what speakers find objectionable in their own speech. Many people are unable to detect marked impairments in their own speech, while others request therapy for speech which is well within the normal range. The speaker's level of personal concern does not always agree with the listener's judgment.

Identification and Diagnosis of Speech Defects

Many people are identified as speech defectives by their families, their peers, or by themselves. Some people who get to speech clinics and speech correctionists are referred by other professional people, such as doctors, psychiatrists, psychologists, and teachers. In schools, many children are referred by their regular classroom teachers. Others are identified by systematic screening procedures. Many schools, in addition to requesting referrals by teachers, systematically screen one or two grades each year.

Individuals thus identified as probable speech defectives usually undergo more thorough diagnostic examinations before treatment is started. Depending on the nature of the referral and the amount of information available, the diagnosis may be made either by a single person—the speech correctionist—or by a team of specialists. A complete diagnostic evaluation involves a complete physical examination, including a dental examination to disclose any oral, dental, or other organic factors contributing to the disorder. An assessment of intellectual level, an audiometric evaluation of hearing, and sometimes a psychiatric examination are also made to disclose any intellectual, auditory, or personality deviations which may complicate the picture.

There are several screening and diagnostic scales and tests available to aid in the speech assessment (Barker and England, 1962; Fletcher, 1953). Some of these are the Wood Index of Defective Articulation, the Templin-Darley Screening and Diagnostic Tests of Articulation, and the Boston University Speech Sound Discrimination Picture Test. For evaluation of the severity of speech impairment there are scales of phonographically recorded samples of defective speech graded in terms of severity, with which a particular person's speech can be compared (Curry et al., 1943; Perrin, 1954). Tikofsky and Tikofsky (1965) have shown that fairly objective ratings of speech intelligibility can be made with the aid of such devices.

Prevalence of Speech Disorders

Surveys of the prevalence of speech disorders are not very reliable because of the varying purpose served by the surveys, the different standards applied, the diverse populations sampled, and the biases of the investigators. When all degrees and categories of speech defects are included, the total of speech impaired schoolchildren identified is estimated at around 10 percent. Several surveys have reported from 7 to 8 percent of school-age children with speech defects (Pronovost, 1951). Two committees of the American Speech and Hearing Association (1952, 1959) have independently estimated that a minimum of 5 percent of school-age children have defects of speech sufficiently serious to warrant speech correction or therapy, and that an additional 5 percent suffer from noticeable but less serious defects. A breakdown of the estimated prevalence of speech problems and accompanying disorders is given in Table 14-1.

TABLE 14–1

Distribution of Speech Defects of Various Types and Causes in Public School Children

Type of Defect	Percentage
Articulatory defects	81.0
Stuttering	6.5
Delayed speech	4.5
Hard-of-hearing	2.5
Voice problems	2.3
Cleft palate	1.5
Cerebral palsy	1.0
Bilinguality	
Mental retardation }	0.7
Aphasia	
Total	100.0

Data from American Speech and Hearing Association (1961).

There are more people with speech defects than with any other type of exceptionality, with the possible exceptions of the emotionally disturbed, the "slow learners," and the culturally disadvantaged. Many more males than females have speech defects—two to five times as many, depending on the type of disorders. The full explanations of these sex differences are not known.

Causes of Speech Defects

Speech defects are caused by a wide variety of organic and functional (social and psychological) factors. The organic causes include cleft palate, maldevelopment of other parts of the mouth and jaw, dental irregularities including missing or maloccluded teeth, muscular paralysis of the larynx, tumors or ulcers in or around the larynx, loss of the larynx, brain damage (in cerebral palsy and aphasia) and nasal obstructions.

Functional causes include failure to learn adequate speech, fixations, regressive speech patterns, and general personality and emotional disturbances.

Many speech specialists do not find the dichotomy between organic and functional a very useful one. Speech difficulties which are originally strictly organic in origin usually acquire a large functional component as a result of the way the person reacts to the difficulty, and prolonged functional disorders may have organic consequences. Although it is possible for organic disorders to remain on that level with relatively little functional component, and for functional disorders to continue without any specific organic components, they rarely do so. Most speech defects have both functional and organic components.

Recently, attention seems to be shifting from the organic to the functional as the most significant factors in the etiology of most speech defects (Van Riper and Irwin, 1958).

Recent developments in psycholinguistics may provide a new approach or a new emphasis to the study of deviant speech and language. The more complete understanding of normal psycholinguistic processes may throw light on the nature of the disturbances of speech and language. For example, Menyuk (1964) using a conventional linguistic model compared the syntactic structures of children with "infantile" speech with those of otherwise comparable normal-speaking children. Her analysis indicated that at no age level did the grammatical forms used by the deviant speakers resemble the grammar used by younger normal speakers. She concluded that "infantile speech" is a misnomer. The linguistically impaired children had disordered or disorganized rather than delayed linguistic development.

Nonlanguage Characteristics of the Speech Impaired

Like most types of handicapped people, persons with speech defects often have other disabilities. Many of them, at least more than those with normal speech, are mentally retarded, brain-damaged, or have developmental anomalies such as cleft palate and cleft lip. Therefore, in asking what the speech impaired are like, we need to define the population. If all individuals with defective speech are included, we obtain a very heterogeneous population, some subgroups of which are characterized by deviant physiques or intellectual levels, i.e., the cerebral-palsied and the mentally retarded. Since the group with defective speech contains a disproportionate number of physically and intellectually handicapped individuals, we would expect the mean level of the entire group to be below that of the general population. On the other hand, if we inquire into the physical, intellectual, and personal characteristics of people whose only handicap is their speech impairment, the answer may be quite different. There are few, if any, studies of such groups; consequently, our discussion must deal with the entire group of people with defective speech.

PHYSICAL CHARACTERISTICS OF THE SPEECH IMPAIRED

Most individuals with defective speech are physically normal. That is, most speech defects are primarily functional in nature and are unaccompanied by marked organic impairments. However, about 16 percent of the children with the more serious types of speech defects also have physical disabilities, and this group is large enough to bring the entire group of speech-impaired individuals below the norm of the entire population in general physique (Eisenson, 1963).

The performance of speech-impaired children is slightly below normal on tests of motor proficiency (Jenkins and Lohr, 1964). Children who retain their speech errors are more inferior in these same tests than are those who outgrow their speech errors (Dickson, 1962). Speech-impaired children—even those with no apparent organic defects—are inferior in tests of rhythm, motor coordination, and strength (Bilto, 1941). Most of the children in the studies cited had severe articulatory defects. It is possible that children from the lower socioeconomic levels are represented disproportionately in such groups, and that they are below par in physique and motor proficiency partly because of related factors, such as poor nutrition and inadequate medical care. Children who do not outgrow speech errors may not do so because of the presence of fewer models of good speech in their homes and communities. It seems probable that the inferior physical status of speech defectives as a group is the result of the presence of the 16 percent who also have physical disabilities, such as cleft palate and cerebral palsy, and the additional fact that some speech defects, such as poor articulation, are more common and more persistent in children of the lower class, who are also somewhat below the normal in physique because of related factors.

SENSORY CAPACITIES OF THE SPEECH IMPAIRED

We find a larger incidence of speech defects among the severely visually and aurally impaired than among the population at large. When we exclude these extreme subgroups, the relationship between speech defects and sensory capacities largely disappears. Although many speech correctionists believe that speech-impaired individuals—particularly those with defective articulation—are weak in auditory discrimination (Van Riper,

1954; 1963), the studies of basic sensory acuity fail to show such a relationship (Eisenson, 1963).

INTELLIGENCE LEVEL OF THE SPEECH DEFECTIVES

Studies have consistently found a positive relationship between language proficiency and intelligence level. Therefore, it is not surprising to find that children with speech defects fall below the norms in measured intelligence (Everhart, 1953; Garrison and Force, 1965). Defects such as the absence of speech, marked delay in acquiring speech, and poor articulation, which may be caused by the child's failure to learn are, of course, very common among the mentally retarded. However, when the mentally retarded are excluded, there is still a slight relationship between measured intelligence and the incidence of speech defects (Eisenson, 1963). It is possible that differences in socioeconomic level may be a causal factor here also.

EDUCATIONAL ACHIEVEMENT OF THE SPEECH IMPAIRED

Even excluding the mentally retarded and the cerebral-palsied, children with speech defects are relatively retarded in school (Berry and Eisenson, 1956; Carrell, 1936). Speech defectives are retarded scholastically even out of proportion to expectations based on their intelligence test scores (Eisenson, 1963). Social-class differences can hardly account for the greater educational than intellectual retardation of children with speech defects. It would seem that speech defects constitute a greater handicap in formal learning than they do in acquiring the more general intellectual skills and information required for satisfactory intelligence-test performance.

Classifications of Speech Disorders

Speech defects are classified in several ways, depending on the purpose of the classification and the interest of the writer. As previously indicated, a broad twofold classification of speech defects into the organic and the functional is commonly used when etiology is considered. Surveys of speech problems typically classify defects according to the forms they take and according to other associated and causal factors. Accordingly, we have articulatory disorders, disturbances of rhythm, voice disorders, delayed or retarded speech, mutism, and aphonia as types of defects. In a third type of classification, we list speech disorders associated with cleft palate, brain damage (cerebral palsy and aphasia), deafness, and mental retardation.

These various classifications cut across each other. Most of the classes of disorders based on symptoms (articulatory, voice, rhythm, delayed speech, and so forth), with the possible exception of aphasia, can be either organic or functional. Speech disorders of mentally retarded, cleft-palated, or cerebral-palsied individuals may take any of the forms listed, although certain types are more common than others.

DISORDERS OF ARTICULATION

Disorders of articulation consist of omission ("at" for "cat"), substitution ("gog" for "dog"), distortion or additions ("furog" for "frog") of speech sounds. They may involve the mispronunciation of an entire word or words.

Certain articulatory disorders are referred to as *immature speech* (baby talk) since all children make these errors in the early stages of language development. Table 14-2 shows the age levels when children are normally able to properly articulate certain sounds. More recent studies (Mecham, Berko, and Berko, 1960) indicate that *p, b, m,* and *o* are usually the easiest sounds for children to articulate. Additional sounds, in order of chronological development, are *h, w, d, k, g, j, f, v, t, z, l, s, u,* and *r.* This order agrees quite well with Davis's (1938) norms. A large percentage of errors of articulation are eliminated by the time children reach the fourth grade, i.e., by the age of nine or ten (Roe and Milisen, 1942). After this age, defects of articulation seldom diminish without specific remedial measures.

TABLE 14–2
Ages at Which Children Are Normally Able to Articulate Certain Sounds

Age (In Years)	Sounds
3.5	b, p, m, w, h
4.5	t, d, g, k, ng, y
5.5	f, v, s, z
6.5	sh, l, th (as in then)

Data from Davis (1938).

Lisping is another common form of articulatory defect among preschool and lower-grade children. Its frequency decreases rapidly as children get older, but its persistence beyond the first or second grade warrants corrective procedures. *Lalling* (distortions of *r* and *l* sounds) is sometimes listed as an additional form of articulatory disorder.

Disorders of articulation are the most common form of speech defects, accounting for from 60 to 80 percent of diagnosed speech disorders.

DELAYED SPEECH

The age at which normal children begin to speak varies so widely that it is impossible to set a specific age beyond which delay in speaking is exceptional. However, when a child of three or four does not talk, it should become a matter for study. There are many causes of delayed speech. Table 14-3 indicates the principal causes of delayed speech in a fairly large group of children.

TABLE 14–3
Delayed Speech in 278 Children

Cause of Delay	Number of Children
Deafness	110
Developmental aphasia	72
Mental deficiency	71
Cerebral palsy	22
Mental illness	3

Data from Morley et al. (1955).

In addition to the major causes of delayed speech listed in Table 14-3, some children do not learn to speak at the usual age because of lack of motivation. When doting parents or nurses anticipate every wish, or when gestures, grunts, or cries are effective in controlling others, children may have no need for words. Children with delayed speech because of insufficient motivation may be otherwise quite normal. They may be well-behaved and seem to have made a satisfactory adjustment to the world without speaking. However, some nonverbal children who are not deaf, mentally retarded, brain-damaged or seriously mentally ill, display other patterns of deviant behavior. Some isolate themselves as far as possible from other people, and others seek out close physical contact with both adults and inanimate objects. They rub their bodies along the walls or on furniture, rub their faces against toys, climb on laps and snuggle up even to strangers (McWilliams, 1959). The significance of these activities is not known, but they are often considered symptomatic of personality disorders.

DISORDERS OF VOICE PRODUCTION: PHONATION

Voice disorders consist of marked deviations in the loudness, pitch, quality, duration, or flexibility of sounds. In addition to the relatively simple variations of each, there are other voice defects, such as breathiness, harshness, hoarseness, and nasality. Voice disorders have the lowest incidence of all categories of speech disorders among children. They are difficult to correct in children, principally because the speech mechanism is still developing and the voice quality is changing. Voice disorders are more often diagnosed and treated in adults than in children, whereas the opposite is true of articulatory disorders and delayed speech.

DISTURBANCES OF RHYTHM: STUTTERING, STAMMERING, AND CLUTTERING

Although some workers (Weiss, 1964) claim that stuttering, stammering, and cluttering should be differentiated, most authors do not discriminate among them. We shall use the term *stuttering* to cover the entire range of rhythmic disorders, and leave any differentiations within the group to the specialists.

The literature on stuttering is voluminous and often contradictory. More research has been done and more material written on stuttering than on any other type of speech disorder. Theories about the causes of stuttering range from the organic, through social learning, to mental hygiene. Therapy has varied from routine drills and breathing exercises, through individual and group psychotherapy, to hypnosis and faith cures. There are no forms of treatment that cannot claim a sizable number of successes. We shall briefly summarize the principal research findings and indicate, as best we can, the current theories of stuttering and methods of treatment.

Definitions of Stuttering. It is easier to describe stuttering than to define it. Stuttering is one of the major forms of nonfluency. It is primarily a disturbance of the normal flow and rhythm of speech. It involves blocks, hesitations, and prolongations, and repetitions of sounds, syllables, words, or phrases. It is frequently accompanied by muscular tension, rapid eye-blinking, irregularities of breathing, and facial grimacing. No two stutterers have the same secondary symptoms.

Causes of Stuttering. The alleged causes of stuttering have been as diverse as the theories, and are often related to them. The earlier conceptions stressed organic factors such as heredity and lack of hemispheric brain dominance (Travis, 1931). The social learning, mental hygiene, or psychological conceptions have stressed habit, personality, and emotional factors as the primary causal factors. No one cause or set of causes has been discovered to date. Stuttering probably has multiple causation.

The types of evidence usually presented in support of the alleged organic etiology are:

1. The incidence of stuttering in the family lines of stutterers is much greater than in the families of nonstutterers, suggesting a possible genetic basis (Nelson, 1939; West, Nelson, and Berry, 1939).
2. Stuttering is more frequent among left-handed people and among people shifted from their original left-hand preference (West, Nelson, and Berry, 1939). This fact has been used to support a lack-of-brain-dominance conception of the cause of stuttering.
3. Stuttering has a number of physiological components or accompaniments (Kopp, 1934).
4. Stuttering is associated with multiple births (twinning, and so forth), and with prematurity (Berry, 1937).
5. There is a greater-than-chance incidence of central nervous system disorders among stutterers (Gregory, 1964).

The functional conceptions of stuttering seem to be supported by the following facts:

1. Stuttering varies tremendously as a function of situational factors (Siegel and Haugen, 1964).
2. Stuttering (secondary stuttering) has profound emotional components (Sheehan, 1958b; Glauber, 1944).
3. Nondirective and psychoanalytic psychotherapy which improves general adjustment, reduces conflicts, and decreases anxieties often helps or cures stuttering.
4. Stuttering most often develops at times when the child experiences considerable social pressures (when learning to speak, on entering school and, to a lesser degree, at adolescence).
5. The parents of stutterers display a characteristic pattern of traits consisting of perfectionism and high levels of aspiration for their children (Goldman and Shames, 1964; Kinstler, 1961).

Johnson's (1942, 1956) "diagnosogenic" conception of the origin of stuttering is typical of the functional, social-psychological point of view. According to Johnson, when the young child experiences normal nonfluencies while learning to speak, his parents often fail to recognize that he is passing through a normal transitional stage of language learning. They label the child's normal blockings, hesitations, and repetitions as "stuttering," and become concerned about his "defective" speech. The label associated with manifestations of parental anxiety becomes a stigma. The child eventually becomes concerned about his own speech, believing that he is a stutterer. He then becomes fearful of not speaking properly and establishes a vicious cycle of fear—anxiety—nonfluency—increased fear

—higher levels of anxiety—greater nonfluency, and so forth. According to this conception, stuttering begins in the mind or ears of the listener, and is transferred to the child as concern for his own speech. The child comes to anticipate stuttering, dreads it, tries to avoid it, becomes tense, and so stutters.

Cross-cultural studies lend some support to Johnson's contention. Certain cultures with very tolerant and accepting attitudes toward speech (Ute and Pilagra Indians and native Polynesians) are said to have little, if any, stuttering, and their languages contain no words for it. In cultures with strict standards of speech (the Cowickan and Japanese societies), the incidence of stuttering is high and they have specific names for the disorder (Stewart, 1960; Lemert, 1962; Henry and Henry, 1940).

Studies of the parents of stutterers also report results which are consistent with Johnson's "diagnosogenic" conception of the origin of stuttering. These studies indicate that the parents of stutterers and nonstutterers differ in their patterns of parent-child interaction. The parents of stutterers are more critical and intolerant of deviant behavior in their children. They are more perfectionistic and hold higher levels of aspiration for their children. Furthermore, these attitudes are specifically related to the speech area (Goodstein, 1958). Readers interested in a good presentation of Johnson's theory, as well as several other conceptions of stuttering, should read the books by Luper and Mulden (1964), and by Robinson (1964). Wingate (1962a, 1962b, 1964) in a series of three articles and Lanyon and Duprez (1970) in a more recent study review the evidence bearing on the Johnson diagnosgenic or evaluational theory of stuttering and question the adequacy of this conception of the etiology of stuttering. On the other hand, Sander's (1963) experiment concerned with listener's evaluations of simulated disfluent speech yields results which are consistent with the proposition that stuttering may well have its genesis in the ears of the listener.

Continued interest in the possible organic basis for stuttering is reflected in studies such as Gregory's (1964) hypothesis that stuttering may be related to a "central auditory disturbance" and Martin's (1962) testing of the hypothesis that stuttering may derive from a "constitutional tendency to perseverate." However, the data derived from these studies support neither hypothesis.

Primary and Secondary Stuttering.   The distinction between primary and secondary stuttering made by Bluemel in 1932 has proven to be a useful one even though the dichotomy has been criticized by others and has been somewhat modified by Bluemel himself (Bluemel, 1932, 1957; Bloodstein, 1961; Garrison and Force, 1965). As we have already indicated, all children experience a degree of nonfluency when learning to speak. A large number—some say as many as 30 percent—of children between the ages of two and four show blockings, hesitations, and repetitions of sounds or words. From an objective standpoint, they stutter. However, at this age —the so-called primary stage—the child is not aware of his speech difficulties. He is not self-conscious about his speech. He does not experience the secondary symptoms of increased muscular tension, fear, and struggle that characterize the secondary stage of stuttering.

In the secondary stage of stuttering, the individual has been labelled by himself and others as a stutterer. He approaches speech in general, and certain words or sounds in particular, with anxiety. He is afraid that he will stutter. His fear increases the probability of his stuttering. Some speech therapists claim that only secondary stuttering is "true stuttering." Primary stuttering is only "normal nonfluency."

Irrespective of their theoretical commitments, all speech specialists agree that social factors are important, if not crucial, in the development of stuttering (Adams and Dietze, 1965; Stromsa, 1965; Luper and Mulden, 1964; Johnson, 1959). Most of the psychogenic or social-learning conceptions of stuttering also assign a crucial role to fear or anxiety in the genesis of stuttering. Social attitudes and anxiety are both essential components of most functional (mental hygiene) conceptions of the origins of stuttering.

The Treatment of Primary Stuttering. Even though the distinction between primary and secondary stuttering is difficult to make, the initial hesitations, blockings, and repetitions of the two-to-four-year old require different treatment than the secondary symptoms of the confirmed stutter. Here are some general suggestions for parents and other adults concerned about the nonfluencies of the child who is in the early stages of language acquisition:

1. Measures taken should be indirect and not concerned with the speech deviations as such.
2. Keep the child in good physical condition.
3. Provide a pleasant, relaxed home atmosphere.
4. Provide as many good speech models as possible.
5. Try to develop feeling of adequacy and self-confidence (a satisfactory self-concept) in the child by utilizing his assets and minimizing his liabilities.
6. If referred to, child's nonfluencies should be acknowledged but accepted as normal. The impression that they are bad or that other people are anxious about them should be avoided.

Symptomatic Treatment of the Secondary Stutterer. Symptomatic treatment may attempt to either teach the person to stutter in a way that is tolerable to himself and to others (controlled stuttering) or to talk without stuttering (inhibition of stuttering).

Controlled stuttering is attained by teaching the stutterer rate-controlled speech techniques of breathing and controlled phrasing, through the repetition of what is said, reading in unison, negative practice (practice in stuttering) and various distracting devices (Van Riper, 1954). Remedial procedures are intended to develop tolerance of stuttering, emotional desensitization, anxiety reduction, and controlled speech. Treatment designed to make it possible for the person to talk without stuttering consists in teaching him analytically, step by step, to articulate properly and gradually to build up fluency. Many of the same techniques used in teaching controlled stuttering may also be used to develop speech which is relatively fluent. The treatment of stuttering, as well as of many other types of speech defects, seems to be shifting away from mechanical drills and devices (speech correction) toward therapeutic relationships (speech therapy). One manifestation of this shift in emphasis is a preference for the term *speech therapist* rather than *speech correctionist*.

Psychotherapy for the Stutterer.   Psychotherapy is used with stutterers on the assumption that the nonfluency is either a symptom of, or is accompanied by, personality maladjustment and that the way to handle the stuttering is to deal with the underlying personality defects. Speech pathologists have recommended and used psychotherapy ranging all the way from directive counseling and group discussion to the nondirective, psychoanalytic, and hypnotic therapies. The goals of psychotherapy for stutterers are essentially the same as those for individuals with normal speech. These include the development of insight (self-understanding), changes in the self-concept (ego building), self-acceptance, emotional desensitization (the reduction of fears and anxieties), and the improvement of personal relations (Wyatt and Herzon, 1962).

Psychotherapy attempts to go beyond the removal of the symptom, and deals with the more basic problems and conflicts on the assumption that speech will improve with personality reorientation and improved adjustment.

The Personality Traits of Stutterers.   Prescribing psychotherapy for stutterers implies that they are in need of personality reorganization. However, a survey of the studies of the personality traits and characteristics of stutterers does not show them to be markedly maladjusted. Goodstein (1958) and Sheehan (1958a) have surveyed the literature on the topic published over a twenty-five-year period. They found opinions ranging all the way from the contention that stutterers are essentially normal people except in speech, to the notion that stuttering is the manifestation of a basically neurotic personality. These two extensive surveys disclosed little evidence to support the contention that either children or adults who stutter have a particular pattern of personality traits, are neurotic, or are otherwise severely maladjusted. Stutterers certainly do not appear to be severely maladjusted when compared with psychiatric patients. However, they are significantly different from nonstutterers in being more tense, anxious, and withdrawn. Stutterers also have lower levels of aspiration. They have significantly more personal and social problems than nonstutterers, but it is impossible to tell whether these problems were responsible for the stuttering or developed as a consequence of social reactions to the speech defect.

SPEECH DEFECTS ASSOCIATED WITH NEURAL IMPAIRMENT

Impairment of brain functioning may be due to maldevelopment, traumatic injury, hemorrhage, infections, abscesses, and tumors. Such pathology may result in localized injury and the impairment of language functions (aphasia) or it may produce widespread neural damage, with language disorders constituting only a part of a total syndrome which includes widespread muscular paralysis or dysfunction and mental subnormality.

The Aphasic Child. Aphasia literally means loss of speech. As a clinical entity, it is an impairment in the understanding or expression of language due to brain injury. Aphasia is a disturbance of one's ability to handle language symbols. Traditionally, the term has been applied to adults and children who have suffered brain damage *after* language has been acquired. Here the meaning is clear, for there is a loss or impairment of a previously acquired habit system. However, the concept of "congenital aphasia" discussed in a later section implies something quite different.

Aphasia is typically subdivided into these types: (1) *sensory or receptive aphasia,* in which the person can hear and see, but cannot understand spoken or written language; (2) *motor or expressive aphasia,* in which the vocal apparatus is not paralyzed but the individual cannot formulate speech properly nor write properly; (3) *conceptual aphasia,* in which the person is unable to formulate concepts (less frequently listed as a category); and (4) *global or mixed aphasia,* in which all language forms are affected.

The loss of the language function due to brain injury in a child who has already acquired language skills does not differ from aphasia in adults, except that the language disturbance is milder than in adults with comparable brain damage and recovery is both more rapid and more complete (Benton, 1962; 1964.) The prognosis for postnatally acquired aphasia in children is good (Kleffner, 1959).

Congenital Aphasia. As early as 1866, some cases of marked language impairment in children who were neither deaf nor mentally retarded were called "congenital aphasia," but the concept never gained general acceptance. However, the question of the existence of such a clinical entity has recently received considerable attention. Despite a persistent controversy concerning the existence of the syndrome, the term has received widespread publicity and several clinics are so labelling certain children with communication disorders (McGinnis, 1963; Hull, 1963).

Congenital aphasia is often diagnosed by a process of exclusion and inference. When certain language deficits are present in the absence of mental retardation, sensory impairments, or emotional disturbances (autisms), neural pathology is postulated as the probable cause and the child is labelled "aphasic." Some of these children show evidence of central nervous system impairment, but there are many children called "aphasic" whose language impairment is the first and only manifestation of central nervous system deficit (Hull, 1963; Bay, 1964; Benton, 1964). However, most workers feel that the term should be reserved for children with positive evidence of cerebral impairment. Failure to develop language, in and of itself, is not presumptive of congenital aphasia.

None of the behavioral symptoms listed as characteristically accompanying childhood aphasia is *peculiar to this syndrome.* The most commonly mentioned symptoms (Barry, 1955; Eisenson, 1963; Edwards, 1965) are:

1. Erratic responses to the same stimulus
2. Distractibility
3. Abnormal fixation on unimportant details
4. Perseveration
5. Hyperactivity
6. Emotional lability
7. Mixed laterality
8. Abnormal delays in responding
9. Perceptual disturbances
10. Poor motor coordination

All of these are symptoms of brain damage in general. Congenital aphasia, as compared with the postnatally acquired condition, is said to be more severe, less likely to disappear spontaneously, less readily corrected by educational and therapeutic programs, and different in the nature of the neural impairment. The last point refers to the fact that ordinary postnatally acquired aphasia is supposed to result from damage to the *dominant cerebral hemisphere.* Children with demonstrable injury to the speech area of *either hemisphere alone,* either congenital or occurring in infancy, are not aphasic, so it is assumed that congenital aphasia involves damage to both hemispheres.

Educators are proposing to substitute the term "verbal communication disorders" for "aphasia," and to avoid neurological implications by referring to these children simply as "children with learning disabilities" (Bateman, 1964; Capobianco, 1964).

Speech Defects Associated with Cerebral Palsy.   About 90 percent of children with cerebral palsy are said to have significant speech disorders. Their speech impairments are part of a larger syndrome including abnormal sucking, chewing, swallowing, breathing, and tongue movements. Language training is typically a part of their total rehabilitation program. Because of the widespread nature of the neural impairment and the number of accompanying handicaps, speech correction is often quite difficult. It is recommended that speech training be started when the child normally begins to speak (one to one-and-a-half years of age), and in most cases it will continue for years (Mecham, Berko, and Berko, 1960).

Tests with the Illinois Test of Psycholinguistic Abilities indicate that athetosics—a subcategory of cerebral palsy in which the neural damage is subcortical—are superior to spastics, whose brain injuries are cortical, on the representational level, while the spastics are superior to athetoids on the automatic-sequential levels (Myers, 1965). In general, spastics are superior to athetoids in general language level (Hammill and Irwin, 1965). Speech correctionists working with cerebral-palsied children will find the monograph *Speech Therapy for the Cerebral Palsied,* by Westlake and Rutherford (1961), helpful.

SPEECH DEFECTS ASSOCIATED WITH MENTAL RETARDATION

The relationship between mental retardation and speech level is high. Table 14-4 shows this relationship as indicated by a typical study.

TABLE 14–4
Speech Defects as Related to Degrees of Mental Retardation

IQ	50–69	21–49	20 and below
Percentage with speech defects	43	73	100

Data from Sirken and Lyon (1941).

There are several reasons for the close relationship between language proficiency and intellectual level. The most obvious is that the individuals of lower levels of intelligence lack the capacity for acquiring language. Prior to the advent of intelligence testing, idiots were defined as those individuals who were so low in mental level that they did not learn to speak. In addition to the inability of the most severely mentally retarded to acquire speech, mental retardation and speech defects may both have a common cause, i.e., brain damage or defective development of the nervous system. Critical reviews of the relationships are given by Goertzen (1957) and Smith (1962). The mentally retarded seem to suffer from the same *types* of speech defects as do the mentally normal, although the frequency of defects is greater (Gens, 1951).

SPEECH DEFECTS ASSOCIATED WITH CLEFT PALATE

Cleft lip and cleft palate are prenatal in origin. They represent a failure of the bones and the soft tissues of the roof of the mouth and the lips to develop normally. A complete cleft of the palate creates an abnormal opening between the mouth and the nasal cavities. This opening interferes with normal sucking, chewing, swallowing, and speaking. In speaking, the air and speech sounds normally expelled through the mouth can pass without control through the nose. The cleft may involve one or both sides of the upper lip in varying degrees. The American Dental Association estimates that 1 child in every 700 is born with cleft palate (Hull, 1963). Surveys show that the incidence varies from 1 in 276 to 1 in 1,030 in different populations (Tretsven, 1963). The causes of cleft palate are not clearly established. A genetic factor seems to be involved (Schwartz, 1954). Maternal nutrition, the Rh factor, and maternal illness during pregnancy are among the possible environmental factors (Goodstein, 1961).

The incidence of defective hearing is higher in those with cleft palates than in the normal population. The intelligence level of these children seems to be slightly below that of comparable normal children (Goodstein, 1961).

Corrective surgery, with or without the insertion of a false palate, is quite successful in closing the cleft palate and cleft lip. However, the upper lip is frequently scarred, immobile, or short. The border of the lip may also be irregular. It is recommended that corrective surgery on cleft lips be done at ten to fourteen days of age, and that surgery on the cleft palate start at eighteen to twenty months (Dingman, 1963). Even with corrective surgery, the voice is frequently so hypernasal and articulation so faulty that speech correction and therapy are necessary. Because dental problems are usually involved, the rehabilitation of cleft palates often requires the combined services of pediatricians, surgeons, dentists, orthodontists, otologists, speech therapists, and sometimes psychologists or psychiatrists (Westlake, 1955).

Behavior Problems Associated with Speech Defects

What was said about the personality traits of stutterers applies equally well to speech defectives as a group. They are not typically seriously maladjusted or neurotic. However, they do have more than their share of adjustment problems. They tend to be less acceptable to their peers than are children with normal speech (Woods and Carrow, 1959). Like stuttering, other functional speech defects are associated with a set of high standards imposed on the children by the parents in an atmosphere of emotional tension (Wood, 1946; Moncur, 1952; Marge, 1965).

Ways in which children with problems of articulation differ from children with normal speech in the areas of conduct and behavior disorders are shown in Table 14-5. In the study reported in Table 14-5 (Fitz-Simons, 1958), seventy children with normal speech were compared with a group of children with nonorganic articulatory problems.

TABLE 14–5

The Relative Incidence of Conduct and Behavior Disorders among Children with Defects of Articulation and among Normal Children

Conduct and Behavior Disorders	Frequency of Occurrence		
	Articulation Sample	Normal Sample	Differences Between Groups
1. Eating and food problems	39	2	37
2. Nervousness	53	22	31
3. Temper tantrums	35	8	27
4. Showing off	30	6	24
5. Refusal to obey	27	7	20
6. Thumb sucking	34	15	19
7. Shyness	31	13	18
8. Destructiveness	18	2	16
9. Fears	21	10	11
10. Jealousy*	6	3	3
11. Sleeplessness	6	1	5
12. Lying	6	1	5
13. Eneuresis	9	3	6
14. Fingernail biting	7	11	4
15. Hurting pets	1	0	−1

*All differences above this level are statistically significant at or above the .05 level. Data from FitzSimons (1958).

FitzSimons (1958) also reports that more of the children with speech problems had experienced: abnormal birth conditions; bottle feeding; early weaning; early toilet training; and delay in walking and talking. In school, they were inferior in reading readiness, reading, health habits, and work habits. Projective test performances indicated that they exceeded the normal children in aggressive tendencies, fears, anxieties, and in perception of parents as authoritarian.

School Programs for Speech Correction

Although speech correction is done in hospitals, clinics, and private offices, by far the bulk of speech therapy is done in the schools. Many universities operate speech clinics as both training and service centers, but the largest number of speech correctionists are employed in public school systems.

The most common administrative educational arrangement is to use itinerant teachers. In this type of organization, each teacher serves several schools and the children remain in their regular schools and classes. The itinerant teacher visits each school regularly and provides group or individual therapy as frequently as the workload permits. This plan is easily administered and can be easily adjusted to meet changing needs (Steer, 1961). The teacher's maximum case load is often specified by state or local codes or regulations. The recommended maximum case load ranges from 70 to 100. However, a survey made in 1961 found that the average case load was 130 children. Accepting 100 as the normal case load means that any school district enrolling 2,000 students could utilize the services of a speech therapist (Hull, 1963).

In some school systems, speech specialists handle the most difficult cases and train regular teachers to work with the less seriously defective children. The American Speech and Hearing Association has set standard qualifications which speech therapists should meet and has delineated the role of public school therapists in their statement on "Services and Functions of Speech and Hearing Specialists in Public Schools" (1962).

About 75 percent of the children receiving speech therapy in the average school are in the first three grades. Each child is typically seen at least weekly for individual or group work. Maximum carryover from session to session is gained when the regular teachers and the parents cooperate. Very often definite school, home, and private practice exercises are required. Studies have indicated that parents can participate effectively in speech improvement programs (Tufts and Holliday, 1959; Backus and Beasley, 1951).

SCHOOL PROGRAMS WITHOUT A SPEECH THERAPIST

In-service training programs can aid the regular classroom teachers in handling the children with the less serious speech defects, although they probably will not attempt formal therapy. Every teacher is, to a degree, a teacher of speech. Each teacher can be a good speech model. The classroom teacher can make referrals to private, hospital, or university clinics when they are available. The teacher can handle children with all types of speech defects in the ways suggested earlier for the general treatment of the primary stutterer. Some additional suggestions for the classroom handling of the child with a major speech defect are:

1. Complete acceptance of the child as a completely worthy individual is most important.
2. Accept the child's nonfluencies in a relaxed and unembarrassed fashion. Try to get the children to do likewise.
3. Do not look away from the child, or take over and speak for him.
4. Encourage, but do not force, the child with serious speech defects to speak before the class.
5. Provide the child with nonverbal assignments and responsibilities to keep him from capitalizing on his disability.
6. Capitalize on the child's assets and provide recognition for his accomplishments to increase his self-confidence.
7. Provide as much group participation as possible for the child. If he will not participate verbally, let him participate in a nonverbal way.
8. Provide some daily oral experience for the child, such as group singing, reading in unison, or ordinary conversation.

Summary

Speech is defective whenever the manner of speaking interferes with communication, calls undue attention to itself, or causes the speaker concern to the degree that special remedial measures are deemed necessary. Initial identification of speech defects is made both informally and by systematic screening procedures. Diagnosis and treatment may involve parents, teachers, speech therapists, psychologists, psychiatrists, pediatricians, surgeons, dentists, and orthodontists. It is conservatively estimated that 5 percent of school-age children have speech defects sufficiently serious to require therapy, and that an additional 5 percent with less serious disorders should probably receive some speech correction. The causes of speech defects are both organic (cleft palate, auditory defects, brain damage, and so forth) and functional (learning failure and emotional blocking).

As compared with normal people, those with speech defects are slightly inferior in physical characteristics, motor facility, sensory functions, intelligence, school achievement, and general behavioral adequacy. This inferiority is partially the result of the high incidence of speech defects among the organically impaired and the greater prevalence of speech problems (particularly defects in articulation) among persons of the lower socioeconomic levels.

Speech defects are usually classified according to major symptoms, as disorders of articulation, delayed speech, voice disorders, and disturbances of rhythm. Additional classes of speech disorders are based on accompanying defects. Thus we have speech disorders associated with mental retardation, cleft palate, and brain damage (cerebral palsy, aphasia). On the basis of etiology, speech defects are classified as organic or functional.

Speech disorders are treated in hospitals, clinics, schools, and private offices. The largest number of children are treated in the public schools. Treatment is given both individually and in groups, and concerns itself primarily either with symptoms (speech correction) or with underlying causes (speech therapy). In the schools, the speech therapist typically serves several schools. Her case load should normally not exceed one hundred.

References

ADAMS, M. R., AND D. A. DIETZE, "A Comparison of the Reaction Times of Stutterers and Non-stutterers to Items on a Word Association Test," *J. speech hearing res.*, VIII (1965), 195–202.

AMERICAN SPEECH AND HEARING ASSOCIATION, COMMITTEE ON THE MIDCENTURY WHITE HOUSE CONFERENCE ON CHILDREN AND YOUTH, "Speech Disorders and Speech Correction," *J. speech hearing disord.*, XVII (1952), 129–37.

———, Committee on Legislation, "Need for Speech Pathologists," *Amer. speech hearing assoc.*, I (1959), 138–39, 161–67.

———, "Public School and Hearing Services," *J. speech hearing disord.* (1961) Mono. Suppl. 8.

———, "Services and Functions of Speech and Hearing Specialists in Public Schools," *Amer. speech hearing assoc.*, IV (1962), 99–100.

BACKUS, O. L., AND J. BEASLEY, *Speech Therapy with Children*. Boston, Mass.: Houghton Mifflin Company, 1951.

BARKER, J., AND G. ENGLAND, "A Numerical Measure of Articulation: Further Developments," *J. speech hearing disord.*, XXVII (1962), 23–27.

BARRY, H., "Classes for Aphasics," in *Special Education for the Exceptional*, eds. M. E. Frampton and E. D. Gall, Vol. II. Boston: Porter Sargent, Publisher, 1955.

BATEMAN, B., "Learning Disabilities: Yesterday, Today, and Tomorrow," *Except. child.*, XXXI (1964), 167–77.

BAY, E., "Present Concepts of Aphasia," *Geriatrics*, XIX (1964), 319–31.

BENTON, A. L., "Aphasia in Children," in *Readings on the Exceptional Child*, eds. E. P. Trapp and P. Himmelstein. New York: Appleton-Century-Crofts, 1962.

———, "Developmental Aphasia (D.A.) and Brain Damage," *Cortex*, I (1964), 40–52.

BERRY, M. F., "Twinning in Stuttering Families," *Human biol.*, IX (1937), 329–46.

———, AND J. EISENSON, *Speech Disorders*. New York: Appleton-Century-Crofts, 1956.

Bilto, E. W., "A Comparative Study of Certain Physical Abilities of Children with Speech Defects and with Normal Speech," *J. speech disord.*, VI (1941), 187–203.

Bloodstein, O., "The Development of Stuttering: III. Theoretical and Clinical Implications," *J. speech hearing disord.*, XXVI (1961), 67–82.

Bluemel, C. S., "Primary and Secondary Stuttering," *Quart. j. speech*, XVIII (1932), 187–200.

————, *The Riddle of Stuttering*. Danville, Ill.: Interstate Publishers, 1957.

Capobianco, R. J., "Diagnostic Methods Used with Learning Disability Cases," *Except. child.*, XXXI (1964), 187–93.

Carrell, J. A., "A Comparative Study of Speech-Defective Children," *Arch. of speech.* I (1936), 179–203.

Curry, R., et al., "A Phonographic Scale for the Measurement of Defective Articulation," *J. speech disord.*, VIII (1943), 123–26.

Davis, J. P., "The Speech Aspects of Reading Readiness: Newer Practices in Reading in the Elementary School," in *Seventeenth Yearbook, Department of Elementary School Principals.* Washington, D.C.: National Educational Association, 1938.

Dickson, S., "Differences between Children Who Spontaneously Outgrow and Children Who Retain Functional Articulation Errors," *J. speech hearing res.*, V (1962), 263–71.

Dingman, R. O., "Modern Concepts of the Treatment of Cleft Lip and Cleft Palate," *Rehabil. lit.*, XXIV (1963), 144–46.

Edwards, A. E., "Automated Training for a 'Matching-to-Sample' Task in Aphasia," *J. speech hearing res.*, VIII (1965), 39–43.

Eisenson, J., "The Nature of Defective Speech," in *Psychology of Exceptional Children and Youth* (2nd ed.), ed. W. M. Cruickshank. Englewood Cliffs, N.J.: Prentice-Hall, Inc., 1963.

Everhart, R. W., "The Relationship between Articulation and Other Developmental Factors in Children," *J. speech hearing disord.*, XVIII (1953), 332–38.

FitzSimons, R. M., "Developmental, Psychosocial, and Educational Factors in Children with Articulation Problems," *Child devel.*, XXIX (1958), 481–89.

Fletcher, H., *Speech and Hearing in Communication*. Princeton, N.J.: D. Van Nostrand Co., Inc., 1953.

Garrison, K. C., AND D. G. Force, *The Psychology of Exceptional Children* (4th ed.). New York: The Ronald Press Company, 1965.

Gens, A., "The Speech Pathologist Looks at the Mentally Deficient Child," *Train. sch. bull.*, XLVIII (1951), 19–27.

Glauber, I. P., "Speech Characteristics of Psychoneurotic Patients," *J. speech disord.*, IX (1944), 30–32.

Goertzen, S., "Speech and the Mentally Retarded Child," *Amer. j. ment. defic.*, LXII (1957), 244–53.

Goldman, R., AND G. H. Shames, "Comparisons of the Goals that Parents of Stutterers and Parents of Nonstutterers Set for Their Children," *J. speech hearing disord.*, XXIX (1964), 381–89.

GOODSTEIN, L. D., "Functional Speech Disorders and Personality: A Survey of the Literature," *J. speech hearing res.*, I (1958), 359–76.

———, "Intellectual Impairment in Children with Cleft Palates," *J. speech hearing res.*, IV (1961), 287–94.

GREGORY, H. H., "Stuttering and Auditory Central Nervous System Disorder," *J. speech hearing res.*, VII (1964), 335–41.

HAMMILL, D. D., AND O. C. IRWIN, "Speech Differences among Cerebral Palsy Subclasses," *Except. child.*, XXXI (1965), 277–80.

HENRY, J., AND Z. HENRY, "Speech Disturbances among Pilagra Indian Children," *Amer. j. orthopsychiat.*, X (1940), 99–102.

HULL, F. M., "Speech Impaired Children," in *Exceptional Children in the Schools*, ed. L. M. Dunn. New York: Holt, Rinehart & Winston, Inc., 1963.

IRWIN, R. B., "Speech Disorders," in *Special Education for the Exceptional*, eds. M. E. Frampton and E. D. Gall, Vol. II. Boston, Mass.: Porter Sargent, Publisher, 1955.

JENKINS, E., AND F. E. LOHR, "Severe Articulation Disorders and Motor Ability," *J. speech hearing disord.*, XXIX (1964), 286–92.

JOHNSON, W., "A Study of the Onset and Development of Stuttering," *J. speech hearing disord.*, VII (1942), 251–57.

———, *Speech Handicapped School Children*. New York: Harper & Row, Publishers, 1956.

———, *Children with Speech and Hearing Impairment*, United States Office of Education Bulletin 3. Washington, D.C.: Government Printing Office, 1959.

KINSTLER, D. B., "Covert and Overt Maternal Rejection in Stuttering," *J. speech hearing disord.*, XXVI (1961), 145–55.

KLEFFNER, F. R., "Teaching Aphasic Children," *Education*, LXXIX (1959), 413–18.

KOPP, G. A., *Metabolic Studies of Stutterers*, Speech Monograph 7. Bloomington, Ind.: Speech Association of America, 1934.

LANYON, R. I., AND D. A. DUPREZ, "Non-fluency, Information and Word Length," *J. abnor. psychol.*, LXXVI (1970), 93–97.

LEMERT, E. M., "Stuttering and Social Structure in Two Pacific Societies," *J. speech hearing disord.*, XXVII (1962), 3–10.

LUPER, H. L., AND R. L. MULDEN, *Stuttering Therapy for Children*. Englewood Cliffs, N.J.: Prentice-Hall, Inc., 1964.

MCGINNIS, M. A., *Aphasic Children: Identification and Education by the Association Method*. Washington, D.C.: Alexander Graham Bell Association for the Deaf, 1963.

MCWILLIAMS, B. J., "The Non-Verbal Child," *Except. child.*, XXV (1959), 420–23.

MARGE, M., "The Influence of Selected Home Background Variables on the Development of Oral Communication Skills in Children," *J. speech hearing res.*, VIII (1965), 291–309.

MARTIN, R., "Stuttering and Perseverations in Children," *J. speech hearing res.*, V (1962), 332–39.

MECHAM, M. K., M. J. BERKO, AND F. G. BERKO, *Speech Therapy in Cerebral Palsy*. Springfield, Ill., Charles C Thomas, Publisher, 1960.

MENYUK, P., "Comparison of Grammar of Children with Functional Deviant and Normal Speech," *J. speech hearing res.*, VII (1964), 107–21.

MONCUR, J. P., "Parental Domination in Stuttering, *J. speech hearing disord.*, XVII (1952), 155–64.

MORLEY, M., et al., "Delayed Speech and Developmental Aphasia," *Brit. med. j.*, XX (1955), 463–67.

MYERS, P., "A Study of Language Disabilities in Cerebral Palsied Children," *J. speech hearing res.*, VIII (1965), 129–36.

NELSON, S. E., "The Role of Heredity in Stuttering," *J. pediat.*, XIV (1939), 3–15.

PERRIN, E. L., "The Rating of Defective Speech by Trained and Untrained Observers," *J. speech hearing disord.*, XIX (1954), 48–51.

PRONOVOST, W., "A Survey of Services for the Speech and Hearing Handicapped in New England," *J. speech hearing disord.*, XVI (1951), 148–56.

ROBINSON, F. B., *Introduction to Stuttering*. Englewood Cliffs, N.J.: Prentice-Hall, Inc., 1964.

ROE, V., AND R. MILISEN, "The Effect of Maturation upon Defective Articulation in Elementary Grades," *J. speech hearing disord.*, VII (1942), 37–50.

SANDER, E. K., "Frequency of Syllable Repetition and 'Stutterer' Judgments," *J. speech hearing disord.*, XXVIII (1963), 19–30.

SCHWARTZ, R., "Familial Incidence of Cleft Palate," *J. speech hearing disord.*, XIX (1954), 228–38.

SHEEHAN, J. G., "Conflict Theory of Stuttering," in *Stuttering: A symposium*, ed. J. Eisenson. New York: Harper & Row, Publishers, 1958. (a)

———, "Projective Studies of Stuttering," *J. speech hearing disord.*, XXIII (1958), 18–25. (b)

SIEGEL, C. M., AND D HAUGEN, "Audience Size and Variations in Stuttering Behavior," *J. speech hearing res.*, VII (1964), 381–88.

SIRKEN, J., AND W. LYON, "A Study of Speech Defects in Mental Deficiency," *Amer. j. ment. defic.*, XLVI (1941), 74–80.

SMITH, J. O., "Speech and Language of the Retarded," *Train. sch. bull.*, LVIII (1962), 111–24.

STEER, M. D., "Public School Speech and Hearing Services," United States Office of Education, Coop. Research Project 649 (8191) *J. speech hearing disord.*, Monog. Suppl. 8 (1961).

STEWART, J. L., "The Problems of Stuttering in Certain North American Indian Societies," *J. speech hearing disord.*, Monog. Suppl. 6 (1960), 61–87.

STROMSA, C., "A Procedure Using Group Consensus in Adult Stuttering Therapy," *J. speech hearing disord.*, XXX (1965), 277–79.

TIKOFSKY, R. S., AND R. P. TIKOFSKY, "Intelligibility Measures of Dysarthric Speech," *J. speech hearing res.*, VIII (1965), 325–33.

TRAVIS, L. E., *Speech Pathology*. New York: Appleton-Century-Crofts, 1931.

TRETSVEN, V. E., "Incidence of Cleft Lip and Palate in Montana Indians," *J. speech hearing disord.*, XXVIII (1963), 52–57.

TUFTS, L. R., AND A. R. HOLLIDAY, "Effectiveness of Trained Parents as Speech Therapists," *J. speech hearing disord.*, XXIV (1959), 395–401.

VAN RIPER, C., *Speech Correction: Principles and Methods* (4th ed). Englewood Cliffs, N.J.: Prentice-Hall, Inc., 1954.

———, *Speech Correction* (4th ed.). Englewood Cliffs, N.J.: Prentice-Hall, Inc., 1963.

———, AND J. R. IRWIN, *Voice and Articulation.* Englewood Cliffs, N.J.: Prentice-Hall, Inc., 1958.

WEISS, A., *Cluttering.* Englewood Cliffs, N.J.: Prentice-Hall, Inc., 1964.

WEST, R., S. E. NELSON, AND M. F. BERRY, "The Heredity of Stuttering," *Quart. j. speech*, XXV (1939), 23–30.

WESTLAKE, H., "Understanding the Child with a Cleft Palate," in *Special Education for the Exceptional*, eds. M. E. Frampton and E. D. Gall, Vol. II. Boston, Mass.: Porter Sargent, Publisher, 1955.

———, AND D. RUTHERFORD, *Speech Therapy for the Cerebral Palsied.* Chicago, Ill.: National Society for Crippled Children and Adults, 1961.

WINGATE, M. E., "Evaluation and Stuttering. Environmental Stress and Critical Appraisal of Speech," *J. speech hearing disord.*, XXVII (1962), 244–57. (a)

———, "Evaluation and Stuttering. Identification of Stuttering and the Use of a Label," *J. speech hearing disord.*, XXVII (1962), 368–77. (b)

———, "Recovery from Stuttering," *J. speech hearing disord.*, XXIX (1964), 312–21.

WOOD, K. S., "Parental Maladjustment and Functional Articulatory Defects in Children," *J. speech disord.*, XI (1946), 255–75.

WOODS, F. J., AND M. A. CARROW, "The Choice-rejection Status of Speech Defective Children," *Except. child.*, XXV (1959), 279–83.

WYATT, G. L., AND J. M. HERZON, "Therapy with Stuttering Children and Their Mothers," *Amer. j. orthopsychiat.*, XXXII (1962), 645–59.

SOCIAL DEVIANCE

V

15

Social Deviance

In the course of daily living, all individuals are subjected to frustration and stress in various forms. Children and adults suffer from fatigue, pain, disease, and injury, as well as from frustration, conflict, anxiety, and fear. The reactions to these facets of life are many and varied. The reactions to the frustrations and stresses of existence are, no doubt, a function of a complex matrix of biological, social, and psychological factors. There are, of course, genetic and constitutional determinants of behavior, but the adaptive behaviors of greatest concern to psychologists and educators are those that are learned. Biological considerations may, in part, establish the ease or difficulty with which certain behavior can be acquired and determine the nature of treatment to be employed in behavioral correction, but social-psychological principles of behavior acquisition and modification are applicable within these genetic and biological limitations.

People with differing physiological characteristics have adjustive problems that vary with their physical conditions. Without denying the existence and influence of biological factors, emphasis will be placed on social-psychological factors in this consideration of social deviance.

Habits of Adjustment

Ways of coping with environmental stress and strain are learned in the same general way as other responses. No unique principles of learning are required to account for the acquisition of behavior that is socially or personally unfortunate or inadequate, as opposed to behavior that appears to be essentially adaptive and effective. The *circumstances* of learning will differ for the two, but the *principles* involved are probably identical.

Given the commonality of physical structures of human beings and the commonality of experiences that they have as a result of living within a culture, it is not surprising that people develop a number of ways of dealing with the environment that are essentially alike. The means of coping with environmental situations that are learned and employed frequently have been classified and labelled as "mechanisms" (Freud, 1938). Behavioral mechanisms are used by everyone, and nothing really "mechanistic" or "abnormal" is implied by the term. They are behaviors that are learned in the course of ordinary living. When they become extremely routinized and are employed excessively, they become unusual. The various mechanisms were developed within psychoanalytic theory and have subsequently been employed by psychologists in general as labels for describing behavior. The labels designate descriptive categories of behavior and are not intended to be explanatory. The so-called defense mechanisms have become well known, and therefore no detailed treatment of them will be attempted. They form the basis for the development of certain behavior that may be considered as deviant, however, and a review of them may prove helpful.

MECHANISMS OF BEHAVIOR

Rationalization has been selected to illustrate the operation of mechanisms in general. *Rationalization* is the process of presenting more personally or socially acceptable motives for one's behavior than those that actually exist. Children soon learn that certain reasons for doing things are more acceptable, and therefore better, than others. They learn that rewards and punishments, both obvious and subtle, are frequently administered on the basis of motives underlying their activity rather than the activity itself. The child in our culture learns that to act on the basis of impulse, emotion, desire, or revenge is not socially approved, but that acting on the basis of reason, deliberation, generosity, and kindness is socially approved. In the child's attempts to behave in accordance with the demands of society, he learns to offer "rational" excuses for his seemingly inappropriate behavior. If this is done in a sufficient variety of instances, and over a long enough period of time, the child may come to believe his own rationalizations. In this case, the rationalizations are self-deceptive as well as socially deceptive. Excessive habits of rationalization derive perhaps from excessive familial, cultural, and social demands for logical, rational motives for behavior, and from our essential unwillingness to accept emotional and irrational excuses.

With practice, a child can become quite adept in rationalizing his behavior and in deceiving others. When he comes to believe his own rationalizations, he forgets what the real and original motives were and loses sight of the fact that his behavior is face-saving and ego-inflating. His rationalizations then become habitual, unconsciously motivated—a way of life. Verbal expressions of appropriate motives for socially inappropriate behavior are learned because they are rewarded.

There are a goodly number of mechanisms whose development can be understood through essentially this same pattern of learning, reinforcement, social deception, and self-deception. The usual mechanisms—such as projection, identification, sublimation, withdrawal, aggression, daydreaming, regression, compensation, and repression—are to be viewed as usual habits of responding. But they are habits that can get out of hand and become dominant and consistent ways of behaving that are detrimental to society and to personal effectiveness.

EMOTIONAL DISTURBANCE AND SOCIAL MALADJUSTMENT

When socially or personally unsatisfactory modes of behavior are acquired in the course of living, and the manner of acquisition is relatively easy to discern, we generally refer to this as "social maladjustment." When the reinforcements are subtle and the behavior not obviously adaptive, the individual is said to be "emotionally disturbed."

Emotionally disturbed children are children with emotional problems severe enough to prevent them from making the necessary adjustments for effective functioning in the culture. They have acquired habits of behavior sufficiently different from other children reared in similar circumstances so that their behavior is considered to be personally and socially deviant. Their behavior may range from aggressive destruction to complete withdrawal. They are unable to do what is expected of their normal peers and are to be found in any social class and in a variety of families. Their social and personal learning has been inappropriate, but the reasons for this are vague.

Socially maladjusted children are chronic violators of broad cultural mores and social values. They have learned to behave in accordance with a set of values and rules that may be shared by their immediate peers, but not by the broader culture. Delinquent gangs are constantly in trouble with constituted authority because the code of conduct acceptable to the immediate group is not accepted by the broader society. Their accepted code of conduct involves truancy, fighting, and defiance of constituted authority. They are handicapped by having learned a provincial pattern of social values, by their conformity to a code that differs from that of the general population. Socially maladjusted children learn their behavior in families and communities that do not conform to the more widely accepted values. The families are typically multiproblem families from the point of view of the rest of society, and many of these families are fostered in urban slum areas.

Some chronic violators of broad cultural mores are emotionally disturbed, and some emotionally disturbed individuals are to be found in gangs of the socially maladjusted. There is some overlap between the two. The same overt behavior can stem from either emotional disturbance or social maladjustment. When the behavior pattern derives rather directly from the obvious social-learning situation and other aspects of personality malfunction are not present, it is generally called "social maladjustment." When the behavior of the individual is unlike that of his immediate peers and it is not apparent how the behavior was learned, it usually comes under the category of "emotionally disturbed." Many children who are delinquent are really victims of unfortunate social situations and have learned inappropriate behavior, but they are not emotionally disturbed. It has been estimated that no more than 25 percent of delinquent acts can be attributed to emotionally disturbed children (Kvaraceus and Miller, 1959). Among groups of delinquent children, it is difficult to discern any distinctive personality patterns (Richardson and Roebuck, 1965).

Children who are problems to themselves and to society, and whose behavior apparently arises from emotional disturbance (inappropriate emotional learning), will be treated under three headings: Anxiety, Withdrawal, and Aggression. Under the heading of Aggression, we shall discuss some aspects of delinquency that may derive from either emotional disturbance or social maladjustment.

Anxiety

Anxiety is probably basic to all forms of maladjustive behavior, to the so-called behavior mechanisms as well as to the neuroses and the more severe functional psychoses. Certain varieties of behavior which appear to be more directly the consequence of anxiety than others have been designated as anxiety reactions.

Anxiety can be conceptualized as fear with a future reference. If a frightening stimulus is present and observable in the environment, the reaction is usually called "fear." A person can be anxious about an impending circumstance or event and be fearful in the presence of the actual stimuli. The elimination of anxiety in the world in which we live is impossible. It is inevitable that the child growing up in our culture is exposed to anxiety-evoking situations. The infant experiences frustration and conflict as an inevitable consequence of being cared for and developing in the family. Inconsistency and incompatibility of disciplinary techniques are bound to occur. Various restrictions are placed on behavior by adults, and some of these restrictions are not consistent with demands placed on the child. A child is encouraged to become independent and to stand up for his rights, but he is punished for aggressiveness. Threats are our constant companions throughout childhood, adolescence, and adulthood. Parents and other persons in positions of authority learn that threats are an effective means of controlling behavior, regardless of how much anxiety is evoked by them.

ANXIETY AND CULTURE

The importance of the cultural situation in the development of anxiety reactions has been emphasized by a number of investigators. Karen Horney (1937) emphasized the importance of the feeling of helplessness, isolation, and fear a child experiences in being reared in an essentially hostile world. She referred to the reactions from such stress as "basic anxiety," and considered the feeling of anxiety deriving from such situations as basic to the later development of neurosis. The basic causes of anxiety were seen as deriving from the rejection and disapproval a child receives from adults.

Patterns of child rearing in the middle and upper classes have been viewed as a source of anxiety (Lundin, 1965). Among these classes, overprotection, excessive mothering, and pampering are found, and the child is likely to be overly dominated by his parents. When this occurs, the child has little opportunity to learn appropriate methods of adapting to the problems of life. The aggression that usually arises from frustration is discouraged, and expressions of hostility are punished. Striving toward higher social status by the middle class, and the consequent use of children to gratify parental desires for improved social position, may also have a confusing and frustrating effect on children (Seward, 1956).

All individuals are subjected to frustration and punishment from time to time. The anxiety-ridden individual fails to learn adequate means for reducing or avoiding his anxiety. His cultural situation may make it nearly impossible for such learning to occur. The subtleties of reinforcement of behavior within a given family are such that one child may have sufficient opportunity for such learning while another may not. The possibilities for reduction of anxiety and resolution of conflict in ways condoned by family and society may be more numerous for one child in a family than for another, and such possibilities are more numerous for children from certain social classes than for others.

CHRONIC ANXIETY

The chronically anxious person presents a rather complex array of symptoms. He is fearful and apprehensive. He is worried and frightened, without knowing exactly why he feels as he does. The level of anxiety that he experiences is pathological, in the sense that it appears to be out of proportion to any realistic causal factors. He often recognizes that his anxiety is unrealistic. The anxiety is often constantly with him, though varying in intensity, and it is not tied to any particular situation or set of stimuli. Such anxiety has been termed "free-floating" (Freud, 1936). The anxiety state may be described as a fear, and ascribed by the sufferer to a specific cause or situation; however, the causes and situations shift from time to time and are not the real causes of the anxiety. Chronic anxiety is a persistent nonadaptive reaction arising from a failure to acquire personal and social responses adequate for self-protection.

Chronic-anxiety sufferers are jumpy, irritable, and easily upset by irregularities in routine. Trembling sometimes occurs for no apparent reason. Problems of sleep are chronic, with frequent nightmares and anxious dreams of being pursued. Anxious children may awaken in the night frequently, and tell of troubled dreams. Adults are often fatigued, in spite of the fact that they have not engaged in excessive activity. Excessive tiredness and feelings of fatigue following sleep and apparent rest are common.

Children's appetites may suffer, and their bladder control may become erratic. Adults may lose interest in food and find that they must urinate frequently. Gastro-intestinal disturbances are common. The attention span of anxious children becomes exceedingly short, and concentration becomes difficult for adults. Absentmindedness is rather common in anxious adults, and if heavy demands are placed on them they may become quite confused. Anxious children cry rather readily, many times for no observable reason. Ordinary demands seem excessive to the anxious child, and may result in tears.

The neurotically anxious adult reports feelings of apprehension, uncertainty, and dread. The precise situations that produce these reactions cannot be identified, but the feelings are constantly with him. His job efficiency may become impaired. He is unhappy and disturbed, and his family is distraught with his ineffectiveness and unhappiness. Anxiety-ridden children suffer from a lack of energy and inability to direct what little they can muster toward the demands of school and home. They are intense and fearful of failure, but cannot direct energy toward its avoidance. School becomes a heavy burden and they are beset by feelings of tenseness, apprehension, loneliness, and discouragement.

The chronically anxious are made anxious by so many stimuli that the individual cannot discriminate among them and respond in a manner that would be effective in their reduction. The stimuli cannot be identified and, therefore, the person can do little about them. From time to time the chronically anxious person may suffer *acute* anxiety. These anxiety attacks present an exaggerated picture of the chronically anxious person. The individual cannot identify the stimuli or situation that immediately produces these attacks, and they may occur sporadically and be frightening and demoralizing for the person. His usual feeling of apprehension becomes magnified; he becomes suddenly restless, cannot continue what he is doing, and gets up and moves about; his heart begins to pound; his mouth may feel dry; he begins to perspire; he may gasp for breath, tremble, and wring his hands. He doesn't know where to go or what to do, and his disorganization is quite intense. He may think there is something seriously physically wrong, such as a heart attack, and seek assistance. Subsequently, he suffers embarrassment and doubt when told that there is nothing physically wrong.

If the anxiety attack is particularly severe, the person may become seriously disorganized and disoriented. He may become aggressive and abusive, or self-destructive. The attack may last for a number of days. Such extreme attacks of anxiety have been termed *panic reactions* (Cameron, 1947). They are difficult for the individual to cope with, and psychiatric attention is indicated.

PHOBIC REACTIONS

Phobias are intense, specific fears that have no apparent rational basis. The number of specific phobias that have been given descriptive titles is legion. A phobia is an anxiety reaction, but it differs from chronic anxiety in that the specific stimuli that give rise to the feelings of uneasiness and apprehension are known to the individual. He does not know why he is frightened of these events, however, and his fear is out of all proportion to the real danger. He may feel embarrassed and self-conscious about his feelings of panic, but they are very real and intense. When a person is confronted with the phobic object, he may suffer acute anxiety or even panic. In the extreme, phobias may become quite incapacitating; the individual may devote so much time and energy to the avoidance of the fearful situation that he cannot carry on many of his usual functions.

People exhibiting phobic reactions probably have had a goodly number of anxiety-evoking experiences and are thus somewhat predisposed to chronic anxiety. If they encounter situations which are frightening or anxiety-producing for them, their anxiety becomes conditioned to the stimuli of the situation. They usually cannot recall the conditions under which they learned to respond with fear. The fear is perpetuated by avoiding the stimuli that induce it, and the phobic reaction may spread to a variety of tangentially related stimuli. In such instances a person may develop a number of anxiety reactions of sufficient severity and specificity to be called "phobias."

COMPULSIONS AND OBSESSIONS

Some individuals acquire ways of reducing anxiety that are temporary expedients. That is, they learn patterns of thought and action that serve to reduce anxiety, but only on a temporary basis. The behavior keeps overt anxiety at a relatively low level and serves to keep acute anxiety and panic from developing.

Compulsions and obsessions are coercive, recurrent acts, or impulses to act, in rather specific ways. The person is quite aware of what he is doing or feels compelled to do, recognizes it as irrational, silly, or even dangerous, but is unable to stop doing it (*compulsion*) or get rid of the impulse to perform the act (*obsession*). The impulse to act is sometimes situational, in that it occurs whenever the stimuli are appropriate. In other instances the impulse to act seems to build up as the result of a variety of stimuli, until the act is performed. The individual feels more and more anxious until finally he commits the compulsive act which affords him some measure of anxiety reduction.

An obsession is a thought or idea which keeps recurring to the person. It is usually coercive, irrational, and anxiety-laden, but cannot be disposed of. For example: A mother cannot stop thinking that if she had administered proper medication to her child it would be alive today; the idea that she has killed a loved one keeps recurring. A person is obsessed with the notion that he will lose his keys or wallet, and must reassure himself by checking on their presence every few minutes. An example of the combining of an obsession and compulsion is the behavior of the person who is obsessed by the thought that he did not lock his house when he left in the morning. He cannot get rid of the idea and feels compelled to return to check. He does so nearly every morning of his life! If he didn't return to check on it, he would feel uneasy and preoccupied all day.

The list of possible compulsive-obsessive reactions is an imposing one. They range all the way from excessive neatness, excessive cleanliness, and counting steps, posts, and cracks in the sidewalk to criminal acts such as kleptomania (compulsive stealing) and pyromania (compulsive fire setting). The manias are all technically compulsions.

Combinations of phobic and obsessive-compulsive reactions are more common than their occurrence in isolated form. All have a strong component of anxiety. For example: A person may be mysophobic (have a morbid fear of dirt). He is obsessed with the idea that he is being contaminated with dangerous germs by everything he touches, and has an accompanying handwashing compulsion. These elements are all consistent and mutually supportive. Other combinations of phobia, obsession, and compulsion may occur in the same person.

It has been suggested (Portnoy, 1959) that the anxiety neurotic is really the most psychologically healthy of all neurotics because he is attempting to cope with life in the face of multitudinous threats. He is able to endure great amounts of anxiety without employing the massive defensive reactions and other distorted behavior typical of other psychiatric syndromes. In spite of this contention, it is probably true that great numbers of anxious people seek drugs or use alcohol to attain temporary relief from their feelings of anxiety.

Withdrawal

Some people learn to adjust to social situations through withdrawal. Such habits of adjustment are probably learned in the same manner that other social responses are learned. The individual has found that withdrawal and isolation are rewarding for him. Withdrawal is a relatively easy response to make. It requires less effort than aggressive behavior, and it is rather immediately rewarding. Withdrawal from social contacts can act as a kind of insurance against social failure. If one does not try, he cannot fail, and it is better never to have tried at all than to have tried and failed, as far as the individual involved is concerned.

Withdrawal and timidity are of particular educational concern because they are not as disruptive and attention-getting as aggressive behavior. The child who is overly aggressive and combative stands out as an individual whose adjustment to the school situation is not adequate. The withdrawing student, however, is likely to go unnoticed, because his behavior never disrupts the classroom procedures. He annoys no one, minds his own business, and does his own work. The teacher busy with problems of instruction and classroom control can easily overlook the withdrawn student. Perhaps one of the reasons why psychologists consider seclusiveness so serious is the tendency for it to go unnoticed and undealt with until it becomes very serious. Studies indicate that teachers are becoming more and more aware of the significance of shyness and withdrawal as symptoms of maladjustment (Thompson, 1940). Early studies showed a great discrepancy between the attitudes of teachers and psychologists toward social withdrawal and sensitiveness. The greater agreement between the two shown in later studies (Fitzsimmons, 1958) reflects the teachers' increased understanding of the concepts of mental hygiene.

A word of caution is here in order. Not all quiet and retiring people are pathologically involved in withdrawal. The great emphasis on the possible pathological effects of excessive repression and introversion has led to a tendency, in some circles, to view all quiet, unpretentious and meditative people as emotionally disturbed. Because some of the major psychotic syndromes are dominantly withdrawal behavior patterns, unaggressive and introverted people are sometimes in danger of being considered ill and in need of psychological help. It should be indicated, at this point, that children reared in families where parents are quiet and reflective are likely to learn patterns of behavior that are quiet and reflective. The same thing might be said of children in families where the parents are relatively socially withdrawn and shy. The learning of such responses under such conditions is precisely what is to be expected, and we should not regard behavior of this sort as pathological. Withdrawal becomes of pathological concern when it stems from emotional disturbance rather than from family tradition. The reticent and quiet child may be quite happy, and so long as he is not seriously damaging his own personal effectiveness or does not harm the well-being of others, it would seem that the rubric of "individual differences" should cover the situation.

CAUSES OF WITHDRAWAL

It has been indicated that withdrawal may stem from convention and from family patterns of living (Sawrey and Telford, 1971). The person whose socially isolated behavior results from a prolonged series of reality-oriented learning experiences is not necessarily maladjusted. For many people, moderate social withdrawal and a certain degree of social isolation may represent good adjustments.

The more severe defensive withdrawal stems from emotional maladjustment and serves to reduce anxiety. In the broadest terms, the individual who perceives others as sources of pain and discomfort, and who finds that social isolation is less painful or less threatening than social contact, will develop withdrawn and seclusive habits of adjustment. Abusive discipline, excessive physical punishment, verbal mistreatment, and the withholding or withdrawal of affection as the dominant methods of control in childhood are conducive to the development of fear, timidity, and withdrawal.

Children are very resilient, and they can withstand a good deal in the way of physical punishment, neglect, and abuse. There is some evidence that inconsistencies in treatment are more conducive to anxiety and withdrawal than are perpetually painful or punishing situations. A given level of abuse or punishment is less disturbing to a child when the abuse is part of the social culture to which he is subjected, than if the same treatment is given to him when he is the only individual in his family or community who is so treated. When punishment is universal and apparently inevitable, it is perceived as part of a rough world that can and must be endured. When a child is sometimes punished and sometimes rewarded by the same people and for the same activity, he has little opportunity to learn how to avoid the punishment. He can, however, learn to avoid the people who administer it. He can withdraw as much as possible from them, and the response of withdrawal becomes reinforced by the avoidance of abuse. There is evidence that predictable punishment is more tolerable and less fear-arousing than is random and unpredictable punishment (Sawrey, 1961). Severity and inconsistency would appear to be two aspects of punishment that are particularly conducive to withdrawal. If the pattern of withdrawal is intense or if the number of persons and circumstances to be avoided is great, a generalized habit of withdrawal can emerge.

WITHDRAWAL FROM REALITY

Schizophrenia. The schizophrenias are the most severe varieties of withdrawal. The term *schizophrenia* is currently used to include a large number of psychotic reactions in which there are fundamental disturbances in reality relationships and in emotional and intellectual processes. A variety of symptoms may be displayed by the patient and, because of this, some investigators feel that the label *schizophrenia* is relatively meaningless. Nevertheless the term persists, and a constellation of behavior patterns is subsumed under the label. The picture of schizophrenic reactions seems to be one of emotional apathy, indifference, and withdrawal. There is a marked reduction of interests and attachments and, of course, an impoverishment of human relationships. In some instances, delusions and hallucinations develop. It has been observed that the schizophrenic appears to have withdrawn from reality, constructed his own inner reality, and moved into it.

This reaction is more characteristic of adults than of children, the typical age of onset being reported as between seventeen and twenty-four years (Kant, 1948). When a comparable reaction occurs before puberty, it is often designated as "childhood schizophrenia" and is characterized by severe withdrawal, disorganization, lack of affect, and distorted emotional reactions. The schizophrenic patient has found ways of reducing or avoiding anxiety, but the means of doing so are unsatisfactory to others. Their adjustments are extreme and result in personal and social isolation and insulation. Childhood schizophrenia is not too common, but quite dramatic. The symptoms are essentially like those occurring in adolescents and adults, and the withdrawal tends to be quite severe.

Autism.   Childhood schizophrenia may not be an appropriate category in which to include some schizophrenic-like behavior by children. As a consequence, some early patterns of behavior have been designated as "autistic." Thus, a pattern of early severe withdrawal in children has been termed *infantile autism* (Kanner and Lesser, 1958). Early infantile autism is rarely diagnosed until the second or third year, when it becomes apparent that something has gone awry. Parents of such children frequently report that the infant did not welcome, or resisted, physical contact from a very early age, or that it was a "good" baby and did not require handling or fondling, and that it seldom cried or expressed anger. That is, the child failed to develop normal relationships with others. The vocabulary of such children is small, and they may have developed a language of their own. Frequently, these children repeat words or phrases that are spoken to them but make no other response. Their repetition of words and phrases that they hear appears to be mechanical and without intent to communicate. The child resists changes in his routine or in his environment in general. He arranges his own world the way he wants it, without regard to the wishes of others. He frequently becomes engaged in apparently meaningless, routine activity, and is preoccupied with it. Such children react so inadequately to speech and other noises that they are frequently thought to have impaired hearing. They are quite successful in shutting out the external world and responding only to themselves. Autistic children pay little attention to others, including their parents. There seems to be no emotional or personal relationship between mother and child. The child neither seeks nor accepts the usual comforts of maternal companionship, but may wander about aimlessly, even in strange surroundings.

As autistic children approach school age, their condition begins to resemble mental retardation and they are not infrequently so diagnosed. Interruptions in the child's routine, or attempts to establish new ones, may result in temper tantrums and essentially unmanageable behavior. Treatment of such children is difficult, and the prognosis is not very good.

Affectional and social development are almost absent in autistic children. Such behavior is usually considered to be learned very early within the family—particularly in interaction with the mother. It would appear that cold or indifferent personal relationships might be characteristic of the family, and indeed this is reported to be the case in a sizable number of cases. Many children grow up in such families, but not all become autistic. Each child, however, does have a unique climate in which to develop, and each does have unique learning experiences. In spite of our tendency to ascribe a dominant role in personality formation to early learning experience, a recent review of forty years of research on the problem concludes that the research has identified no factors in the parent-child interaction of schizophrenics, neurotics, or those with behavior disorders which could be identified as unique to them or which could distinguish one group from the others, or any of the groups from the families of control subjects (Frank, 1965).

Infantile autism has been described, by some workers, not as severe emotional disturbance or a form of mental illness but rather as a form of mental retardation (Rimland, 1964). According to this position, the autistic child suffers from a cognitive deficiency, from an inability to relate present sensations to past experience. Thus, the child's bizarre and socially inappropriate behavior stems from his neurological impairment, an impairment in the function of the reticular system, possibly produced by neonatal hypoxia resulting in vascular damage to genetically predisposed individuals.

The etiology of infantile autism is vague, the symptoms severe and complex, the diagnosis uncertain, treatment not clearly understood, and the prognosis poor. This is not a very rosy picture! The frequency of occurrence of severe infantile autism is not very great, but the dramatic nature of the disorder and its resistance to treatment have caused a great deal of attention to be focussed on it. Conditioning the child to respond more appropriately has been used with some success (Ferster and De Myer, 1962), and investigations of these procedures for treatment of autistic children continue. Several investigators have reported varying degrees of success in their treatment (Graziano and Kean, 1967; Lovaas et al., 1966; Zaslow, 1969).

Regression.   Other forms of withdrawal that may seriously impair personal and social effectiveness include *regression.* Regression, if defined as a return to earlier or less mature behavior, has been called *retrogression* by some investigators. Regression has also been defined as a manifestation of more primitive behavior after having learned and behaved in a more mature fashion. If "primitive behavior" is conceived as behavior that has not necessarily been in the earlier response repertoire of the individual, but is simply a more primitive or rudimentary response, it is probable that regression in this second sense does not occur. The existence of a reservoir of inherited racial or primitive behavior patterns which are potentially arousable under adequate stress, and which display themselves in an individual for the first time after the person is old enough to "regress," is a doubtful hypothesis.

Regression and *regressive behavior* will be used to designate the occurrence of less mature behavior after having learned more mature forms. When regression is motivated by the desire to withdraw, the behavior tends to become rigid, compulsive, and persistent. That regression does occur when recent, efficient habits are severely thwarted has been demonstrated in lower animals (Hamilton and Krechevsky, 1933; Mowrer, 1940; Masserman, 1946). Children experimentally frustrated during play have been shown to reduce their subsequent play to a much less mature and constructive level. Children differed tremendously in the extent of their regression, but on the average, they regressed to a play level about one-and-one-half years below their previous play patterns (Barker et al., 1941).

Children, as well as adults, may, when faced with severe stress, adopt previously successful or useful behavior. Children are said to regress when they utilize patterns of behavior under stress that they had previously abandoned. Thus, the child faced with the frustrations of school and separation from mother may cry readily, resume the abandoned habit of thumb-sucking, engage in baby talk, have temper tantrums, wet his pants, or do whatever has been heretofore successful in obtaining attention and affection.

At later ages, frustration may produce behavior that was previously used and abandoned. Adults may weep over tragedy and become extremely dependent on others. Adults who were overprotected when young may readily return to their earlier overdependency as a means of avoiding hardship and discouragement. Severe regressive reactions may occur under conditions of great stress, and then the individual regresses to a state of rather infantile dependency and helplessness.

Daydreaming and Fantasy. Daydreaming and fantasy are apparently universal human activities (Singer and McCraven, 1961). Daydreaming and fantasy, in and of themselves, are not to be considered as symptomatic of disturbance. However, when they become excessive and wish-fulfilling (autistic) they become effective ways of withdrawing. One can learn to satisfy many of one's desires by such activity, and they can become dominant ways of reacting to threat and stress. The frequency and popularity of daydreaming is understandable in terms of its availability. It can be engaged in by anyone at anytime, unless he is otherwise preoccupied.

Classrooms are particularly conducive to daydreaming because the presence of many children in the same classroom dictates that they all remain relatively inactive and quiet. Children can vicariously satisfy many of their wants, wishes and desires through imaginary activities and fanciful social situations. Dull children and children with visual or auditory handicaps frequently find that they cannot grasp the instruction and tend to cease trying. Bright children find much extra time with little to do. Daydreaming provides a convenient escape from the possibilities of loss of prestige and self-respect because of failure. It is also an adventurous escape from boredom and monotony. Daydreams are the imaginative fulfillment of wishes and are, therefore, always satisfying. They can be tough competition for the school routines. Daydreaming actually does little to aid in the solution of problems, but it serves as an effective temporary escape from the unpleasant impingement of reality. In the extreme, fantasy and daydreaming can provide the individual with a comfortable imaginary world of his own in which to live.

Aggression

Aggressive behavior may be designated either as being a type of overt behavior or as a particular kind of motivated activity. If the emphasis is on the motivation for the activity, as opposed to the overt behavior itself, aggressive behavior implies hostility It represents activity intended to injure or destroy a person or his possessions. In the broader sense, aggressive behavior can be conceived of as *approach*, as contrasted with *avoidance* behavior. In this sense, aggressive behavior is not necessarily hostile, and may simply derive from the learning of aggressive (approach and attack) responses from cultural experience.

Much aggressive behavior results from social practices which reinforce the behavior. Behavior may be viewed by the general public as aggressive and hostile, even though it results from social learning and is not necessarily emotion-laden or emotional in origin. Aggressive behavior that exceeds socially approved limits may be the manifestation of response patterns acquired in a family, community, or subculture which encourages such behavior. When patterns of aggression are so acquired, the children are taught to be aggressive. Boys gain status with their parents, family, and peers through aggression and attack. Not only does the boy defend himself aggressively, he may seek out opportunities to assert himself and improve his status by dominating others. Such aggression may become a way of life and a means of seeking status. In the broader culture, the aggressive responses so acquired (fighting, sexual aggressiveness, legal misdemeanors) may meet with resistance and punishment. As a result of such frustration, he may respond with increased aggression. His increased aggressiveness, resulting from frustration, may be hostile in nature, whereas the original behavior may not have been hostile or emotionally instigated.

HOSTILE AGGRESSION

Hostile aggression is probably always the result of some kind of frustration. It was early hypothesized that frustration invariably resulted in aggressive behavior (Dollard et al., 1939). This position was revised a short time later by the same investigators to allow for other types of responses to frustration (Miller, 1941). Although aggression is not the inevitable consequence of frustration, real or threatened frustrations remain the principal causes of hostile aggression.

Frustration.   There are a great variety of circumstances that are frustrating. Frustrating events and circumstances can be divided into three varieties for purposes of study (Sawrey and Telford, 1971): frustration by delay; frustration by thwarting; and frustration by conflict.

Frustration by *delay* is produced by withholding from an individual the rewards that he has previously learned follow a given sequence of behavior. Small or short delays are more frustrating to children and young adults than to older persons, and they react more dramatically. Delays may result in vigorous protests. The infant, particularly, is in a pretty helpless condition. He has not yet learned that delay may be unavoidable or that it is only temporary. He may react emphatically, with protest, crying, temper, or attack. As he matures, the severity of the consequences of delay diminish, but delay remains an important cause of frustration. Experimental investigations confirm the frustrating effects of delay of rewards on animals (Amsel, 1958) and on humans (Sears, Hovland, and Miller, 1940).

Frustration by *thwarting* occurs when purposeful behavior is interfered with, interrupted, or prevented. The physically restrained infant struggles and cries. Many rules, regulations, and restrictions imposed by society may prevent or interfere with motivated behavior and result in frustration. Some frustrating obstacles to performance may be physical characteristics of the individual himself—a physical handicap, being too small or too large, ineptness, obesity, clumsiness, or illness. Social and economic sources of thwarting are many and varied, and constitute important barriers to motivated behavior.

Motivated behavior may also be thwarted by *conflict*. The basic conflictual situation involves the presence of two incompatible possibilities of response in a situation when each, if present alone, would yield a response (Verplank, 1957). Conflict is an inevitable consequence of life. The frustrations resulting from conflict cannot be avoided completely, even in the best organized and regulated of societies. Choices must be made, decisions must be rendered, and behavior frequently may be difficult to reconcile with values. Conflict, as an important source of frustration, has received a great deal of attention from psychologists, and the interested reader will have no difficulty in locating literature relevant to the topic.

As children grow up, they are conditioned to become frustrated by an expanded series of stimuli. Stimuli accompanying or preceding actual physical thwarting agents operate as conditioned stimuli for frustration. Words, gestures, facial expressions, intonations, and threats that accompany or precede thwarting come to act as effective agents of frustration. Thus, actual delay, thwarting, prevention, or conflict need not occur in order to produce the response. The threat of any of these produces frustration.

Forms of Aggression.   Aggressive responses to frustration may take a variety of forms. Apparently, the initial and original response to thwarting is a diffuse, chaotic, emotional outburst. This angry outburst seems to be neither purposive nor directive. It consists of squirming, twisting, throwing the arms and legs about, and crying. With maturity and experience, the aggressive response to frustration becomes less random and more *directed, purposeful, and retaliative.* The responses come to be directed toward the thwarting agent and are intended to eliminate, remove, or diminish the effectiveness of the restriction. The child physically attacks the restricting agent by hitting, kicking, or biting.

Most children soon learn that an *indirect* attack on the thwarting agent is often more strategic than is a direct attack. Consequently, a child may hide a possession of his mother or father, or may destroy something of theirs, in retaliation for being thwarted. When big brother restricts the child's activities, he may appeal to mother or father to punish the brother, rather than personally attack him. Some children learn to feign injury at the hands of a brother or sister in order to get father or mother to punish the older or younger sibling. Children learn to use threats aggressively, as does the two-year-old boy who, on being prevented from doing something by his father, pulls at the lamp cord and pretends that he will tip it over. When orderliness is emphasized by the mother, she may find that her child, when frustrated, will create chaos in a room by moving furniture and throwing or scattering objects around. When children are frustrated, they make indirect physical attacks by engaging in disapproved behavior calculated to annoy their frustrators.

Indirect physical attack may take the form of the well-known temper tantrum. Young children, when frustrated, may cry, scream, fall to the floor, thrash and kick, and even violently bang their heads on the wall or floor. Parental alarm over such behavior may reinforce it, and the behavior may be perpetuated either by their alarm or by their acquiescence to their child's demands. Some severe tantrums may also be interpreted as representing a failure of the child to learn more sophisticated ways of responding to frustration. Viewed in such a fashion, the *diffuse, chaotic, emotional outburst,* characteristic of early responses to frustration, persists as a consequence of immaturity and derives from an absence of social learning rather than results from it.

Children usually learn through experience that either direct or indirect physical attack on the person restricting one's activity is not always the wisest approach to the problem. If the person who is causing the frustration is larger, stronger, or more skillful, direct physical attack invites counterattack, resulting in further frustration and increased punishment. Consequently, with the development of language, a verbal attack on the thwarting agent may be substituted for the direct or indirect physical retaliation. This is really attack at a symbolic level. Calling the person names, swearing at him, and "cutting him down to size" verbally are symbolic aggressive responses to frustration. In addition to verbal responses to thwarting, other symbolic retaliative aggressive responses, such as making faces, sticking out one's tongue, or thumbing one's nose, may be employed. A further extension of symbolic aggression evolves when it is learned that *indirect symbolic aggression* can serve to damage others without immediately endangering oneself. Instead of swearing at or calling someone names to his face, we tell derogatory stories, start malicious rumors, and otherwise undermine his reputation. We attack the status and the good name of the person thwarting us, rather than make a direct attack on him. We may also attack another person indirectly by belittling or discrediting his possessions, his family, his friends, his beliefs, his ideas, or his ideals.

In the extreme, indirect hostile responses toward one's own family whom one believes to be thwarting him may take the form of personal immorality, delinquency, or criminality. The behavior serves to discredit the family and to besmirch its otherwise good reputation. The delinquency and distressing eccentricity of some adolescents and adults may represent such indirect hostile forms of aggression.

Pathological Aggression.   Children displaying pathological aggressiveness as a way of life have been described dramatically by Bettelheim (1950) and by Redl and Wineman (1951; 1952). The children described by these authors are largely incapable of rational control of their own behavior. They have either failed to develop any inner controls, or their normal behavior controls have been destroyed by the inconsistencies of their social environment when they were young. They have become victims of their own aggressive impulses and are largely controlled by them. Aggression seems to be their only way of reacting to life and its stresses. They erupt into reckless destruction or blind rage at the slightest provocation. Their anxieties, fears, and guilt feelings all manifest themselves in aggressiveness which often involves repeating the same acts which produced their guilt feelings in the first place.

Having had a pleasurable social experience, they do not seem to be able to remember it and realize the possibility of its repetition. They seem incapable of profiting from social experience despite normal intelligence. They cannot delay satisfaction. If their desires are not immediately gratified, they react with hostility and violence. The causes of their failures and their hostilities are all projected outward, in paranoid fashion. Everyone and everything is perceived as threatening, and they react to the perceived hostile and punishing world with counterhostility.

Manifestations of affection and goodwill toward these individuals are interpreted either as signs of an enemy's weakness or as tricks designed to deceive them. Offers of assistance are met with unreasonable demands for more and, if the demands are not met, the inevitable explosion of hate is set off. They neither request nor accept help. These "psychopaths" have proved to be resistant to treatment because of the consolidation of their intense hostility into a pattern of defensive reactions against any offers of help from others. They are seriously emotionally disturbed, behave in ways that are socially and personally destructive, and resist treatment and overtures of assistance.

Familial Correlates of Aggression.   Overaggressive, antisocial individuals have been consistently reported to have come from early environments characterized by parental rejection, permissiveness of aggression, lack of parental supervision, a low level of parental expectation, parental social deviance, parental dissatisfaction with the child's role in life, family discord, inconsistent treatment, and the use of physically painful punishment or threats of physical punishment (Glueck and Glueck, 1950; Bandura and Walters, 1959; McCord, McCord, and Zola, 1959; McCord, McCord, and Howard, 1961; Berkowitz, 1958, 1962).

These research findings are consistent with the interpretation of overaggression as either a reaction to excessive frustration or a product of social learning. The list of parental practices found in the background of aggressive children provides a picture of a background for the learning of aggression as a way of life. Patterns of aggression developing under such conditions can be considered essentially nonhostile in nature and social in origin. Several of the familial correlates of aggression also constitute excessive frustration of a kind that instigates hostile aggression. The use of physically painful punishment, frequent threats, parental rejection, and parental bickering and disagreement about methods of child rearing with resulting inconsistencies in treatment, provide a favorable background for the development of hostile, retaliative aggression.

The studies of aggression in children uniformly disclose that both social learning and excessive aggression-instigating factors in the home contribute to the development of overaggressiveness in the child. When aggressive behavior is thwarted by the broader society, the person's cultural aggressiveness may become confounded with hostile and retaliative behavior. The result is both personally and culturally damaging. A more complete discussion of aggression can be found in Sawrey and Telford, (1971).

Delinquency

Delinquency may derive essentially from the social learning of deviant patterns of response or from hostility arising from frustration. The two are probably never discrete categories of delinquent behavior, but the social aspects have been emphasized by certain researchers (Cloward and Ohlin, 1960; Gibbons and Garrity, 1962) and the essentially psychological factors by others (Glueck and Glueck, 1950; Argyle, 1961). It is no doubt true that both psychological and sociological factors are significant in the etiology of juvenile delinquency (Hathaway and Monachesi, 1963). It is extremely difficult to determine when the principal influences are sociological factors and when they are psychological, because of the difficulties in distinguishing between the two classes of factors. It would seem that when the social-learning factors considered to be primarily responsible for the subsequent behavior are readily discernible, there is a tendency to call the delinquency social. When the factors are subtle and cannot be readily identified, psychological or personality variables are invoked. One method of classification has to do with whether the delinquency can be classified as "social" or "solitary." However, some delinquents are neither purely social nor solitary in their delinquent acts.

If the delinquent comes from a background of social, economic, and educational deprivation where delinquency is common (a "bad" family background), social-learning factors are invoked and it is found that such delinquents are more likely to commit delinquent acts in groups or gangs (i.e., social delinquency). If the delinquent comes from a family which provides adequate social, economic, and educational opportunities (a "good" family background), psychological explanations are offered, and it is found that there is a tendency for such delinquency to be solitary. But the "good" family may be providing a social learning situation that is no better than that of the "bad" family. The two familial situations are grossly different, but each may be the training ground for social deviance.

THE COMPLEXITY OF DELINQUENCY

Whether juvenile delinquency be defined in a legalistic manner (behavior on the part of a child between seven and seventeen which violates existing law) or simply as engaging in antisocial or asocial aggressive behavior unapproved by the community, the problem is a complex one. As we have already indicated, overaggressiveness and delinquency may stem from either social learning or frustration. The available statistics on delinquency pose problems both of reliability and validity. There is tremendous variation in the laws of the several states, policies of courts, police, schools, and other social agencies. There is no universally accepted method of identifying, classifying, or treating delinquent behavior. The incidence of hidden, or undiscovered, delinquency is not known. Many, if not most, adult males tell tales of their youth that involve undetected delinquent acts. In a study by Murphy, Shirley, and Witmer (1946), case studies of 114 boys over a five-year period were reported. Of these boys, only 13 had been involved in no delinquent activity, to the case worker's knowledge. The remaining 101 had been involved in 6,416 legal infractions, although only 95 of these infractions had led to legal complaints involving police or court action. Other investigators report essentially the same sort of findings. In an investigation of 1,700 law-abiding men and women, it was reported that almost all admit to having committed legal offenses, and two-thirds had engaged in behavior legally defined as felonious (Wallerstein and Wyle, 1947). It is contended that although all juvenile delinquents participate in some kind of antisocial behavior, the majority mature into socially conforming adults.

It has already been indicated that delinquency involves both social and psychological factors. Factors in the home, the family, the school, and the community, as well as the psychological factors of frustration, hostility, and aggressive retaliation, are all involved. There seems to be no one clear picture of delinquency or the delinquent. Children from lower, middle, and upper classes become delinquent, as do both sexes. Boys are much more frequently identified as delinquent than are girls—four or five times as frequently. Girls are more likely to be involved in drunkenness and problem sex behavior than are boys (Bowman, 1959).

One of the problems of the delinquent is the social climate of the American culture. We place great emphasis on achievement and competition. Aggressiveness is thus rewarded, but at the same time our culture insists on conformity and cooperation. Learning when and how to compete and to conform is not an easy task for many children, or for adults.

Early investigators saw delinquency as being spawned in the underprivileged and lower-class environments. Others have emphasized faulty home factors, child rearing practices, and parent-child relationships as productive of delinquency. Still others have emphasized the excessive competitive striving in our culture. Personality variables have been studied, with conflicting results. Attempts to predict delinquency and to develop delinquency predicting instruments have been less than promising (Bothman, Hartinger, and Richardson, 1965). Delinquency is becoming more common in the so-called better homes and communities. New patterns of delinquency are attributed to our changing times. Communications media are said to influence the young toward greater competitiveness, aggressiveness, and delinquency. A search for simple causes of delinquent behavior seems doomed to failure, for the causes appear to be many.

Considering the many-faceted background of the development of delinquency, it would appear that corrective approaches and preventive approaches will also have to be many-faceted. Recent emphasis on the education and behavior correction of delinquents has been on the individual treatment of the individual deviate. Although there may be a certain commonality of background among overly aggressive and delinquent youngsters, each still has his own wants, wishes, desires, frustrations, and ambitions. Emphasis on understanding the individual delinquent in his unique circumstance should prove helpful in both corrective and educational practice.

Prevalence of Maladjustment

The frequency of occurrence of maladjustment in our society is difficult to determine. There is no universal agreement as to what constitutes a disturbed child. A child is said to be emotionally disturbed when his reactions are so personally unrewarding and inappropriate as to be unacceptable to his peers and to adults. Educators must be concerned with a school program for the emotionally disturbed as well as for other children. To the educator, a child is disturbed when his behavior is so inappropriate that regular class attendance would be harmful to the child or would disrupt the class.

Mental health is recognized as a serious social problem. The estimated frequency of emotionally disturbed people in our culture varies from one source to another, but all agree that it is too high. Some have estimated that at least 10 percent of the school-age population is in need of psychiatric help (Bower, 1961). Some half-million severely disturbed youngsters are excluded from school by expulsion or refusal of admission (Southern Regional Education Board, 1961). There are about 13,000 young people of school age in state mental hospitals on any given day (Southern Regional Education Board, 1961). Despite the estimates that 10 percent need psychiatric help, only 0.34 percent of the school-age population served are seen as new admissions to community mental health clinics (Bahn and Norman, 1959). There is probably a tendency to overestimate the actual number of seriously disturbed children. Not all children in need of psychiatric services can be said to be seriously disturbed. Some of them suffer from minor, transitory, or situational maladjustment, and although they might profit from supportive psychiatric services, they should hardly be thought of as having serious emotional disturbances.

A common estimate is that 0.5 percent of school-age children are emotionally disturbed. This would mean that out of 100,000 persons of school-age there would be about 500 emotionally disturbed school-age children. Disturbed children are found in all social classes, but the lower classes produce far more in proportion to their number. In Bower's (1961) California study, families in which the fathers' occupations were classified as "service" or as "semiskilled" produced more than twice as many emotionally disturbed children than would be expected by their proportion in the state population. Families in occupational categories of "professional and managerial," "clerical and sales," "skilled," and "unskilled" produced fewer than expected. In general, the lower social areas provide less stability and security, and therefore are more conducive to emotional disturbance (Hollingshead and Redlich, 1958).

Special schools and classes are provided for socially maladjusted youths. Classes for the socially maladjusted make up the third largest area of special education in Chicago and Philadelphia (Kvaraceus and Ulrich, 1959). The programs for the mentally retarded and the speech-impaired are the only ones exceeding those for the socially maladjusted, and programs and services for the emotionally disturbed and socially maladjusted are being expanded at a very rapid rate. The need for teachers with special training and for psychological services for these youngsters is a pressing one.

Summary

All individuals are subjected to frustration and stress in the course of daily living. People develop a variety of means for coping with frustration and stress. The more routinized of these have come to be known as "defense mechanisms." If this behavior does not become too rigid or exclusive, it can be considered as a portion of adaptive living. If it becomes a dominant way of responding to social stimuli, it is symptomatic of emotional disturbance.

A distinction is generally made between the emotionally disturbed and the socially maladjusted. The emotionally disturbed exhibit patterns of behavior sufficiently different from other children reared in similar circumstances so that their behavior is considered personally and socially deviant. Their behavior may range from aggressive destructiveness to rather complete social withdrawal. Socially maladjusted children are chronic violators of broad cultural mores and social values. They acquire their behavior patterns through social learning. They behave according to the standards of their subgroup, but those standards and values are deviant from those of the broader culture.

Responses generated by emotional disturbance were grouped under three broad headings: anxiety; withdrawal; and aggression.

Chronically anxious people present a complex array of symptoms. The individuals are fearful and apprehensive, without really knowing why. Chronic anxiety sufferers are irritable, jumpy, and easily upset by disturbances in their routine. They have problems in sleeping, suffer from chronic fatigue and gastro-intestinal disturbances, and may tremble or perspire for no apparent reason. Many stimuli produce anxiety in the chronically anxious. They may suffer attacks of acute anxiety. Phobic reactions—acute, specific fears—are not uncommon among the highly anxious. Compulsions to commit particular acts and obsessive thoughts are also common among persons suffering from anxiety.

Withdrawal is learned in the same way that other social responses are learned. In withdrawal, the individual learns to avoid social contacts. Withdrawal and timidity have received extra attention because they may be symptomatic of severe emotional problems. It should be remembered, however, that shy, unobtrusive behavior may be learned in families that are essentially quiet and withdrawn. Not all withdrawn persons are emotionally disturbed. They may have learned to live a less socially oriented existence and be quite well-adjusted to it.

Serious withdrawal may be precipitated by abusive discipline, excessive physical punishment, verbal mistreatment, and the withholding of affection. The most serious form of withdrawal is withdrawal from reality, as in schizophrenia. A pattern of early severe withdrawal in children has been termed *infantile autism*. Such withdrawal patterns are extremely personally damaging and resistant to treatment. The background of both schizophrenia and infantile autism is but vaguely understood.

Daydreaming and fantasy were treated as minor forms of withdrawal. Withdrawal in the form of regression to earlier modes of acquired responding has been experimentally demonstrated. It is not an uncommon, transient phenomenon in children who are frustrated and overly dependent on parents for emotional support.

Much aggressive behavior results from social practices that reinforce aggression. Such patterns of behavior are best understood as social aggression that does not necessarily entail frustration or hostility. It is simply a learned way of coping with the world. Some subcultural patterns of social behavior are predominantly aggressive, and overt aggression is a way of life.

Hostile aggression is a result of frustration. It has an emotional basis and may be retaliative. Frustration can be divided into three classes for purposes of study. Basically, frustration is produced by delay, thwarting, and conflict.

The initial response to thwarting is a diffuse, chaotic, emotional outburst. As development and learning take place, direct attack and means of indirect attack are acquired. The temper tantrum may be conceived of as either an indirect physical attack or as a primitive emotional outburst. Symbolic and indirect symbolic aggression develop as the person becomes more sophisticated. Aggressiveness can develop into a severely damaging way of life. Such pathological aggression has received a good deal of investigative attention. Psychopathic behavior, once developed, is difficult to change.

The familial correlates of aggression have been extensively investigated. Researchers are fairly well agreed about the kinds of family relationships giving rise to excessively aggressive behavior. The studies of aggression in children uniformly disclose that both social learning and excessive aggression-instigating factors in the home contribute to over-aggressiveness in children.

Delinquency, like aggressive behavior in general, can be understood as aggressive, hostile behavior or as a culturally acquired way of life. *Social delinquency* is the label usually applied to the latter form. Delinquency is an ill-defined research area, and one to which a variety of disciplines can and do contribute. The phenomenon is not well understood, and a great deal of research is needed to clarify the concept and shed better light on its etiology, prevention, and treatment.

References

AMSEL, A., "The Role of Frustrative Nonreward in Noncontinuous Reward Situations," *Psychol. bull.*, LV (1958), 102–19.

ARGYLE, M., "A New Approach to the Classification of Delinquents with Implications for Treatment," *Inquiries Concerning Kinds of Treatment for Kinds of Delinquents*, Monog. 2, Board of Corrections, State of California (July, 1961), 15–26.

BAHN, A., AND V. B. NORMAN, "First National Report on Patients of Mental Health Clinics," *Publ. health rep.*, LXXIV (1959), 943–56.

BANDURA, A., AND R. WALTERS, *Adolescent Aggression*. New York: The Ronald Press Company, 1959.

BARKER, R., T. DEMBO, AND K. LEWIN, "Frustration and Regression: an Experiment with Young Children," *Univ. iowa stud. child welf.*, XVIII, No. 1 (1941).

BERKOWITZ, L., "The Expression and Reduction of Hostility," *Psychol. bull.*, LV (1958), 257–83.

———, *Aggression: A Social Psychological Analysis*. New York: McGraw-Hill Book Company, 1962.

BETTELHEIM, B., *Love Is Not Enough*. New York: The Free Press, 1950.

BOTHMAN, R. W., W. HARTINGER, AND H. RICHARDSON, "A Comparison of Two Delinquency Predicting Instruments," *J. res. crime delinq.*, II (1965), 45–48.

BOWER, E. M., *The Education of Emotionally Handicapped Children*. Sacramento, Calif.: California State Dept. of Education, 1961.

BOWMAN, P. H., "Effects of a Revised School Program on Potential Delinquents," *Ann. amer. acad. pol. sci.*, CCCXXII (1959), 53–61.

CAMERON, N., *The Psychology of Behavior Disorders*. Boston: Houghton Mifflin Company, 1947.

CLOWARD, R. A., AND L. E. OHLIN, *Delinquency and Opportunity*. New York: The Free Press, 1960.

DOLLARD, J., et al., *Frustration and Aggression*. New Haven, Conn.: Yale University Press, 1939.

FERSTER, C. B., AND M. K. DE MYER, "A Method for the Experimental Analysis of the Behavior of Autistic Children," *Amer. j. orthopsychiat.*, XXXII (1962), 89–98.

FITZSIMMONS, M. J., "The Predictive Value of Teachers' Referrals," in *Orthopsychiatry and the School*, ed. M. Krugman. New York: American Orthopsychiatric Association, 1958.

FRANK, G. H., "The Role of the Family in the Development of Psychopathology," *Psychol. bull.*, LXIV (1965), 191–205.

FREUD, S., *Inhibition, Symptoms and Anxiety*. London: The Hogarth Press, Ltd., 1936.

———, *A General Introduction to Psychoanalysis*. Garden City, N.Y.: Garden City Publishing Company, 1938.

GIBBONS, D. C., AND D. L. GARRITY, "Definition and Analysis of Certain Criminal Types," *J. crim. law criminol. police sci.*, LIII (1962), 27–35.

GLUECK, S., AND E. GLUECK, *Unraveling Juvenile Delinquency*. New York: Commonwealth Fund, 1950.

GRAZIANO, A. M., AND J. E. KEAN, "Programmed Relaxation and Reciprocal Inhibition with Psychotic Children," in *Proc. 75th Annu. Conv. of Amer. Psychol. Assoc.*, II (1967), 253–54.

HAMILTON, J. A., AND I. KRECHEVSKY, "Studies on the Effects of Shock upon Behavior Plasticity in the Rat," *J. comp. physiol. psychol.*, XVI (1933), 237–53.

HATHAWAY, S. R., AND E. D. MONACHESI, *Adolescent Personality and Behavior: MMPI Patterns of Normal, Delinquent, Dropout, and Other Outcomes*. Minneapolis, Minn.: University of Minnesota Press, 1963.

HOLLINGSHEAD, A. B., AND R. C. REDLICH, *Social Class and Mental Illness*. New York: John Wiley & Sons, Inc., 1958.

HORNEY, K., *The Neurotic Personality of Our Time*. New York: W. W. Norton & Company, Inc., 1937.

KANNER, L., AND L. LESSER, "Early Infantile Autism," *Pediat. clin. n. amer.*, V (1958), 711–30.

KANT, O., "Clinical Investigations of Simple Schizophrenia," *Psychiat. quart.*, XXII (1948), 141–51.

KVARACEUS, W. C., AND W. B. MILLER, *Delinquent Behavior: Culture and the Individual*. Washington, D.C.: National Education Association, Juvenile Delinquency Project, 1959.

———, AND W. C. ULRICH, *Delinquent Behavior: Principles and Practices*. Washington, D.C.: National Education Association, Juvenile Delinquency Project, 1959.

LOVAAS, O. I., G. FREITAG, M. I. KINDER, B. D. RUBENSTEIN, B. SCHAEFFER, AND J. Q. SIMMONS, "Establishment of Social Reinforcing in Two Schizophrenic Children on the Basis of Food," *J. exper. child psychol.*, IV (1966), 109–25.

LUNDIN, R. W., *Principles of Psychopathology*. Columbus, O.: Charles E. Merrill Books, Inc., 1965.

McCORD, W., J. S. McCORD, AND A. HOWARD, "Familial Correlates of Aggression in Nondelinquent Male Children," *J. abnorm. soc. psychol.*, LXII (1961), 79–93.

————, J. S. McCord, and I. Zola, *Origins of Crime*. New York Columbia University Press, 1959.

Masserman, J. H., *Principles of Dynamic Psychiatry*. Philadelphia, Pa.: W. B. Saunders Co., 1946.

Miller, N. E., "The Frustration-Aggression Hypothesis," *Psychol. rev.*, XXXVIII (1941), 337–42.

Mowrer, O. H., "An Experimental Analogue of 'Regression' with Incidental Observations on 'Reaction-Formation,'" *J. abnorm. soc. psychol.*, XXXV (1940), 56–87.

Murphy, F. J., M. M. Shirley, and H. L. Witmer, "The Incidence of Hidden Delinquency," *Amer. j. orthopsychiat.*, XVI (1946), 686–96.

Portnoy, I., "The Anxiety States," in *American Handbook of Psychiatry*, ed. S. Arieti. New York: Basic Books, Inc., Publishers, 1959.

Redl, F., and D. Wineman, *Children Who Hate: The Disorganization and Breakdown of Behavior Controls*. New York: The Free Press, 1951.

————, *Controls from Within*. New York: The Free Press, 1952.

Richardson, H., and J. Roebuck, "Minnesota Multiphasic Personality Inventory and California Psychological Inventory Differences between Delinquents and Their Nondelinquent Siblings," in *Proc. 73rd Annu. Conv. of Amer. Psychol. Assoc.* (1965), 255–56.

Rimland, B., *Infantile Autism: The Syndrome and Its Implications for a Neural Theory of Behavior*. New York: Appleton-Century-Crofts, 1964.

Sawrey, J. M., and C. W. Telford, *Psychology of Adjustment* (3rd ed.). Boston, Mass.: Allyn & Bacon, Inc., 1971.

Sawrey, W. L., "Conditioned Responses of Fear in Relationship to Ulceration," *J. comp. physiol. psychol.*, LIV (1961), 347–49.

Sears, R. R., C. I. Hovland, and N. E. Miller, "Minor Studies of Aggression: 1. Measurement of Aggressive Behavior," *J. psychol.*, IX (1940), 275–95.

Seward, G., *Psychotherapy and Culture Conflict*. New York: The Ronald Press Company, 1956.

Singer, J. J., and V. G. McCraven, "Some Characteristics of Adult Daydreaming," *J. psychol.*, LI (1961), 151–64.

Southern Regional Education Board, "The Emotionally Disturbed Child," *Ment. health form.* (Atlanta, Ga., South. reg. Educ. bd.) IV, No. 2 (1961).

Thompson, C. E., "The Attitudes of Various Groups toward Behavior Problems in Children," *J. abnorm. soc. psychol.*, XXXV (1940), 120–25.

Verplank, W. S., "A Glossary of Some Terms Used in the Objective Science of Behavior," *Psychol. rev.*, Suppl. VIII, No. 6, Part 2 (1957), 1–42.

Wallerstein, J. S., and C. J. Wyle, "Our Law-abiding Law Breakers," *Probation*, XXV (1947), 107–12.

Zaslow, R. W., "A Theory of Infantile Autism and Its Implications for the Treatment of Behavior Disorders in Children," in *Cognitive Clinical Psychology*, ed. L. Breger. Englewood Cliffs, N.J.: Prentice-Hall, Inc., 1969.

16

The Culturally Disadvantaged

As indicated in an earlier chapter, behavioral and developmental deviations have significance only within a given cultural context. Variations in physique, intellect, and personality are universal; the society dictates which of these constitute disabilities or assets, impairments or enhancements of personal worth. Each culture assigns tasks, attaches meanings to deviations, and classifies people according to the demands and expectancies of that culture. Thus individuals able to function quite adequately in one culture or subculture or family situation may be handicapped in another. It is these individuals who are "culturally deprived," "culturally disadvantaged," or caught in "cross-cultural streams."

The Concept of Cultural Disadvantage

On a broad conceptual level, it is possible to define the culturally disadvantaged. However, on the practical level, it is usually impossible, in the present state of our knowledge, to differentiate between those individuals who function inadequately primarily because of their impoverished or deviant cultural background, on the one hand, and those who function similarly because of inherent lack of capacity for learning, on the other. The latter are those individuals functioning as the "slow learners," the "dull normals," the "borderline," or the mentally retarded primarily because of genetic limitations. The culturally disadvantaged are those individuals with presumably adequate intellectual potentiality, who function inadequately socially and educationally because of a culturally deprived or culturally inappropriate background.

The distinction between these two groups of handicapped individuals is important. The handicap of the culturally disadvantaged can be prevented by social change; it can be remedied by the cultural enrichment of the child's life. It is conceivably reversible. Society presumably has the option of diminishing or eliminating it. At least, society can do this more readily than it can eliminate the handicap of those individuals who are either inherently deficient or are suffering from irreparable neural impairment. This is because limitations of the constitutionally deficient individuals are primarily neural deficits, of either genetic or environmental origin, while the handicaps of the culturally disadvantaged are socially induced. The dichotomy between the genetic and the environmental origin of a handicap cannot be equated with the irreversible-reversible characteristics of the conditions. The inability of the brain-damaged child to profit from environmental opportunities is just as real and irreversible, in the present state of our knowledge, as is that of the microcephalic child, for example, who is equally mentally deficient, but from genetic causes. Brain damage is exogenous (environmental) while microcephalia is endogenous (hereditary) in origin. There are also conditions of irreversible mental subnormality which are created by a combination of both *genetic* and *environmental* factors. For example, phenylketonuria results in mental retardation only when the genetic inability to metabolize phenylalanine (one of the amino acids and a normal constituent of most proteins) and the presence of phenylalanine above a critical amount in the diet (an environmental factor) are both present. The specific environmental deficit responsible for the handicap of the culturally disadvantaged child, as the name indicates, is in the broad cultural area.

Subnormal educational and social functioning can result form either lack of capacity to learn, or from cultural disadvantage, or from the combination of both. The problem of distinguishing between the two or assigning adequate weights to them in specific cases is still largely unsolved. Potentiality for learning is never measured directly, but inferred from behavior. And behavior is the product of inherent potential and the total impact of environment on the individual. Therefore, if we start with individuals of equal potentialities (identical twins), differences in their achievement can be ascribed to their different environments. Similarly, individuals of different potentialities (a normal boy and his microcephalic brother) raised in the same, or comparable, environments will differ in achievement, but largely because of their inherent differences. In such extreme cases, the primary causes of marked deficiencies in aptitudes can be assigned. However, in most cases it is impossible to differentiate between the environmental and genetic determinants of achievement. The relative emphasis placed on nature and nurture usually reflects the bias of the person making the judgment more than it reflects the preponderance of the evidence.

The question of the primary determinants of social status in America points up this question. Are the bulk of the people making up the lower socioeconomic class in America on this level because of low inherent aptitude, or are they there because of the type of environment in which they were raised? Environmentally induced handicaps can perpetuate themselves generation after generation, in much the same way as genetic deficiencies. In the 1920s and '30s, most people accepted the hereditist interpretation. More recently, the environmental factor has received increasing emphasis. Those people accepting the genetic emphasis believe that the bulk of the lower class will maintain or gravitate to this status no matter what is done to or for them. The environmentalists, on the other hand, insist that these people are potentially adequate, normal individuals who will so function if the vicious circle of poverty and deprivation can be broken.

Probably most people do not subscribe to either of these propositions. They believe that some people function inadequately primarily because of lack of potentiality, and that others do so largely because of environmental deprivation. It is undoubtedly true that, in most cases, the two reinforce each other. Individuals of limited potentiality gravitate to the slums, there to live in cultural deprivation and poverty which further accentuate their handicap. Likewise, individuals with normal potentiality who are socially and vocationally handicapped end up in these same areas, sometimes intermarry with those of lower genetic potential, and raise their offspring under the same culturally deprived conditions.

In most cases of educational and social inadequacy, it is practically impossible to determine the relative importance of the genetic and cultural factors. Consequently, in our discussion of the culturally disadvantaged we will be talking about the nature, origin, and significance of the social disadvantage which the members of designated groups experience. We do not imply that social disadvantage is their only handicap, and it does not follow that cultural enrichment will make them all normally adequate individuals. Many of the characteristics of the culturally disadvantaged are common to the "slow learners," many of whom are presumably so classified because of constitutional limitations. If we may expand the meaning of an educational term, the culturally disadvantaged person is an "underachiever" in terms of his potentialities. Because of cultural disadvantage he functions educationally, economically, and socially, not only below his potential level (most people do that), but also less adequately than the average person with equal potentiality. Probably no child has an environment which maximally fosters the development of his potentialities, and no one today can identify such an environment, but we can specify some of the cultural conditions which produce gross functional impairments.

Who Are the Culturally Disadvantaged?

Anyone living long enough in a culture, subculture, or family to acquire the basic skills, value systems, attitudes, and ways of life of that society and family may find himself culturally disadvantaged when he is either required or elects to live and compete in a markedly divergent culture. The population of the culturally disadvantaged has diverse origins. Some of the subgroups making up this segment of the population are ethnic minorities, people from isolated rural areas, migrant laborers, people inhabiting some self-contained urban villages, and most of the big, heterogeneous, poverty-stricken groups of people living in the slums of our cities.

While most of these people are poor, not all the poor are culturally impoverished. Rapid social change (e.g., automation) may make obsolete the skills of formerly competent men and women and relegate them to the ranks of the unemployed poor. Many people are poor—the blind, the deaf, the orthopedically handicapped, and the mentally ill—because of personal inadequacies, without their own environments or that of their offspring necessarily being culturally disadvantaged in terms of its behavioral outcomes. Lack of money becomes truly handicapping when it is linked to attitudes of apathy, resignation, and hopelessness. Having no job is less of a handicap than looking forward to and accepting the reality of an entire life with no job for either oneself or one's children or than living in a world which has changed so much that one cannot even understand it. There are many poor people living in skid-row environments who maintain organized, stable family lives, and who hope for something better for themselves or their children. They expect to move—preferably to the suburbs. They do not identify themselves with the neighborhood, and they display many of the characteristics of the middle-class status for which they are striving. Many of the lower-paid working-class families are not significantly culturally disadvantaged. While it is true that most of the culturally disadvantaged are poor, the poverty stricken also include the old, the recently unemployed, the physically, mentally, and emotionally handicapped, the downwardly mobile drifters, and the upwardly mobile individuals, many of whom are not culturally deprived. People who lose their wealth do not thereby acquire the psychological accompaniments of cultural disadvantage; conversely, increases in income do not always lead to a diminution of the psychological consequences of cultural deprivation.

The many ramifications of economic deprivation and cultural disadvantage in present-day America are only now becoming widely recognized. Poverty and social disadvantage typically involve the stigma of "social welfare living," under- or malnutrition, disorganized patterns of family life, educational deprivation, vocational incompetence, poor medical care, high rates of drug usage, delinquency, and urban crime—and the personal consequences of these experiences of apathy, hopelessness, and either resignation or resentment and rebellion.

Cultural Disadvantage Related to National Origin

Not all minority groups become culturally disadvantaged when transplanted from their native countries to contemporary American society. Most western Europeans acculturate quite readily. With some exceptions, second- and third-generation British, Scandinavians, Germans, Slavs, and French merge into American society and become indistinguishable from the "typical" Anglo-Americans. Individuals of Oriental—principally Chinese and Japanese—background have fared quite well in the United States. However, studies indicate that the Italians (principally the southern Italians) and the Spanish-Americans (largely Mexican-Americans and Puerto Ricans) assimilate Anglo culture less readily. This difference in rate of acculturation may be more a matter of the different social levels of the immigrants' subcultures than a reflection of basic cultural differences having to do with their country of origin. There is some evidence that immigrants to the United States are not representative samplings of their national populations. Some culturally disadvantaged groups in America have brought with them the cultural disadvantage they acquired and experienced in a subculture of their native country. For example, the Italian-Americans studied by Strodtbeck (1958) and Gans (1962) and their descendants are immigrants from the south of Italy and Sicily. These are very poor rural areas compared with the more industrial northern parts of Italy.

It is certainly true that the average Spanish-American immigrant or his forebears came from a culture whose economic and educational level is closer to that of the average slum dweller than the typical middle-class American. We have no studies of the acculturation of upper-class Italians, Puerto Ricans, or Mexican-Americans. It is probable that at least a part of the handicap of some of these groups is the persistence of a culture of poverty which cuts across ethnic and racial lines. At any rate, studies indicate the existence and persistence of some ethnic, national, and religious differences in immigrants and their children which are significantly related to achievement in contemporary America.

Cohen (1970) has documented the fact that the children of first-generation immigrants to America during the first two or three decades of this century had difficulties in school comparable to those currently experienced by Negroes, Mexican-Americans, and Puerto Ricans. The discussions and debates concerning the causes and significance of the educational deficits of these children parallel quite precisely the current discussions and differences of opinion over these questions. The current questions concerning the linguistically and culturally biased tests and school curricula and the nature-nurture issue were debated in almost identical terms during this earlier period. The studies of the first three decades of this century indicated that the children of Italian and Polish farm parents obtained mean IQ's of 85 on conventional intelligence tests. This is about the same value given currently for Afro-Americans.

The Negro population of America constitutes a unique ethnic group. Although most of them are native Americans, as were their forebears for several generations, they remain one of the largest culturally disadvantaged ethnic groups in the country today. When ethnic background is said to be one source of cultural disadvantage, it is not implied that all such handicaps are alike. The nature and origin of the cultural disadvantage seems to be quite different for the various ethnic and national groups. We shall discuss the Negroes, Puerto Ricans, and Mexican-Americans as examples of *disadvantaged* groups, the Jews as a group with some decided cultural *advantages* in contemporary American society, and the Italians as *intermediate*.

The early life of the child seems to be critical in the development of motivation for later achievement. We will, therefore, concentrate on those family conditions which funnel the ethnic, neighborhood, community, and general cultural influences into the child's life.

THE NEGROES

The Negroes constitute the largest nonwhite group in America, and an increasing proportion of the population. In the 1950s, one in ten Americans was nonwhite (predominantly Negro). In the 1960s, one in nine is nonwhite, and in the 1970s, it is anticipated, one in eight will be nonwhite. In 1960, Negro women were having children at a rate 40 percent higher than that of white women in America (Glazer and Moynihan, 1963; White, 1965).

The fact that the Negroes are found in disproportionate numbers among the educationally, socially, and economically disadvantaged hardly

requires documentation. Negroes have a high proportion of school failures, dropouts, and low educational achievement. They also contribute
disproportionately to the delinquent and socially deviant populations.
Negroes were rejected for military service in World War II on the grounds
of mental deficiency (largely illiteracy) at a rate over six times that of
whites (Ginzberg and Bray, 1953). The widely publicized Negro ghettoes
of New York and Los Angeles perpetuate many of the facets of cultural
disadvantage, but efforts to desegregate housing and to eliminate the
ghettoes of the cities have made little headway. Laws forbidding discrimination in renting and selling have been countered by massive, if covert,
evasion. Perpetual shortages of low-cost housing produce as much segregation by "discrimination for" as by "discrimination against." Just as jobs
are obtained by the friends or relatives of the employed, so good low-cost
apartments descend through a chain of relatives, friends, and other in-
siders, year after year and decade after decade. In many cities, even without racial discrimination, Negroes get a poor share of the better low-cost
housing because they are, in large measure, latecomers. For example, it is
said that the rent-controlled housing in New York City discriminates
against anyone who came into the city after 1943. The bulk of the rural-to-
urban migration and South-to-North Negro migration has occurred since
1940. Desegregation of a white residential area, up to now, has meant a
period of transition ending with the simple extension of the all-Negro
neighborhood into the previously all-white area. It has seldom resulted in
a stable racially mixed area. The pattern of white withdrawal before in-
coming Negro residents is found everywhere in the nation (Glazer and
Moynihan, 1963). Economic disadvantage and widespread discrimination
combine with other factors to restrict Negroes to the poorest housing the
country provides.

Vocationally, the Negroes are predominantly unskilled. They are the
last to be hired and the first to be fired. Their unemployment rate is
regularly two or more times that of the general population. The Negroes
are the prime example of a minority group suffering profound cultural
disadvantage in contemporary America. The Negro is *in, but not of,*
American society. He has been called "America's internal alien" (Harrington, 1963).

The roots of the cultural handicaps of the Negro segment of the population are varied, but probably the most important is the nature of the
Negro's family and his chronic poverty. The weakness of the Negro family
in America probably dates from slavery. Most vestiges of native African
life were left behind when white traders and African chieftains tore families apart, sold the individuals as slaves, and brought them to America.
For two hundred years under slavery, Negro women bore children—often
fathered by white men—which were taken from them and sold to other

plantation owners. Legalized marriages and intact families were the exception under slavery.

The free Negro, with no established pattern of normal family life, and living on the periphery of the white culture, has perpetuated an unstable family structure. The weak family organization manifests itself in a high rate of illegitimacy, many common-law marriages, and widespread desertion (the poor man's divorce). One-fourth of the Negro families in the New York metropolitan area in 1960 were headed by women, whereas less than one-tenth of the white households were in this category. The rate of illegitimacy among Negroes was between fourteen and fifteen times that among whites. Most of the large numbers of infants abandoned in the hospitals of New York by their mothers, and forced to live there for extended periods because there is no room for them elsewhere, are Negro children (Glazer and Moynihan, 1963). A disproportionate number of Negro children live apart from parents and relatives, live in overcrowded homes, have roomers and other related and unrelated persons living with them, suffer chronic poverty, and have mothers who are forced to work because their fathers are unable to find work.

There is evidence that Negro males suffer most from these social and economic circumstances. The Negro man has been demasculinized. His sex role has become ambiguous. Negro men under slavery and, to a lesser degree since, have seen white men defile Negro women and been powerless to protest. That Negro women find more jobs available to them than do Negro men in the cities has added to the indignities heaped on the Negro husbands and forced them to play subordinate roles. Men are expected to be masterful and powerful, and the consequences of powerlessness and economic impotence are greater for them.

In families in which the father is ineffectual as a breadwinner and head of the family, in which he periodically leaves home whether in search of work or simply to disappear, and in which the mother is the breadwinner, the authoritarian figure, and the only constant and stable parent, the Negro boy has a much greater chance of establishing an inappropriate sex role and an inadequate self-concept. His knowledge of the adult male world is inadequate, his social and vocational aspirations inappropriate, and his self-image ambiguous. Negro girls are generally found to be better students, report a more satisfactory family situation, and have more positive self-concepts than do Negro boys (Deutsch, 1960).

The Negro, unlike many European immigrants has been largely cut off from his own culture and language. The extended family and clannishness of the Italian, the Puerto Rican, and the Mexican has no counterpart among the Negro. Lacking a common known historical background, deprived of his native language, value system, and culture, there was little to create a cohesive group and to support morale in the face of adversity.

Consequently, the Negro communal organizations are weak, just as the family is weak. Experiencing loneliness and a sense of isolation from the mainstream of life, with others looking upon him as inadequate and as not belonging, the Negro has looked upon himself in the same way.

Negro parents want their children to go to school, to become well educated, to be moral, law-abiding citizens, and to become personally competent, but it is only a wish. It remains largely in the realm of fantasy. It is not an expectation. That which slavery began has been perpetuated by prejudice and discrimination affecting education, employment, housing, self-respect, and the whole motivational system of the American Negro. Migration, urbanization, technological unemployment, and poverty always create problems, but when family patterns and communal organizations are already weak the problems are greatly magnified.

THE SPANISH-AMERICANS

The Spanish-American immigrants to the United States are concentrated in two areas—the Puerto Ricans in the New York metropolitan area, and the Mexican-Americans in the southwestern United States. The 1961 census figures showed that 613,000 people of Puerto Rican birth or parentage were in New York City and that three-fifths of the migrants to the mainland were settling in the city. In 1961, more than one-seventh of the children born in the city were of Puerto Rican parents. In this same year, the birth rate of Puerto Ricans was 40 per 1,000, for all nonwhites it was 30, and for whites it was 20 per thousand. It is estimated that the Puerto Ricans comprised one-eighth of the population of the city in 1970.

While we distinguish between the Puerto Ricans and the Negroes, the two groups are not discrete. There has been a great mixture of ethnic groups in Puerto Rico. In 1860, almost half the Puerto Ricans in the United States were listed in the census as Negro. By 1900, only two-fifths, and, in 1950, only one-fifth were so listed. The proportion of Negro Puerto Ricans in New York continues to drop from census to census for unknown reasons. It is estimated that in 1966 only about 4 percent of Puerto Ricans were clearly Negro, so we shall discuss them as two separate ethnic groups despite the fact of considerable mixture. This is no more paradoxical than considering the Negro population of America as an ethnic group, when the typical member of this group probably has almost as much white as Negro ancestry.

The economic disadvantage of the Puerto Ricans in New York City is comparable to that of the Negroes. The per-family income of Puerto Ricans in 1960 was 63 percent of the median income of all New York families. In this same year, 5 percent of all New York males, 6.9 percent of all nonwhite males, and 9.9 percent of all Puerto Rican males were unemployed. One-half of all the families in the city receiving supplemental aid from the Department of Welfare were Puerto Ricans. They constituted one-half of the home-relief cases and one-third of the aid-to-dependent-children cases (Glazer and Moynihan, 1963).

As among the Negroes, there is a good deal of leaving school at the earliest possible age. In 1960, 18 percent of the elementary school pupils, 17 percent of the junior high school students, and only 8 percent of the high school students were Puerto Ricans. This indicates a high dropout rate below the high school level. The proportion of Puerto Ricans in the *academic high school* was only 5 percent in 1960. The Puerto Ricans have fared better than the Negroes in terms of upward economic and social mobility, although they still constitute a big group of the ethnically disadvantaged.

Puerto Rican family life has some strengths and some weaknesses. In some ways, the native Puerto Rican family was similar to that of the European peasant. It was patriarchal and authoritarian. The husband demanded respect and obedience from wife and family. The marriages, unlike those of European peasants, however, included many consensual, or common-law, marriages. Consequently, as among the Negroes, about one-third of the births were technically illegitimate. The consensual marriage was unstable and was made even more so by the existence of additional mistresses and the considerable sexual adventurism of the Puerto Rican men.

The position of children in the Puerto Rican family was better than the marriage practices suggest. Most observers report that mothers were very much attached to their children, often loving them to the point of overprotection. Although men might have children by a number of women, they typically took responsibility for all of them. The custom of having godparents (co-parents) for each child provided a second set of parents to take over the responsibility of parenthood when necessary. Children may have been overprotected; certainly, they were seldom abandoned, rejected, or neglected.

Whether because of less prejudice and discrimination or because of different personal and social motivations, the prognosis for improvement in the status of the Puerto Ricans seems to be better than that of the Negroes. In 1960 there were an estimated 4,000 Puerto Rican-run businesses in New York City. This is considerably more than the much larger Negro population has established, even though the major Negro migration was years ahead of the Puerto Ricans. The 1960 census showed more Puerto Ricans than Negroes in the category of "managers, officials, and proprietors."

In 1966 there were an estimated 3,500,000 Mexican-Americans in the United States. They are found predominantly in Texas, New Mexico,

Colorado, Arizona, and California. In all of these states, the Mexican-Americans constitute the largest ethnic group of culturally disadvantaged (Busma, 1954).

The cultural disadvantage of the Mexican-Americans, like that of the Puerto Ricans and Italian-Americans, is more the result of their having cultural traits which handicap them in American society than it is the result of enforced segregation, prejudice, and discrimination. Many Mexican-American communities, like the Italian-American, reproduce in a modified form the *barrio* of Mexico. People from the same villages in Mexico have settled together in the same localities and maintained a life similar to that found in Mexico. Inhabitants of the Mexican-American community have a strong feeling of kinship with each other, and a feeling of separation from the English-speaking community.

Families and godparents are the most important social ties among the people of the Mexican-American community. The extended family, including grandparents, aunts, uncles and cousins, is closely tied together and provides mutual aid and counsel. Four kinds of godparents are recognized, one for each of the sacraments of baptism, communion, confirmation, and marriage. These godparents enter into a special social and religious relationship, not only with their godchild but also with the child's parents. This relationship formalizes friendship, extends the size of the kinship group, and enhances neighborhood solidarity.

The Mexican family is authoritarian and patriarchal. Both parents express deep affection and concern for their children. Men are expected to have extramarital amorous adventures, often of a rather permanent sort, but like the Puerto Ricans, they accept responsibility for their illegitimate offspring. Children are seldom deserted, nor do they lack care and affection (Clark, 1959; Lewis, 1959, 1960, 1961, 1964).

Clark (1959), studying a poor Mexican-American community of the Santa Clara Valley in California, reported that practically all the people spoke Spanish, about half were bilingual, and less than half could read or write their native tongue. The cultural disadvantage of the Mexican-Americans manifests itself in, or derives from, poverty, low levels of educational and social status, and little expectation that their level or that of their children will improve. The studies intended to clarify the nature of these disadvantages have not been very helpful, but the better-controlled ones indicate that the attitudes of Mexican-American children toward education and social advancement are considerably less positive than are those of Anglo-American children, even when the groups are matched for socioeconomic level, intelligence, age, grade, and sex (Demos, 1962).

A comparison of seventy-five delinquent Mexican-American and seventy-five Anglo-American delinquents, whose names were drawn at random from the list of juvenile hall residents in Los Angeles, California, reveals some interesting differences (Harvey, 1949). The typical delinquent Mexican boy in Los Angeles is Catholic and bilingual. His parents have little education. Although over half the parents of the boys in both groups were separated, death was the main cause of the broken homes in the Mexican families, while most of the American families were broken by divorce. The Mexican families were larger—6 children as compared with 4.2 in the American families. Fifty-seven percent of the Mexican boys had a history of truancy, as compared to 36 percent of the American boys. While only one Mexican boy was rated as "incorrigible," this was the third highest offense for the Americans. The mean Stanford-Binet IQ for the Mexican boys was 77.2, while the American boys averaged 91.1. Only 17 percent of the Mexican boys were judged to have "psychiatric aberrations," whereas 46 percent of the American boys were so categorized.

THE ITALIAN-AMERICANS

The Italian-Americans are not an impoverished group like the Negroes or the Puerto Ricans. They are gradually being absorbed into the mainstream of American society. However, they typify the failure of even the third and fourth generation of certain groups to blend into a standard, national, American type. The grandchildren and great-grandchildren of Italian immigrants still think of themselves on many occasions, and for certain purposes, as Italian. There is also a persistence of many old-country attitudes and values which tend to circumscribe their achievements in education, business, politics, and even in crime.

The Italian immigrants to America came in two waves. The earlier and smaller one consisted of workmen from northern Italy. They came between 1860 and 1900, when the western part of the United States was experiencing its early growth. Those early Italian immigrants to California played an important part in the development of the mining industry, in fishing, in truck gardening, and in the construction industry. After 1900, the *big* migration from Italy began. These immigrants were largely illiterate peasants from southern Italy and Sicily. They had seldom travelled beyond the confines of their own villages. All people outside their own villages, or even outside their own families, were *foresteri*—strangers (Foerster, 1919). Between 1899 and 1910, 2,300,000 Italian immigrants entered the United States. Of these, 1,900,000 were from southern Italy or Sicily. Seventy-seven percent were either farm workers or unskilled laborers, 15 percent were skilled or semiskilled workers, and only 1 percent were professionally trained. More than half were illiterate.

In America, as in Italy, the traditional bounds of family and neighborhood (the counterpart of the small Italian village) continued to circumscribe the life and achievements of many American-Italians (Strodtbeck, 1958; Gans, 1962; Glazer and Moynihan, 1963). The Italian immigrants congregated with others from the same province or village and settled in the same blocks or small industrial areas around the cities. These Italian neighborhoods have been remarkably stable and remain so even today, as Gans has indicated in his book, *The Urban Villagers* (1962). In these Italian neighborhoods, the conservative village of southern Italy is, in part, recreated and maintained. The typical ethics of the peasant of southern Italy and Sicily has been called "amoral familism" (Banfield, 1958). This means that a person owes nothing to anyone outside his extended family. Morality is largely limited to family members and close friends. Strangers are outsiders. They are not to be trusted, and it is legitimate to advance one's family's interest, or one's own, at the expense of strangers.

The education of Italian youth is restricted by the outlook of the family and neighborhood. The typical peasant of southern Italy is pretty well resigned to fate. He sees little possibility of advancement for himself or for his children. Education is only for priests, who leave home never to return and are thus lost to the family and to the community. A satisfying family life, pleasant social contacts with one's friends, and the possible attainment of some local political power constitute the extent of the normal aspirations of the bulk of the population. Formal education is devalued. Too much reading is bad for people. Education makes people lazy and opens the mind to unhealthy beliefs. "Do not make your child better than you are," says an old south Italian proverb (Glazer and Moynihan, 1963). Such beliefs persist, only somewhat attenuated, to the second and third generation in America, and limit the influence of formal education which is the principal channel to vocational and social success in contemporary American culture.

The Italian family is strong. Divorce, separation, and desertion are rare. Family life is highly valued, and family ties are tenacious. Italian parents keep their children close to them, both physically and emotionally. Education and vocational advancement must not threaten either the family's interests or the family relationships. Social mobility for the Italian youth must be individual mobility, since the group is conservative and moves slowly, but the child's socialization makes it painful for him to leave family and neighborhood. The good son and daughter are content to work hard, hope for a lucky break, marry a neighborhood boy or girl, raise a family, and not spend too much time in school.

Whereas the problems of present-day Negroes derive partially from the weaknesses and disorganization of the family, the failures of Italian children to strive for better education and upward mobility stem from a strong, highly organized family life which devalues these goals. The effects of this heritage are diminishing among the elementary and secondary school children. The incidence of truancy and dropping out is decreasing, but the proportion of children of Italian ancestry graduating from college is still far below their proportion in the population (Glazer and Moynihan, 1963). The gap between the occupations pursued by first- and second-generation Italians is smaller than that of any other European immigrant group, indicating their relatively slow rate of upward mobility (Cohen, 1970).

THE JEWS AND JAPANESE IN AMERICA

We discuss the Jews only for purposes of contrast. They are not a culturally disadvantaged group. On the contrary, the Jews and Japanese stand in marked contrast to the Negroes and Puerto Ricans and, to a lesser degree, with the Italian-Americans. Certain components of old-world Jewish and Japanese culture, family life, and experience make it possible for the Jews and Japanese in America to take advantage of the opportunities provided them and achieve phenomenal success.

The Jewish characteristics which seem to work to their advantage in contemporary American culture are: (1) a strong, closely knit family and communal organization; (2) a passion for education and upward socio-economic mobility; (3) a long-range time orientation; and (4) broad, liberal, humanitarian interests.

Studies have repeatedly documented the strengths of the Jewish family. Like the Italians, the Jews have a low incidence of families broken by desertion, separation, or divorce. Child neglect is virtually nonexistent, and the rate of juvenile delinquency is low. If anything, Jewish children suffer from maternal overprotection. Intermarriage between Jews and non-Jews is comparatively rare. The disapproval of intermarriage is remarkably strong, even among the native-born. Jewish parents favor residence in predominantly Jewish neighborhoods in order to increase the probability of their children marrying a Jewish person. In America the closeness of the Jewish family, unlike that of its Italian counterpart, has never restricted the child's achievement. The Jewish boy finds it easier than the Italian boy to leave home. The Jewish family participates symbolically in the accomplishments of its members. The Jewish child is also a part of a community that is rapidly moving upward, and so he experiences no conflict between individual achievement and occupational mobility, on the one hand, and family or communal loyalty, on the other. Jewish mobility is a mass phenomenon and is socially approved.

Jewish tradition and culture has always placed a high value on education. Intellectual attainments carry high prestige. The preschool Jewish boy receiving religious instruction is already a serious student. "Parents will bend the sky to educate their sons," is an old Jewish saying. It is therefore not surprising that the Jews have displayed a passion for education unparalleled in American history. The free city colleges of New York were largely Jewish by the turn of the century. With the increasing prosperity of the Jewish community, the admissions officers of the high-prestige universities became busily engaged in devising ways of keeping the Jewish segment of their student bodies down to what they considered reasonable proportions. The professional schools—notably the medical schools—set tight quotas for Jewish students. Cornell University Medical School, located in New York City, in 1940 admitted only one of every seventy Jewish applicants, whereas it accepted one out of every seven non-Jewish applicants of equivalent qualifications (Bloomgarden, 1957). The Jews have become the best educated ethnic group in America. At times they have been overeducated in proportion to the vocational opportunities open to them. The brute facts of discrimination maintained the bans on higher levels of employment long after they had been lowered within the educational institutions. This meant that highly educated Jews were unable to obtain employment in areas for which they were well trained and qualified. The same thing happened to the Japanese in California before World War II. This meant frustration and disappointment for these overtrained individuals, but it also meant that when the barriers of discrimination were lowered, many of these people were ready and waiting for the jobs that became available. The opposite of this is true of the Negro. As the barriers of discrimination were being lowered for them in the 1960s, there were more places in college and industry available to Negroes than there were qualified applicants to occupy them. The major task of the Scholarship Service and Fund for Negro Students was to find qualified Negro students to accept the available scholarships and college openings. The president of this organization said, in 1960, that there were places in northern colleges for five times as many Negro students as were found available and qualified to accept them. Companies willing and anxious to hire Negro engineers are unable to find qualified applicants (Plaut, 1960).

While the Jewish family is a closely knit one and family identifications are high, the entire Jewish community is in many respects the important social entity. The present and future status of all Jews is the really significant variable. The accomplishments of the individual Jew are meritorious in themselves, add to the prestige of the individual, and reflect credit on the family, but more important, they enhance the status of all Jews. The entire community—and all Jews, in a very real sense—participates in the achievements of its members. One generation sacrifices to educate and push the next generation up the ladder, and the generation which benefits is expected to pass along this advantage with an additional increment to the next. Parental and community gifts and benefits provided young people are not given in anticipation of reciprocal gifts in the present, but are expected to elicit corresponding assists to each succeeding generation. Thus assistance progresses in an ascending spiral which blesses the giver and helps the recipient, but more significantly, enriches the community and the entire ethnic group (Strodtbeck, 1958; Kramer and Leventman, 1961; Srole and Langner, 1969; Yaffe, 1961). The emphasis on the desirability of long periods of formal education, the benefits of which accrue to the family, to succeeding generations, and to the community, reflects a long-range time orientation, a delayed-gratification pattern in an extreme form. Thus we find many components of traditional Jewish family and communal life contributing to the motivation of the individual. These cultural values instilled in the developing child largely account for the fact that a Jewish boy is much more likely to graduate from college than is an Anglo-American boy of equal intellectual ability and social status. The Anglo-American boy, in turn, is more likely to graduate from college than is an Italian-American, Puerto Rican, or Negro boy of comparable social and intellectual levels (Halsey, Floud, and Anderson, 1961).

Superficially, the Japanese would seem to be ideal candidates for the category of culturally disadvantaged in America. Japanese language, culture, religion, and family organization seem to be very different from those of other Americans. The background of the typical Japanese immigrant to America was rural-peasant. His vocational background was that of subsistence farming. He came to the United States with only temporary residence in mind. He established and maintained special part-time schools to perpetuate his native language, religion, and culture. He was a member of a highly visible, socially deviant group. He met prejudice, discrimination, and restrictive legislation in America. However, in a comparatively short time the Japanese have attained a surprisingly high level of education; they have moved from unskilled migrant farm laborers, to renters, and finally, as the legal restrictions concerning land ownership were removed, they became highly competent independent farmers. As the social barriers were lowered they also became successful businessmen and professional people. In both education and income the Japanese rank higher than all other identifiable ethnic groups as defined by the United States Census; more than 50 percent of Japanese children of college age (18–24) are attending college. This percentage is well ahead of that of WASPs (Kitano, 1969b).

Although different in many respects, there is apparently a significant compatibility, not necessarily identity, between the value systems of the Japanese and American cultures which has made it possible for the Japanese-American to progress rapidly in current American society. Some of these compatibilities are the personal characteristics of diligence and hard work, a belief in the importance of attaining and maintaining a good personal and family reputation in the community, and an unquestioned expectation that children will fulfill their obligations to self, family, and race (Kitano, 1969b). The Japanese emphasis on strong communal and family ties and their style of life have resulted in a low rate of identified and diagnosed mental illness (Kitano, 1969a). Nair (1970), in a comparative study of farming practices in the United States, Japan, and India, claims that the small Japanese farmer has not changed essentially from the skillful and diligent practices of 500 years ago. She claims that their practices derive from the purest "Protestant" work ethic, although they have never known either Calvin or Knox.

Divergence within Ethnic Groups

Mere group membership in the Negro, Puerto Rican, Mexican-American, Italian-American, or any other similar group should not be equated with cultural disadvantage. Many members of all of these groups are not disadvantaged and function very adequately in contemporary American society. Conversely, not all Jews are culturally advantaged. The individual differences within any group far exceed the difference between the norms of any two groups. Group differences should not be overgeneralized. For example, that the Jews in Israel apparently have their culturally deprived subcultures is indicated by their establishing special kindergarten programs designed to improve the educational readiness of their low-status Jewish children (Smilansky, 1965).

The Negro subgroup which came to New York City from the British West Indies—principally from Jamaica—seems to have suffered considerably less cultural disadvantage than the main stream of Negro migrants from the South. In 1930, the West-Indian immigrants and their children constituted between a fifth and a fourth of the Negro population of New York City (Reid, 1949). This group, for a time, was highly distinctive in language, religion (Anglican), and general outlook. They reacted vigorously to the greater prejudice and discrimination they encountered in the United States. As a consequence, many of them turned radical. Negro communists and labor leaders in the 1930s were disproportionately frequently West Indians.

The culture of the native West-Indian Negroes seems to have emphasized the values of hard work, social advancement, saving, and education much more than did that of the typical Negro culture of the American South. The incidence of illiteracy among the West-Indian immigrants was low, and they contributed disproportionately to the number of Negro leaders. In the late 1930s, it was estimated that one-third of the Negro professional population was foreign-born, largely West Indian (Reid, 1949). We can only guess why the West Indians were superior to the native

Negroes in business enterprise, leadership, and education. Perhaps the aspirations and self-concepts of Negroes coming from islands where all positions in society, except the very highest, were held by Negroes were sufficiently high to maintain motivation in the new society for a few generations. By now the West Indians have merged into the larger Negro group, and probably have succumbed to the feelings of inadequacy, inferiority, and hopelessness of the Negro subculture.

There are also tremendous sectional differences within the Negro population of the United States. The rejection rates for military service in World War II for mental deficiency (really primarily illiteracy) were five times as high (202 per 1,000 registrants) in the southeast United States as in the northwest (40 per 1,000). The rejection rates for Negroes in the northwest and the far west (40 and 50 per 1,000) were actually below the white rates in the southeast and the southwest (52 and 54 per 1,000) (Ginzberg and Bray, 1953).

Madsen (1967), in a study of several hundred Mexican children, found those from upper-class urban homes to be much more competitive, and they consequently scored considerably higher than lower-class urban and rural children on tasks where high levels of motivation for *individual achievement* led to success. However, in tasks where progress depended upon the cooperation of all four members of a team and where success required each person to defer in turn to the others, the urban poor and the rural children did about equally well and both groups were far superior to the children from urban upper-class homes. These results raise the question: Is the low level of achievement motivation of Mexican-American children a reflection of their rural and lower social-class origins, or is the more competitive attitude of urban upper-class Mexican children the product of a relatively new industrial and educational order which has not yet affected the rural and lower-class urban children? This same author has reported more recently that children of the kibbutzim (Israeli rural communal settlements) are more cooperative than middle-class Israeli children reared in the regular family setting (Shapira and Madsen, 1969). He has also found dramatic differences between Mexican village children, on the one hand, and urban Afro-American, Anglo-American, and Mexican-American children, on the other (Madsen and Shapira, 1970).

Many of the differences among social classes of Anglo-Americans are in the same direction and are comparable in extent to those found between typical Anglo-Americans and any of the disadvantaged ethnic groups (Battle and Rotter, 1963; Bloom, Whiteman, and Deutsch, 1963). There is some evidence that, within the Negro group, social class and ethnic group membership interact in such a way that, as social-class level increases, the influence of ethnic group membership increases (Deutsch and Brown, 1964), whereas in other ethnic groups—the Jews for example—

this does not occur (McClelland, 1961). This means that when Negro and white children of the same socioeconomic levels are compared, the superiority of the whites increases at each higher socioeconomic level, while the superiority of the Jews over Anglo-Americans stays fairly constant at all socioeconomic levels. Apparently American-Jewish culture is sufficiently powerful to wipe out the effects of social class on achievement, which are marked in other ethnic groups.

Being a Negro in America leads to social disadvantage, and being both Negro and lower-class produces additional increments of cultural handicap. This leads one to wonder to what extent other characteristics—such as disorganized family life, high rates of illegitimacy, and low levels of communal organization—arise from the cumulative effects of such things as poverty and general environmental deprivation and are not uniquely related to ethnic group membership. They may be the result of discrimination and segregation, rather than, as we previously suggested, the outcome of their unique ethnic history.

Subcultures of the Disadvantaged

Because of the widespread concern with the large population of poverty-stricken Negroes, Puerto Ricans, and Mexican-Americans in the United States it is easy to overlook the fact that most of the poor (80 percent) are white (Riessman, Cohen, and Pearl, 1964). A large proportion of the poor whites are native Anglo-Americans. As we indicated earlier, members of a social class are shaped first by their families, second by their subculture, and third by the larger culture of which they are a part. Since the 1930s it has become increasingly clear that the United States is not a classless society. On the contrary, it has many subcultural disadvantaged groups, even among the native Anglo-American population. It is therefore necessary to consider the subcultures and families of the disadvantaged lower social classes, in order to understand the nature and origins of their handicaps.

The most striking feature of the culturally disadvantaged in America is that they are poor. Not all the poor are culturally deprived, but certainly most of the culturally disadvantaged live in poverty. Most of them are unemployed, many are "on welfare." Poverty drives them to the slums where they congregate and live in inadequate, overpriced housing which they resent. The poor live among those who, like themselves, are unemployed and have lost touch with the working world. They are not in a position to learn of job openings. Everything around them tells them that there are no jobs and little hope. The tips and information leading to new jobs are known and transmitted mostly by those already employed. For example, a 1956 study of over 4,000 men laid off when the Packard

Motor Company closed down in Detroit disclosed that three-fourths of those who obtained new jobs did so through friends, neighbors, or relatives. Only 14 percent obtained work in the supposedly conventional way of submitting applications and making oral inquiries at company personnel offices (Bagdikian, 1965).

The slum, for the unemployed, rapidly becomes a circumscribed area permeated by attitudes either of despair and apathy or hostility and rebellion. Poverty becomes truly handicapping when combined with the conviction that the lack of money is irremediable.

Because of the ever-increasing demands of our culture, many people who could have functioned quite adequately in American society fifty years ago now find themselves overwhelmed by social circumstances which they can neither understand nor control. The prerequisites of a constructive and satisfying life are constantly being raised. With the educational level of the general population constantly increasing, formal education—not necessarily the ability to perform certain tasks—is the credential required for entry into the economic life of twentieth-century America. However, large numbers of culturally deprived children are unable to take advantage of the educational programs available to them (Hess and Shipman, 1965). The jobs that the lower-class child might find available require little formal education. The curriculum of the school seems remote from the world of work as he knows it. He does not perceive education as an economic asset. Despite these negative factors, the average lower-class child is initially willing to try, and he hopes to do well in school. Many of his initial attitudes are positive.

However, the typical child with a culturally disadvantaged background has handicaps which insure his failure at school. Most of these originate in his home and his subculture. The lower-class family has many of the characteristics of the culturally disadvantaged Negro. It is broken by divorce, desertion, or forced separation because of the location or nature of available work. The family constellation is unstable. Father leaves home for extended periods, in search of work, or because he finds temporary employment elsewhere, or because he simply deserts his family periodically. Older brothers and sisters leave to get married or to take jobs, only to return when unemployed, or separated or divorced. More distant relatives or friends come to stay, either during times of domestic or economic crisis or more permanently, when it becomes necessary to double up in housing.

Poverty places additional burdens on the lower-class child. All components of family life lack the long-range uniformity and predictability of the average middle-class family. One eats well when one's parents are employed, but at other times meals may be rather unpredictable. Not only the family constellation and the amount of food, but housing, clothing, and one's whole pattern of life, may change without warning. The disorganization of the lower-class child's life influences his time orientation. For such children, the future becomes a vague, diffuse region where anything can happen and whose possible rewards are too uncertain and remote to mean much. The child's discipline typically involves physical rewards and punishments which are designed to get him to do or not do specific, immediate things. Life is a series of critical situations in which irritable and tired adults use physical punishment in an erratic way to maintain discipline. With such a background it is not surprising that few lower-class children develop the deferred-gratification pattern of life required for the commitment to a long-range life plan which the middle or upper-class child assumes as part of his world. The lower-class person is not at all sure that it is rational for him to trade impulsiveness for restraint, spontaneity for self-discipline, play for work, immediate satisfactions for remote and uncertain rewards. The costs of the middle-class way of life are immediate and clear; the rewards are remote and problematic. He lacks interested adults who help to link past, present, and future by recalling prior shared experiences, relating them to present occurrences, and predicting future ones. Caught in the present, they do not plan ahead. They take their pleasure on a moment-to-moment basis.

The culturally disadvantaged child lives in a world that is dominantly physically, rather than ideationally and verbally, controlled. He, in turn, learns to live and act in a physical rather than ideational way. His religion comes to be loud singing, hand-clapping and shouting, rather than the reasoned consideration of ethical and moral issues. His neuroses take the form of organic conversion reaction and catatonia (motor forms) rather than the more mental forms of obsessions, depressions, and anxiety reactions. Language is used to control other people more than to carry information. The manipulation of objects and people is more important than the manipulation of ideas or the transmission of information.

Rural-Urban Migrants

Many of the twenty million immigrants who came to the United States between 1880 and 1920 had a rich culture heritage. As we have indicated, some found their old-world culture an asset in America (the Jews did), while for others (i.e., the Italian peasants) it was a liability. In the forty years between 1920 and 1960, twenty-seven million rural Americans migrated to our cities (Bagdikian, 1965). Some of these may have found the rural subcultures from which they came to be an advantage in the urban culture, but more of them have found it to be a handicap. The earlier

European immigrants found lots of unskilled jobs waiting for them. When the initial language barriers were overcome, most of them—or their children or their grandchildren—were able to emulate models of success and finally merge indistinguishably into the population. This has not been true of the rural-urban migrants.

The more recent migrants from the rural areas have come as refugees to a society in which unskilled jobs are few and getting fewer. The man with only the strength of his back and arms to offer is unproductive. The only housing available to him is in block after block of slums filled by older, impoverished, and hopeless or new and bewildered migrants like himself.

The rural-to-urban migrant finds new demands placed upon him. His plumbing, heating, and lighting must conform to municipal and state codes. He can no longer put up a tar-paper shanty for shelter, use an open privy in the back yard, carry water from the stream across the road, and dispose of his garbage by feeding it to his chickens and pigs. He cannot create a health hazard, his children must be vaccinated, and he must join social security. If he is to get a job without the intervention of relatives or friends, he must fill out complicated application forms, follow printed directions, and be judged by his record of educational and occupational achievement.

To the man accustomed to a small rural community where he knew everyone and dealt with others on an individual and personal basis, the impersonality of urban life is sinister and threatening. Because the city treats him impersonally, he regards it as hostile. The impoverished rural migrant becomes bewildered and lost in a world where he must deal with big government, big industries, and large masses of impersonal people. When he desperately needs help, he finds that the agencies designed to provide that help are cold and formidable. He is skeptical of the agencies' usefulness, ignorant of their procedures, and too confused to try. Finally from necessity, he may succumb to the expectancy of his new environment and accept a state of situational dependency. He is helpless to affect the most significant social aspects of his life. He is dependent on the operation of agencies and forces which he does not understand. He feels that he has become the victim of arbitrary and irrational forces. Urban renewal programs disrupt his neighborhood and force him to move, compulsory school-attendance laws require his children to attend school when they should be out earning money, settlement houses impose set arbitrary criteria for their use, high-pressure salesmen persuade him to agree to high-interest installment financing he cannot afford, and then his furniture is repossessed or his check garnisheed. Reduced to relief, he meets deliberate rudeness and complicated procedures sometimes designed to discourage applicants. All of these experiences combine to place the displaced rural poor at the mercy of completely incomprehensible forces.

Weller (1965) has shown how the isolated mountaineer's way of organizing his life, his way of looking at things, his relationship to other people, the basic direction of his thinking—in short, his cultural life, which was quite satisfactory for his isolated, agrarian existence in his mountain area—are quite inadequate in the urban world. Members of different subcultures and social classes, by virtue of their different conditions of life, come to perceive the world differently, to develop different conceptions of social reality, different aspirations and expectations, different conceptions of the desirable and the possible. And these differences often constitute barriers to integration and progress in changing society.

The Linguisitic and Cognitive Consequences of Cultural Disadvantage

A person's perceptual and conceptual systems reflect that individual's peculiar experiential history. Language is the most sensitive index of one's experiential background, particularly one's social history. Linguistic limitations not only reflect experiential deficits, they also constitute blocks to the realization of the individual's intellectual potentiality. Language can be conceived of either as a "cloak" which covers one's percepts and concepts or as a "mold" which fashions and limits one's thinking. It probably functions in both of these ways. Limited linguistic categories and usages reflect deprivations in one's social history. They also both reflect the individual's ideational limitation and impose restrictions on his thought processes. We shall briefly summarize the consensus of a large number of studies of the linguistic characteristics of individuals growing up in a typical lower-class family and subculture (Cutts, 1962).

Such a person's sentences are short, grammatically simple, and often incomplete. Requests or commands are curt and brief, with a minimum of explanation or elaboration and no offer of alternatives. For example, the lower-class mother talking on the telephone tells her noisy child to "Shut up" or "Stop that noise," whereas her middle- or upper-class counterpart is more likely to say, "Please, Johnny, you are making so much noise I can't hear." The implications of these utterances may be the same, but their ideational outcomes may be quite different. In the second case, the child has alternatives which he may consider and act upon. He can simply continue what he is doing but reduce the noise level, he can turn to some other less noisy activity, he can engage in the same activity in another room, or if he is already in another room he can close the door. The implied request is also time-limited; the noise is objectionable only when the mother is talking on the telephone. As soon as she finishes telephoning he can resume his activity. He makes choices and responds in a rational way within a reasonable framework.

The lower-class child's questions are answered by "Yes," "No," a nod, a shake of the head, or a shrug of the shoulder, while the middle-class parent is more inclined to elaborate, explain, qualify, and rationalize his answers. Language is of limited usefulness to the lower-class child. His world is not verbally organized. His world may be noisy, with a lot of people shouting and talking, but the function of speech is limited. Much of the noise is not meaningfully related to the child and is not instructive. Verbal exchanges consist largely of orders, requests, and threats expressed in single words, short sentences, and abbreviated idiomatic expressions. There is little reason for careful listening in order to make fine auditory discriminations. The detection of gross cues addressed specifically to him is sufficient for the child to function satisfactorily in the lower-class culture.

The noisy environment with a minimum of informational content is ideal for teaching the child to be inattentive. When only a small portion of language is instructive and gross conventional cues are sufficient to convey general meanings, the child gets little practice in learning to make fine verbal distinctions and to develop precise speech. When so much speech is noise, he learns to respond to tone of voice and emotional overtones, rather than to the words which are used.

Lower-class speech involves extensive use of simple dogmatic statements and gross dichotomous classifications, with a minimum of reservation, qualifications, and withholding of judgments. Because the speaker fails to particularize, to make characterizations and differentiations, lower-class language is essentially impersonal. People are either "good ones" or "bad ones." You must be either for or against. Things are black or white. The impersonal characteristic of lower-class speech results from the speaker forcing all people and acts into a few simple categories. Distinctions are blurred, small but significant differences are disregarded, and fine but important discriminations are not made. To illustrate this we will borrow an example we have used before (Sawrey and Telford, 1968):

> "What kind of a person is he?"
> "He is a stinker."
> "Yes, but tell me precisely what kind of a person he seems to be."
> "He is just a stinker and nothing else."
> "But he is gracious and well-mannered; he is a good worker and co-operates well with others. The only objection I have to him is that he tries to be all things to all people, which makes him seem to be two-faced. Isn't that so?"
> "Well, that's just what I said. He's two-faced, and anyone that is two-faced is a stinker."

The more restricted speech of the lower classes makes use of a narrow range of idiomatic expressions which emphasize the general feelings of the speaker rather than the rationality of that which is said. Convenient, abbreviated tags are hung on people and their acts which serve to catalog them according to the speaker's emotional reactions. Such speech makes maximum use of simile, analogy, and nicknames, or of slang, profane, and obscene language. The use of similes, analogies, and nicknames, in place of rational, critical evaluation, results in caricatures of reality. It typically magnifies superficial differences and categorizes people and actions on the basis of characteristics with high visibility, and either glosses over, or disregards entirely, more fundamental similarities or differences.

Slang, profanity, and obscenity do not make language more informative. They do not impart information. They signify how the speaker feels, his social origins, or the poverty of his vocabulary. The person whose speech is restricted to the lower-class linguistic code attempts to carry conviction by the emotional overtones and exaggerated emphasis of words and manner of speaking, rather than by the informational impact of what is said. The final phrases of statements made within the framework of a restricted code serve to emphasize the impact of what is said or to test to see if the desired effect is being registered. ("Imagine that!" "Isn't that awful?" "You see?" "Isn't that so?") The restricted language pattern is often vivid and abbreviated. Its liberal use of nicknames, its shortened words and phrases, its liberal use of slang and profanity give an earthiness, a simplicity, and a picturesqueness which make it seem richer than the more formal and precise speech of the educated middle- or upper-class person. However, the apparently freer use of language, the seeming originality, and the graphic quality often obscure the poverty of its content.

Language serves different functions for the lower-class than for the typical middle- or upper-class person. For the lower-class individual, language serves to control others and to express feelings more than to convey information, and the force of the language derives from the power and status of the speaker rather than from the information it imparts. Behavior is regulated not by the probable consequences of the act itself, but according to the relationship of the speaker and the listener. The child obeys not because of the instructional content of what he is told, but because the speaker is his father, mother, teacher, policeman, or someone else with power or authority. What is said is less important than who says it. When the child responds to a demand by saying, "Who says I have to?" he is making an explicit reference to this. When the child's "Why?" is answered either implicity or explicitly by, "Because I say so," or "Because I am your mother," the emphasis is on a status or power relationship rather than on the rationality of the request.

The following conversational exchange illustrates several of these characteristics.

SON: "Can I go to town tonight?"
FATHER: "No, you certainly can not!"
SON: "Why not?"
FATHER: "You are always going to town."
SON: "Well, why shouldn't I?"
MOTHER: "Didn't you hear your father?"
SON: "Yes, but there is no reason why I shouldn't go."
FATHER: "I said you are not going and that's reason enough. Now shut up!"

Such a verbal exchange is characterized by the total lack of information exchanged, the emphasis on authority, and the use of language to control behavior rather than to instruct.

Bernstein (1958, 1964) has called speech having the characteristic listed above a "public," "restricted," or "limited" linguistic code, as contrasted with the "formal" or "elaborated" code of the typical educated middle or upper-class person. Although we have referred to typical lower-class language as a restricted or public linguistic code, Bernstein (1964) points out that a restricted code is not necessarily social-class linked. It will arise in most closed communities or subgroups, such as prisons, armed-forces units, and peer groups. Much adolescent jargon is of this nature. Whenever speech is peculiar to a given group, whenever unique meanings develop which tend to be implicit and vague and are not verbally elaborated, you have the components of a restricted linguistic code. Members of a family may develop such codes. Twins often develop words and phrases with unique meanings.

The restricted linguistic code becomes cognitively significant *when it is the only code available to the individual.* It seems that many lower-class children and adults use only a restricted code and have access to no other. So long as the restricted lower-class language is used within a limited social context, it functions quite adequately. However, its usefulness is limited to a subculture where all members have somewhat the same frame of reference and the same code. This frame of reference is one in which power, status, and authoritarian relationships are controlling factors. When language functions largely to control behavior, ambiguity concerning status and power disturbs the persons involved. People using exclusively a restricted linguistic code attempt to structure social situations according to a hierarchy where age, sex, size, position, authority, or power provide clear prescriptions for appropriate behavior. Such people are greatly concerned with "Who is in charge around here?"

The middle- and upper-class cultures are more conducive to the development of multiple, elaborated linguistic codes. Such people can understand and use the more restricted language of the "street," but they are equally at home with alternative, more precise, and more discriminating language. In an elaborated linguistic code, language is primarily a medium for communicating relatively precise meanings. It makes explicit the similarities and differences among people, acts, percepts, and concepts. A speaker's skills, information, and unique personal traits are more significant than the status and power he represents. Expecting that speakers will play many roles and use different language systems, the listener depends on the precise verbal transmission of meaning and less on the status of the speaker, his tone of voice, and the emotional impact of his speech. An elaborated linguistic code focusses attention on the consequences of behavior and on the rational relationships between behavior and its consequences, rather than on the power and status relationships of the people involved.

The child using an elaborated linguistic code, or alternate language codes, comes to perceive other people as sources of information rather than as controllers of behavior. When the other person rationalizes his behavior in terms of information and his sources of information, the child is learning one of the social skills of the successful man in his culture. He is learning to seek information from books, magazines, and libraries, as well as from other people. The child learns that knowledge, as well as people, has power to control the social and physical world.

Rationalizing one's behavior in terms of probable consequences emphasizes a long-range time orientation. When language is used to relate what was done yesterday to today's events, and the probable consequences of today's occurrences to what will happen tomorrow, it makes the child aware of the consistencies and continuities involved in his life. Out of such experiences grow well-ingrained expectations of reward for starting jobs promptly, performing well, and completing tasks.

Apart from the use of linguistic codes which minimize the instructional functions of language, the free time that might be used by the lower-class parent in instructing the child is limited. Economic stress requires that all adults work long hours. Homes are overcrowded, and the parents are so preoccupied with life's insistent demands that they discourage questions. Unaware of the child's needs and unable to serve as sources of information themselves, they do not provide alternate sources or encourage the child to use books, libraries, and schools.

When the linguistically limited child enters school and does not understand the instructions or information provided, he does not ask questions which might help him and so he falls farther and farther behind. His habits of inattention, and his dependence on gross cues and status relationships as guides to conduct, keep him from perceiving the precise meaning of what is said, and so he fails to understand. His inattention is, in turn, perpetuated by his failure to comprehend what is going on. There is evidence that social-class differences in the general environmental orientation and in the perceptual abilities of schoolchildren *decrease* with chronological age, whereas social *language differences tend to increase* (Deutsch, 1964).

Early linguistic patterns are more resistant to change by ordinary educational experiences than are general perceptual and orientational processes. Social-class differences in language are not entirely accounted for in terms of measured intelligence. They persist even when groups of children are matched for both verbal and nonverbal mental age and school grade (Robinson, 1965). Many lines of evidence indicate that language is the area most sensitive to the impact of the multiplicity of problems associated with experiential deprivation and cultural disadvantage.

It is easy to misunderstand the distinction between a "public," "restricted," or "limited" and a "formal" or "elaborated" linguistic code. Because the restricted language is predominantly that of the lower classes and because it makes maximum use of monosyllabic words, short and grammatically simple sentences, and little use of subordinate clauses and qualifying terms, it seems to be a very parsimonious and direct form of speech. On the other hand, the "formal" or "elaborated" language of the school and of the middle and upper classes uses more polysyllabic words, more complex and involved sentence structures, and more qualifying terms and phrases. Many people, therefore, perceive formal speech as simply a complicated, involved, high-toned, and stilted way of saying the same things that are said more simply and directly in public speech. The people whose only linguistic code is a restricted one perceive the person using formal language as saying things that everyone knows in ways that are unnecessarily hard to understand. Conversely, many people view public, restricted speech as the coarse, vulgar language of the gutter, which is simply not used by nice people. To use formal language identifies one as belonging to a superior social and intellectual class. While differences in language usage may carry such connotations, these are not the essential cognitive differences.

Perhaps a distinction between ostentatious or pedantic speech, on the one hand, and what Bernstein (1958) and others have called "formal" or "elaborated" language, on the other, should be made. When a person says "He arrived prematurely" instead of "He came too soon," "What is your destination?" instead of "Where are you going?" or "In the event that he comes" instead of "If he comes," he is only being ostentatious or pedantic. The simpler speech is just as precise and informative as the more involved. These linguistic differences may have some sociological significance, but their cognitive differences are minimal. Certain words are not preferred because of their differing emotional connotations. For example: "spit" is less preferred than "saliva," "naked" than "nude," and the many four-letter Anglo-Saxon words than their polysyllabic equivalents of Greek or

Latin origin. Why the Anglo-Saxon terms have come to be considered coarse, ugly, vulgar, obscene, and therefore to be avoided is a question quite apart from their cognitive differences, which in many cases are nonexistent.

Every academic discipline, to a degree, has its own elaborated linguistic code. The language system related to a particular field consists of the terms and concepts which have specific, precise meanings and usages for that field. Sometimes these terms and concepts are developed within, and limited to, a given field of study. Other terms are borrowed from common usage but are given limited and precise definitions within the discipline. The uninitiated often mistakenly perceives the technical scientific vocabulary of medicine, for example, as the more erudite and complex equivalents of the words in common usage. However, the "streptococcal infection of the pharynx" of the physician is not the medical equivalent of the layman's "sore throat." The "sore throat" of the nonmedical person may be an allergic phenomenon, an inflammatory reaction, a bacterial or viral infection, or a benign or a malignant tumor. The differences are very important to the physician. To a degree, becoming proficient in a specialized field of knowledge consists in learning to observe and learn the significance of differences which are disregarded by the untrained person. The complex technical vocabulary which develops within a field of knowledge is required to indicate and communicate fine differences, minute discriminations, and differentiating characteristics which seem insignificant or nonexistent to the layman but are of great significance to the specialist.

When the teacher and student see the problem of the culturally disadvantaged child with a limited language system as that of acquiring a new vocabulary or new set of terms and expressions for things the child already knows, they are probably mistaken. If the educational problem is perceived to be one of vocabulary building, the memorization of words becomes the remedy. However, so long as the child simply learns equivalent terms for his inadequate percepts and concepts, he is not attacking the primary difficulty. The child, in addition to learning new terms, also needs to change his perceptual and conceptual categories. He must learn to note and attach significance to differences which he has previously disregarded. He must learn to differentiate in areas which were previously undifferentiated. He must become aware of, and learn to deal with, the complexities of the world without forcing it into a few simple categories which can be labelled with convenient tags. He must learn to consider other people and what they say as sources of information, rather than simply as restricting and controlling his behavior. When he learns that what is said is at least as important as who says it, he will discover that behavior can be guided by relevant information as well as by power and status relationships.

Social and Educational Needs of the Culturally Disadvantaged

The roots of motivation toward achievement in contemporary American culture are many and diverse. McClelland (1961), in an extensive series of studies, has rather convincingly linked strong motivation for achievement and national economic growth. He has also indicated, as we have in earlier sections, that a complex network of ethnic, religious, economic, and family influences are involved in producing an individual's unique motivational system. We cannot be sure just what economic factors, cultural and sub-cultural influences, and aspects of family life are effective in motivating people toward achievement. However it seems clear that strong motivation arises from a cluster of personal factors, including levels of aspiration and expectation, independence and self-reliance, adequacy of self-concept, and optimism of general outlook. Any programs devised to reduce cultural disadvantage need to be very broad.

ECONOMIC FACTORS IN CULTURAL DISADVANTAGE

While cultural disadvantage is not solely a matter of family financial status, it is one important factor. Oscar Lewis (1959; 1961) writes of "a culture of poverty," the patterns of which are amazingly similar whether the poor are in Mexico, the United States, or Israel. Although poverty is relative, it may be that when people in any dominant culture live near the subsistence level they are all reduced to a least common denominator and become very much alike. When life is a constant struggle for existence, when subsistence must be striven for, all values and all motives may merge into one.

Most poverty in the United States is relative. It is relative to the culture and to the expectations of the culture. When, in order barely to maintain a home, both parents are either working or looking for employment, when the home is overcrowded, when children are neglected, when parents are unemployed and without hope, or when parents are anxious and irritable, the prerequisites for instilling high levels of aspiration in the children are certainly lacking. Riessman, Cohen, and Pearl (1964) have estimated that ten billion dollars (less than 10 percent of our annual federal expenditures) would lift all the families in the United States above the poverty level. This alone would probably not solve the problems of cultural disadvantage. When the poor are not suffering acute deprivation, supplying more money makes no impact on their dependency and their basic attitudes. Increasing income above a certain minimum level will affect the motivational systems of the poor only when it diminishes their feelings of powerlessness and hopelessness, rather than because of the material things it provides. More money, when bestowed and controlled by others, does not reduce the recipients' feelings of isolation and incompetence. They still feel powerless. Poverty is cyclical for several reasons. The poor of one generation establish conditions—material, social, and psychological—which perpetuate poverty in the next. Increased money only makes possible the breaking of this cycle; it does not in itself reduce dependency or prevent the perpetuation of the expectancy of dependency.

If parents, despite their poverty, have maintained high levels of aspiration for their children and are sufficiently motivated, more money may make it possible for them to realize their aspirations. Potentiality does not generate its own motives. Potentiality requires both opportunity and incentives for its realization. Money only provides the opportunity.

EDUCATIONAL FACTORS

It is clear that conventional schooling has not been successful in overcoming the cultural disadvantage of the bulk of the lower-class children. The difference between the advantaged and the disadvantaged child, relatively small in the kindergarten and first grade, becomes larger with each additional school year (Bloom, Whiteman, and Deutsch, 1963). The disadvantaged child's deficit becomes cumulative. The typical lower-class child enters school so poorly prepared that initial failures are almost inevitable, and so school experiences are negative. As we have already indicated, the disadvantaged child's preschool environment has not provided the necessary background for education. His life has had little systematic ordering of experiences. He has not learned to make pertinent discriminations. He has failed to develop habits of sustained attention. He has not learned about sources of information—adults, books, newspapers, magazines, and libraries. He has not built up expectations of reward for being informed, acquiring skills, starting promptly, doing one's best, completing tasks, and delaying gratification. His home has failed to provide a rich language experience and the good models of speech with the constant corrective feedback from interested adults which are necessary to adequate language development. Because of these deficiencies, the lower-class child enters school handicapped by a pattern of socially induced disabilities.

When a child enters school with such handicaps, and experiences failure, he becomes discouraged and his deficiencies become accentuated. Each year produces increasing frustration and failure. Eventually he becomes alienated from the school and seeks satisfactions elsewhere.

The first years of school are critical in the child's life. If learning at this time is not successful and satisfying, the person's entire educational career is jeopardized. Repeated failure instills in the child an unsatisfactory self-concept and an antagonistic attitude toward school and learning in general. To increase the probability of success, the handicaps of cultural disadvantage must be attacked before the child enters school. Caldwell (1970) has provided a good discussion of the importance of early intervention if the deleterious effects of cultural disadvantage are to be reduced.

Some educational programs designed specifically for the culturally disadvantaged were begun in the early 1960s. The Economic Opportunities Program instituted in 1965, and particularly the Operation Head Start portion of it, were designed specifically to provide preschool programs for these children. These programs are based on the assumption that early intervention in the child's life will significantly reduce the handicapping influence of a culturally impoverished environment. While these programs are still developing, most of them are modified nursery school and kindergarten programs.

The first nursery school on record was organized in a London slum area to meet the needs of just such a disadvantaged population (Spodek, 1965). The first kindergarten established by Maria Montessori in Rome was for the children living in the San Lorenzo section of Rome—a slum district. It is interesting that the early 1960s witnessed a revival of the Montessori kindergartens in America and a return of part of the nursery school and kindergarten movements to the purpose for which many of them were originally developed (Montessori, 1964).

SPECIAL PROGRAMS FOR CULTURALLY DISADVANTAGED CHILDREN

The special educational programs for the culturally disadvantaged are designed to develop intellectual and social competencies, positive self-concepts and social attitudes, and marketable vocational skills—appropriate objectives for all children. The principal difference between the programs designed for disadvantaged children and those for the more advantaged is that in the former many things must be specifically and formally taught whereas more advantaged children are taught these same things in the home and culture as a part of the normal developmental process. Programs specifically designed for the disadvantaged also attempt to prevent the development of expectations of failure and low levels of self-esteem which often arise from the child's failure to achieve in accordance with the expectations of the dominant culture.

In the area of intellectual and social competences, the special programs are designed to develop and enlarge the child's perceptual and conceptual repertoire and his communicative skills. This typically involves an enrichment of the child's experiences in an expanded nursery school or kinder-garten setting. At older ages field trips, audio-visual aids, and wide reading provide additional sources of enriched experience.

The special programs attempt to engender positive attitudes toward self and others, as well as toward the school and other social institutions. Experiences are provided which, it is hoped, will raise levels of aspiration and expectations and develop favorable self-images. The development of marketable skills is considered to be of paramount importance for these children since learning for its own sake, for leisure-time activities, or for aesthetic appreciation is considered to have little meaning and motiva-tional potency.

The home, the subculture, and the community are considered to be the primary sources of the child's cultural disadvantage. Consequently, efforts are often directed at involving the home in the "total push" program which is considered to be necessary if these programs are to have a signifi-cant impact on the child. Programs which are typical of many which have attempted to effect changes in disadvantaged children through their homes are Gray and Klaus (1965), Radin and Weikart (1967), and Klaus and Gray (1968).

TYPES OF EDUCATIONAL PROGRAMS
FOR THE OLDER DISADVANTAGED

In addition to the programs for the preschool child referred to above, some have covered the entire age range. Others have been designed pri-marily for school dropouts and adults (Bloom et al., 1965; Witty, 1967; Kohlberg, 1968; Hess and Bear, 1968).

VARIETIES OF PRESCHOOL PROGRAMS

Preschool programs for the culturally disadvantaged tend to be either of the traditional nursery-school type or of a more highly structured cogni-tively-oriented type. In a critical evaluation of these two types, Weikart (1967) placed the Alpern (1966) and Henderson (1965) projects and most of the early "Operation Head Start" programs in the first category. He placed such programs as the early Dawes (1942) program for orphanage children, the Kirk (1958) program for the mentally retarded, the Gray and Klaus (1965) program for disadvantaged black children, the Deutsch (1964) preschool and early education project, his own (Weikart, 1967), and the Bereiter programs developed at the University of Illinois in the more formally structured cognitively-oriented category.

Weikart (1967) concludes that the first-listed programs, following more or less traditional nursery-school practices, do improve the social and emotional adjustment of the child. However, the more highly structured and more task-oriented programs obtain social and emotional development as well as the more conventional nursery-school procedure does, and, in addition, produce significant intellectual development. Capobianco (1967) concurs in Weikart's evaluation.

Several studies published since Weikart's 1967 review support his contention that the more highly structured, cognitively-oriented programs have been more successful in compensating for the deficits of the disadvantaged child than have the more socially oriented conventional nursery school-like programs. Karnes et al. (1968a) found that a highly structured seven month program of language training for culturally disadvantaged three-year-olds produced substantial gains in measured intelligence (Stanford-Binet IQ) and psycholinguistic skills as measured by the Illinois Test of Psycholinguistic Abilities. Karnes et al. (1968b) in a second study found that a highly structured program focussed on the development of linguistic and cognitive skills produced significantly greater improvement in intellectual functioning (Stanford-Binet test scores), linguistic abilities (ITPA scores), perceptual development, and school readiness than did a more traditional program stressing personal, social, and motor development. McConnell et al. (1969) found comparable advantage for a daily program of specific linguistic and sensory perceptual instruction administered to disadvantaged children in two community day centers as compared with comparable children receiving a traditional kindergarten type program. Kodman (1970) obtained significant gains in Stanford-Binet IQ's of Appalachian disadvantaged children provided a program aimed at improving sensorimotor skills, language, perceptual, and cognitive development for a period of three-and-a-half school years.

The most recent report on the pioneering Klaus and Gray (1968) project shows that while their program was a rather intensive and extended one and produced gains which they characterized as modest, the gains have been maintained at a significant level for four years. Di Lorenzo and Salter (1968) in a two-year follow-up study of three groups of prekindergarten children through kindergarten, first, and second grades found the kindergarten experience to be beneficial for the disadvantaged children as indicated by significant differences between the total experimental and comparable control groups on the Stanford-Binet, Peabody Vocabulary Test, and the Illinois Test of Psycholinguistic Abilities. The authors claim that the most effective prekindergarten programs were the more structured cognitively oriented ones. The prekindergarten experience proved to be more effective for disadvantaged whites than for disadvantaged nonwhites. The white children maintained the advantage they enjoyed at the end of the prekindergarten but did not show any additional accumulative effects. On the other hand, the nonwhites did not maintain their advantage over the controls. This suggests that for long-term effectiveness nonwhites (more disadvantaged?) children require continued special programing to counteract the effects of the adverse circumstances of their lives.

It should be pointed out that the question of the relative efficacy of the more highly structured, cognitively-oriented as compared with the more personal, social, and motor development-oriented traditional nursery-school programs is by no means settled. Zigler and Butterfield (1968) claim that the increase in IQ following the highly structured programs is due to the reduction in debilitating motivational factors rather than to changes in rate or level of intellectual development. Likewise, Kohlberg (1968), after reviewing many of the same studies referred to above, claims that the changes obtained were more a result of changes in "cognitive motivation" than changes in "cognitive capacity." He insists that these changes soon reach a ceiling rather than moving continuously upward and that the motivational changes themselves do not lead to increased cognitive capacity.

Americans have always had great faith in the efficacy of education. Consequently it is not surprising that more and better education has been perceived as the answer to the problems posed by a large segment of the population which is economically and socially disadvantaged. In an advanced industrial society occupational success and social advancement are increasingly dependent upon intellectual competence. Where knowledge is power, education provides the key to social and economic status. The problems of poverty and social disadvantage were originally perceived as primarily an educational problem involving pedagogical concern with the basic questions of effective teaching and learning. However, the initial attempts to improve the performance of the disadvantaged by changing the quality of physical facilities, increasing the personnel assigned, and providing auxiliary services did not significantly improve the quality of learning. When the effects of family background are controlled for, school characteristics account for little of the remaining school achievement differences (Coleman, 1966). The findings of the Coleman report were discouraging to many people as have been the apparent educational effect of racial desegregation.

THE EFFECTS OF DESEGREGATION

The 1954 Supreme Court desegregation decision and opinions claimed that school segregation per se is harmful to children. However, at the time of this decision the empirical evidence supporting this claim was quite tenuous (Deutscher and Chein, 1948; Clark, 1953). Almost 20 years later the data supporting this claim are still meager. "Before and after" studies of school systems subsequently desegregated are almost universally poor in design and involve many uncontrolled variables. For example, segregation often was accompanied by an upgrading of the quality of education and many other changes which could well explain the gain in achievement.

However, such studies as we have suggest that, following segregation, children generally perform no worse and in most instances better than before. The studies show a strong effect of social class integration on achievement but the evidence is less clear for a residual relationship between ethnic group integregation and achievement. This is consistent with the finding that achievement is more closely correlated with social class than with race per se.

The laboratory studies (such as Katz, 1964; 1968) and inferences drawn from them together with the tenuous data from uncontrolled field studies suggest that the academic performance of disadvantaged minority ethnic group children is higher in integrated than in equivalent segregated schools provided the children are accepted and supported by peers and staff. In other words, improvement is dependent upon the presence of social and psychological rather than upon the mere fact of physical integration.

There is some evidence that a higher percentage of white students in the integrated classroom has a beneficial effect on the achievement of the disadvantaged minority. The earlier the Negro children have white classmates the higher their achievement (Coleman, 1966; U.S. Commission on Civil Rights, 1967). McPortland (1968) has also shown that school desegregation is significantly associated with higher achievement for black pupils only if they are in predominantly white classrooms, but classroom integration is to a degree favorable irrespective of what percentage of the school is white.

Program Evaluation

Even though attempts to upgrade education, desegregation of the schools and the development of programs designed specifically for the educationally and socially disadvantaged have been carried out extensively over the past fifteen years, it is still difficult to make any valid overall statements concerning their efficacy. It is generally agreed that the educational modifications and new programs have not lived up to the hopes and promises of their early advocates. Increasingly, it is recognized that the problems involved are much broader and more complex than originally assumed. It is becoming evident that the problems are not purely pedagogical but involve all aspects of the communities and the individuals involved. Reversing the negative impact of social insulation, ethnic discrimination, economic deprivation, low levels of social and self expectations has proved to be much more difficult than was anticipated.

Despite the expenditure of vast amounts of money and the establishment of a large number and wide variety of programs, surprisingly few positive findings which are of general applicability have emerged. The positive findings have been so frequently offset by negative ones, and the positive effects found immediately following training so often wash out in a few years (Plant and Southern, 1970; Shriver, 1967; Wilkerson, 1965), that some investigators have concluded that the compensatory education programs have failed (Blatt and Garfunkel, 1967; Jensen, 1969; Robinson, 1968; Kohlberg, 1968; Shriver, 1967; Fowler, 1968). "Explanations" for these failures range all the way from the claim that the resistance of intellectual functioning to change is because intelligence is primarily genetically determined (Jensen, 1969), through "critical period" hypotheses which claim that the basic processes underlying intellectual functioning rapidly lose their plasticity following about the third year of life (Bloom, 1964; Caldwell, 1970) resulting in a decreased susceptibility to environmental influences, to the contention that with increasing age the individual simply becomes increasingly "locked in" by his previously established patterns of thinking, feeling, and acting. However, the largest group of workers in the field remain convinced that the intellectual functioning of all children can be significantly modified if only the proper combination of learner characteristics and teaching methods can be evolved.

Some Philosophical Considerations

Since everyone to some extent is ethnocentric, each person sees his own unique way of life and his set of values as the best. Consequently, Americans typically view high levels of motivation for social and economic advancement as good.

There are many people who believe that, in certain ways, the south-Italian, Mexican, and Puerto-Rican peasant cultures are superior to that of middle-class American society. Their lack of concern with time, their sensitivity to and regard for personal feelings, their lack of reverence for power, their high evaluation of family and communal relationships, their high "affiliation motivation" and relatively low "achievement motivation" —to use McClelland's (1961) terminology—seem to be admirable traits. The extended family-godparent relationships, in which each member assumes responsibility for every other member, seems to be superior to the more highly competitive, egocentric American pattern. Weller (1965) has described the satisfactory and personally rewarding way of life of the independent Appalachian mountaineer who lacks interest in making money, in buying shiny new cars, or in keeping up with the Joneses. Confronted with a rugged and niggardly physical environment, the mountaineer has turned to the intimate personal relationships of his family and his local community as the primary sources of his satisfactions. In the urban factory the employer is, of course, mystified when the immigrant mountaineer returns to his job after an absence of a week and says that he had to go home for the funeral or marriage of a neighbor or second cousin. Work, efficiency, and money are subordinate to personal relationships and loyalties. Such values seem superior to the typical "market morality" of contemporary America.

Even the "familial amorality" of the Italian and the sexual adventurism of the Italian and Mexican male have their compensatory close affectional relationships. The lower-class, slum-dwelling Anglo-Americans have developed a somewhat unique subculture, with picturesque aspects and protective devices.

Cross-cultural studies indicate that no one society has a monopoly of those characteristics which contribute to personal satisfaction and social betterment. Consequently, many people ask why the typical middle-class virtues of hard work, thrift, and diligence, its high regard for formal education, its emphasis on the desirability of upward social mobility, and its belief that virtue carries its own reward must be imposed upon all people. Other cultures may be equally good, and a diversity of cultural patterns and values can add to and enrich a society.

In practice, only certain limited components of divergent cultures have been found to be sufficiently compatible with the mainstream of American life to persist relatively unchanged for long periods of time without the subcultures and individuals suffering because of them. The isolated, rural Appalachian and Cumberland mountain communities that have been by-passed by urbanization, industrialization, and tourism are ultimately penalized for their backwardness. They cannot remain untouched by national and world markets, federal and state legislation concerning schools, public health, taxation, social security, and public welfare. They ultimately find that even their limited needs and low levels of aspiration cannot be maintained as the differential in the price of the farm produce they sell and the things they buy becomes greater. The farmer with five acres and a mule is pushed below the subsistence level when he must compete with mechanized, large-scale, scientific agricultural practices. In order to survive, such people gravitate to the welfare rolls or migrate to the cities and merge with the hordes of culturally disadvantaged already there.

The religious groups which have tried to maintain their subcultures by insulating themselves in self-contained communities have been only partially successful. The Amish, Dukhobors, and Hutterites, for example, find that they are fighting a losing battle in trying to maintain their ways of life within a divergent culture. Because of the impossibility of completely insulating themselves from the dominant society, and either the impracticability of or dangers involved in excluding them from legal requirements concerning education, public health, taxation, fire and police regulations, these people find themselves continually on the move, seeking more congenial countries in which to live or conforming more to the demands and expectancies of the dominant culture.

There seems no practical alternative to judging, punishing, and rewarding people according to the dictates of the dominant cultural pattern within which they elect to or are forced to live. Whenever a group's subcultural practices and values place it at a significant disadvantage and either threaten or become a burden to the dominant culture, measures will be taken to change the situation. One basic way of doing this is to change the value systems and cultural patterns of the subgroup. Consequently, it is generally recognized that more money, compulsory school attendance, desegregation, and the elimination of discrimination, prejudice, and intolerance alone will not eliminate the handicap of the culturally disadvantaged. Their fundamental values, levels of aspiration, and expectations must be modified. The only practical approach to the basic problems of cultural disadvantage is the replacement of one set of values by another.

Are Intelligence Tests Unfair to the Culturally Deviant Child?

Tests and test scores in themselves are, of course, neither fair nor unfair. Tests have reliability and validity and are appropriate or inappropriate for particular purposes. It is only the treatment of individuals pursuant to the obtaining of test scores that can be appropriately labelled fair or unfair. Discussions concerning the use and misuse of psychological tests usually focus on intelligence tests. They are really scholastic aptitude tests. If we conceive of intelligence as the effective dealing with one's environment, intelligence tests are devised to indicate an individual's level of competence in dealing with the academic environment, the subworld of formal education. Intelligence is not an entity but an attribute of an individual, like beauty or speed. People function more or less adequately, i.e. intelligently, in terms of the demands and expectancies of the culture and situations in which they live.

All tests are culturally biased. Starting over a quarter of a century ago, and continuing up to the present, there have been periodic attempts to develop "culture free" or "culture fair" tests (see Steckle et al. (1969) for a recent effort). Today we recognize that there is no such thing. It is possible to decrease the specific cultural content in the development and validation of a given test but in doing so we diminish its usefulness in the social context where it is designed to be used. No single set of aptitudes is the paragon or prerequisite of survival and adaptability in all environments. Every society requires individuals capable of performing the necessary social and economic functions of that society, and inevitably will favor and reward aptitudes, behavior, and values contributing to those capabilities.

The intelligent and highly valued person in a hunting society is the person with keen vision and hearing, great strength and endurance, and good motor coordination so that he can detect, track down, and either capture or kill the animals of prey. These are the aptitudes upon which their survival depends. Successful living on the terms dictated by current industrialized society increasingly requires a background of success in school. Intelligence tests are designed to tap the scholastically relevant characteristics of the individual for use in educational placement and guidance.

In the school, welfare, or court situations where questions of intellectual competence arise, we do not start with mental test scores. We start with inadequacies in adaptive behavior. These inadequacies most often take the form of marked retardation in the development of sensorimotor, language, and self-help skill in the preschool period, failures in school learning during the school age period, and gross inadequacies in the broad social and economic competence realm in adulthood. We start with the observation that some individuals have acquired markedly less socially useful things or have learned them significantly less well than their peers. Systematic sampling of the individual's perceptual, learning, memory, and reasoning processes and the products of past learning (his repertoire of information and linguistic skills) by means of standardized tests help determine whether or not these demonstrated failures are due to deficiencies in the cognitive-learning realm.

In the senior author's experience screening children referred by teachers as probably mentally retarded, 20 percent of the time children so referred score within normal ranges on conventional mental tests. The educational inadequacies of such children are the result of something other than lack of scholastic aptitude. Scoring within normal ranges on such tests means: (1) that the perceptual, memory, judgmental, and reasoning aptitudes, (2) the fund of information acquired as the result of experiences common to children of comparable age and circumstances, and (3) the repertoire of specifically taught skills and information which are a necessary prerequisite to additional school learning are on too high a level for the individual's difficulties to be due to lack of intellectual competence. Today, children scoring within normal ranges on intelligence tests but who are markedly retarded in school achievement may be classified as "educationally handicapped," or as having "learning disabilities" and provided help as indicated in earlier chapters. When failures in adaptive behavior are accompanied by evidences of gross cognitive-intellectual inadequacies, the child may be identified as mentally retarded and become eligible for special assistance in a program more appropriate to his competences and level of functioning.

Is it fair to label and stigmatize a culturally deviant child as mentally retarded when his failures in learning are the result of his cultural deviancy? The components of his cultural deviancy which handicap him are (1) his different language, attitudes, values, and fund of information, (the ethnically different), (2) his lack of sufficient opportunity or incentive to acquire the necessary skills and information (the white ghetto child), or (3) his acquisition of maladaptive behavior patterns, values, and attitudes which operate to deter him from learning the more adaptive ones required by the dominant culture within which he either elects, or is forced, to live (either of the above mentioned groups).

In this context, we would insist that it is unfair to provide any child anything less than that program of education and training which will make it possible for him to function maximally in terms of (1) his own needs for autonomy and self-realization and (2) his need to deal effectively with the social and economic demands of his environment. What is "best" for a given child can be determined only by an appropriate matching of what he is with that program of education and training which will maximally facilitate his living and growing within the context of the demands and expectancies of his culture. This match is never perfect. The ideal program to fulfill these requirements is often either unavailable, nonexistent, or unknown.

In practice, the fairness or unfairness of educational practices can only be determined by people's judgments as to the relative appropriateness of the alternatives available. Most of the heated current discussions of this question focus on the placement of culturally deviant, disadvantaged, and/or minority ethnic group children in classes for the mentally retarded. The unfairness of such placements can only be judged in the context of the reasons for the placement and the available alternatives.

In the past the only alternatives open to a child who was failing to learn in school was either to leave him in the regular class or assign him to a special class for the mentally retarded. To take a specific example: Juan, age 12, fifth grade, bilingual, Mexican-American; educational achievement: reading, low first grade (practically a nonreader), arithmetic, second grade, geography, history and science, second to third grade; intelligence test scores: group test IQ's 50, 62, 49, 63, WISC verbal 55, performance 85, Full Scale 68, Stanford Binet IQ 65. Teachers' comments consistently indicate failure in all courses but periodical promotions because of age. Teachers' judgments indicate repeated failures possibly due to poor home conditions, lower social class, bilingualism, and Mexican-American background. Suggested category: culturally disadvantaged and/or mentally retarded. Teachers and principal recommend special class placement. Should Juan be certified as mentally retarded and placed in the special class?

If he is placed in the special class he will have the advantages of a small and ungraded class making possible much more individual help, a specially trained teacher who is more understanding and knowledgeable concerning children with special educational problems, an increased likelihood of having more success and fewer failure experiences, a more manually and vocationally oriented program terminating in a work-study program to assist in his transition from school to work, and a lessened likelihood of being a school dropout since the holding power of the special classes for the mentally retarded is greater than that of the regular class.

On the negative side, Juan in the special class will be officially designated mentally retarded. Although it is true that the mentally retarded are stigmatized and unofficially labelled in the regular classroom, the official labelling and segregation adds to the social devaluation. There is also a probability of his getting locked into the mentally retarded "track" and remaining there despite improvement sufficient to warrant his reassignment to a regular class. The assignment may become a self-fulfilling prophecy if Juan succumbs rather than strives to cope with his specific deficiencies and overcome them.

Of course, there is no objective way of drawing a balance between these relative advantages and disadvantages. It must be done in terms of one's subjective evaluation of each specific situation and individual. The senior author has often made recommendations for placement of such children because of considerations such as the following: Juan is in an impossible situation in the regular class. He cannot read and until he learns to read his outlook is hopeless. His fifth-grade teacher is neither competent nor has the time to teach him to read. If he remains in the regular class he will be a school dropout at the earliest possible time and he will not have even the minimal educational competences required to compete in the present world. The teacher of the class for the mentally retarded is bilingual, she understands and has been successful in working with children of this type, she has two other children in her class like Juan who are on about the same educational level. This teacher will probably be able to teach him to read, and this may make it possible for him to progress in the other school subjects. We will refer Juan to the special class, with the teacher's understanding that, in our opinion, Juan has the inherent potential for achieving; if he can learn to read and gain some confidence in himself he may be able to progress in his other subjects also. We recommend that he be retested every year and that if he progresses sufficiently he be transferred back into a regular class.

Today, many children who are educationally retarded primarily because of social and cultural deficits can be placed either in the classes for the educationally handicapped (learning disabilities) or in classes specifically set up for the culturally disadvantaged. This situation provides a wider variety of alternative special programs and/or teachers for children with educational problems which are primarily cognitive-learning in nature than was previously the case.

The senior author on several occasions has been asked to render a judgment as to the appropriateness of placement of individuals who as children were in classes for the mentally retarded but who, as adults, are now functioning intellectually and socially as either completely normal or as superior individuals. The request for such an opinion typically carries implications of malpractice, incompetence, or at least gross error on someone's part. The author has usually avoided the request by suggesting an alternative to the implied interpretations. This is to the effect that maybe such an individual was able to attain the status that he now enjoys because in the past someone in authority recognized that the individual was in need of help, and that the class for the mentally retarded was the only place where he could get it. He consequently was certified as mentally retarded as the only way to make the assistance available to him. He was assigned, received the needed assistance, and was then shifted out as able to progress to normal or greater heights because of, and not in spite of, the experience. Today, the need for this sort of assignment is much less than it was formerly, but because special programs and assistance are usually still restricted to certain specific categories or rigidly defined groups for legal and administrative purposes, it is often necessary to stretch the categories, definitions, and labels in order to provide the assistance to students who need it but do not qualify in terms of a literal interpretation of the administrative codes.

Maybe it is unfair to discriminate against the disadvantaged ghetto or minority ethnic group child by denying him the benefits of the special class and condemning him to continue in a completely hopeless and frustrating situation where he has been for the past four or five years because he is not "truly" mentally retarded while we freely provide these services to the equally retarded socially advantaged child whose mental deficiency is of genetic or organic etiology. If the special program is more effective in eradicating or diminishing the educational, social, and vocational handicap of the intellectually subnormal, it should be equally available to all, irrespective of etiology. Individuals can be either genetically or environmentally, organically or functionally handicapped, and there is no evidence that the etiology or the fact that at some point in the child's life the deficiency was preventable is relevant to his eligibility for special help nor, at the present state of our knowledge, do they call for differential educational, remedial, or rehabilitative programs or procedures.

If the minority ethnic child should not be placed in the special program because the benefits are so small or problematical that the child will be better off to remain in the regular class, the same thing may be equally true of all the mentally subnormal, and special classes as such should be eliminated. We have previously indicated that some people are saying just this (Lilly, 1970).

Shall We Reduce the Cultural Bias of Tests, School Curricula, and Society?

Current proposals to eleminate the cultural bias of tests, school curricula, and society usually oversimplify the problem. Scholastic aptitude tests are culturally oriented because schools are culturally oriented, and schools are culturally oriented because they are creatures of that culture and are designed to prepare the individual for successful living within that culture. Cultures are not changed by the decisions of test makers or teachers. They are not changed by the rational decisions or votes of sizable minorities or numerical majorities. Cultural changes involve the modification of a wide range of evaluative feelings and attitudes as well as individual and institutional practices. These attitudes and practices are acquired largely incidentally and unconsciously as a part of the individual's normal developmental processes. Cultures develop and change slowly.

We would like to suggest the types of changes that will be necessary before the orientation of schools and scholastically oriented tests can be changed. On an intermediate level, we must change our beliefs that certain categories of human activities are better than others and that people who, either inherently or because of early conditioning, are more proficient in these activities are more valuable than other people. People engaging in activities perceived as more immediately life-saving, life-perpetuating, and life-enhancing are considered more valuable than are people less directly concerned in these kinds of activities. Thus, medicine men and physicians, sages and teachers, holy men and priests are more highly valued than are peasants and unskilled workers. The skills and aptitudes which are necessary to attain these superior positions are also highly valued. The educational subgoals leading to these professions also borrow a part of the prestige enjoyed by the professions for which they are the prerequisites. So, reading, writing and arithmetical skills, as well as the knowledge necessary to attain these professional goals, are more highly valued than are physical strength and endurance, manual dexterity and motor skill required in the occupations with less prestige.

As modern technology phases out more and more of the "lower level" skills, only the more intellectual endeavors that are more difficult to replace by machines remain, with formal education and intellectual skills constituting increasingly the only avenue to monetary rewards and social prestige. However, it is obvious that factors such as scarcity also determine monetary rewards for skills and services and may increase the prestige and social status of previously devalued occupations. If plumbers, carpenters, electricians, maintenance, and service men continue in short supply, and their incomes soar (many now make more money than school superintendents and college presidents), the social value of the worker may cease to be symbolized by the color of his collar or how clean he can keep his hands. So long as the culture values highly the more intellectually demanding activities, the educational programs designed to train people to engage in these activities will continue to have high prestige, and tests designed to provide information concerning an individual's scholastic aptitudes and relevant skills will maintain their current intellectual orientation and cultural bias. The problem is not one of diminishing the cultural bias in school curricula and scholastic aptitude tests but to make sure that they are compatible with each other.

The authors feel that much of the current concern with test "overselecting" the disadvantaged for special class placement is misplaced. In practice, tests will not overselect the disadvantaged unless the educational tasks and teacher's judgments have already overselected them. Almost uniformly, tests are used to determine the eligibility of children for special class placement only *after* the child's school failures and teacher's judgments have identified them. Because of biased stereotypes teachers may over- or underselect in terms of educationally irrelevant variables such as social class, ethnic group membership, or sex. Tests and test items are inappropriate only if they differentiate between categories of students such as majority and minority group members and culturally advantaged and disadvantaged individuals either more or less sharply than do the broader social- and educational-success criteria. Educational success, teacher judgments, and test scores as criteria are valid to the extent that they select those, and only those, children who need special help or special class placement and subsequently profit from the experiences. These criteria are invalid to the extent that they certify and place in special classes or programs those who will actually profit more from continued attendance in regular classes (overselection) or fail to certify and place in special classes children who will profit additionally from such placement (underselection). The fact that more minority ethnic group children are certified for placement in special classes for the educationally handicapped and the mentally retarded can be variously interpreted. One explanation is that these individuals are caught in cross-cultural streams. Early learning is irrelevant or inconsistent with current learning. When discontinuities or inconsistencies between early and late environments exist, previous learning may be useless or handicapping in the new context.

An alternative interpretation is that the social and educational systems have been unable or unwilling to provide a sufficient variety of alternative programs or techniques to educate the diverse populations they serve within the regular school classes. Maybe "overselection" is really undereducation or inappropriate education. Despite frequent and cogent criticisms and occasional passionate and irrational tirades levelled against intelligence tests, a child's IQ obtained by a competent examiner has more significant educational and other behavioral correlates than any other single psychological measure (Kohlberg and Zigler, 1967).

It seems that the cultural bias will remain an essential component of scholastic aptitude tests. If we have a radical revision of educational programs as advocated by some people (Gordon and Wilkerson, 1966), the nature and bias of educationally oriented tests will change accordingly. Taking education as it is, conventional tests are as predictive of success in schools predominantly black as in schools predominantly white (Boney, 1966; Stanley and Porter, 1967; Roberts, 1962; Hills, Klock, and Lewis, 1963; Kendrick and Thomas, 1970). Studies directed specifically at an evaluation of the bias of conventional scholastic aptitude tests have found no difference in predictability for blacks and whites in either integrated or segregated schools (Cleary, 1968; Kendrick and Thomas, 1970). These tests also have been found to be equally useful for predicting the school achievement of both socially advantaged and socially disadvantaged students (Munday, 1965; Kendrick and Thomas, 1970).

Devising tests tailored to particular minority ethnic groups or to various disadvantaged subcultures will, of course, show differences in favor of the members of the various minorities. Although proposals to develop such tests have been recently presented anew, the senior author is sure that an "intelligence test" based on the culture of southwestern American Indians was developed in the late 1920s or early 1930s. However, we have been unable to locate a reference to it in the literature. This test, when administered to whites and American Indians, produced the anticipated differences in favor of the Indian children. Scores on such tests will presumably be predictive of success in the cultures for which they are designed but will be less indicative of aptitude for functioning in different cultures.

Adjust the School to the Child Rather Than the Child to the School

Some are suggesting that the adjustments to the disadvantaged school groups must be made by the educational system rather than adjusting the child to fit the school. This suggestion has an apparent reasonableness which makes it quite convincing. However, such statements can refer to two quite different things. On the one hand, it sometimes means that we must start where the child is in our attempts to educate him. The more we know about the family background, social status, ethnic group membership, and language, as well as the perceptual, conceptual, memory, and rational processes of the learner and his repertoire of educationally relevant meanings, information and skills, the more we will be able to relate what he is to his educational experiences. These are more or less self-evident truths which have been part of practically every good educational practice and technique for a long time.

On the other hand, adjusting the school to the child as applied to disadvantaged minority group children has sometimes meant not only accepting the child as an individual and understanding him in terms of his social experiences, but accepting his culture as a given and facilitating the child's development in that cultural direction. Most often the notion of maintaining the child's cultural heritage has centered on his deviant language.

The question is often raised as to the significance of the language deficit of socially disadvantaged children. Some workers see the deviant language of disadvantaged children as constituting the greatest hazard to academic success and subsequent life achievement. Some linguists perceive the deviant language as an impoverished linguistic code reflecting an equally impoverished underlying cognitive and intellectual mental organization. Other workers perceive the linguistically limited child as simply lacking the most important tool for learning. There are also those who maintain that children from culturally disadvantaged homes and communities are not really language handicapped. They insist that such children have functionally complete and adequate, although different, language systems of their own. These people claim that, from a purely linguistic point of view, nonstandard English is just as valid a language as standard English and it is only a kind of intellectual snobbery and provincialism that keeps us from recognizing this fact. The problem is seen by these linguists as being, not that of the speaker of nonstandard English, but that of the standard English speaking majority.

While it is theoretically a fact that an infinite variety of nonstandard English is just as functionally complete and equally legitimate as standard English, it is also true that deviant languages are not equally useful. If customers and clients prefer to patronize, if personnel officers prefer as employees, and fellow-workers are biased in favor of, people whose language they understand and who readily understand them, and if printed instructions and reports written by an employee all require the understanding and use of standard English, then the educational tolerance and/or encouragement of nonstandard English is of doubtful utility. If restriction to a nonstandard form of speech, for whatever reason, shuts off these individuals from significant social and economic opportunities the tolerance and even romanticizing of ghettoese and other deviant languages may be misguided. Deviant linguistic codes may be equally functional within their limited contexts but they are not equally negotiable. English is just as complete linguistically and just as "good" as French; but in France French is more useful and the Englishman who lives in a section of France where no one speaks or understands English will continue to function at a disadvantage until he learns to understand and speak French.

Until customers, clients, fellow-workers, personnel officers, and employers are all fluent in, and tolerant of, the various nonstandard forms of English, and until books, newspapers, magazines, and instructional materials are written in various nonstandard English dialects the linguistically different individuals will be at a disadvantage. Nonstandard English is less useful because less people understand, accept, and value it. It is not "bad," it is simply less negotiable, and linguists who point out the beauties of ghettoese and insist that the disadvantaged should not be required to learn anything else must either make all others multilingual so the ghetto child can remain monolingual or the disadvantaged minority will continue to function at a disadvantage in their search for greater economic and social opportunities.

However, language is only a part of one's culture and many components of deviant cultures can be maintained without handicapping those who elect to retain them. The minority ethnic groups can retain their unique forms of family organization—the extended family and close family ties of the Spanish-Americans and the Jews. They can keep their family traditions and practices, their native dress to be worn either for special occasions or as much and for as long as they wish, celebrate their national holidays and honor their national heroes either within their own group or in public with others joining in, perpetuate their folklore, perform their national dances and sing their songs, maintain special full- or part-time schools, if necessary, to teach the young concerning their native culture, history, and traditions as the Japanese and Jews did until they felt it was no longer necessary. They can live within their "urban villages" as Gans (1962) has shown some Italian-Americans have done. The perpetuation of these practices produces what we have always had to a degree in America, a cultural pluralism (Glazer and Moynihan, 1963).

Ideally such a cultural pluralism permits each individual and group either to integrate and assimilate into the larger culture or to maintain as much of his native culture as he wishes, every person and group being free to give up or maintain as much of his group or ethnic identity as he chooses. Every person should have free access to all the rights, opportunities and be equally obligated to assume the obligations and responsibilities of society. He may marry across color and ethnic group lines at his own discretion and without penalties. He should be able to live wherever he chooses and on any standard he can afford. Children of all races, social classes, intellectual levels, and with all degrees of handicap should be provided that type of training and educational program which will make it possible for them to attain maximum self-realization and satisfaction and to deal most effectively with the social and economic demands of their world. In a broader context, society should insure a minimum standard of living for all, with maximum opportunities for self-realization and socialization, with incentives to work and satisfactions from work for all those able to produce, and minimum indignity for those unable to do so.

Summary

Individuals may function inadequately either because they lack the potentiality for learning or because of inadequate or inappropriate experiential backgrounds. The latter are the culturally disadvantaged. Cultural disadvantage is always relative to the demands and expectancies of the dominant culture of the society in which the person either elects or is required to live.

The culturally disadvantaged in contemporary American culture consist predominantly of certain minority groups with different national origins (Negroes, Puerto Ricans, Mexican-Americans), people inhabiting culturally impoverished rural areas, and most of the big, heterogeneous group of poverty-stricken slum dwellers. While most of the culturally disadvantaged are poor, not all of the poor are culturally impoverished.

The largest groups of different national or ethnic origins experiencing current cultural disadvantage are the Negroes, Puerto Ricans, Mexican-Americans, and to a lesser degree, the Italian-Americans. The Negro's disadvantage seems to stem predominantly from weakness in his family and communal life and his chronic poverty, which interact. The stresses of migration, urbanization, and unemployment always create problems, but when poverty is already chronic and patterns of family life and community organization already weak, the problems are greatly magnified.

Whereas the problems of the Negroes in America derive partially from the weakness of their family and communal structure, the failure of the Italians to strive for upward mobility and higher education stems from a strong, highly organized family and communal life which devalues these goals. The family life of the Puerto Rican and Mexican-Americans has some strengths and some weaknesses. The high percentage of consensual marriages and the sexual adventurism of the males constitute weaknesses of these families. However, the male responsibility for the support of his illegitimate as well as his legitimate children, the custom of providing godparents (co-parents) for each child, and the close affectional ties between parent—particlarly the mother—and child are elements of strength in these families.

The lower and lowest classes in America constitute the largest subgroups of the culturally disadvantaged. Some of the roots of, or concomitants of, the disadvantages experienced by this group are:

1. The constantly increasing educational and occupational demands and expectancies of the culture
2. The increased urbanization of the population resulting from mechanized, large-scale scientific farming, which has forced the marginal farm owners, share-croppers, and farm laborers to migrate to the cities
3. The increased proportion of the economically impoverished who have gravitated to the ghettoes of the poor, where they educate or miseducate each other
4. The people's distrust of impersonal agencies such as educational systems, public health departments, fire departments, public and private welfare agencies, and police departments designed to help them
5. The lack of stable family patterns, appropriate models of behavior, and incentive to achieve
6. The relatively low level of formal education as well as a lack of appropriate occupational skills
7. The lack of social skills and knowhow which make possible the use of the available sources of information, education, training, and assistance
8. The emphasis on fate or bad luck or the connivance of other people as the causes of their misfortunes
9. A more present than future time-orientation
10. The restriction of their perceptual and cognitive categories and systems, as evidenced by their dependence upon a restricted or public language system which has the following characteristics:
    a. It is more imperative than instructive. It is intended to control other people rather than instruct them.
    b. It is power and status-oriented. The power of language derives from the age, position, size, or strength of the speaker, rather than from the information imparted. Children learn to relate to the status of the speaker more than to the logic of the propositions or to the probable consequences of the acts.
    c. Public language makes extensive use of a limited range of dogmatic statements, and gross dichotomous classifications with a minimum of reservations and qualifications.
    d. The limited language code emphasizes and reinforces group solidarity by emphasizing similarities and minimizing individual differences.

e. The use of a restricted and unique linguistic code induces a sense of social identity and conformity at the expense of personal identity and individual uniqueness.

f. "Public" language is temporally limited, poorly structured, and informationally impoverished. Much of it is noise and encourages inattention.

Programs for the remediation of cultural disadvantage include:

1. Diminishing the restrictive influences of poverty, discrimination, and segregation.
2. Providing more and better educational and vocational training programs
3. Establishing preschool programs which intervene early enough in the child's life to have a major effect on the child's perceptual, conceptual, linguistic, and motivational systems

References

ALPERN, G. D., "The Failure of Nursery School Enrichment Programs for Culturally Disadvantaged Children," *Amer. j. orthopsychiat.*, XXXVI (1966), 244–45.

BAGDIKIAN, B. H., "National Poverty and National Rehabilitation," *J. rehabil.*, XXXI (1965), 34–40.

BANFIELD, E., *The Moral Basis of a Backward Society*. New York: The Free Press, 1958.

BATTLE, E. S., AND J. B. ROTTER, "Children's Feeling of Personal Contrast as Related to Social Class and Ethnic Group," *J. personal.*, XXXI (1963), 482–90.

BEREITER, C., AND S. ENGLEMANN, *Teaching Disadvantaged Children in the Preschool*. Englewood Cliffs, N.J.: Prentice-Hall, Inc., 1966.

BERNSTEIN, B., "Social Class and Linguistic Development: A Theory of Social Learning," *Brit. j. sociol.*, IX (1958), 159–74.

———, "Social Class Speech Systems and Psychotherapy," in *Mental Health of the Poor*, eds. F. Riessman, J. Cohen, and A. Pearl. New York: The Free Press, 1964.

BLATT, B., AND F. GARFUNKEL, "Educating Intelligence: Determinants of School Behavior of Disadvantaged Children," *Except. child.*, XXXIII (1967), 601–8.

BLOOM, B. S., *Stability and Change in Human Characteristics*. New York: John Wiley and Sons, Inc., 1964.

———, A. DAVIS, AND R. HESS, *Compensatory Education for Cultural Deprivation*. New York: Holt, Rinehart & Winston, Inc., 1965.

BLOOM, R., M. WHITEMAN, AND M. DEUTSCH, "Race and Social Class as Separate Factors Related to Social Environment." Paper read at Amer. Psychol. Assoc., Philadelphia, 1963.

BLOOMGARDEN, L., "Medical School Quotas and National Health," *Commentary*, XXIII (1957), 506–15.

BONEY, J. D. "Predicting the Academic Achievement of Secondary School Negro Students," *Personnel and guidance j.*, XLIV (1966), 700–703.

BUSMA, J. H., *Spanish Speaking Groups in the United States*. Durham, N.C.: Duke University Press, 1954.

CAPOBIANCO, R. J., "A Pilot Project for Culturally Disadvantaged Pre-School Children," *J. spec. edu.*, I (1967), 191–96.

CALDWELL, B. M., "The Rationale for Early Intervention," *Except. child.*, XXXVI (1970), 717–26.

CLARK, H. B., "Desegregation: An Appraisal of the Evidence," *J. soc. issues*, IX (1953), 1–76.

CLARK, M., *Health in the Mexican-American Culture*. Berkeley, Calif.: University of California Press, 1959.

CLEARY, T. A., "Test Bias: Prediction of Grades of Negro and White Students in Integrated Colleges, *J. educ. meas.*, V (1968), 115–24.

COHEN, D. K., "Immigrants and the Schools," *Rev. educ. res.*, XL (1970), 13–27.

COLEMAN, J. S., *Equality of Educational Opportunity*. U.S. Dept. of Health, Education, and Welfare. Office of Education, Washington, D.C. Superintendent of Documents, Government Printing Office, Washington, D.C. 1966.

CUTTS, W. G., "Special Language Problems of the Culturally Deprived Child," *Clearing house*, XXXVII (1962), 80–83.

DAWES, H. C., "A Study of the Effect of an Educational Program upon Language Development and Related Mental Functions in Young Children," *J. exper. educ.*, XI (1942), 200–209.

DEMOS, G. D., "Attitudes of Mexican-American and Anglo-American Groups toward Education," *J. soc. psychol.*, LVII (1962), 249–56.

DEUTSCH, M. P., "Minority Group and Class Status as Related to Social and Personality Factors in Scholastic Achievement," *Soc. appl, anthr.*, Monog. No. 2 (1960).

———, "The Disadvantaged Child and the Learning Process," in *Mental Health of the Poor*, eds. F. Riessman, J. Cohen, and A. Pearl. New York: The Free Press, 1964.

———, AND B. BROWN, "Social Influences in Negro-White Intelligence," *J. soc. issues*, XX (1964), 24–35.

DEUTSCHER, M., *Institute for Developmental Studies: Annual Report.*, New York: New York Medical College, 1965.

———, AND CHEIN, I., "The Psychological Effects of Enforced Segregation: A Survey of Social Science Opinion," *J. psychol.*, XX (1948), 259–87.

DI LORENZO, L. T., AND R. SALTER, "An Evaluative Study of Prekindergarten Programs for Educationally Disadvantaged Children: Follow-up and Replication," *Except. child.*, XXXV (1968), 111–19.

FOERSTER, R. F., *The Italian Emigrant of Our Times*. Cambridge, Mass.: Harvard University Press, 1919.

FOWLER, W., "The Early Stimulation of Cognitive Development," in *Preschool Education: Theory, Research, and Action*, eds. R. Hess and R. Bear. Chicago, Ill.: Aldine Press, 1968.

GANS, H. J., *The Urban Villagers*. New York: The Free Press, 1962.

GINZBERG, E., AND D. W. BRAY, *The Uneducated*. New York: Columbia University Press, 1953.

GLAZER, N., AND D. P. MOYNIHAN, *Beyond the Melting Pot*. Cambridge, Mass.: Massachusetts Institute of Technology Press, 1963.

GORDON, E. W., AND D. A. WILKERSON, *Compensatory Education for the Disadvantaged.*, New York: College Entrance Examination Board, 1966.

GRAY, S., AND R. A. KLAUS, "An Experimental Preschool Program for Culturally Deprived Children," *Child develop.*, XXXVI (1965), 887–98.

HALSEY, A. H., J. FLOUD, AND C. A. ANDERSON, eds., *Education, Economy, and Society*. New York: The Free Press, 1961.

HARRINGTON, M., *The Other America*. New York: The Macmillan Company, 1963.

HARVEY, L., "The Delinquent Mexican Boy," *J. educ. res.*, XLII (1949), 417–24.

HENDERSON, A. S., *1965–66 Annual Progress Report to the Ford Foundation on the Preschool and Primary Education Project*. Harrisburg, Pa.: Council for Human Services, 1965.

HESS, R., AND R. BEAR, eds., *Preschool Education: Theory, Research, and Action*. Chicago, Ill.: Aldine Press, 1968.

———, AND V. SHIPMAN, "Early Blocks to Children's Learning," *Children*, XII (1965), 189–94.

HILLS, J. R., J. C. KLOCK, AND S. LEWIS, *Freshmen Norms of the University System of Georgia, 1960–1962*. Atlanta, Ga.: Office of Testing and Guidance, Regents of the Univ. System of Ga., 1963.

JENSEN, A. R., "How Much Can We Boost IQ and Scholastic Achievement?" *Harvard educat. rev.*, XXXIX (1969), 1–123.

KARNES, M. B., A. S. HODGINS, R. L. STONEBURNER, W. M. STUDLEY, AND J. A. TESKA. "Effects of a Highly Structured Program of Language Development on Intellectual Functioning and Psycholinguistic Development of Culturally Disadvantaged Three-Year-Olds," *J. spec. educat.*, II (1968a), 405–12.

———, A. S. HODGINS, AND J. A. TESKA, "An Evaluation of Two Preschool Programs for Disadvantaged Children: A Traditional and a Highly Structured Experimental Preschool," *Except. child.*, XXXIV (1968b), 667–76.

KATZ, I., "Review of Evidence Relating to Effects of Desegregation on the Intellectual Performance of Negroes," *Amer. pschol.*, XIX (1964), 381–99.

———, "Academic Motivation and Equal Educational Opportunity," *Harvard educat. rev.*, XXXVIII (1968), 57–65.

KENDRICK, S. A., AND C. L. THOMAS, "Transition from School to College," *Rev. educat. res.*, XL (1970), 151–79.

KIRK, S. A., *Early Education of the Mentally Retarded*. Urbana, Ill.: University of Illinois Press, 1958.

KITANO, H. H. L., "Japanese-American Mental Illness," in *Changing Perspectives in Mental Illness*, eds. S. C. Plog and R. P. Edgerton. New York: Holt, Rinehart & Winston, Inc., 1969a.

———, *Japanese-Americans: The Evolution of a Subculture*. Englewood Cliffs, N.J.: Prentice-Hall, Inc., 1969b.

KLAUS, R. A., AND S. W. GRAY, *The Early Training Project for Disadvantaged Children: A Report After Five Years. Monograph of the Society for Research in Child Development.* XXXIII, No. 4 (1968), Serial No. 120.

KODMAN, F., "Effects of Preschool Enrichment on Intellectual Performance of Appalachian Children," *Except. child.,* XXXVI (1970), 503–7.

KOHLBERG, L., "Early Education: A Cognitive-Developmental View," *Child develop.,* XXXIX (1968), 1013–62.

―――, AND E. ZIGLER, "The Impact of Cognitive Maturity on the Development of Sex Roles in the Years Four to Eight," *Genet. psychol. monog.,* LXXV (1967), 89–165.

KRAMER, J. R., AND S. LEVENTMAN, *Children of the Gilded Ghetto.* New Haven, Conn.: Yale University Press, 1961.

LEWIS, O., *Five Families: Mexican Case Studies in the Culture of Poverty.* New York: Basic Books, Inc., Publishers, 1959.

―――, *Tepoztlán: Village in Mexico.* New York: Holt, Rinehart & Winston, Inc., 1960.

―――, *The Children of Sanchez: Autobiography of a Mexican Family.* New York: Random House, Inc., 1961.

―――, *Pedro Martinez: A Mexican Peasant and His Family.* New York: Random House, Inc., 1964.

LILLY, M. S., "Special Education: A Teapot in a Tempest," *Except. child.,* XXXVII (1970), 43–49.

McCLELLAND, D. C., *The Achieving Society.* Princeton, N.J.: D. Van Nostrand Co., Inc., 1961.

McCONNELL, F., K. B. HORTON, AND B. R. SMITH, "Language Development and Cutural Disadvantage," *Except. child.,* XXXV (1969), 597–606.

McPORTLAND, J., *The Segregated Student in Desegregated Schools.* Baltimore, Md.: Johns Hopkins University, 1968.

MADSEN, M. C., "Cooperative and Competitive Motivation of Children in Three Mexican Subcultures," *Psychol. rep.,* XX (1967), 1307–20

―――, AND A. SHAPIRA, "Cooperative and Competitive Behavior of Urban Afro-American, Anglo-American, Mexican-American and Mexico Village Children," *Develop. psychol.,* III (1970), 16–20.

MONTESSORI, M., *The Montessori Method.* New York: Schocken Books, 1964. First published in English in 1912.

MUNDAY, L. A., "Predicting College Grades in Predominantly Negro Colleges," *J. educ. meas.,* II (1965), 157–60.

NAIR, K. *The Lonely Furrow: Farming in the United States, Japan, and India.* Ann Arbor, Mich.: University of Michigan Press, 1970.

PLANT, W. T., AND M. L. SOUTHERN, *Effects of Preschool Stimulation Upon Subsequent School Performance Among the Culturally Disadvantaged.* U.S. Dept. of Health, Education, and Welfare, Office of Education Project No. 5–0590, 1970.

PLAUT, R. L., "Increasing the Quantity and Quality of Negro Enrollment in College," *Harvard educ. rev.,* XXX (1960), 273–77.

RADIN, N., AND D. P. WEIKART, "A Home Teaching Program for Disadvantaged Preschool Children," *J. spec. educat.,* I (1967), 183–87.

REID, I. D., *The Negro Immigrant: His Background Characteristics and Social Adjustment, 1899–1937*. New York: Columbia University Press, 1949.

RIESSMAN, F., J. COHEN, AND A. PEARL, eds., *Mental Health of the Poor*. New York: The Free Press, 1964.

ROBERTS, S. O., *Studies in Identification of College Potential*. Nashville, Tenn.: Fisk University Dept. of Psychology, 1962.

ROBINSON, H., "The Problems of Timing in Preschool Education," in *Preschool Education: Theory, Research, and Action*, eds. R. Hess and R. Bear. Chicago, Ill.: Aldine Press, 1968.

ROBINSON, W. P., "Cloze Procedures for the Investigation of Differences in Language Usage," *Lang. speech*, VIII (1965), 42–55.

SAWREY, J. M., AND C. W. TELFORD, *Educational Psychology* (3rd ed.). Boston: Allyn & Bacon, Inc., 1968.

SHAPIRA, A., AND M. C. MADSEN, "Cooperative and Competitive Behavior of Kibbutz and Urban Children in Israel," *Child develop.*, XL (1969), 609–17.

SHRIVER, R. S., "After Head-Start, What?" *Child. educ.*, XLIV (1967), 2–3.

SMILANSKY, S., Progress Report on a Program to Demonstrate Ways of Using a Year of Kindergarten to Promote Cognitive Abilities, Impart Basic Information and Modify Attitudes of Culturally Deprived Children in Their First Two Years of School. Jerusalem: Henrietta Szold Institute, 1964. Reported in Bloom, B. S., A. Davis, and R. Hess, *Compensatory Education for Cultural Deprivation*. New York: Holt, Rinehart & Winston, Inc., 1965.

SPODEK, B., "Poverty, Education and the Young Child," *Educ. leadership*, XXII (1965), 593–604.

SROLE, L. AND T. S. LANGNER, "Protestant, Catholic, and Jew: Comparative Psychopathology," in *Changing Perspectives in Mental Health*. eds. S. G. Ploz and R. B. Edgerton. New York: Holt, Rinehart & Winston, 1969.

STANLEY, J. C., AND A. C. PORTER, "Correlation of Scholastic Aptitude Test Scores with College Grades for Negroes versus Whites. *J. educat. meas.*, IV (1967), 199–218.

STECKLE, L. C., R. W. HENDERSON, AND B. O. MURRAY, *WLW Culture-Fair Inventory*. New York: Personal Growth Press, 1969.

STRODTBECK, F. L., "Family Interaction, Values, and Achievement," in *Talent and Society*, ed. D. McClelland. Princeton, N.J.: D. Van Nostrand Co., 1958.

WELLER, J. E., *Yesterday's People: Life in Contemporary Appalachia*. Lexington, Ky.: University of Kentucky Press, 1965.

WEIKART, D. P., "Pre-school Program: Preliminary Findings," *J. spec. educ.*, I (1967), 163–81.

WHITE, T. H., *The Making of the President: 1964*. New York: Atheneum Publishers, 1965.

WILKERSON, D. A., "Review of Preschool Programs," *Rev. educat. res.*, XXXV (1965), 240–46.

WITTY, P. A., ed., *The Educationally Retarded and Disadvantaged*. The Sixty-sixth Yearbook of the National Society for the Study of Education. Chicago, Ill.: University of Chicago Press, 1967.

YAFFE, J., *The American Jew.*, New Haven, Conn.: Yale University Press, 1961.

ZIGLER, E., AND E. C. BUTTERFIELD, "Motivational Aspects of Changes in I.Q. Test Performance of Culturally Deprived Nursery School Children," *Child develop.*, XXXIX (1968), 1–14.

PROBLEMS OF
THE AGED

VI

17

The Aged

Age is an important variable in determining how individuals behave in relationship to each other. Young people's behavior in interaction with young people is different from young people's behavior with middle-aged or older people. The same is true for old people. Their behavior in regard to each other differs from their behavior relative to young people or middle-aged persons.

In speaking of the behavior of the aged it is recognized that there is an interaction between age and behavior. It is true, too, that there is an interaction between the variables of sex, age, and behavior. Old men behave differently toward other old males than they do toward elderly females and differently yet in relationship to the middle-aged and young of each sex. This is true also of older females. The behavior of the aged of both sexes is influenced by the social class within which they have lived and this influence is not identical for the two sexes. Social class is also a partial determinant of how long one will live. The interacting variables of concern have now grown to four—age, sex, social class, and behavior. Variables such as economic status, health, educational level, and others interact with age and sex in the determination of behavior and as a part of social-class determination. The interactive effects of many variables are to be found in the investigations of the aged. The effects of age alone, isolated from all other variables, are difficult to determine.

Who Are the Aged?

It is well recognized that there are individual differences among people as they develop, mature, and age. Some individuals are active, alert, and involved in this culture at seventy-five or eighty years of age while others at these ages may be sedentary, preoccupied, and introverted. The various capacities of the individual also age at different rates. It must be recognized that age can be considered biologically, psychologically, and sociologically. There are many indices of age and aging but for our purposes we shall take chronological age as the indicator. In the past the chronological age of sixty has been used as a convenient point at which to begin identification of the aged. More recently age 65 has been employed as the beginning of the period of old age. This number is probably utilized because it is a frequent age for compulsory retirement and the age at which eligibility for certain social benefits ensues. We shall use 60–65 as the beginning of the age of concern when considering the old-age group in the culture.

At mid-century there were 10 million people in the United States over 65 years of age; by 1960 there were about 16 million; in 1970 about 20 million, and by 1980 it is estimated that there will be 25 million over the age of 65. This will constitute roughly 10 percent of the total population (White House Conference on Aging, 1961). As life is prolonged by advances in social and medical science, the U.S. is becoming a greater older population than it has ever been before. There were five or six times as many people over 65 in the United States in 1970 as there were in 1900. The greater number of older people in the population does not reflect a prolongation of life for the aged but rather the greater proportion of the population which lives to old age. In 1900 the life expectancy for an American male was 49 years. It is almost 70 today. However, the life expectancy for men at the age of 65 is 14 additional years, compared to 13 additional years in 1900. Man is not living to be older and older but more men are living long enough to reach old age (Burger, 1969). The life expectancy for women is greater than for men and therefore women are disproportionately represented in the aged population.

Socioeconomic Status of the Aged

The median annual income for the single person over 65 years of age has been reported to be $1,055 with 30 percent of those over 65, single or married, living in poverty (Burger, 1969). The 1963 Social Security Survey of the Aged indicated that two-thirds of the married persons over 62 years of age had a median equity of $10,000 in nonfarm homes and median assets of $11,180 (including homes). Among couples with at least one of the partners over 65, 41 percent were classified as poor (i.e. they had an income of less than $2,500 per year). If all the assets of individuals are prorated as annual income over expected life, the median income for married couples over 65 would be $3,795 (Birren, 1970). These data indicate that a very high proportion (30 to 40 percent) of the aged readily can be classified as poor. In 1969, there were approximately 4.8 million people aged 65 and over who were living in poverty according to a United States Senate Special Committee on Aging report entitled "Economics of Aging" (Associated Press, 1971). Rapidly rising health costs also were reported as a serious problem for the elderly. Limited income is a serious obstacle to living the kind of life that they would like to live, for a high proportion of the aged. It is rather obvious that not enough is being done to provide for the social and economic security of our citizens over 65 years of age. Progress has been made in this regard, but certainly a nation cannot be content with over a third of its elderly citizens living on budgets so limited as to produce serious problems of insecurity, unhappiness, and even poor health.

INDIVIDUAL DIFFERENCES AMONG THE AGED

There is a danger when speaking of the aged to speak and think as if they really comprised an homogeneous group. About the only way this could be done with any semblance of accuracy would be with regard to chronological age.

An interesting and extensive investigation of old people in industrial societies reports that a large proportion of the aged in the United States, Great Britain, and Denmark are reasonably active and involved in the culture. They have continuing contacts with relatives and friends and appear to have made adequate social and personal adjustments. Their social role and declining physical status appear to have become an acceptable part of their lives. Remarkable similarities among the three industrial cultures were reported (Shanus et al., 1968). It has been indicated that a danger in reports of such investigations may be to deemphasize the heterogeneity of the aged population. It is easy to lose sight of the fact that there are minorities of significant size, within the group designated as aged, that lead lives of low quality and of relative isolation (Mechanic, 1969). The heterogeneity of the aged was given emphasis by the President's Council on Aging (1963) when their report was prefaced by the observations that:

The older American has nearly 18 million faces. The faces are those of:

Three ex-Presidents
Nearly ten percent of the entire United States population
Nearly 1-1/2 million people living on farms
More than one out of four United States Senators
Almost 2 million people working full time
Two of the nine United States Supreme Court Justices
More than 10,000 people over 100 years old
Over 12-1/2 million people getting social security benefits
Over 2.3 million war veterans
More than 3 million people who migrated from Europe to the United
    States

The following mosaic of probabilities was presented as a composite picture of the older American:

He may be between 65 and 70 but he is probably older;
He may have an adequate income but probably not;
He may be working but it is unlikely;
He may have a high school education but probably doesn't;
He may be in good health but probably isn't;
He may not receive social security but probably does;
He would like to have more to do but the opportunities don't exist;
He may collect a private pension but probably not;
He may have adequate health insurance but probably doesn't;
He may live alone but probably not.

It has been indicated that the following observation might be added: "He is probably a she." (Koller, 1968).

It is important that we not lose sight of individual differences when the aged are being discussed. Indeed they do have in common the fact that they are in the later years of life but wide differences do exist among them.

Stereotypical Views of the Aged

Stereotypical views of the aged emphasize one or more of the following negative qualities to a considerable degree. The aged are ineffective; they are cross, cranky, or critical; they are worn out physically as well as mentally (Lane, 1964). They are preoccupied with death or dying (Kogan and Shelton, 1962); most older people have "senile" qualities. These stereotypes seem to persist in the face of evidence that the beliefs are not true. The beliefs appear to derive in part, at least, from the study of institutionalized aged persons. When noninstitutionalized aged persons are investigated, there is little evidence to support the stereotypes (Swenson, 1962; Wiggins and Schoeck, 1961). Young people report that they believe that one of the greatest fears of many old people is of death and dying, while old people indicate that one of their greatest fears is of lack of money and financial insecurity (Kogan and Shelton, 1962). Older people appear to be more concerned with living conditions than with fear of death attributed to them by the young. This investigation reports greater similarities than differences in the beliefs of younger and older subjects relative to the aged but it also reports some important differences. The authors compare the relationship to that of a majority-minority group conflict in which the older persons are depicted as having the less desirable characteristics, e.g., they need financial assistance and affective support. However, the older group is not viewed as power oriented as is the typical minority. Indeed, they are judged as having few characteristics to support the view that power is desirable. The aged really do not fit the picture of a typical minority group for this and other reasons. For example, they are not identifiable from an early age and do not have prolonged experience with minority status. Everyone is a potential member of the group classified as "aged" and many factors influence his attitudes, beliefs, and behaviors besides those of chronological age. In commenting on the finding that independently living older people had less negative feelings of self worth than did an institutionalized group (Mason, 1954), Birren (1964, p. 247) observes that the personal circumstances of those over age sixty may be more important in determining attitudes and level of functioning than is chronological age. Personal circumstances (i.e. socioeconomic status, health, strength, availability of relatives, friends) may be sufficiently uniform within a group of the aged to produce some uniformity of attitude, belief, or behavior. It is tempting to assume that these attitudes are a function of age rather than personal circumstances. Caution should be used in interpreting the results of investigations where there are such confounding variables.

Problems of Investigating the Aged

In any area of research there are problems involved that are either exaggerations of problems associated with research in general or that are unique to particular research under consideration. Investigation of the aged is no exception. A very real and serious problem has to do with obtaining a sample of the aged that is large enough and representative enough so that adequate generalizations can be made. Recent research efforts have been undertaken with greater cognizance of this problem than was common a short while back. A great number of studies of old people have been conducted using institutionalized aged as the subjects. The vast majority of older people are not institutionalized. Less than 5 percent of the aged reside in institutions (Bader and Hoffman, 1966). It seems obvious that public institutions for the aged house those who are alone or rejected, isolated, of less good health, and the dependent as residents more frequently than those people would be represented in the entire population of the aged. Certainly, the 5 percent who are institutionalized cannot be taken as representative of the aged in general. Such investigations, if the sampling and other research variables are adequate, can yield information about the population of institutionalized aged, but not much on the rest of the aged population.

Many older persons are unwilling to serve as subjects in research investigations. This may be because they are suspicious that some of their capacities are diminishing and they do not want to be embarrassed by such a disclosure. It may be, too, that the aged simply feel that there is little that they personally can gain from research, the results of which will not be available for some period of time.

There have been few studies that are longitudinal in nature. That is, most investigations have dealt with a population of the aged and have compared the group of aged persons studied to groups of younger people. Such cross-sectional investigations fail to take into account the influence of cultural changes. What has been interpreted as changes occurring with age may be only differences among age groups due to cultural change. In order to really determine what psychological changes are attributable to age, aging must be studied within a group of individuals. This takes time. Investigations of the characteristics of a group of persons over time will have to be carried out by an institute or organization since the time lapse involved will often exceed the adult life of a single investigator. The best known of the longitudinal studies is probably the one on the gifted started by Terman at Stanford University. Terman and Oden (1959) have already reported on the gifted group at mid-life. Subsequent reports on this group should prove to be most enlightening. Until the results of such longitudinal investigations are reported, much of our knowledge of change due to aging must be extrapolated from cross-sectional investigations.

Characteristics of the Aged

The period of old age is characterized as a period of slowing down; a period of decline of certain abilities; a period requiring social, psychological and physical adaptation to changed or changing circumstance.

That physiological changes occur with aging appears to be self-evident. Infants are different from children who differ from young adults who in turn are different from the middle aged. Old age would seem to be an arbitrarily designated span toward the end of the life cycle of the individual in which physical signs of decline in function and structure become noticeable. These aspects of decline due to aging are to be distinguished from those due to injury, disease, or other pathological processes.

Longevity is a function of a great number of influences. These include what appear to be heritable predispositions in survival for given periods of time. Genetic influences on longevity are operative throughout the lifespan of the individual as are environmental influences. The damage incurred by injury, disease, and nutritional deficiency is probably cumulative over the life span and is irreversible in its effects as far as the longevity of the individual is concerned.

There is a tendency for children to have length of lives similar to their parents. Even more convincing of the genetic bases for longevity are the studies of aging in twins by Kallman and Jarvik (1959). They found the causes of death to be more similar in one-egg than in two-egg twins and the difference in age of death among those dying past the age of sixty was found to be less for one-egg twins than two-egg twins. Such evidence strongly suggests that longevity is a partial function of genetics. One-egg twins show a remarkable similarity in intellectual functioning as well as appearance in later life. It is well recognized that environmental circumstances tend to have greater communality in kinship groups than in the population in general, but, the influence of these factors notwithstanding, the genetic influence is strongly indicated. It could be that if humans mated selectively according to ancestral age, a longer life span would evolve. The physical condition of the elderly depends upon inheritance factors, manner of living, accident, injury, disease factors and other environmental influences.

PHYSICAL CHANGES AMONG THE AGED

Physical stature declines with age. This results primarily from the stooping of the shoulders which gives the appearance of being smaller. There is also some shrinking of the vertebral cartilages which reduces actual height. Arms and legs may have wrinkles and appear to be flabby. Changes in the appearance of the skin can be rather marked. The epidermis thins and becomes more flexible and flaccid with age. Under the skin, tissues become less elastic because of the atrophy of elastic fibers from the intercellular matrix. The skin appears to sag and wrinkle. Sweat and oil glands atrophy with age and tend to make the skin somewhat dry and coarse. These factors are superimposed on those of diminution of secondary sex characteristics, loss of muscle tone, and muscular and joint stiffness. The movement of the aged is characterized by shortened stride, a widened base, and a slight leaning forward.

Tremors in the hands and face of older people are not at all uncommon. These tremors are more noticeable when the individual is tired or is emotionally aroused. Loss of hair that results in a sparsely haired scalp or in baldness, especially in men, is a common characteristic of the aged as is loss of hair color that results in gray or white hair. Hair in the opening of the ear and in the nostrils is usually coarse and bristly. The eyebrows may become somewhat bushy and bristly as well.

Facial appearance is affected by dryness and wrinkles of the skin along with other factors. Many older people have lost their teeth or they have worn down and give a pinched expression to the mouth and face. The cheek muscles sag a bit, eyelids are baggy, and the eyes may appear lusterless and watery due to inadequate tear gland function.

The changes in physical appearance of the aged are reflections of changing physiological structures and functions. Changes that occur at the cellular level in the skeleton produce bones that are brittle, become subject to fractures which are slow in healing. Visceral changes, particularly atrophy of the testes, liver, lungs and kidneys, are a part of aging. The central nervous system does not go unaffected. There appears to be a decrease in brain weight with advancing age. However, great brain weight loss is probably a function of pathological processes rather than of the normal aging process (Bondareff, 1959). Loss of cells in the nervous system with aging occurs in the human cortex (Brody, 1955).

Changes in physiological functions are of great significance in the lives of the aged. There tends to be a decrease in the amount and quality of sleep among older people and they tend to suffer from insomnia (Roffwarg et al., 1966). Difficulties with teeth and chewing coupled with a decline in taste sensitivity with age (Cooper et al., 1959) result in changes in food intake among the aged. They tend to eat less and to eat more frequently.

Blood pressure increase because of the rigidity of arterial walls is rather common (Master and Lasser, 1964). Shortness of breath and increased heart beat rate take longer to return to normal following exertion than they do for younger people. The aged cannot tolerate extremes of temperature and are particularly sensitive to reduced temperatures (Hurlock, 1968). General strength and work capacity decline in old age and recuperation from fatigue takes longer among those of advanced age (Hurlock, 1968).

SENSORY CHANGES

It has already been indicated that changes in taste sensitivity occur with aging. In general, this is true of the other sensory functions. This decrease in sensory acuity with age is not as devastating in its consequence as might first be imagined. First of all in normal sensory function there is more than adequate sensory input for usual personal and social functioning. Considerable diminution of acuity can occur without producing incapacity. Moreover, except where the loss is extreme, adaptation to reduced sensory functioning is usually possible because the decline of efficiency occurs on a gradual basis. In addition, certain of the sensory processes (vision and hearing) can be given assistance with mechanical devices (glasses and hearing aids).

Vision is less efficient among older people than it is among younger adults. Ability to discriminate small objects decreases in the aged as does color sensitivity (Kleemeir, 1951); the pupil size of the eye diminishes with age (Birren et al., 1950) resulting in a reduced amount of light reaching the retina. Older persons require more light for good vision and, as a result, their vision shows more relative improvement than does the younger person when illumination is increased. Visual accommodation (the ability to focus on objects at varying distances) is less good among the aged. The eye accommodates to nearby objects by shortening the focal distance of the lens. With age the muscular system weakens and the lens loses its elasticity thus decreasing accommodation to objects close to the eye.

Loss of hearing efficiency is as common with aging as are changes in vision. Deterioration in hearing is greater for high frequencies than it is for others. Such loss of efficiency may be produced by prolonged exposure to high level noise but loss of sensitivity in the aged cannot be wholly explained by such injury. Reduced acuity is found among the aged who have no history of either acoustic injury or disease. Most of the aged, even though they do have reduced auditory acuity, can hear speech and have little difficulty in personal conversations. Loss of hearing is greater for males than for females in advanced years and older people are likely to blame their hearing deficiencies on the "mumbling" of others rather than on their own loss of hearing (Schaie et al., 1964). Sensitivity to pain diminishes with age. Beginning at about age 15 and becoming marked after age 60 (Schulderman and Zubek, 1962), this loss of pain sensitivity may be sufficient so that pain as a danger signal may become impaired.

The aged must adapt to the physical changes that occur with aging. Changes in physical appearance that may be rather profound can be of particular importance in a culture such as ours with its emphasis on youthful beauty. The general decrease in sensory acuity that comes with aging must be accommodated for by the aged. This may prove harder than a first glance would indicate. Information about the world is filtered through the sensory equipment. Moreover, much of the enjoyment of living is derived from sensory functioning. If sights, sounds, and tastes are diminished or distorted much of their enjoyment is gone. If sensory efficiency becomes sufficiently reduced, social isolation is likely to occur and the aged must then adjust to social isolation in addition to reduced physical capacity and sensory efficiency.

INTELLECTIVE FUNCTIONING OF THE AGED

Changes in intellectual functioning with age may not be as great (Bayley, 1965; Bayley and Oden, 1955) or as important as is popularly assumed. While it is true that the performance of the aged on certain tests of intellectual functioning is not at as high a level as is the performance of younger persons, the importance of high performance in these areas in the lives of the aged has not really been established. Intelligence tests have been devised very largely to predict academic success. It is the young who attend school and must achieve therein. It is not clear that the same complex of abilities that contributes to the academic success of the young contribute equally to successful adult living in the later years. The cultural role of the aged is grossly different from that of the young and the complex of abilities required for success in the culture no doubt is different for the two groups.

The study of changes in intellect is best accomplished in studies of the same individuals over time (longitudinal studies) rather than the comparing of one age group with another at the same time (cross-sectional studies). Longitudinal investigations of mental abilities generally report significant decline in individuals after seventy years of age. Recent research findings have supported the hypothesis that decrements in learning among older people are not simply a function of structural changes in the central nervous system. The decrement, partially at least, is associated with heightened arousal of the autonomic nervous system that occurs when the learning situation is presented (Eisdorfer et al., 1970). There, of course, are pronounced individual differences in both rate and amount of decline. There is relatively less loss of mental efficiency among those of initially high intellect than among those of initially lower levels (Birren, 1961; Owens, 1966) and those who continue to be engaged in work tend to do better on intelligence tests than those who do not (Busse, 1955). It would seem that those who keep actively involved in their culture rather than become disengaged from it tend to maintain better intellective functioning. Rate of decline among those who continue to engage in learning tasks is not as great as for those who do not continue to get practice in learning (Berkowitz and Green, 1965).

Tests of general intelligence indicate a slight general decline as individuals approach sixty years of age (Owens, 1966). In tasks involving learning, older subjects tend to be more cautious, require more time to integrate their responses, and do not deal so readily with novel material as do younger ones (Birren et al., 1961). As task complexity increases older subjects require more time and sometimes do not understand the complex instructions that are required. They do less well even when they slow down (Birren et al., 1954). When tests of inductive and deductive reasoning are administered there is a decline in performance with age that has been interpreted as partially due to an increase in cautiousness with age (Birren et al., 1961; Botwinick, 1964; 1966). Memory for recent events is said to decline in old age, while memory for more remote events remains good. Motivation is an important factor in memory and recall and older people may not be motivated as strongly to remember as are the young. Because of lack of interest, poor habits of attention, and decline of sensory efficiency older people may not get as distinct an impression of what they see and hear as they should. This would contribute to apparent forgetting (Friedman, 1966). Greater difficulty is encountered in *recall* than in recognition by the aged, with the loss in ability to recall being considerable (Schonfield and Robertson, 1966). Of all of the measures used in tests of general intelligence, the one showing the least decline is vocabulary (Botwinick, 1964; Fox and Birren, 1950). Those intellectual activities that are dependent on verbal comprehension and language are less affected by aging than are those activities that are less language and vocabulary dependent. Tasks involving speed are particularily affected by aging. It has been suggested that the general decline in performance on speed measures is more than the slowing down of physical functioning and that they imply changes in control over the way stored information is used (Birren et al., 1962).

A certain amount of inflexibility or rigidity of perception as well as approach to problems is characteristic of older people. Such conceptual rigidity may begin in middle age and become more and more pronounced as age advances (Botwinick, 1964).

Creative work and scientific publication tend to be concentrated more among younger than older populations. Lehman's (1953) important studies of age and achievement indicate that both quality and quantity of output decline with age and that quality is likely to deteriorate more rapidly than is quantity of production. Dennis and Girden (1954) report that scientists in their sixties publish about half as much as those in their thirties and forties.

INTERESTS AND ACTIVITIES OF THE AGED

Changes in physical strength, sensory acuity, health and general level of energy of the aged are reflected in the decrease of activities requiring energy and exertion and an increase in sedentary activities (Kent, 1966). The narrowing of interests among the aged is a partial function of social class.

Lower-class individuals do not have as great a variety of interests as do those from higher social classes (Rose, 1966). Lower-class aged have less interest in community organizations and their forms of recreation are more limited (Rosenblatt, 1966). Interests and activities of the aged tend to be extensions of the interests and activities that were common at an earlier age. Those interests that offer the greater satisfactions tend to be retained as circumstances permit. Women tend to have a wider range of interests during adulthood and old age than do men. This could be due to the more frequent focusing of interests on vocational pursuits by men than women. Men frequently have difficulty in occupying their time when their vocational lives are interrupted by retirement (Rose, 1966; Rosenblatt, 1966).

Self-interest and self-centeredness tend to increase as people grow older. Thoughts about themselves, how they feel, and what they want to do occupy a significant portion of the life of the aged (Henry and Cummings, 1959). Concern for themselves, their health, and the past are parts of being self-centered that may contribute to unfavorable attitudes toward older people (Henry and Cummings, 1959). In spite of the tendency toward self-interest with age there appears to be, at least for many, a decrease in interest in clothing and appearance. The lack of interest in appearance results in carelessness in grooming habits and a failure to make the best possible appearance. Older men, probably because of previous habits of careful grooming as a vocational asset, tend to be more concerned for personal appearance than do older women. Socially active older people, of course, tend to be more appearance conscious and more interested in clothing than are those who are socially withdrawn. Styles and fashions seldom are as appropriate for the physiques of the older citizen as they are for the younger person and they may become discouraged with attempts to improve appearance with clothing that is ill-designed or ill-fitting for the figure that has been changed by aging (Ryan, 1966). Though some older people are much interested in dressing in the latest of fashions, they tend to be a small minority of the aged. Many of the elderly are deterred from manifesting their interest in clothing and appearance by limited income. Many older people simply do not have sufficient funds for the purchase of other than the absolute essentials. Such poverty mitigates against interest in clothing and motivation to make an attractive appearance (Ryan, 1966). In spite of the difficulties of maintaining attractive appearance, some older people realize that lack of neatness and good grooming are more easily overlooked in the young than the aged and maintain high motivation to be neatly and appropriately dressed. Many older people, from both rural and urban settings, read fashion magazines and shop around to see what are the latest fashions (Ryan, 1966).

It is popularly believed that as people become elderly they become more religious. For the average elderly person this is not particularly true. There is no strong tendency for an increase in religiousness of people as they grow older (Havighurst and Albrecht, 1953; Orbach, 1961). Most older people tend to maintain their religious beliefs and habits formed earlier in life (Orbach, 1961; Covalt, 1965).

Retirement

An outstanding feature of American culture has been that of striving for social and economic gain. A real dedication to the idea that upward social, educational, and economic mobility were available to those who would strive has been a part of Americans' traditional belief system. Emphasis on gainful employment, hard work, individual effort, and striving as conditions or qualities to be revered has long been part of the culture. Such a dedication to upward social and economic mobility is quite understandable when coupled with the fact that this nation is one that possesses good natural resources for the rewarding of effort. Paid employment (e.g., "having a good job") not only comes to be a symbol of "success" but also having a "good job" becomes a moral value. The revered position that "work" has held in the lives of elderly people makes it quite understandable that the older person may feel a considerable loss of meaning in his life when he is forced into retirement. Dedication to the values of work and employment has not served the same desirable ends for the elderly in retirement as it did when they were young. It matters little if the aged worker's pension is adequate if paid employment is the only kind that is considered meaningful. Retirement, particularily if it is compulsory, can present serious problems of adjustment for those who live in a "work-and-production" oriented culture. Significant attitude changes toward work, employment, and productivity became noticeable in some of the "youth cultures" of the 1960s and early 70s. The affluence of society was partially rejected by some of the subgroups within the culture. This rejection of the values of cultural involvement, work, and material productivity, if maintained and if it should become a real part of the broad culture, no doubt would bring about significant attitudinal changes toward retirement and reduce many of the adjustment difficulties currently associated with the retirement of those having lived under very different work orientation.

The young or middle-aged worker involved in rearing a family and living a busy social and personal life may look upon early retirement as a time for the real enjoyment of leisure. He may look forward to having time to do those many things for which time has been lacking in the past. He can remove himself from the competitive "rat-race" and sit back and enjoy the remainder of his years in quiet contentment. This picture changes considerably however, for those for whom retirement is imminent. The rosy picture of retired life may change rather markedly. Will there be adequate funds to continue to live in the manner to which he has grown accustomed? Will he be able to find part time work if desired and necessary? What will he do with the time heretofore devoted to work? Changing lifetime patterns of living is not easy for most and they have had little experience with uncommitted time (Kent, 1966).

Retirement as a social problem is of relative recent vintage in the culture. Compulsory retirement at a preestablished age, is in part, a result of scientific and technological development in the culture. Compulsory retirement systems have derived from attempts to control the labor supply, from humanitarian concerns, and technological advances that require adjustments of which the young are deemed most capable (e.g., new production methods and emphasis on speed of performance). There has been a trend away from self-employment and toward the development of larger enterprises that employ great numbers of people on fixed or relatively fixed incomes. The requirements of work and the conditions of retirement are under control of associates and employers and only remotely and partially controlled by the individual. Only those who are successfully engaged in business for themselves or are successfully self-employed in the professions can decide, individually, when they want to retire. Not only are more and more people retiring but the length of the retirement period grows longer as well (Report of President's Council on Aging, 1963). It has been estimated that a twenty-year-old male worker in 1975 may expect to spend 10 years in retirement. In 1940 that worker could expect to spend five-and one-half years in retirement and in 1900 only 3 years (Claque, 1949). Whether significant changes in the length of time spent in retirement will continue in the near future is dependent upon changes in the age of compulsory or voluntary retirement as well as changes in longevity of the working population.

ATTITUDES TOWARD RETIREMENT

A great many attitudes toward retirement exist. They range from highly favorable to very unfavorable. For many of the currently retired, who were born into, grew up, and matured in a work oriented culture, retirement from work is something they do not value. Many would prefer to work, even at a less satisfactory job than their previous employment (Report of President's Council on Aging, 1963). Some of this reluctance to retire or the desire to return to work stems from the economic situation in which the elderly find themselves. Many retired persons are in need of money to provide for the necessities of life and must depend upon economic aid from governmental sources, charitable institutions, friends, or relatives. This is not very attractive in prospect nor is it an attractive way to live for the aged.

Some of the various attitudes toward retirement by those who are retired can be examined rather openly. Retirement may be resisted and resented if it means a drastic reduction in living standard for the individual. This is particularily true if the money available in retirement is only enough to meet the necessities of existence or even less!

While some older workers look forward to being freed from the routines and pressures of work, they do not want to quit work completely. To do so would deprive them of income, feelings of usefulness, social contacts, and various other values associated with work. For many, a partial retirement plan or even reassignment is preferable to complete retirement as such. Being forced into retirement by reaching compulsory retirement age, by dismissal, or by illness is emotionally disturbing and constitutes a serious problem in adjustment to retirement. Voluntary retirement leads to better adjustment in retirement (Thompson et al., 1960). This is probably because those who voluntarily retire have planned for it, are psychologically ready for it, and can afford it. Many workers do not want to retire, resist the whole idea of retirement, and do not prepare themselves psychologically, socially, or economically for retirement. Attitudes toward retirement vary all the way from angry resentment "at being discarded" or "being unjustly kicked out of the working world," through "turning the old horse out to pasture" (a reward for the no longer useful) to welcome relief from the work-a-day world and its steady pace (just reward for valuable services rendered).

Adequate planning for retirement in terms of the social, psychological, economic, and vocational factors of life after retirement should bring about more favorable attitudes toward retirement and enhance adjustment to the role of the retired person. The cessation of work for the person who has derived much of life's satisfaction from work is a difficult task. Plans that include activities designed to compensate, in part, at least, for the satisfactions heretofore realized from work should be a part of retirement plans. Idleness and inactivity for the previously active can be a traumatic experience. Leisure time when it is not planned for can lead to boredom and indifference to life and living. Adult education programs designed to encourage the development of interests and skills that will enable the retired person to feel his life is meaningful and useful should be encouraged (Chown and Heron, 1965). The role of the retired person must be such that social contacts and companionship are available, feelings of usefulness result, and prestige is provided (Kent, 1966).

Just "finding something to do" becomes a problem for some men in retirement. They may become involved in assisting with household tasks. These activities are usually not too satisfactory but do provide at least a feeling of being useful (Kent, 1966). One of the more overrated activities in terms of real satisfactions or substitute for satisfaction derived from work is the hobby. Hobbies, often advocated as aiding adjustment during adult life and as a solution to retirement problems, seldom prove to be work substitutes and do not necessarily facilitate adjustment in retirement, because they usually result in solitary activity. Hobbies tend to be "time-killers" and do not usually contribute to feelings of usefulness, to prestige, or to the economic welfare of the retired (Johnson, 1958). Men adjust less well to the role changes produced by retirement than do women (Kent, 1966). This is probably due to the involvement of women more intimately in the tasks of homemaking. These tasks must be performed even in retirement. Then, too, the woman has usually had more experience with the domestic role than has the man. The role, therefore, is not so foreign to her and does not involve as much of an adjustment.

When there are healthy attitudes toward aging as well as toward retirement on the part of the worker and his family the chances of satisfactory adjustment to retirement are the greatest (Turner, 1955). Those retired persons who live in homes for the aged have more opportunities for social contacts and recreational activities than those who remain in their own homes or live with relatives. These homes, in addition to providing social contacts and recreational facilities, must also provide opportunities for the aging to engage in tasks that will provide prestige and feelings of usefulness in order to promote good adjustment. Those who remain in their home community after retirement and have adequate money to live about as they lived before retirement make the best adjustments because they have fewer adjustments to make.

Sexual Role of the Aged

Sexual activity among the aged when opportunity for sexual expression is at hand, is probably more common than it is popularly believed. It is a common belief that with old age comes a loss of interest in sex as well as sexual impotence. It is true that men as well as women undergo physical changes in bodily functions, but this does not mean that either sexual interest or potency is destroyed. Sexual activity is a function of a number of factors besides those of health and physical condition. Particularly for the aged, compatability with the spouse is an important factor in the maintenance of sexual activity. The aged have difficulty in obtaining sex partners if they do not have a spouse and few single aged maintain an active heterosexual life (Christenson and Gagnon, 1965; Swartz, 1966). Patterns of sexual behavior developed earlier in life have important influences on sexual behavior in old age. Those that have been relatively sexually active continue to be relatively more active in old age than those who were less active earlier (Freeman, 1961; Kinsey et al., 1953).

Sexual behavior among the aged is, no doubt, inhibited by some popular attitudes toward sex and aging. Many of the aged expect to be impotent. Psychological factors are sufficiently important in sexual functioning that such an expectancy frequently leads to impotence (Kinsey et al., 1948). Then, too, attitudes toward sexual functioning of the elderly frequently are antagonistic. Some believe that by the time they are past middle age they ought to be through with sex. Many aged people feel that showing any interest in sex is inappropriate for them and sex should be limited to the young who are capable of reproduction. There is a tendency among some people to regard sexual interests and behavior after middle age as pathological in spite of its being widespread and recognized as a legitimate function by those with the most information (Geriatric Focus Report, 1966).

Intercourse among men and women in their sixties and seventies is to be expected for most couples in good health. Frequency of sexual relations decreases with age but when intercourse is discontinued it is most usually because of illness of one of the spouses or because of diminished desire in the husband. When health conditions are adequate there is a gradual diminution of sexual activity in the aged rather than a sudden cessation (Christenson and Gagnon, 1965).

A great deal of interest and emphasis on sexual freedom and functioning has come about in the past decade or so. With an increase in the acceptance of sexual behavior as not involving shame and guilt and as being a legitimate means of human expression, continuance of sexual activity into the period of old age should be expected to increase.

WIDOWHOOD

Learning to live without a spouse after years of being married presents serious problems for the aged, who have more difficulty adjusting to changes than do younger persons. When death or divorce of the spouse comes at a late age the results can be particularly traumatic and require a good deal in the way of adaptive behavior in order for the widowed to continue to live an adequate life. Loneliness becomes an important problem for the aged and particularly for the widowed (Kent, 1966).

Men tend to marry women their own age or younger than they are and women tend to live longer than do men. When these two factors are combined it can be expected that there will be a great deal more women than men who are widowed in their advanced years. There is a ratio of better than 5 females for every 4 males in the older population. It is estimated that this will rise to about 6 to 4 by 1985 (Geriatric Focus Report, 1966). Only one-third of American women sixty-five years of age and older live with their husbands in their own household. It has been estimated about half of the women sixty years of age are widows. It is probable that the percentage of men who are classified as widowed by age sixty is far less because men who are widowed tend to remarry more frequently than do women (Geriatric Focus Report, 1966). Most married women spend their last years living without a spouse. This presents problems for the aging woman in the culture. She may have to live on less money, move to less adequate quarters, or live with children or relatives. The probability is high that she does not want to do this.

Relatively few older people fully appreciate the problems that are produced by widowhood; even though the possibility of widowhood is recognized and some planning for it does take place, most have difficulty adjusting to being alone.

Loneliness can be considered a major problem of widowhood (Tanenbaum, 1967). Remarriage is one of the ways by which older people deal with the problem of loneliness in widowhood. Older women do not remarry as frequently as do older men. This is true because there are more elderly women than men, some women are reluctant to give up their own pension rights, and older men tend to select women who are younger when they remarry.

SINGLENESS

It is popularly believed, by those who are married, at least, that an old person who has never married and has no "family" will face an unhappy and lonely old age. This does not appear to be the case. People who live alone for years adjust to living without family. They develop interests and activities independent of family ties and companionship. They are probably better equipped to face old age than are those people who have been married for the major part of adult life and then have to adjust to living without a spouse. There is no reason why a bachelor or spinster should not live happily and actively in old age (Lowenthal, 1964).

Social-Personal Living

The aged are to be found living under the same variety of circumstances that are common to the culture in general. The aged belong to all educational and socioeconomic levels of society. There are, however, special needs of the aged that should be met. Their need for convenient services, housing, health and recreational services are most likely to be adequately met among the more affluent families. Income limitations may severely restrict the kinds of housing and services available to the aged.

SOCIAL LIFE

Social theorists have indicated that one of the effects of industrialization on the family has been to produce social isolation. This has been particularly true for the aged who have been described as isolated from kinship and community ties. This picture may be somewhat more gloomy than that which actually exists. A rather lengthy investigation of the aged in the United States, Britain, and Denmark (Shanus et al., 1968) presents a somewhat rosier picture of the aged than previously had been common. They depict a relatively large proportion of the aged in all three countries as maintaining reasonably active and culturally involved lives. The aged in these countries apparently continue to maintain kinship contacts and mingle with other older persons in the community as well as with the young. They are further depicted as making quite satisfactory personal adjustments to their role in society and to their declining physical status. This no doubt is true for large numbers of the aged. In focusing attention on the poor and dependent minorities of aged it easily can be overlooked that a great majority of the elderly do quite well in the culture.

It cannot and should not be ignored, however, that the aged are heavily and disproportionally represented in the ranks of the poor. Then, too, 4 to 6 percent of the aged are institutionalized. Many of these aged people are in essentially custodial institutions or in mental hospitals not because of mental illness but because of the lack of appropriate community facilities (Mechanic, 1969). Ralph Nader has urged the elderly to form a retired people's liberation movement to resist "geriatric segregation" that forces many to exist in shabby nursing homes (UPI, 1970).

Housing. Many of the aged poor live in the central city in inadequate, unattractive, and relatively expensive housing (Birren, 1970). Although the aged often appear to dislike their housing, they do not move as frequently as the young. A Los Angeles investigation revealed that 90 percent of individuals over fifty were dissatisfied with their living arrangements, but that only 13 percent actually moved during a one year period (Birren, 1970). The aged are less mobile than the young and many may be unable to move because of lack of funds. Urban redevelopment has failed to relieve the plight of the aged and in some cases has made matters worse for them. Frequently the aged are displaced by redevelopment programs that build housing and shopping facilities that are beyond the economic grasp of the aged poor. There are serious psychological consequences to the relocation of any group of people. This is particularly true of the aged. People are often extremely unhappy about losing their homes and neighborhoods. This grief may turn into depression for older residents whose self-identity is maintained through stable physical surroundings and social relationships. What may look like deterioration and disorganization of a community to city planners, may represent low rent, interaction with friends, and proximity to relatives to the aged. Birren (1970) has argued convincingly that city structure should be dictated by function rather than function being dictated by structure. Cities, he asserts, are primarily social organizations and only secondarily are they collections of concrete, steel, and wooden structures. An adequate environment should offer many options and opportunities for individual self-expression and for individual development and activity. This is true for the aged as well as for the young.

Birren (1970) has urged that city planning take into account the needs of the aged. Older people may be quite overwhelmed by environmental obstacles that are really not obstacles at all for the young. Such things as high steps to get into a bus or street car, busy streets, fast changing traffic lights, inadequate street signs and lighting, and poor labeling of buildings can present problems of such magnitude as to produce real discouragement. The aged may do without goods and services that they should have when they are too inconvenient or troublesome. Services of banks, medical doctors, dentists, shops, lawyers, repair service and recreational facilities may be forgone because they are too inconvenient or require too much energy to obtain.

With advancing age there occurs a shrinking in one's "life-space." That is, objects and events that are near at hand and immediately available provide more and more of a person's psychological support. Thus, the immediate environment assumes great importance for the aged. This concept of "life-space" and its diminution with time should be employed in the design of personal and community facilities to accommodate the aged (Birren, 1970).

The partial segregation of the aged provided by retirement communities and retirement homes may be advantageous for some, because older persons do enjoy the companionships of other older people just as the young enjoy the young. However, many elderly should live in communities that are designed to enhance the quality of living for all ages. Familiar people, familiar objects, and buildings designed to facilitate living are an advantage to the aged as well as to the rest of society.

Adjustment and Behavioral Disorder

Behavioral disorders and adjustment of the aged have not been given the investigative attention that has been given these processes in the young. It is known that older people undergo psychological changes. The physical decline of aging poses adjustment problems as do the changes that occur in the social life of the aged. The friends of the aged die, many of the aged will outlive their friends and many of their relatives, including some of their children. These events, occurring with passage of time, add to the problems of adjustment presented by the physical processes of aging that were described earlier in this chapter. It is possible that if more research attention were paid to adjustive problems of the aged we would discover that their problems are of comparable magnitude with those of the young. Psychological changes tend to come about gradually and many of them do not interfere in the processes of effective living for the aged.

BEHAVIORAL DISORDERS

Aged persons must respond to the stresses and strains of living and they probably become a bit less adaptable to stress with age. The aged person who was neurotic when he was younger may develop additional behavioral patterns of a neurotic nature in his old age as life stresses accumulate. Aged persons suffer from anxiety, exaggerated concern for health and well being (hypochondriacal reactions), depressive reactions, and other neurotic behaviors. Severe depressions and feeling of persecution (paranoid reactions) are the most common disorders of the severely disorganized aged person (Straker, 1963).

The two major severe disorders of older people are those associated with physical deterioration. *Senile brain disease* (senile dementia) and *cerebral arteriosclerosis* account for about 80 percent of the behavioral disorders of the aged (Marks, 1961). The brain changes in senile dementia (cerebral atrophy and degeneration) and in cerebral arteriosclerosis (blocking or rupture of cerebral arteries occurs) are held to be directly causative of the behavior disorganization and aberrations that occur. However, it is now recognized that there is little relationship between amount of neurological damage and the severity of the behavioral disorganizations.

Senile Dementia. Typically it is gradual in onset and involves a general slowing up of physical and mental functioning. The symptoms vary from one patient to another. They appear to depend upon the personality organization of the patient, his life situation, and the nature and extent of cerebral degeneration. There is usually a gradual personal-social withdrawal, a narrowing of interest and activity, a loss of alertness and a general resistance to innovation and changes in routine. Periods of confusion and loss of memory for recent events are common. Insomnia is common as is a preoccupation with bodily processes and well-being. As the condition becomes advanced there is a lack of interest in appearance, depression that is severe, reduced comprehension, confusion, and disorientation.

Senile psychoses account for about 8 percent of the first admission to mental hospitals. Average age of first admission is about 75 years for both men and women. Average age of onset is no doubt considerably less than this because of care in the home before the decision to hospitalize (Coleman, 1964).

Senile dementia typically is classified into several types depending upon the predominant symptoms. If the clinical picture is much like that described above (an exaggeration of normal changes in aging) it is called simple deterioration. If a dominant feature is that of delusions of persecution it is classified as paranoid reaction. The *presbyophrenic* type is characterized by a marked impairment in memory. The patient is amiable, talks a great deal, and fabricates events to fill in his loss of memory. Many senile dementia patients are extremely confused and subject to spells of delirium. These are the *delirious and confused*. The patient who is severely depressed and excessively and morbidly hypochondriacal is designated as *depressed and agitated*.

Although there may be some remission of symptoms in some patients, the prognosis for those classified as senile dementia is one of continued decline in psychological and physiological function until death. The decline may occur over a period of months or years.

Behavior disorders associated with cerebral arteriosclerosis do not differ greatly from those of senile dementia. Cerebral arteriosclerosis involves a hardening of the arteries of the brain. Senile plaques (deposits of fatty and calcified substance) in the inside layers of the blood vessels produce a gradual closing of the artery and its consequent impairment of circulation. The arteries can become blocked by a blood clot or by blocking from a piece of fatty or calcified material. The vessel may then rupture and bleeding will occur.

If there is a sudden blockage, or if a small blood vessel ruptures, this is termed a small stroke. The behavioral symptom will be dependent upon the severity and location of the resultant damage. A major stroke (one in which there is a generalized impairment of brain function) results from massive damage. Generally, arteriosclerotic brain diseased patients do not show the profound deterioration found in senile patients.

In over half of the cases the onset of cerebral arteriosclerosis is sudden (a stroke). The patient is confused, disoriented as to time and place, incoherent, and suffering from some paralysis. This acute confusional state may last for several days or even months before there is a remission of symptoms. There are varying amounts of brain damage resulting in impairment of functioning. Rehabilitative measures can be instituted and some of the physical and mental handicaps can be improved or compensated for by the patient.

When the onset of the disorder is gradual there may be a slowing of activity and involvement in living. The person may complain of being chronically tired, of being dizzy, or of having a headache. Frequently there are periods of depression, confusion, and loss of memory. By the time the person is eventually hospitalized the symptoms are much the same as for senile dementia.

About 15 percent of all first admissions to mental hospitals are classified as psychoses associated with cerebral arteriosclerosis. Average age of first admission is about 74 years (Coleman, 1964).

Successful Aging

One of two conditions is inevitable for all people. Either one dies before he becomes classifiable as being old or he lives to be so classified and experiences some aspects of aged living before death. Attention can be focused on the life and living of the aged but the life and living of the aged cannot be divorced from the processes of life and living that have preceded being aged. Adequate living as an elderly person is a function of adequate preparation for life as an older person. Education and planning for aging, retirement, old age, and eventual death can probably enhance the quality of life for all when they grow older.

It is difficult if not impossible to describe, identify, or define successful aging. The goals, the purposes, and the functions of aged living are probably not different, in principle from those for any other group. However, there are special problems that exist for the aged that are unlike those of most other people. Old age is the period of decline. It is the period preceding life's termination. It is a period when physical and mental powers are declining. It is a period when family life changes and many who have lived life as married persons must now live alone. Loneliness may be a problem. Financial uncertainty or inadequacy may be severely limiting as an inflationary economy continues. Most social benefits to the aged are not currently designed to be other than "assists" in the lives of the aged. Social security was not designed as a complete supportive system but as a supplementary or auxiliary part of retirement. Most pensions are considerably less than they should be because of either inflation or the fact that they too were designed to be supplemental. Supplemental services are fine if there is something to supplement, but large numbers of the aged have little in the way of savings or other assets. Financial inadequacy and loneliness are two problems that many of the aged must contend with that many do not plan to have to contend with in their latter years.

Successful aging involves the personal element of self-satisfaction. If the person is reasonably satisfied and content with his life and regards himself positively, his *personal* aging can be regarded as successful. In addition to the personal element of successful aging there is a *social* aspect that is interactive with it. If society is reasonably satisfied with the individual's fulfillment of his social roles and cultural obligations, the individual can be said to be aging successfully in a social sense. These two aspects to successful aging are of necessity mutually supportive but they are not completely interdependent.

Successful aging results in successful living as an old person. Throughout life motivational changes occur, goals change, and personality changes. Each portion of life offers its own aspects of living that can result in feelings of fulfillment, adequate self-regard, social acceptance, and dignity. Living for the aged should be as filled with these qualities as their earlier lives and their culture can provide.

Summary

Aging can be considered biologically, sociologically, and psychologically as well as chronologically. Age 65 has come to be fairly well accepted as the beginning of the period of old age. This is an arbitrary designation that coincides with a frequent age for compulsory retirement and for eligibility for the receipt of certain social benefits. There are about 20 million people over 65 years of age in the United States. There is a greater proportion of the population which lives to old age than there ever has been before. Man is not living to be older but more are living long enough to reach old age.

The aged do not fare well economically in our culture. Thirty to forty percent of the aged readily can be classified as poor. The aged are to be found in all economic strata, however, just as they are to be found among all intellectual levels and social classes.

Many of the research investigations of the aged have been conducted using institutionalized elderly people as subjects. The generalizability of such findings to the aged population in general is highly questionable. Only about five percent of the aged reside in institutions and nursing homes and they cannot be said to be representative of the aged as a group. The aged are a very heterogeneous group of people on most variables except chronological age.

The aged suffer a loss of physical status, a diminution of certain sensory functions and a general slowing down of various intellectual functions. They become more vulnerable to injury and disease and they are less mobile than younger individuals.

As people age they tend to become a bit more self-centered and have an enhanced concern for health and general well-being. Retirement, widowhood, and loneliness are serious problems for the aged. The aged have difficulty functioning in an environment that is not too kind to them. The aged are heavily and disproportionally represented among the ranks of the poor. Urban housing costs are high and the housing tends to be inadequate. The aged are subject to the stresses of living the same as are other groups in the culture. The adjustment of the aged has received less investigative attention than has the adjustment of the young. The aged are subject to the additional stresses of physical deterioration and do suffer from some disorders that tend to produce adjustment problems and behavior disorders. Even with these handicaps, most of the aged apparently adjust rather well to their personal-social situation.

References

ASSOCIATED PRESS, "Elderly Poor Ranks Grow," *San Jose Mercury*, Jan. 18, 1971, p. 8.

BADER, I. M., AND D. M. HOFFMAN, "Research in Aging," *J. home economics*, LVIII (1966), 9–14.

BAYLEY, N., "Research in Child Development: A Longitudinal Perspective," *Merrill-Palmer Quarterly*, XI (1965), 183–208.

————, AND M. H. ODEN., "The Maintenance of Intellectual Ability in Gifted Adults," *J. geront.*, X (1955), 91–107.

BERKOWITZ, B., AND R. F. GREEN, "Changes in Intellect with Age: v. Differential Changes as Functions of Time Interval and Original Score," *J. genetic psychol.*, (1965) , 179–92.

BIRREN, J. E., *The Psychology of Aging*. Englewood Cliffs, N.J.: Prentice-Hall, Inc., 1964.

————, "The Abuse of the Urban Aged," *Psychology today*, III, No. 10 (1970), 36–38, 76.

————, "Research on the Psychology of Aging: Concepts and Findings," in *Psychopathology of Aging*. eds. P. H. Hock and J. Zubin. New York: Grune and Stratton, 1961, 203–22.

————, M. W. BICK, AND M. YIENGST, "The Relation of Structural Changes of the Eye and Vitamin A to Elevation of the Light Threshold in Later Life," *J. exp. psychol.*, XXXX (1950), 260–66.

————, W. R. ALLEN, AND H. G. LANDAU, "The Relation of Problem Length in Simple Addition to Time Required, Probability of Success, and Age," *J. geront.*, IX (1954), 150–61.

————, E. A. JEROME, AND S. M. CHOWN, "Aging and Psychological Adjustment: Problem Solving and Motivation," *Rev. educ. res.*, XXXI (1961) 487–99.

————, K. F. RIEGEL, AND D. F. MORRISON, "Age Differences in Response Speed as a Function of Controlled Variations of Stimulus Condition: Evidence of a General Speed Factor," *Gerontologia*, VI (1962), 1–18.

BONDAREFF, W., "Morphology of the Aging Nervous System." In *Handbook of Aging and the Individual*, ed. J. E. Birren. Chicago, Ill.: University of Chicago Press, 1959, 136–172.

BOTTWINICK, J., "Research Problems and Concepts in the Study of Aging." *Gerontologist*, IV (1964), 121–29.

————, "Cautiousness in Advanced Age," *J. geront.*, XXI (1966), 347–53.

BRODY, J., "Organization of the Cerebral Cortex: III. A Study of Aging in the Human Cerebral Cortex," *J. comp. neurology*, CII (1955), 511–56.

BURGER, R. E., "Who Cares for the Aged?" *Saturday Review*, January 25, 1969, pp. 14–17.

BUSSE, E. W., "Studies in the Process of Aging: The Strengths and Weaknesses of Psychic Functioning in the Aged," *Am. j. psychiatry*, CXVI (1955), 896–901.

CHOWN, S. M., AND A. HERON, "Psychological Aspects of Aging in Man," *Ann. rev. psychol.*, XVI (1965), 417–50.

CHRISTENSON, C. V., AND J. H. GAGNON, "Sexual Behavior in a Group of Older Women," *J. geront.*, XX (1965), 351–56.

CLAQUE, E., "The Working Life Span of American Workers," *J. geront.*, IV (1949), 285–89.

COLEMAN, J. C., *Abnormal Psychology and Modern Life*, (3rd ed.). Chicago, Ill.: Scott, Foresman and Company, 1964.

COOPER, R. M., I. BILASH, AND J. P. ZUBEK, "The Effect of Age on Taste Sensitivity," *J. geront.*, XIV (1959), 56–58.

COVALT, N. K., "The Meaning of Religion to Older People," in *Problems of the Aged*, eds. C. B. Wedder and A. S. Lefkowitz. Springfield, Ill.: Charles C Thomas, 1965.

DENNIS, W., AND E. GIRDEN, "Current Scientific Activities of Psychologists as a Function of Age," *J. geront.*, IX (1954), 175–78.

EISDORFER, C., J. NOWLIN, AND F. WILKIE, "Improvement of Learning in the Aged by Modification of Autonomic Nervous System Activity," *Science*, CLXX (1970), 1327–29.

FOX, C., AND J. E. BIRREN, "The Differential Decline of Wechsler Subtest Scores in 60–69-Year-Old Individuals," *Amer. psychol.*, V (1950), 467.

FREEMAN, J. T., "Sexual Capacities in the Aging Male," *Geriatrics*, XVI (1961), 37–43.

FRIEDMAN, H., "Memory Organization in the Aged," *J. genet, psychol.*, CIX (1966), 3–8.

GERIATRIC FOCUS REPORT, "Menopause Not End of Sex," *Geriatric focus*, V, No. 5 (1966), 1, 6.

————, "Widowhood in Old Age," *Geriatric focus*, V, No. 9 (1966), 1–5.

HAVIGHURST, R. J., AND R. ALBRECHT, *Older People*. New York: Longmans, 1953.

HENRY, W. E., AND E. CUMMINGS, "Personality Development in Adulthood and Old Age," *J. projective techniques*, XXIII (1959), 383–90.

HURLOCK, E. B., *Developmental Psychology*. New York: McGraw-Hill Book Company, 1968.

JOHNSON, D. E., "A Depressive Retirement Syndrome," *Geriatrics*, XII (1958), 314–19.

KALLMAN, E. J., AND L. F. JARVIK, "Individual Differences in Constitution and Genetic Background," in *Handbook of Aging and the Individual*, ed. J. E. Birren. Chicago, Ill.: University of Chicago Press, 1959.

KENT, D. P., "Social and Cultural Factors Influencing the Mental Health of the Aged," *Amer. j. orthopsych.*, XXXVI (1966), 680–85.

KINSEY, A. C., W. B. POMEROY, AND C. E. MARTIN, *Sexual Behavior in the Human Male*. Philadelphia, Pa.: Saunders, 1948.

————, W. B. POMEROY, C. E. MARTIN, AND P. H. GEBHARD, *Sexual Behavior in the Human Female*. Philadelphia, Pa.: Saunders, 1953.

KLEEMEIR, R. W., "The Relationship Between Orthorator Tests of Acuity and Color Vision in an Aged Population," *J. geront.*, VI (1951), 372–79.

KOGAN, N., AND F. C. SHELTON, "Beliefs About Old People: A Comparative Study of Older and Younger Samples," *J. genet. psychol.*, C (1962), 93–111.

KOLLER, M. R., *Social Gerontology*. New York: Random House-Knopp, 1968.

LANE, B., "Attitudes of Youth Toward the Aged," *J. marriage and family*, XXVI (1964), 229–31.

LEHMAN, H. C., *Age and Achievement*. Princeton, N.J.: Princeton University Press, 1953.

LOWENTHAL, M. F., "Social Isolation and Mental Illness in Old Age," *Amer. soc. rev.*, XXIX (1964), 54–70.

MARKS, H, II., "Characteristics and Trends of Cerebral Vascular Disease," in *Psychopathology of Aging*. eds. P. H. Hock and J. Zubin. New York: Grune and Stratton, 1961, 69–99.

MASON, E. P., "Some Correlates of Self-Judgments of the Aged," *J. geront.*, IX (1954), 324–37.

MASTER, A. M., AND R. P. LASSER, "Blood Pressure After Age 65," *Geriatrics*, XIX (1964), 41–46.

MECHANIC, D., "The Social Condition of the Aged," *Science*, CLXIII (1969), 1049–50.

ORBACH, H. L., "Aging and Religion," *Geriatrics*, XVI (1961), 530–40.

OWENS, W A,, "Age and Mental Abilities: A Second Adult Follow-Up," *J. educ. psychol.*, LVII (1966), 311–25.

Report of President's Council on Aging. Washington, D C,; Government Printing Office, 1963.

ROFFWARG, H. P., J. N. MUZIO, AND W. C. DEMENT, "Ontogenetic Development of the Human Sleep-Dream Cycle," *Science*, CLII (1966), 604–19.

ROSE, A. M., "Class Differences Among the Elderly: A Research Report," *J. soc. res.*, L (1966), 356–60.

ROSENBLATT, A., "Interests of Older Persons in Volunteer Activities," *Soc. wk.*, XI, No. 3 (1966), 87–94.

RYAN, M. S., *Clothing: A Study in Human Behavior*. New York: Holt, Rinehart & Winston, Inc., 1966.

SCHAIE, K. W., P. BATES, AND C. R. STROTHER, "A Study of Auditory Sensitivity in Advanced Age," *J. geront.*, XIX (1964), 453–57.

SCHULDERMAN, E., AND J. P. ZUBEK, "Effect of Age on Pain Sensitivity," *Perceptual and motor skills*, XIV (1962), 295–301.

SCHONFIELD, D., AND B. A. ROBERTSON, "Memory Storage and Age," *Canadian j. psychol.*, XX (1966), 228–36.

SHANUS, E., P. TOWNSEND, D. WEDDERBURN, H. FRIIS, P. MILHOJ, AND J. STEHOUWER, *Old People in Three Industrial Societies*. New York: Atherton Press, 1968.

STRAKER, M., "Prognosis for Psychiatric Illness in the Aged," *Amer. j. psychiatry*, CXIX (1963), 1069–75.

SWARTZ, D., "The Urologist's Viewpoint," *Geriatric focus*, V, No. 5 (1966), 1, 5.

SWENSEN, W. M., "The Many Faces of Aging," *Geriatrics*, XVII (1962), 659–63.

TANENBAUM, D. E., "Loneliness in the Aged," *Mental hygiene*, LI (1967), 91–99.

TERMAN, L. M., AND M. H. ODEN, *The Gifted Group at Mid-Life*. Stanford, Calif.: Stanford University Press, 1959.

THOMPSON, W. E., G. F. STREIF, AND J. KOSA, "The Effect of Retirement on Personal Adjustment: A Panel Analysis," *J. geront.*, XV (1960), 165–69.

TURNER, A. N., "The Older Worker: New Light on Employment and Retirement," *Personnel*, XXXII (1955), 246–57.

UNITED PRESS INTERNATIONAL, "Nader Blisters Elder's Neglect," *San Jose Mercury*, Dec. 18, 1970, p. 4.

WIGGINS, J. W., AND H. SCHOECK, "A Profile of the Aging: USA." *Geriatrics*, XVI (1961), 336–42.

WHITE HOUSE CONFERENCE ON AGING, *The Nation and Its Older People; Report of White House Conference on Aging*, Jan. 9–12, 1961. Washington, D.C., 1961.

APPENDIX

Specialist Organizations
and Agencies

Agencies and Organizations Concerned with Problems Associated with All or Most Categories of Exceptionality

Very often the greatest service the nonspecialist can render an exceptional individual or the parents and counselors of such people is to put them into contact with agencies and organizations that can provide authoritative information and counseling on a continuing basis. Consequently, we have provided lists of appropriate national or world agencies and organizations. We list here the names and addresses of agencies dealing with the entire range of exceptional people. Following this general list we also provide lists of the principal agencies concerned with each of the special areas of exceptionality.

AMERICAN ASSOCIATION FOR HEALTH, PHYSICAL EDUCATION, AND RECREATION
1201 16th St., NW
Washington, D.C. 20036

AMERICAN OCCUPATIONAL THERAPY ASSOCIATION, INC.
251 Park Avenue S.
New York, New York 10010

AMERICAN REHABILITATION COUNSELING ASSOCIATION OF THE AMERICAN PERSONNEL AND GUIDANCE ASSOCIATION
1607 New Hampshire Ave., NW
Washington, D.C. 20009

THE ASSOCIATION OF REHABILITATION CENTERS, INC.
7979 Old Georgetown Rd.
Washington, D.C. 20014

THE COUNCIL FOR EXCEPTIONAL CHILDREN
1411 S. Jefferson Davis Highway, Suite 900
Arlington, Virginia 22202

INFORMATION CENTER—RECREATION FOR THE HANDICAPPED
Outdoor Laboratory, Little Grassy, Southern Illinois University
Carbondale, Illinois 62901

NATIONAL ASSOCIATION OF SHELTERED WORKSHOPS AND HOMEBOUND PROGRAMS
1522 K St., NW
Washington, D.C. 20005

GOODWILL INDUSTRIES OF AMERICA, INC.
9200 Wisconsin Ave.
Washington, D.C. 20014

INTERNATIONAL SOCIETY FOR REHABILITATION OF THE DISABLED
219 E. 44th St.
New York, New York 10017

NATIONAL ASSOCIATION FOR MUSIC THERAPY, INC.
Box 610
Lawrence, Kansas 66055

NATIONAL REHABILITATION ASSOCIATION
1522 K St., NW
Washington, D.C. 20005

NATIONAL COMMITTEE FOR MULTI-HANDICAPPED CHILDREN
    339 14th St.
    Niagara Falls, New York 14303

NATIONAL CATHOLIC EDUCATION ASSOCIATION
    Special Education Dept.
    4472 Lindell Blvd.
    St. Louis, Missouri 63108

NATIONAL RECREATION AND PARK ASSOCIATION
    1700 Pennsylvania Ave., NW
    Washington, D.C. 20006

NATIONAL THERAPEUTIC RECREATION SOCIETY
    1700 Pennsylvania Ave., NW
    Washington, D.C. 20006

THE PRESIDENT'S COMMITTEE ON EMPLOYMENT OF THE HANDICAPPED
    U.S. Department of Labor
    Washington, D.C. 20210

SOCIAL AND REHABILITATION SERVICE, CHILDREN'S BUREAU
    330 C St., SW
    Washington, D.C. 20201

SOCIAL AND REHABILITATION SERVICE, REHABILITATION SERVICES ADMINISTRATION
    330 Independence Ave., SW, Rm. 3139 D
    Washington, D.C. 20201

SOCIAL AND REHABILITATION SERVICE, OFFICE OF RESEARCH, DEMONSTRATIONS,
    AND TRAINING
    HEW North Bldg., Rm. 3315
    Washington, D.C. 20201

U.S. OFFICE OF EDUCATION, BUREAU OF EDUCATION FOR THE HANDICAPPED
    7th and D St., SW
    Washington, D.C. 20202

Organizations Concerned with the Intellectually Gifted

THE NATIONAL ASSOCIATION FOR GIFTED CHILDREN
    8080 Springvalley Dr.
    Cincinnati, Ohio 45236

NATIONAL COUNCIL FOR THE GIFTED
    700 Prospect Ave.
    West Orange, New Jersey 07052

Agencies and Organizations Concerned with Mental Retardation

AMERICAN ASSOCIATION ON MENTAL DEFICIENCY
    5201 Connecticut Ave., NW
    Washington, D.C. 20015

INTERNATIONAL LEAGUE OF SOCIETIES FOR THE MENTALLY HANDICAPPED
      12, rue Forestiere
      Brussels-5, Belgium

JOSEPH P. KENNEDY, JR. FOUNDATION
      719 13th St., NW, Suite 510
      Washington, D.C. 20005

NATIONAL ASSOCIATION FOR RETARDED CHILDREN
      420 Lexington Ave.
      New York, New York 10017

PRESIDENT'S COMMITTEE ON MENTAL RETARDATION
      Washington, D.C. 20201

Association Concerned with Learning Disabilities

ASSOCIATION FOR CHILDREN WITH LEARNING DISABILITIES
      2200 Brownsville Rd.
      Pittsburgh, Pennsylvania 15210

Organizations and Agencies Concerned with Visual Defects

AMERICAN ASSOCIATION OF WORKERS FOR THE BLIND, INC.
      1511 K St., NW, Suite 637
      Washington, D.C. 20005

AMERICAN FOUNDATION FOR THE BLIND
      15 W. 16th St.
      New York, New York 10011

AMERICAN PRINTING HOUSE FOR THE BLIND
      1839 Frankfort Ave.
      Louisville, Kentucky 40206

ASSOCIATION FOR EDUCATION OF THE VISUALLY HANDICAPPED
      711 14th St., NW
      Washington, D.C. 20005

NATIONAL SOCIETY FOR LOW VISION PEOPLE, INC.
      2346 Clermont
      Denver, Colorado 80207

DIVISION FOR THE BLIND AND PHYSICALLY HANDICAPPED
      The Library of Congress
      Washington, D.C. 20542

Organizations and Agencies Concerned with Defects of Speech and Hearing

ALEXANDER GRAHAM BELL ASSOCIATION FOR THE DEAF, INC.
      1537 35th St., NW
      Washington, D.C. 20007

AMERICAN ACADEMY OF PRIVATE PRACTICE IN SPEECH PATHOLOGY AND AUDIOLOGY
P.O. Box 53217, State Capital Station
Oklahoma City, Oklahoma 73105

THE AMERICAN SPEECH AND HEARING ASSOCIATION
9030 Old Georgetown Rd.
Washington, D.C. 20014

CONFERENCE OF EXECUTIVES OF AMERICAN SCHOOLS FOR THE DEAF
c/o Dr. Howard M. Quigley
5034 Wisconsin Ave., NW
Washington, D.C. 20016

THE CONVENTION OF AMERICAN INSTRUCTORS OF THE DEAF
c/o Dr. Howard M. Quigley, Executive Secretary
5034 Wisconsin Ave., NW
Washington, D.C. 20016

COUNCIL OF ORGANIZATIONS SERVING THE DEAF
4201 Connecticut Ave., NW, Suite 210
Washington, D.C. 20008

COUNCIL ON EDUCATION OF THE DEAF
c/o Dr. George T. Pratt, President
Clarke School for the Deaf
Northampton, Massachusetts 01060

NATIONAL ASSOCIATION OF HEARING AND SPEECH AGENCIES
919 18th St., NW
Washington, D.C. 20006

NATIONAL ASSOCIATION OF THE DEAF
2025 Eye St., NW, Suite 321
Washington, D.C. 20006

WESTERN INSTITUTE FOR THE DEAF
215E. 18th Ave.
Vancouver 10, British Columbia, Canada

Organizations and Agencies Concerned with Orthopedic Handicaps and Epilepsy

AMERICAN ACADEMY FOR CEREBRAL PALSY
University Hospital School
Iowa City, Iowa 52240

AMERICAN CORRECTIVE THERAPY ASSOCIATION, INC.
811 St. Margaret's Rd.
Chillicothe, Ohio 45601

AMERICAN PHYSICAL THERAPY ASSOCIATION
1740 Broadway
New York, New York 10019

HUMAN GROWTH, INC.
307 5th Ave.
New York, New York 10016

LITTLE PEOPLE OF AMERICA, INC.
   P.O. Box 126
   Owatonna, Minnesota 55050
MUSCULAR DYSTROPHY ASSOCIATION OF AMERICA, INC.
   1790 Broadway
   New York, New York 10019
THE NATIONAL EASTER SEAL SOCIETY FOR CRIPPLED CHILDREN AND ADULTS
   2023 West Ogden Ave.
   Chicago, Illinois 60612
THE NATIONAL FOUNDATION—MARCH OF DIMES
   800 2nd Ave.
   New York, New York 10017
UNITED CEREBRAL PALSY ASSOCIATIONS, INC.
   66 E. 34th St.
   New York, New York 10016
NATIONAL EPILEPSY LEAGUE, INC.
   203 N. Wabash Ave., Rm 2200
   Chicago, Illinois 60601

Organizations and Agencies Concerned with Mental Health

AMERICAN ASSOCIATION OF PSYCHIATRIC CLINICS FOR CHILDREN
   250 W. 57th St., Rm 1032, Fish Bldg.
   New York, New York 10019.
AMERICAN ORTHOPSYCHIATRIC ASSOCIATION, INC.
   1790 Broadway
   New York, New York 10019
AMERICAN SCHIZOPHRENIA FOUNDATION
   Box 160
   Ann Arbor, Michigan 48107
THE NATIONAL ASSOCIATION FOR MENTAL HEALTH, INC.
   Suite 1300, 10 Columbus Circle
   New York, New York 10019
U.S. PUBLIC HEALTH SERVICE, HEALTH SERVICES AND MENTAL HEALTH
   ADMINISTRATION, NATIONAL INSTITUTE OF MENTAL HEALTH
   5454 Wisconsin Ave.
   Chevy Chase, Maryland 20015

Association Concerned with Crime and Delinquency

NATIONAL COUNCIL ON CRIME AND DELINQUENCY
   44 E. 23rd St.
   New York, New York 10010

Name Index

AAMD classification, 253, 262
AAMD project, 57, 60, 61, 93
Aase, B. H., 61, 62
Abel, G. L., 320
Abel, T. M., 235, 242, 248
Abraham, W., 133, 150
Adams, M. R., 403, 412
Albrecht, R., 517, 530
Alexander the Great, 380
Alexander, F. G., 58, 93
Albright, M., 342, 355
Allen, W. R., 515, 529
Alpern, G. D., 478, 496
Alt, H., 61, 93
Amatruda, C. S., 185, 219
American Association on Mental Deficiency
    (AAMD), 58, 93, 182–85
American Dental Association, 408
American Foundation for the Blind, 302,
    309, 325
American Medical Association, 331, 355
American Psychiatric Association, 188–89
American Speech and Hearing Association,
    394, 410
Ammons, C. H., 311, 325
Amsel, A., 434, 443
Anastasi, A., 197, 213, 214, 217, 230, 448
Anaxagoras, 6
Anderson, C. A., 461, 498

Anderson, V. M., 344, 355
Andres, J. G., 311, 312, 328
Andrews, J. S., 235, 251
Apgar, V., 209, 217
Arey, L. B., 295
Argyle, M., 438, 443
Aristotle, 6
Asch, S., 32, 54
Ashcraft, S. C., 302, 310, 316, 317, 319, 325,
    327
Asher, E. J., 213, 217
Asher, P., 367, 386
Associated Press, 507, 529
Axelrod, S., 315, 316, 325

Backus, O. L., 410, 412
Bader, I. M., 510, 529
Bagdikian, B. H., 465, 466, 496
Bahn, A. K., 63, 94, 95, 440, 443
Bailey, C. J., 260–69
Bajema, C. J., 230, 248
Baker, C., 199, 223
Baker, H. J., 6, 25, 267, 386
Balken, E. R., 212, 217
Baller, W. B., 229, 248
Bandura, A., 437, 443
Banfield, E., 458, 496
Bannatyne, A., 281, 295
Bansch, R., 108, 121

541

Barbe, W. B., 120, 121, 139, 150
Barge, C. F., 316, 328
Barker, J., 393, 412
Barker, R. G., 45, 54, 432, 443
Barnett, C. D., 293, 295
Barnett, M. R., 321, 325
Barnette, W. L., 137, 144, 150
Barraga, N. C., 322, 325, 326
Barron, F., 156, 157, 165, 166, 168, 178, 180
Barry, H., 406, 412
Barsch, R. H., 279, 286, 287, 294, 295
Bateman, B. D., 277, 280, 292, 295, 297, 314, 326, 407, 412
Bates, P., 513, 531
Battle, E. S., 463, 496
Bauman, M. K., 313, 317, 326
Bay, E., 406, 412
Baylev, N., 53, 54, 514, 529
Bear, R., 478, 497, 498
Beasley, J., 410, 412
Behrens, M. L., 98, 121
Belden, K. H., 255, 271
Belden, R. H., 194, 221
Bell, N. W., 97, 121
Benda, C. E., 203, 210, 217, 368, 387
Bender-Gestalt Test, 276
Bender, L., 276, 296
Bensberg, G. L., 267, 268, 269
Bentley, J. E., 130, 150
Benton, A. L., 405, 406, 412
Bentzen, F. A., 283, 293, 296
Bereday, B., 150
Bereiter, C., 478, 496
Bergman, J., 61, 93
Bering, E. A., Jr., 209, 210, 217
Berko, F. G., 398, 407, 415
Berko, M. J., 398, 407, 415
Berkowitz, B., 514, 529
Berkowitz, L., 437, 443
Bernhardt, K. S., 212, 217
Bernstein, B., 471, 473, 496
Berry, M. F., 397, 401, 412, 416
Bettelheim, B., 436, 443
Betwee, M. C., 89, 95
Bice, H. V., 367, 370, 371, 387, 388
Bick, M. W., 513, 529
Biddle, M. D., 314
Biel, W. C., 212, 217
Bilash, I., 512, 530
Bilton, E. W., 346, 413
Bingley, T., 382, 387
Birch, J. W., 131, 132, 152, 323, 328
Birren, J. E., 507, 509, 513, 514, 515, 523, 524, 529, 530
Bixler, R. H., 320, 326
Blank, H. R., 315, 326
Blatt, B., 482, 496
Blizzard, R. M., 258, 272
Blodgett, H., 107, 121
Blom, G. E., 278, 296
Bloodstein, O., 402, 413
Bloom, B. S., 199, 217, 478, 482, 496, 500
Bloom, R., 463, 476, 496
Bloom, S. E., 255, 269

Bloomgarden, L., 460, 497
Blue, C. M., 66, 93, 264, 270
Bluemel, C. S., 402, 413
Blumberg, A., 66, 95
Boag, T. J., 62, 93
Boas, F., 200, 217
Bodmer, W. F., 198, 217
Boffey, P. M., 207, 217
Bogarty, W., 176, 180
Bogman, S. K., 351, 352, 356
Boles, G., 104, 121
Bonaparte, N., 380
Bond, H. M., 142, 150
Bondareff, W., 512, 529
Boney, J. D., 491, 497
Bonsall, M., 139, 150
Bord, M., 48, 54
Bothman, R. W., 439, 443
Botwinick, J., 515, 529
Bower, E. M., 440, 443
Bowman, P. H., 439, 443
Boyles, I. J., 362, 387
Braille, L., 302, 319
Branch, C. L., 260, 270
Bray, D. W., 234, 249, 452, 463, 498
Breger, L., 176, 180, 445
Brent, R. L., 206, 207, 217
Brerston, B. L., 350, 355
Brett, G. S., 6, 25
Bridge, E. M., 375, 378, 380, 383, 387
Bridgman, L., 323
Bridgmann, A. S., 128, 150
Brieland, D., 312, 313, 326
Brigham, C. C., 200, 217
Brill, R. B., 352, 355
Brimhall, D. R., 140, 150
Brody, J., 512, 530
Broida, D. C., 363, 381, 382, 387
Brookover, W., 89, 93
Brown, A. W., 262, 270
Brown, B., 463, 497
Brozek, J., 212, 219
Burger, R. E., 506, 530
Burks, A. J., 236, 251
Burks, B. S., 135, 139, 150, 214, 217, 228
Burt, C., 128, 142, 150, 166, 179
Busma, J. H., 456, 497
Busse, E. W., 514, 530
Butterfield, E. C., 480, 501
Byrne, D., 48, 54

Caesar, J., 380
Cain, L. F., 264, 270
Caldwell, B. M., 477, 482, 497
California Association for Neurologically Handicapped Children, 278
California Psychological Inventory (CPI), 146
California Test of Mental Maturity, 147
Calovini, G., 362, 387
Calvert, D. R., 345, 357
Calvin, J., 462
Cameron, N., 425, 443
Capobianco, R. J., 407, 413, 479, 497
Carmichael, L., 220

Carp, F. M., 315, 326
Carrell, J. A., 397, 413
Carrow, M. A., 409, 416
Carter, C. O., 193, 217
Carter, J. D., 374, 387
Casper, M., 188, 221
Casterline, D., 348, 357
Cattell, J. McK., 129, 140, 150
Cattell, R. B., 159, 161, 179
Cavalli-Sforza, L. L., 198, 217
Centers, L., 103, 121
Centers, R., 103, 121
Cerva, L., 211, 218
Chambers, N. S., 120, 121
Chamove, A. S., 257, 270
Chandler, A. H., 204, 223
Chein, I., 480, 497
Chevigny, H., 12, 25, 47, 54
Chicago Hearing Society and Clinic, 67
Chown, S. M., 515, 519, 529, 530
Christenson, C. V., 520, 521, 530
Claque, E., 518, 530
Clark, A. D., 278, 296
Clark, H. B., 480, 497
Clark, M., 456, 497
Clark, P. M., 162, 179
Clarke, A. D., 207, 214, 218, 236, 249
Clarke, A. M., 214, 218, 239
Clarke, C. M., 194, 218
Clarke, E. L., 140, 150
Cleary, T. A., 491, 497
Clements, D. S., 280, 296
Cloward, R. A., 438, 443
Coates, C., 161, 179
Cobb, M. V., 137, 151
Cobb, S., 373, 375, 388
Coffey, V. P., 257, 270
Cohen, D. K., 451, 459, 497
Cohen, J., 464, 475, 497, 500
Cohen, M. F., 308, 328
Cohler, M. J., 137, 150
Cole, C. C., 140, 150
Coleman, J. C., 526, 527, 530
Coleman, J. S., 480, 481, 497
Collins, A. L., 381, 388
Collmann, R. D., 254, 270
Colton, K., 367, 370, 371, 388
Conant, J. B., 133, 150, 243, 249
Conference of Executives of American
      Schools for the Deaf, 331, 355
Conn, J. C., 211, 218, 262, 270
Connor, L. E., 74, 93, 352, 355
Converse, H. D., 118, 122
Cooper, R. M., 199, 218, 512, 530
Copper, A., 193, 222
Cotzin, M., 311, 326, 328
Coughlin, E. W., 363, 387
Covalt, N. K., 517, 530
Covington, M. V., 176, 177, 179
Cowen, D., 203, 204, 224
Cowie, V., 193, 222
Cox, C. C., 159, 168, 179
Cram, C., 378, 388
Crane, M. M., 304, 326

Crome, L., 259, 271
Croneberg, C. G., 348, 357
Crothers, B., 371, 390
Crowder, T. H., 139, 140, 151
Cruickshank, W. M., 25, 85, 93, 95, 273, 283,
      284, 285, 293, 363, 367, 369, 370, 389,
      413
Cruse, D. B., 293, 296
Crutchfield, R. S., 176, 177, 179
Culley, W. J., 227, 249
Cummings, E., 516, 530
Curry, E. T., 333, 355
Curry, R., 393, 413
Cushner, I. M., 206, 218
Cutts, W. G., 468, 497
Cuttsforth, T. D., 313, 326

Dahlstein, D. H., 245, 250
Dale, D. M., 336, 355
Dallenbach, K. M., 311, 325, 326, 328
Dalton, M. M., 306, 326
Daly, F. M., 242, 246, 247, 249
Dann, M., 208, 218
Darke, R. A., 209, 218
Davis, A., 232, 249, 478, 496, 500
Davis, H., 335, 355
Davis, J. P., 398, 413
Davis, K., 215, 218
Dawes, H. C., 478, 497
Dawson, S., 211, 218, 262, 270
Day, M. F., 205, 218
Dayan, M., 267, 270
Dayton, N. A., 229, 249
DeGroat, L. J., 257, 270
DeHaan, F., 133, 150
De Haan, R. F., 133, 151
Dejong, R. N., 261, 270
Delacato, C. H., 286, 287, 288, 290, 294, 295,
      296
Delhanty, J. D., 193, 222
de Maupassant, G., 380
de Paul, V., 7
Dembo, T., 432, 443
Dement, W. C., 512, 531
Demeroth, N. J., 198, 201, 221
DeMille, R., 166, 179
Demos, G. D., 456, 497
DeMyer, M. K., 431, 444
Dennis, W., 215, 218, 515, 530
Denny, L. A., 176, 179
Deutsch, L., 380, 383, 387
Deutsch, M. P., 453, 463, 473, 476, 478, 496,
      497
Devereux, G., 247, 249
Diamond, G. L., 48, 54
Dickson, S., 396, 413
Dietze, D. A., 403, 412
DiLorenzo, L. T., 479, 497
Dinger, J. C., 245, 249
Dingman, H. F., 227, 249, 262, 270
Dingman, R. O., 408, 413
Diogenes, 6
Dix, M., 336, 355
Dobzkansky, T., 197, 218

Dolbear, K. E., 128, 151
Doll, E. E., 66, 93, 182, 183, 195, 218, 231,
    249, 367, 387
Doll, R., 205, 218
Dollard, J., 433, 443
Dolphin, J. E., 363, 387
Doob, A. N., 31, 54
Douglas, F. M., 335, 355
Downs, M. P., 355
Dramer, M., 63, 95
Dreger, R. M., 201, 218
Drevdahl, J. E., 159, 179
Drillien, C. M., 208, 218
Driscoll, K. W., 257, 271
Dubin, H. N., 66, 93
Duetscher, M., 480, 497
Dunn, L. M., 89, 91, 93, 143, 151, 244, 245,
    249, 263, 264, 270, 306, 325, 326, 414
Dunsdon, M. I., 367, 369, 370, 387
Duprez, D. A., 402, 414
Durea, M. A., 237, 249

Eames, T. H., 317, 326
Edgerton, R. P., 498
Educational Policies Commission, 75, 93
Edwards, A. E., 406, 413
Edwards, A. S., 213, 218
Edwards, J. H., 194, 218
Efron, R., 383, 387
Eichenlaub, J. E., 211, 218

Falek, A., 193, 220, 255, 271
Farber, B., 102, 122
Farrant, R. H., 341, 356
Farris, L. P., 317, 326
Feinstein, S. H., 311, 328
Fernald, D., 293, 297
Fernald, G., 291, 292, 296
Ferrara, R. P., 91, 93
Ferster, C. B., 431, 444
Fertsch, P., 319, 326
Fiedler, M. F., 11, 25, 342, 356
Field, A. M., 212, 223
Fierro, B., 257, 270
Fillmore, E. A., 214, 223
Finestone, S., 310, 326
Fishler, K., 108, 122
Fishman, S., 36, 39, 54
Fitzgerald, P. H., 194, 219
Fitzhugh, K. B., 291, 295, 296
Fitzhugh, L., 291, 295, 296
Fitzsimmons, M. J., 428, 444
FitzSimons, R. M., 409, 413
Fletcher, H., 393, 413
Floud, J., 461, 498
Floyer, E. B., 371, 387
Foote, F. M., 304, 326
Footlick, S. W., 293, 297
Force, D. G., 362, 387, 397, 402, 413
Forester, R. F., 457, 497
Forssman, H., 193, 219
Foulke, E., 320, 326
Fowler, E. P., Jr., 335, 355
Fowler, W., 231, 249, 482, 497
Fox, C., 515, 530

Foxe, A. N., 376, 387
Frampton, M. E., 324, 325, 326, 328, 352,
    355, 412, 414, 416
Frank, G. H., 431, 444
Frank, M., 212, 219
Fraser, F. C., 202, 219
Frazier, A., 53, 54
Freedman, A. M., 98, 122
Freedman, J. L., 31, 54
Freeman, F. N., 197, 199, 214, 219, 222
Freeman, J. T., 521, 530
Freitag, G., 431, 444
Freud, S., 5, 420, 424, 444
Friedman, H., 515, 530
Frierson, E. C., 130, 151
Friis, H., 507, 523, 531
Fritz, M. F., 212, 219
Frostig, M., 290, 294, 295, 296, 297
Fry, P. C., 212, 218
Furth, H., 341, 356
Fusfeld, I. S., 342, 356

Gagnon, J. H., 520, 521, 530
Galen, 6
Gall, E. D., 324, 325, 326, 328, 352, 355, 412,
    414, 416
Gallagher, J. J., 134, 139, 140, 151
Gallaudet College, 350
Gans, H. J., 450, 458, 493, 498
Garfunkel, F., 482, 496
Garrett, H. E., 201, 219
Garrett, J. F., 25, 54
Garrison, K. C., 362, 387, 397, 402, 413
Garrity, D. L., 438, 444
Gates, A. I., 203, 220
Gauger, A. B., 368, 387
Gebhard, P. H., 521, 531
Geist, H., 381, 388
Gens, A., 408, 413
Gentile, A., 344, 356
Geriatric Focus Report, 521, 522, 530
Gesell, A., 185, 215, 219
Getman, G. N., 287, 288, 296
Getzels, J. W., 160, 162, 166, 167, 171, 172,
    173, 175, 179
Geyer, M. L., 333, 356
Gibbons, D. C., 438, 444
Gibbs, E. L., 379, 388
Gibbs, F. A., 379, 388
Gibby, R. G., 195, 220
Gibson, D., 194, 219, 254, 255, 270
Gibson, J. B., 198, 223
Giliberty, F. R., 61, 93
Gillingham, A., 292, 296
Ginzberg, E., 234, 249, 452, 463, 498
Girden, E., 515, 530
Gitlin, D., 257, 272
Gladwin, T., 195, 204, 205, 208, 221, 222,
    231, 232, 234, 251
Glasser, F. B., 205, 219
Glauber, I. P., 401, 413
Glazer, N., 452, 453, 455, 458, 459, 493, 498
Glueck, E., 437, 438, 444
Glueck, S., 437, 438, 444
Goddard, H. H., 195, 236, 249

Goertzen, S., 407, 413
Goffman, E., 42, 43, 47, 54, 59, 93
Golberg, M. L., 89, 90, 93, 94
Goldman, R., 41, 54, 401, 413
Goldstein, H., 266, 270
Goldstein, K., 274, 277, 296
Goldstein, L., 206, 219
Golton, F., 128, 151
Goodenough, F., 245, 249
Goodstein, L. D., 402, 404, 408, 414
Goodwill Industries, 66
Gordon, E. W., 491, 498
Gordon, H., 213, 219
Gorelick, J., 264, 272
Gottesman, I. I., 192, 193, 219
Gough, H. G., 168, 179
Graham, D. F., 247, 249
Graham, F. K., 210, 219
Graliker, B. V., 108, 122
Gray, S., 478, 479, 498, 499
Graziano, A. M., 431, 444
Green, R. F., 514, 529
Greenberg, M., 204, 219
Greenblatt, M., 61, 94
Gregg, M. M., 204, 219
Gregor, W. P., 270
Gregory, H. H., 401, 402, 414
Grupp, E., 207, 222
Guetzkow, H., 212, 219
Guilford, J. P., 156, 160, 165, 179
Guldager, L., 324, 327

Haines, A., 205, 218
Halgren, M. R., 287, 288, 296
Hallpike, C. S., 336, 355
Halsey, A. H., 461, 498
Halstead, W. C., 276, 296
Hamilton, J. A., 432, 444
Hammer, E. G., 173, 179
Hammill, D. D., 407, 414
Hannah-Alava, 194, 220
Haring, N. G., 281, 293, 297
Harlow, H. F., 257, 270
Harrell, M. S., 236, 249
Harrell, R. F., 203, 212, 220
Harrell, T. W., 236, 249
Harrington, M., 452, 498
Harshman, H. W., 90, 94
Hartinger, W., 439, 443
Harvey, L., 457, 498
Harvey, O. J., 161, 179
Hasse, K., 344, 356
Hatfield, E. M., 305, 327
Hathaway, S. R., 438, 444
Hatten, P. H., 320, 327
Hauck, B. B., 143, 151
Haugen, D., 401, 415
Havighurst, R. J., 133, 141, 150, 151, 232,
      249, 517, 530
Hayes, S. P., 314, 315, 317, 326, 327
Heber, R. A., 182, 183, 220
Heber, R. F., 94, 245, 250
Heck, A. O., 130, 151, 319, 327
Heckleman, R. G., 297
Hefner, R., 379, 388

Heinze, S., 157, 180
Hellmuth, J., 277, 295, 296, 297
Henderson, A. S., 478, 498
Henderson, P., 377, 388
Henderson, R. W., 484, 500
Henry, J., 402, 414
Henry, W. E., 516, 530
Henry, Z., 402, 414
Heron, A., 519, 530
Herzon, J. M., 404, 416
Hess, R. D., 231, 249, 465, 478, 496, 497, 498, 500
Higgins, J. V., 230, 249
Hildreth, G. H., 89, 90, 94, 137, 151
Hill, A. B., 205, 218
Hill, G., 34, 38, 54
Hills, J. R., 491, 498
Himmelstein, P., 412
Hippocrates, 6
Hock, P. H., 529
Hodgins, A. S., 479, 498
Hodgson, F. M., 74, 83, 94
Hoeltke, G. M., 89, 94
Hoffmann, D. M., 510, 529
Hoffmeister, J. K., 161, 179
Holland, J. L., 164, 179
Holland, J. S., 160, 181
Holliday, A. R., 410, 416
Hollingshead, A. B., 441, 444
Hollingworth, L. S., 130, 135, 137, 151, 152
Holt, K. S., 257, 270
Holzinger, K. J., 197, 199, 214, 219, 222
Hood, P. N., 367, 389
Hoover, R. E., 237, 302
Hopkins, T., 367, 370, 371, 388
Horn, A., 144, 151
Horne, D., 290, 296
Horney, K., 423, 444
Horstmann, D. M., 204, 220
Horstmann, P., 258, 270
Horton, K. B., 479, 499
Hovland, C. I., 434, 445
Howard, A., 437, 444
Howe, S. G., 323
Hsia, D. Y., 257, 271
Hughes, H. H., 118, 122
Hughes, R. B., 341, 356
Hull, F. M., 406, 408, 410, 414
Hurlin, R. G., 306, 327
Hurlock, E. B., 512, 530
Huseth, B., 64, 94
Hutt, M. L., 195, 220
Hyman, D. J., 91, 93

Ingram, C. R., 227, 242, 250
Institute for Personality Assessment and
      Research (IPAR) 157, 158, 159
Irwin, J. R., 395, 416
Irwin, O. C., 407, 414
Irwin, R. B., 391, 414
Itard, 274, 287
Iyengar, K. S., 91, 93
Izard, C. E., 363, 387

Jackson, P. W., 160, 162, 166, 167, 171, 172,
      173, 175, 179

Jacobs, M., 205, 219
Jacobson, C. B., 194, 221
James, I. P., 382, 388
Jarvik, L. F., 193, 220, 255, 271, 511, 530
Jenkins, E., 396, 414
Jenkins, M. D., 136, 151
Jenkins, R. W., 262, 270
Jensen, A. R., 198, 199, 201, 220, 482, 498
Jensen, D. W., 135, 139, 150
Jerome, E. A., 515, 529
Jessen, M. S., 294, 297
Johnson, D., 242, 245, 250, 275, 297
Johnson, D. E., 520, 530
Johnson, G. O., 89, 93, 94, 95, 296
Johnson, G. R., 238, 250
Johnson, H. G., 137, 151
Johnson, J. C., 350, 356
Johnson, O. J., 139, 151
Johnson, R. C., 98, 122
Johnson, W., 401, 402, 403, 414
(The) John Tracy Clinic, 67
Jolly, D. H., 227, 249
Jones, A. M., 135, 136, 151
Jones, H. E., 212, 213, 220
Jones, J. W., 303, 327
Jones, L., 213, 218
Jones, M. C., 53, 54
Jordon, A. M., 213, 220
Jordon, S., 49, 54, 122
Jubenville, C. P., 62, 94
Jucknat, M., 241, 250
Justman, J., 90, 94

Kain, L. M., 242, 246, 247, 249
Kallmann, E. J., 511, 530
Kalter, H., 202, 220
Kane, E. R., 287, 288, 296
Kanner, L., 374, 388, 430, 444
Kant, O., 429, 444
Kariger, H., 89, 93
Karnes, M. B., 147, 148, 151, 479, 498
Karres, M. B., 314, 327
Kass, C. E., 277, 281, 297
Kates, F. F., 341, 356
Kates, S. L., 341, 356
Katz, I., 481, 498
Kean, J. E., 431, 444
Keller, H., 323
Kellogg, W. N., 311, 327
Kelsey, F. O., 208, 220
Kendrick, S. A., 491, 498
Kennedy, W. A., 89, 95
Kent, D. P., 515, 518, 519, 520, 521, 530
Kephart, N., 273, 279, 285, 286, 294, 295, 297
Keppel, G., 11, 25
Kerby, C. E., 303, 305
Kershner, J. R., 294, 297
Kidd, J. W., 182, 183, 220
Kinder, E. F., 242, 248
Kinder, M. I., 431, 444
Kinsey, A. C., 521, 531
Kinstler, D. B., 401, 414
Kirk, S. A., 89, 94, 242, 243, 245, 250, 264, 271, 273, 280, 281, 297, 478, 498
Kirman, B. H., 258, 271, 367, 371, 388

Kitano, H. H. L., 461, 462, 498
Klaus, R. A., 478, 479, 498, 499
Kleemeier, R. W., 513, 531
Kleffner, F. R., 405, 414
Klein, S. P., 156, 186
Klineberg, O., 200, 220
Klock, J. C., 491, 498
Knoblock, H., 254, 271
Knox, J., 462
Koch, A. M., 212, 220
Koch, R., 108, 122
Kodman, F., 333, 356, 479, 499
Kogan, N., 508, 509, 531
Kohlberg, L., 478, 482, 491, 499
Kohnky, E., 213, 220
Koller, M. R., 508, 531
Kopp, G. A., 401, 414
Kosa, J., 519, 532
Kough, J., 133, 151
Kramer, B. M., 62, 94
Kramer, J. R., 461, 499
Kreshevsky, I., 432, 444
Krugman, M., 444
Krush, T. P., 81, 94, 297
Kugel, R. B., 59, 94, 228, 250
Kugelmass, I. N., 192, 202, 221
Kulkmann-Anderson Intelligence Test, 238
Kurtzman, K. A., 172, 179
Kvaraceus, W. C., 238, 250, 422, 441, 444

Lamb, C., 380
Land, S. L., 327
Landau, H. G., 515, 529
Lane, B., 508, 531
Langdon, J. N., 236, 252
Langner, T. S., 461, 500
Lanyon, R. I., 402, 414
Larve, C. M., 122
Lasser, R. P., 512, 531
Lauwerys, P., 150
Lawson, D., 257, 271
Laxer, R. M., 105, 122
Laycork, S. R., 118, 122
Lea, H. C., 6, 7, 25
Leahy, A. M., 228, 250
Lee, E. S., 200, 220
Lefkowitz, A. S., 530
Lefver, W., 297
Lehman, H. C., 138, 151, 231, 250, 515, 531
Lehman, O., 193, 219
Lehtinen, L., 276, 279, 283, 295, 298
Lejeune, J., 193, 221
Lemert, E. M., 402, 415
Lemkau, P. C., 188, 221
Lennox, W. G., 372, 373, 375, 376, 377, 379, 381, 388
Lenz, T., 228, 250
Lesser, L., 430, 444
Lessinger, L. M., 131, 152
Leu, D., 89, 93
Levan, A., 193, 223
Leventman, S., 461, 499
Levin, H., 99, 122
Levine, E., 342, 356
Levine, E. S., 25, 54

Levine, M., 293, 297
Levine, S., 264, 270
Levine, S. Z., 208, 218
Lewin, K., 432, 443
Lewis, E. O., 195, 221
Lewis, O., 456, 499
Lewis, S., 491, 498
Lewis, W. D., 136, 151
LeZok, R. J., 312, 327
Lieberman, R., 205, 206, 224
Lilienfeld, A. M., 208, 222, 254, 271
Lilly, M. S., 489, 499
Linduska, N., 46, 54
Ling, T. L., 315, 328
Lisanbee, L. K., 53, 54
Locke, J., 4, 5
Lohr, F. E., 396, 414
Loquist, L. H., 11, 25
Los Angeles City School Districts, 83, 94,
    137, 144, 152
Lovaas, O. I., 431, 444
Lovell, C., 237, 250
Lowe, G. M., 213, 221
Lowenbach, H., 379, 388
Lowenfeld, B., 306, 310, 313, 315, 317, 320,
    327
Lowenthal, M. F., 522, 531
Lubs, H. A., 255, 271
Lucito, L. J., 137, 152
Luecking, E. M., 133, 153
Lukoff, I. F., 49, 54, 310, 326
Lunde, A. S., 351, 352, 356
Lundin, R. W., 423, 444
Luper, H. L., 402, 403, 414
Lurie, L. A., 211, 221, 262, 271
Luterman, D. M., 308, 328
Lycette, R. R., 194, 219
Lyon, W., 407, 415

McCandless, B. R., 213, 221
McCarthy, J. F., 283, 297
McCarthy, J. J., 230, 250, 283, 297
McCarthy, J. M., 277, 297
McClelland, D. C., 464, 475, 482, 499, 500
McClure, H. M., 194, 221, 255, 271
Maccoby, G. E., 99, 122
McConnell, F., 479, 499
McCord, J. S., 437, 444, 445
McCord, W., 437, 444, 445
McCord, W. M., 198, 201, 221
McCormick, D. D., 293, 297
MacDermot, P. N., 211, 222
McDonald, W. B., 258, 271
McGinnis, M. A., 406, 414
McGowan, J. F., 117, 122
McGraven, V. G., 432, 445
MacGregor, R., 99, 122
McIntire, J. T., 367, 370, 388
MacIntire, M. S., 254, 271
Mackay, R. P., 378, 388
McKee, G. W., 287, 288, 296
Mackie, R. P., 245, 250
MacKinnon, D. W., 157, 165, 170, 179
Macmeeken, A. M., 136, 152
McMenemy, R., 292, 297

MacMillan, T. ., 61, 62, 94
McNemar, Q., 165, 166, 167, 179, 232, 250
McPortland, J., 481, 499
McWilliams, B. J., 399, 414
Macy, A. S., 323
Madsen, M. C., 463, 499
Magnifico, 242, 250
Malherbe, E. H., 134, 152
Malzberg, B., 377, 389
Maltzman, I., 156, 176, 180
Maltzman, M., 344, 356
Mandelbaum, D. G., 215, 221
Marge, M., 409, 414
Marks, H. H., 525, 531
Marsh, R. W., 166, 180
Martin, C. E., 521, 531
Martin, H. P., 259, 271
Martin, R., 402, 414
Martinson, R. A., 89, 94, 131, 132, 143, 149,
    152
Masland, R. L., 204, 205, 208, 221, 222
Maslow, A. H., 156, 180
Maslow, P., 297
Mason, E. P., 509, 531
Massmerman, J. H., 432, 445
Master, A. M., 512, 531
Masters, F. H., 246, 250
Mathias, E., 212, 221
Matson, D. D., 260, 271
Mauncy, J., 311, 312, 328
Maurer, S., 212, 217, 221
May, F. B., 166, 180
Mearns, H., 177, 180
Meeham, M. K., 398, 407, 415
Mechanic, D., 507, 523, 531
Medinnus, G. R., 98, 122
Mednick, S., 156, 176, 180
Meeker, M., 144, 152
Mellin, G. W., 204, 221
Mellman, W. J., 193, 221
Menkes, J. H., 257, 271
Menolascino, F. J., 254, 271
Menyuk, P., 395, 415
Merlis, S., 376, 390
Merrifield, P. R., 160, 166, 179
Merrill, M. A., 226, 238, 250
Metfessel, M., 237, 250
Meyer, V., 368, 389
Meyers, P., 407, 415
Meyerson, L., 332, 336, 338, 339, 341, 356
Michael, J. L., 336, 341, 356
Michaels, R. H., 204, 221
Mickelson, P., 235, 250
Miles, C. C., 135, 137, 152
Milisen, R., 398, 415
Miller, E., 370, 389
Miller, E. A., 107, 122
Miller, K. S., 201, 218
Miller, N. E., 434, 435
Miller, R. W., 207, 221
Miller, V., 139, 152
Miller, W. B., 422, 444
Millhoj, P., 507, 523, 531
Minnesota Multi-phasic Personality Inventory
    (MMPI), 170

Minto, A., 204, 221
Mirels, H. L., 162, 179
Mitchell, B. C., 197, 214, 219
Mohr, J., 228, 250
Monachesi, E. D., 438, 444
Monahan, J. E., 135, 152
Moncur, J. P., 409, 415
Montessori, M., 287, 477, 499
Moorhead, P. S., 193, 221
More, H., 212, 221
Morgan, C. T., 212, 221
Morkowin, B. V., 348, 357
Morley, M., 399, 415
Morris, J. E., 320, 327
Morrison, D. F., 515, 529
Moss, J. W., 335, 357
Moss, M., 335, 357
Motto, J., 350, 357
Mowrer, O. H., 432, 445
Moynihan, D. P., 452, 453, 455, 458, 459, 493,
    498
Mulden, R. L., 402, 403, 414
Mullen, E. A., 238, 250
Mullen, F. A., 380, 388
Munday, L. A., 491, 499
Murphy, D. P., 206, 219, 221, 258, 271
Murphy, F. J., 438, 445
Murray, B. O., 484, 500
Muzio, J. N., 512, 531
Myers, E., 11, 25
Myerson, L., 11, 25, 46, 54
Mykelbust, H. R., 275, 297, 341, 357

Nader, R., 523
Nair, K., 462, 499
Nass, M. L., 341, 356
National Association for Children with
    Learning Disabilities, 277
National Association for Mental Health, 58
National Association for Retarded Children, 67
National Council on Crime and Delinquency,
    580
National Safety Council, 362–89
National Society for the Prevention of
    Blindness, 304
Nelson, S. E., 401, 415, 416
Nelson, V., 199, 223
New, E. V., 208, 218
Newell, N., 119, 123
Newman, H. H., 199, 222
New York State Department of Mental
    Hygiene, 188, 222
Nickerson, G., 211, 222
Niehn, B. F., 66, 94
Nisbet, J. D., 229, 230, 231, 250
Nolan, C. Y., 316, 318, 320, 322, 327
Norman, V. B., 63, 94, 440, 443
Northway, M. L., 212, 217
Novack, K., 211, 218
Nowlin, J., 514, 530
Nowrey, J. E., 6, 7, 25
Nuffield, E. J., 382, 389
O'Connor, N., 187, 188, 222, 264, 271
Oden, M. H., 129, 138, 139, 140, 141, 142,
    145, 150, 152, 153, 160, 181, 197, 223,
    510, 514, 529, 532

O'Hanlon, G. S., 212, 222
Ohlin, L. E., 438, 443
Olsen, K., 69, 95
Olshansky, S., 66, 67, 94
O'Niell, J. J., 335, 336, 346, 357
Orbach, H. L., 517, 531
Orlansky, H., 98, 122
Orton, S. T., 275, 297
Otto, H. J., 130, 152
Otto, W., 292, 297
Oughterson, A. W., 206, 222
Owens, W. A., 514, 531

Paine, R. S., 257, 271, 371, 390
Painter, G., 294, 297
Palm, H. J., 170, 180
Paracelsus, 7
Parnes, S. J., 143, 152
Pasamanick, B., 208, 222, 254, 271
Passow, A. H., 89, 90, 93, 94
Paterson, D. G., 339, 357
Patric, A. D., 257, 271
Patterson, R. M., 273
Pearl, A., 464, 475, 497, 500
Pegnato, C. V., 131, 132, 152
Pelleteri, O., 204, 219
Penafiel, R. W., 257, 270
Penfield, W., 377, 379, 389
Penrose, L. S., 192, 193, 205, 210, 222, 255,
    259, 263, 271, 377, 380, 389
Perestein, J. A., 367, 389
Perrin, E. L., 393, 415
Peter, L. J., 292, 298
Peters, R. S., 25
Pfantz, H. W., 63, 95
Phelps, H. R., 243, 250, 366, 367, 389
Philleo, C., 273
Phillips, E. L., 293, 297
Pickett, B. H., 353, 357
Pickett, J. M., 353, 357
Pieper, W. A., 194, 221, 255, 271
Pierce, J. V., 146, 152
Pierson, W. P., 193, 220, 255, 271
Pinel, 7
Pintner, R., 261, 277, 339, 357, 381, 389
Plant, W. T., 482, 499
Plaut, R. L., 460, 499
Plog, S. C., 498
Plummer, G., 258, 272
Pollock, H. M., 377, 389
Pomeroy, W. B., 521, 531
Porter, A. C., 491, 500
Porteus, D. S., 237, 251
Portnoy, I., 427, 445
Poulos, T. H., 349, 357
Pozesonyi, J., 194, 219, 255, 270
Pozony, L., 254, 270
Prechtl, H. F., 210, 222
President's Council on Aging, 507, 518, 531
Proctor, B., 343, 357
Project Talent, 167
Pronovost, W., 394, 415
Pryor, M., 293, 295
Radin, N., 478, 499
Radke, M. J., 99, 122
Ramirez, I., 257, 270

Ratzburg, 283, 293, 296
Raus, S., 367, 369, 387
Reddell, R. C., 345, 357
Redl, F., 436, 445
Redlich, R. C., 441, 444
Reed, E. W., 230, 249, 251
Reed, S. C., 230, 249, 251
Reichstein, J., 336, 357
Reid, I. D., 462, 500
Reynolds, M. C., 341, 357
Rice, C. E., 311, 328
Richards, C. J., 278, 296
Richardson, H., 422, 439, 443, 445
Ricketts, B. M., 100, 123
Rickey, A., 213, 222
Ridgway, R. W., 281, 297
Riegel, K. F., 515, 529
Riessman, F., 464, 475, 497, 500
Riley, L. H., 308, 328
Rimland, B., 431, 445
Ringness, T. A., 241, 251
Ripple, R. E., 166, 180
Robbins, J. E., 229, 251
Robbins, M. P., 294, 298
Robbins, N., 324, 328
Roberts, F. J., 204, 221
Roberts, J. A., 191, 192, 222, 229, 251
Roberts, S. O., 491, 500
Robertson, B. A., 515, 531
Robinson, F. B., 402, 415
Robinson, H., 482, 500
Robinson, H. B., 193, 202, 203, 204, 205, 206,
    208, 211, 222, 227, 251, 254, 260, 265,
    272, 380, 383, 388
Robinson, N. M., 193, 202, 203, 204, 205, 206,
    208, 211, 222, 227, 251, 254, 260, 265,
    272, 380, 383, 388
Robinson, W. P., 473, 500
Rock, D. A., 156, 180
Roe, E. D., 312, 313, 328
Roe, V., 398, 415
Roebuck, J., 422, 445
Roffwarg, H. P., 512, 531
Rogers, C. R., 99, 122, 156, 175, 176, 180
Rogers, M. C., 213, 222
Roos, P., 267, 272
Rose, A. M., 516, 531
Rosen, B. M., 63, 94, 95
Rosenblatt, A., 516, 531
Rosenfeld, G. B., 370, 389
Rosenstein, J., 336, 355, 357
Ross, A. O., 11, 24, 25, 110, 122
Rost, K. J., 293, 298
Rothschild, J., 18, 25
Rotter, J. B., 463, 496
Rubenstein, B. D., 431, 444
Rubin, E. Z., 89, 95
Ruch, F. L., 212, 222
Ruddle, F. H., 255, 271
Rugh, R., 207, 222
Rundle, A. T., 191, 193, 222, 256, 257, 258, 272
Rupp, C., 372, 389
Rusk, H. A., 46, 54
Rutherford, D., 407, 416
Ryan, G. M., 335, 355
Ryan, M. S., 516, 531
Rytard, D. A., 270

Saffian, S., 363, 389
Sakel, M., 372, 389
Sakula, J., 205, 218
Salter, R., 479, 497
Sander, E. K., 402, 415
Sarason, S. B., 110, 122, 195, 204, 205, 208,
    221, 222, 231, 232, 234, 235, 251, 366,
    368, 369, 377, 381, 389
Satir, V. M., 99, 122
Sawrey, J. M., 17, 20, 26, 54, 154, 180, 242,
    251, 363, 389, 428, 434, 437, 445, 469
Sawrey, W. L., 429, 445
Schaefer, E. S., 99, 122
Schaefer, V. G., 237, 251
Schaeffer, B., 431, 444
Schaie, K. W., 513, 531
Schain, R., 205, 219
Scheerenberger, R. C., 265, 272
Scheerer, M., 276, 296
Schein, J. D., 344, 356
Scheinberg, I. H., 257, 272
Schlacgel, T. F., Jr., 315, 328
Schmidt, L. D., 117, 122
Schnobrick, J. N., 293, 297
Schoeck, H., 509, 532
Schonell, F. E., 367, 370, 386, 389
Schonfield, D., 515, 531
Schulderman, E., 513, 531
Schunoff, H. F., 350, 357
Schur, E. M., 40, 55
Schusterman, R. J., 311, 328
Schwartz, R., 408, 415
Scott, R. A., 301, 307, 308, 328
Seagoe, M. V., 132, 152
Sears, R. R., 99, 122, 434, 445
Seashore, C. E., 315, 328
Selesnick, S. T., 58, 93
Senison, C. B., 89, 95
Sequin, 274, 287
Seward, G., 423, 445
Seymour, A. H., 212, 222
Shames, G. H., 401, 413
Shannon, D. C., 137, 144, 152
Shanus, E., 507, 523, 531
Shapiro, A., 463, 499, 500
Shaw, M. C., 147, 152
Shaycoft, M. F., 167, 180
Shea, P. D., 142, 152
Sheehan, J. G., 401, 404, 415
Shelton, F. C., 508, 509, 531
Shere, M. D., 108, 122
Shield, J., 229, 251
Shipman, V., 231, 249, 465, 498
Shirley, M. M., 438, 445
Shriver, R. S., 482, 500
Shuey, A. M., 201, 223
Siegel, E., 90, 95
Siegel, G. M., 401, 415
Silver, A. G., 34, 38, 54
Simmons, J. Q., 431, 444
Simpson, J. A., 258, 272
Singer, J. J., 432, 445
Singh, J. A., 215, 223
Sirken, J., 407, 415
Sisler, L. E., 262, 270
Skeels, H. M., 214, 223, 228, 233, 251
Skinner, C. W., Jr., 204, 223

Skodak, M., 228, 233, 251
Slater, E., 229, 251
Smallpace, V., 194, 218
Smilansky, S., 462, 500
Smith, A., 254, 272
Smith, A. J., 212, 223
Smith, B. R., 479, 499
Smith, D. W., 258, 272
Smith, E., 100, 123
Smith, H., 100, 123
Smith, H. W., 89, 95
Smith, J. O., 408, 415
Smith, M. B., 49, 51, 55
Smith, M. F., 236, 251
Smock, C., 363, 389
Soddy, K., 202, 208, 223
Somerfield-Ziskund, E., 383, 390
Sontag, L., 199, 223
Southern, M. L., 482, 499
Southern Regional Education Board, 440–45
Spar, H. J., 310, 328
Specht, L. F., 139, 152
Speer, G. S., 214, 223
Spivak, G., 293, 297
Spodek, B., 477, 500
Springer, K. J., 174, 181
Srole, L., 461, 500
Stanburg, J. B., 258, 272
Stanford-Binet, 132, 148, 202, 209, 238, 381,
      457, 479, 486
Stanley, J. C., 491, 500
Stanton, M., 381, 389
Stanton, N., 261, 272
Starbuck, H. B., 312, 327
Stecht, T. G., 320, 326
Steckle, L. C., 484, 500
Steer, M. D., 410, 415
Steffire, B., 139, 150
Stehouwer, J., 507, 523, 531
Stein, M., 157, 180
Stemlicht, M., 255, 272
Stenquist, G., 324, 328
Stephen, E., 365, 366, 371, 390
Stephens, T. M., 323, 328
Sterritt, G. M., 355
Stevens, H. A., 61, 66, 94, 95
Stewart, J. L., 402, 415
Stillman, B., 292, 296
Stock, F. G., 236, 252
Stokol, W. C., 348, 357
Stoller, A., 254, 270
Stolurow, L. M., 320, 326
Stoneburner, R. L., 479, 498
Stouffer, S. A., 142, 152
Stout, G. H., 212, 223
Straker, M., 525, 531
Strauss, A. A., 273, 274, 275, 276, 278, 279,
      283, 285, 287, 295, 298
Streif, G. F., 519, 532
Streng, A., 330, 350, 351, 357
Strodtbeck, F. L., 450, 458, 461, 500
Stromsa, C., 403, 415
Strother, C. R., 513, 531
Studley, W. M., 479, 498
Sugar, O., 378, 388

Sumption, M. R., 133, 153
Supa, M., 311, 328
Swan, C., 204, 223
Swartz, D., 520, 532
Swenson, W. M., 509, 532
Syden, M., 244, 251

Tanenbaum, D. E., 522, 532
Tanner, J. M., 200, 223
Tarjan, G., 227, 249, 265, 270
Tatham, C. M., 212, 217
Taylor, C. W., 157, 160, 168, 169, 180
Taylor, E. J., 46, 54
Taylor, G. J., 237, 249
Taylor, H., 69, 95
Taylor, J. G., 312, 328
Telford, C. W., 17, 20, 26, 53, 54, 104, 123,
      154, 180, 201, 223, 242, 251, 363, 389,
      428, 434, 437, 445, 469
Tenny, J. W., 45, 55, 378, 390
Terman, L. M., 129, 130, 134, 135, 136, 137,
      138, 139, 140, 141, 145, 153, 160, 181,
      197, 223, 510, 532
Terry, T. L., 304
Teska, J. A., 479, 498
Thelly, F., 26
Therman, E., 193, 223
Thoday, J. M., 198, 223
Thom, D. A., 119, 123, 372, 390
Thomas, C. L., 491, 498
Thompson, C. E., 428, 445
Thompson, G. B., 260, 270
Thompson, W. E., 519, 532
Thorne, F. C., 235, 251
Tietze, C., 188, 221
Tiffany, R. K., 341, 356
Tijo, J. H., 193, 223
Tikofsky, R. P., 393, 415
Tizard, J. P., 187, 188, 222, 235, 241, 251, 257,
      264, 271, 371, 377, 382, 383, 390
Tobias, J., 264, 272
Tolkin, S. H., 238, 252
Tomlinson, H., 213, 223
Torrance, E. P., 156, 161, 162, 166, 169, 170,
      174, 175, 176, 177, 181
Towbin, A., 208, 223
Tower, D. B., 384, 390
Towne, C. H., 235, 251
Townsend, P., 507, 523, 531
Trapp, E. P., 412
Travis, L. E., 400, 415
Treadgold, A. F., 195, 202, 208, 223
Tretsven, V. E., 408, 415
Tuddenham, R. D., 232, 251
Tufts, L. R., 410, 416
Tulkin, S. R., 201, 223
Turner, A. N., 520, 532
Turner, W. J., 376, 390
Turpin, R., 193, 221
Ullman, M., 123
Ulrich, W. C., 441, 444
United Cerebral Palsy Association, Inc., 67,
      367
United States Children's Bureau, 67

United States Department of Health, Education and Welfare, 337, 357
United States Office of Education, 306
UPI, 523, 532

Vail, D. J., 59, 95
Valett, R. E., 292, 298
Van Itallie, P. H., 344, 357
Van Riper, C., 395, 396, 404, 416
Van Wyle, M. K., 346, 357
Vernon, M., 336, 341, 358
Verplank, W. S., 434, 445
Villey, P., 310, 328
Vineberg, S. E., 327
Vineland Training School, 195
Vocational Rehabilitation Agency, 65
Voelker, P. H., 64, 95
Vogel, E. F., 97, 121
Volta Bureau, 67

Waisman, H. A., 257, 270
Wallach, M. A., 161, 181
Wallerstein, J. S., 439, 445
Wallin, J. E., 195, 202, 208, 215, 229, 220, 237, 238, 240, 252, 254, 261, 272, 378, 390
Walter Reed Army Institute of Research, 211
Walters, R., 437, 443
Wandever, Z. W., 255, 272
Ward, L. F., 129, 153
Warden, C. J., 212, 220
Warfield, F., 41, 55
Warfield, G. J., 107, 121
Warkany, 202, 220
Waters, W. J., 205, 223
Wawrzaszek, F. J., 350, 357
Wayne County Training School, 273
Weber, A., 6, 7, 26
Wechsler-Bellevue, 381
Wechsler, D., 226, 238, 252
Wechsler, H., 64, 65, 95
Wechsler Intelligence Scale for Children, 133
Wedder, C. B., 530
Wedderburn, D., 507, 523, 531
Wedeking, L. P., 237, 252
Wedenberg, E., 332, 358
Weikart, D. P., 478, 479, 499, 500
Weinman, D., 204, 223
Weisberg, P. S., 174, 181
Weiss, A., 400, 416
Weller, J. E., 468, 482, 500
Wellman, B. L., 232, 252
Wenan, C., 193, 221
Wenar, C., 37, 55
Werner, H., 273, 275, 283, 285
Wertheimer, K. N., 276, 298
Wesselhoeft, C., 258, 272
West, R., 401, 416
Westenberger, E. J., 213, 224
Westlake, H., 407, 408, 416
Wheeler, L. R., 214, 224
Whitaker, J. E., 212, 222
White, B. J., 161, 179
White House Conference on Aging, 506, 532

White House Conference on Child Health and Protection, 331, 358
White, T. H., 451, 500
Whiteman, M., 49, 54, 310, 326, 463, 476, 496
Whittlesey, J. R. B., 297
Whyte, W. H., Jr., 154, 181
Wiener, L. L., 380, 383, 387
Wiengest, M., 513, 529
Wiggins, J. W., 509, 532
Wilkerson, D. A., 482, 491, 498, 500
Wilkie, F., 514, 530
Wilkins, L., 258, 272
Williams, D., 324, 328
Windle, W. F., 269
Winebrenner, D. K., 303, 328
Wineman, D., 436, 445
Wingate, M. E., 402, 416
Winich, C., 61, 95
Wiseman, D., 292, 298
Witmer, H. L., 99, 123, 438, 445
Witmer, L., 291, 292, 298
Witty, P. A., 130, 135, 136, 137, 138, 139, 153, 231, 250, 478, 501
Wolf, A., 203, 204, 224
Wolfensberger, W., 59, 77, 78, 79, 94, 95, 298
Wolfle, D., 144, 153
Wollersheim, J. P., 314, 327
Wolman, B. B., 292, 298
Wood, K. S., 409, 416
Woods, F. J., 409, 416
Woodward, E., 203, 220
Worchel, P., 311, 312, 325, 328
World Health Organization, 188–89
Wortis, S. B., 378, 388
Wright, B. A., 11, 26, 33, 42, 45, 53, 55, 363, 390
Wunsch, W. J., 255, 272
Wyatt, G. L., 404, 416
Wyatt, S., 236, 252
Wyle, C. J., 439, 445
Wyley, J. H., 254, 271
Wyllie, W. S., 366, 390
Wynburn, G. M., 336, 337, 358

Yaffe, J., 461, 501
Yankauer, A., 333, 356
Yannet, H., 191, 205, 206, 224, 364, 368, 369, 390
Yerkes, R. M., 200, 224
Yudin, L., 341, 356

Zajonc, R. B., 48, 55
Zarfas, D. E., 254, 270
Zaslow, R. W., 431, 445
Zehnder, J. R., 66, 95
Zigler, E., 480, 491, 499, 501
Zimals, V., 211, 218
Zingg, R. M., 215, 223
Ziskund, E., 383, 390
Zola, I., 437, 445
Zubek, J. P., 199, 218, 512, 513, 530, 531
Zubin, J., 529
Zuk, G. H., 104, 123
Zweibelson, L., 316, 328

Subject Index

AAMD classification, 188, 225
Achievement motivation, 482
Acrocephaly, 259
Adjustment
  habits, 420–22
  impairment of, 183
  intelligence and, 15
  school, 491–94
Afro-Americans, 451–53
Aged
  activities, 515–17
  adjustments, 524, 527
  appetite, 512
  behavior disorders, 524, 527
  blood pressure, 512
  characteristics, 510–17
  creativity, 515
  hobbies, 520
  housing, 523–24
  identity, 506
  individual differences, 507–8
  insomnia, 512
  institutionalized, 523
  intellectual changes, 514
  intelligence, 514–15
  interests, 515–17
  "life-space", 524
  loneliness, 522
  longitudinal studies, 510
  minority group, 509

physical changes, 511–12
  recall, 515
  relegiosity, 516–17
  research problems, 509–10
  rigidity, 515
  self-centeredness, 516
  sensory changes, 512–14
  sex activity, 520–21
  sex roles, 520–22
  single, 522
  skin, 511
  social living, 522–24
  socioeconomic status, 506–8
  stereotypes, 508–9
Aggression
  familial correlates, 437
  forms, 435–36
  hostile, 432–34
  pathological, 436–37
  retaliative, 435
  social learning, 436–37
  successful, 506, 527–28
  symbolic, 435–36
Agraphia, 275
Akinetic epilepsy, 395
Amaurotic familial idiocy, 257
American Association of Mental Deficiency,
  23
Amino acid, 256
Amputees, 39

Analgesia, 16
Anaphia, 16
Anencephaly, 203, 259
Anesthesia, 16
Anosmia, 16
Anoxia, 368
Anticonvulsant drugs, 383
Anxiety
  acute, 425
  chronic, 424–25
  "free-floating", 424
  general, 422, 427
  Oedipal, 174
Aphasia, 274–75, 397, 405–7
Architects, 157–59
Arthritis, 364
Articulation, 398–99
Artists, 173
Asthma, 364
Astigmatism, 317
Asylums, 56–57
Attack, 435–36
Audiometer, 13, 334
Audiometry, 330–31
Auditorially handicapped
  educational achievement, 341–42
  intelligence, 339–41
  personal characteristics, 337–42
  rigidity, 341
Auditory acuity, 335–36
Auditory defects
  causes, 336
  childhood diseases, 336
  incidence, 336
  postnatal causes, 336
Auditory testing
  conditioned response methods, 336
  GSR, 335
Aural acuity, 333–36
Aural handicaps
  definitions, 330–32
  significance of, 229–30
Aural impairment
  audiometric definitions, 332
  GSR, 335
  tuning fork, 334
Aurally handicapped
  additional handicaps, 338–39
  articulation, 333
  college, 350–51
  deaf, 330–32
  education, 347–51
  finger spelling, 348
  hard-of-hearing, 330–31
  hearing aids, 332
  individual differences, 332
  language learning, 346–47
  nursery schools, 349
  occupations, 351–52
  prospects, 353
  sign language, 348
  special teacher, 348–49
  speech, 333
  vocational training, 352–53

watch test, 333–34
whisper test, 333–34
Aurally impaired
  adjustment, 342
  children, 345–47
  tests, 333–36
Autism, 262, 430–31

Barrio, 456
Basic anxiety, 423
Beauty, 34–35
Behavior mechanisms, 420–21
Beri-beri, 213
Bilingualism, 486–87
Black Muslim, 41–42
Blind
  additional handicaps, 323–24
  adjustment, 313–14
  cane travel, 310
  cognitive functions, 315–17
  conceptual processes, 315–17
  congenitally, 304–6, 312, 315
  education
    arithmetic, 320
    audio aids, 320
    Braille, 318–20
  educational needs, 318–20
  employment, 321
  face vision, 311–12
  guide dogs, 310
  handicaps, 306–8
  kinethesis, 316
  mental map, 310
  mentally retarded, 324
  misconceptions, 307
  mobility, 308–12
  mobility training, 309–10
  motor memory, 310
  obstacle sense, 311–12
  orientation, 310
  perceptual processes, 315–17
  rubella, 324
  sensory acuity, 315
  stereotypes, 307
  stigma, 307
  typewriting, 320
  vocational training, 320–21
Blindisms, 308, 313–14
Blindness
  cortical, 275
  educational, 302
  functional definitions, 302
  mind, 275
  partial, 302
  vocational, 302
  word, 275
Blood type, 196–97
Boarding home, 64
Boredom, 433
Braille, 75–76, 317, 319–20
Brain damage
  linguistic problems, 275
  Strauss syndrome, 274

Brain-injured, 278
   distractability in, 293
   minimally, 277
   reading and, 293–94
Brain injury, 274–75

Caesarian delivery, 368
Cerebellar ataxia, 191
Cerebral arteriosclerosis, 525
Cerebral palsy
   classification, 364–66
      ataxia, 366
      athetoid, 365–66
      limb involvement, 366
      spastic, 365
   epilepsy, 371
   etiology, 368–69
   genetic origin of, 260
   hearing disability, 371
   incidence, 366–67
   intelligence, 369–71
   mental deficiency, 367, 370–71
   natal causes, 368
   postnatal causes, 369
   prenatal causes, 368
   speech defects, 407
   speech disorders, 371
   treatment, 371
Child abuse, 236
Child rearing practices, 423
Chromosomes, 193
Chronic anxiety, 424–25
Cleft palate, 408
Clinics, 63
Community Hospital, 61
Compulsions, 426–27
Conflict, 434
Congenital aphasia, 405–6
Congenital deafness, 336
Congenital defects, 193, 203
Congenitally blind, 315
Convergent thinking, 162–64
Convulsive disorders
   early childhood, 372
   epilepsy, 371–86
Cottage plan, 58
Creative adolescents
   conformity and, 171–72
   families of, 172–73
   goals of, 171–72
   I Q, 171–72
   mothers of, 172–73
   risk taking, 172–73
   vocational choices, 172
Creative adults
   artists, 169
   identification, 157–59
   motivation, 170
   scientists, 168–69
   values, 167–68
   writers, 169
Creative children
   identification of, 159–60, 173
   projective tests and, 174

Creative person, 156
Creative process, 156
Creative thinking, 163–64
Creativity
   adult, 515
   Berkeley studies of, 157, 159
   conformity and, 175–76
   convergent thinking in, 160
   definition, 155–56
   development, 175–77
   divergent thinking in, 160–64
   fostering of, 175–77
   generality of, 156
   humor, 171–72
   I Q, 164–67
   level, 157
   living-in assessment, 158–59
   nonconformity, 176
   practice and, 176–77
   psychological freedom and, 175
   psychological safety and, 175
   social utility, 165
   special talent as, 156
   tests, 160–62
Cretinism, 191, 197, 211, 257–58
Crippled children
   adjustment, 362–64
   cerebral palsied, 364–71
Cultural bias
   curricula, 489–91
   inevitable, 490–91
   tests, 489–91
Cultural disadvantage
   cognition, 489–94
   comparative, 482–84
   concept, 446–49
   coping, 487
   economic factors, 475–76
   educational factors, 476–77
   linguistics, 468–75
   Mexican-American, 455–57
   national origin, 450–51
   Negro, 451–54
   rural, 467
   stigma, 486–87
Cultural isolation, 483–84
Cultural pluralism, 493–94
Culturally disadvantaged
   background, 465–66
   children's programs, 477–78
   desegregation, 480–81
   educational needs, 475–81
   identity, 449–50
   intelligence testing, 226, 484–89
   learning and, 276–77
   neuroses, 466
   older people, 478
   philosophical considerations, 482–84
   preschool programs, 478–80
   program evaluation, 481–82
   rural-urban migrants, 466–68
   social needs, 475–81
Custodial retarded
   classification, 264–65
   training of, 267–68

Day centers, 62–63, 264
Daydreaming, 432–33
Day hospitals, 264
Deaf
  adventitiously, 331
  cognition, 316–17
  conduction, 332
  functional, 332
  linguistic handicap, 317
  neural, 332
  organizations, 352
  rubella, 324
  social life, 352–53
  special classes, 350
  special schools, 349–50
  speech problems, 346–47
Deafness
  hereditary, 340
  word, 275, 290
Deductive reasoning, 163–64
Defective children, 101–8
Delayed speech, 399
Delinquency
  complexness, 437–40
  family, 438
  sex differences, 439
  social climate, 422, 439
Delusions, 429
Denial, 102
Depression, 105–7
Desegregation, 480–81
Desensitization, 404
Developmental levels, 287–88
Deviance
  anxiety and, 36–37
  concealment of, 40–41
  intellectual, 16
  motor, 17
  overlapping areas of, 18
  personality, 17
  sensory, 16–17
  social, 17–18
  social attitudes and, 27–30
  stigma and, 37
Deviancy
  family nature, 96–97
  reactions to, 31–33
Deviant people
  fear of, 7
  naturalistic conception, 6–7
  prescientific conception, 5–7
Deviation, 16–20
Diabetes, 364
Diagnostic service, 77–82
Diplegia, 366
Disability
  acceptance of, 39–43
  age and, 108–10
  congenital, 109
  coping with, 44–45
  denial of, 39–43
  handicap and, 33–35
  succumbing to, 43–44
  teaching to, 284–85

Disabled
  assistance for, 50–51
  demeaning of, 50–51
  dependency and, 50–51
  prejudice against, 47–48
  stereotyping, 47–48
Disadvantaged, 464–66
Discrimination, 48–50
Divergent thinking, 162–64
Doppler effect, 311
Down's syndrome, 193, 254–55
  intelligence in, 255
  physical signs, 254
Dull normal, 447
Dwarfism, 4, 206, 258
Dyslexia, 274–75

Early blind, 316
Eczema, 364
Educationally deaf, 331
Educationally disadvantaged, 488–89
Educationally handicapped (EH), 226, 278
EEG, 379–80
Emotionally disturbed, 421
Encephalitis, 210, 261–62, 368
Environmental factors
  infections, 203–5
  physical trauma, 203
  prenatal, 201–2
  prenatal nutrition, 202
  superior, 197
Epilepsy
  attitudes toward, 384
  aura, 374
  brain damage, 260
  brain lesions, 372–73, 378
  cerebral dysrythmia, 372
  drug therapy, 383
  EEG, 379–80
  emotional factors, 380
  emotional problems, 382–83
  etiology, 378–80
  family, 378–79
  focal, 378
  grand mal, 373–74
  incidence, 377–78
  intellectual deterioration, 381
  intelligence, 380–81
  Jacksonian, 375
  mental deficiency, 377–78
  personality, 382–83
  petit mal, 375
  prognosis, 383–84
  psychogenic factors, 380
  psychomotor, 376–77
  sex differences, 377
  treatment, 383–84
Epileptic equivalency, 376–77
"Epileptic personality," 22, 383
Ethnic groups, 462–64
Exceptional adults, 18, 51–52
Exceptional children, 51–52
  parental counseling, 110–11

public understanding, 68
sibling reaction, 108
special classes, 70–72
Exceptional people
beauty, 34–35
educational programs, 28–29
employer acceptance, 68
humanitarian values in, 29
minority status, 46–48
overachievement, 12
qualitative conception, 7–10
rehabilitation, 29
societal help for, 28–29
superiority, 19
trait patterns in, 8–9
Exceptionality
athletic prowess, 19
current conceptions, 13–16
definitions, 13–14
degree of, 20
extensiveness of, 22–23, 52–53
individual differences, 22
individuality, 30–31
I Q, 20
social criteria, 14–16
stereotypes, 22–23
terminology used, 23–24
values, 15

Family
care, 63–64
counseling, 99
deviancy effect, 97
emotional climate, 99
relations, 96–108
size, 230–31
subsystems, 97–98
verbal stimulation, 231
Fantasy, 432–33
Fear, 425–26
Feebleminded, 188, 190
Fighting, 433
Foster children, 233
Foster home, 63–64
Freidreich's ataxia, 191
Frustration, 432, 434

Galactosuria, 192, 211
Gallaudet College, 350
Gargoylism, 192, 257
Garveyites, 40
Gaucher's disease, 257
Geniuses, 169
German measles, 203
Gestalt psychology, 276, 279
Gifted
acceleration, 144
achievement, 131, 147
achievement testing, 137
adjustment, 118–20, 146
adult accomplishment, 145–46
class honors, 138
college, 141

cultural background, 140–42
cultural influences, 197
definition, 129–31
democratic families, 141–42
early studies, 128–29
educational achievement, 136–38, 142–43,
148–49
extra curricular activities, 138
group intelligence test, 131–32
incidence, 133–34
individual intelligence testing, 132
marital status, 146
occupational background, 141
parental education, 141
parental exploitation, 119
parental fear, 118–19
personal characteristics, 138–40
physical characteristics, 135
school achievement, 144–45
school grades, 132
sex, 135–36
social class, 141–42
special programs, 143
synonyms, 130–31
teachers' ratings, 152–53
terminology, 139–31
underachievement, 142–48
Gigantism, 4
Glaucoma, 305–6
Glycogenosis, 256
Godparents, 455–56
Grand mal, 21
Group counseling, 116–17
Guilt, 105–6

Halfway houses, 64–65
Hallucinations, 429
Handicap
acceptance of, 41–43
coping, 43
denial, 45
disability and, 33–35
secondary gains in, 44
visibility of, 38–39
vocational discrimination, 47
Handicapped
counseling, 67–68
home training of, 67–68
recreation for, 66–67
secondary, 37–38
segregation of, 49
Handicapped children, 102
Handicapped people, 87
Head start, 28–29
Hearing aids
amplification, 343–44
limitations, 344–45
Hearing loss
medical aspects, 342–45, 408
surgery, 343
symptoms, 332–33
Hellers's disease, 262
Hemiplegia, 366
Heredity, 195

Hobbies, 520
Home instruction, 73–74
Homogeneous grouping, 90
Home teachers, 73–74
Hospital instruction, 72–73
Huntington's chorea, 191–92
Hurler's disease, 257
Hydrocephaly, 203–4, 259
Hyperopia, 317
Hypoglycaemia, 256
Hypoparathyroidism, 258

Identical twins, 447
Idiopathic epilepsy, 372
Idiot, 188, 190, 263
Illinois Test of Psycholinguistic Abilities
     (ITPA), 479
Imbecile, 188, 190, 263
Immigrants, 467
Individual differences, 3–5
Inductive reasoning, 163–64
Infantile autism, 430–31
Innate response system, 287
Institutionalization, 58–60
Institutional placement, 100–101
Institutional routines, 59
Institutional schools, 266
Institutions
   colonies, 58
   cottage plans, 58
   indictment, 58–60
   multipurpose, 57
   non-residential, 61–64
   residential, 56–58
   short term, 57–58
   special purpose, 57
Intelligence
   aged, 514–15
   borderline, 184, 447
   cerebral palsy, 370–71
   correlates, 165–66
   correlation studies, 228–29
   creativity, 164–67
   crime, 237–38
   "culture fair" tests, 484–85
   delinquent, 457
   dental hygiene, 213
   dull normal, 184
   education, 233
   family, 228–32
   heritability, 198–201
   infection, 213
   language deficit, 339–40
   longitudinal studies, 514–15
   nonverbal, 339–40
   nutrition, 212–13
   occupations, 236
   protein, 212
   race, 198–201
   range restriction, 166–67
   speech defectives, 397
   urban vs. rural, 234–35
   visually impaired, 314
   vitamins, 212
Interest, 516

Isolation, 483–84
Italian-Americans
   education, 458
   family, 457–59
Itinerant teacher, 72

Japanese
   culture, 459–62
   family, 461–62
   value system, 461–62
Jews
   cultural advantage, 459–62
   discrimination, 460
   family, 459–60
Job requirements, 47

Kibbutzim, 463
Kleptomania, 427
Kwashiorkor, 212

Lalling, 399
Language
   authority, 471–72
   handicap, 492–93
   lower class, 469–70
Late blind, 316
Learning disabilities
   behavioral, 279–80
   behavioral deficits, 283
   brain damage, 280
   definitions, 280–81
   diagnosis, 282
   educational appeal, 281–82
   educational programs, 283–92
      Barsch, 286–87
      Delacato, 288–90
      Fernald, 292
      Fitzhugh, 291
      Frostig, 290–91
      Getman, 287–88
      Kephart, 285–86
      Strauss-Lehtinen-Cruickshank, 283–85
      Witmer, 291–92
   etiology, 276–77
   evaluative studies, 293–94
   legal status, 277–78
   new category, 279
   nonstigmatizing, 282
   parents and, 278
   perceptual motor, 283–85
   perceptual-motor practice, 286
   popularity, 277
   pragmatic approaches, 292–93
   specific deficit, 282
   Straussian legacy in, 273–74
   visual motor, 287–88
   visual perception, 290–91
"Left-over" children, 281
Linguistic code
   deviant, 493
   elaborated, 472
   lower-class, 470–71
   restricted, 471–74
Lip reading, 347–48

Lisping, 398
Little's disease, 364
Longevity, 511

Magic, 6
Maladjustment
  emotional, 421–22
  prevalence, 440–41
  situational, 440
  special schools, 441
Meningitis, 211, 260–61, 336, 368
Mental deficiency, 188
Mental level
  education, 232–33
  geographic area, 234–37
  occupation, 233–34
Mental retardation
  asphyxia, 209–10
  asssessment, 186–87
  bio-chemical anomalies, 256–57
  blood incapatibility, 205–6
  brain infections, 260–62
  brain injury, 198, 210
  carbohydrate metabolism, 256
  chromosomal aberrations, 193–95
  criteria, 13, 187–88
  cultural factors, 190–91, 213–15
  definitions, 182–84
    AAMD, 182
    developmental, 185
    functional, 183–84
    learning ability, 185–86
    quantitative, 183–84
    social adjustment, 186
  degree, 20–21
  diversity, 215–16
  diet, 211–13
  discipline, 238
  education, 187, 243–44
  encephalitis, 210
  endocrine disturbances, 257–58
  environmental factors, 201–15
  etiology, 190–92
  extreme deprivation, 214–15
  familial, 190–91
  fat metabolism, 257
  galactosaemia, 256
  home environment, 214
  identification, 184–85, 187
  illegitimacy, 235
  institutional effects, 215
  irreversibility of, 182–83, 213
  isolation, 215
  meningitis, 211
  metabolism, 192–93
  moderate, 225
  motivation, 241–42
  multi-genetic, 194–95
  mutations, 207
  natal causes, 208–10
  nature-nurture, 195–98
  physical education, 245–46
  postnatal causes, 210–15
  postnatal infections, 210–11
  prematurity, 208–9

  profound, 225
  protein metabolism, 256–57
  protozoal infection, 204
  radio activity, 206–7
  recessive gene, 192–93
  Rh factor, 205–6
  secondary curricula, 244–45
  severe, 225
  single gene, 191–92, 256
  social expectancy, 238–40
  social training, 245
  speech defects, 407–8
  sporadic, 192
  table of terminology, 189
  toxic agents, 207–8
  viral diseases, 205
  vitamins, 202
  vocational training, 245–46
Mexican-Americans
  child studies, 463
  delinquency, 456–57
  family, 455–57
Microcephaly, 192, 203–4, 206, 258–59, 447
Middle Ages, 6
Mild retardation
  administration for, 243–44
  attention span, 242
  borderline intellect, 227
  crime, 237–40
  curriculum, 240
  delinquency, 237–40
  educational level, 232–33, 242–43
  incidence, 226–27
  industrial accidents, 236–37
  job expectancy, 236–37
  learning, 240–41
  legal protection, 238–39
  level of aspiration, 241
  poverty, 235–36
  sex, 238
  socio-economic background, 232–46
  verbal facility, 240–41
Mildly retarded
  adjustments, 235
  draft rejection, 234
  education, 240–44, 246–47
  employment, 246–47
  family, 228–32
  fertility, 229–30
  physical characteristics, 227–28
  physical handicaps, 228
Mongolism
  chromosomal anomalies, 192–94
  mosaicism, 255
  physical appearance, 203, 254–55
  translocation, 255
  trisomy, 193, 255
Monoplegia, 366
Montessori schools, 477
Moron, 188, 190, 263
Mosaicism, 194
Mother-child relationship, 98–99
Motor training, 285
Movigenics, 286–87
Mumps, 205, 336

Muscular dystrophy, 364
Myopia, 317

Nature-nurture, 198–201
Negative discrimination, 48
Negative practice, 404
Negro
  family, 453–54
  slavery, 452–53
  socioeconomic status, 452
  West Indian, 462
Nephrogenic diabetes insipidus, 258
Neurofibromatosis, 191
Neurological impairment, 275–77
Niemann-Pick disease, 257
Non-residential institutions, 61–63
Nursing homes, 253, 264

Obsessions, 426–27
"Open admittance", 51
Operation Head Start, 478
Originality, 155–56, 177
Orthopedic handicap
  incidence, 361–62
Orthopedically disabled
  emotional disturbance, 11
Orthopedically handicapped
  adjustment, 362–64
  congenital defects, 362
  limitation, 364
  parental attitudes, 363–64
  self-concept, 363
Osteomyelitis, 364
Overselection, 490–91
Oxycephaly, 259

Panic reactions, 425
Paraplegia, 366
Parental Counseling
  acceptance, 113
  attitudes, 114
  gifted, 120
  group, 116–17
  information, 115–16
  interpretation, 114–15
  listening, 111–12
  planning, 116
  principles of, 111–20
  terminology, 112–13
Parental Reactions
  ambivalence, 101, 104
  coping, 102
  denial, 102–3
  dependency, 107–8
  depression, 105–7
  guilt, 105–7
  projection, 104–5
  self pity, 103–4
  shame, 105
Parkinson's disease, 210, 261
Partially sighted, 302
  education, 321–23
  educational aids, 322–23
  magnification for, 322–23

Pellagra, 213
Permissiveness, 98
Personality, 17
Petit Mal, 21
Phenylalanine, 196, 256–57
Phenylketonuria (PKU), 192, 211, 256–57,
  447
Phenylpyruvic amentia, 196
Phobias, 425–26, 427
Poliomyelitis, 362, 364
Polydactylism, 203
Postencephalitis, 261–62
Poverty, 448–50, 465–66, 475–76
Prejudice, 49–50
Prematurity
  cerebral palsy, 208, 368
  neurological damage, 209
Prenatal infection, 203–4
Prenatal nutrition, 202–3
Presbycusis, 336–37
Projection, 104–5
Prosthetic devices, 39
Psycholinguistics, 395
Psychological freedom, 176
Psychological safety, 176
Pubentas praecox, 4
Pyknoepilepsy, 375
Pyromania, 427

Quadriplegia, 366

Racial discrimination, 50–52
Rationalization, 420–21
Reading disability, 275
Recreational programs, 66–67
Regressive behavior, 431–32
Regular Classroom
  acceptance, 84
  exceptional children, 83–91
Remediation Services, 77–82
Renaissance, 7
Residential facilities, 265–66
Residential institutions, 264–67
  Community hospital, 61
  role, 60–61
  size, 59–61
  training centers, 60
Resource center, 91
Resource teacher, 71–72
Retirement, 518–20
Retirement homes, 524
Retrogression, 431
RH factor, 205–6, 368, 408
Rubella, 203–4, 336, 368
Rural-urban migrants, 466–68

Schizophrenia, 262, 429–30
School failure, 186
Seizure, 371–76
Self-concept, 35–36, 39–40, 106, 109
Self-pity, 103–4
Senile dementia, 525–26
Senile psychoses, 525–26
Sensory limitations, 21

Severe retardation
  chromosomal aberrations, 254–55
  clinical types, 253
  cultural causes, 262–64
  definition, 253
  deprivation and, 262
  distinguishing characteristics, 253–54
  genetic syndromes, 254–62
  I Q, 253
  psychological causes, 262–63
Severely retarded
  conditioning of, 267–68
  custodial, 264–65
  emotional problems of, 262
  habit training of, 267
  residential institutions, 265–67
  training, 263–64
Sexual adventurism, 483
Sexual infantilism, 258
Shame, 105–7
Sheltered workshops, 65–66, 264
"Sight saving", 321–22
Sign language, 348
Slow learners, 184, 117, 448
Snellen Test, 304
Social change, 449
Social climate, 439
Social deviance, 21–22, 41–42
Social programs, 66–67
Social welfare, 450
Socioeconomic class, 448
Spanish-American
  Mexican-American, 455–57
  Puerto Rican, 454–55
Spastic paralysis, 364
Special classes
  civil rights and, 86
  itinerant teacher, 72
  modifications of, 71–72
  resource teacher, 71–72
  segregation and, 86–87
Special day schools, 69–70
Special education
  administration of, 82–83
  auxiliary services for, 76–77
  goals, 75
  integration, 77
  placement in, 76
Speech
  nonstandard, 492–93
  normal, 401
  public, 471
Speech Correction
  multidisciplinary involvement, 391–92
  school program, 404, 410–11
Speech correctionist, 404
Speech defects
  behavior problems, 408–9
  causes, 394–95
  cleft palate, 408
  criteria, 392
  definitions, 392
  diagnosis, 393
  identification, 393
  neural impairment, 405–7

  organic, 394–95
  parental standards, 409
  prevalence, 393–94
  social, 394–95
  tests, 393
Speech development, 312
Speech disorders
  articulation, 398–99
  cerebral palsy, 396
  classification, 396–408
  cluttering, 400
  delayed speech, 399
  educational achievement, 397
  intelligence, 397
  lalling, 399
  lisping, 398
  motor coordination, 396
  nonlanguage characteristics, 395–97
  phonation, 400
  physical characteristics, 396
  rhythm disturbances, 400–405
  sensory capacities, 396–97
  stammering, 400
  stuttering, 400–405
Speech pathology, 21
Speech perception tests, 335
Speech reading, 346
Speech therapist, 410–11
Speech therapy, 404
Spina-bifida, 364
Status epilepticus, 375
Stigma, 27–30
Strauss syndrome, 278–79
Stroke, 526
Structure
  environmental, 284–85
  program, 285
  relationship, 284
Stuttering
  causes
    diagnosogenic, 401–2
    functional, 401–2
    organic, 401
  controlled, 403–4
  definitions, 400
  personality, 104–5
  primary, 402–3
  psychotherapy, 404
  secondary, 401, 402, 404
  social factors, 402–3
  treatment, 403–4
Sucrosia, 256
Symptomatic epilepsy, 372
Syphilis, 203, 210, 368
Syphilitic brain infection, 260

Tay-Sach's disease, 192, 257, 314
Teaching material, 285
Television instruction, 74
Terminology, 23, 24
Thalidomide, 103, 207
Thyroid deficiency, 257–58
Timidity, 427
Tolerance, 51

Trainable retarded, 263, 264
Tremors, 511–12
Triplegia, 366
Tuberous sclerosis, 191
Tuning forks, 334
Twins, 511

Underachievers, 146–47
Union League of the Deaf, 45

Verbal stimulation, 230–31
Vision
    aged, 513
    distance, 302
    shadow, 302
    travel, 302
    tunnel, 302
Visually handicapped
    functional definitions, 302
    quantitative definitions, 302–3
Visual imagery, 315
Visual impairment
    cataracts, 305–6
    excessive oxygen, 304
    heredity, 305
    incidence, 306
    injuries, 305
    intelligence, 314–15
        symptoms, 303–4
        tests of, 304
Visual motor training, 287–88
Visual speech, 347–48
Visually handicapped
    definitions, 301–3
Visually impaired
    education, 317, 318, 323
    educational plans, 323
    speech disorders, 312–13
Vocational rehabilitation, 65
Voice disorders, 400

WASP, 461
Wechsler Intelligence Scale for Children
    (WISC), 10–11
Welfare, 464
White House Conference Report, 361–90
Widowhood, 521–22
Withdrawal
    causes, 428–29
    normal, 428
    punishment, 429
    reality, 429–33
"Work camp houses", 64–65
World Conference of the Deaf, 46
World Deaf Olympics, 46

X-ray, 207